# Canon Law Society of America

Proceedings
of the
Seventy-Ninth
Annual Convention

Indianapolis, Indiana
October 16-19, 2017

Canon Law Society of America

© Copyright 2018 by the Canon Law Society of America

ISBN 978-1-932208-49-8
ISSN 0277-9889
SAN 237-6296

The Canon Law Society of America's programs and publications are designed solely to help canonists maintain their professional competence. In dealing with specific canonical matters, the canonist using Canon Law Society of America (CLSA) publications or orally conveyed information should also research original sources of authority.

The views and opinions expressed in this publication are those of the individual authors and do not represent the views of the CLSA, its Board of Governors, staff or members. The CLSA does not endorse the views or opinions expressed by the individual authors. The publisher and authors specifically disclaim any liability, loss or risk, personal or otherwise, which is incurred as consequence, directly or indirectly, of the use, reliance, or application of any of the contents of this publication.

Unless otherwise noted, all canons quoted are from the *Code of Canon Law, Latin-English Edition* (Washington, DC: Canon Law Society of America, 2012) and the *Code of Canons of the Eastern Churches, Latin-English Edition* (Washington, DC: Canon Law Society of America, 2002).

Printed in the United States of America.

Canon Law Society of America
Office of the Executive Coordinator
415 Michigan Avenue NE, Suite 101
Washington, DC 20017-4502

# TABLE OF CONTENTS

*Foreword* ............................................................................................................. vii

*Keynote Address*

Mercy, Justice and the Law: In the Spirit of the Jubilee Year of Mercy
Fifteen Years after the Dallas Charter and Essential Norms:
State of the Question
    *Reverend Robert J. Geisinger, SJ* .................................................................. 1

*Major Addresses*

Mercy, Justice and Law in Francis' Interpretation of Vatican II
    *Professor Massimo Faggioli* ........................................................................ 22

*Seminars*

When the Tribunal Is Not An Option, Is There Another? What Hath Francis Wrought?
    *Reverend John P. Beal* ................................................................................ 37

Insufficient Faith Leading to Simulation or Error
    *Most Reverend Monsignor Kenneth Boccafola* ......................................... 61

Raking the Embers, to Extinguish Or Start A Fire: Some Thoughts on the Possibilities for the Future of Apostolic Religious Life
    *Sr. Maria Casey, RSJ* .................................................................................. 80

Silver and Gold We Have Not: Balancing Conflicting Values in Diocesan Bankruptcy
    *Dr. Barbara Anne Cusack* .......................................................................... 92

Religious Sponsors, Ministry Leaders and Diocesan Bishops: Together in Communion
    *Sr. Sharon Euart, RSM* ............................................................................. 107

Canonical Exclusionary Rules and the Just Adjudication of Delicts against the Sacrament of Penance
    *Reverend Monsignor Ronny E. Jenkins* ................................................... 122

Circumstances Allowing the Use of the *Processus Brevior*: Some Exegetical Considerations
    *Reverend Monsignor John G. Johnson* .................................................... 142

Current Priestly Formation: *Status Quæstionis*
   *Reverend Robert Kaslyn, SJ*.................................................................. 164

Harmony and Solicitude: Recent Canonical Changes and the Catholic Eastern Churches
   *Reverend Alexander M. Laschuk* ......................................................... 189

Canonical Developments in the Personal Ordinariates Established under the Auspices of the Apostolic Constitution *Anglicanorum coetibus*
   *Most Reverend Steven J. Lopes* ........................................................... 208

Some Canonical and Pastoral Considerations in Causes of Canonization
   *Jeannine Marino* ................................................................................... 218

Called to be a Missionary Church: How the Missionary Experience Can Inform the New Evangelization
   *Reverend Ricardo Martín-Pinillos*....................................................... 242

Structural Reorganization of the Metropolitan Appellate Structure and Approval Process
   *Very Reverend Joseph L. Newton*........................................................ 253

Diocesan Administration *Sede Vacante*: Practical Principles and Questions
   *Reverend Aaron Nord*........................................................................... 272

Social Media and Its Relationship to the *Communio*
   *Matthew Palmer* ................................................................................... 289

Reception into Full Communion of Those in Irregular Marriages: Pastoral Realties and a Canonical Solution
   *Reverend Monsignor Michael A. Souckar*........................................... 292

*Officers' Reports*

President
   *Reverend Bruce Miller* .........................................................................307
Treasurer
   *Sister Nancy Reynolds, SP* ...................................................................314
   Independent Auditor Report
   *Linton Shafer Warfield & Garret, P.A.* ................................................318
   Fiscal Year 2017-2018 Budget ................................................................335
Executive Coordinator
   *Reverend Patrick J. Cogan, SA* ...........................................................352

General Secretary
  *Colleen Crawford*..................................................................................352

*Committee Reports*
Constitutional Standing Committees
  Nominations ..........................................................................................354
  Resolutions............................................................................................355
  Resource and Asset Management..........................................................355
  Professional Responsibility ..................................................................356

On-Going Committees
  Church Governance................................................................................358
  Clergy.....................................................................................................358
  Convention Planning..............................................................................361
  Institutes of Consecrated and Apostolic Life ........................................363
  Laity .....................................................................................................365
  Publications Advisory Board.................................................................366
  Research and Development....................................................................369
  Sacramental Law....................................................................................373

*Varia*

Business Meeting Minutes
  *Mary Gen Blittschau* ...........................................................................375

Homily, Convention Liturgy
  *Reverend Bruce Miller* ........................................................................384

Role of Law Award Citation
  *Reverend Bruce Miller* ........................................................................387

Role of Law Award Response
  *Sister Victoria Vondenberger, RSM* ....................................................390

Tribunal Statistics 2016 .............................................................................395

Contributors ...............................................................................................403

2017 Convention List of Participants .......................................................405

# FOREWORD

The Canon Law Society of America is pleased to publish the *Proceedings* of the Seventy-Ninth Annual Convention which was convened in Indianapolis, Indiana, on October 16-19, 2017 at the Westin Hotel. The convention *Proceedings* have been published for almost fifty years, thus providing a significant volume of presentations and reports.

We are grateful to the presenters who have submitted their text for publication, even when their presentation was in power-point or other electronic medium. The texts have been edited to be in conformity with the CLSA Style Sheet and publication guidelines. Included in this edition are the annual Tribunal Statistics collected from participating (arch)dioceses and (arch)eparchies and also a listing of the participants in the Indianapolis convention.

The CLSA, established on November 12, 1939 as a professional association, presently has more than 1100 members who minister in more than thirty-five countries. Additional copies of this 2017 volume of *Proceedings* may be purchased from the CLSA website: www.canonlawsocietyofamerica.org at the Bookstore link.

Information on how to become a member of the CLSA may be found from the CLSA website or contact the administrative office.

Canon Law Society of America
415 Michigan Avenue NE, Suite 101
Washington, DC 20017-4502
(202) 832-2350

# Keynote Address

## Mercy, Justice, and the Law:
## In the Spirit of the Jubilee Year of Mercy

## Fifteen Years After the Dallas Charter and Essential Norms: State of the Question
### Reverend Robert J. Geisinger, S.J.

Thank you for the kind welcome. I am honored to be asked to offer this Keynote Address[1] in a city so dear to me. Two of the happiest and most challenging years of my life were spent here in Indianapolis teaching high school (1985-1987). I will always be grateful for my ordination to the priesthood here on 14 September 1991 in the chapel of Brebeuf Preparatory School, our primary Jesuit apostolate in this marvelous archdiocese. It is good and fulfilling to be back, not only because of that history, but much more so because today I am among colleagues and friends in the law, because I am among colleagues and friends in Christ.

### Prologue

*Walking. Building. Professing.*

**MISSA PRO ECCLESIA**
**with the Cardinal Electors**
**Homily of Pope Francis in the Sistine Chapel**
**Thursday, 14 March 2013 (the day after his election)**

In these three readings, I see a common element: that of movement. In the first reading, it is the movement of a journey; in the second reading, the movement of building the Church; in

---

[1] I regret that circumstances did not allow a substantive question-and-answer exchange to follow this forty-five minute address, as had been long planned. I mention this only because I looked forward to incorporating thoughtful and enriching observations into this printed text as a result of that conversation among colleagues, as would be usual for published papers following convention presentations. I consider these reflections, always fully my own, lesser for not having been fed by critical peer interaction following the address itself.

the third, in the Gospel, the movement involved in professing the faith. Walking, building, professing.[2]

Let's stay with this image of movement for a moment. Let us presume that if we are walking, building, and professing well the vocation as canon lawyers that we have been given, we are already immersed in the waters of mercy and justice.

Our presumed starting point is that we serve the Gospel truth because every one of us in this room is a servant of the Gospel and therefore a lover of God and of what is true.

As we serve the Lord and the Church, as we serve mercy, justice, and the law in a particular, lively way because we are canonists and participants in the life of the law (practitioners, academics, staff, notaries, advocates, judges, bishops) ... as we so serve, all of us are preachers and holders of truth, justice, mercy, and the law.

Let us examine – in these days, and beginning now – well and carefully how we are indeed serving as best we can these principles, these norms of mercy and justice, as we live the law. In doing so, we do not fear self-criticism or shared internal criticism, among friends in the Lord, which discussion and critique can only be healthy presuming that it be reasoned and spoken in love. Spoken in love, and lived in love. I'll get to that later, in the Epilogue.

Hence for our point of departure, let's note this year's convention theme: *Mercy, Justice, and the Law: In the Spirit of the Jubilee Year of Mercy.*

Since I am presuming that if we are doing good and doing well – or at least as best we can – what we're doing, then the mercy and justice pieces are part of the composite as they should be, whether naturally or because we put them there. We can presume them the mortar between the bricks of this afternoon's topic.

Let's move now from the general to the specific. In the next 40 minutes, let us touch upon the theme *Fifteen Years After the Dallas Charter and Essential Norms: State of the Question*. One cannot work this issue without considering *Sacramentorum sanctitatis tutela (SST)* of 2001 and its May 2010 revision.

*SST*, and the *Essential Norms* with their uniquely (to this day) granted *recognitio*, didn't come from nowhere ... they came in some shape or form from the Legislator's examined conscience, from a lived and digested awareness

---

2   *In queste tre Letture vedo che c'è qualcosa di comune: è il movimento. Nella Prima Lettura il movimento nel cammino; nella Seconda Lettura, il movimento nell'edificazione della Chiesa; nella terza, nel Vangelo, il movimento nella confessione. Camminare, edificare, confessare.* Accessed from http://w2.vatican.va/content/francesco/it/homilies/2013/documents/papa-francesco_20130314_omelia-cardinali.html.

of sin, from a corporate examination of the work of the Evil One, however imperfect that digestion may have been in recent decades. The aforementioned two documents represent a remarkable effort to get it right.

A state of the question evaluation includes an examination of the body's life, the circumstances, truth, and reality which shape our understanding and application of law even when existing law (*CIC* 1983, *CCEO* 1990) has seemed insufficient, thus warranting (which I take to be a given) the *Essential Norms* and *SST*.

A state of the question assessment is a type of judgement, not leading of course to definitive resolution but leading toward judgement, not univocal or uniform but a composite of different (sometimes dramatically or even violently different) opinions. Every *notitia criminis* reception leads to a judgement of some type (is this pursuable or not?); every first investigation is a judgement (is there *fumus delicti*, or not?); every trial is a judgement, every process based on an extra-judicial decree approach (i.e., an administrative penal process) is a judgement; and really every penal precept, every "placement on administrative leave", every response by way of press bulletin, every letter read to the faithful from a pulpit about an accusation is in some form a judgement.

Fifteen years later, we take a moment now to examine where we are on this issue, in a state of the question evaluation, with our own individual judgements in this sensitive, volatile area in which the *Essential Norms* and *SST* figure so prominently. I'll return to the "personal evaluation" by each of us in the Epilogue. As you have already heard, there's lots to happen in the Epilogue ... my heart will be there at our point of arrival, but I now turn to the "in-between".

I have a series of six themes which I offer post-Prologue and pre-Epilogue. They are, in order: (1) Premises and Presumptions; (2) Priorities; (3) Persons; (4) Processes; (5) Potholes and Potential Potholes; and (6) Possibilities. My sweep through this power point presentation is to offer a running commentary of where I think we are fifteen years later with the *Essential Norms* and *SST*, in light of positions I've held and ministry offered since 1994 in this area. There's no walking back the *Essential Norms*. We are canonists, and we respect what is written in the *Essential Norms*, in *SST* / *Norms 2010*, *CIC*, and *CCEO*. We are canonists, and so we also live in a flowing context of evaluation, to say nothing of the flow of change. Under the flow we have some premises and presumptions.

### PREMISES AND PRESUMPTIONS

1. While in common parlance we refer to the "Dallas Charter" and may intend both the "Charter for the Protection of Children and Young People" and the *Essential Norms*, our canonical interlocutor today (in terms of juridic import) will be the *Essential Norms* and not the "Charter".

2. We have recognized in these fifteen years that the human damage and the ecclesial damage to the Universal Body caused by the sexual abuse of minors by clerics is incalculable. Among the debatable points under discussion in these minutes, this is not one.

3. We have learned that we may not, cannot tire of an issue which exhausts us. We can't not be vigilant. Protection of young people and prosecution of perpetrators among ecclesiastics must not lighten up. Declining numbers of fresh cases must not allow us to think that some sort of victory has been won. The stakes – above all the human stakes (our young people, and those equivalent to them in law) – are too high. We can't become comfortable.

4. The United States Conference of Catholic Bishops and those assisting with *Essential Norms* implementation, especially within the community of canonists, should be deeply proud for having faced what needed to be faced, not only 15 years ago but certainly even before in many places. Exceptional times called for exceptional measures and exceptional persons. One can debate the propriety of the "how" and the reality of "too late" while still acknowledging that the clear directives of the *Essential Norms* required a resoluteness and a quick application in chaotic times. Leadership and canonists did their best fifteen years ago (as just noted, in many places even earlier) and have not stopped since.

5. The general unity of the USCCB these last 15 years on *Essential Norms* / *SST – Norms 2010* issues has been a remarkable blessing, especially as regards putting protection first. Increasingly over the last 15 years, we have been able to take this wonderful unity for granted.

6. In my opinion, with and since the *Essential Norms* and the Charter, we have gotten much more right (in the moral realm) than wrong. There is no going backward. Later I will point to some areas which invite attention or considered reflection as we go forward.

7. Our *Essential Norms* do not always transport and translate well. We may be right on levels moral and canonical, and have culturally sound ways of proceeding in our USA context, but unintended colonialism can be counterproductive. Without giving way to relativism (what is *wrong by way of abuse is wrong, period, full stop*), cultural sensitivity is needed in

understanding how abuse is understood, how accusations are best made, and how resolution can be pursued in an equitable manner. Again, I am speaking beyond the United States on this point.

8. Our jurisprudence – USA, Congregation for the Doctrine of the Faith (CDF), internationally in other episcopal conferences – in an ongoing way is in slow development on one level or another, and this is not likely to change as implementation responds to culture and to times. In some ways, we may better speak of praxis (the "how-to" or the doing) rather than jurisprudence (the philosophic system) as such, especially since regrettably the CDF does not publish much of the latter except for the occasional paper given at a workshop, convention, or academic conference.

9. We may hold the presumption 15 years later that the *CIC* and *CCEO* did not get something right or were lacking, and that *SST / Norms 2010* and the *Essential Norms* necessarily responded to that. If true (and I believe it is), this invites two related questions: What was the problem with these codes, and why? There continue to be not a few *Essential Norms* and *SST / Norms 2010* critics who hold that we always had what was canonically necessary already without this other special legislation, if we only could have figured out how to apply existing law rightly. I tend to believe that if such an application were obvious or easy, we would have found our way toward it. Because we couldn't or didn't, *SST* and the *Essential Norms* entered in, to great advantage in my opinion.

10. The Church is no longer a law unto itself on prosecution and protection issues; we were, and we didn't do so well with it. This is something the *Essential Norms* helpfully saw and inhered into a way of proceeding. The insistence that problems of clerical sexual abuse of minors could be handled exclusively in the Church by internal leadership – especially just clerical leadership – is now in the past. Cooperation with state authorities as appropriate and warranted is now a given.

11. The Church lives under pressure from civil and government authorities in ways advantageous, though not without raising concerns (e.g., when does the need for accountability and transparency bleed over into government invasion and restriction of internal ecclesiastical freedom).

12. We as canonists serve well when we offer Ordinaries a reasonable range of opinions and options based in ecclesiastical law, including those not always easy to hear, with due respect for those responsible for the decision. This is

true especially in protecting the rights of the accused. This is not contrary to the *Essential Norms*.

### Priorities

1. Our top priority remains the protection of young persons and those equivalent to them in law.

   ***Address of His Holiness Pope Francis to the Participants in the Congress on "Child Dignity in the Digital World"***
   Sala Clementina
   *Friday, 6 October 2017*

   "As all of us know, in recent years the Church has come to acknowledge her own failures in providing for the protection of children: extremely grave facts have come to light, for which we have to accept our responsibility before God, before the victims and before public opinion. For this very reason, as a result of these painful experiences and the skills gained in the process of conversion and purification, the Church today feels especially bound to work strenuously and with foresight for the protection of minors and their dignity, not only within her own ranks, but in society as a whole and throughout the world."[3]

2. Every allegation must be heard, every accuser deserves attention, *every true victim comes first.*

3. Advocacy and the right of defense are to be assured at each stage of a canonical process.

4. Fair prosecution, whether in the civil / criminal forum or in the ecclesiastical forum, is now taken for granted in a way that it was not a short thirty or even

---

[3] *Come tutti sappiamo, la Chiesa Cattolica negli anni recenti è diventata sempre più consapevole di non aver provveduto a sufficienza al proprio interno alla protezione dei minori: sono venuti alla luce fatti gravissimi di cui abbiamo dovuto riconoscere le responsabilità di fronte a Dio, alle vittime e alla pubblica opinione. Proprio per questo, per le drammatiche esperienze fatte e per le competenze acquisite nell'impegno di conversione e purificazione, la Chiesa sente oggi un dovere particolarmente grave di impegnarsi in modo sempre più profondo e lungimirante per la protezione dei minori e la loro dignità, non solo al suo interno, ma in tutta la società e in tutto il mondo.* http://w2.vatican.va/content/francesco/en/speeches/2017/october/documents/papa-francesco_20171006_congresso-childdignity-digitalworld.html

twenty years ago. This is a huge step forward, as long as truth is held as sacred and justice is applied fairly.

5. We must cooperate appropriately and to the fullest with civil / criminal authorities; we do not discourage disclosure (*Essential Norms* 9 and especially 11).

6. The spirit of *Essential Norm* 8 is firm ("When even a single act of sexual abuse") as is the spirit of *Essential Norm* 9 ("even one act of sexual abuse"). This was considered a priority when the *Essential Norms* were composed and ratified as particular law.[4] An important *Essential Norm* 8 phrase to keep in mind here is "if the case so warrants" when considering dismissal from the clerical state. The CDF has forthrightly supported such dismissals when warranted, in my time in that dicastery and as best I know before that, even under criticism from some quarters that the CDF is harsh, extreme, unwilling to give the accused a fair shake, too quick to dismiss or approve dismissal. Dismissal from the clerical state remains a real option, supported and implemented when right and just.

7. When the evidence does not lead to a penal canonical conviction, the matter is remanded to the ordinary exercise of governance of local canonical authority (bishop or major religious superior) to define or delineate the exercise of ministry (or lack thereof) by the accused party in accord with norms of ecclesiastical law. This is left to the prudent governance of local competent ecclesiastical authority, who may restrict the exercise of ministry of clerics subject to him by use of that authority according to the norm of law. Depending on circumstances, another Vatican dicastery other than the CDF may be helpful in assisting parties toward an equitable solution that keeps unsuitable clergy out of active ministry while assuring that the norm of law and the rights of the affected cleric are respected.

PERSONS

1. The respectful and sympathetic treatment of accusers has a rightly prominent place in practice, as stated in *Essential Norm* 3 when mandating "immediate

---

[4] The phrase "zero tolerance" is not canonical parlance and so is not used in this address. The *Essential Norms* point to the idea, in particular law enjoying the *recognitio*, and so that is the language employed here. Along these lines, the position of the Congregation for the Doctrine of the Faith is that "the return of a cleric to public ministry is excluded if such ministry is a danger for minors or a cause of scandal for the community." http://www.vatican.va/roman_curia/congregations/cfaith/documents/rc_con_cfaith_doc_20110503_abuso-minori_en.html

pastoral care of persons who claim to have been sexually abused when they were minors by priests or deacons."

2. *Essential Norms* 6 and 13 rightly speak to the presumption of innocence and the restoration of a good name for unsubstantiated claims against clerics.

3. Particular issues can arise in cases of "unsubstantiated" claims or accusations. If moral certitude cannot be reached, the accused enjoys the benefit of the doubt (*in dubio pro reo*). However, notoriety arising from the accusation and public measures already taken may make it difficult to restore what was lost. Yet more delicate it would be if there are legitimate reasons apart from the unfounded accusation to limit the cleric's ministry, which as noted above is to be done by ordinary administrative measures within the competence of the Ordinary. Of note here is the last sentence of *Essential Norm* 13: "When an accusation has been shown to be unfounded, every step possible will be taken to restore the good name of the person falsely accused." One could argue that there is a nuance between "unfounded" and "falsely accused", with the latter being more fully exonerating (i.e., innocence) and the former being closer to a finding of "unsubstantiated".

4. *Essential Norm* 6 reads that "When there is <u>sufficient evidence that sexual abuse of a minor has occurred</u>, the Congregation for the Doctrine of the Faith shall be notified." For its part, *SST / Norms 2010* do not speak of evidence: "Whenever the Ordinary or Hierarch receives a report of a more grave delict, <u>which has at least the semblance of truth, once the preliminary investigation has been completed</u>, he is to communicate the matter to the Congregation for the Doctrine of the Faith … " (Article 16). This may help to account for the fact that so many *SST / Norms 2010* Article 6 cases arrive at the CDF from the United States with a preliminary investigation which often looks already like a completed administrative penal process. The "semblance of truth" can often be ascertained with facility and little documentation. The question here for CDF purposes is simply credibility: could it reasonably be true?

5. Regarding the imposition of precautionary measures, *Essential Norm* 6 speaks of the obligation to apply precautionary measures following the report of the accusation to the CDF: "The bishop / eparch *shall then apply* the precautionary measures mentioned in *CIC* canon 1722 or *CCEO* canon 1473 … ". In contrast, both *CIC* canon 1722 and *CCEO* canon 1473 speak of what can (*potest*) happen, as does *SST / Norms 2010* Article 19 (*iure imponendi / habet potestatem*). Once again this underlines the desire that the *Essential Norms* go the extra step to assure protection of young people.

6. Precautionary measures cease when the process or cause ceases (*CIC* canon 1722, *CCEO* canon 1473. What if no process eventuates for whatever reason,

whether reasonable or not (e.g., the denunciation is not seriously pursued by the accuser; lack of personnel resources; leadership inertia; likelihood that a process would not lead to a definitive conclusion)? The accused remains in limbo. May this continue indeterminately in light of the *Essential Norms*? Justice would indicate not.

7. One among the most severe yet mercy-oriented canonical norms concerns religious clerics. *CIC* canon 695 (alluded to in *Essential Norms* footnote 1) tells us that religious must be dismissed (*dimitti debet*) from the institute if guilty of sins against the sixth commandment committed with a minor. However (a *nisi* clause), superiors may judge "that dismissal is not absolutely necessary, and that sufficient provision can be made in some other way for the amendment of the member, the restoration of justice, and the reparation of scandal."

8. It can happen that an Ordinary takes a fresh look at a previously treated, decided, or adjudicated case, and may pursue a different finding or penalty, perhaps dismissal from the clerical state. Apart from the risk of double jeopardy (*ne bis in idem*), the cleric involved has only gotten older since his case was taken up the first time. To impose a more severe (or even the most drastic) penalty late in his life – if he is living peacefully – opens a human and perhaps even moral question. On the other hand, if the cleric is not living peaceably but rather is disobedient to imposed measures, this is serious and further penalties may be applied, including of course dismissal. If directly related to risks to minors (with any such risk not being tolerable), this disobedience remains the competence of the Congregation for the Doctrine of the Faith. If the matter concerns other discipline issues, the competence may well rest with another dicastery (e.g., the Congregation for the Clergy or the Congregation for Institutes of Consecrated Life and Societies of Apostolic Life).

9. A problem occasionally encountered concerns unassignable clerics, i.e., clerics who for various reasons largely unrelated to abuse of minors cannot be assigned to public ministry. If there is an alleged offense regarding possible abuse of minors which is prescribed, and its canonical prosecution is not at all promising by any objective measure, it perhaps might well be better for the CDF not to derogate from prescription, thereby leaving canonical action before another dicastery possible (without calling into question the CDF's exclusive competence in *graviora delicta* cases which are canonically actionable). In this way, the resolution is truer (his "unassingability" is larger than the accusation which cannot be pursued in a promising manner, and of which accusation the cleric could well be exonerated) and protects the CDF from overstepping itself in disciplinary matters beyond those directly foreseen in *SST / Norms 2010*. In other words, this practice when appropriate may help the Ordinary from receiving an unhelpful response

from the dicastery less able to assist, leading him toward sounder help with a more defensible result before a dicastery perhaps more able or competent to assist. What has just been said is not meant to soften in any way that in cases so warranting, derogation is granted by the CDF and the case is prosecuted canonically, as justice demands.

### Processes

1. In my opinion, *CIC* canon 1341 is simply exquisite in its content and in its expression. I recall during my licentiate studies, I twice had Velasio DePaolis as an examiner in the oral portion of the Gregorian comprehensive exams concluding each of the two years of the canon law licentiate. Both years he asked me about this canon: *"An ordinary is to take care to initiate a judicial or administrative process to impose or declare penalties only after he has ascertained that fraternal correction or rebuke or other means of pastoral solicitude cannot sufficiently repair the scandal, restore justice, reform the offender."* Fifteen years after the *Essential Norms* and with the public reckoning and thumping (so much of it more than well-deserved) that we continue to live, this canon may seem softly relevant but more so quaint. The tougher line, and perhaps the more healing line, is that justice demands punishment (period), and we get to punishment through penal procedures (period). True victims may have an understandable goal in mind as to what will rest their spirits in terms of punishment. Protection of young persons and restoration of trust are primary. At the same time, and taking nothing away from the prior phrases, if a *CIC* canon 1341 solution is plausible it bears consideration. The *Essential Norms* are approved law. How they interface with *CIC* canon 1341 should remain a point of interest. Raising this point does not, may not in any way chip away at the protection of young persons and those equivalent to them in law, which is paramount – on this point, there is no going back.

2. *CIC* canon 1344 and *CCEO* canon 1409 §1[5] lead us to the principles of weighing punishment already experienced in other *fora*, and an otherwise clean record (rare as that may be). Guilt is guilt, and mercy need not impede justice, but what is one to do with the idea of (possibly) tempering the punishment as implicit in the canons. This does *not* mean that one is reinserted into active public ministry. The *Essential Norms* are law, and if that one act is judged sufficient to keep the cleric from the public exercise of sacred ministry, so be it.

3. One of the thornier questions when weighing proportionality in penalties is found in *Essential Norms* footnote 2: "If there is any doubt whether a specific act qualifies as an external, objectively grave violation, the writings of recognized moral theologians should be consulted and the opinions of recognized experts should be appropriately obtained ... Ultimately, it is the responsibility of the diocesan bishop / eparch, with the advice of a qualified review board, to determine the gravity of the alleged act." This is where diversity among cultures invites flexibility, i.e., what is weighed as grave in one culture might not be in another. With the *Essential Norms*, we are speaking of U.S. culture, with all its internal rich diversity. The criteria on this point ("whether a specific act qualifies as an external, objectively grave violation") have developed over recent years, ever more insistent on a low-bar in favor of the protection of young persons and those equivalent to them

---

[5] *CIC* canon 1344: "Even if the law uses preceptive words, the judge can, according to his own conscience and prudence: 1° defer the imposition of the penalty to a more opportune time if it is foreseen that greater evils will result from an overly hasty punishment of the offender; 2° abstain from imposing a penalty, impose a lighter penalty, or employ a penance if the offender has reformed and repaired the scandal or if the offender has been or, it is foreseen, will be punished sufficiently by civil authority; 3° suspend the obligation of observing an expiatory penalty if it is the first offense of an offender who has lived a praiseworthy life and if the need to repair scandal is not pressing, but in such a way that if the offender commits an offense again within the time determined by the judge, the person is to pay the penalty due for each delict unless in the interim the time for the prescription of a penal action has elapsed for the first delict." *CCEO* canon 1409: "§1. In the application of penal law, even when the law is expressed in preceptive terms, the judge, in accord with his own conscience and prudence, can: 1° defer the imposition of the penalty to a more appropriate time, if it is foreseen that greater harm will ensue from a hasty punishment of the guilty party; 2° abstain from imposing a penalty or impose a lighter penalty if the offender has reformed and reparation of the scandal and harm has been adequately provided, or if the guilty party has been, or it is foreseen, will be sufficiently punished by civil authority; 3° moderate the penalties within equitable limits if the guilty party committed several offenses, and the cumulative burden of the penalties appears excessive; 4° suspend the obligation of observing the penalty in favor of him who has committed an offense for the first time, after having been commended heretofore by an upright life, as long as the need to repair scandal is not pressing. The suspended penalty is lifted entirely if the guilty party has not repeated the offense within the time set by the judge; otherwise such a one shall be more severely punished as the perpetrator of both offenses, unless in the meantime time has run out for initiating a penal action for the prior offense."

in law. In this area, too, there is no going back. Yet the very wording of the footnote rightly and justly notes that there is no one measuring rod or any one definition which will apply equally to all situations. Prudential judgement enters in, to be examined in light of the law at the various procedural levels afforded in law.

4. Every so often a parenthetical phrase is rich. Continuing on this point of proportionality in penalties, let's take another look at *Essential Norm* 8b: "If the penalty of dismissal from the clerical state has not been applied (e.g., for reasons of advanced age or infirmity), ...". With historical cases, the matter of advanced age or infirmity is real. I also am aware of how many accused find themselves in that aged-or-infirm situation without definitive resolution of their cases, perhaps because of the slowness of Rome. We've been doing the best we can, which I realize is small comfort by way of response. Though an extreme case may call for putting it aside, "reasons of advanced age or infirmity" is an opportune phrase sometimes useful. To this end, *Essential Norm* 9's reference to "the executive power of governance" (*id est*, the ordinary exercise of the Ordinary's *potestas* through an administrative act, e.g., warning; penal precept) is a helpful insertion.

5. Staying with *Essential Norm* 8b, we have lived now for a decade and a half with the phrase that one option in *SST / Norms 2010* Article 6 cases is that if not dismissed from the clerical state, "the offender ought to lead a life of prayer and penance." We know that this is not the canonical nomenclature associated with a penalty (which would more likely refer to the permanent removal from the public exercise of all sacred ministry). Experience has demonstrated that vigilance is not easy to guarantee if residential arrangements are not respected. Further, there is the real question of finances and sustaining a cleric (who has offended) for what may even be decades. Also, there is the moral and spiritual question in the case of true perpetrators: if there is no genuine repentance, and prayer is difficult to come by, it may be that the so-called "life of prayer and penance" may be little more than an extended paid absence resembling an open-ended vacation. The predicament is exacerbated if the offender is relatively young.

6. This coming spring (May 2018) will mark the conclusion of the first triennium of the recourse *Collegio* instituted by the Supreme Legislator. This College is an instance of the CDF's Feria IV to judge final recourses in administrative penal *delicta graviora* processes. The Moderator of the body is the dicastery's Prefect, and its current President is former CDF Promoter of Justice Archbishop Charles J. Scicluna. The College's principal focus is the adjudication of impugned CDF decrees issued by the dicastery's *Congresso*, weighing both the decision regarding guilt or not (i.e., the overall merits of the case) and the penalty (i.e., if guilty, the proportionality of the penalty). I

don't think it would be breaking any confidences to say that this *Collegio* is a work in progress.

### POTHOLES AND POTENTIAL POTHOLES

1. The nature of a more grave delict via social media continues under discussion. The 2010 revision of *SST* (*Norms* Article 6, §1) explicitly included and brought to the level of law as *delicta graviora* "the acquisition, possession, or distribution by a cleric of pornographic images of minors under the age of fourteen, for purposes of sexual gratification, by whatever means or using whatever technology". Beyond child pornography (clearly and unambiguously an evil, to say nothing of a crime), what is the proportionate penalty for the offender if there has been no skin-to-skin contact and the material is <u>not</u> graphic? Here I am speaking, by way of example, of leading yet ambiguous text messages sent by a cleric to a minor, or exchanges of fully clothed persons in photographs which may be interpreted as imprudent. Disciplinary measures are warranted, no doubt, as are warnings threatening prompt action against the cleric in the face of continued activity. How explicit must the proposed abuse be before crossing the *graviora delicta* line?

2. The Holy Father has not been shy about revising portions of *CIC* and *CCEO* to serve the greater good as he so judges in the exercise of his Petrine Office. As to what effect a possible *Liber Sextus* revision could have on the *Essential Norms* and *SST / Norms 2010* will make for an interesting phase of the journey we are on, should such a revision be promulgated.

3. *SST / Norms 2010* Article 30, §1 reminds us that "Cases of this nature are subject to the pontifical secret." It is becoming increasingly difficult on all continents to keep the Acts of *SST / Norms 2010* Article 6 cases truly under the pontifical secret, as civil authorities demand access under threat of prosecution. The phrase ("pontifical secret") as phrases go, just sounds bad. By its nature the pontifical secret can be perceived as an operation against proper transparency which contributes to a culture of secrecy. On the other hand, this high level of confidentiality is meant to protect accusers and witnesses as they come forward, and to protect the good names and security of all involved. However practically difficult it may be to maintain proper secrecy in light of vigilance by non-ecclesiastical entities, the moral worth of this confidentiality is clear. The question of "mandated reporting" is a distinct one, as this generally applies "pre-process". On this point, former CDF Prefect Cardinal William Levada wrote clearly in a 3 May 2011 circular letter to episcopal conferences regarding development of *SST / Norms 2010* protocols, on behalf of the dicastery: "Sexual abuse of minors is not just a canonical delict but also a crime prosecuted by civil

law. Although relations with civil authority will differ in various countries, nevertheless it is important to cooperate with such authority within their responsibilities. Specifically, without prejudice to the sacramental internal forum, the prescriptions of civil law regarding the reporting of such crimes to the designated authority should always be followed. This collaboration, moreover, not only concerns cases of abuse committed by clerics, but also those cases which involve religious or lay persons who function in ecclesiastical structures." A distinct question concerns those accusers / victims who wish to speak, but only under promise of firm confidentiality (i.e., those willing to speak in the ecclesiastical forum and only that). The CDF position, however, is clear and unambiguous: "the prescriptions of civil law regarding the reporting of such crimes to the designated authority should always be followed."

4. No mention of potholes or potential potholes in cases concerning sins against the Sixth Commandment committed by clerics against minors would be complete without noting that 2017 has been a year of staff changes internal to the CDF. This has not been easy. We have an excellent staff with fine canonists. The Holy Father has been generous in encouraging us to hire the staff needed, and has assured us of the funding, as long as we can find qualified persons (which can be a challenge). We have particular needs in terms of English mother-tongue. Also, we are reviewing our internal methods for moving cases along in a timely manner, as the question is not only one of staff numbers but also of management systems.

### POSSIBILITIES

1. In the 1990s and following the birth of the *Essential Norms*, we found ourselves in the United States without much praxis-based penal law expertise, yet we were better off than in many parts of the world simply because of the depth of talent in our bench. Looking back, how did this happen: why didn't we train ourselves in penal law? Looking ahead, what aren't we training ourselves for now?

2. The possibility of shifting *Essential Norms* cases from the CDF to another dicastery or tribunal has been rumored at various moments of the current pontificate. It seems that the Holy Father has determined that there will be no imminent change.

3. What would a revision of the *Essential Norms* look like? What would a revision of *SST / Norms 2010* look like? The difficulty is that once the lid is taken off to allow reconsideration of *some* facets, indeed *all* facets can be reconsidered in a way that in the end could result in taking steps backward rather than forward. As noted above, there can be no going backward on

issues concerning the protection of young persons and the prosecution of offenders.

4. If we all had more staff and money and time and creative energy, restorative justice is a theme inviting attention in our work. If the phrase is new to you, google it. I first learned of initiatives in this area through a Jesuit companion, Father Michael Kennedy on the west coast of the United States. As I have looked and followed from a distance the ministry of the Jesuit Restorative Justice Initiative, I have wondered what this could possibly look like in the area of broken relationships covered by the *Essential Norms*. So many of us in this convention hall do our best to adapt, without knowing it, some of the good elements of restorative justice initiatives. I wish more could be done.

5. As we celebrate the centenary of the Pio-Benedictine Code, Book Four's Title 33 (canons 2186-2194) makes for an interesting read. The *onerata conscientia* of that code finds some spiritual and juridical parallel in its 1983 and 1990 successors, but its concrete essence does not carry over, i.e., application of discretionary authority in specific circumstances. Was something lost? It may be argued that if that discretionary authority were better employed a half century ago in handling matters pertaining to what we now know as *Essential Norms – SST / Norms 2010* cases, we'd have been better off for it.

6. The fuller involvement of non-clerics, non-doctorates in penal processes is inevitable and – I strongly believe – necessary. The first reason is practical in that there are not enough clerics and not enough doctorate-bearing canonists to go around. The second reason is moral, in that I truly am a son of what this crisis bore in the United States and so therefore must say that the clerical veil need be further lifted. At the CDF, we currently have only two lay canonists (out of roughly a dozen) who are working directly on *graviora delicta* cases. Both have canon law doctorates. For the time that remains for me in my current position, I encourage expanding that number, especially in light of the case backlog. Again, that's practical. Beyond the practical, I simply think it is healthy to have non-cleric canonists involved in working through these materials (always in accord with the norm of law), as of course this episcopal conference learned already well back in the 90s in some parts of the country. I can also add that when dispensations are requested of the CDF for lay participation in penal cases, the strong tendency is to say "yes" if the person is qualified. This is not new, as it has been the CDF's practice now

for years. Qualified non-clerics working in this material raise credibility, I believe.[6]

7. I'd like my closing slide in this layered romp through various "P" issues to take us to another "P" word: pendulum. Fifteen years ago the pendulum needed to swing, hard. Put baldly, we needed to crack through a prejudice in favor of clerical inability to do wrong, or if wrong was done and known to be done, we needed to work through a system which found *CIC* and *CCEO* sometimes used discreetly (no doubt often unknowingly) as tools available for complicit participation in hindering the search for truth and, based on that, justice. Clerics had all the rights in the face of these accusations; perhaps I overstate, but not by much. That was wrong and remains loudly wrong to this day, and in the office I hold there will be no complicity along those lines. We learned the hard way that "protection" can be a bad word when mixed with clericalism, and the *Essential Norms* and *SST / Norms 2010* revision helped the pendulum to adjust as was woefully needed at that time. Really, let's just say it: they gave the pendulum a huge shove. What does the pendulum need now? I myself don't know, except to say that I'd like it to move center, to not swing more than a few degrees in either direction, and to have *CIC* and *CCEO* as glued-to companions of the *Essential Norms* and *SST / Norms 2010*. The protection of young persons and those equivalent to them in law must always and unambiguously be the point of departure and the point of arrival. Fair application of law follows closely behind.

### Epilogue

Let's undertake a type of discernment now, an examination of conscience.

Returning to the current Supreme Legislator's triptych in his first full day in office, in our *walking*, in our *building*, and in our *professing* the Gospel in its justice and in its mercy, how is Lady Justice doing?

Is blindfolded Lady Justice less ... or more ... a functional image than prior to the *Essential Norms* or *Sacramentorum sanctitatis tutela*? We may think we are coming out the other end (at least in this part of the world) of the worst of *SST / Norms 2010* Article 6 cases, though vigilance asks us to never leave the tunnel. Diminishing numbers of cases nationally must not tempt us to minimize, minimize the import of the issue. Every fresh (i.e., not historical) case reminds us not to think that we have made the Church great again on this issue.

As we look behind us in this tunnel, what do we see?

---

6   Along these lines, the consultative / advisory review boards of *Essential Norms* 4 and 5 are now part of our praxis-DNA. The predominantly lay presence on these boards is key to their proven success.

First, I see (with the occasional sleepless night) the utter devastation of lives: whether called accusers or presumed victims or victims or survivors; whether called accused or offenders or perpetrators or a "good man who never could have done that". These latter are real abusers who did real, horrible damage. Further, I see damage to ecclesiastical authority morally (which is now being rebuilt, which is so encouraging and must continue to be encouraged). I see damage to particular churches in incalculable ways, and while it's not about the money, the money matters because of how – at least in public perception – it may lessen enthusiasm for financial support in doing what we're good at – e.g., evangelization, charity, education, immigration, health care. Fifteen years ago, strong canonically-relevant action was needed, and *Deo gratias* was taken, on both sides of the ocean, by the USCCB and John Paul II, and their collaborators (most notably then-CDF Prefect Joseph Ratzinger). Strong yet advised action continues to be needed, though we are no longer in 2002. Looking back at these last fifteen years, I see the devastation caused by abusers. This utter devastation cannot be repeated, and inasmuch as the *Essential Norms* assist with that avoidance, they serve.

Second, I see that the politics, the polar and polarizing differences of opinions extraneous to law at the local level and at the highest level, can impede a more pristine pursuit of (1) justice as a realizable goal in general and (2) the well-pondered application of justice in each specific case. This polarization continues even to this day, with victims and victimizers whose true number will never be known.

Third (and here I speak from my current assignment which allows me an international view), I sometimes observe how layers of sin, sickness, narcissism, mendaciousness, and pride may obscure ways forward for caring rightly above all for the true victim who must be heard and whose rights must be vindicated ecclesially, but also for the true offender who must be dealt with by competent Church authority justly and in accord with existing canon law and ecclesiastical norms. Even if perhaps significantly on the decrease, any knowing and intentional hindering of the pursuit of truth and justice in the canonical forum in this area is at least seriously wrong. Because Christ can redeem even this, I know He truly is Lord.

In this maelstrom, how is our blindfolded Lady Justice doing? Her statue is placed at my office door, under the photo of Pope Francis common to our offices. She's a statue so fragile ... whether ceramic or porcelain, I don't know these things. Before leaving Rome to come here, I picked her up to look underneath and was surprised to see that she was actually made in China. But I keep her there because I worry about her – not the statue, although I do hope she never falls, and the occasional visitor who brushes up too closely to her is gently encouraged by me to a few inches distance. Her reality was not made in any country. For our purposes as Catholic Christian canonists, her reality is made in Christ.

As you saw stated differently as presented in the slides, I worry sometimes that we have painted ourselves into a place where the law can't breathe quite as much or as freely as it would or should – so often for explainable reasons, but the law can't breathe if all rights – from the 5 year old to the 95 year old – are not given the attention, patience, advocacy, and voice which arise from the *CIC* canon 208 and *CCEO* canon 11 essence of personal dignity, i.e., the personal dignity of all involved. These in turn more fundamentally arise from natural and acquired rights pertinent to adjudicating guilt and innocence.

The mirror must be an instrument in any assessment, including the one we now discuss. Looking into the mirror of justice and seeing who we are as bearers, what do we see of mercy? How in law have we failed to allow mercy tempering justice in *CIC*, *CCEO*? In the allowed corrections of the *Essential Norms* and *SST* and in the application of tools available, have we made for just space for the reality of how our law can inform the human heart, and how the human heart can inform our law, always in balanced and measured ways?

*Mercy, Justice, and the Law: In the Spirit of the Jubilee Year of Mercy* is the theme of this year's convention. As CDF Promoter of Justice since 2014, this is a daily dilemma for me, in this ministry I enjoy and am so grateful to be called to in various forms already since 1994. Veterans here might share my opinion in looking back, that had the soundly and indisputably useful *Essential Norms* been in place earlier, it would have been so helpful because somewhere along the line common sense got dangerously fogged in those closing decades of the last century, in so many dioceses and religious institutes across this country. As a result, truth was buried in the fog, and justice for true victims was too long denied. The *Essential Norms* were and remain a forceful step forward.

As we seek clarity and light in the dilemmas, we might turn not to Lady Justice but to *Sedes Sapientiae* and in the mirror which this assessment invites, even demands, we turn to *Speculum Iustitiae*.

### Homily, Pope Francis, *Domus Sanctae Martae*
### Mass with a group of clergy sex abuse survivors,
### Monday, 7 July 2014

"Dear brothers and sisters, because we are all members of God's family, we are called to live lives shaped by mercy. The Lord Jesus, our Savior, is the supreme example of this; though innocent, he took our sins upon himself on the cross. To be reconciled is the very essence of our shared identity as followers of Jesus Christ. By turning back to him, accompanied by our most holy Mother, who stood sorrowing at the foot of the cross, let us seek the grace of reconciliation with the entire people of God. The loving intercession of Our Lady of Tender Mercy is an unfailing source of help in the process of our healing."[7]

*To be reconciled is the very essence of our shared identity as followers of Jesus Christ.* What norm could be more essential?

I would hope that 15 years after the *Essential Norms* and *SST*, we can't be but where Pope Francis would want us ... seeking to be reconciled, seeking healing for all of us, and for every person (accused, accuser, friend, relative), every dossier we ever met in this horrid mess, never not loved by Jesus Christ.

We seek healing at the foot of the Cross: with tears of the heart that need to be repaired because the seamless garment needs to be re-sewn as best we can, with tears of the heart that need to be dried even if we do so alone at night with only the back of our hand available. We have been through so much together on this issue, in this country, among ourselves as ministers of justice on behalf of Ordinaries, on behalf of accusers, on behalf of true victims, on behalf those young persons yet untouched and yet unharmed who must remain that way. As canonists, in these 15 years we have gone places in the law where perhaps we'd have rather not gone, and have pushed – or been pushed by – shifting contours in the application of penal law in these tough cases, a pushing which at times has been bruising, or worse. In this, we try to stand proudly together as peers, but not without cost as each has her or his own perspective of the damage and the damaged. We seek healing at the foot of the Cross.

As canonists, we seek truth which on our best days leads to justice. With Francis and his two immediate predecessors, let us also ever push toward healing, as so many in this room do, day in and day out. Let us seek the intercession of Our Lady of Tender Mercy as Francis says. We know that she is an unfailing source, but it is our Lord Jesus Christ who offers the *ultimate* salve as we seek to heal, and to allow the law to heal, and the law to *be* healed.

It is good in God our Lord that we serve as we do. However, I recognize that in the area of which I have been speaking, quite specifically, we live with some juridic imperfections in the *Essential Norms* and *SST / Norms 2010*. Still, the

---

7   *Hermanos y hermanas, siendo todos miembros de la Familia de Dios, estamos llamados a entrar en la dinámica de la misericordia. El Señor Jesús nuestro salvador es el ejemplo supremo, el inocente que tomó nuestros pecados en la Cruz; reconciliarnos es la esencia misma de nuestra identidad común como seguidores de Jesucristo. Volviéndonos a El, acompañados de nuestra Madre Santísima a los pies de la Cruz, buscamos la gracia de la reconciliación con todo el Pueblo de Dios. La suave intercesión de nuestra Señora de la Tierna Misericordia es una fuente inagotable de ayuda en nuestro viaje de sanación.* http://w2.vatican.va/content/francesco/en/homilies/2014/documents/papa-francesco_20140707_omelia-vittime-abusi.html

system has worked and is working, and we will continue to make it work. With the system we have, we need to help the law heal and be implemented beyond extraneous pressures ... from the local to the highest level ... which pressures may work contrary to what is true, what is just, what is right.

You and I, we are the protectors charged with not allowing truth and justice ... in law ... to be betrayed.

So in your heart, how are we doing with that? In your mind, in your learning, in your love of the law and of our Lord; in your love of accusers and accused; in your love of true, hurting, defiled victims, and of true offenders who are authors of repugnant actions; in your love of those accusers and accused who fabricate for whatever reason, sometimes unknowingly or unintentionally; and, yes, in your love of those falsely or insubstantially accused who can't get their lives fully back, ever: how are we doing as protectors charged with not allowing truth and justice in law to be betrayed?

In this keynote I wish to invoke a chord (I've just been using the word) which brings together the elements of our theme, namely: mercy, justice, and the law. That unifier is love.

This concluding portion of my address you've just heard was long prior composed when I was pleased to see that Pope Francis raised this theme a little over a week ago, as raised yet earlier by Benedict XVI, in his Message for the 16th International Congress of the *Consociatio Internationalis Studio Iuris Canonici Promovendo* in Rome. In a message read by Secretary of State Pietro Parolin on 4 October 2017, the Supreme Legislator was speaking more generally to the centenary of the 1917 Code, as he specifically recalled how "the invitation of Benedict XVI in his *Letter to Seminarians* returns as impelling, valid not just for seminarians but for all the faithful: 'Learn to understand and – dare I say it – to love canon law in its intrinsic necessity and in the forms of its practical application: a society without law would be a society deprived of rights. Law is the condition of love' (18 October 2010). *Nulla est caritas sine iustitia.*"[8]

---

8  *Sotto questo punto di vista, ritorna impellente l'invito di Benedetto XVI nella Lettera ai seminaristi, ma valido per tutti i fedeli: «Imparate anche a comprendere e – oso dire – ad amare il diritto canonico nella sua necessità intrinseca e nelle forme della sua applicazione pratica: una società senza diritto sarebbe una società priva di diritti. Il diritto è condizione dell'amore» (18 ottobre 2010). Nulla est caritas sine iustitia.* https://press.vatican.va/content/salastampa/it/bollettino/pubblico/2017/10/06/0674/01482.html. Pope Francis earlier linked justice with love in number 21 of his bull *Misericordia vultus* (11 April 2015): "God does not deny justice. He rather envelops it and surpasses it with an even greater event in which we experience love as the foundation of true justice." http://w2.vatican.va/content/francesco/en/bulls/documents/papa-francesco_bolla_20150411_misericordiae-vultus.html.

But what about the inverse: let's turn this around. I propose from my deepest self that the setting not be of law being the condition of love, but rather that love be the condition of law.

Mercy, justice, and the law unite under love. Love is the highest, the first, the greatest, the last, and the most enduring. It is the surest source for the healing of which Francis spoke.

May this be a rich convention, on so many important topics – of roundness and of holy provocation – of import in our ministry. *We're all in this together.* Let grace do what grace does. We pray our way forward. Let us walk, let us build, and let us profess, in love of the truth, in love of justice, and in love of the law. As we assist those in need and prosecute those deserving; as we seek to re-establish ecclesiastical and ecclesial credibility, a slow process at which this canon law society and this episcopal conference are exemplary in the effort; as we seek to restore what one can of broken lives of true victims and of true offenders; and as we continue to hope and work that pendulum to where it needs to be, albeit always in motion: I say let love unite mercy, justice, and law.

Let us replace fake love, abusive love, polemical love, defensive love, media love, money love, unreasoned love with the one and only love which Jesus Christ alone can offer.[9] In this mess, He alone supplies. Let love – human love, and the love of Christ – unite mercy, justice, and law.

May the loving intercession of Our Lady of Tender Mercies, as Francis invokes, be an unfailing source of help in the process of our healing ministry of which the *Essential Norms* and *SST* are law.

I greet you and I love you in Christ, and I thank you for your attention.

Let the convention begin.

---

9   Early the same month in which this address was delivered, a wave of adult sexual harassment accusations began in the United States, most notably in the entertainment, journalism, and government industries. My reference here in this series of paired words is entirely unrelated to that (as it only could be given the chronology), yet this secular reality is not without parallel to what we have lived through with *Essential Norms* cases, especially in terms of public reaction and media influence. I hasten to add that one cannot compare sexual harassment accusations in the adult realm to sins against the Sixth Commandment committed by clerics against minors. The latter is of a notably weightier qualitative and quantitative gravity because minors are involved. I merely wish here to extract my language in this sentence from a cultural moment which happened by coincidence to be starting contemporaneously with the delivery of this Keynote Address.

# MAJOR ADDRESS

## MERCY, JUSTICE, AND LAW IN FRANCIS' INTERPRETATION OF VATICAN II
### *Professor Massimo Faggioli*

1. *Introduction*

This invitation to speak about Pope Francis and the law is most welcome because of how important canon lawyers' roles are in the present life of the Church. It is part of a theologian's vocation and profession to talk with canon lawyers. For some time, especially during the post-Vatican II period, canon lawyers have been criticized for not talking to theologians and pastors. However, I believe that something similar could be said about theologians not talking to pastors and canon lawyers – a phenomenon that is part of the growing knowledge fragmentation of ecclesial experiences in the contemporary Church. The pontificate of Francis means a new season of dialogue within the Church; and I welcome this wonderful opportunity to do this during the convention of the Canon Law Society of America.

I would like to open my remarks with a short story: Pope Francis' visit to the Apostolic Penitentiary of March 17, 2017. Before concluding his visit by telling a popular story about the "Madonna of the Tangerines" in southern Italy (the Madonna patron saint of the thieves in that part of Italy) Francis started his address by saying something very typical of his approach to the law in relation to mercy:

> In fact, I have to confess, this Penitentiary is the type of tribunal I really like! Because it is a 'court of mercy', to which we are directed to obtain that indispensable medicine for our soul, which is Divine Mercy![1]

---

[1] Pope Francis during his visit to the Apostolic Penitentiary, March 17, 2017: "In realtà, ve lo confesso, questo della Penitenzieria è il tipo di Tribunale che mi piace davvero! Perché è un 'tribunale della misericordia', al quale ci si rivolge per ottenere quell'indispensabile medicina per la nostra anima che è la Misericordia divina!": https://w2.vatican.va/content/francesco/it/speeches/2017/march/documents/papa-francesco_20170317_corso-foro-interno.html.

This anecdote relates to my lecture, which will not be one on the pontificate of Pope Francis and canon law. This is something that would require a canon lawyer, or a legal scholar, which I am not. Certainly, there are canon lawyers who criticize his approach to the law and legislative technique. For example, the two *motu proprii* of August 15, 2015, *Mitis Iudex Dominus Iesus* and *Mitis et Misericors Iesus,* a lower-ranking kind of canon law amending the Code of Canon Law on marriage law. Instead, my approach will be focused on the analysis of the relationship between Francis' theology in the major documents: *Evangelii Gaudium, Laudato Si',* and *Amoris Laetitia,* his approach to canon law, and the law in general.

This is one of the key issues to understanding Francis' pontificate in the next few decades. However, there is also a short-term relevance of this topic. The relationship between Francis' theology and the law, which will become more important as we approach an important milestone of this pontificate – according to the announcements made by the C9 (Council of nine Cardinals), that is, the reform of the Roman Curia through an apostolic constitution, which reportedly should be published in 2018.

For now, this lecture will focus on Francis' approach to three key notions for his pontificate: *mercy, justice, and law* – from the point of view of Bergoglio's interpretation of Vatican II. In other words, how Vatican II refers to mercy, justice, and law; and what are the trajectories and parameters of Francis' reception for these three pontifical concepts. This will also say something about Francis and the role of the law in his ecclesiology.

2. *Mercy in Vatican II and in Francis*

"Mercy" (*misericordia*) is the most important key word to understanding Francis' pontificate. During the first Angelus prayer of his pontificate, on Sunday March 17, 2013, the newly elected pope from Argentina mentioned the book that Cardinal Walter Kasper gave him as a present during the conclave, *Mercy,* which had just been published in Italian.[2] Kasper's book is a very interesting one because, among other things, it begins by pointing out the silence of Catholic systematic, theological reflection on mercy. This silence is partially and indirectly improved at Vatican II, according to Kasper, with the famous passage in the pastoral constitution *Gaudium et spes* at paragraph 22: "Christ's goal of human history, focal point of longings of history and of civilization."

It is fair to say from the outset that mercy is not a particularly evident focus in the debate and teaching of Vatican II *per se*. However, we find *misericordia*

---

2   See Walter Kasper, *Mercy. The Essence of the Gospel and the Key to Christian Life.* Transl. William Madges (New York: Mahwah NJ, 2014). Italian edition: *Misericordia. Concetto fondamentale del vangelo – Chiave della vita cristiana* (Brescia: Queriniana, 2013).

in interesting passages of the conciliar corpus. The mention of *"misericordia Dei"* in *Lumen gentium* 11 (the chapter on "the people of God" as well as the sacraments); in *Lumen gentium* 40 on the "universal call to holiness;" in *Nostra Aetate* 4 on Judaism and the relationship between the two Covenants, as well as the God of the Old Testament being already a God of mercy. In *Apostolicam Actuositatem* 8 there is a passage about "mercy for the needy and the sick" (wherein the English translation on the Vatican website says "pity" and not "mercy"), and similarly in *Apostolicam Actuositatem* 19 and 31 on the works of charity and mercy.

The pastoral constitution, *Gaudium et spes* mentions mercy in terms of *"opera in servitium omnium"* ("works at the service of all") according to the goal to "structure and consolidate the human community according to the divine law." The decree on the pastoral ministry of the bishops *Christus Dominus* at par. 16 talks about "active mercy [with which] bishops should pursue priests who are involved in any danger or who have failed in certain respects."[3]

For Francis, mercy's role expands significantly from the treatment received at Vatican II. Firstly, a key, necessary element towards understanding the Pontificate is that Francis' reception of Vatican II is *not* based on the final documents only, but on a broader understanding of the "Documents of Vatican II," which pertains to the theological reception of the entire conciliar event. In two important passages, the exhortation, *Evangelii Gaudium*, at paragraphs 41 and 84, Francis quotes from St. John XXIII's opening speech of Vatican II, *Gaudet Mater Ecclesia*, of October 11, 1962. This speech gave a new direction to the council agenda, as well as thanks, wherein the Pope talks about the Church and modern world errors:

> Often errors vanish as quickly as they arise, like fog before the sun. The Church has always opposed these errors. Frequently she has condemned them with the greatest severity. Nowadays however, the Spouse of Christ prefers to make use of the medicine of mercy rather than that of severity. She considers that she meets the needs of the present day by demonstrating the validity of her teaching rather than by condemnations.[4]

*Gaudet Mater Ecclesia* is one of Francis' favorite Vatican II passages. Interestingly, it is not from one of the sixteen final council documents, but rather from the document that hermeneutically and historically represents the first step in understanding the Vatican II institution. It is also a passage that plays a key

---

3   See also: "Mater Jesu" in *Lumen gentium* 58; "Pater misericordiae" in *Lumen gentium* 56 and *Presbyterorum Ordinis* 18; "Viscera misericordiae" in *Lumen gentium* 40.
4   For the complete text of John XXIII's opening speech, "Gaudet Mater Ecclesia," see *The Documents of Vatican II*, ed. Walter M. Abbott (London: Chapman, 1966), 710-719.

role, once again, in the recent speech given on October 11, 2017 for the 25th anniversary of the *Catechism of the Catholic Church*, where observers find very powerful statements about the need for the Church to change the passages of the *Catechism* addressing the death penalty.[5]

Francis' use of the texts of Vatican II is more cautious and less abundant, compared to St. John Paul II especially. It is typical of this pontificate that Francis does not make a strictly textual case when he mentions Vatican II, even though there is a patterned manner in the way he approaches the Vatican II documents.[6]

On the other hand, there is a connection between the way Francis uses the term "mercy" in his major documents and the theology of Vatican II. In *Evangelii Gaudium*, Pope Francis mentions mercy 30 times to describe the Church as "a community that has an endless desire to show mercy, the fruit of its own experience of the power of the Father's infinite mercy" (*EG* 24); also quoting Thomas Aquinas (*Summa*, II-II) saying that "as far as external works are concerned, mercy is the greatest of all the virtues" (EG 37) about mercy as a gift of God (*EG* 112).

More directly related to the theology of Vatican II there are other passages, with a special ecclesiological focus, in terms of the priorities of the Church: for instance, "The Church must be a place of mercy freely given, where everyone can feel welcomed, loved, forgiven and encouraged to live the good life of the Gospel" (*EG* 114). *Evangelii Gaudium* talks often about the inclusiveness of the Church and a preferential option: "The Church has realized that the need to heed this plea is itself born of the liberating action of grace within each of us, and thus it is not a question of a mission reserved only to a few;" also "The Church, guided by the Gospel of mercy and by love for mankind, hears the cry for justice and intends to respond to it with all her might" (*EG* 188).[7]

Francis' Church is a poor Church and a Church for the poor, where mercy (much more than *justice*) is the gate for this ecclesiological change: "We

---

5  That was not the first time Francis addressed the issue of the death penalty. He had done already in his speech to the delegates of the International Association of Penal Law, on October 23, 2014, when he talked about the death penalty and Church teaching in the context of what he called a culture of "incitement to revenge and penal populism": https://w2.vatican.va/content/francesco/en/speeches/2014/october/documents/papa-francesco_20141023_associazione-internazionale-diritto-penale.html.

6  See Massimo Faggioli, "'Evangelii Gaudium' as an Act of Reception of Vatican II," in *Pope Francis and the Future of Catholicism: Evangelii Gaudium and the Papal Agenda*, ed. Gerard Mannion (Cambridge UK: Cambridge University Press, 2017), pp. 38-54.

7  Interestingly, the quotation in *EG* 188 is from the 1984 instruction of the Congregation for the Doctrine of the Faith "On Certain Aspects of the 'Theology of Liberation", *Libertatis Nuntius*, August 6, 1984, http://www.vatican.va/roman_curia/congregations/cfaith/documents/rc_con_cfaith_doc_19840806_theology-liberation_en.html.

incarnate the duty of hearing the cry of the poor when we are deeply moved by the suffering of others. Let us listen to what God's word teaches us about mercy, and allow that word to resound in the life of the Church. The Gospel tells us: 'Blessed are the merciful, because they shall obtain mercy' (*Mt* 5:7)" (*EG* 193).

Mercy is part of the non-ideological way for Francis to make an ecclesiological case for Church change: in *EG* 198 he writes that "for the Church, the option for the poor is primarily a theological category rather than a cultural, sociological, political or philosophical one. God shows the poor 'his first mercy'." (*EG* 198).

In *Amoris Laetitia*, the use of "mercy" follows an ecclesiological emphasis that is similar to the first exhortation of Francis. In the exhortation on love in the family, "mercy" is used 34 times, and its use is topical especially in chapter 8 entitled "Accompanying, Discerning, and Integrating weakness." In *AL* 296 Francis writes: "The Church's way, from the time of the Council of Jerusalem, has always been the way of Jesus, the way of mercy and reinstatement...The way of the Church is not to condemn anyone forever" (*AL* 296). Immediately after, in *AL* 297, Francis talks about mercy and the life of "Logic of the Gospel:"

> It is a matter of reaching out to everyone, of needing to help each person find his or her proper way of participating in the ecclesial community and thus to experience being touched by an 'unmerited, unconditional and gratuitous' mercy. No one can be condemned forever, because that is not the logic of the Gospel! Here I am not speaking only of the divorced and remarried, but of everyone, in whatever situation they find themselves. Naturally, if someone flaunts an objective sin as if it were part of the Christian ideal, or wants to impose something other than what the Church teaches, he or she can in no way presume to teach or preach to others; this is a case of something which separates from the community (cf. *Mt* 18:17). Such a person needs to listen once more to the Gospel message and its call to conversion.

In *Amoris Laetitia*, Francis reminds us that mercy is a call for *all* Church members: "Mercy is not only the working of the Father; it becomes a criterion for knowing who his true children are. In a word, we are called to show mercy because mercy was first shown to us" (*AL* 310). Francis' use of mercy is consistent with Vatican II's because it is rooted intentionally and explicitly in the Gospel message. Francis reenacts the turn to Jesus Christ as operated by the theology of Vatican II – something German-French Jesuit Christoph Theobald has recently called the "generative grammar" of Vatican II.[8]

---

8    About this, see Christoph Theobald, *Le Concile Vatican II. Quel avenir?* (Paris: Cerf, 2015) 159-180.

3. *Justice in Vatican II and in Francis*

Compared to mercy, the use of the term "justice" is less typical of Francis' vocabulary. Interesting to note, the difference between the background intellectual and socio-political is the use of "justice" at Vatican II and Pope Francis' usage.

*"Ius"* and *"iustitia"* are terms used very frequently in Vatican II, which is a rediscovering moment by the Catholic Church of the sensible concept of "right" and "rights:" especially in the constitution *Gaudium et spes*; in the decree on the pastoral ministry of the bishops *Christus Dominus*; and in the declaration on religious liberty *Dignitatis Humanae*. For Vatican II, it is one method towards ending the theological paradigm of political anti-liberalism, which is typical of the "long nineteenth century" reign of Catholicism between the French Revolution and World War II.[9]

There was at Vatican II a newly discovered idea of "rights" with important intra-ecclesial and general ecclesiological consequences, not merely with *"ius fidelium"* in *Lumen gentium* 36-37 and *"ius ad participationem liturgicam"* in *Sacrosanctum Concilium* 14, but with a very visible acquisition of the Vatican II vocabulary about "justice" and "right." There is also *"ius gentium,"* "law of nations," in *Dignitatis Humanae* 6 and *Gaudium et spes* 79, as well as an idea of justice as part of overall human progress: "all that men do to obtain greater justice, wider brotherhood, a more humane disposition of social relationships has greater worth than technical advances" (*GS* 35). There is a link between justice and peace in *Lumen gentium* 36, in *Dignitatis Humanae* 6, and in *Gaudium et spes* 38, 77. There is also a call for secular authorities to "govern in justice" (*"regere in iustitia"*) in *Gaudium et spes* 34.

Notably, there is also a theological understanding of the difference between God's justice and human justice in *Dignitatis Humanae* 11 (*"iustitia Dei superior"*) concerning the paragraph of the declaration on religious liberty explaining the Gospel passage "Render to Caesar the things that are Caesar's and to God the things that are God's" (Matthew 22:21).

There is also an interesting link between *"veritas et iustitia"* in *Christus Dominus* 11 (quoting *Ephesians* 5:9: "until finally all men walk 'in all goodness and justice and truth'"). In *Dignitatis Humanae* 1 there is a passage about the regard of the Church for the relationship between freedom, truth, and justice:

> This demand for freedom in human society chiefly regards the quest for the values proper to the human spirit. It regards, in the first place, the free exercise of religion in society. This

---

[9] About this see John W. O'Malley, *What Happened at Vatican II* (Cambridge, MA: Belknap Press of Harvard University Press, 2008).

Vatican Council takes careful note of these desires in the minds of men. It proposes to declare them to be greatly in accord with truth and justice. To this end, it searches into the sacred tradition and doctrine of the Church-the treasury out of which the Church continually brings forth new things that are in harmony with the things that are old.

In *Gaudium et spes* 55, truth and justice are part of the birth of a "new humanism:"

Throughout the whole world there is a mounting increase in the sense of autonomy as well as of responsibility. This is of paramount importance for the spiritual and moral maturity of the human race. This becomes clearer if we consider the unification of the world and the duty which is imposed upon us, that we build a better world based upon truth and justice. Thus we are witnesses of the birth of a new humanism, one in which man is defined first of all by this responsibility to his brothers and to history.

Vatican II talks also about *"veritatis iustitia,"* "justice of truth." In *Ad Gentes* 21 there is a link between mission, justice and holiness: "Their main duty, whether they are men or women, is the witness which they are bound to bear to Christ by their life and works in the home, in their social milieu, and in their own professional circle. In them, there must appear the new man created according to God in justice and holiness of truth (Eph. 4:24) [*novus homo qui secundum Deum creatus est in iustitia et sanctitate veritatis*]."[10]

In the corpus of Vatican II there seems to be no discernable tension between *ius, iustitia,* and *misericordia*: this can be interpreted as part of the council's attempt to give credit to the earthly realities, as well as to the Church's witness for the progress of justice in this world. In *Gaudium et spes* the idea of "justice" is articulated in terms of social, economic, and international justice looking at the possible applicability of Catholic social doctrine to the political realm. It is part of the positive view of Vatican II on the world - positive in the sense of a still limited awareness of the complex relationship and tensions between the law, the Gospel, and the world.

There is a difference between Vatican II and Francis' use of "justice" and "right." In this pontificate, the occurrence of "justice" and "right" is in the

---

10  The English translation on the Vatican website says "true holiness". A similar passage about "the new man" (in the non-inclusive translation of the Vatican website) in *Gravissimum Educationis* 2: "the new man created in justice and holiness of truth (Eph. 4:22-24)".

context of a prophetic denunciation of the existing order and of the social-political consensus. In *Evangelii Gaudium* Francis connects justice to the concrete application of other values. At paragraph 54, he talks about "justice and inclusiveness in the world." At paragraph 180, Francis explains the Gospel announcing a Kingdom of justice: "The Gospel is about the kingdom of God (cf. *Lk* 4:43); it is about loving God who reigns in our world. To the extent that he reigns within us, the life of society will be a setting for universal fraternity, justice, peace and dignity."

There is in Francis a more visible distinctiveness of the Church in the world today and this distinctiveness is also about justice. In *Evangelii Gaudium* 183, Francis articulates his vision of the relationship between Church and politics to the ordering of society: "If indeed the just ordering of society and of the state is a central responsibility of politics," then the Church cannot and must not remain on the sidelines in the fight for justice" (here quoting Benedict XVI's encyclical *Deus Caritas Est*). In *Evangelii Gaudium* the Church's role in the fight for social justice is a recurring theme (paragraphs 184, 194, 201, 204, 219, 221).

Francis keeps the focus on the socio-political realities and their impact on family and marriage in *Amoris Laetitia*, where a series of tensions is visible: a tension between love and justice (paragraph 102: "love can transcend and overflow the demands of justice"); between truth and justice (paragraph 311: "It is true, for example, that mercy does not exclude justice and truth, but first and foremost we have to say that mercy is the fullness of justice and the most radiant manifestation of God's truth"); and between culture and the Christian embodiment of the love command in terms of a fight for justice (paragraph 183: "this love [in the family] is called to bind the wounds of the outcast, to foster a culture of encounter and to fight for justice").

4. *Law in Vatican II and in Francis*

The use of law by Vatican II must be understood in the context of the decision of the council to postpone many issues to the post-conciliar Code, which would be promulgated in 1983 after the failed attempt, in the early 1970s, to approve a *Lex Ecclesiae Fundamentalis*.[11] This decision – which in part reflected John XXIII's announcement of January 25, 1959, but more importantly reflected the strategy of the Roman Curia to defend the status quo – had a significant impact on the concept of law elaborated at Vatican II.

The use of law, *lex* by Vatican II, is mostly in terms of law of the Church: fifteen times between "*lex ecclesiastica*" (*Lumen Gentium* 24, 27, 45; *Orientalium Ecclesiarum* 21; *CD* 44; *Perfectae Caritatis* 4; *Optatam Totius* 1, 10;

---

11  See Daniel Cenalmor Palanca, *La ley fundamental de la iglesia. Historia y análisis de un proyecto legislative* (Pamplona: EUNSA, 1991).

*Presbyterorum ordinis* 16, 17, 21) and "*lex ecclesiae*" (*Sacrosanctum Concilium* 13, *Lumen gentium* 26, *Christus Dominus* 8; "*lex canonica*" in *Lumen gentium* 45). There is also an abundant use of "*lex civilis*" (*Inter Mirifica* 12; *Christus Dominus* 12,19; *Apostolicam Actuositatem* 14; *Dignitatis Humanae* 6,13; GS 7, 53, 79). Despite the assumptions of an anti-legalistic sentiment of Vatican II, much more scarce is the use of "*lex conscientiae*" (only once, but in a very important and famous passage in *Gaudium et spes* 16). Other uses of *lex* are more indicative of the trajectories of Vatican II: "*lex caritatis*" (*Presbyterorum Ordinis* 6), "*lex evangelica*" (*Gaudium et spes* 74), "*lex evangelizationis*" (*Gaudium et spes* 44) and "*lex oeconomiae christianae*" (*Gaudium et spes* 41).

It is undeniable that there is something distinctive in the sources of Francis' thought, and especially the encounter between the Gospel and human experience – an experience that is considered by the Church.

One of the most frequent ways for Francis to use "law" in his texts (especially in his homilies during the Mass he celebrates at Santa Marta every morning) is the contraposition between the Gospel of Jesus and the "doctors of the law" – in a way that sometimes becomes stereotypical and unfortunate about the law (and especially in his referring to the Pharisees). This is something we see not only in the colloquial language of Francis, but in his formal teachings as well: law versus reality and law versus grace.

Quoting the final document of the Aparecida Conference of the Latin American episcopates in 2007, in *Evangelii Gaudium* 10 Francis talks about the "law of reality."[12] Law is used to give an idea of the need of rebalancing the language of the Church:

> First, it needs to be said that in preaching the Gospel a fitting sense of proportion has to be maintained. This would be seen in the frequency with which certain themes are brought up and in the emphasis given to them in preaching. [...] The same thing happens when we speak more about law than about grace, more about the Church than about Christ, more about the Pope than about God's word (*EG* 38).

In *Evangelii Gaudium* there is a conversion between law and love, like at paragraph 101: "Let us ask the Lord to help us understand the law of love. How good it is to have this law!". Francis frames this in Pauline terms in *Evangelii Gaudium* 161: "'The one who loves his neighbour has fulfilled the whole law... therefore the love of neighbour is the fulfilling of the law' [*Rom* 13:8, 10]".

---

12 "Here we discover a profound law of reality: that life is attained and matures in the measure that it is offered up in order to give life to others. This is certainly what mission means:" *Evangelii Gaudium* 10.

More prominent, for obvious reasons given the focus on family and marriage, is the role of the law in the exhortation *Amoris Laetitia*, especially for the implications for canon law. *Amoris Laetitia* 295 talks about the law in biblical terms, as a gift: "For the law is itself a gift of God which points out the way, a gift for everyone without exception; it can be followed with the help of grace". *Amoris Laetitia* acknowledges the tension and the gap between law and discernment, especially at paragraph 304: "It is reductive simply to consider whether or not an individual's actions correspond to a general law or rule, because that is not enough to discern and ensure full fidelity to God in the concrete life of a human being."

Interestingly, in the text of *Amoris Laetitia,* law is mostly "God's law," much less "natural law," and even less in terms of "canon law" – as it is typical of a document meant to be pastoral and reaching the lay faithful.

As part of the hermeneutical context for the interpretation of *Amoris Laetitia*, it is necessary to recall briefly the speech of October 24, 2015 for the conclusion of the Synod on the family. The second half of the speech opens with a paragraph that synthesizes Francis' view of the relationship between law and mercy:

> The Synod experience also made us better realize that the true defenders of doctrine are not those who uphold its letter, but its spirit; not ideas but people; not formulae but the gratuitousness of God's love and forgiveness. This is in no way to detract from the importance of formulae – they are necessary – or from the importance of laws and divine commandments, but rather to exalt the greatness of the true God, who does not treat us according to our merits or even according to our works but *solely* according to the boundless generosity of his Mercy (cf. *Rom* 3:21-30; *Ps* 129; *Lk* 11:47-54). It does have to do with overcoming the recurring temptations of the elder brother (cf. *Lk* 15:25-32) and the jealous labourers (cf. *Mt* 20:1-16). Indeed, it means upholding all the more the laws and commandments which were made for man and not vice versa (cf. *Mk* 2:27).[13]

## 5. *Francis' use of Vatican II and the law*

From this brief comparative analysis of the use of the three concepts of mercy, justice, and law in Vatican II and in Francis' major documents, I will now try to draw some conclusions about Francis' use of Vatican II and the law and what this says about this pontificate.

---

13  Pope Francis, speech for the conclusion of the Bishops' Synod, October 24, 2015 http://w2.vatican.va/content/francesco/en/speeches/2015/october/documents/papa-francesco_20151024_sinodo-conclusione-lavori.html.

## 5.1. *Crisis of metaphysics-based theology and the law: mercy and transcendence*

Francis' emphasis on mercy is not just a new concept on the role of Christians and of the Church in society. It is also a further step of the Catholic magisterium in the rebalancing of Catholic grammar and vocabulary towards a presentation of the faith that is less "propositional," and more "sacramental" and "testimonial." The four principles articulated in *Evangelii Gaudium* 222-237 ("time is greater than space; unity prevails over conflict; realities are more important than ideas; the whole is greater than the part") represent a different philosophical framework from the recent past of the Catholic magisterium. The emphasis on mercy shifts the burden of Christian viability from an intellectual argument to a more transcendental, or spiritual one, but always firmly rooted in a reality assumed in its concrete, existential dimension.

This has significant consequences on the kind of Catholic approach to the law issue. Francis' approach is much more based on a Christological focus that is traditionally used in a way that is not afraid of being critical. In this sense, Francis quotes, *Dei Verbum*, especially in its chapter II about revelation and tradition.[14] Francis' approach to the role of the law is much less based on natural law, reason, and tradition. It is not a coincidence that this aspect of Francis' pontificate meets resistance, especially from some Catholic intellectual and clerical circles in the United States where the sense of the tradition is shaped in a particular way (more often than in other Catholic Churches around the world) by a lack of historical consciousness and confidence on the law's literal application.

### 5.1.1. *Francis as an example of post-Vatican II theology*

Francis' approach to the law casts a light on his usage of revelatory sources and Catholic theological work. It is not that Vatican II is more important than canon law, the Catechism, or Catholic tradition, nor merely a primacy of spiritual discernment on religious law. Rather, each is read considering an understanding of the whole Catholic theological and magisterial tradition that extended from Vatican II. For Francis, *ressourcement* does not merely apply to the ancient and medieval Christian sources, but to the Gospel of Jesus Christ, as well. This has drastic consequences for his usage and understanding of the law.

Traditional theology's key role as contained in the second chapter of *Dei Verbum*, and especially paragraph 8 in this regard, was evident in his October 11, 2017 speech for the 25th anniversary of the *Catechism of the Catholic Church*. It

---

14 About this see Joseph Ratzinger, "Dogmatic Constitution on Divine Revelation," in *Commentary on the Documents of Vatican II*, ed. Herbert Vorgrimler, vol. III (New York: Herder and Herder, 1969) pp. 155-198.

detailed the importance for the need to change the Catechism in certain passages about the death penalty, and along the lines of Francis' thinking.[15]

### 5.1.2. *Church, law, and globalization*

Francis, in some sense, departs from Vatican II with his take on the relationship between the Gospel, the Church, and the law that is more naively aware of the "optimistic" and positivistic equation between law and justice. In this perception, which does not merely apply to Francis but across the universal Catholic Church today, the new global system of socio-economic relations is equally merciful and just as it was at the time of the council.

At the time of Vatican II, there was apparently less need for a Church focused on mercy and its political consequences. The focus of Vatican II was rather about rejecting Catholic integralism and "Christian totalitarianism," and leaving behind the historical-political model of medieval Christendom. In the words of Walter Kasper, "[Vatican II] advocated the legitimate autonomy of politics as well as the autonomy of all other secular matters belonging to the sphere of culture".[16] Now, more than fifty years after the end of Vatican II, Francis' approach to the shortcomings of the law are part of a different perception of "the world of this time" – different from Vatican II and *Gaudium et spes*. There is no nostalgia of Christendom, and no idealization about the world of today, especially seen with the eyes of the poor and marginalized. The eyes of the marginalized in today's world are the eyes with which Francis looks at the law – both the ecclesial law, and civil or secular law.[17]

### 5.1.3. *Francis and Vatican II as "western liberal consensus"*

Francis' approach to the law challenges the idea that Vatican II can be easily interpreted as the "liberal" turn of Catholicism. Francis has proven that every counter-narrative about Vatican II (as in the beginning of the decay of Catholicism and of Western civilization because of the embrace of Vatican II for the "western liberal consensus"[18]) is a narrative that can proceed only from a Western and North-Atlantic political perspective; and one that makes limited sense historically and theologically for global Catholicism.

---

15 Pope Francis, speech to the participants of the meeting organized by the Pontifical Council for Promoting the New Evangelization, October 11, 2017 http://en.radiovaticana.va/news/2017/10/11/pope_francis_the_dynamic_word_of_god_cannot_be_mothballed/1342352.
16 Walter Kasper, *Mercy*, p. 187.
17 About this, see Massimo Faggioli, *Catholicism and Citizenship. Political Cultures of the Church in the 21st Century* (Collegeville: Liturgical Press, 2017).
18 See here the famous thesis by Richard John Neuhaus, *The Catholic Moment* (San Francisco: Harper and Row, 1987) 37-69.

This turn must be seen together with Francis' "meta-doctrinal shift" (the primacy of pastoral) as the most important theological shift of Vatican II. "The pastorality that marks Vatican II can be defined as the art of giving men and women access to the one source of the Gospel message."[19] In the post-modern world, our contemporaries must face a variety of sources, as was stated in his 2013 interview with Antonio Spadaro, SJ, in *Civiltà Cattolica*:

> Vatican II was a re-reading of the Gospel in light of contemporary culture [...] Vatican II produced a renewal movement that simply comes from the same Gospel. Its fruits are enormous. Just recall the liturgy. The work of liturgical reform has been a service to the people as a re-reading of the Gospel from a concrete historical situation. Yes, there are hermeneutics of continuity and discontinuity, but one thing is clear: the dynamic of reading the Gospel, actualizing its message for today—which was typical of Vatican II—is absolutely irreversible.[20]

There is not only a geographical and geopolitical shift in the magisterial reception and interpretation of Vatican II under Francis, but rather a new relationship between the interpretation of Vatican II and that of the post-Vatican II period. A different geography of the Church implies a different historical interpretation of the recent past, of Vatican II, and especially of the post-Vatican II period, for which there is yet an easily fixable universal narrative, much less an interpretation.

The whole history of the post-conciliar period is interpreted not from the perspective of the myth of medieval Christendom and loss of Christendom to secularization,[21] but from the emancipatory perspective of Catholicism in Latin America, precisely from the appreciative myth of the secular and cosmopolitan that is quite the opposite of the ecclesiastical, institutional-hierarchical interpretation of the post-Vatican II period in the US. If it is true that there is a mission-logical reframing (as in Theobald's French, *recadrage*) from a geographical to a cultural

---

19 Christoph Theobald, *La réception du concile Vatican II. Vol. I: Accéder à la source* (Paris: Cerf, 2009), 697. About this see also Christoph Theobald, *"Dans les traces…" de la constitution "Dei Verbum" du Concile Vatican II. Bible, théologie, et pratiques de lecture* (Paris: Cerf, 2009).
20 Pope Francis, interview with Antonio Spadaro SJ, in *America*, September 19, 2013 https://www.americamagazine.org/faith/2013/09/30/big-heart-open-god-interview-pope-francis (published as a book-length interview as *A Big Heart Open to God: A Conversation with Pope Francis*, New York: Harper Collins, 2013).
21 For the resilience of the myth of medieval Christendom in the 20th century, see the seminal work of Giovanni Miccoli, *Fra mito della cristianità e secolarizzazione. Studi sul rapporto chiesa-società nell'età contemporanea* (Genova: Marietti, 1985).

and relational understanding of the missionary activity of the Church,[22] then for Francis there is also a geographical *recadrage* that is deeply felt at the cultural-economic centers of the world, like in America.

It is necessary to understand the different receptions of Francis' "anti-legalism" in different areas of the world, with significant differences between European and Latin American Catholic episcopates and clergy-- one side filled with large sectors of the American Catholic episcopate and the other side with clergy. These differences largely overlap with the receptive differences of *Amoris Laetitia*. This must do with the law idea, and not just with different theological cultures and traditions.

## 6. Conclusions

Very recently, in his message to the 16th International Congress of Canon Law which took place in Rome, on 6th October 2017, Francis addressed, again, the issue of the law and Church governance – yet another major text of Francis that begins by quoting John XXIII's *Gaudet Mater Ecclesia*. In this speech, Francis linked canon law and Vatican II in a way:

> Collegiality, synodality in Church governance, valorization of the particular Church, responsibility of all lay faithful in the mission of the Church, ecumenism, mercy and proximity as the primary pastoral principle, personal, collective and institutional religious freedom, open and positive secularity, the ecclesial and civil communities in its various expressions: these are some of the great themes where canon law can also carry out an educational function, facilitating in the Christian

---

22 See Christoph Theobald, "L'exhortation postlude *Evangelii Gaudium*. Esquisse d'une interprétation originale du Concile Vatican II", *Revue Théologique de Louvain*, 46/3 (2015), 328.

people the growth of a shared feeling [in Italian: *sentire*] and of a culture that corresponds to the teachings of Vatican II.[23]

Francis is reserving here an important role for canon law in conversation with theology and magisterium. In some sense, Francis is here much closer, paradoxically, to Benedict XVI than to John Paul II and Paul VI, whose pontificates were much more attentive to the update need and canon law reform.

These few reflections are just a minimal contribution to the debate on Pope Francis' theological reception. This is clearly an important time for the future of Catholic theology. For all one can say about Francis' "anti-legalistic" mentality, there is a new necessary consciousness to make an argument for a more robust presence of theological education in Catholic scholastic institutions. Canon law has an extremely important role to play in the still ongoing theological reception of Vatican II, as well as an awareness of the role of law in the history and life of the Church as a critical part of a corrective sense of the Catholic tradition.

Despite all the appearances of what Francis has said and done, the model Church that Pope Francis has in mind requires a robust presence of canon law in Catholic theological education. Not only because turning Catholicism and Catholic ecclesiology towards a more collegial and synodal Church requires a key contribution from canon law, but rather canon law and specifically the scholarship on the history of canon law has much to say and teach Catholics today about the environment of neo-traditionalism and anti-traditionalism. In this situation of extremes, namely neo-traditionalism versus anti-traditionalism, we cannot underestimate the importance of the intellectual, traditional retrieval of the Catholic Church in canon law.

---

23 Pope Francis, *Message to the XVI International Conference of "Consociatio Internationalis Studio Iuris Canonici Promovendo"*, September 30, 2017: https://w2.vatican.va/content/francesco/it/messages/pont-messages/2017/documents/papa-francesco_20170930_codice-diritto-canico.html. The entire speech is important, and also this passage: "Guardando al secolo che ci separa da quell'atto di promulgazione, non si può negare che il Codice pio-benedettino abbia reso un grande servizio alla Chiesa, nonostante i limiti di ogni opera umana e le distorsioni che, nella teoria e nella pratica, le disposizioni codiciali possono aver conosciuto, ivi compresa qualche tentazione positivistica. In sostanza, la codificazione attrezzò la Chiesa per affrontare la navigazione nelle acque agitate dell'età contemporanea, mantenendo unito e solidale il popolo di Dio e sostenendo il grande sforzo di evangelizzazione, che con l'ultima espansione missionaria ha reso la Chiesa davvero presente in ogni parte del mondo. Da non sottovalutare poi è il ruolo svolto dalla codificazione nella emancipazione dell'istituzione ecclesiastica dal potere secolare, in coerenza col principio evangelico che impone di 'dare a Cesare quel che è di Cesare e a Dio quel che è di Dio' (cfr *Mt* 22,15-22). Sotto questo profilo, il Codice ha avuto un doppio effetto: incrementare e garantire l'autonomia che della Chiesa è propria, e al tempo stesso – indirettamente – contribuire all'affermarsi di una sana laicità negli ordinamenti statali."

# SEMINAR

## WHEN THE TRIBUNAL IS NOT AN OPTION, IS THERE ANOTHER? WHAT HATH FRANCIS WROUGHT?
*Reverend John P. Beal*

I. Introduction

    Christian communities have struggled from the very beginning to know how to accompany their divorced members. Jesus' unqualified and seemingly exceptionless condemnation of divorce[1] so shocked even his disciples that, at least according to the Gospel of Matthew, they responded by throwing up their hand and remonstrating, "If that is the case of a man with his wife, it is better not to marry."[2] Discomfort with Jesus "hard saying" on divorce did not end there. Already in the New Testament we see local churches squirming to find a little "wiggle room" that would allow them to be faithful to Jesus' word but still find room in their communities for at least some of those who had divorced. We may never be certain what the phrase "except in the case of *porneia*" inserted into Jesus' logion by the evangelist we know as Matthew may have meant to his original audience.[3] Nevertheless, it is clear that this phrase that launched a thousand doctoral dissertations was meant to shield some divorced people from Jesus' withering reproach. In a similar way, Paul's response to the question raised by the community in Corinth about a Christian woman unjustly deserted by her still unbelieving husband has been understood as an exception to Jesus' unqualified condemnation of divorce,[4] an exception that has come down to us as the "Pauline Privilege." And the search for "wiggle room" did not end with the close of the New Testament era. Every subsequent generation has struggled to discern how to be, at once, faithful to the teaching of Jesus and merciful to those who have fallen short of his exacting norm.

For most of the last millennium, the Catholic Church of the Christian West has observed a discipline that upholds the principle of Jesus' teaching by refusing

---

[1] See John P. Meier, *A Marginal Jew, Vol 4: Law and Love* (New Haven, CT: Yale University Press, 2009) 74-181.
[2] *Mt* 19: 10.
[3] *Mt* 5: 31-32 and 19: 9. See the discussion in Raymond F. Collins, *Divorce in the New Testament* (Collegeville, MN: Liturgical Press, 1992) 184-213 and the bibliography in Meier, 136-138.
[4] 1 Cor 7: 12-15. See the discussion in Collins, 9-39.

to admit divorced and remarried faithful to Holy Communion. Three principal reasons have been adduced for this exclusion:

> [First] they live in open contradiction to the meaning of the Eucharist as expressing the [faithful and indissoluble] bond between Christ and the Church; [second] admitting them would cause scandal, that is, would lead people to think that the Church was abandoning its teaching on indissolubility; and [third] they are not able to have access to penance, the door for them to the Eucharist, because this requires a firm purpose of amendment. Unless they are willing to separate from their present spouses, or to live without making use of properly marital acts, their purpose of amendment is not sufficient.[5]

However, the traditional discipline has tempered the rigor of this principle by admitting to the sacraments those divorced and remarried faithful whose previous unions have been judged fundamentally flawed from the very beginning and so invalid or have met the fairly narrow criteria for dissolution or, as the traditional canonical language puts it, "dispensation." With the passage of time, both the grounds recognized as giving rise to the nullity of marriages and the criteria under which marriages can be dissolved or dispensed have expanded and the procedures according to which marriages can be declared invalid or dissolved have been simplified and made more "user friendly." As a result, in recent years the number of marriages declared null or dissolved by Church authority have proliferated to the point that critics inside and outside the Church have complained that the mushrooming number of annulments is compromising the Church's witness to the indissolubility of marriage.

Despite the proliferation of declarations of nullity in the last fifty years, there has been a persistent undercurrent of dissatisfaction with the highly juridical (some would say, "legalistic") way in which the Church has been trying to deal with the phenomenon of divorce and suggestions of alternatives to the tribunal process for divorced and remarried faithful who want to return to the sacraments.[6] This dissatisfaction has tended to focus on two rather different situations. On the one hand, some divorced people are convinced that their now broken marriages were invalid but are unable to demonstrate the invalidity, either because they cannot meet the burden of proof required by tribunals or because no tribunals

---

5  James H. Provost, "Intolerable Marriage Situations: A Second Decade," *The Jurist* 50 (1990) 607. This rationale for exclusion is expressed magisterially in John Paul II, apostolic exhortation *Familiaris consortio*, §84, December 15, 1981: *AAS* 74 (1982)184.
6  See the summary of the theological and canonical discussion of these alternative approaches in James H. Provost, "Intolerable Marriage Situations Revisited," *The Jurist* 40 (1980) 141-196; Id., "Intolerable Marriage Situations: A Second Decade," *The Jurist* 50 (1990) 573-612; and John P. Beal, "Intolerable Marriage Situations Revisited: Continuing the Legacy of James H. Provost," *The Jurist* 63 (2003) 253-311.

are available. Such people find themselves is what has been called "the conflict situation," that is, there is a conflict between what they know in their hearts and what they can demonstrate in the Church's external forum. On the other hand, some divorced people have no basis for claiming or even thinking that their prior marriages were invalid but find being barred from the reception of the sacraments because of their current canonically irregular unions a real hardship. Such people find themselves in what has been termed "the hardship situation."

## II. Alternative Scenarios

### A. *"Internal forum" solutions: a misnomer*

Canonists and theologians have proposed ways to resolve both the "conflict" and the "hardship" situations. These approaches have often been lumped together under the rubric of "internal forum solutions." This characterization is unfortunate. Such promiscuous usage suggests that there is a well-defined understanding of what the phrase "internal forum solution" entails that is widely shared by scholars and other knowledgeable people, part of the arcane lore that is vouchsafed to cognoscenti but withheld from the masses. In fact, the phrase is a technical and canonical sounding term for which there is no generally accepted technical meaning in canon law. Misunderstanding and confusion stem from the fact that the phrase "internal forum" is understood quite differently by moral theologians and canon lawyers. For moralists, the terms "internal forum" and "forum of conscience" are essentially interchangeable. The internal forum signifies "a *subjective judgment* concerning the morality of an act or even conscience itself as the place where this subjective judgment is exercised." Thus, forum of conscience "means simply the moral relation of the soul to God."[7] As Anthony Kosnik explained in a paper for a CLSA symposium on alternatives to the marriage tribunal in 1978:

> The characteristic of the internal forum is that it is directed primarily, although not exclusively, to the immediate welfare of the individual person. The medium which it employs to reflect this concern and render its judgments is that of personal conscience. Its decisions are expected to take into account all the particularities and uniqueness involved in concrete situations. Its role is to provide a practical response to the

---

[7] Urban Navarette, "Conflictus inter forum internum et externum in matrimonio," in *Investigationes Theologico-Canonicae* (Rome: Gregorian University Press, 1978) 334. Emphasis in the original. Navarette was quoting without attribution Antonius Mostaza Rodriguez, "De foro interno iuxta canonistas postridentinos," in *Investigationes Theologico-Canonicae*, 292. Mostaza Rodriguez presented a much more detailed account of the emergence of the distinction between internal and external fora in "Forum internum—forum externum: En torno a la naturaleza juridica del fuero interno," *Revista Española de Derecho Canonico* 24 (1968) 253-331; 339-364.

existential needs that confront an individual in the here and now.[8]

Thus, the internal forum is the sphere not of law but of personal moral decisions made by individuals before God, perhaps, but not necessarily, with the assistance of a confidant like a confessor who does not judge or exercise governance power but serves as a sounding board and offers counsel. Such subjective moral judgments are purported to provide a sufficient basis for responsible action even when they lead to acting in pursuit of one's personal spiritual good in ways that conflict with the general law of the Church.[9] When applied to the situation of the irregularly married, such "internal forum solutions" are said to authorize such people to receive the sacraments of penance and Eucharist as if the general law of the Church did not apply to their cases.

Whatever may be the merits of this understanding of the "internal forum" in moral theology, it is not how canon law understands the phrase. In canon law, the internal forum is "a *secret judgment* on the part of a judge of a public society (the confessor with respect to sins, an ecclesiastical superior with respect to penalties and other juridic bonds), or even the place where this judgment is rendered."[10] Thus, it is not true to say that the external forum is juridic and concerned with external observance while the internal forum is not juridic and touches only on matters of conscience. Rather, actions in both fora always "concerns a relationship to some act of ecclesiastical power [of governance]."[11] Despite the somewhat misleading language of canon 196 of the 1917 Code of Canon Law, canon law does not recognize two types of power of governance,

---

8   Anthony Kosnik, "The Pastoral Care of Those Involved in Canonically Invalid Marriages," *The Jurist* 30 (1970) 32.
9   Ibid., 32-33.
10  Navarette, 334. Emphasis in the original. See also, Francisco Urrutia, "Internal Forum—External Forum: The Criterion of Distinction," in *Vatican II: Assessments and Perspectives Twenty-Five Years After (1962-1987)*, ed. René Latourelle (New York: Paulist Press, 1987) 1: 632-647; Id., "The 'Internal Forum Solution:' Some Comments," *The Jurist* 40 (1980) 128-140; Juan Ignacio Arrieta, "The Internal Forum: Notion and Juridical Origin," *Studia Canonica* 41 (2007) 27-45; Velasio de Paolis, "Natura e funzione del foro interno," in *Investigationes theologico-canonicae* (Rome: Gregorian University Press, 1978) 115-142; René Naz, s.v., "For," in *Dictionnaire de Droit Canonique*, 5: 871-873; Helmut Pree, "Forum externum und forum internum: Zu Sinn und Tragweite der Unterscheidung," in *Gnade und Recht: Beiträge aus Ethik, Moraltheologie und Kirchenrecht*, ed. Stephan Haering, Josef Kandler and Raimund Sagmeister (Frankfurt: Peter Lang, 1999) 497-512; Id., "Forum externum und forum internum: Zur Relevanz des Gewissensurteil im kanonischen Recht," *Archiv für katholisches Kirchenrecht* 168 (1999) 25-50; Id., "Kirchenrecht und Barmherzigkeit—Rechtstheologische und rechtstheoretische Aspekte," Vortrag auf der Tagung "Kirchenrecht und Barmherzigkeit," 15 Juli 2015, www.kath-akademie-bayern.de/aktuelle-mitteilung/itemsBarmherzigkeit_pree%20red%20.pdf..
11  Ibid.

one for the external forum and the other for the internal forum.[12] Rather, the power of governance or jurisdiction exercised in the internal forum is exactly the same power that is exercised in the external forum. Nor is the distinction between the internal forum and the external forum determined by whether the exercise of power of governance is oriented, respectively, to the private good of the individual faithful or to the common good of the Church.[13] The internal and external fora are not distinguished by the matters over which the Church's jurisdiction is exercised so that some matters are the exclusive preserve of one forum or the other. Thus, although sins are usually dealt with and absolved in the internal sacramental forum of penance, they can be, and sometimes are, dealt with in the external forum, either judicially[14] or administratively.[15] What distinguishes the two fora is the manner in which the power of governance is exercised: power of governance is exercised for the external forum in a manner that is overt, public and susceptible to proof; it is exercised for the internal forum in a manner that is hidden, "occult" in the technical sense of that term, and not susceptible to proof   Nevertheless, conflicts between the two fora can sometimes arise. For canon law, these conflicts between the external and the internal fora are not conflicts between the law on one hand and personal conscience on the other but "between two juridical norms within the same legal system."[16] Such conflicts often result when one legal norm is applicable to facts as they are publicly known and knowable and the other to facts that are occult, at last in the sense that they are not known or likely to become known to the community. For this reason, exercises of jurisdiction for the external forum have their effects and are binding for both fora; exercises of jurisdiction for the internal

---

12   Canon 196 of the 1917 CIC stated: "Potestas iurisdictionis seu regiminis, quae ex divina institutione est in Ecclesia, *alia est fori externi, alia fori interni*, seu conscientiae, sive sacramentalis sive extra-sacramentalis." Emphasis added.

13   Carlo Sebastian Berardi, *Commentarium in Jus Ecclesiasticum Universum* (Turin: Ex typographia Regia, extant apud G.D.M Moranum bibliopolum, 1766) 1: 12-13. As a result of these criteria for the distinction between the two fora, Berardi held that administration of the sacraments, public prayer and canonical warnings were activities belonging to the internal forum. This distinction had enough resonance in canonical literature that it was adopted by some commentators on the 1917 Code, most notable Wernz and Vidal. See Francis Xavier Wernz and Peter Vidal, *Ius canonicum* (Rome: Gregorian University, 1928) 2: 357, n. 365: "Jurisdiction *of the external forum* is that which refers primarily and directly to the public good, whether the *common* good of the faithful or that of the Church. . . . Jurisdiction *of the internal forum* (forum of conscience) is that which concerns *primarily* and *directly* the private good of the faithful. It regulates the private relations with God. . ., not the social relations with the Church as a visible society." Emphasis in the original.

14   CIC, canon 1401, 2°: "Ecclesia iure proprio et exclusive cognoscit. . . de violatione legum ecclesiasticarum deque omnibus in quibus inest ratio peccati."

15   CIC, canon 915: "Ad sacram communionem ne admittantur excommunicati et interdicti post irrogationem vel declarationem poenae aliique in manifesto gravi peccati obstinate perseverantes."

16   De Paolis, 140.

forum, however, "are not recognized" for the external forum, unless the law provides otherwise.[17] Thus, an exercise of power of governance for the internal forum cannot authorize the one on whose behalf the power was exercised to act in the external forum. For example, a dispensation from the obligation of observing a matrimonial impediment by a confessor for the internal forum in an occult case frees the penitent to enter marriage validly but, since the fact that the dispensation was granted is not subject to public proof, a conflict between the internal and external fora would result should the existence of the impediment become public. As a result, a new dispensation for the external forum would be necessary.

This limitation on the scope of jurisdiction exercised for the internal forum severely restricts the usefulness of attempts to resolve the dilemma of the divorced and remarried by so-called "internal forum" solutions. Since a person's marital status is generally public, a true "internal forum" approach to an irregular marriage situation could not allow a divorced and remarried person to receive Holy Communion publicly, unless that person's status was, in fact, occult or not known in a particular locale, and only for as long as it remained so. Yet, those who propose generic "internal forum" solutions to irregular marriage situations seem to assume that these approaches can authorize access to the sacraments for their beneficiaries regardless of how well their marital status may be known in the community. Moreover, an "internal forum" solution to any dilemma necessarily entails an exercise of power of governance. A confessor, for example, is authorized to dispense from occult impediments to marriage for the internal forum in situations of danger of death[18] and to dispense from matrimonial impediments in occult cases in situations where everything has been prepared for the wedding and grave harm would result from delaying the celebration.[19] However, the law does not empower confessors or any other ecclesiastical authority to dispense from the obligations of a valid marriage or to declare the invalidity of a marriage for the internal forum.[20]

B. *Approaches to the "conflict situation"*

Despite their rather awkward fit with the canonical understanding of the internal forum, so-called "internal forum solutions" have been proposed to meet the pastoral challenge posed by the divorced and remarried who were caught in the "conflict situation," i.e. certain of the invalidity of their prior union but unable to prove it, and so beyond the tender mercies of the judicial marriage nullity process. Although successive waves of procedural reforms permitting judges to give ever greater probative weight to the confessions and other declarations of the parties themselves and the testimony of even a single witness

---

17  CIC, c. 130.
18  CIC, c. 1079, §3.
19  CIC, c. 1080, §1.
20  Pree, "Forum externum und forum internum," 510, n.41.

have considerably diminished the number of people who fall into the "conflict situation" in North America and parts of Europe, the same cannot be said for much of the rest of the world. In many places, tribunals have long been either non-existent or under-performing and will continue to be non-existent or under-performing for the foreseeable future. Consequently, even the new streamlined marriage nullity procedures will leave thousands, those to whom the late Victor Pospishil referred as "the Damned Millions," with no hope for a return to the sacraments as long as their ex-spouses live.[21]

Traditional canonists of unquestioned orthodoxy have offered an approach to resolving the "conflict situation."[22] According to these authors,

> for "conflict situations," in which it is objectively speaking certain that the prior marriage was invalid but there is no possibility of producing proof of this in the external forum before the tribunal, there is the theoretical possibility of an internal forum solution that meets the requirements of the external forum, even if in practice this possibility remains decidedly hypothetical. It amounts to the consideration that neither the need for proof before the tribunal, nor the need for canonical form for the new union, are binding in the specific case. This is a valid position entailing a reasonable application of canonical fairness, as this is formulated in the classical principle that ecclesiastical legislation does not oblige in the case of disproportionately severe penalties.[23]

Proponents of this sort of "internal forum" solution for the true "conflict situation" hasten to add that this approach is quite theoretical since most members of the faithful and even the confessors who may guide them lack sufficient grasp of the intricacies of the canonical grounds for nullity of marriage to reach certainty about the invalidity of their prior unions.[24] Even when such certitude is reached, perhaps with the counsel of a canonically astute spiritual guide, the "solution" could "be applied only where the fact of the prior union and the fact that its nullity has not been declared are not known by the ecclesial community."[25]

---

21 Victor Pospishil, "Response to the Role of Law Award," *CLSA Proceedings* 56 (1994) 270.
22 Urrutia, "Internal Forum—External Forum," 651-653; Navarette, 339-340; Marcelino Zalba, "Cooperatio materialis ad malum morale," *Periodica* 71 (1982) 437-440.
23 Urrutia, "Internal Forum—External Forum," 652.
24 Navarette, 338-339.
25 Urrutia, "Internal Forum—External Forum," 652.

C. Approaches to the "Hardship Situation"

1. *Three German Bishops in 1993*

Perhaps as a result of the relatively limited utility of this traditional sort of "internal forum" solution, the distinction between the "conflict situation" and the "hardship situation" has gradually disappeared from canonical discussions. Instead, many have pushed for a less juridic approach to irregular marital situations, whether the broken marriages were arguably invalid or not. One of the boldest, or at least the most highly publicized, such initiative was the pastoral plan announced in 1993 by three bishops of the Upper Rhine Province of Germany, Archbishop Oskar Saier of Freiburg, the Bishop Karl Lehman of Mainz and then Bishop Walter Kasper of Rottenburg-Stuttgart. The three bishops affirmed the Church's teaching on the indissolubility of marriage and the prudence of the Church's discipline that divorced and remarried people "generally cannot be admitted to the Eucharistic feast as they find themselves in life situations that are in objective contradiction to the essence of Christian marriage." However, they immediately qualified this acknowledgement with the recognition that the general norms of canon law "cannot regulate all of the very often very complex individual cases." For these very difficult cases, the bishops proposed a structured pastoral dialogue between the divorced-remarried couple and a priest to determine whether the general prohibition on the reception of the sacraments applied to their case. In the course of this pastoral dialogue, certain criteria for re-admission to Holy Communion were judged indispensable:

--When there is serious failure involved in the collapse of the first marriage, responsibility for it must be acknowledged and repented.

--It must be convincingly established that the return to the first partner is really impossible and with the best will the first marriage cannot be restored.

--Restitution must be made for wrongs committed and injuries done insofar as this is possible.

--In the first place this restitution includes fulfillment of obligations to the wife and children of the first marriage. . . .

--Whether or not a partner broke his or her first marriage under great public attention and possibly even scandal should be taken into account.

--The second marital partnership must have proved itself over a long period of time to represent a decisive and publicly recognizable will to live permanently together and also according to the demands of marriage as a moral reality.

--Whether or not fidelity to the second marriage has become a moral obligation with regard to the spouse and children should be examined.

--It ought to be sufficiently clear—though not to any greater extent than with other Christians—that the partners seek truly to live according to the Christian faith and with true motives, i.e., moved by genuinely religious desire, to participate in the sacramental life of the Church. The same holds true of the children's upbringing.[26]

The bishops foresaw that the result of this pastoral dialogue might be that one or both of the partners would reach the conclusion that there was no obstacle to their return to Eucharistic fellowship. If this were the case, the role of the participating priest was not "to pronounce any official admission in the formal sense" but to "respect the judgments of the individual's conscience" and to "defend such a decision of conscience against prejudice and suspicion," while taking "care that the parish does not thereby take offense."[27]

2. The Response of the Holy See

The response of the Holy See to this pastoral initiative was swift and sharp. The three bishops were summoned to meet with the Congregation for the Doctrine of the Faith in February and again in June of 1994. In September of 1994, the Congregation issued a letter to the bishops of the Catholic Church which reaffirmed the traditional discipline of barring the divorced and remarried from the reception of Holy Communion[28] and rejected as "inadmissible" and as inconsistent with the "public reality" of marriage pastoral processes of discernment like those proposed by the three German bishops (without mentioning them by name) since they depend on "the mistaken conviction" that divorced and remarried persons themselves are able, "on the basis of [their] own convictions, to come to a decision about the existence or absence of a previous marriage and the value of the new union" and so to judge their own fitness to approach holy communion.[29] The letter insisted that the divorced and remarried can be admitted to Holy Communion only after the invalidity of the previous marriage has been "discerned with certainty by means of the external forum established by the church."[30]

---

26  Three German Bishops, "Pastoral Ministry: The Divorced and Remarried," *Origins* 23 (March 10, 1994) 674. The complete German version appeared as Bischöfe der Oberrheinischen Kirchenprovinz, "Zur seelsorglichen Begleitung von Menschen aus zerbrochenen Ehen, Geschiedeenen und Wiederverheirateten Geschedienen. Einführung, Hirtenwort und Grundsätze," *Herder-Korrespondenz* 47 (1993) 460-467.
27  Three German Bishops, 675.
28  Congregation for the Doctrine of the Faith, letter "Ad catholicae ecclesiae episcopos de reception communionis eucharisticae a fidelibus qui post divortium novas inierunt nuptias," September 14, 1994: *AAS* 86 (1994) §4.
29  Ibid., §7.
30  Ibid., §9.

This position of the Congregation was reinforced by the 2000 "Declaration" of the Council for Legislative Texts, which held that the divorced and remarried were, without exception, among those "obstinately persisting in manifest grave sin" who were to be barred from the reception of Holy Communion in accord with the norm of canon 915.[31] What was remarkable about both the Congregation's letter and the Council's declaration was not their ringing defense of the general discipline excluding the divorced and remarried from Holy Communion but their insistence that this general norm is exceptionless, save in cases where couples were willing and able to embrace the "brother-sister" situation. By this insistence, they branded as illegitimate the views of "approved authors" of unquestioned orthodoxy who had advocated the legitimacy of admitting to Holy Communion divorced and remarried spouses who were subjectively convinced of the invalidity of their prior marriages but unable to prove this invalidity in a church tribunal.[32] As a result, these two Roman interventions not only squelched the pastoral plan of the three German bishops, but effectively squelched public discussions of non-tribunal solutions of the pastoral problem posed by thousands of divorced and remarried Catholics for over a decade.

III. If at first you don't succeed. . . . .

A. Cardinal Kasper and the 2014 and 2015 Synods

The issue of a path to Holy Communion that did not pass through the marriage tribunal for the divorced and remarried resurfaced in a lecture given by Cardinal Walter Kasper at the request of recently elected Pope Francis to the Extraordinary Consistory of Cardinals on February 20 and 21, 2014. Without explicitly mentioning the pastoral plan he and the other two German bishops had put forward in 1994, Kasper made the case for it or something very much like it. He asked rhetorically:

> Is this path beyond rigorism and laxity, the path of conversion, which issues forth in the sacrament of mercy—the sacrament of penance—also the path that we can follow in this matter? Certainly not in every case. But if a divorced and remarried person is truly sorry that he or she failed in the first marriage, if the commitments from the first marriage are clarified and a return is definitely out of the question, if he or she cannot undo the commitments that were assumed in the second civil marriage without new guilt, if he or she strives to the best of

---

31 Pontifical Council for Legislative Texts, "Dichiarazione," June 24, 2000, *Communicationes* 32 (2000) 159-162. English translation in *Origins* 30 (August 17, 2000) 174-175.
32 See Federico R. Aznar Gil and José R. Flecha Andrés, *Divorciados y eucharistia*, Colleción Relectiones 22 (Salamanca: Universidad Pontificia Salamanca, 1996) 39-72 and James H. Provost, "Internal Forum Marriage: Some Reflections on a Study by Urban Navarrete," in *Magister Canonistarum* (Salamanca: Publicaciones Universidad Pontificia de Salamanca, 1994) 199-217.

> his or her ability to live out the second civil marriage on the basis of faith and to raise the children in the faith, if he or she longs for the sacraments as source of strength in his or her situation, do we then have to refuse or can we refuse him or her the sacraments of penance and communion, after a period of orientation?[33]

Kasper insisted that the "way of penance" he was proposing was not a "general solution" to the problem of the divorced-remarried, but

> a narrow path by arguing that admission to penance and Holy Communion requires "*discretio,* spiritual discrimination, pastoral prudence, and wisdom. . . . Such *discretio* is no cheap compromise between the extremes of rigorism and laxity, but rather—like every virtue—the path of the responsible middle and the right measure.[34]

This lecture to the cardinals gathered in extraordinary consistory soon "went viral" and reignited discussion of "a way of penance" as a possible alternative to the marriage tribunal for the divorced and remarried. As a result, this "way of penance" quickly made its way to the agenda for the extraordinary synod of bishops devoted to "Pastoral Challenges to the Family in the Context of Evangelization" that Pope Francis had already convoked for 2014 and the discussion continued in the ordinary synod of bishops on "The Vocation and Mission of the Family in the Church and in the Contemporary World" that met in 2015.

Discussion of the pastoral care of the divorced and remarried at both Synods—and outside of them-- was intense and heated. In the end, a proposal to recommend to the Holy Father a "way of penance" for divorced and remarried faithful failed to receive the necessary two-thirds vote. As a result, the Synod's Final Report limited itself to saying:

The path of accompaniment and discernment guides the [divorced and remarried] faithful

> to an awareness of their situation before God. Conversation with a priest, in the internal forum, contributes to the formation of a correct judgment on what hinders the possibility of fuller participation in the life of Church and Church practice which can foster it and make it grow. Given that gradualness is not in the law itself (cf. FC 34), this discernment can never prescind

---
33 Walter Kasper, *The Gospel of the Family* (Mahwah, NJ: Paulist Press, 2014) 32.
34 Ibid., 32-33.

from the Gospel demands of truth and charity as proposed by the Church. This occurs when the following conditions are present: humility, discretion and love for the Church and her teaching, in a sincere search for God's will and a desire to make a more perfect response to it.[35]

### B. *Amoris Laetitia*

Pope Francis' post-synodal apostolic exhortation *Amoris Laetitia* of March 19, 2016 picks up where the synodal discussion left off and subtly nudges it forward.[36] After making clear that "not all discussions of doctrinal, moral or pastoral issues need to be settled by interventions of the magisterium,"[37] the Pope invited the Church, clergy and laity alike, to seek ways of addressing the pastoral care of the divorced."[38] The Pope sets the context for this discussion by affirming the traditional Christian vision of marriage.[39] "In order to avoid all misunderstanding," he insists, "in no way must the church desist from proposing the full ideal of marriage, God's plan in all its grandeur."[40] Indeed, "a lukewarm attitude, any kind of relativism or an undue reticence in proposing that ideal would be a lack of fidelity to the Gospel and also of love on the part of the Church,"[41] and "any breach of the marriage bond 'is against the will of God.'"[42] As a result,

> if someone flaunts an objective sin as if it were part of the Christian ideal or wants to impose something other than what the church teaches, he or she can in no way presume to teach or preach to others; this is a case of something that separates from

---

35 Synod of Bishops, XIV Ordinary General Assembly, "The Final Report of the Synod of Bishops to the Holy Father, Pope Francis, October 24, 2015, §86: *Origins* 45 (January 14, 2016) 565.
36 Francis, apostolic exhortation *Amoris Laetitia*, §4, March 19, 2016: English translation in *Origins* 45 (April 21, 2016) 778. This apostolic exhortation had as its stated intention "to gather the contributions of the two recent synods on the family, while adding other considerations as an aid to reflection, dialogue and pastoral practice and as a help and encouragement to families in their daily commitments and challenges."
37 Ibid. §3.
38 Ibid., §291.
39 Francis, *Amoris Laetitia*, §292; 819: Marriage "as a reflection of the union between Christ and his church, [which] is fully realized in the union between a man and a woman who give themselves to each other in a free, faithful and exclusive love, who belong to each other until death, and are open to the transmission of life, and are consecrated by the sacrament that grants them the grace to become a domestic church and a leaven of new life for society."
40 Ibid., §307; 822.
41 Ibid.
42 Ibid., §291; 819.

the community (cf. Mt 18:17). Such a person needs to listen once more to the Gospel message and its call to conversion.[43]

Nevertheless, the Holy Father recognizes "the frailty of many of her children" and the church's responsibility to "accompany with affection and care the weakest of her children. . . , by restoring in them hope and confidence."[44] Although their love may be described as "wounded and troubled" and their situations "irregular," these faithful are not beyond God's mercy. In some cases, their unions may "radically contradict" the Christian ideal, but, in others, they "realize it in at least a partial and analogous way."[45] It is these "constructive elements" in unions that "do not yet or no longer correspond" to the Church's ideal that provide the basis for "a constructive response seeking to transform them into opportunities that can lead to the full reality of marriage and family in conformity with the Gospel"[46] according to what Francis (with a nod to John Paul II) calls "the law of gradualness."[47]

To address the situations of those in irregular situations, and especially those who are divorced and remarried, Francis sets forth a pastoral strategy of accompaniment, discernment and integration. The ultimate aim of this accompaniment is to help those in irregular situations to "understand the divine pedagogy of grace in their lives and offering them assistance so they can reach the fullness of God's plan for them, something that is always possible by the power of the Holy Spirit." When they are truly accompanied on their spiritual journeys by other members of the faithful, including priests and bishops ready to do what good they can "even if in the process [their] shoes get soiled by the mud of the street,"[48] the divorced and remarried cannot just know intellectually but "feel" viscerally that they are "not excommunicated members of the church, but instead [are] living members able to live and grow in the church and experience her as a mother who welcomes them always, who takes care of them with affection and encourages them along the path of life and the Gospel."[49]

Accompaniment inevitably leads to discernment. Like Pope John Paul II, Francis recognizes that the divorced and remarried "can find themselves in a variety of situations that should not be pigeonholed or fit into overly rigid classifications leaving no room for suitable personal and pastoral discernment."[50] The situations of spouses who made every effort to salvage their marriages but

---

43  Ibid., §297; 820.
44  Ibid., §291; 819.
45  Ibid., §292; 819.
46  Ibid., §§292-294; 819.
47  Ibid., §294; 819.
48  Ibid., §308, 822.
49  Ibid., §299; 820. Here Francis is quoting from 2015 Synod of Bishops, Final Report, §84, 564.
50  Ibid., §298; 820.

were unjustly abandoned, for example, are quite different from the situations of those who consistently failed in [their] obligations to the family. While all of these possible scenarios fall short of the Gospel ideal, they demand "an approach that 'carefully discerns situations'" and an awareness that "no 'easy remedies exist.'"[51] Unlike Pope John Paul II, however, Francis does not propose that this variety of situations needs to be addressed by a uniform discipline.[52] This personal and pastoral discernment of individual cases needs to take into account not only the dizzying variety of concrete circumstances in which the divorced and remarried find themselves but also the many complex factors that can diminish or even extinguish a person's imputability or moral responsibility for an irregular situation in which he or she is involved.

> Hence it can no longer simply be said that those in any "irregular" situation are living in a state of mortal sin and are deprived of sanctifying grace. More is involved here than mere ignorance of the rule. A subject may know full well the rule, yet have great difficulty in understanding "its inherent values" or be in a concrete situation that does not allow him or her to act differently and decide otherwise without further sin.[53]

Since situations are so diverse and complex, the faithful and their pastors need to engage in a process of discernment "that 'guides the faithful to an awareness of their situation before God. Conversation with the priest, in the internal forum, contributes to the formation of a correct judgment on what hinders the possibility of a fuller participation in the life of the church and what steps can foster it and make it grow.'"[54]

The most obvious way for divorced and remarried faithful to remove obstacles to their fuller participation in the life of the church is to submit their situation to the marriage tribunal for a possible declaration of nullity. Although the marriage tribunal is only addressed peripherally in the apostolic exhortation *Amoris Laetitia*, there is nothing in the tenor of the exhortation that suggests that a successful encounter with the marriage tribunal is the only way of surmounting "the various forms of exclusion currently practiced in the liturgical, pastoral, educational and institutional framework" and allowing the divorced and remarried "to be more fully integrated in Christian communities in the variety of

---

51  Ibid., §298; 820.
52  Ibid., §300; 820: "If we consider the immense variety of concrete situations. . . it is understandable that neither the synod nor this exhortation can be expected to provide a new set of general rules, canonical in nature and applicable in all cases. What is possible is simply a renewed encouragement to undertake a responsible personal and pastoral discernment of particular cases."
53  Ibid., §301; 821.
54  Ibid., §300; 821. See 2015 Synod of Bishops, Final Report, 86.

ways possible, while avoiding any occasion of scandal."[55] Francis is insistent that his call for discernment does not mean that individuals can decide unilaterally which forms of exclusion apply to themselves or "that any priest can quickly grant 'exceptions' or that some people can obtain sacramental privileges in exchange for favors."[56]

Such misunderstandings can be avoided only by discernment that consists in a structured dialogue between a divorced and remarried person (or perhaps couple) and their spiritual advisor which is characterized by "'humility, discretion and love for the church and her teaching, in a sincere search for God's will and a desire to make a more perfect response to it.'"[57] Part of this dialogue may entail "an examination of conscience through moments of reflection and repentance"[58] during which the divorced and remarried might well ask themselves such questions as: "How did they act toward their children when the conjugal union entered into crisis; whether or not they made attempts at reconciliation; what has become of the abandoned party; what consequences the new relationship has on the rest of the family and the community of the faithful; and what example is being set for young people who are preparing for marriage."[59] Francis expresses confidence that "when a responsible and tactful person who does not presume to put his own desires ahead of the common good of the church meets with a pastor capable of acknowledging the seriousness of the matter before him, there can be no risk that a specific discernment may lead people to think that the church maintains a double standard."[60]

In the logic of the apostolic exhortation, these specific discernments can eventually promote the "integration" of divorced and remarried faithful more fully into the life and mission of the church. When a divorced and remarried person has acknowledged and repented for their responsibility for the failure of the prior marriage, when he or she has made restitution in so far as possible for harm done especially to the former spouse and children, when the new partnership

---

55  Ibid., §299; 820. Much of the recent discussion of the situation of the divorced and remarried in the Church has focused on their exclusion from the reception of Holy Communion. However, this is not the only form of exclusion from participation in the life of the church to which they have been subjected. For example, the divorced and remarried are generally barred from serving as sponsor at baptism and confirmation, from most liturgical ministries, and from serving as teachers in Catholic schools and even as catechists in religious education programs. It is not unheard of that the children of those in irregular unions are refused admission to Catholic schools or to baptism and the other sacraments of initiation. Francis assigns to personal and pastoral discernment to ascertain whether these and other forms of exclusion from participation in the life of the Church can be surmounted in individual cases.
56  Ibid., §300; 821.
57  Ibid. The passage is taken from 2015 Synod of Bishops, Final Report, 86.
58  Ibid.
59  Ibid., 300; 821.
60  Ibid.

has proven itself as a publicly recognizable permanent commitment, and when it seems clear that he or she is truly striving to live the faith, it would seem possible that at least some of usual forms of exclusion can be surmounted.[61] In such discernment, of course, consideration must be given not only to the personal desires of the divorced and remarried person but also to "the common good of the church," especially insuring that overcoming some forms of exclusion in individual cases does not lead to misunderstanding on the part of the faithful or even to compromising the Church's witness to the Gospel ideal.

Can the accompanying, discerning and integration to which Francis calls the Church result eventually in the return of some divorced and remarried faithful to Holy Communion even without a favorable decision by a marriage tribunal? It is hard to read *Amoris Laetitia* without coming away with the conclusion that it might. Hidden away in footnote 351 is the affirmation that the help provided by the Church to a divorced and remarried person can "in certain cases . . . include the help of the sacraments."[62] The Holy Father does indeed seem to be holding out the possibility of reconciling divorced-remarried Catholics, a "way of penance" like the one promoted by Cardinal Kasper, that did not pass through the Church's marriage tribunals. His defense of the approach to irregular situations he is proposing against the complaints of "those who prefer a more rigorous pastoral care that leaves no room for confusion"[63] and his rejection of "a cold bureaucratic morality" in favor of "a pastoral discernment that is ever ready to understand, forgive, accompany, hope and above all integrate"[64] would make no sense if the integration to which discernment might lead would be limited to such relatively minor exclusions from participation as serving as baptismal sponsor. Nor would there be any reason for concern about misunderstandings "that any priest can quickly grant 'exceptions' or that some people can obtain sacramental privileges in exchange for favors" if discernment could not result at least sometimes in return to Holy Communion.[65]

IV. *Some Questions*

Pope Francis' apparent openness to the return of divorced and remarried faithful to Holy Communion following a process of accompaniment and discernment leaves a number of unanswered questions for canonists:

    1. Are there Precedents for "A Way of Penance"?

---

61  For example, discernment may lead to the conclusion that at least some divorced remarried faithful are "leading a life of faith" that warrants allowing them to serve as baptismal sponsors or exhibit sufficient "integrity of life" to all for their appointment as teachers in schools or religious education programs. See *CIC*, c. 803, §2.
62  Francis, *Amoris Laetitia*, n. 351.
63  Ibid., §311; 823.
64  Ibid.
65  Ibid., §300, 821.

Pope Francis has not called into question the Church's doctrine on the indissolubility of marriage; but he has proposed a mitigation of the Church's discipline aimed at rendering that doctrine "specific in the small details of daily living."[66] Just as the exclusion of the divorced and remarried from Eucharistic fellowship was not an invention of the post-Tridentine Church but part of Church discipline since patristic, perhaps even biblical, times, so the idea of "a way of penance" for readmission of the divorced and remarried to the sacraments is not a creation *ex nihilo* of three German bishops in 1993 or of liberal theologians and canonists in the post-conciliar era but a discipline with roots in the patristic era. Although all of the Fathers of the Church condemned divorce as a grave moral evil, it does seem that, at least in some places, a way of penance was available to divorced and remarried person and that, at the end of this penitential path, was reconciliation with the Church and return to Eucharistic communion. Although the historical data is murky and its meaning contested, this way of penance may be the disciplinary approach that canon 8 of the Council of Nicea characterized as "the teaching of the Catholic and Apostolic Church" which Novatian schismatics had to agree to "make. . . the rule of their conduct" as a condition for their own reconciliation with the Great Church.[67] This penitential path seems to have provided the trajectory from which the present discipline of the Eastern non-Catholic Churches emerged. Thus, the way accompaniment, discernment and integration now put forth by Pope Francis is not without precedent.

The key question to be resolved is not is an alternative discipline possible, but whether the alternative proposed adequately protects the integrity of the Church's teaching. Unfortunately, the fate of this easier softer way discipline in the discipline of non-Catholic Churches of the East is not especially reassuring. The Churches of the East firmly adhere to the doctrine that marriage is indissoluble while following a less restrictive disciplinary policy for admitting divorced and remarried persons to penance and Holy Communion and even to a new marriage in the Church. This mitigation of the rigor of the law lest its weight be more than weak humans can bear is characterized by the Orthodox as the exercise of *oikonomia*. Critics of the Orthodox practice, including Pope Benedict XVI when he was still Prefect of the Congregation for the Doctrine of the Faith, have claimed that this discipline dangerously, and therefore unacceptably, undermines the Church's witness to the indissolubility of marriage.[68] The example of the efforts of the communities of the Anglican communion to hold the line against

---

66 Aidan Kavanagh, *On Liturgical Theology* (Collegeville: Liturgical Press, 1984) 142.
67 Giovanni Cereti, "The Reconciliation of Remarried Divorcees According to Canon 8 of the Council of Nicea," in *Ius Sequitur Vitam: Studies in Canon Law Presented to P.J.M. Huizing*, ed. James Provost and Knut Walf (Leuven: Peeters, 1991) 193-207. This article is based on a larger study: Giovanni Cereti, *Divorzio, Nuovo nozze e penitenza nella Chiesa primitive* (Bologna: EDB, 1977).
68 Joseph Cardinal Ratzinger, "Introduzione," in Congregation for the Doctrine of the Faith, *Sulla pastorale dei divorziati risposati* (Vatican City: Libreria Editrice Vaticana, 1998) 22-24.

admission of divorced and remarried people to new marriages, much less to Holy Communion, is even less reassuring.

2. How Much Repentance is Enough?

Faithful to the word of the Lord himself, the Church has traditionally held that those who remarry after a divorce are guilty of adultery and that the subsequent marriage is itself an adulterous relationship. The sin is understood to be compounded each time the divorced and remarried parties engage in conjugal relations. To be reconciled to God and the Church through the sacrament of Penance, sinners must be genuinely repentant. True repentance entails "a firm purpose of amendment," that is a genuine commitment to ceasing the sinful activity. For divorced and remarried persons such repentance has been understood to mean either separating from the new consort or, if grave reason counsel against separation, committing themselves to living together while forsaking conjugal intimacy.[69] Observers more sympathetic to Pope Francis' approach argue that some divorced and remarried people may be truly repentant but morally unable to either to separate or to live together in continence. To demand the impossible of such people would be excessively rigid.[70] However, the critics respond that such tenderhearted appeals to mercy discount the power of grace to give the truly repentant the strength to endure the hardships of separation from an adulterous relationship or to embrace the yoke of continence. Pope Francis, however, is clearly on the side of the "tender hearted." The integration of the divorced and remarried that Pope Francis foresees requires repentance but neither a commitment to separate nor an agreement to live "as brother and sister" on the part of divorced and remarried as a condition for their return to Holy Communion. Rather, Francis holds that, in some cases, divorced and remarried faithful are already "giving what for now is the most generous response they can give to God" and that it is what God himself is asking amid the concrete complexity of [their] limits."[71] Commenting on this section of *Amoris*

---

69  See, for example, John Corbett, Andrew Hofer, Paul J. Keller, Dominic Langevin, Dominic Legg, Kurt Martens, Thomas Petri and Thomas Joseph White, "Recent Proposals for the Pastoral Care of Divorced and remarried: A Theological Assessment," *Nova et Vetera* 12 (2014) 601-630.

70  More recently, it has even been suggested that the traditional characterization of the adultery resulting from remarriage after a divorce as a continuing offense is not an accurate moral assessment of the person's situation. See Cathleen Kaveny, "Mercy for the Remarried: What the Church Can Learn from Civil Law," *Commonweal*, August 14, 2015, 18: "[N]othing in Jesus' words or conduct demands that in our broken world, the sin involved in divorce and remarriage be treated as one continues indefinitely, without possibility of repentance. To impose such a requirement in every case confounds the mercy that is the touchstone for the divine lawgiver." This article is based on a larger study, see Cathleen Kaveny, "Mercy, Justice, and Law: Can Legal Concepts Help Foster new Life?" in *Familie: Auslaufmodell oder Garant userer Zukunft?,* ed. Georg Augustin and Rainer Kirchendorfer (Freiburg: Herder, 2014) 298-326.

71  Francis, *Amoris Laetitia*, §303; 821.

*laetitia*, Cardinal Coccopalmiero observes: "The Church, therefore, could allow access to Penance and the Eucharist, for the faithful who find themselves in an irregular union, which, however, requires two essential conditions: they desire to change their situation, but cannot act on their desire."[72]

### 3. Are Divorced and Remarried Still "Publicly Unworthy"?

The possibility of a route for divorced and remarried faithful to the return to Holy Communion that does not pass through the marriage tribunal is, of course, at odds with 2000 Declaration of the Pontifical Council for Legislative Texts which lumped all divorced and remarried Catholics among the "publicly unworthy" who were to be barred from the reception of Holy Communion in accord with the norm of canon 915. In principle, a teaching document like the apostolic exhortation does not of itself change the law as it has been authoritatively interpreted. Nonetheless, the 2000 Declaration purports to be less an interpretation of the law than an exposition of the theological underpinnings for the blanket exclusion of the divorced and remarried from Holy Communion and a firm rejection of an opinion bubbling up in the canonical world at the time that held that the sort of discernment for which Pope Francis is now calling was necessary to determine whether the traditional exclusion applied in an individual case.[73] As a result, Pope Francis' exhortation has substantially eroded the rationale of the Declaration.

Nonetheless, Francis acknowledges that the concern for scandal resulting from the reception of Holy Communion by the divorced and remarried which is an underlying concern of the 2000 Declaration will also be a concern with return to Holy Communion at the end of a process of accompaniment and discernment. Dealing with the problem of scandal is not, of course, a new problem. The Pontifical Council for Legislative Texts declaration had conceded that even in the case of those who had agreed to live together as "brother and sister," since

---

72  Francesco Coccopalmerio, *A Commentary on Chapter Eight of Amoris Laetitia* (Mahwah, NJ: Paulist Press, 2017) 25.
73  See, for example, the argument on behalf of a discerning approach by Patrick Travers, "Reception of the Holy Eucharist by Catholics Attempting Remarriage and the 1983 Code," *The Jurist* 55 (1995) 187-217; Alphone Borras, "The Canonical Limits of Catholic Identity: Some Problematic Situations," *Concilium* 5 (1994) 47-59; Klaus Lüdicke, "Tathaftung und Schuldhaftung? Zum Problematik der wiederverheirateten Geschiedenen angesichts der Grundprizipien der kirchlichen Sanktionsrechtes," in *Geschiedenen-Wiederverheiratet-Abgewiesen?* Ed. Theodore Shneider (Freiburg: Herder, 1995) 254-266; and Jean Werkmeister, "L'Accès des divorcés remarries aux sacraments," *Revue de Droit Canonique* 48 (1998) 59-79. For the contrary point of view, see John J. Myers, "Divorce, Remarriage and Reception of the Sacraments," *The Jurist* 57 (1997) 485-516; Michael Manning, " Reception of Holy Communion by Divorced and Remarried Catholics," *Canon Law Society of Great Britian and Ireland Newsletter* (September 1997) 3, 63-71; and Ignatius Gramunt, "Non-Admission to Holy Communion: The Interpretation of Canon 915 (CIC)," *Studia Canonica* 35 (2001) 175-190.

this fact "is per se occult, while their condition as persons who are divorced and remarried is per se manifest, they will be able to receive Holy Communion only *remoto scandalo.*"[74] Moreover, it might as well be conceded, that, although the "annulment process" is in principle a public matter, the process and even the outcome is usually shrouded in secrecy. Consequently, the return of the divorced and remarried to the sacraments after their marriages have been declared invalid or dissolved often raise more than a few eyebrows. Avoiding scandal will also have to be a consideration if the integration of divorced and remarried faithful after accompaniment and discernment includes their return to Holy Communion.

### 4. How is This Approach Going to Work?

Although Francis foresees that fuller integration into the life of the Church may result from the process of accompaniment and discernment he calls for, he clearly does not foresee that the discernment will be a purely solitary and personal matter for the divorced and remarried person himself or herself. It involves a process, perhaps a lengthy process, with a pastor or spiritual guide willing "to enter into the reality of other people's lives and to know the power of tenderness."[75] The role of this spiritual companion is "to guide the faithful to an awareness of their situation before God" and contribute "to the formation of a correct judgment on what hinders the possibility of fuller participation in the life of the church and on what steps can foster it and make it grow."[76] But how is this process of integration after discernment going to work in practice? In some cases, the overcoming of exclusions to participation in the life of the Church by divorced and remarried Catholics after discernment will inevitably entail an action by a church authority. A pastor or sacramental minister would admit a divorced-remarried member of the faithful as baptismal sponsor and a pastor or principal would hire one as a teacher in a Catholic school or engage one as a catechist in a religious education program. The role of authority in the return by divorced and remarried faithful to Holy Communion after a process of discernment is not nearly as clear. Of course, a minister would have to refrain from refusing Holy Communion to a divorced and remarried faithful who came forward with hands outstretched, but refraining from refusing is not the same as authorizing admission. Nor does it seem that the pastor or spiritual guide who accompanies the person on the journey of discernment will give official authorization for the reception of Holy Communion. A confessor may absolve a penitent from sins, but actions taken in the internal forum generally do not have effects in the external forum. Francis' process of accompaniment, discernment and integration is reminiscent of the process outlined by the three German bishops in 1993 and resurrected more recently by Cardinal Kasper. If so, the decision to return to Holy Communion rests with the parties and the role of the pastor or spiritual guide is not "to pronounce any official admission in the

---

74  PCLT, Declaration, §2,
75  Francis, *Amoris Laetitia*, §310; 822.
76  Ibid., §300; 821.

formal sense" but to "respect the judgments of the individual conscience" and "to defend such a decision of conscience against prejudice and suspicion," while taking "care that the parish does not thereby take offense."[77]

> Cardinal Coccopalmiero helpfully suggests:
>
>> Clearly, the essential conditions above must be carefully and authoritatively discerned by the ecclesiastical authority. . . . The ecclesial authority will, at least normally, be the pastor, who knows the people directly, and for this reason he can make a proper judgment in these delicate situations. However, it could be necessary, or at least very useful, to have a service of the Curia, in which the diocesan Ordinary, in a similar way to what is provided for difficult marriage cases, offers appropriate counseling or even specific authorization in cases regarding admission to the sacraments of reconciliation and the Eucharist. . . . In any case, it is obvious that the competent ecclesiastical authorities, I would say the Episcopal Conferences, should promptly issue some guidelines to instruct the faithful and their pastors on these matters.[78]

In fact, some episcopal conferences and some diocesan bishops have issued such guidelines since the promulgation of *Amoris Laetitia*, but they are not terribly consistent on the question of whether the divorced and remarried can be admitted to holy communion and are largely silent about how readmission is to be accomplished.[79] Even the guidelines issued on September 5, 2016 by the bishops of the pastoral region of Buenos Aires, Argentina, that Pope Francis has promulgated in the *Acta Apostolicae Sedis* as a kind of approved commentary on chapter eight of *Amoris Laetitia*, while clearly affirming the possibility of admitting the divorced and remarried to the sacraments, are not very helpful in providing criteria for readmission, the process to follow when discerning

---

77 Three German Bishops, 675.
78 Coccopalmerio, 25-26.
79 For the Archdiocese of Philadelphia, see Charles Chaput, "Pastoral Guidelines for Implementing 'Amoris Laetitia," archphila.org/wp-content/uploads/2016/AIOP_AL-guidelines.pdf; for the episcopal conference of Poland, see Komunikat z. 376. Zebranie Plenarnego Konferenci Episkopatu Polski, =; for Malta, see "Criteria for the Application of Chapter VIII of Amoris Laetitia,: http://ms.maltadiocese.org/WEBSITE/2017/PRESS%20RELEASES/Norms%20for%20the%20the%20Application%20of%20Chapter%20VIII%20of%20AL.pdf; for Germany, see Press Release German Bishops' Conference, www.dbk.de?fileadmin/redaktion/diverse_downloads/presse_2017/2017-015a-Wortlaut-Wort-der-Bischofe-Amoris-Laetitia; for Belgium, see Belgian Bishops Conference, "*Amoris Laetitiae* Lettre pastoral, www.cathobel.be%2Fwp-content%2Fuploads%2F2017%2F05%2F2017-05-09-Amoris-laetitia-Lettre-pastorale.pdf&edit-text=.

readmission or suggestions on how to explain readmissions to the local community.[80] Those like me who feel the pull of what Francis disparagingly calls a "bureaucratic morality" would feel more comfortable with clearer criteria for readmission and a more structured decision-making process. However, Francis calls us to "stop looking for those personal or communal niches that shelter us from the maelstrom of human misfortune and instead to enter to the reality of other people's lives" and realize how "wonderfully complicated" they can be.[81] He seems much more comfortable getting his shoes dirty in the messiness of human life than many of us are.

## 5. Are We on the Slippery Slope?

Pope Francis does not propose that this process of accompaniment, discernment and integration should be seen as providing "a new set of general rules, canonical in nature and applicable to all cases"[82] or that "what is part of practical discernment in particular circumstances cannot be elevated to the level of a rule," something "that would not only lead to an intolerable casuistry but would endanger the very values that must be preserved with special care."[83] Nevertheless, it is hard for me to see how this regime of mercy can long coexist with the Church's traditional discipline without the former ultimately eroding the latter.

First, Catholics in North America are notorious for transforming processes into programs and transmuting exceptions to the rule into the rule itself. Under the American Procedural Norms approved in 1970, tribunals were allowed to seek dispensations from the then-mandatory second instance process for affirmative decisions in marriage nullity cases. It was understood when these norms were approved that dispensations would be sought only in rare, "open-and-shut" cases. However, dispensations were soon sought in 90% or more of cases which received affirmative decisions. Within a short time after the restoration of the catechumenate with the promulgation of the Order of Christian Initiation of Adults, what had been envisaged as an extended process of conversion was transmuted into a six month program with "graduation" at the Easter Vigil. Is it realistic to think that the process of discernment called for by Pope Francis will not soon become another program?

---

80 Bishops of the Pastoral Region of Buenos Aires, "Criterios basicos para la applicación del capitulo VIII de Amoris laetitia," *Acta Apostolicae Sedis* 108 (2016) 1072-1074. See also Francis, apostolic letter ad excellentissimum Dominum Sergium Alfredum Fenoy, delagatum Regionis Pastoralis Bonaerensis, September 5, 2016: *Acta Apostolicae Sedis*, 108 (2016) 1071-1072 AND Peter Cardinal Parolin, "Rescriptum ex Audientia SS.Mi," June 5, 2017: *Acta Apostolicae Sedis* 108 (2016) 1074.
81 Francis, *Amoris Laetitia*, §308; 822.
82 Ibid., §300; 820.
83 Ibid., §304; 821-822.

Second, the careful discernment of situations on a case by case basis inevitably entails judgments about the sincerity of a person's repentance and readiness to move to a greater degree of participation in the life of the Church and of the readiness of the community to integrate that person. The "careful discernment of situations" that will inevitably admit some divorced and remarried faithful but not others to the sacraments is not likely to survive long in a culture like ours that champions equality at every turn and for which "judgmentalism" is the one remaining unforgiveable sin.

Third, Francis seems to envision his approach of accompaniment, discernment and integration of divorced and remarried faithful as a sort of "way of penance and conversion" like the one sketched by Cardinal Kasper. However, one can wonder whether our current culture can support such a penitential way. While the 2015 Synod of Bishops was debating whether to recommend to the Holy Father "a way of penance" for the divorced and remarried, one commentator in a national newspaper opined: "Most divorced people are 'guilty' only of being human" and recommended that the synod "simply call on Pope Francis to proclaim to the divorced and remarried: 'Thank you for sharing with the rest of God's people your faith-filled longing to join us at the feast of the Lord's mercy. We have missed you for too long. Welcome home!'[84]" Such willingness to welcome the divorced and remarried home unconditionally does not bode well for maintaining a sense that their return is the final stage on a journey of penance. While there may be some precedent in the Church's tradition for dealing with divorce and remarriage through the discipline of penance, there is no precedent in the tradition for treating Jesus' teaching as an anachronism.

V.   Conclusion

I really don't know where the process of accompanying, discerning and integrating on which Pope Francis has set us forth is going to lead. The Church's discipline or canon law is the flawed, fragile, and always subject to revision effort to spin out the norms and processes to keep the ecclesial community faithful to the Gospel in the small details of daily living. This discipline is certainly not beyond criticism and, like all things human, it is always in need of reform. And we canonists have heard plenty of such criticism during the last half-century. Nevertheless, as the late Aidan Kavanagh pointed out:

> Canonical laws, which are often denigrated as being unimportant [or worse], attempt to render the [three canons of Holy Scripture, Creed, and Eucharistic Prayer] specific in the small details of faithful daily life. When canonical laws are overlooked too long, the other three canons are likely to drift away from the church's consciousness and to be honored

---

84   George B. Wilson, "Policy Fails the Test of Pastoral Wisdom," *The National Catholic Reporter*, September 11-24, 2015, 36.

only in the breach. When this happens, such a church will invariably discover its apostolate to be compromised, its faith dubious, its worship more concerned with current events than with the presence of the living God, and its efforts bent more on maintaining its own coherence than to restoring the unity of the world to God in Christ.[85]

Despite my reservations about where Pope Francis is pointing us in *Amoris Laetitia,* I am challenged by his admonition that "we should always consider 'inadequate any theological conception that in the end puts in doubt the omnipotence of God and, especially, his mercy.'"[86]

---

[85] Kavanagh, *On Liturgical Theology,* 142.
[86] Francis, *Amoris Laetitia,* §311; 823.

# Seminar

## Insufficient Faith Leading to Simulation or Error
*Most Reverend Monsignor Kenneth Boccafola*

The question of lack of faith and its effect on the validity of the matrimonial consent of the baptized is one of the subjects currently being studied by bishops, theologians and canonists. The present paper would hope to contribute to the current discussion by recalling certain basic principles of the accepted magisterium which have then been absorbed into and further elaborated by Rotal jurisprudence. Accordingly, I would first like to examine the reasons for maintaining that insufficient faith, *per se* and in itself, *should not be considered as an* independent or autonomous ground of marital nullity. Hence our attention will then be focused on insufficient faith as a disposing cause possibly leading to nullity, but nullity based on the grounds of simulation or an error which determines the will.

I. Fundamental Question

The question of the lack of faith has been enjoying quite a rebirth of interest at the present time, especially due to the 2014 Synod on the Family. In the *Relatio Synodi* [n. 48] the Bishops made this suggestion: "Among other proposals, *the role which faith plays in persons who marry* could possibly be examined in ascertaining the validity of the Sacrament of Marriage, all the while maintaining that the marriage of two baptized Christians is always a sacrament."

Then too the *motu proprio Mitis Iudex Dominus Jesus* in Art. 14:1 says: "Among the circumstances of things and persons which can allow a case for nullity of marriage to be handled by means of the briefer process according to cann. 1683-1687, are included, for example: *the defect of faith which can generate simulation of consent or error that determines the will*".

This matter had also been confronted by theologians and canonists in the aftermath of the Second Vatican Council and during the revision period leading to the 1983 Code. A fundamental question was posed: "If one lacks faith in marriage as a sacrament can he or she celebrate the marriage validly?" Or: "Do baptized non-believers contract a sacramental marriage? Are they capable of full matrimonial consent in the sense of the sacrament?". Or another canonical way of posing the same question: "Is the lack of faith, in and by itself, an autonomous ground of matrimonial nullity?"

The classic response to such questions had already been formulated in the ordinary Papal magisterium and then further elaborated in Rotal jurisprudence. Pope Benedict XVI succinctly summed up this response in an observation on this subject in his last allocution to the Roman Rota in January of 2013: "*The indissoluble pact between a man and a woman does not, for the purposes of the sacrament, require of those engaged to be married, their personal faith*; what it does require, as a necessary minimal condition is the intention to do what the Church does".

Such a conclusion was quite generally accepted until the post Vatican II era when certain scholars, e. g., such as Julio Manzanares, began to question the prevailing opinion that faith was not essential for marital consent. Then too at a meeting of the International Theological Commission in 1976 the matter was also considered. The Commission noted: "... in the case of one who has no trace of faith as such [in the sense of a disposition to believe] nor any desire for grace and salvation, the question arises whether the general intention to contract which we have discussed is truly sacramental or not, that is, is the marriage validly contracted or not.[1]

So let us first examine the classic response to the question elaborated by the ordinary magisterium and Rotal jurisprudence on the basis of the underlying theological principles. In the course of this we can address some of the difficulties raised against this position. Then we will go on to consider some possible scenarios in which a lack of faith or insufficient faith, while not being an autonomous ground of nullity, can still constitute a contributing cause for nullity on other familiar grounds such as simulation and error. And finally we will reflect on some newer developments.

II. Theological Presuppositions as well as the Need for Precise Terms and Definitions

As one seeks to address this question it becomes necessary to understand the underlying presumptions that will affect one's formulation of an answer. It is also very necessary to understand and define as well as one can the exact terms of the inquiry. In this discussion it is presupposed that baptism effects an ontological change in the person's soul. It seals the soul with a permanent character. The baptized person is in Christ and the Holy Spirit dwells within him or her. A second presupposition is that the spouses are the ministers of the sacrament to each other. The official witness of the Church merely receives their consent, i. e., testifies to the fact that they have exchanged marital consent.

---

1 Commissio Theologica Internationalis, "Propositiones de quibusdam quaestionibus doctrinalibus ad matrimonium christianum pertinentibus," *Gregorianum* 59 (1978) 458.

Furthermore, everyone realizes that the celebration of a sacrament, an outward sign which signifies and effects grace, is intimately connected with faith. Faith is presupposed and is the *causa dispositiva* of a fruitful reception of a sacrament.

Yet it is legitimate to ask whether or not those raising the question of the lack of faith or insufficient faith have adequately defined their terms for this debate. Faith is first of all a theological virtue, and traditional Catholic doctrine has held that the three theological virtues are infused into the soul at the moment of baptism. So it could be asked how, then, can a baptized person be totally without faith? [Pope Francis makes an oblique reference to this point in his discourse to the Rota in 2015: *"Indeed the habitus fidei is infused at the moment of Baptism and continues to have a mysterious influence on the soul, even when faith has not been developed, and psychologically speaking, seems to be absent"*].

Of course, more generally, faith is considered as a psychological phenomenon, that is, as a conscious attitude of belief. I suppose in this sense it would be referred to as living faith. Accordingly, even the very term used to present the question, i. e., "baptized non-believers, is ambiguous and even contradictory, since the phrase seems to consider faith or belief only as a psychological phenomenon (which therefore would also be subject to various grades of intensity) and to leave no room for considering faith in its ontological aspect as an infused virtue. In any event it is certainly quite an arduous and almost impossible task to individuate and evaluate the degree of intensity of the psychological phenomenon which would mark it as sufficient to provide the minimum faith necessary for valid matrimonial consent. [Pope John Paul II in *Familiaris Consortio*, says pastors for example, cannot refuse to celebrate the sacrament based simply on their evaluation of the spouses' lack of intensity of faith].

Then, too, the very way a question is formulated and presented often times has a decisive influence on the response expected, because of the underlying presupposition that manifests itself in the way the question was presented. For example, to pose the question whether non-believers or those who lack faith are capable of full matrimonial consent in "the sense of the sacrament" seems to presuppose a real difference between simple consent to matrimony and a consent to the Sacrament of Matrimony. It seems to take for granted that the baptized who enter marriage must be conscious of and embrace not only the natural reality of marriage, but also something considered additional, i. e., the *Sacrament* of Marriage.

III. Theological Principle from the Magisterium: For the Baptized, the Sacrament of Marriage is Inseparable from the Natural Matrimonial Pact.

A) The natural nuptial pact is a not merely profane reality.

Marriage is described in c. 1055 as a covenant by which a man and a woman establish between themselves a partnership of the whole of life and which is ordered by its nature to the good of the spouses and the procreation and education of offspring and which, between the baptized has been raised by Christ to the dignity of a sacrament.

We are all aware that great numbers of the youth of our day, though they may be baptized, live in a secular world and are either ignorant of or in error about the above definition of marriage. Yet even in our own modern day, marriage is still predominantly understood as a natural human institution, that is, as a stable commitment between a man and a woman to share their lives in an intimate loving relationship with one another, committing themselves to faithfulness to one another, and which looks forward to the happiness of the spouses and the good of children.

The Church has always understood that marriage is precisely this natural pact (*matrimonium in fieri*) and institution (*matrimonium in facto esse*) which has been present in all times and in all cultures, even though perhaps in slightly different forms in different places and times. But this natural institution is not something merely profane and alien from God. The Second Vatican Council reminds us that marriage is: "An intimate community of life and conjugal love founded by the Creator and imbued with his laws ... God himself is the author of marriage."[2]

Such a conciliar statement was not something new, but rather it reflected the previous Magisterium.[3] Massimo Mingardi has expressed it this way: "Right from Creation marriage could not be considered a profane reality, and not simply because it takes its origin from God (something which is true of all creation) but because in it, is manifested in a privileged way that man is the image and likeness of God [in so far as He is life as relationship and gift of himself] and also because in the call to establish a relationship with another human being man finds in his inner self his true vocation, that of being in a relationship with God,

---

2    Vatican II, pastoral constitution *Gaudium et spes*, December 7, 1965 AAS (1960) 1967, n .48.: "Intima communitas vitae et amoris coniugalis a Creatore condita suiisque legibus instructa ... Ipse Deus est auctor matirmonii."
3    Leo XIII, letter to the Archbishops and Bishops of the ecclesiastical provinces of Turin, Vercelli and Genoa *Ci siamo*, June 1, 1879: ASS 12 (1879) 4-5, 11: "La connubiale unione non e' opera o invenzione del uomo: Iddio stesso, supremo Autore della natura, sin dalle prime con detta unione ordino' la propagazione del genere umano e la costituzione della famiglia l'origine e la sanctificazione delle nozze e' da Dio".

a relationship which finds its full and definitive fulfillment in the relationship of Christ to His Church."[4]

B) What, Then, is the Sacrament Of Marriage, or in other Words, What Constitutes the "Sacramentality" of Marriage?

Some authors such as J. Manzanares[5] [Correcco, Moneta] in the period before the new Code was promulgated, have held that the question of the separability of contract and sacrament remained open, Some even proposed a two step process for the Sacrament of Matrimony: first a couple would have a valid natural marriage before the State, and then later on, if the couple had sufficient faith and desire for the sacrament there could be a sacramental celebration in Church.

Nonetheless, the promulgation of the new Code of Canon Law reiterated the Church's perennial teaching that no valid matrimonial contract can exist between baptized persons without it being at the same time a sacrament. This absolute inseparability of contract and sacrament in the baptized has certainly been authoritatively taught in the ordinary Magisterium[6] [and reiterated by the Synod Fathers, as we have seen].

In fact, it would seem that nowadays, with the new research that has been done, that the debate no longer principally concerns whether or not the natural matrimonial pact can be separated from the Sacrament, but rather whether or not the natural contract is actually identical with the Sacrament. The constant Magisterium, as reflected in these words of Pope Leo XIII, has always maintained:

> Christ the Lord raised marriage to the dignity of a sacrament; for marriage is the very contract itself, providing it is done according to law, and thus it follows that for this reason marriage is a sacrament because it is a sacred sign producing grace and an image recalling the mystic marriage of Christ with His Church. The form and figure of those nuptials are

---

4   Massimo Mingardi, "Identitas contractum inter et sacramentum," *Periodica* 87 (1998) 225 226: "Già a livello della creazione perciò il matrimonio non può essere considerato realtà profana: e non semplicemente perché trae origine da Dio (questa vale per tutta la creazione), ma perché in esso si manifesta in modo privilegiato che l'uomo e' immagine e somiglianza di Dio (il quale e' vita relazionale e dono di sé), e insieme perché nella chiamata a rapportarsi con un altro essere umano l'uomo scopre nel suo intimo la sua vocazione profonda, quella di essere in relazione con Dio, una relazione che trova il suo compimento pieno e definitivo nell'unione di Cristo e della Chiesa."
5   Julio Manzanares, "Habitudo matrimonium baptizatorum inter et sacramentum: omne matrimonium duorum baptizatorum estne necessario sacramentum?" *Periodica* 67 (1978) 35 80.
6   Pius IX, allocutio *Acerbissimum vobiscum* diei 27 septembris 1852: Denz. 1640 "... inter fideles matrimonium non dari posse, quin uno eodemque tempore sit sacramentum ... ". Pius IX, Pontifex Maximus Acta I, Romae s. a 393. See also Mingardi, 216-217.

expressed by the very bond itself of this highest union by which a man and woman are mutually joined together, which is nothing else than marriage itself. Therefore it is clear that, among Christians, a true union is *in se et per se* a sacrament. And therefore nothing is more abhorrent to the truth than to consider the sacramental dignity as an added something, or as a property extrinsically attached to it, which can be distinguished from the contract and made to disappear by the will of men.[7]

[Because of this identity of contract and sacrament, the Rota for many years did not entertain the ground of nullity consisting in exclusion of the sacramental dignity of marriage, but rather immediately converted such a claim of nullity into that of total simulation, Only more recently has exclusion of sacramental dignity been accepted as a ground of nullity because it was recognized that one could psychologically distinguish and exclude the sacramental dignity even though this would still in effect ontologically constitute a total simulation of marriage].

Thus it seems clear that the Church teaches that "sacramentality" or the "sacrament" is that *natural pact* between the spouses that we have spoken about above,"" i.e., the stable commitment between a man and a woman to share their lives in an intimate relationship with one another, committing themselves to faithfulness to one another, and which looks forward to the happiness of the spouses and the good of children. It is the *"res"* of matrimony and it becomes *"res et sacramentum"* in the baptized because on account of their baptism the spouses have already been joined to Christ. Christ is not strange or alien to them even if they might not consciously be aware of Him.

The Sacrament of Matrimony, or the sacramentality of matrimony consists therefore in the fact that the natural marital covenant or contract itself between a baptized man and baptized woman has been transformed into a sign and source of grace, i.e. one of the seven sacraments of the New Law. The sacramental dignity is the essential matrimonial covenant itself. Sacramentality adds nothing to this

---

7    Leo XIII, encyclical *Arcanum, divinae sapientiae*, February 10, 1880: ASS 12 (1879) 394: "Nam Christus Dominus dignitate sacramenti auxit matrimonium; matrimonium autem est ipse contractus, si modo sit factus iure. Huc accedit, quod ob hanc causam matrimonium est sacramentum, quia est sacrum signum et efficiens gratiam, et imaginem referens mysticarum nuptiarum Christi cum Ecclesia, Istarum autem forma ac figura illo ipso exprimitur summae coniunctionis vinculo, quo vir et mulier inter se conligantur, quodque aliud nihil est, nisi ipsum matrimonium. Itaque, apparet, omne inter christianos, iustum coniugium in se et per se esse sacramentum: nihilque magis abhorrere a veritate, quam esse sacramentum decus quoddam adiunctum, aut proprietatem allapsam extrinsecus quae a contractu distingui ac disparari hominum arbitratu queat."

natural pact except the fact that for the baptized who have consummated their marriage, this pact, besides being naturally intrinsically permanent, becomes extrinsically indissoluble because it is also a sign of the union of Christ and His Church.

> IV. Logical Corollary: The Validity or Invalidity of a Sacramental Marriage Is Determined by Exactly the Same Principles Used For Deciding Whether Or Not the Natural Human Matrimonial Pact Is Valid or Invalid.

From an analysis of the principles of Thomistic rational psychology illustrated in Rotal jurisprudence we know that an act of matrimonial consent placed with sufficient general knowledge of what marriage naturally consists of - even though this knowledge might be somewhat vague and incomplete - and placed with free consent of the will, is all that is necessary to create the natural marital pact, which in the baptized is *eo ipso, ex opere operato*, elevated to the Sacrament of Marriage. It would seem that nothing additional with regard to the content of the spouses act of the will is required for consent to the Sacrament of Matrimony than that which is required for the natural pact of marriage.

> V. Classic Response to the Question Posed: Faith is not Required for Validity, Only Right Intention.

As long as one freely seeks to enter a real, true natural nuptial pact, such consent is sufficient to enter a valid contract. Nothing more specifically religious needs to be *included* in that consent; and once the consent has been exchanged the favor of the law regards it as valid until proven otherwise. Thus it would seem that a baptized non-believer who willed to enter a true marriage would also by that fact contract a valid sacramental marriage. Faith is always to be fostered and hoped for as a living and vital element of the spouses choice. It is necessary as a *causa dispositiva* for *fruitfully* receiving the Sacrament, but it is hard to see why, according to the principles just explained, it would be absolutely necessary for the *validity* of the matrimonial consent. Even the International Theological Commission in its *Propositiones* of 1977 said simply that a *dubium facti* [in an individual case therefore, and not a general *dubium iuris*] can arise about the validity of a marriage *ubi nullum vestigium fidei qua talis ... invenitur.*

With regard to the intention required to confect or administer the sacrament, granted that the general principles of sacramental theology require that the minister of the sacrament have the intention of *faciendi id quod Ecclesia facit*, no real problem exists because, according to the principles explained, the minimum that the Church requires for the sacrament of matrimony is simply that the spouses will to enter a natural human nuptial pact.

Of course if one of the spouses should deliberately advert to and *exclude* by a positive act of the will, marriage itself, or the sacramental dignity of marriage, or one of marriage's essential properties such as unity or indissolubility, then the marriage would be invalid because of this deliberate exclusion.[8]

VI.  Possible Scenarios Involving Lack of Faith:

A practical way to understand the diverse consequences on the validity or invalidity of marital consent that a spouse's lack of faith might give rise to, is to envision the range of distinct possible attitudes that someone with a weak faith entering marriage might have concerning sacramentality.

A) The first and hopefully most common attitude, is, of course, that of the devout and faithful Catholic who with a full understanding and acceptance of the Church's teaching, knowingly embracing the duties and obligations of marriage out of true love for his or her partner, consciously marries in the Lord, fervently seeking the benediction of the Church and the grace of the sacrament. In this situation, of course, there is no obstacle to the lawful and valid exchange of consent, which consent brings into existence the marriage sacrament, whose fruitfulness then will depend on the state of grace of the parties.

B) A second possible attitude is that of the baptized person entering marriage who is indifferent to the sacramental dignity of marriage. He has little or no faith, and is concerned principally with the things of this world; he simply intends to marry as others in society do, although he is not particularly hostile or adverse to religion or to the Church.

In this case traditional Rotal jurisprudence holds that the marriage would be valid. For the principle is clearly, although rather bluntly, stated in a sentence *coram* Doheny of 17 April 1961: "Between baptized persons no marital contract exists which is not by the fact itself a sacrament, whatever the parties feel, or hold or believe, for the sacrament comes into existence by the will of Christ, not by the will, or the desire, or the opinion, or the faith, of the parties. Therefore every Christian, even though he lacks true faith, contracts validly and enters a true sacrament along with the contract in so far as he wills what is of the essence

---

8  Cf. *c.* Fiore July 17, 1973: *RRDec* 65 (1973) 592-593: "... etiamsi matrimonium baptizatorum irritari posset ob exclusam a contrahente in unda baptismali renato sacramentalem dignitatem, eo quod inter baptizatos iugalis contractus consistere nequeat suo robore, quin eo ipso sit sacramentum (c. 1012, #2), attamen, ut huiusmodi irritatio fiat, requiritur semper ut dignitas sacramentalis excludatur actu positivo voluntatis, quo ipsum matrimonium excluderetur si esset separabile a sacramento. Hinc, in fonte baptismi lotus, qui non vult sacramentum matrimonii, sed vult verum contractum iugalem, in facie ecclesiae, in re seu de facto  haud excludit sacramentum; contractus matrimonialis pro baptizatis, in re, seu de facto  a sacramento separari non potest, idcirco nupturiens christifidelis sacramentum a contractu matrimoniali seiungere non valet."

of the contract, and does not exclude, by a positive act of the will, any essential element."[9]

But immediately an important objection is raised: how can something that is not known, or is not appreciated, be willed? The spouse in the case in question is indifferent to the sacramental and religious nature of marriage; perhaps he does not even know what a sacrament is, how can he therefore will to receive it?

This objection is answered by recalling certain scholastic principles; it is true that nothing can willed without having been known beforehand, *nihil volitum quin praecognitum* That is, something *volitum in se* has to be first known before it can be willed. But something which is inseparably connected with something else may not necessarily be *volitum in se*, but can be *volitum in alio*. What is directly willed or intended therefore is the marriage contract, and having willed this, a baptized person can also be said to have willed, even though only implicitly, the sacrament.[10]

The same objection is raised in yet another form, this time under the guise of intention: It is asked how can a sacrament be conferred on someone if he has no intention of receiving it? Once again the response is the same: since the natural contract and the sacrament are inseparable, the intention to truly marry is, *eo ipso*, even if only implicitly, the necessary and sufficient intention to receive the sacrament. As Cardinal Pompedda has put it: "All the sacramental categories do not have to be applied to marriage, and in particular the intent to receive a sacrament, because the only intent required is the intention to contract, that is because by the divine institution, the intention to contract is the intention to receive the sacrament. Thus it is clear that there is a vast difference between a mere lack of intention to receive the sacrament and the actual exclusion of sacramental dignity.[11]

---

9   *Coram* Doheny, April 17, 1961: *RRDec* 53 (1961) 185: "inter baptizatos non datur contractus matrimonialis, quin eo ipso sit sacramentum, quidquid sentiant, quidquid teneant, quidquid credant contrahentes: nam sacramentum voluntate Christi fit, non voluntate partium, aut earum desiderio, aut earum opinione, aut earum fide. Ideo quisquis christianus, etsi recta fide carens ... valide contrahit, ac verum sacramentum, simul cum contractu, init, quoties id, quod de essentia contractus est, velit, seu, positivo voluntatis actu, non excludat."
10   Zenon Grocholewski, "Crisis doctrinae et iurisprudentiae rotalis circa exclusionem dignitatis sacramentalis in contractu matrimoniali", *Periodica* 67 (1978) 288: "... factum quod intentio non necessarie debet dirigi in sacramentalitatem expresse, seu obiectum volitum in se non significat eius exclusionem, positivo actu factam, et ideo non reddere matrimonium nullum."
11   Cf. Mario Pompedda, *Studi di Diritto Matrimoniale Canonico* (Milan, Giuffrè, 1993) 419: "Non devono pertanto applicarsi univocamente al matrimonio tutte le categorie sacramentali, ed in specie l'intenzionalità sacramentale: l'unica intenzionalità richiesta è la volontà di contrarre, cioè la intenzionalità contrattuale è, per istituzione divina, intenzionalità sacramentale."

The same basic objection is raised once again in a slightly different form by those who highlight the fact that the spouse is not only the *recipient* of the sacrament, but that he or she is also the *minister* of the sacrament. Furthermore, although sacramental theology in general as well as the documents of the Council of Trent do not require *fides* or *probitas* in the minister of a sacrament, they do require him to have at least a minimum intention, i. e. *faciendi id quod facit Ecclesia*. It is therefore asked: how can a minister who is indifferent to the rites of the Church, who has no concern for the sacrament, be said to be doing *id quod facit Ecclesia?*

In response, I would ask you once again to imagine the case we have before us. The spouse in question, although he does not have a living faith, is not opposed to the faith or in rebellion against it; in fact he can be said to have a certain amount of respect for the Church in so far as he has consented to enter the Church building, to submit himself to its discipline and ceremonies. This very acceptance of the ceremony can be looked upon, itself, as fulfilling that minimum intention of doing what the Church does.[12]

Is this not the same kind of attitude that a pagan neighbor or a Jewish nurse in a hospital might have when she might administer baptism to a newly born infant in danger of death, because she knows that such an action would be important to her Catholic neighbor. Is this not the same kind of attitude that a non-Catholic Christian marrying a Catholic in the Church, with a dispensation from mixed religion, would have? If such an attitude were not sufficient to manifest valid matrimonial consent, how could the Church grant such dispensations and permit such mixed marriages?

But in the final analysis, if the spouse in question truly consents to marriage, he is doing *id quod facit Ecclesia* because the Church only requires him to have a true and proper intention, that is, the intention to contract a real and true marriage.

C) A third possible attitude is that of the baptized person who presents himself in Church, truly intending to marry, but with an attitude of opposition or aversion to the faith and to the sacramental dignity of marriage. It can be said that he is in a state of rebellion against the sacramental order of redemption, and desires only the simply natural order of creation. On the one hand he wants a true marriage, on the other hand he wants nothing to do with religion or with sacraments.

In order to decide on the validity of marriage in this case I believe one would have to fall back on the classic jurisprudential approach: determining the prevailing will of the spouse. We must discover what he *primarily* intends and

---

12 Ibid., 416: "nel fatto stesso di presentarsi davanti il parroco per celebrare il matrimonio, dovrebbe essere implicito l'intendimento del nubente di volere il matrimonio quale disciplinato dalla Chiesa."

wills. If he wills a true marriage above all, then he has true marital consent and the marriage is valid, and it is also a sacrament.

But his frame of mind could be: I want marriage, but I refuse to accept marriage as the Church presents it, i. e., as a sacrament. In that case his will and his consent are directed to a phantom or impossible object, since no true marriage which is not at the same time a sacrament is possible for a baptized person. If such a will act de facto persists it amounts to total simulation of consent, because the person, whether he is conscious of it or not, is willing something impossible and unreal. His opposition to sacramentality is strong enough to exclude, in the particular circumstances, the will to contract; therefore the will not to contract prevails over the will to contract and we have a situation of total simulation.

Similarly, if he should determine: I want marriage, but only if it is the way I envision it, i. e. non-sacramental and dissoluble, this would amount to his placing a condition on his consent, and the marriage would be invalid according to c. 1102 #1 or #2 (*conditio contra substantiam*). However, doctrine and jurisprudence require that such an attitude may not be presumed but must be clearly demonstrated.

VII. Lack of Faith as a Cause of Error about the Nature of Marriage? Is This the Basis of the Possible *Dubium Facti* Envisioned by the Theological Commission?

One's act of consent can also be null and invalid because of substantial error. But here too principles derived from rational psychology and reflected in Rotal jurisprudence point out that a simple error, that is, one which does not determine the will because it remains merely in the sphere of the intellect, does not affect the validity of the act of consent. Thus a baptized non-believer's simple error about the indissolubility of marriage, would not have an invalidating effect on his matrimonial consent.

The possibility, however, also exists that a spouse's consent could be affected by *error pervicax seu error pervadens*.

A) Hence in this scenario we are dealing with *a spouse who is in error* about the sacramental dignity of marriage or its essential elements. The spouse in this case is one who has formed a false judgment and believes that marriage, even for a Christian, is merely a terrestrial reality, that it has only civil effects and that it does not have to be permanent, indissoluble or sacramental. And it is with this mindset that he presents himself before the priest.

Canonical jurisprudence sees, in such a case, the possibility of two species of error: a)*non determinans voluntatem* and b) *error pervicax or radicatus*, which can be sufficiently pervasive to influence the will and thus be an error which determines the will.

In the case of *error non determinans voluntatem* (or as it was known in the code of 1917, *error simplex*) the marriage would be valid, as we explained above. The reasoning behind this conclusion is the fact that the intellect and will are separate entities and each operates in its own sphere; error has its effect in the intellectual sphere, but not necessarily in the volitional sphere. And so the intellect might rest perhaps in the erroneous conviction that marriage is simply a terrestrial non-sacramental reality, but at the same time the will is directed toward marriage as such, that is, as it is with its true object; the will simply consents to marriage. Thus the simple error in the intellect does not have a determining influence on the will, and the marital consent is valid.[13]

To prove that one is no longer dealing with simple error one must demonstrate in some fashion that the error has not remained in the intellect, but has entered the field of operations of the will. This may be done by pointing out concrete deeds, actions or for example, a state of mind perhaps in rebellion against the Church and society etc, which have caused the will to be determined to choose only a non-sacramental marriage. In many Rotal cases the absence of Christian education or an upbringing contrary to the tenets of the faith is often seen as a remote cause of nullity since absorbed erroneous ideas might possibly have influenced the spouse to limit the object of his consent; but as long as these ideas are only generic and vague, they are not seen to have sufficient force to determine the will. But if a precise reason, and therefore a probable element of proof, can be indicated as to why a spouse would definitely have applied these particular ideas to his own specific marriage, this can be a sufficient demonstration that the error has determined the will.

A law section c. Stankiewicz illustrates two ways in which error can determine the will.

a) The first occurs when a baptized person with little or no faith is so imbued with a *false judgement*, for example about the indissolubility of the bond that *he or she is truly functioning out of an invincible error that presents to the will marriage only as a dissoluble institution*. Thus the error is truly leading the will to consent only to dissoluble marriage and *determines the will to choose only that kind of marriage*. We see in this situation that such an error, so rooted in the person that it is considered the truth, determines the object of the internal

---

13   Ibid., 411: "A tale principio si aggiunge la teoria della volonta' generale presupposta nel nubente, cosi come i canonisti di grande nome hanno cercato di puntualizzare. L'errore, cioe', circa le proprieta' essenziali o la dignita' sacramentale non induce nullita' nel consenso purche' si abbia la volonta' generale di contrarre un vero matrimonio: e per il favor matrimonii si presume che tale volonta' generale esista e con essa i nubenti accedano a contrarre."

will in such a way that this will accepts, under the appearance of good, the object proposed. So the will determined by error is actually directed toward the attainment of another object which is essentially different from the true formal object of matrimonial consent, by substituting, although unknowingly, one for the other. The spouse in this case did not consent to marriage as it is but only to his own false notion of marriage.

Accordingly, it is also clear that such tenacious error is actually determining *the will by a positive act*. For in the case of determined error there is not merely ignorance, or an inertia of the will or the absence of willing. As we read in a sentence c. Funghini of 22 February 1989, *Dec* 81 (1989), p. 30: "[my translation] There is no act of the will unless the will wants something. In order for an act of the will to happen it is necessary that the inclination from which it arises encounter a resistance either internal or external, and overcome it." So in our case the one erring positively seeks and intends the substitute object determined by his own will, and if he should de facto erroneously consent to an object substantially different from that which he intended, his act of consent would be vitiated by substantial error.

Thus to prove this determining error one must in some way demonstrate a reason to hold in the particular case that the person's will was positively seeking and intending, e. g. only to accept dissoluble marriage. One has to prove not only a general inclination towards the substitute object, but also an adherence to that object tenacious enough to overcome some sort of internal or external resistance. One would have to present some reason why the error should be considered an invincible rather than a merely simple error. The one erring should be so convinced of his own object of consent [dissoluble marriage] that he would be willing to bid farewell to marriage itself, rather than be required to accept indissoluble marriage.

Another method of verifying such determined error would be found in the *criterium reactionis*. It would seem that the spouse who erred, upon discovering his error, namely that he had entered a marriage which society and the other spouse considered indissoluble, he would have to have had some reaction. Most probably he would have denounced the fact that anyone would have expected him to be in a permanent marriage etc., or he would have protested, or manifested his dissent in some way.

Another way in which determining error can lead to simulation is also explained by Stankiewicz.

b) A positive erroneous consent, determining the will according to the substitute object specified by the error, operates autonomously as long as the error remains invincible. But the mind's firm adherence to that substitute object (a sort of dissoluble pseudo-marriage) can be weakened by doubt or the fear that the opposite (acceptance of permanent marriage) might possibly be required for a real valid marriage. In that case, then, the loss of the state of certitude brings about *a conscious divergence* between the internal will and the objective reality of the canonical matrimonial order that must be expressed by an external declaration at the time of the contract.

Because of this conscious divergence the person either accepts marriage according to the meaning of the words he outwardly expresses (indissoluble and faithful) or else his tenacious adherence to his own concept becomes the proportionate and grave reason for his excluding indissolubility by a positive act of the will. In this case his rooted error has caused him to simulate, although only partially, because he wishes marriage but positively intends to exclude one of its essential elements, indissolubility.

But also in this situation the partial simulation has to be carried out by a positive act of the will. *Such a will act cannot be just presumed but must be shown to have been truly elicited either explicitly or implicitly.* It is not necessary to show that the contractant absolutely understood that the bond would be broken, but it suffices to show that he or she retained the faculty of dissolving the bond if it should become necessary.

Since it is a question of a positive act of the will operating in both of the hypotheses of the way determined error invalidates matrimonial consent, the normal ways to prove such a positive act of the will are relied on. The first of these is either a judicial or extrajudicial confession of the person who is erring or simulating. Of course one in invincible error might not be conscious of having positively excluded indissolubility, but should at least be conscious of the divergence between his internal conception of marriage and the words expressed in the ceremony. Establishing the proximate and remote causes of the simulation, that is showing why the error made the transition from intellect to will, is another means of proof. Antecedent, concomitant and subsequent circumstances can also provide arguments that demonstrate the contractant's real internal will and show how it was determined by certain facts and events.

So in the situation of rooted error or error *pervicax* the error is maintained with such vehemence and has so invaded the personality and way of thinking of a spouse that a presumption now seems to exist that the intellectual error has indeed penetrated and determined the will so that the will can only intend an object in conformity with its own intellect.

Cardinal Pompedda has described this error giving it a new and more precise descriptive name, *error pervadens*. It is in this context of error that he discusses the lack of faith and its possible effects on the validity of marriage. One must distinguish between the faith which is necessary for the sacrament to be received fruitfully and the minimum intention needed to administer the sacrament. No *explicit* intention to wish or to accept matrimony as a sacrament is needed because the only intention needed is the intention to truly contract marriage. In other sacraments there must be a religious intention because one is creating a efficacious grace giving sign. In marriage, however, a created natural reality has already by the institution of Christ been converted into a sacrament, and the spouses need merely to embrace that reality.

In so far as they are also ministers of the sacrament the spouses must have at least the implicit will to consent in what the Church intends when it celebrates the marriage. Where there is however a real contrast between this general intention of doing what the Church does and the spouses' own contrary intention, the contrary intention prevails because it is the intention that is actually determining the spouses' will act.

Thus, until recently lack of faith was seen to have a role to play only in either of two ways: 1) in so far as it can be a contributing factor or cause that induces the will to positively exclude the sacramentality of marriage [simulation], or 2) in so far as it involves an *error pervadens*, or better, an *error specificans obiectum*.

VIII. New Insight on the Role of Faith in Marital Consent Presented by Pope Benedict XVI in His Last Allocution to the Roman Rota.

In an allocution given in January of 2013 to the Judges of the Roman Rota, Pope Benedict XVI discussed how lack of faith can have an impact on the validity of matrimonial consent. As we have seen, he specifically stated: "The indissoluble pact between a man and a woman *does not require*, as far as the sacrament is concerned, *the personal faith of the spouses*". And he went on to quote Saint Pope John Paul II who told the Rota in 2003 that "... an attitude on the part of the spouses which does not take into account the supernatural dimension of marriage *can render it null, only if it impairs validity on the natural level"*.

Nevertheless, Pope Benedict, with a new and profound insight based on a consideration of the cultural situation of modern man, then went on to illustrate a new way in which a spouse's lack of faith might possibly affect his capacity to enter even the natural nuptial pact. He pointed out that contemporary culture is so imbued with accentuated subjectivism and ethical and religious relativism that some people question whether or not contemporary man is capable of actually binding himself. If that were true, then modern man could not bind himself definitively in the natural nuptial pact. And even if one should admit that a bond which lasts for an entire lifetime is truly possible and corresponds to the nature of man, those same people would argue that such a bond is in contrast with man's natural liberty and with his self-realization. Such a notion is part of widely disseminated mentality which holds that a person becomes himself only by remaining autonomous and entering into contact with another only by means of relationships which can be interrupted at any time. In such a context a person's choice to link himself with a bond which lasts an entire lifetime does not seem possible on the merely human level; only with opening himself to the light of faith in the Lord would such a choice be possible. Thus one can understand how the closing of oneself to God or a refusal of the sacred dimension of the conjugal union and its value in the order of grace, makes it very hard to accept and to choose even the natural matrimonial covenant itself.

And so Pope Benedict hypothesizes that the lack of faith can perhaps have an effect on marital consent in so far as the lack of faith might make one incapable of truly donating oneself to the other and incapable of acting for the *bonum coniugum*. One must not prescind from the consideration that there can be cases in which, specifically by reason of an absence of faith, the good of the spouses becomes compromised and, in fact is excluded from consent itself. For example there could be a refusal to accept the equal dual union which contradistinguishes the matrimonial bond. And so he concludes: "With the present considerations, I certainly do not intend to suggest any facile automatism between lack of faith and invalidity of the matrimonial union, but more particularly I wish to point out how such a *lack of faith may even, albeit not necessarily, have a compromising effect on the very goods of matrimony*, since a referral back to the natural order as willed by God is inherent in the nuptial pact.

IX. Need for Caution in the Treatment of This Complex Question in Order To Avoid Creating Illegitimate Personal Presumptions of a General Nature That Are Not in Accord with Recognized Jurisprudence.

Since there does not appear to be a real solid *dubium iuris* about the application of the traditional principles of determining validity of consent to the marriage of baptized non-believers, and since furthermore each particular case in which the validity of consent is actually challenged should be determined individually on its merits according to the approved jurisprudence, it does not seem legitimate for a canonist or a tribunal to hold that there is a general presumption of invalid consent in a situation involving lack of faith.

The establishment of a general presumption contrary to the approved jurisprudence about the effects on the validity of marriage of the lack of faith would have several serious repercussions. How would such a statement or presumption affect the Church's doctrine on baptism? At present we allow infant baptism even though the recipients do not have actual living faith at the moment of the reception of the sacrament. If the Church should require living faith for the valid reception of the sacrament of marriage, why would it not require the same in the case of baptism? Do we wish to call into question the validity of infant baptism?

Ready acceptance of a general presumption that baptized non-Catholics lack faith in or deny the Sacrament of Marriage, or that they are in a state of *error pervadens* about the essential properties of marriage would lead to the conclusion that millions of marriages entered into by baptized non-Catholics are not valid or sacramental. What ecumenical effect would this have? Would most Anglicans, Methodists etc. be happy to hear that the Catholic Church no longer considers their marriages to be sacramental? The result would be that the Sacrament of Marriage would no longer seem to be something that all the baptized might attain to, but rather the special prerogative of an elite group of truly devout Christians, mostly belonging to the Catholic Church.

Greater pastoral problems would result from such a general presumption than could be solved by such a presumption. At present the Church grants the permission to marry in the case of mixed religion since it presumes that the baptized non-Catholic who wishes to marry a Catholic is entering marriage with a naturally valid and sufficient consent. If it is now presumed [because of his lack of living faith in the sacrament] that he does not have the minimum sufficient intention to do what the Church does, and that there is the probability of an invalid celebration, how would the Church justify granting this permission? Would not greater pastoral problems for priests be caused by calling into question the current praxis of granting permissions for mixed marriages? [for unworthy Catholics, c. 1071, n. 4].

X. Conclusion

In this discussion we have had the chance to focus our attention on the meaning of sacramentality or the sacramental dignity of marriage. We have seen that while closely connected with the *bonum sacramenti,* sacamentality itself should not be confused with or considered identical with the indissolubility or permanence of marriage. It can best be defined, as c. 1055 seems to define it, as *the elevation of the natural covenant* by which a baptized man and a baptized woman constitute a partnership of their whole life (ordered by its nature to their reciprocal good and to the generation and education of offspring) to the dignity of a sacrament, that is, to be *a sign of the salvific and eschatological order* into which the baptised person has been already been inserted by his baptism. It is thus the very essence of marriage, that is the natural pact between the spouses both *in fieri* and *in facto esse*, which is elevated to be a life-giving sign and source of grace.

Hence it would seem that lack of faith *per se* cannot constitute a legitimate autonomous ground of marriage nullity. Rather lack of faith can be a contributing factor or disposing cause which would impact on marital consent in three ways: 1) as a contributing cause for the grounds of partial or total simulation 2) as a contributing cause for the grounds of error determining the will, or 3) possibly as a contributing cause for the grounds of incapacity to accept and discharge the essential obligations of marriage.

It seems correct to say that one can directly exclude sacramentality by a positive act of the will as a result of a deliberate intention contrary to sacramentality, so that in the psychological order such an act might be described as a partial simulation; however, one must on always be mindful that in the ontological order a true partial simulation becomes in fact a total simulation, in so far as consent to an impossible object is inefficacious and totally invalidates true matrimonial consent. The exclusion of sacramentality, then, results in the exclusion of the essence of marriage, and the marriage ceremony itself effects only an implicit act of simulation or an implicit act of conditioned consent.

Next, we have seen that, in order to determine the invalidity of the consent, one must prove that an error concerning the essential elements of marriage is an error that has truly determined the person's will in the individual case. One can not generally presume that such error has determined the person's will, but rather the acts of the case must show that the error did not simply remain in the person's intellect but actually passed over and had an influence on his will.

Yet in some cases the facts and the circumstances of the case are such that they do demonstrate the presence of a deeply rooted *error pervicax et pervadens*, which has so pervaded the person's personality and mentality that it is also seen to have determined and affected his will.

Lack of faith can be taken as a conditioning factor which helps one to determine if the error concerning sacramentality has truly determined the person's will. In the case of *error pervadens* where the lack of faith may have prevented the spouse from intending and willing a specifically religious act, one must examine the *seriousness* and *internal sincerity* with which the spouse lets himself be involved in the religious ceremony, that is, with which he consents to truly contract marriage in that setting.

As much of what has been said above follows the line of thought proposed by Cardinal Pompedda. I will end by restating his conclusion: "From what has been said so far, it does not seem to me that one could agree with the proposal of a new ground of nullity based on a lack of faith. ... I think that the question of sacramentality should be proposed for judgment under the twofold ground of nullity a) either as an exclusion of an essential element of marriage or b) as an error about an essential element which has determined the will."[14]

---

14 Pompedda, *Studi di Diritto Matrimoniale Canonico,* 446: "Il fin qui detto, se bene inteso, non mi sembra che eventualmente potrebbe consentire di proporre un nuovo capo di nullità, concepito come 'mancanza di fede'. ... ritengo che l'aspetto sacramentale potrebbe essere sottoposto a giudizio sotto il duplice capo di nullità b) come exclusio elementi essentialis matrimonii b) ovvero, come error circa elementum essentiale voluntatem determinans.

Finally, Pope Benedict XVI has recently suggested that lack of faith might possibly in some cases constitute an incapacity to accept and discharge the obligations connected with the *bonum coniugum* or the three *bona Augustiniana*, and thus have an impact on the natural nuptial pact. Accordingly, such a case might be judged under the grounds of nullity of c. 1095 n. 3. But even he noted how arduous it is to determine such matters on both the practical and juridical levels and therefore recommends that each case be decided based on the factual investigation of the particular case, and not by means of a facile general presumption.

# Seminar

## Raking the Embers, to Extinguish or Start a Fire: Some Thoughts on the Possibilities for the Future of Apostolic Religious Life
### *Sister Maria Casey, RSJ*

When I was a child my grandparents lived with us. One of my earliest and enduring memories is that of my grandfather taking responsibility for keeping the turf fire alive always and burning healthily for cooking and heating in our large kitchen which doubled as a living room and was really the heart as well as the hearth of our home. Each evening he raked the fire, spreading out the dying embers carefully and covering them with ashes, saved from the morning, in a manner that I would now call very scientific. The following morning, he was first up and would remove the ashes and reclaim the embers to start a new fire. Only on extremely rare occasions would the fire have gone out – usually when a lesser skilled member of the family raked the embers the previous night.[1]

In dark times for the Chosen People, Isaiah reminded them, "Cease dwelling on days gone by and brooding over past events! Look! Here and now I am doing something new; at any moment it will break from the bud. Can you not see it?" (Isaiah 43:18-19). At the Annunciation, the same loving, caring God sent a messenger to Mary, a virgin, to tell her that she would conceive and give birth to a son and that she should call him Jesus (Luke 1.31). At his last meal with his Apostles Jesus gave them the promise "I will ask the Father and he will give you another helper who will stay with you forever (John 14: 16). He is the Spirit who reveals the truth about God and is in each one. Later that evening Jesus, told them, "It is my own peace I give you ... Do not be worried and upset; do not be afraid." Later still Jesus went out to seal his fate – passion, crucifixion and finally, resurrection. From the suffering in this Paschal Mystery the Church was born.

Into this Church which suffered through persecution and many other vicissitudes, the Holy Spirit always was generous with "the newness" that Isaiah foretold and that Jesus had promised till the end. In particular times of need, there came to the Church from the same loving God special charisms which "broke from the bud" and blossomed in the guise of different forms of consecrated life.

---

1  See Joan Chittister, *The Fire in These Ashes: A Spirituality of Contemporary Religious Life*, (Kansas City: Sheed & Ward, 1996) 36-37. Chittister calls the process "grieshog" – the gaelic word.

Out of the ashes of sorrow there arose a new fire of love enabling the children of the Father and gifting them with a newness that alleviated their needs at that particular time in history.

A charism, that particular gift for a specific time and place, was given to a person or a group, to respond to a call to further the mission of Jesus in the world, often through living a consecrated life. The response is expressed in a closer following of Christ who is the Way, the Truth and the Life, leading all to the Father under the guidance of the Holy Spirit who "awakens the desire to respond fully; it is he who guides the growth of this desire, helping it to mature into a positive response and sustaining it as it faithfully translates into action".[2]

This is a special gift of the Spirit to the Church, a gift that Paul VI, in *Evangelica testificatio*,[3] was the first to label "charism" specifically in relation to religious institutes.[4] He explains, "the charism of the religious life, far from being an impulse born of flesh and blood or derived from a mentality which conforms itself to the modern world, is the fruit of the Holy Spirit, who is always at work within the Church" (*ET*, 11). The Second Vatican Council recognised that a charism is a gift that the Lord gave to the Church. "This gift determines the identity of the institute, its nature, its spirit, its finality and its particular character: terms the code of Canon Law uses to indicate the elements of a charism of consecrated life.[5] The Code itself does not use the term "charism" there being great difficulty in defining its nature.

Pope Francis in many of his homilies speaks of the gift that the particular charisms are to the Church. During his three hour meeting with the Leaders of male religious institutes on November 29, 2013, he said, in discussing relations with bishops, "The charisms of the various institutes need to be respected and fostered because they are needed in dioceses".[6] In his homily for the feast of the

---

2  John Paul II, Post-synodal Exhortation *Vita consecrata*, (=*VC*), 25 March 1966, in *AAS* 88 (1996) 377-486; English translation, *Consecrated Life* (Sherbrooke, QC: Médiaspaul, 1996).
3  Paul VI, Apostolic Exhortation on the Renewal of Religious Life, *Evangelica testificatio*, (= *ET*), 29 June 1971, in *AAS* 63 (1971) 497-526; English translation in A. Flannery (ed.) vol. 1, *Vatican Council II: The Conciliar and Post-Conciliar Documents*, (= Flannery 1), New Revised Edition (Dublin: Dominican Publications, 1992) here at *ET* 11, p. 685.
4  See B.J. Sweeney, *The Patrimony of an Institute in the Code of Canon Law; A Study of Canon 578* (Rome: Pontificia studiorum Universitatis a S. Thoma Aquinate in Urbe, 1995) 46-51. While Vatican Council II did not use "charism", the author says that, in placing consecrated life within the context of life and holiness of the Church, it placed it within the charismatic structure of the Church.
5  Jean Beyer, "Charisms, Religious Institutes and Particular Churches," *Consecrated Life* 15 (1990) p. 317
6  Pope Francis quoted in http://www.catholicherald.co.uk/news/2014/01/03/pope-francis-calls-on-religious-orders-to-wake-up-the-world/ accessed July 10, 2017.

Presentation, February 2, 2015, he considers that members of consecrated life must walk the path of Jesus. He says, "This path, then, takes *the form of the rule*, marked by *the charism of the founder*".[7]

In the history of the development of apostolic institutes of religious the Vatican did not always honour the significance of a charism. As is well known the early form of consecrated life was monastic with women religious being enclosed. When there was a proliferation of new institutes, the Fourth Lateran Council in 1215 decreed that, henceforth, all new institutes should follow one of previously approved rules.[8] In 1298 Boniface VIII decreed in the Constitution, *Periculoso,* that all vows taken in a community approved by the Holy See were solemn vows.[9] Moreover, it imposed cloister on all women religious without exception. The concept of imposed cloister was confirmed by Pius V in a Constitution *Circa Pastoralis* (May 29, 1566).[10] Women who could only leave the cloister if fire, leprosy or an epidemic warranted it.[11] Eventually, the Holy See took control for approving new institutes and the edict requiring that their rule be one of the four approved, namely that of Benedict, Augustine, Basil and Francis, stifled the expression of new charisms and removed the authority to approve new institutes from bishops and placed it in the hands of the pope.

As society developed and there was a move from a largely rural community to urban ones, new problems and new needs arose both in the church and society. New institutes for men appeared where members could move freely from the cloister to meet the needs and have recognition for simple vows. It was the era that saw the flourishing of mendicant orders, whose members went out to preach and assist the poor. As the male monastics moved out to minister in the "world" women did not have this privilege and, in fact, women who wanted to follow the example of Francis and Ignatius were not permitted to do so.

For women, the first foundresses who sought to follow suit met with serious difficulty. For Angela Merici and her Ursulines and Mary Ward and her Loreto sisters, life was not merely difficult but horrendous. In spite of the pain, they

---

7   Pope Francis, http://www.news.va/en/news/pope-francis-opens-year-for-consecrated-life-homily, accessed July 8, 2017.
8   J.D. Mansi (ed), *Sacrorum conciliorum nova et amplissima collectio,* vol. 22, col. 1002.
9   A. Friedberg, *Corpus iuris canonici* (Lipsiae: ex Officina B. Tauchnitz, 1879-1881) vol. 2, cols. 1053-1054.
10  *Bullarum diplomatum et privilegiorum sanctorum romanorum pontificum, Taurinensis editio (cura Tomassetti), locupletior facta collectio novissima plurium brevium, epistolorum, decretorum actorumque, Sedes a S. Leone Magno usque ad praesens (1740)* (A. Taurinorum, S. Franco et H. Dalmazzo editoribus, 1857-1872) vol. 7, 447-448.
11  See L. Jarrell, *The Development of Legal Structures for Women Religious between 1500 and 1900: A Study of Selected Institutes of Religious Life for Women,* Canon Law Studies 513 (Washington, DC: Catholic University of America, 1984) 22.

founded the first institutes of apostolic women with central government. Over the years, other apostolic institutes sprang up and managed to have their constitutions, which included simple vows, approved but not their institutes. The institutes were technically "tolerated" but the women were not recognised as true religious, even though they worked in the Church for the poor in a great variety of ways. It was not until December 8, 1900 that Pope Leo XIII issued the Constitution, *Conditae a Christo,* adapting the law to life and recognising congregations with simple vows as religious.[12] This Constitution also clarified that there were two classes of congregations with simple vows, those with *diocesan* approval and those with *pontifical* approval.

On June 28, 1901 the Congregation of Bishops and Regulars issued *Normae* which set out the procedures for all institutes with simple vows seeking full papal approbation and, while they were not law, they were often adhered to slavishly giving all institutes a uniform pattern. The *Normae* had stated that there was no place in constitutions for material that was not juridic. Hence, the Constitutions of various congregations did not express anything of their distinctive character and spiritual motivation.[13] The 1917 Code of Canon Law relied on the constitution, *Conditae a Christo* and the *Normae* for their sources. The recovery of the distinctive charisms of institutes did not occur until the Second Vatican Council[14] and the promulgation of the 1983 Code of Canon Law.[15]

The first document of great significance for Religious was *Perfectae caritatis.* It stated that "The adaptation and renewal of the religious life includes both the constant *return to the sources of all Christian life* and to *the original spirit of the institutes* and their *adaptation to the changed conditions of our time.*" These three aspects together with the directive to adapt constitutions, directories, custom books, books of prayers and ceremonies, the manner of living, praying and working as well as taking into account the modern physical and psychological circumstances of members brought about a flurry of unprecedented activity in most religious institutes. Special general chapters were called, the concept of subsidiarity was widely embraced with everyone possible being consulted on changes, constitutions were updated, habits were simplified, the manner of

---

12   Leo XIII, Apostolic Constitution *Conditae a Christo,* in *Acta Leonis XIII Pontificis Maximi,* (Romae: ex Typographica Vaticana, 1881-1905) vol. 20, 317-327.
13   See Mary Wright, *Mary Ward's Institute: The Struggle for Identity* (Sydney: Crossing Press, 1997) 29.
14   See Second Vatican Council, "Decree on the Up-to-Date Renewal of Religious Life," *Perfectae caritatis,* (= PC), 28 October 1965, *AAS* 58 (1966) 702-712; English translation in Flannery 1, 611-623. See also Paul VI, *Ecclesiae sanctae II,* in Flannery 1, 624-633.
15   *Codex iuris canonici auctoritate Ioannis Pauli PP. II promulgatus,* Libreria editrice Vaticana, 1983. British Commonwealth version of English language translation: *The Code of Canon Law in English Translation,* new revised edition prepared by The Canon Law Society of Great Britain and Ireland, in association with The Canon Law Society of Australia and New Zealand and The Canadian Canon Law Society, (London: Collins; Ottawa: Canadian Conference of Catholic Bishops, 1997).

living was modified and the accretions of unsuitable customs from years or even centuries past were cut away. Members of institutes strode bravely into a new world arena.

It must be noted that religious life, while not of the world, is embedded in the world and the Church, both of which were undergoing profound change in the scientific, political and social scenes. Sputnik had gone into space with huge ramifications for the space race, education and world views. The Church was experiencing the heady days of the post Vatican times with changes unheard of and, even, undreamt of. Experimentation was the rallying call of the day. Mass could be celebrated in the vernacular and facing the people, vestments were adapted and church architecture was modified.

By the time the Code of Canon Law was promulgated, religious institutes were somewhat surprised to see that "charism" was not mentioned but the essence was codified under patrimony in canon 578 which reads, "

> The whole patrimony of an institute must be faithfully preserved by all. This patrimony is comprised of the intentions of the founders, of all that the competent ecclesiastical authority has approved concerning the nature, purpose, spirit and character of the institute, and of its sound traditions.

While religious institutes continued to meet the needs of the people, by the 1980s there was a new inward-looking approach to the living of religious life. There was an increasing sense of entitlement to freedom in the way that it was lived. Some institutes alienated themselves from Church bureaucracy and attempted to function separately. Many institutes began to lose members and some, in fact, were said to haemorrhage. Moreover, in an era of great change and more opportunities for women to function well in society, there was a real decline, especially in western cultures in the numbers entering religious institutes.

In individual institutes there is a lifecycle that incorporates various stages:[16]

- *the foundation period* when the vision/charism of the founder is "contagious". A small group follows the expression of the charism to meet specific needs in a particular moment of history for the love of God and the poor.
- *The expansion period*: many new members join the group so that there is an effort to establish an organisational template and constitutions and specific way of life together.

---

16   L. Cada et al., *Shaping the Coming Age of Religious Life* (Seabury Press: New York, 1979) 53.

- *The stabilisation period*: the institute is at its peak, becomes fully structured and has a tendency to depend on customs and tried ways of operating.
- *The breakdown period*: the customary ways of living and acting no longer meet newer expressions of need. Numbers decline and are generally ageing.
- *The critical period*: Decline in numbers and an ageing cohort no longer indicate a viable institute. There are choices to be made.

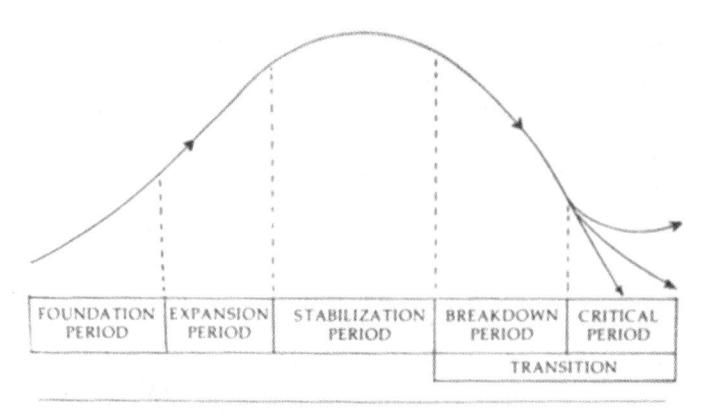

FIGURE 2.2: Life Cycle of a Religious Community

Arbuckle, recognises three models for religious life: the monastic, mendicant and apostolic but he introduces another, the therapeutic model for this post-Vatican II critical period for apostolic religious institutes. He describes the model as one where members are no longer looking outward to the needs of their time but are focussed on the primacy of the individual over apostolic needs; the centrality of the human person to the neglect of the common good; too many meetings for decision making; encouraging people to be over-dependent on community life. He claims that "*the therapeutic community is designed precisely to respond first and foremost to the individual needs of clients, only indirectly of course to the needs of the world beyond them.*" [17]

Arbuckle makes clear that he does not imply that members are mentally ill but that some of the processes accepted in institutes in response to the call after Vatican II for renewal and subsidiarity have been mis-used or undertaken without due assessment.

The renewal that was so enthusiastically embraced after the Vatican Council has now impacted on the effectiveness and relevance of institutes. The move

---
17  G. Arbuckle, "Suffocating Religious Life: A New Type Emerges", in http://www.theway.org.uk/Back/s065Arbuckle.pdf accessed July 15, 2016.

from a more monastic, totally "community" oriented lifestyle to one that is more individualistic where members chose to live alone for the most part, to pursue individual ministries and not be involved in what was once described as congregational or "corporate" works may have led to this diminishment of numbers and effectiveness as a congregation. That is not to say that members are not still being individually very effective and pastorally involved. He believes, too, that community decisions are often plagued with over consultation and that superiors are hampered in their decision-making as a result.

The implication is that institutes with ageing and diminishing numbers need to look again at the gift of the charism that motivated their founders. Pope Francis, at the vigil for the Year of Consecrated Life, said:

> *Leave your nest and head for the margins of humanity today! To do this, let Christ meet you. The encounter with Him will inspire you to encounter others and will lead you toward the neediest, the poorest. Reach all the peripheries that are in need of the light of the Gospel. This will ask of you vigilance to discern the novelties of the Spirit; lucidity in recognizing the complexity of the new frontiers; discernment in identifying the limits and the appropriate manner to proceed; and immersion in reality, 'touching the suffering flesh of Christ in others'.*[18]

While Pope Francis repeatedly challenges members of consecrated life to re-visit their charism, he is careful to remind them that "with Christ, always start from the Gospel! Take it on as your way of life and translate it into daily actions marked by simplicity and coherence, thus overcoming the temptation to transform it into an ideology." He warns that the charism of institutes of consecrated life is one facet of the Gospel and must not be operated apart from the Gospel or the Church. However, the ministry must be one of "service" and not one of "servitude".[19]

While this "going out to the peripheries" once more may revitalise an institute it is not merely a matter of attracting more members. In 2015, Pope Francis warned formators to ensure that "the eventual crisis of quantity does not result in a much graver crisis of quality."[20] He advised formators not to accept members who were not suitable for the institute.

---

18  Pope Francis, November 29, 2014 in http://beforeitsnews.com/religion/2014/11/pope-francis-to-consecrated-men-women-leave-your-nests-2481992.html accessed July 20, 2017.
19  Ibid.
20  Pope Francis, April 13, 2015 addressing Formators, https://www.ncronline.org/news/vatican/pope-francis-warns-religious-orders-not-accept-unbalanced-people     accessed, October 3, 2017.

What then are the options for an institute that is ageing and diminishing to the stage that it is almost totally therapeutic? Are the embers of the charism being smothered with the ashes of diminishment, age or non-engagement in the Gospel as expressed in the Church and the world of the now?

There are the solutions offered in the Code of Canon Law. Canon 582 provides two options which are fusions and unions of institutes of consecrated life. Both processes are reserved to the Apostolic See alone.

Fusion occurs when a small congregation with diminishing and ageing members decides to join a larger more viable congregation with a similar charism. The small congregation loses its identity and its members become part of the larger congregation together with all its assets and liabilities.

Union occurs when two congregations with similar charisms or with a common founder are both suppressed and form one new congregation with a new constitution and combined assets and liabilities. For both of these actions what is important is Christ's mission and not just the survival of either congregation. There needs to be a realistic hope that the members can continue to work and minister on the prophetic edge of the church and the world. If, however, the new entities die out, this is a chance to enter the mystery of the suffering and death of Christ.

In more recent years, other solutions have been tried. In Australia two small diocesan congregations that were no longer able to provide their own leadership requested their respective Archbishops to suspend the requirement in their constitutions to hold elections for a congregational leader and council. This request was made, in both cases, after a lengthy preparation and discernment by the members. They reviewed their history and the expression of their charisms, examined what they wished to retain and what they would need to let go, mulled over which of their ministries might survive and which would not. They consulted some congregations with similar charisms and ministries with a view to reaching a decision to request outside leadership. The final General Chapter was held, the suspension of the relevant part of the constitution was granted by the Archbishops. Discernment proceeded to decide on who would provide leadership. When the decision was finally taken, the Archbishops and both congregations were involved in drawing up a Memorandum of Understanding that would give a framework for the future. One congregation completed this journey some years ago and the second one is now on the way.

A third diminishing diocesan congregation followed a different path. It was always a small congregation with ministry of outreach to the poor. When the sisters reached the critical stage when they no longer could hold a valid chapter they divested themselves of their ministries to a larger congregation. They invited this congregation to companion them until such time as there are no more members. The companioning congregation treats them as though they were members – inviting them to events and community celebrations of prayer, ministries and events such as birthdays and jubilees. These companioned sisters continue to live in a house of their own knowing that if they need aged care their companion congregation will provide it.

In other congregations where the grieshog is extinguishing the embers of the charism there are different arrangements for their end of life and eventual demise. Francis Morrisey, OMI, has written widely on the pathways undertaken in Canada and the USA. While all the solutions above are canonically acceptable, what is not acceptable is treating associates or other lay persons (by whatever other names) as members – either of general councils or chapters. Certainly, they assist in many facets of an institute but not in the same manner as vowed members.

History provides us with many examples where the raking of the embers led to a new fire and a resurrection of ailing congregations such as the Loreto sisters, who were suppressed and their foundress jailed for her efforts. The embers were kept alive and, today, there are two congregations that arose from the vision of a few members.[21] Another example of the tenacity and faith in their charism was that that experienced in the re-vitalisation of the Hospitaller Order of St John of God in Spain by Brother (now Saint) Benedict Menni. Brother Menni went alone to Spain to re-instate the order "which to all intents and purposes ceased to exist as a result of the Laws of Suppression passed by liberal governments" in the mid-nineteenth century. Among the many congregations that were suppressed was that of the Spanish Hopitallers. Through the untiring and faith-filled efforts of St Menni the Spanish province of the Hopitallers was not only refounded, with approval granted in 1884, but a new congregation of women, Sisters Hospitallers, had their constitutions approved in 1882.[22]

Institutes of Consecrated life came into being with an impulse of the Holy Spirit who gifted a person or persons to respond to particular needs in a given moment of history by living a particular facet of the Gospel for the sake of the Mission. Pope (now Saint) John Paul II reminded us, "The purpose of a charism as a gift to consecrated life is to share in the mission of Jesus which is the realisation of the Reign of God through the Church given to the world as sacrament and servant."[23]

---

21　See Mary Wright, *The Canonical Development of the Institute of the Blessed Virgin Mary* (Sydney: Crossing Press, 1997).
22　A. Montonati, *The Courage of a Prophet; Saint Benedict Menni* (Milan: Ancora S.r.I., 2000) 160 p. .
23　John Paul II, Encyclical Letter, *Redemptoris missio,* (=*RM*), 7 December 1990, in *AAS* 83 (1991) 249-340; English translation in *Origins,* 20 (1990-1991) 545.

There are two schools of thought concerning the life-time of a charism. There are some who say that a charism dies when the original need is met and the congregation is in decline and moves towards extinction. There are others who say that the charism is a gift to the Church from the Holy Spirit who does not take back a gift. It is a call to live a facet of the Gospel and the expression of this facet can be adapted to a continuing need, or to a new need not necessarily identical to the original need.

What is needed for those congregations desiring to rake the embers to re-kindle the flame of the first impulse? Let us look at an example from the secular world of business. Recall the story of Kinky Boots[24] briefly. A manufacturing company, for generations, produced the best product that served a particular group within society. Not only did the excellent product not change, the culture of the company, its approach to leadership and the service did not change over several generations. Consequently, when society's needs changed with changing fashions the company found itself facing bankruptcy and closure with consequences for the owners and employees. With help from an unexpected quarter, and a daring change to the usual patterns both of product and approach the company came back to life. The young owner had been advised, "find the niche that is not served and look to it!". After much discussion, planning and trial the new product led to a success that could not have been imagined.

How may ageing congregations learn from this experience? The head of the company had to consider its ultimate purpose, how he could care for employees some of whom had been with the company all their lives, how he could keep up morale, how he could fan the flame of new ideas while still retaining the integrity of the company's original vision. He knew he had to consider the extent to which he could take risks, accept opposition and face unknown outcomes along the path he wanted to go. He had to accept the challenges of leadership in a venture hitherto unknown or even tested in the factory. Moreover, he had to address the complexities of relationships, the prejudices of staff and the uncertainty of the outcome.

In a congregation facing an uncertain future, there may only be one or a few members who can recognise the niche not being served and see the need for a new expression of the original charism that is suitable for the present and the future. These persons need not necessarily be members of the leadership group but they will ultimately need the co-operation of the leadership. The leadership would have a dual role at this time. They would have to refine, through good discernment, what current needs could be met while still retaining the essence of the original charism. In addition, they could not neglect the care of the ageing members of or making provision for the needs of those who can no longer work at the coal-face. Pope Francis reminds us that "these ones are the memory of

---

24  See one version of the story at https://en.wikipedia.org/wiki/Kinky_Boots_(musical) accessed July 25, 2017.

the institute, these sisters are those who have sowed, who have worked... These sisters pray for the institute...These sisters also have very extensive experience... Let them feel consulted, and from their wisdom will come good advice. Be sure of it."[25] Pope Francis also warned against a temptation to ignore poverty at this period.

He advises, "when a religious institute feels that it is dying, feels that it no longer has the ability to attract new members, feels that perhaps the time for which the Lord had chosen that congregation has passed, there is the temptation to greed"[26] and simply to focus on a very comfortable lifestyle for members.

Those members seeking to "re-kindle the flame" could face opposition and non-acceptance in a congregation whose members could well say, "that is not how we always did it!" They would have to overcome allegiance to tradition, customs and other accretions of practice as regards the how and the why that "mission" was carried out. Arbuckle explains that while "congregations desperately need outward-looking, faith-oriented evangelisers" they are not always accepted since they often cannot give all the details required for concretising new pastoral insights. This inability to give precise details and possible outcomes demands both trust and faith in an ever-leading, beckoning God.

Such a new initiative in response to current unmet needs could well be inspired by re-visiting the trust and faith of founders who often began alone and faced many obstacles even to being banished from the congregation they founded. There is quite a list. Our foundress, Saint Mary of the Cross MacKillop was excommunicated (albeit invalidly and later re-instated), faced difficulties with some of her own members and with bishops who were accustomed to one type of religious life. She was so convinced of her calling to alleviate the needs of the day, in a hitherto unknown way, that she worked untiringly to bring education to the outback children and solace to the uncared-for aged as well as orphans and prostitutes. She listened attentively to the will of God becoming a holy woman persevering despite obstacles of many kinds. She could do so with calm and peace because, as one person said recently, the Holy Spirit shone through her.[27]

Moreover, new expressions of a charism are encouraged today since it is claimed that "in a church that defends the poor and marginalised, it is clear that the religious orders are a prime example of a church that is not a flight from the world but a prime example of 'a flight from the power structures of

---

25  https://w2.vatican.va/content/francesco/en/speeches/2016/may/documents/papa-francesco_20160512_uisg.html accessed September 24, 2017.
26  Ibid.
27  See https://brisbanecatholic.org.au/articles/homily-feast-st-mary-cross-mackillop-2/ accessed September 22, 2017.

the Empire' of today.[28] Religious, despite a certain amount of criticism, are in a position to live the strong message of *communio* coming from Vatican II because they are not so tightly bound to hierarchical structures as are the clergy and bishops. Cardinal Joseph Tobin speaking at a Religious Life event in Heythrop College on the future of religious institutes said that while numbers are a reality the future should not be about statistics. "Hospitality lies at the heart of religious life, welcoming all as a way of welcoming Christ." [29]

In conclusion, while the numbers in apostolic religious congregations are declining, the gift of the charism hidden/smoored under the ashes of time and change can be raked at this moment to start a new fire. With a clarity of vision, a certain risk, a strong will to innovate and a firm belief in the call of a loving God, this fire of His love and care can be started once more to reveal "something new" to His suffering people. As Pope Francis exhorted us in *Evangelii gaudium,* "Let us be realists, but without losing our joy, our boldness and our hope-filled commitment. Let us not allow ourselves to be robbed of missionary vigour!"[30] Let us rake the embers and start a fire!

---

28  Massimo Faggiolo, *Catholicism & Citizenship: Political Cultures of the Church in the Twenty-First Century* (Collegeville: Minnesota, 2017) 22.
29  See http://www.indcatholicnews.com/news.php?viewStory=21151 accessed October 5, 2017.
30  Pope Francis, *Evangelii Gaudium* : Apostolic Exhortation on the Proclamation of the Gospel in Today's World (24 November 2013) http://w2.vatican.va/content/francesco/en/apost_exhortations/documents/papa-francesco_esortazione-ap_20131124_evangelii-gaudium.html accessed October 9, 2017.

# SEMINAR

## SILVER AND GOLD WE HAVE NOT: BALANCING CONFLICTING VALUES IN DIOCESAN BANKRUPTCY
### *Dr. Barbara Anne Cusack*

I. Introduction

Throughout the almost five-year period that the Archdiocese was involved in Chapter 11 bankruptcy, Archbishop Listecki's constant reminder was: "Prayer and patience." So much so that at the conclusion of the case and the acceptance of the Plan of Reorganization, he met with all those who had been involved and gave them a token of gratitude – "Prayer and Patience."

Let me highlight some background for this presentation:

- Sources: canon law, civil law (especially relevant law in Wisconsin), experience;
- Public record only – not information from claims because they were filed under seal with only a few people, myself included, permitted by the judge to review the contents;
- When you've seen one case, you've seen one case; not commenting on what transpired in other dioceses because there is so much that goes on in the background and I am not privy to that information.

I learned that there is a lot of technical language in bankruptcy law! I will try to keep the jargon to a minimum and, when it is necessary to use that terminology, I will attempt to define the terms. But remember, I am a mere canon lawyer. I am not a civil attorney and do not play one on TV!

II. Context and Chronology

Let us look at the context and chronology within which the Archdiocese of Milwaukee case unfolded.

*Diocesan and Parish Legal Structure*

In 1883, the legislature of the State of Wisconsin provided the opportunity for Catholic parishes to incorporate. The parishes in the Archdiocese of Milwaukee began establishing themselves as civil corporations from that time to the present. Under the provisions of Wisconsin Statute §187.19, each parish has its own corporate identity, board of directors, officers, and structure. Each parish corporation owns legal title to its property. The Archdiocese has respected the status of the parish corporation through various procedures and policies.

The Archdiocese of Milwaukee has been a civil corporation since 1903. It, too, is structured under the provisions of State of Wisconsin Statutes, this time according to Chapter 181. The Archbishop is the sole corporate member.[1]

*Chronology of events leading up to the Chapter 11 case*

In the late 1980's it became clear that the Archdiocese needed to set up some structures for addressing reports on sexual abuse by clergy. One structure came to be known as project Benjamin. It had several facets including a full-time professional to receive reports and make referrals for therapy. It also had a Board that brought together professionals from mental health, law enforcement, survivors and advocates. They worked on setting up policies and procedures. Other sub groups looked at various topics such as protection of the rights of clergy, review system to ensure quality therapy, support groups, etc.

In 2002, when the USCCB issued the Charter for the Protection of Children and Youth, most of its provisions had been in effect in the Archdiocese of Milwaukee for many years. A Code of Ethical Standards for church leaders had been in place since 1994. Although not mandated by state law, all church employees and volunteers with regular contact with minors were required to have criminal background checks completed and were advised that, again not by state law but by diocesan policy, they were mandatory reporters and were trained as such. This is just to mention a few requirements under the Charter that were already in place in the Archdiocese of Milwaukee.

However, when the publicity about clergy sexual abuse of minors went viral, the Archdiocese was painted with the same broad brush strokes as was every diocese.

---

1  Attorney Bruce Arnold, Husch Blackwell, LLP, provided much of the civil law citations and background. For more from a civil attorney's perspective see his presentation: "The Archdiocese of Milwaukee," National Diocesan Attorneys Association, 49th Annual Meeting, Phoenix, Ariz., April 2013

*Legal Landscape*

The civil law context in the State of Wisconsin is quite unique. In a series of decisions, beginning in the mid-1990's the Wisconsin State Supreme Court ruled that negligent supervision claims against the Church are barred by the Establishment Clause of the First Amendment. (As an aside, the Archdiocese had not argued its cases on that ground – the judges said they chose to "extend" their ruling on statutes of limitations – which was the legal argument our counsel had presented – and include a ruling on the First Amendment.) The court also ruled that the statute of limitations is not tolled (i.e., the clock stops running) by repressed memory.

In January 2004, then-Archbishop Timothy Dolan introduced an Independent Mediation System. It was designed by an outside consultant and its purpose was to provide a means by which survivors of sexual abuse by clergy could have their stories heard, be offered apologies and provided some manner of compensation. The system was set up to try to achieve some justice since the civil courts were not available to them. The system was designed to take case reports over a four month period and then move to mediation sessions. It quickly became apparent that the system needed to be open-ended and it continued in place for over five years, only shutting down when the Archdiocese filed for bankruptcy.

In 2004, the Archdiocese made the decision to publish the names of all clergy who have been (or would be if they were still alive) restricted from all priestly ministries, may not celebrate the sacraments publicly, or present themselves as clergy in any way. I will return to this point later and review how possibly conflicting values needed to be balanced.

Despite the court rulings, plaintiff's counsel continued to file cases against the Archdiocese for clergy sexual abuse. In 2007, one such case made its way to the State Supreme Court. Once again, the precedent set in earlier cases with regard to negligent supervision was upheld. However, this time the judges were also presented with a claim of fraud on the party of the Archdiocese. The claim was made that the underlying act of the Archdiocese that led to the plaintiffs' injuries was the alleged fraudulent misrepresentation that the plaintiffs would be safe in the presence of priests. The statute of limitations for fraud is six years in the State of Wisconsin. The case was remanded for further discovery to determine when the six years began to run. A claim is not deemed to accrue until the aggrieved party's discovery of the facts constituting the fraud. We will not go into all of the civil law proceedings and rulings. Suffice it to say, that with this door opened for potential lawsuits, lawsuits began to be filed.

By the summer of 2010 the Archdiocese was the defendant in twelve lawsuits brought by 17 defendants. All claimants were clients of the Anderson Law Firm in Minneapolis. In October 2010 the Archdiocese participated in mediation with counsel for the claimants using the services of an out-of-state judge. The mediation was not successful. The archdiocese made an offer of $4.6 million in an attempt to reach a resolution, but that offer was rejected in December 2010. At that point it was clear that the only way to bring about some closure and finality would be to do so under Chapter 11 reorganization.

In January 2011, one year to the day after his installation as Archbishop of Milwaukee, Archbishop Jerome Listecki filed a voluntary petition for relief under Chapter 11 of the United States Bankruptcy Code. Thus began a massive discovery order, whereby the Archdiocese was required to search for and produce what eventually resulted in 60,000 documents. These were 60,000 documents, not pages. Various depositions were ordered. An extensive notification process was required by the court so that anyone who possibly had a claim of sexual abuse of a minor could be asked to file a claim. Local and national notices were required along with mailing of thousands of notices. In addition to the notice required of and conducted by the Archdiocese, various attorneys did their own advertising seeking clients.

III. Contested Issues

Having set that background context and having reviewed the chronology of related events, we can examine what were the contested issues during the bankruptcy process. Many of them have both civil law and canon law considerations. I will be using the term "Creditors" often. This is the technical term for all those who filed claims. They are represented by a committee and have their own legal counsel. Another point to keep in mind, in a Chapter 11 bankruptcy case, the Debtor (the one who filed for bankruptcy) pays both sides' legal fees, its own and those of the Creditors' Committee. Payment to plaintiff counsel is usually a percentage of whatever is paid to the claimant.

During the previously cited mediation in October 2010, the Archdiocese presented its complete balance sheet of available assets. The Archdiocese was also still paying off a loan that had been taken out when lawsuits involving two former priests of the Archdiocese were filed in California during the time of the so-called roll back period. Plaintiffs' counsel challenged the accuracy of the financial statements provided in the Fall of 2010, claiming that other assets were property of the estate. Thus began the extensive litigation of these contested issues.

*Parish Property*

As noted before, parishes in the Archdiocese of Milwaukee have been separately incorporated since 1883. This structure parallels that in canon law where parishes are ipso iure public juridic persons in their own right. These facts notwithstanding, efforts were made for what is called "substantive consolidation."

A declaratory judgement was sought that parishes were the alter egos of the Archdiocese and that parish assets are property of the bankruptcy estate, that is, property of the Archdiocese. That effort was vigorously defended. Almost as soon as the Archdiocese filed for Chapter 11 protection, a group of pastors convened a meeting of all pastors and the group decided to hire their own counsel. Every parish put forth a modest amount as a retainer. The Archdiocese was able to show that consistently parishes were treated as separate corporations. Because the Archdiocese was diligent in requiring parishes to follow applicable corporate law, to elect their trustees in accord with the requirements of state statutes, that actions of the corporate directors were properly recorded and kept on file, among other corporate acts, the Archdiocese prevailed in keeping parish assets out of the estate. The court found that parishes own their own property, finance their own activities and manage their own assets. Funds of the Archdiocese were not used to fund or support parish activities unless or except when funds were donated to the Archdiocese with the attached restriction that they be distributed to a parish or parishes. Proper record – keeping to demonstrate these facts to the court was essential. [2]

*Parish Deposit Fund*

In order to assist parishes with economies of scale and administrative functions relative to their investments, the Archdiocese managed what was called the Parish Deposit Fund. It was a voluntary program that parishes and other Catholic entities within the territory of the Archdiocese utilized to manage their investments. Each parish or entity has a separate and identifiable account and the funds were not used as a savings and loan operation. Eventually the Fund had accumulated $75 million of parish assets.

With staffing cuts in the mid-2000's, it was no longer possible for the Archdiocese to offer this service to parishes and the Fund was closed. Participants could either remove their funds and manage their investments themselves or move their investments to a new trust management vehicle. In the end, all funds were identified and transferred to one of these options.

When creditors, in the course of the bankruptcy, saw this history, they attempted to argue that these funds were really funds of the estate, the Archdiocese. "The Archdiocese transferred in excess of $35 million from the 'Parish Deposit Fund' to the fund participants. The Creditors sought what is called "derivative standing" (that is, the theory that the assets of the Parish Deposit Fund were owned by the Archdiocese and since the Archdiocese would not bring action to recover the funds from the parishes, the Creditors could acquire standing to bring action in the place of the Archdiocese.) They tried to do this to recover the

---

[2] In re Archdiocese of Milwaukee, Debtor. United States Bankruptcy Court, E.D. Wisconsin. December 7, 2012 Memorandum Decision on the Committee's Motion for Standing on Alter Ego And Substantive Consolidation Claims.

transferred funds which belonged to the individual participants in the program. The Court found that the Archdiocese was justified in not bringing action against the parishes and, thus, the Creditors were not afforded derivative standing and could not sue to bring these funds into the estate."[3]

*The Cemetery Trust*

One contested dimension of the bankruptcy that drew considerable national attention was The Cemetery Trust. The Archdiocese had set money aside since the early 1900's for the perpetual care of cemeteries. Initially it was money for individual lot care. By 1969, it was a fund that was called the Income Care Fund (the income from the fund was to pay for the cemetery upkeep) or Perpetual Care Fund. Eventually, all grave purchases included perpetual care. Again, diligent record-keeping resulted in the production of the sales forms which had two sections, one of which was the contract for perpetual care. Funds were set aside by the Archdiocese in amounts that the Archdiocese viewed as necessary for perpetual care, generally corresponding to the number of grave and mausoleum sales. The funds were always separately accounted for, separately audited, and separately managed. In 2008, the funds were placed in a formal trust. The funds went from be a de facto trust to a de iure trust. The Trust was established in accord with both canon and civil law. (We will look later at the canon law structures and processes used.)

Because of the sizeable amount of these funds, they were very attractive to the Creditors. Despite the fact that the Trust was a separate civil and canonical entity, the Creditors early on signaled their intent to draw these funds into the estate.

The Archbishop, in his capacity as Sole Trustee of the Cemetery Perpetual Care Trust, took the pre-emptive step. The Trust hired its own counsel and commenced an adversary proceeding against the Creditors seeking a declaration that the Cemetery Trust, as well as the funds contained there, are not property of the estate. The Archbishop, as Sole Trustee, contended that the Cemetery Trust funds are a charitable trust, and funds cannot be diverted without legal and possible criminal charges. Counsel for the Trust further argued that the funds are protected by canon law and the Religious Freedom Restoration Act ("RFRA") and the First Amendment. The findings on this issue were split by district court and the 7th Circuit Court. Counsel for the Trust filed a **Petition for Writ of Certiorari** with the U.S. Supreme Court asking the Court to review the decision of a lower court. This Petition was still pending at the time the Plan of Reorganization was filed and accepted. This question of First Amendment rights remains an unresolved issue.

---

3   See Arnold.

*Faith in Our Future Trust*

In 2007, then Archbishop Dolan created the Faith In Our Future Trust ("FIOF"), and launched a campaign to raise $105 million for Catholic education and faith formation. The FIOF Trust is a section 501(c)(3) charitable organization created for the purpose of raising funds for Catholic education and faith formation. This Trust was also established as a canonical entity, separate from the Archdiocese. Sixty percent (60%) of the pledges received by the FIOF Trust were, when paid by the donor, distributed to the donor's parish to be used only for the restricted purposes permitted by the Trust (as made applicable in each parish's unique circumstances and case statement) in support of Catholic education and faith formation. Some examples of the restricted use of the FIOF Trust funds include scholarships for elementary and high school students who could not otherwise afford a Catholic education, support for men studying for the priesthood and the formation of adult lay leaders, and support for the expansion of Catholic campus ministry at both public and private campuses in Southeast Wisconsin.

The Creditors again filed a motion seeking derivative standing to sue the FIOF Trust. They asserted that the Archdiocese "fraudulently transferred" the *goodwill* (not any money, just "goodwill") of the Archdiocese by allegedly providing the FIOF Trust with the names, addresses and/or donor histories of the registered Catholics and other potential donors. Choosing to ignore the underlying facts, the Committee alleged (incorrectly) that the Archbishop and others of the Archdiocese's employees spent time, effort and energy, while being paid by the Archdiocese, to develop the FIOF Campaign and solicit donations to it. The Committee alleged that the donor lists, and employee time along with the goodwill of the Archdiocese they represent were transferred to the FIOF Trust with the intent to hinder, delay or defraud creditors and/or for which the Archdiocese did not receive reasonably equivalent value. Finally, the Committee made the unprecedented claim that the FIOF Trust's solicitation of the Archdiocese's donors interfered with the Archdiocese's ability to raise additional donations and was intended to place the money beyond the reach of the Archdiocese's creditors. None of these arguments were based on any factual information. The parishes provided the list of parishioner names and addresses to an outside consulting firm which was running the campaign. The Trust reimbursed the Archdiocese for any and all staff time used to assist the consultants. And finally, not only did this campaign not hinder the Archdiocese's ability to raise funds, but it met its annual appeal goal every year.

However, the Archdiocese, in the interests of judicial economy, and to avoid the expenses of responding to further frivolous claims by the Creditors, entered into an agreement with the Creditors and the FIOF Trust to put a hold on all litigation related to the Trust while not affecting the ability to adjudicate claims later. Again, the FIOF Trust was represented by its own counsel.

*Insurance Issues*

Another contested arena was insurance coverage. A considerable amount of time, energy, and expense went into negotiating and litigating over insurance. First of all, we needed a road map to ascertain who provided the coverage for which years because the claims went back decades. We did a very careful job of charting the years of coverage for various insurers, knowing that some had gone out of business with their coverage transferring to a successor insurer. It was worth the effort because no insurance carrier denied that they were, in fact, responsible for the years designated; what they objected to was whether they were responsible for providing any payment under the coverage.

When the Independent Mediation System went into effect, the Archdiocese was immediately notified that there would be no coverage for any settlements because the Archdiocese was taking on this process voluntarily, not in response to lawsuits. We accepted that consideration but proceded anyway, using non-restricted reserves, interest on investments, sale of property and other assets, cut staff and expenses to cover the cost of almost 200 settlements at an average of $50,000 each.

When the lawsuits and claims were filed under the allegation of fraud, again the insurance companies denied coverage. Fraud is an intentional tort, a deliberate wrong action against someone. Insurance does not cover you for intentional wrong acts. If someone accidentally trips on my property and is injured, my insurance should cover the claim. If I deliberately trip someone and they get injured, there is no coverage for my bad act.

We will not go into the very technical process used to counter the insurance companies' positions. Needless to say, after very protracted mediation sessions, the insurers agreed not to pay for the settlements but to buy back all their insurance policies. I think they never wanted to hear the words "Archdiocese of Milwaukee" ever again! To the surprise of many attorneys and other business leaders, we reaped $7.4 million to be used for abuse survivors and to pay the expenses of the Chapter 11. The insurance companies also held coverage for all of the parishes and some other Catholic institutions. They insisted that these policies be bought back as well. In order to obtain what is called a "channeling injunction" where non-debtor entities (e.g., parishes which were ruled to be legally separate) receive the same permanent release from future claims that the debtor (the Archdiocese) would receive in the Plan of Reorganization, the judge indicated that the parish should have to make some form of payment into the Plan. The attorney for the parishes advised them to weigh the benefit / loss to such an action. It would cost them a nominal amount and the benefit of a future without fear of these lawsuits would be very beneficial. All the parishes contributed to the plan. There was some consternation on the part of plaintiffs' counsel because the channeling injunction would mean that they could not go parish by parish and sue them. All parishes would be included in the release. However, they also knew that the insurance companies had no obligation to provide any funding and the funding was coming in only if the parishes participated in the buy-back plan.

*Plan of Reorganization*

With all of these moving parts in play, just what did the Plan of Reorganization do? Through a combination of insurance money, parish contributions, a settlement with the Cemetery Trust and a loan from the Cemetery Trust using unoccupied land as collateral, the Archdiocese was able to fund the Plan at $21.5 million. Slightly less than half of that money went for attorney fees for both sides and well as other administrative expenses such as forensic accountants, hired by the Creditors to try to prove the Archdiocese was hiding money; they found none.

I will highlight a few dimensions of the Plan:

- Established a $500,000 therapy fund to provide lifetime therapy payments and support to those abused by diocesan priests. These funds came from the parish contributions to the Plan. Paying for the good of others was more palatable to them than lining lawyers' pockets.

- Settled litigation against Insurers which will be paid out to abuse survivors and be used to pay part of the accrued administrative expenses.

- Provided a financial settlement for abuse survivors with eligible claims, using the classification of claims established by the court. Funds were transferred into a Plan Trust. Decisions about the distribution of funds from that Trust were given over to a court-appointed administrator.

- Provided funds to pay for litigation against other archdiocesan insurance companies for the recovery of additional monies to benefit abuse survivors.

- Outlined a feasible operational plan for the archdiocese to continue its ministry in the community, providing the worship, outreach and service that make up the work of the Catholic Church in southeastern Wisconsin

- Affirmed the archdiocese's commitment to preventing child sexual abuse within the Church and within our society by outlining its voluntary action plan of non-monetary commitments to keep children safe.

- Ensured that no priest with a substantiated allegation of sexual abuse of a minor can ever serve in ministry in any capacity in the Archdiocese of Milwaukee.

- Affirmed the archdiocese's commitment to open and candid communication by making public the names and related documents of any diocesan priest with a substantiated allegation of sexual abuse of a minor.

- Will convert five parcels of undeveloped real estate owned by the archdiocese into cash at more than their loan or sale value by using the property as collateral to secure the loan to pay administrative expenses of the proceeding.

- Utilize the loan as a way to come up with the cash needed to pay the estimated $5 million in accrued professional fees as required by the U.S. Bankruptcy Code.

- Restructured the debt on the Pastoral Center property to allow for repayment of the mortgage to Park Bank, a secured creditor, and utilize the property for archdiocesan offices because it is less expensive than relocating the operational offices.

- Renegotiated the Pastoral Center lease with the Milwaukee Bucks who use the facility for training, increasing annual revenue to help offset building operations.

- The Plan Respects and honors the donor restrictions and designations of funds held by the diocese to be used for specific designated purposes.

IV. Canonical Considerations

Along the way of the five-year process, there were various junctures where not only civil law but also canon law needed to be considered. We will take a look at what those canonical considerations were.

*Pre-petition Issues*

Periodically diocesan bishops need to review with their Finance Officer and Finance Council to ensure that proper structures and procedures are in place. Some questions to be asked:

- Are structures and procedures in place that genuinely respect the provisions of canon 515, §3: "A lawfully established parish has juridic personality by virtue of the law itself." As such they are "subjects of obligations and rights which accord with their nature" (c. 113, §2). Among those rights are the right to own and administer the property it has legitimately acquired. Do structures and procedures exist which respect that right to ownership and make clear that the assets of parishes are not the assets of the diocese?

- Is there a periodic review of funds that have been restricted by a donor to ensure that those restrictions are being observed? Are the norms of canon 1284, §2, 3° being followed, namely to "observe the provisions of canon and civil law, and the stipulations of the founder or donor or lawful authority [and]to take special care that damage will not be suffered by the Church through the non-observance of the civil law"?

- If funds are being held for a designated or restricted purpose, is there a value in converting a de facto trust or endowment into a de iure one? If so, are the appropriate civil laws being observed? Has consideration been given to having a parallel canonical structure such as an autonomous pious foundation established? (c. 1303, §1, 1°) Since the resulting juridic person is bound by the norms on ecclesiastical goods, are those norms being observed?

- Are the norms for the operation of the Diocesan Finance Council up-to-date and being observed? Do the members of the Finance Council understand their role and do they have the necessary orientation when they are appointed?

- Is the College of Consultors properly established and are their statutes up-to-date and being observed?

- Are records properly maintained and easily retrievable? Where are clergy records maintained and who has access to them?

*Canonical Considerations when Filing for Bankruptcy*

*Coming to the Decision:*

The archdiocese had already liquidated most available assets not in use for education, charitable or other ministry, to provide financial and psychological support to survivors and cover related costs. When it was clear that efforts to resolve pending and future lawsuits through mediation and settlements would continue to be fruitless, plans began unfolding for filing the petition for Chapter 11 bankruptcy relief with the Federal Court. Recognizing that such a filing would constitute an act of extraordinary administration, the required canonical consultation took place with both the College of Consultors and the Diocesan Finance Council. Since both groups had received regular updates on the legal challenges the Archdiocese faced, this action came as no surprise. That does not mean that there were not extensive and wide-ranging discussions, especially exploring whether or not any other options might be available.

Once these consultations were complete and a record made of them, the Archbishop approached the Congregation for Clergy. He explained the background and included a financial analysis of archdiocesan assets as well as a financial overview of assets. The latter document provided information about assets that are not available for settlement and resolution of these cases. It was shown that the amount being demanded by plaintiff's counsel far exceeded the available assets of the Archdiocese. He further stated that he had been assured that other funds held in trusts, along with parish assets, pensions, and other permanently restricted funds could not be accessed by the courts, but that he would have to see if that fact held. (From what we've seen earlier in this presentation – it did not!)

Since these two consultative bodies will have important roles to play throughout the bankruptcy process, open and candid communication with them is essential. In order for that tenor to exist, it may be useful to have legal counsel present at meetings to grant them privilege. Since every note, letter, document, set of minutes can become part of a discovery motion, minutes of these minutes need to be carefully written so that they accurately convey the substance of the meeting but do not leave remarks open to interpretation that could harm the diocese or bishop in court. Having legal counsel review a draft of minutes may be useful.

When it is clear that the time for filing a Plan of Reorganization is close, it will become clear what extraordinary administration (e.g., taking out a loan), alienation (e.g., selling land holdings), or canon 1295 transactions (e.g., mortgaging property) will be necessary. These same consultative bodies should be given full information so that they can properly give their consent to the filing of the Plan and to its elements. Again, contact with the Congregation for Clergy will most probably be necessary given the nature of the acts and the value of the transactions. In our experience, the response from the Congregation was prompt and did not cause any delays.

*Diocesan Bishop as Steward*

Diocesan bishops are mindful of their roles as stewards of the assets entrusted to the local church. A diocesan bishop is never more conscious of those responsibilities than when preparing for and living through bankruptcy. Canon 1284 becomes a key canon for him then if not before! He becomes even more vigilant that goods placed in his care in no way perish or suffer damage. (c, 1284, §2, 1°) He becomes painfully aware that even having arranged for insurance contracts, he is not guaranteed that coverage will be available. If he followed the expectation that the ownership of ecclesiastical goods would safeguarded in ways which are valid in civil law (c, 1284, §2, 2°), he may have to take the contentions to court but he has more of a chance at prevailing than if he had done nothing. Being diligent about the observance of the provisions of canon and civil law, and the stipulations of the founder or donor will go a long way to seeing that damage will not be suffered by the Church (c, 1284, §2, 3°). With the volume of reporting required and the expanse of document production, the keeping of accurate records of income and expenditure, becomes eminently clear (c, 1284, §2, 7°). Likewise, keeping in order and preserving in a convenient and suitable archive the documents and records establishing the rights of the Church to its goods (c, 1284, §2, 9°) not only saves time and energy and money, it also can help bring the necessary legal arguments before the court with documentation to back them up.

*Juridic Personality*

While most bankruptcy judges do not want to hear arguments based solely on canon law, being able to show by our policies, procedures and protocols that we have respected the canonical distinctions between and among juridic persons can be helpful. Diocesan bishops should review their procedures, especially any commingling of assets of separate juridic persons, and make the necessary changes or those assets will be considered conjoined in the estate of the diocese and lost to their rightful owners. Diocesan policies that require parishes to deposit excess funds with the diocese may hand to the Creditors just the argument they need to show substantive consolidation, that the assets of one are the assets of the other and all are attainable to the estate.

V. Values in the Balance

*Seeking the Truth*

At all stages of the bankruptcy process, there is a balancing of values that occurs. We can never be after any pursuit that is not the pursuit of truth. But seeking the truth may look like a lack of compassion for survivors because we are "fighting" for clarity about the assets of the estate. Taking the time to present the facts can do just that, take time. And with the clock ticking on billable hours all the time, that clock is costly. Many comments have been made about the fact that the bankruptcy process in Milwaukee took so long. It did – arguably the longest diocesan bankruptcy to date. But the decision was made and followed, not to back down and roll over on claims by the creditors that were simply not true.

*Non-Economic Considerations*

In every bankruptcy Plan of Reorganization, there will be economic and non-economic considerations written in. The economic ones can be so long in coming that it would be easy to agree too quickly to the non-economic conditions with the finish line in sight. In our case, we had the non-economic conditions spelled out and agreed to long before the litigation on economics was complete. The non-economic conditions that were settled upon largely included actions we had already taken, many of them part of the Charter requirements. Bishops need to be cautious that they do not relinquish any of their governance authority in the non-economic considerations. We have seen efforts to have bishops relinquish their right to make priestly assignments or hand over to civil officials oversight of their activities. There is a value in coming to an amicable agreement about non-economic considerations but there has to be the counterbalance of retaining the integrity of the bishop's governance authority.

*Claims Objections*

It may be tempting in trying to resolve claims in a bankruptcy case, to simply accept any and all claims in order to speed up the process. Again, the pursuit of truth and commitment to justice also has to come into play. The Archdiocese chose to object to some of the claims filed. Many of the claims involved religious order priests, brothers and sisters. A number of the claims brought allegations against lay people who worked at a parish or school or elsewhere. Some claims did not allege any sexual abuse. Other claims did not involve minors. The archdiocese objected to these claims and decided it could not satisfy claims involving individuals outside its jurisdiction. Because the archdiocese had limited money, it was important that financial payments were reserved for those sexually abused by Archdiocese of Milwaukee priests. In the end, balancing the value of providing some relief to survivors, claims against non-archdiocesan priests were given secondary consideration if the abuse occurred at an archdiocesan site.

In addition, claims objections were filed on these grounds:

- People who had already received a previous settlement from the archdiocese;
- People who claimed fraud when there is no evidence fraud was possible;
- Claims that had no connection to the archdiocese;
- Claims that were not sexual abuse of a minor.

With a limited pool of funds available, it did not seem just to provide additional funding to those who had already received a settlement. In the end, the amount of the average settlement through the claims process was about the same as the average amount in the settlements through the mediation process.

*Disclosure of Names*

One of the non-economic demands made by the Creditors was the release of names of all alleged perpetrators. Having made the difficult decision to release those names years prior to the filing of bankruptcy, we did not need to re-visit that demand. However, it may be helpful to share what criteria were used for deciding whose name to list and why the disclosure was ultimately made. In order for a name to be listed it was required that we had substantiation of abuse of a minor while the individual was a cleric. We posted only the names of those clergy who were fully restricted form ministry (or would be if they were alive) for sexual abuse of minors. What values did we consider?

1. Protecting children is our primary concern and obligation. Making public these names was another layer of assurance that they would not present themselves as clergy.

2. By releasing this information, the Church of southeastern Wisconsin reaffirmed its commitment to seeking, reaching out to, and encouraging any survivors of clergy sexual abuse of minors who had yet to come forward to do so, knowing that they will be believed. Seeing the name of one's abuser can be validating for a survivor, especially one who believes he or she was the only victim.

3. We wanted to affirm the faithful, holy, and wholesome service of the vast majority of priests who serve Catholics and the community in southeastern Wisconsin and remove any doubt any of them might be an offender.

We did not ignore the norm of canon 220: "No one may unlawfully harm the good reputation which a person enjoys, or violate the right of every person to protect his or her privacy." It was our firm belief that we were not acting unlawfully and that these individuals had harmed their own reputation by the acts they committed against children and youth.

There are multiple other values that need to be weighed and held in the balance during bankruptcy. I return to the motto we used and recommend it to others should they find themselves in the choppy waters of bankruptcy: Prayer and patience!

# SEMINAR

## Religious Sponsors, Ministry Leaders and Diocesan Bishops: Together in Communion
*Sister Sharon Euart, RSM*

**Introduction**

Over the past several years, we have become aware of an increasing number of situations within Catholic institutions throughout our country, particularly in Catholic schools and parishes, arising from conflicts with the Church's teachings – such as the termination of a female high school teacher who married her lesbian partner, a male parish music director who married his same-sex partner, an unmarried middle school teacher who was pregnant, a Catholic school teacher who was pregnant via artificial insemination, the introduction of morality clauses in employee contracts in Catholic institutions, transgender issues for faculty and students in Catholic schools, and the examples continue to grow. Such conflicts as well as the legal challenges that follow raise serious and difficult questions for religious sponsors, ministry leaders, and diocesan bishops, thereby highlighting the importance of this relationship and the need at times for clarification.

During this seminar, I hope to offer a canonical framework for dialogue and decision-making on the part of sponsors, ministry leaders, and bishops should situations arise involving a matter for which the diocesan bishop has oversight. In this context, I will focus my comments on three key themes: sponsorship and public juridic personality; Catholic identity and charism; and the roles and relationships between ministry leaders, religious sponsors and diocesan bishops in the spirit of communion.

**Relevant Conciliar, Canonical and Papal Documents**

There are three key documents emanating from the Second Vatican Council that are particularly relevant for our topic: *Lumen gentium* (Dogmatic Constitution on the Church), *Christus Dominus* (Decree on the Pastoral Office of Bishops in the Church), and *Perfectae caritatis* (Decree on the Renewal of Religious Life). Each of these documents provides a theological foundation for the canonical provisions on bishops and religious men and women that have been incorporated into the code. The 1978 post-conciliar instruction *Mutuae relationes*, the Directives for Mutual Relations Between Bishops and Religious in the Church (April 23, 1978), currently being updated under Pope Francis, was developed as a practical means to ensure an orderly and fruitful cooperation and collaboration between bishops and religious at all levels. The relevant canons of the 1983 *Code of Canon Law* reflect the conciliar teaching on the episcopacy and the apostolate of the diocese, the apostolate of religious and juridic persons, and contain norms guiding Catholic identity and the role of church authority. Finally, Pope Francis' *Joy of the Gospel* provides guidance on the authenticity of charism. Each of these documents is helpful in providing a framework for addressing issues related to the relationship between bishops, sponsors and ministry leaders.

**Sponsorship**

The notion of "Sponsorship," beginning in the early 20th century when religious institutes owned and operated their institutional ministries, was advanced in the 1970s by religious institutes as their numbers began to decline and their priorities began to change, along with the recognition of Vatican II on the important role the laity play in the life and mission of the Church. Sponsorship became a commonly used term in regard to church ministries as a way of acknowledging the desire on the part of founding religious institutes to continue to exercise an important role in their ministries.[1] Sponsorship involves three elements: the use of one's name; the exercise of certain governance responsibilities resulting from the use of this name; and some form of accountability to church authorities.[2] It is a flexible term with no precise definition or official status either civilly or canonically.[3] Rather, it reflects an evolving concept with various understandings ranging from those in which the sponsors have minimal involvement in the oversight of the ministry to those totally controlled by the sponsors. Generally, the relationships of sponsoring religious institutes to the sponsored ministries involve governance, influence, and advocacy.

While there is no clear definition of sponsorship, the Catholic Health Association (to which I am most grateful for the numerous resources it has developed on sponsorship and public juridic persons) and later the Canon Law Society of America in its 2006 publication, *Sponsorship in the United States Context: Theory and Praxis*, describe sponsorship of a ministry as "a formal relationship between a recognized Catholic organization and a legally formed entity, entered into for the sake of promoting and sustaining the Church's mission in the world."[4] More simply stated, sponsorship involves a relationship to the

1   See Catholic Health Association, *One Vine, Different Branches: Sponsorship and Governance in Catholic Ministries*, Part II: Practical Components of Sponsorship, (Washington, DC: CHA, 2007) 12.
2   Francis Morrisey, OMI, "Various Types of Sponsorship," in *Sponsorship in the United States Context: Theory and Praxis*, eds. R. Smith, W. Brown, N. Reynolds (Alexandria, VA: Canon Law Society of America, 2006) 19.
3   See, for example, Daniel Conlin, "Sponsorship at the Crossroads," in *Sponsorship: Current Challenges and Future Directions* in *Health Progress* (Catholic Health Association: St. Louis, MO) July/August, 2001, 1-2.
4   Introduction, *Sponsorship in the United States Context: Theory and Praxis,* ii.

Church. It refers to the oversight and guidance of a ministry undertaken on behalf of the Church and through the lens of a particular charism.[5] Through our sponsored ministries, we create an expression of Church, an expression of an ecclesial relationship that is essential to institutional identity.[6]

## Public Juridic Persons

Here is seems appropriate to bring in the concept of a "public juridic person," a canonical notion closely associated with sponsorship and an important aspect of its context.

Apostolic works often transcend the abilities and life span of individual persons. To afford continuity and stability, the legal system of the Catholic Church, like other legal systems, creates artificial entities known as juridic persons on which the law confers certain rights like those of natural persons and on which the law imposes certain obligations. Church ministries are governed by both civil and canon law, with canon law providing a structure that connects a particular group or ministry to the mission of the Church, a structure that protects and sustains what is essential. A public juridic person is similar to not-for-profit corporations in civil law, yet not synonymous with them. It is most often defined by its characteristics.

An ecclesiastical public juridic person is an aggregate (*universitas*) of persons or things in the Church (c. 115 §1); an artificial person, distinct from all natural persons who establish it, administer it, or for whose benefit it exists (c. 114 §1); constituted by church authority or by the law itself to carry out the mission entrusted to it in the name of the Church (c. 116 §§1-2); with a capacity for continuous existence, unless it is legitimately suppressed by competent authority (c. 120§1). It possesses canonical rights and duties conferred upon it (c. 113§2) either by the law itself or by the church authority that establishes it (diocesan bishop or the Holy See) such as the rights to acquire property, enter into contracts, sue or be sued, or incur debts; it is represented by physical persons who are authorized to act on its behalf, either by law or by special statutes; its property is ecclesiastical property (c. 1257§1) and is governed by Book V of the Code of Canon Law on temporal goods. It participates in the mission of the Church and is recognized as Catholic. In turn it must maintain communion with the Church (c. 209) and is subject to some degree of oversight by ecclesiastical authority (c. 116 §1).

---

5     Denise Colgan, RSM, and Doris Gottemoeller, RSM, *Union and Charity: The Story of the Sisters of Mercy of the Americas*, (Silver Spring, MD: Sisters of Mercy of the Americas, 2017) 38.
6     See John Paul II, apostolic constitution *Ex corde Ecclesiae* (August 15, 1990), *Origins* 20/17 (October 4, 1990) n. 27.

The purpose of public juridic persons (c. 114§2) is to carry out the works of the apostolate, works of piety or mercy, both spiritual and corporal, in view of the common good, not just that of individuals (c. 116§1). Examples of public juridic persons established by the law itself include a diocese, parish, seminary, conference of bishops, and a religious institute and its provinces. Church institutions such as hospitals and universities can serve as the substrata for public juridic persons, but juridic personality is not conferred on them by the law. Rather, it can be conferred only be decree of competent ecclesiastical authority.

A religious institute, with approval of its constitutions is erected a public juridic person by the law of the Church with rights and obligations similar to those of natural persons (c. 634). As such, it is perpetual unless suppressed by competent church authority; its assets (temporal goods) are ecclesiastical property subject to the norms of Book V of the Code of Canon Law; and it fulfills its purposes in the name of the Church.

To "function in the name of the Church" is a key characteristic of the relationship of a public juridic person to the Church. It means that the activities of the public juridic person are the work of the Church and not simply the work of the individuals who act on behalf of the public juridic person. To act in the name of another is to act in relationship to the other.[7] In other words, the work of Catholic education, Catholic health care or social services which is entrusted to a religious institute (c. 116) is carried out in the name of the Church through the bond of communion.

**Models of Sponsorship**

Over the years different forms and structures of sponsorship have been developed and tested. There is no single model that has proven to be the best or even the correct one.[8] Traditionally, the sponsorship relationship referred to a position of "corporate strength and independence" exercised through ownership of property and control.[9] For example, when many, if not most, Catholic schools and universities were founded, the governance of the school or university was carried out by the leadership of the religious institute who also served as the Board of Trustees or Directors of the institute's civil corporation. The institute, school, university and other ministries were part of the same civil corporation. In the 1970's the necessity of separating the ministry's civil corporation from that of the religious institute became evident, for example, to enhance eligibility for government funding for education, Medicare and Medicaid, and to protect

---

7   William King, "Sponsorship by Juridic Persons," in *Sponsorship in the United States Context,* 59.
8   Francis Morrisey, OMI, "Our Sponsors, Yesterday, Today and Tomorrow," *Health Progress* 94/ 4 (July-August 2013) 63.
9   Francis Morrisey, OMI, "Various Types of Sponsorship," in *Sponsorship in the United States Context,* 19.

the religious sponsor from liability claims against the institution.[10] In response, religious institutes in the U.S. began to separately incorporate their educational and health care institutional ministries, an action that alone does not change the Catholic character, canonical status or identity of the institution.[11]

At the same time, the governance of many of these ministries moved to a two-tier structure which distinguished between the members of the corporation and the board of directors. In this model certain important decisions were reserved to the "members" tier, which was composed of the leadership of the sponsoring institute (e.g., provincial superior and council).[12] This practice developed in order to ensure the religious institute's continued control over its apostolic works, especially those aspects related to Catholic identity, mission and the administration of ecclesiastical property.[13]

The two-tier model enabled the religious sponsor to carry out its responsibilities for the actions required by canon law on behalf of its apostolic works. This understanding was based on the principle that a religious sponsor would be able to exercise its canonical stewardship responsibilities as the canonical steward over affairs of the civilly incorporated apostolate (c. 1284). This relationship was often expressed by means of "reserved powers" affecting Catholic identity and ecclesiastical property. Initially these reserved powers, also referred to as "faith obligations,"[14] were quite extensive, sometimes numbering as many as fourteen or more. Later, the number was refined and included, for example, approval of the philosophy, mission and identity of the ministry; amendment of articles of incorporation; administration of property; approval of mergers or dissolution; and in some cases, approval of trustees and appointment of the chief executive

---

10 For a discussion of the evolution of the apostolic institutions and the founding institutes, including the McGrath v. Maida debate, see John P. Beal, "From the Heart of the Church to the Heart of the World: Ownership, Control and Catholic Identity of Institutional Apostolates in the United States," in *Sponsorship in the United States Context*, 36-38. For a discussion of the 1963 Higher Education Facilities Act (HEFA), see also Paul Golden, "Sponsorship in Higher Education," in *Sponsorship in the United States Context*, 88-89.

11 Robert T. Kennedy, "Canonical Status of Church-Related Institutions in the United States," in Beal, et al., eds. *New Commentary on the Code of Canon Law* (Mahwah, NJ: Paulist Press, 2000) 176. See also Sharon Euart, RSM, "Church State Implications in the United States of Canon 812 in the 1983 Code of Canon Law (JCD diss.:The Catholic University of America, 1988) 64-65.

12 See Mary Pat Seurkamp, "Who Will Bear this Identity? One Model of Sponsorship," *Current Issues in Catholic Higher Education*, 28/1 (Winter 2007) 85-93. See also The Catholic Health Association, *One Vine, Different Branches: Sponsorship and Governance in Catholic Ministries*, 15-26.

13 Sharon Holland, IHM, "Vatican Expert Unpacks Canonical PJP Process," *Health Progress* (September-October, 2011) 52.

14 Ibid.

officer.[15] In this way, the religious sponsor, through separate civil incorporation and reserved powers provided eligibility for government funding and assured that the mission, values, and the direction of the institution remained faithful to the founding charism and the Catholic nature and identity of the ministry.[16] In other words, the ministry continued to be sponsored canonically by the religious institute. That is, it continued to have a relationship to the Church, through the religious institute which, by definition, functions in the name of the Church (c. 675§3).[17] All the while, a new relationship or partnership between laity and religious and clergy was emerging.

In some other Catholic institutions, the governance was structured with a single-tier board in which the sponsor and the board of directors or trustees share responsibility for the mission of the institution. In this model, the interests and concerns of the religious sponsor are recognized through by-laws, statutes or sponsorship agreements by requiring the board to include as directors or trustees a certain number or percentage of members of the sponsoring institute. Some bylaws require a type of "bloc voting" of the members of the sponsoring group for significant votes.[18] Though separate civil incorporation addressed the issue of government funding for education and medical benefits, for example, it did not resolve the matter of the increasing decline in the number of men and women religious that was unfolding in many religious institutes.

Over time, the distinctions between ownership and control have become less clear, even blurred. For example, it is possible to sponsor a ministry with or without ownership; to have ownership of a ministry with or without control or with minimum control; or to have differing degrees of control as well as different models of sponsorship. In fact, in more recent time, sponsorship efforts have shifted from a focus on ownership to an emphasis on mission and identity. [19]

---

15   See The Catholic Health Association of the United States, *The Search for Identity: Canonical Sponsorship of Catholic Healthcare* (St. Louis, MO: CHA, 1993) 81; Francis Morrisey, OMI, "Basic Concepts and principles," in *Church Finance Handbook*, ed. Kevin McKenna, et al. (Washington, DC: CLSA, 1999) 14.
16   See Robert T. Kennedy, "McGrath, Maida, Michiels: Introduction to a Study of the Canonical and Civil-Law Status of Church-Related Institutions in the United States," *The Jurist* 50 (1990) 351-401. See also, John P. Beal, "From the Heart of the Church to the Heart of the World: Ownership, Control and Catholic Identity of Institutional Apostolates in the United States," 36-38 and Paul Golden, "Sponsorship in Higher Education," in *Sponsorship in the United States Context,* 98.
17   See Sharon Holland, IHM. "A Structure to Sustain Catholic Identity: Sponsorship and Higher Education," Address at the Annual Meeting of the Association of Catholic Colleges and Universities, Washington, DC, January 30, 2011, manuscript, 3.
18   Part II: Practical Components of Sponsorship in *One Vine, Different Branches: Sponsorship and Governance in Catholic Ministries,* 12.
19   Francis Morrisey, OMI, "Various Types of Sponsorship," 29.

Today, sponsorship models under which Catholic institutions have operated are no longer adequate or effective. Factors [20] such as the

- decreasing number of religious, especially women religious, competent and available for ministry and internal governance
- mergers of religious institutes, a rising median age, and the completion of some institutes,
- Increasing complexities and demands in the governance of educational, health care and social service institutions, and
- recognition of the expanded ministry of the laity in partnership with dioceses and religious institutes

have motivated some religious institutes to search for new possibilities and to consider structuring the sponsorship relationship in new ways. Besides the single tier and two tier civil structures, some religious institutes are considering new governing structures such as a systems model or sponsorship council with delegated exercise of reserved powers or transferring sponsorship responsibilities to a diocese, a separate public juridic person (often referred to now as a ministerial juridic person), subsidiaries of public juridic persons, a private juridic person which functions in its own name and whose assets are not considered ecclesiastical property, or a *de facto* Catholic ministry - school or university[21] with a written decree of competent ecclesiastical authority granting consent to identify as Catholic. Some of these options will often involve the sponsor's retaining influence, but not necessarily control, over the mission of the institution.[22] Each of these governing structures is subject to canon law though each has differing requirements for canonical recognition which bring with it the obligation to maintain communion with the Church (c. 209 §1).

It is likely that over the next decade many religious institutes will no longer be able to carry out the responsibilities of canonical stewardship for sponsored institutions (c. 1284); hence, the need for new models of sponsorship as well as new and creative ways of ensuring the continued Catholic identity and mission of Catholic institutions. The separate public juridic person model is one that institutes are increasingly considering as an option for a single or multiple ministries. Building on the experience in Catholic health care, the separate public juridic person is a model that promises there is a future for ministries founded by religious institutes at a time when many institutes can no longer manage them independently. While there are numerous advantages to this model

---

20  John Beal, "From the Heart of the Church to the Heart of the World: Ownership, Control and Catholic Identity of Institutional Apostolates in the United State, 33-35.
21  See CIC canon 803 §3 and John Paul II, apostolic constitution *Ex corde Ecclesiae* (*ECE*) (August 15, 1990), in *Origins* 20/17 (October 4, 1990) Art. 3, 3.
22  See Sharon Holland, IHM, "Vatican Expert Unpacks Canonical PJP Process," 53. See also Holland, "A Structure to Sustain Catholic Identity: Sponsorship and Higher Education" 6, for a listings of possible elements in a decree granting consent to identify as Catholic.

of sponsorship, a major challenge is how best to provide the formation needed for continuing the ministry's charism, mission and Catholic identity by those who will succeed the founding religious leaders. If the ministerial public juridic person is to ensure the member institutions' ongoing Catholic identity and their relationship to the Church, it is critical that initial and ongoing formation be a priority in the establishment of the new public juridic persons. Lay women and men will continue to assume positions of leadership in ministries sponsored by religious institutes and increasingly they will serve as members of the governing body of separate public juridic persons. The engagement of lay men and women in sponsorship roles is profound evidence of the Spirit's involvement in our contemporary life. In these roles, they govern, safeguard, witness to and support continuity of the ministry's charism, mission and identity in building up the communion of the Church.

**Catholic Identity and Charism**

Our charisms are given by the Holy Spirit to renew and build up the Church. In *The Joy of the Gospel*, Pope Francis says that a "sure sign of the authenticity of a charism is its ecclesial character" (*EG* 130), that is, when it is integrated harmoniously into the life of the people of God. He goes on to say - to the extent that a charism is directed toward the Gospel, its exercise will be more ecclesial. Even when it is painful, Francis says that it is in communion that "charism is authentic and mysteriously fruitful."

Catholic identity is at the heart of sponsorship. It recognizes that Catholic institutions participate in the mission of Jesus: the internal faith response to Jesus Christ and the external practicalities of what it means to belong to a visible Church with institutional structures. Identity and mission must be similarly inter-twined in our Catholic institutions if they are to remain in the Church out of whose heart they were born.[23]

Catholic identity should be viewed not as a limiting requirement, but rather as a life-giving connection which involves the ministry leaders, religious sponsor, board of trustees/directors and diocesan bishop in varying degrees and in partnership with one another.

It is not a superficial veneer, mere appendage or add-on to the ministry; nor is it a list of do's and don'ts; rather, it permeates the culture and character of the Catholic institution.[24] Pope St. John Paul II addressed this when speaking to the Catholic academic community in 1979: "The term 'Catholic' will never be a

---

23   John P. Beal, "From the Heart of the Church to the Heart of the World: Ownership, Control and Catholic Identity of Institutional Apostolates in the United States," 32.
24   See Doris Gottemoeller, RSM, "Catholic Identity: Difference or Distinction," CHA Sponsorship Institute, January 2013, 5.

mere label either added or dropped according to pressures of varying forces."[25] It enables a Catholic ministry to make a difference by contributing something important and significant to today's world. Catholic identity cannot be legislated; it is lived. It gives spirit and life to a ministry. (FN. FM)

Finally, Catholic identity is achieved through communion with the Church. Because of the bishop's role to build communion in his diocese and to keep it in communion with the universal church, he exercises oversight for all ministry within his diocese (c.394). Consequently, the identity of a ministry as "Catholic" requires that the institution be in a relationship of communion with the bishop.[26] A ministry cannot be Catholic by itself. Catholic identity requires it to be in an ecclesial relationship beyond itself. [27] In other words, Catholic identity is not only evident in faith and values or name and symbols; it is also evident in its communion with the Church through the local bishop. In an address to Catholic educators at The Catholic University of America in 2008, Pope Benedict said that Catholic identity is not dependent on statistics. Neither can it be equated simply with orthodoxy of course content. It demands and inspires…that each and every aspect of your learning communities reverberates within the ecclesial life of faith.[28]

## Relationships: Religious Sponsor, Ministry Leaders and Diocesan Bishop

### Religious Sponsors

It is important to have a core of people within the ministry who share responsibility for ensuring and promoting the mission identity of the institution. A few brief comments on relationships: sponsors, ministry leaders, boards of trustees and diocesan bishop/ local Church.

Though there is no template for how religious sponsors and ministry leaders should relate to one another, the ministry leaders (e.g. high school head of school, university president, hospital or health system CEO or president) has a right to expect leadership from the sponsor in strengthening the Catholic identity and character of the ministry for it is through the sponsorship relationship that the Catholic institutions are accountable to the Church.[29] Ministry leaders might also expect from sponsors, for example, a clear understanding of the mission and

---

25  John Paul II, quoted in USCCB, *The Application of Ex corde Ecclesiae to the United States*, (Washington, DC: USCCB, 2000) 8.
26  *ECE* II, Art. 5 §1.
27  Francis Morrisey, OMI, "The Church as Communion, Focused on Ministry," CHA Canon Law/Sponsorship Institute, April 2005, 10-11.
28  Pope Benedict, "Address to Catholic Educators 2008," in USCCB Committee on Education, *Catholic Mission and Culture in Colleges and Universities: Defining Documents: 1965-2014* (Washington, DC: USCCB, 2014) 92.
29  Patricia Smith, OSF, "Sponsors and Sponsored Ministries: Mutual; Expectations," in *Sponsorship in the United States Context* 127. See also *ECE* I, 13.

vision of the ministry, a rootedness in the founding charism and Catholic identity, clarity of roles and responsibilities in the context of canon and civil law, ongoing leadership formation, and support.

**Ministry Leaders**

Ministry leaders should be familiar with the charism of the sponsor, aware of and committed to supporting and promoting the Catholic character of the ministry and aware of the responsibility to communicate the ministry's Catholic identity and its implications to the ministry's broader community. They should be familiar with the model of sponsorship governing the ministry and their relationship to ecclesial authority. They should know the church's teaching and law that support Catholic identity and should be aware that they act in the name of the Church in carrying out their responsibilities.[30]

**Boards of Trustees/Directors**

Boards of trustees or directors, as "Keepers of the Mission," cannot be defined solely by canonical rights and obligations. The relationship with the religious sponsor may be more analogous to a partnership in which the sponsor delegates responsibility for governance of the ministry in accord with the articles of incorporation and its bylaws. It is a relationship based on mutual trust and sustained by communication, formation and support.[31] The board has fiduciary responsibility for—holds in trust—what enables the ministry to be what it is. Most importantly, it holds in trust the Catholic identity of the ministry and has a responsibility to understand, ensure, and provide resources to support, promote, and evaluate this identity.

It is important that boards of trustees, as well as ministry leaders, have open dialogue with the leadership of the religious sponsors on a regular basis initiated by the ministry and as requested by the sponsor. This dialogue provides a framework for support of the founding charism, awareness of initiatives of the sponsor and the ministry, and an opportunity for increased understanding of their respective roles and responsibilities. When trustees and ministry administrators view their working together as working *with* rather than working *for* the sponsor in a partnership for carrying out the mission of the Church, they will be better equipped to address mutually the issues involved in the evolution of sponsorship.[32]

---

30  See Smith, 129.
31  See Part II: Practical Components of Sponsorship in *One Vine, Different Branches: Sponsorship and Governance in Catholic Ministries*, 14.
32  See Patricia Smith, OSF, 129.

### Bishops/Local Church

Historically, with the blessing of local bishops, women and men religious established, sponsored and staffed most Catholic colleges and schools in this country. Bishops seldom were involved with the university or school other than for an occasional commencement speaker or celebrant at a special anniversary or to bless new buildings or sports facilities. Generally, both bishops and religious kept a healthy distance from each other. [33] With the Church's conciliar and post-conciliar teaching, especially *Mutuae relationes* and the revised *Code of Canon Law*, we have a renewed understanding of the local Church and the bishop's enhanced role and responsibilities especially in the Church's teaching on the works of the apostolate as ministries not only of the religious sponsor and the institutions, but also of the entire Church. [34] The challenge today is to know how best to work together in a spirit of mutuality and harmony in promoting fidelity to mission.

### Dialogue: Sponsors, Ministry Leaders and Diocesan Bishop

If we ask sponsors and ministry leaders to describe their present experience of episcopal oversight, some would likely say "he doesn't bother us," or "kind neglect" or "generally supportive"; others "suspicion or mistrust"; still others "somewhere in-between." Though some of us might prefer one experience over another, neither extreme is truly helpful. If our goal is to develop an open, honest relationship prior to a crisis or conflict, the starting point is a place of understanding and trust.[35]

As sponsorship of our Catholic institutions by religious institutes takes on new forms in the future (and for many the future is now), issues related to the particular circumstances of the ministry invite the administrators, board of trustees, religious sponsor and the Bishop of the diocese to share insights and experience in a spirit of mutual trust and dialogue around practical yet important issues facing Catholic institutions: for example, as the number of religious in governance roles decreases, what new structures for sponsorship is the religious institute(s) considering? What are the implications of a new sponsorship structure? How can Catholic universities maintain recognition by and accountability to the Church? Are there open lines of communication between the head of a Catholic high school, the sponsor and the diocesan bishop?

33  Joseph L. Bernardin, "Catholic Identity: Resolving Conflicting Expectations," in *Selected Works of Joseph Cardinal Bernardin*, Vol.2: Church and Society, Alphonse P. Spilly, C.PP.S, editor (Collegeville, MN: Liturgical Press, 1991) 171. Also printed in *Origins*, 21:2 (May 23, 1991) 33-36.
34  See Joseph W. Tobin, CSsR, "The Charism and Goods of an Institute and Their Relationship to the Local Church," in *The Management of the Ecclesiastical Goods of Institutes of Consecrated Life and Societies of Apostolic Life: At the service of humanum and the Mission of the Church*, Proceedings of the International Symposium, March 8-9, 2014, (Rome: Libreria Editrice Vaticana, 2014) 58.
35  See Doris Gottemoeller, RSM, "Catholic Identity: Difference or Distinction," 9.

Are there periodic conversations between sponsor of a Catholic hospital and the diocesan bishop? Are there regular opportunities for the theology or religious studies faculty to engage in constructive dialogue with the bishop? Is the diocesan bishop welcomed on campus? How can bishops better serve sponsored ministries? How can sponsored ministries better serve the local Church?[36]

Such a relationship of trust requires openness to mutually respectful dialogue, which Pope Paul VI calls "a form of spiritual communication."[37] In the encyclical *Ecclesiam suam* Paul VI refers to dialogue as a "method of accomplishing apostolic mission" characterized by clarity of language, meekness in communicating the truth, trust in the power of one's words and the integrity of others, and prudence in being attuned to the sensitivities of others (*ES* 81).

The strong exhortation in canon 678§3 to bishops and religious to "proceed through mutual consultation" in organizing ministry suggests that meaningful consultation will happen only if mutual trust, openness and honesty characterize the dialogue and collaboration that take place between bishops and religious.

Pope John Paul II, in the apostolic exhortation following the synod on Consecrated Life *Vita Consecrata*,[38] stresses the importance of cooperation so that there might be an organic development of pastoral programs in local churches (*VC* 48). He speaks of a "constant dialogue" between bishops and religious leaders and describes it as "most valuable" for promoting mutual understanding, a "necessary precondition for effective cooperation" (*VC* 50).

In his address to the U.S. bishops in 2015 in Washington, DC, Pope Francis, said "we are all promoters of the culture of encounter" and "dialogue is our method." "The path ahead," the Pope continued, "is dialogue among yourselves…with your priests…lay persons… families…and society." The same message of Pope Francis might also apply to dialogue between bishops, religious sponsors, and ministry leaders working together to strengthen communion for the Church's mission.[39] More recently Pope Francis, in an address to Vicars and Delegates for Religious, spoke about the need to deepen the value of reciprocity between religious and bishops. He said "mutual relations do not exist where some make demands and others submit out of fear or convenience." Rather, he

---

36  See Association of Jesuit Colleges and Universities, *Some Characteristics of Jesuit Colleges and Universities: A Self-Evaluation Instrument* (Washington, DC: AJCU, 2012)18. See also Joseph Bernardin, "Catholic Identity: Resolving Conflicting Expectations," 174.

37  Paul VI, encyclical *Ecclesiam suam* (August 6, 1964) n. 81 at http://w2.vatican.va/content/paul-vi/en/encyclicals/documents/hf_p-vi_enc_06081964_ecclesiam.html

38  John Paul II, Post-Synodal apostolic exhortation *Vita consecrata*, (March 25, 1996) 48 at http://w2.vatican.va/content/john-paul-ii/en/apost_exhortations/documents/hf_jp-ii_exh_25031996_vita-consecrata.html

39  http://aleteia.org/2015/09/23/francis-to-us-bishops-speak-with-everyone-gently-and-humbly/

said "mutual relations exist wherever dialogue, respectful listening, encounter and understanding, shared search for the truth, the desire of collaboration are cultivated for the good of the Church which is 'house of communion.'"[40]

**Principles of Dialogue**

When conflicts arise in a diocese between the religious sponsor, its ministries and the diocesan bishop, we look for solutions that respect the mutual rights and obligations of all the parties and their respective responsibilities for the mission of the Church. It is critical that sponsors and ministry leaders establish and maintain a relationship with their respective diocesan bishop characterized by mutual trust, dialogue and collaboration so that the first contact is not motivated by a crisis or a problem. If a crisis occurs and there is no prior communication or cooperation with the sponsor, ministry leader and the bishop, the outcome may well be different from a situation in which there have been prior opportunities for dialogue and collaboration.

The application of church teaching in specific situations, whether in a health care facility, school, university, or social service ministry, involves careful discernment of competing goods – the integrity of the ministry, respect for the dignity of individuals, the public perception of an action as faithful to church teaching.[41] Each situation facing religious sponsors, ministry leaders and church leadership is different. Since the diocesan bishop has the authority to determine what is or is not consistent with the church's teaching (cf. cc. 397, 683§1, 803§2, 804§1-2, 805, 806, 827§2) and the right to intervene in exercising responsible oversight of the apostolate, sensitive and at times tense and conflictual dialogue can result.[42]

We know that dialogue is fruitful when it is a struggle to learn from each other, when we have the courage to hear what another might teach us.[43] Perhaps this is where the Catholic Common Ground Initiative, founded by the late Cardinal Joseph Bernardin in 1996, could be helpful. I offer as a consideration seven principles that seem relevant to our discussion and may be helpful in addressing difficult situations and reducing potential conflict as well as in maintaining

---

40   Francis, Address to Participants in the International Congress for Episcopal Vicars and Delegates of Consecrated Life, October 28-30, 2016 at https://w2.vatican.va/content/francesco/en/speeches/2016/october/documents/papa-francesco_20161028_vita-consacrata-convegno.html
41   Colgan, and Gottemoeller, *Union and Charity*, 126.
42   See John Huels, "The Authority of the Diocese over the Schools of Religious Institutes, in S. Euart, et al., eds., *Roman Replies and 2017 CLSA Advisory Opinions* (Washington, DC: Canon Law Society of America, 2017) 81-82. See also Phillip J. Brown, *Restructuring Catholic School Governance for A New Age: Creativity Meets Canon Law* (Arlington, VA: NCEA, 2010) 32-34.
43   Timothy Radcliffe, OP, "To Live Moments of Tension Fruitfully," a presentation to the World Synod of Bishops 1994, 24/19 *Origins* (October 20, 1994) 335.

mutually supportive relationships within the diocese. Not all may be applicable to every situation, but the general notion may provide some guidance.

- We should recognize that no single group or viewpoint in the church has a complete monopoly on the truth.
- We should not envision ourselves or any one part of the Church as a saving remnant.
- We should test all proposals for their pastoral realism.
- We should presume that those with whom we differ are acting in good faith.
- We should put the best possible construction on differing positions.
- We should be cautious in assigning motives.
- We should bring the Church to engage the realities of contemporary culture.[44]

While principles and strategies for dialogue are important for negotiating differences, they are only part of the effort. The other is the attitude and spirit with which we approach the task. Are we truly committed to dialogue as an instrument of communion? Are we convinced that "the truth cannot impose itself except by virtue of its own truth, as it wins over the mind with both gentleness and power"? Are we willing to listen before speaking while teaching? Are we ready to act on the words of Paul VI: "Let us stress what we have in common rather than what divides us" (*ES* 109)? Finally, is our attitude one that reflects a renewed spirit of dialogue that enables us to seek the truth "with fresh eyes, open minds and changed hearts"?[45]

**Spirit of Communion**

The strength of the Church is found in communion, that is, "union with" which is the real source for witnessing the relationship among the disciples of Jesus Christ. Communion ecclesiology is fundamental to the Church's self-understanding; it emphasizes the inter-connectedness that is at the heart of the Church. In calling the Church to realize more fully the communitarian nature of the Church, Pope John Paul II said that the task of making the Church "the home and school of communion" is the "great challenge facing us in the millennium… if we wish to be faithful to God's plan and respond to the world's deepest yearnings."[46]

---

44 See Catholic Common Ground Initiative at http://www.catholiccommonground.org/ resources "Principles of Dialogue.
45 "Called To Be Catholic: Church in a Time of Peril," Statement of the Catholic Common Ground Initiative (New York, National Pastoral Life Center, 1996).
46 John Paul II, apostolic letter, *Novo millennio Ineunte* (January 6, 2001) 43.

Sponsorship is a privileged means of building communion within the Church itself, giving rise to co-responsibility and the potential for collaboration. It is the central unifying theme within the sponsorship relationship.[47] The Church's teaching and its canonical notions can favor a harmonious and fruitful collaboration among religious sponsors, ministry leaders and bishops. But law does not automatically make this happen. Not all the problems presented by life are resolved by the application of norms. Pope Francis, in his recent message to the International Congress of the Consociato Internationalis Studio Iuris Canonici Promovenda, referred to the necessary role of legal norms: "yes," he said, - a role "of service."[48] The Church's law is a servant of communion. While canon Law does not contain specifics as to how sponsors, ministry leaders and bishops should relate to one another, it does provide guidance for carrying out their mutual responsibilities for apostolic activity in a diocese. But more is needed. A search for the common good of the Church, together with a strong sense of interconnectedness and an appreciation for creative dialogue rooted in charity and mercy, can witness to a future unfolding in which sponsors, ministry leaders, and bishops serve the Church's mission together in communion.

---

47    See Francis Morrisey, OMI, "The Church as Communion, Focused on Ministry," 16.
48    See Francis' address to the Consociato Internationalis Studio Iuris Canonici Promovenda at http://press.vatican.va/content/salastampa/en/bollettino/pubblico/2017/10/06/171006h.html

# Seminar

## Canonical Exclusionary Rules and the Just Adjudication of Delicts against the Sacrament of Penance
### *Reverend Monsignor Ronny E. Jenkins[1]*

This presentation addresses two questions. The first is more theoretical: is it possible to achieve a just adjudication of delicts against the sacrament of penance? The answer is significant given that the majority of delicts reserved to the Congregation for the Doctrine of the Faith concern offences against the sacrament of penance. Then, the second question runs more practically: if a just adjudication is possible, how might we conduct such a penal process? Any answer to the questions will necessarily depend one on the other. So, only at the conclusion will I offer my answer to the first question.

From the outset, I note as well that what I offer here is a descriptive study of the questions just raised. It will lead, I believe, to further questions rather than demonstrably sound answers. This is intentional. Given the complexity of this subject, a thorough analytical and synthetic study of the sources will be necessary to achieve that level of robust response to what is, ultimately, a conflict of goods. It is my hope that this first step will at least lay a foundation for what will come afterwards.

To begin, I raise what appears to be a formal contradiction in law. A good starting place for this is usually a foundational principle of the administration of justice. It is essential to the just outcome of any ecclesiastical trial, but most especially one that might result in the condemnation of a criminal defendant, that the most relevant and weighty proofs be proposed and admitted as evidence. To this end, can. 1527 §1 stipulates that, "Proofs of any kind which seem useful for adjudicating the case and are licit can be brought forward." Canon 1452 §2 provides an exceptional way to assure this, "Furthermore," it reads, "the judge can supply for the negligence of the parties in furnishing proofs . . . whenever the judge considers it necessary in order to avoid a gravely unjust judgment. . ."

---

[1] Dean of the School of Canon Law at The Catholic University of America, Washington, DC.

Canon 1600 then adds that the judge may do so even after the conclusion in the cause if injustice would otherwise result.[2]

Among proofs admitted to trial, witness testimony has long stood as a critical tool for establishing the truth regarding a disputed matter. The canonical tradition, in fact, has made a substantial contribution to the legal science regarding the use of witnesses.[3] From it we conclude easily that with no witness testimony, or too strict limitations on its admittance, it is hard to imagine the successful outcome of a penal process. This pertains to both the prosecution presented by the promoter of justice and the defense lodged on behalf of the accused. For this reason, the general principle has always been that all persons are capable of serving as witnesses unless the law indicates otherwise. In penal processes, we include the initial accuser and the victim, if the victim is someone other than the accuser.

Even as our legal tradition has upheld the importance of proof by witnesses, it has also developed doctrine regarding what category of persons should or must be excluded from testifying.[4] Depending on the author and era, the list of those to be excluded grew or shrunk, as did the discretion the judge enjoyed to admit the witness despite an existing cause for exclusion. For instance, historically lay persons were not to be admitted as witnesses in criminal trials against clerics. Yet, prudently, the canon law indicated that they could be – at the judge's discretion – if, by way of one example, no clerical witnesses were available. In this way, the greater harm – a criminal cleric going unpunished – was avoided by allowing the lesser - the testimony of lay witnesses against clerics.[5]

From this, it follows that the just outcome of a criminal process will depend greatly on the degree to which we admit or exclude proofs. Too broad an admission – by the law or the judge - can be as harmful to a just outcome as one that is too restrictive. It is critical, therefore, to find the right balance to allow for the most effective discovery of the truth.

---

2   Can. 1600 §1. After the conclusion of the case, the judge can still summon the same or other witnesses or arrange for other proofs which were not requested earlier, only: 1° in cases which concern the private good of the parties alone, if all the parties consent; 2° in other cases, after the parties have been heard and provided that there is a grave reason and any danger of fraud or subornation is eliminated; 3° in all cases whenever it is likely that the sentence will be unjust because of the reasons mentioned in can. 1645, §2, nn. 1–3 unless the new proof is allowed.

3   For a most recent treatment of the canonical contributions in this area, see: Wilfried Hartmann and Kenneth Pennington, *The History of Courts and Procedure in Medieval Canon Law* (Washington, DC: Catholic University of America Press, 2016).

4   See Charles Donahue, Jr., "The Courts of the Ius Commune," in Hartmann and Pennington, 111-116.

5   Giovanni Devoti provides us with a classic summary of the rules regarding witness testimony under the regime of the Corpus Iuris Canonici: see his *Institutiones canonicae*, vol. 3 (Naples: Tipographia Simoniana, 1852) 116-120.

How does this play out with our current law – and particularly with regard to the adjudication of delicts against the sacrament of penance? Do what I will call our canonical exclusionary rules of evidence promote or hinder just resolution of these delicts?[6] This is our first question.

The 1983 Code of Canon Law stipulates that all persons may serve as witnesses unless the law itself expressly excludes them entirely or partially.[7] Canon 1550 provides one contemporary canonical exclusionary rule. It disqualifies (and thereby excludes) certain persons from serving as a witness in an ecclesiastical judicial process. Paragraph one of the canon excludes minors below the age of 14 and those of limited mental capacity.[8] However, as has been the case for centuries, it offers the judge the discretion to decree their hearing based on the precise condition of the witnesses and the usefulness of the testimony they might offer. In other words, these persons are not excluded because they are always and under all circumstances incapable of testifying or because the content of their testimony is in itself inadmissible under any circumstance.

That is not the case with paragraph two of can. 1550, which is repeated by can. 1231 of the Eastern code. Here the law speaks of those who are incapable (*incapaces habentur*) of testifying in whole or in part. Because they are legally incapacitated, the judge has no discretion to decree their admission due to their particular condition, the need for their testimony or other special circumstances.

The first section declares as *incapaces*, "the parties in the case or those who stand for the parties at the trial," various court officials, including the judge, and others who have assisted the parties in the case at hand.[9] With this provision, the law seeks to avoid bias, confusion of roles and the appearance of injustice.

It is the second section of can. 1550 §2, that concerns our current topic. It forcefully declares as incapable of testifying: "Priests regarding all matters which they have come to know from sacramental confession even if the penitent seeks their disclosure; moreover, matters heard by anyone and in any way on the occasion of confession cannot be accepted even as an indication of the truth."

---

6   I use the phrase "canonical exclusionary rule" to indicate those provisions of the universal law that mandate the total or partial exclusion of certain evidence from a penal process. Here, the evidence will be specifically the identity of an accuser and any information gained on the occasion of the celebration of the sacrament of penance.
7   Can. 1549. All persons can be witnesses unless the law expressly excludes them in whole or in part.
8   Can. 1550 §1. Minors below the fourteenth year of age and those of limited mental capacity are not allowed to give testimony; they can, however, be heard by a decree of the judge which declares such a hearing expedient.
9   Can. 1550 §2. The following are considered incapable: 1° the parties in the case or those who stand for the parties at the trial, the judge and the judge's assistants, the advocate, and others who assist or have assisted the parties in the same case. . .

The 1917 Code already contained this exclusionary rule although with a slight distinction in wording that does not change the substantial equivalence of the two norms. Instead of the current phrase, "even if the penitent seeks their disclosure," the former canon read, "even if he - the confessor - is released from the seal." The change in wording arose from the consultations on the 1976 schema. At the November 1978 meeting of the study group, a consultor suggested the new language was necessary because, "according to the common opinion of theologians, no one can be released from the sacramental seal."[10] His proposal received unanimous acceptance. Still, his was somewhat of a curious recommendation since the opinion of many canonists for centuries was that the penitent can release the confessor from the seal under certain strictly limited conditions.[11] Indeed, the very text of the 1917 code that the consultor sought to modify was used by commentators to demonstrate that fact. Specifically, if confessors were not able to be released, why would the former canon say, "even if [the confessor] is released from the seal"?

At any rate, it is not remarkable that both canons incapacitate the confessor from testifying regarding matters protected by the inviolable sacramental seal. This is not new in our tradition, which developed ever more stringent restrictions on confessor's testifying, most especially when the testimony might in any way betray or disadvantage the penitent.[12] With time, the doctrine developed to forbid any testimony from a confessor - even if there were no danger of betrayal. This was meant mostly to avoid scandal among the faithful and fear arising among penitents that they could not speak freely in the sacramental forum. The same

---

10 "Consultor quidam animadvertit neminem, de communi sententia theologorum, solvi posse a vinculo sigilli sacramentalis confessionis, ideo proponit ut dicatur 'etsi poenitens eorum manifestationem petierit' loco 'etsi a vinculo sigilli soluti sint'. Propositio placet omnibus." *Communicationes* 11 (1979) 110.

11 As Reiffenstuel implies when treating the burden of proof in causes of the violation of the seal: "Si autem fatetur, se quidem peccatum ex confessione, sed cum licentia poenitentis revelasse, onus probandi hanc licentiam incumbit revelanti, saltem in casu, quo poenitens ipsum accusat, aut alias negat se licentiam dedisse." *Jus Canonicum Universum*, vol. 6 (Paris: Ludovicum Vivès, 1869) 567. More recently, Capello maintains [with italics in the original]: "Quare obligatio sigilli vetat, ne confessarius *sine licentia poenitentis* loquatur *extra confessionem* de auditis in confessione tam *cum extraneis* quam *cum ipso poenitente.*" Felix Capello, *Tractatus Canonico-Moralis de Sacramentis*, vol. 2/1 (Turin: Taurinorum Augustae, 1929) 727.

12 Bertrand Kurtscheid, whose historical study on the seal of confession will be cited often here, provides a helpful presentation on this issue. See, *A History of the Seal of Confession*, F. A. Marks, trans. (St. Louis: B. Herder, 1927) 127-169.

has applied with the exclusion of testimony from confessors in causes for the canonization of saints.[13]

Instead, what is more interesting is the extension of the rule to exclude any and all persons other than the confessor from testifying regarding anything at all they know based on the occasion of confession, whether or not that information is otherwise protected by the seal. Here, too, there is no exception to allow the penitent to release these persons bound by the secrecy of confession. We recall that under the former code the term *sigillum* was used for both the confessor and all others with confessional knowledge. We now reserve the term *sigillum* for the confessor and use *secretum* for anyone else. The change in terms does not change the substance or applicability of the law. No one is permitted to betray a penitent, whether a confessor or a third party.

So how did we arrive at such a robust witness exclusionary rule? An early form of this incapacitating norm appears as can. 8, 4° in the 1909 schema of the 1917 Code. It prohibits the use of the forbidden knowledge even as *indicia* of the truth.[14] The first unified schema, presented to the *Congressum* of Cardinals in 1910 left the wording unchanged as can. 294 §2 of the schema.[15] The final version contained in the 1917 Code reflects the substance of the earlier draft but strengthens the intent of the canon to exclude "any and all" information, gained by anyone, and gained in any way.[16] The same wording would be used in the 1936 Instruction on marriage nullity trials, *Provida Mater*.[17]

---

13    Art 101 §1 of *Sanctorum Mater* reads: "A priest must not be admitted to testify about anything that he has come to know through sacramental confession." All others were not excluded from testifying to information gained on the occasion of confession, even if bound by the secret. This is because the cause for canonization is a private process, not a contentious or criminal, public judicial process. Of course, the rule would still apply that the admission of such proof should not cause scandal or otherwise harm the sacrament of penance.

§2. Regular confessors or spiritual directors of the Servant of God must not be admitted to testify concerning anything they have come to know about the Servant of God in the forum of conscience outside sacramental confession (143).

14    "Quin imo quae audita sunt in confessione, si utcumque, etiam de relato aliorum, in iudicio manifestentur, nihil prorsus fiant, adeo ut ne recipe quidem possint qua veritatis indicium." Citation from: Joaquín Llobell, et al., *Il libro De processibus nella codificazione del 1917* (Milan: Giuffrè, 1999) 686.

15    Llobell, 803.

16    Can. 1757 §3. Ut incapaces: 2° Sacerdotes, quod attinet ad ea omnia quae ipsis ex confessione sacramentali innotuerunt, etsi a vinculo sigilli soluti sint; imo audita a quovis et quoquo modo occasione confessionis ne ut indicium quidem veritatis recipi possunt;

17    Art. 119 §3, 2°. Sacerdotes, quod attinet ad ea omnia quae ipsis ex confessione sacramentali innotuerunt, etsi a vinculi sigillo soluti sint; imo audita a quovis et quoquo modo occasione confessionis ne ut indicium quidem veritatis recipi possunt.

I have yet to find historical sources for this forceful and broad norm that excludes any and all information, even if it is not directly protected by the seal. The *fontes* of the 1917 offer none. From Durandus' late 13th century *Speculum iudiciale* onwards, I have found no classical author who discusses this type of mandatory exclusion of witnesses. In fact, few discuss the exclusion of the confessor when the subject matter of testimony would not betray the penitent or create scandal. My consultation with experts in medieval canon law has revealed no source.

Lucio Ferraris in his thorough summary of the doctrine on exclusion makes no mention of it.[18] Neither does Anaklet Reiffenstuel,[19] Giovanni Devoti,[20] or Carl Groß in his major text from 1880, *Das Beweisverfahren im canonischen Proceß*.[21] Michele Lega says nothing when he writes in 1905[22] and neither does Franz Wernz, a very active consultor to the code reform commission, in his 1914 commentary on judicial procedure in decretal law.[23] They all discuss classic exclusionary rules found in the tradition and nothing more. This is but a sampling of available authors.

Bertrand Kurtscheid also remains silent on the matter, at least in the original German version of his standard work on the seal of confession published in 1912.[24] Its remarkably thorough historical treatment of the canon law on the seal says nothing of the exclusion of any and all information gained on the occasion of confession even though, as noted earlier, he does address the question of confession and court testimony. In the 1923 English translation of the work, he offers an update to include the new exclusionary rule of the 1917 code. But he does so without comment as to the sources for the norm. This is unusual given the heavy source annotations that he includes throughout the work. Here alone none appear.

This does not mean, of course, that exclusion did not occur at the request of a party or by order of the judge. Court records over the centuries would provide a more practical view of the question since judges would surely have faced it on occasions. To this point, James Hughes noted in his 1937 doctoral dissertation entitled, "Witnesses in Criminal Trials of Clerics," that, "Church courts have for a long time refused to admit" testimony from any person who has knowledge gained on the occasion of confession. Regrettably, he too offers no sources for

---

18  *Prompta Bibliotheca*, vol. 9 (Venice: Gaspare Storti, 1782) 70-84.
19  Loc. Cit.
20  *Institutiones Canonicae*, vol. 3 (Naples: Simoniana, 1852) 117-119.
21  Innsbruck: Verlag der Wagner'schen Universitäts Buchhandlung, 1880; 11.
22  *De Iudiciis Ecclesiasticis*, vol. 1 (Rome: Typographia Polyglotta, 1905) 419-423.
23  *Ius Decretalium*, vol. 5/1 (Rome: Prati, 1914) 460-464.
24  *Das Beichtsiegel* (Freiburg im Breisgau: Herdersche Verlag, 1912).

this statement, including any of the many court decisions he must have had in mind.[25]

We do find one decision issued by the Roman Rota in 1913, that relates at least indirectly to our search for a source.[26] The case regards a plea for marriage nullity joined on the ground of total simulation on the part of the woman petitioner. She asserts that the evening before her wedding she went to confession and told her confessor that she intended to simulate her consent because her parents were forcing her to marry against her will. She now wished for the confessor to testify to this fact.

The court cites an early 19th century case from the Rota[27] regarding legitimacy of birth that excluded the testimony of a confessor because, as that decision read, "sacramental confession is absolutely foreign to the external forum, in which not only is attention to be paid to the truth, but that truth is to be found only by legitimate means."[28] The decision offers no legal source for this conclusion, although we will see its basis shortly.

In both these cases, the question was only whether the confessor himself could testify, not whether anyone else could if that testimony would in no way betray the penitent. And, oddly enough perhaps, the 1913 decision includes in the decision the woman's statement that she had confessed a grave future sin, the intention to simulate a sacrament. If the sacramental forum is entirely foreign to the external judicial forum, then should the decision have remained largely silent on this matter even though the woman was not a witness, but a party to the case? What she offered still arose in confession and so, by the same rule, should be foreign to the external forum.

In any event, the decision does at least emphasize the principle of law that developed more strongly through the centuries, even if not always in practice: the internal and external fora are or should be entirely foreign to each other. Hence, we can conclude even if the decision does not expressly address the exclusion of any and all information gained in the internal sacramental forum, it can be read to imply as much. In other words, any confessional matter is to be excluded as illegitimate *quoad modum*; that is, because of the way in which it was learned, as well as *quoad substantiam* because the substance of the testimony regards confessional matter.

If it is difficult to find court cases that suggest this broad witness exclusionary rule was in force prior to the 1917 code, perhaps there are legal experts who

---

25  James Austin Hughes, *Witnesses in Criminal Trials of Clerics* (Washington, DC: CUA Press, 1937) 58.
26  *Coram* Prior, March 8, 1913, *RRDec* 6: 210-217.
27  *Coram* D'Avellà, January 20, 1834.
28  Ibid., n. 23. Cited here from *Coram* Prior, 214.

spoke to the matter. Franz Heiner, who served as a rotal auditor from 1908-1919, offers us something. In his work on ecclesiastical criminal processes, published in 1912, he asserts that the confessor cannot testify to anything that he gained on the occasion of confession, whether it was learned directly or indirectly, whether it came from the penitent or a third party. He concludes, "Their attestations, therefore, cannot be admitted even as an indicium of the truth."[29] Here we have the phrase that will make it into the 1917 Code.

Although Heiner does not expressly exclude persons other than a confessor from testifying to anything at all they know from confession, he does say that a judge cannot admit the information they have by way of the confessor's testimony. What follows logically, once more, is that the nature of the information is the disqualifying fact: its relation to sacramental confession – how it was gained and what it contains - is sufficient to exclude it entirely, even as an indication of the truth. It would make little sense, then, to suggest that the confessor is incapable of testifying to such protected information, but anyone else can who comes into possession of it in the same way.

This is, in fact, the position that commentators on the 1917 code will universally propose, even if they also offer no source for the new canon. The exclusion of all information gained on the occasion of confession – even if not directly protected by the seal - intends to safeguard the sacrament and avoid dissuading the faithful from approaching it.[30] By way of example, here are but three of many examples of the strength the former commentators assigned to the exclusionary norm. Pierre Torquebiau writes, "The declarations of witnesses as well must not be taken even as an indication of the truth; one must take them as null and not having been admitted."[31] Alberto Blat repeats the provision of law, adding that such excluded information must be treated as null and as if it had never existed.[32] Conte a Coronata provides the reasoning: "It is a question of protecting in all ways the freedom of conscience so necessary for the sacrament."[33]

---

29 Franciscus Heiner, *De processu criminali ecclesiastico* (Rome: Fredericus Pustet, 1912) 62: "Neque sacerdotes deponere possunt de iis, quae ex confessione aut occasione confessionis directe vel indirecte cognoverint, sive de ipso poenitente, sive de tertiis personis, quamvis a poenitente licentiam loquendi impetraverint. Eorum attestationes igitur ne tamquam indicium veritatis quidem admitti possunt."
30 Most commentators also assert that the provision is of ecclesiastical, positive law, and not of divine law. Some, however, do argue it is of divine law since it relates to the seal of confession and the dignity of the sacrament.
31 "Les déclarations de pareils témoins ne doivent même pas être retenue comme indice de la vérité; on ne doit les tenir pour nulles et non venues." In R. Naz et al., *Traité de droit canonique*, vol. 3 (Letouzey et Ané, Paris, 1948) 246.
32 Alberto Blat, *Commentarium Textus Codicis Iuris Canonicii* (Rome: Typographia Pio X, 1927) 281.
33 "Agitur enim de tuenda omnimoda libertate conscientiae in sacramento tam necessario." Matthaeus Conte a Coronata, *Institutiones Iuris Canonici*, vol. 3 (Rome: Marietti, 1935) 221.

All commentators concur that the judge has no discretion to admit such information and no ecclesiastical authority may dispense from the norm.[34] Moreover, when doubt arises as to the source of the information, the doubt is to be resolved in favor of the sacrament. Authors under the 1983 code maintain these same positions, with one exception that I will mention shortly.

So, given the exclusionary rule regarding witnesses specifically and confessional information generally, is it even possible to hold a fair penal process regarding delicts related to the sacrament? Does the law itself make this almost impossible? And we should recall, that the injured parties and accusers in a penal process serve as witnesses. Presumably, they would have much to say regarding the commission of the crime that took place on the occasion of confession.

Yet, there is an additional provision of law that we need to mention – albeit far more briefly - since it relates directly to the question of our discussion. It arises from Article 24 of the *Norms on the Graviora Delicta* promulgated by the *motu proprio*, *Sacramentorum sanctitatus tutela*, in 2001 and revised in 2010.[35] In all except two of the reserved delicts related to confession, neither the defendant nor his advocate can even know the identity of the accuser without the accuser's express permission.[36] This also functions as a somewhat different type of exclusionary rule. The inadmissibility of this information – the identity of the accuser – results in a denial of the right of the defendant to confront his accuser in cases where that accuser's identity is unknown. This is a serious stipulation of procedural law that cannot help but raise questions of its just nature.

The current formulation of this second exclusionary norm, which is not found in the Code itself, is less strict than the prior one in force until the promulgation of SST in 2001. In the 1922 and 1962 versions of *Crimen sollicitationis*, which set out the law governing the resolution of accusations of solicitation and other more grave delicts, the identity of the penitent could never be made known to the accused, even with the express permission of the penitent. This was meant to avoid as strictly as possible any threat whatsoever to the violation of the seal.

The provision regarding the accuser's anonymity dates back at least to an Instruction of the Holy Office from February 20, 1866. At that time, dioceses and mission territories were still struggling with the implementation of the Constitution of Pope Benedict XIV from 1741, *Sacramentum Poenitentiae*, which dealt generally with the crime of solicitation, but did not issue specific

---

34 Lega can serve as one of numerous examples: *Commentarius in Iudicia Ecclesiastica*, vol. 2 (Rome: Anonima Libraria Cattolica Italiana, 1950) 675.
35 Accessible in English at: http://www.vatican.va/resources/resources_norme_en.html.
36 Art. 24 § 1. In cases concerning the delicts mentioned in art. 4 §1, the Tribunal cannot indicate the name of the accuser to either the accused or his patron unless the accuser has expressly consented.

procedural norms. Because of this, the Holy Office now chose to issue some procedures based on its own jurisprudence and praxis. One of these stated: "Utmost diligence must be taken so that the names of the accusers are not revealed to the defendant and so that the sacred seal is in no way violated."[37]

Whereas neither this Instruction of the Holy Office nor the two editions of *Crimen Sollicitationis* applied this prohibition to any other delicts against the Sacrament of Penance, the current law as found in *SST* applies it to all of them except the delicts of recording or maliciously distributing what was said in confession. This raises a curious point. What if a lay person is accused of a reserved delict, such as attempted celebration of the sacrament: they have no right to know the identity of their accuser?

This leads me to ask again: Does the law truly intend to restrict so forcefully the right to confront accusers or the confessor's ability to testify fully on his behalf, or his ability to call substantive witnesses who might speak in his favor? Alternatively, does the law restrict the promoter of justice to the extent that he would not be able to prosecute crimes effectively in a way that serves justice?

Two authors attempt to avoid this conclusion, each from a different angle. I mentioned earlier Bertrand Kurtscheid's 1927 translation of his work on the sacramental seal. In this edition, he first repeats the common opinion that statements gained on the occasion of confession, "are worthless as evidence, and the judge is not permitted to use them for further investigation."[38] However, he then proffers an exception; namely, he asserts that if testimony does not reveal sinful matter confessed, it may be admitted under certain situations. Here is how he reasons to this conclusion: "If, however, the confessor is guilty of a crime, either regarding faith or morals, this rule does not apply, otherwise punishment would be impossible."[39]

What we see here is an attempt to provide something of an equitable solution for something that the law does not strictly permit. It would be highly unjust for a criminal confessor to escape punishment. Yet, the law cannot intend this outcome. Therefore, barring any violation of the seal, witnesses must be able to testify to what a confessor did or said. Otherwise, justice would not be served and the sacrament (and penitents) would not be protected from offending confessors.

However well intended this conclusion might be, it lacks any corroboration in the authors under the 1917 Code. Moreover, if the intent of the exclusionary

---

37  Benedict XIV, Constitution *Sacramentum Poenitentiae*, June 1, 1741: "Cavetur solertissime, ne denunciantium nomina reo manifestentur et ne sacramentale sigillum quoquomodo violetur." Found in *AAS* 9/II (1917) 505-509. Accessible at: http://www.vatican.va/archive/aas/documents/AAS-09-II-1917-ocr.pdf.
38  Kurtscheid (1927), 300.
39  Ibid., 301.

rule is to protect the sacrament of confession from any harm, then how can an exception be allowed given we can never be absolutely certain no harm will arise? Prosecution of an offending confessor would still be possible without such witness testimony; it might simply be exceedingly difficult to achieve. Most pointedly, the text of the norm under discussion is clear and it is to be interpreted narrowly. This limits our ability to construe the law more broadly as Kurtscheid does.

Professor Klaus Lüdicke has more recently attempted to interpret the exclusionary rule to allow witness testimony under certain conditions. He argues briefly in his commentary on canon 1550 that witnesses who are not confessors are bound by the secret and not by the seal that binds confessors. Therefore, the penitent can permit the witness to testify. The judge would consider whether this permission has been given and then whether the testimony of the witness would harm the sacrament of penance. If it would not, then admission of the witness may be ordered.[40]

Lüdicke presents a clean and simple argument that is worthy of fuller elaboration. This would include discussion of the fact that the canon itself does not apply the distinction between the secret and the seal to the issue of the incapacity of witnesses. Rather, the law's exclusion of both confessor and witness is clear and direct. In this sense, the distinction between the seal and secret is largely terminological rather than substantial, at least when it comes to who may or may not reveal confessional matter in an external forum tribunal. In all cases, neither the confessor bound by the seal nor a third party bound by the secret may betray the penitent (something undisputed), and neither may testify in court regarding anything learned on the occasion of confession.

* * *

With the foregoing in mind, I will move to the second part of my presentation and its principal question: What might a just penal process look like given the exclusionary provisions of the Code? Should we find one that appears to justly resolve an accusation, maybe we find our answer there as well, in practice rather than in theory. To answer this second question, I will present an actual case concerning the violation of the sacramental seal. We will see, perhaps, that the manner in which this case is resolved – especially how witness testimony is used – can provide a general paradigm for resolving the other delicts against

---

40  As Lüdicke puts it: "Die Schweigepflicht jedenfalls der zufälligen Mithörer nach 983 §2 hat nicht denselben Charakter wie die des Priesters. Diese Personen stehen nicht für die Vertraulichkeit des Beichtinstiutes ein, sondern nur für den Schutz des Pönitenten. Bittet er um die Bekanntgabe des Gehörten, kann der Richter den Zeugen zulassen." *Münsterischer Kommentar zum Codex Iuris Canonici*, Klaus Lüdicke, ed. (Münster: Ludgerus Verlag, 1985-) v.s., c. 1550/4.

the sacrament of penance in a just manner that also protects the dignity of the sacrament.

Father Ignatius was a priest and a member of the Capuchin order. He served for some years as the novice master of his community. Father Anastasius, a fellow Capuchin, had been a novice when Father Ignatius served as the novice master. Some years later, Father Anastasius accused Father Ignatius of violating the seal of confession by revealing publically a fault that he had confessed during his time in the novitiate to the novice master. The allegation of misconduct brought about an inquisition to determine whether Father Ignatius was guilty of a violation of the seal.

Father Anastasius stated in his oral accusation that the violation occurred during his novitiate in the Convent of Mondovì, which is located in the Piedmont region of Northern Italy. He claimed that he had revealed a defect to Father Ignatius during confession. Shortly after that, when all the novices gathered for the chapter of faults, Father Ignatius allegedly repeated the defect and reproached him for having committed it. A few days later, Father Anastasius stated he again went to confess to his novice master. This time he mentioned that he was surprised that the confessor had revealed publically the defect confessed previously.

The nature of the accusation brought by Father Anastasius is not uncommon. A penitent hears of a confessor mentioning something the penitent thinks was related only in confession. The immediate sense is that a violation took place. The difficulty becomes, in light of canonical evidentiary rules, how to establish the truth within the limitations of admissible evidence. In this particular case, Father Anastasius testified. A large number of witnesses did as well, including Father Nicholas, the priest the accuser first told of the supposed violation. Circumstantial evidence also played a large role in arriving at the outcome.

The first moment in the process was a comparison of the testimony of Father Nicholas with that of Father Anastasius. As noted, Father Nicholas was the first to hear the accuser's story. He recounted what the Father Anastasius had told him. It mirrored what the accuser stated except for one important fact. Father Nicholas testified that Father Anastasius had told him that when he had confronted Father Ignatius in the confessional about the alleged violation, Father Ignatius was stunned and could not speak. Father Nicholas said that Father Anastasius took this as an acknowledgement of the confessor's guilt.

However, when Father Anastasius was questioned about Father Nicholas' statement he insisted that he could not have made it since he could not recall how Father Ignatius had reacted to the confrontation. He added that he could not even remember what the fault was that Father Ignatius supposedly revealed publically after having learned of it in confession. In fact, he said he had "an impression" that the confessor violated the seal, "a sort of remembrance," and not a certain knowledge. Father Anastasius added in his testimony that he considered Father Ignatius to be a holy man who observed the rule and prayed often.

Witnesses would not speak as highly about Father Anastasius. He supposedly suffered from a negative reputation born partly from the fact that he had earlier been admonished for a lewd act and consigned to penance for it.

Circumstantial evidence also played an important role in the process. The public confession of faults in the novitiate took place usually six times a week. The novices would announce their defects and the novice master would provide appropriate responses. Alternatively, he would simply reproach certain novices for defects they exhibited. This was allegedly what Father Ignatius did regarding the accuser's fault. But if the chapter of faults took place so often, and so many faults were at play, then there is a high degree of likelihood that the fault Father Ignatius mentioned in this case was known to him somehow outside of the sacramental forum.

This becomes more convincing when we note that the novice master was constantly in the presence of and observing the novices. He would easily have recognized their faults without any need to hear their confessions. Here, too, then, the likelihood of knowledge of a fault arising outside of confession becomes much more probable. Another possibility is that Father Ignatius might have learned of it from one of the many friars involved in the formation of the novices.

We saw that Father Anastasius did not recall what the defect was by which the seal was allegedly broken. This implies it was very general in nature and certainly not a serious defect individually attributable to the accuser. This, too, could indicate that it likely was public or shared by several others.

The acts of the case pay considerable attention to the reputation Father Ignatius enjoyed, especially regarding his ministry as a confessor. None of the witnesses provided any indication that he had ever acted improperly with regard to the seal of confession. In fact, he was sought out for the celebration of the sacrament. Others testified that even at the time when he served as novice master he already enjoyed a reputation for a holy life and high degree of maturity. The acts contain highly corroborative testimony that makes it seemingly impossible for Father Ignatius to have committed such a serious offense.

For his part, Father Ignatius remained silent. He provided no statement except the character of his life as a priest, religious and confessor.

In light of the failure of the accusation to stand up under scrutiny, the questionable character of the accuser, his weak memory on specific issues, his own high estimation of the character of Father Ignatius, the circumstantial evidence that fails to support the claim of the accuser, and the quantity and quality of credibility witnesses who speak in favor of the accused, the ruling is, as the acts read, "to vindicate" Father Ignatius from the calumny of his accuser and from the crime of having violated the seal of confession.

\* \* \*

What we see in this brief description of an actual case are the traditional elements of proof used with delicts against the sacrament of penance.[41] We find them most recently in the 1962 document, *Crimen Sollicitationis*. Although this text addressed most specifically the crime of solicitation, and the preliminary investigation into it, the course of proof gathering it lays out can be applied as well to other delicts against confession. The elements of proof in *Crimen* come from the canonical tradition, although we now must consider them with the current exclusionary rules in mind regarding testimony and anonymity. For our purposes, I will presume the accuser claims to be the victim of the accused and is not a third party bringing the accusation.

The first element of proof is the initial accusation or denunciation of the confessor. We saw in the case of Father Ignatius that the accusation as presented by the accuser is of great importance to establishing the truth. Yet, its probative value is weakened considerably if the accusation contains internal or external contradictions or statements that cannot find further corroboration. Because of this, an accuser faces a mighty task: consistency and strength of accusation. If the accusation is not airtight, the conviction of the defendant can quickly become a herculean task for the promoter of justice. This is more so the case since the subsequent testimony of the accuser will often not heal a weak accusation, something we saw with Father Anastasius.

This brings us to the next, particularly sensitive area of proof, the testimony of the accuser and defendant. The accuser is questioned in order to test the accusation and to gain further evidence that might be of value to the process. The responses provided must also conform to canonical exclusionary rules and so not violate the seal and dignity of the sacrament of penance. We should recall as well that if the accuser's identity is to remain anonymous, then any evidence provided that would potentially reveal that identity cannot be included in the acts. We see how this can limit the value of the testimony.

Regarding the defendant, it is worth hearing what *Crimen Sollicitationis* has to say on the matter. It is worth quoting at length: "The questioning of the Defendant takes place . . . with the greatest care being taken on the part of

---

41   They are still applicable, although we can ponder whether Father Anastasius' testimony concerning what he said to Father Ignatius in the second confession would be admissible under today's exclusionary rules.

the judge lest the identity of the accusers and especially of the denouncers be revealed, and on the part of the Defendant lest the sacramental seal be violated in any way. If the Defendant, speaking heatedly, lets slip something which might suggest either a direct or indirect violation of the seal, the judge is not to allow it to be recorded by the notary in the acts; and if, by chance, some such thing has been unwittingly related, he is to order it, as soon as it comes to his attention, to be deleted completely."[42]

To this is added, at least as things were under *Crimen*, the manner in which the interrogation of the defendant is to take place. One example will suffice. When he first appears in the preliminary investigation, the judge delegate is to ask him first, "Whether he knows or can imagine the reason he has been summoned."[43] Only much later, even after several days, will the accused possibly learn of the individual accusations lodged against him. However, he will never have the opportunity to confront his accuser since that identity will remain anonymous.

At any rate, following the questioning of the accuser and accused, the establishment of their credibility and trustworthiness becomes the next central moment in proof. This involves examining the accuser's relationship to the accused (e.g., is there apparent, prior animosity) as well as any evidence that might exist to support or weaken the accuser's general trustworthiness. In cases regarding delicts against confession, where little direct evidence might be available, damage to the accuser's credibility is significant since it removes the probative weight of an essential element of proof.

Yet, if the current law on the *graviora delicta* allows the accuser to remain anonymous is not the confessor as defendant at a serious disadvantage? He cannot present a defense based on the accuser's lack of personal credibility without knowing who that is. The Promoter of Justice, on the other hand, has the advantage of knowing the identity even if he cannot present evidence that directly reveals it. This weakens the procedural parity of the parties, perhaps too far too substantial a degree.

Credibility witnesses will testify to the character – good or bad – of the accuser or the defendant. These witnesses should themselves be of good character. The number of witnesses called by either side is not as critical as is the quality of their testimony and their own personal character. A qualified witness who testifies by virtue of office is especially valuable. All of this is because, as we have seen, direct evidence in the case may be lacking due to its inadmissibility. Often, we are left with a "he said, she said" scenario that can be resolved only by taking into account who is more trustworthy: him or her.

---

42   *Crimen*, 52.
43   Ibid., Formula P.

With regard to the defendant in particular, as thorough an examination as possible should take place with regard to any prior disciplinary issues related to the alleged crime. This would include a search of the archives, personnel files, inquiry of previous jurisdictions where he lived and worked, and inquiries made to religious superiors, if applicable. Anything received becomes part of the acts. Credibility witnesses will then testify to his standing, character, quality of ministry, and so forth, as we also saw happened with Father Ignatius.

Finally, all of the foregoing proofs will be weighed together with the circumstantial evidence that corroborates or weakens the charge against the defendant. Conviction for a delict will result only upon moral certainty regarding the doubt to be resolved. This, in turn, depends on an abundance of probative evidence available to the decision makers so that a miscarriage of justice never occurs.

* * *

From the above-mentioned elements of proof, we saw that the outcome of a process involving delicts against confession will most often depend on the question of who is more credible: the accuser or accused.

Witnesses will certainly testify as they can to facts and circumstances; for instance, whether the confessor was inebriated at the time he entered the confessional. Yet, could a witness testify that he saw the penitent leave the confessional in tears? We might be quick to say yes. However, traditional canonical doctrine holds that the seal protects such an emotional state if its revelation could imply that serious sins were confessed and repented in tears. If a confessor cannot mention the emotional state of a penitent, then should a witness be able to testify to it? Perhaps the exclusionary rule should preclude admission of this type of evidence even if it might be very helpful to ascertaining the truth. I leave that as I pose it: a question.

The canonical tradition has long recognized the importance of credibility in cases involving delicts against the Sacrament of Penance. In fact, it has developed a set of presumptions to assist the judge in coming to a just conclusion. If the accuser is of a much higher character and trustworthiness than the confessor, the accuser prevails. The same goes for the confessor if he enjoys a notably higher credibility. If they are of equal credibility or the credibility of both is doubtful, the confessor prevails.[44]

If we acknowledge the grave importance of arguing matters of credibility, we should also acknowledge the impact the exclusionary rules can have on a successful outcome to such arguments. How can the confessor overcome the unique disadvantage he faces if the identity of the accuser can remain entirely

44  See Ferraris, 374, for one early example.

restricted? Moreover, for both the promoter and defendant, no witnesses may be called who gained any information at all on the occasion of the celebration of confession even if what they will testify to, while not violating the seal, impacts directly the question of credibility and so of guilt or innocence.

Which brings me back, at last, to my initial question. Is it possible to adjudicate justly delicts against the Sacrament of Penance? Of course, I could answer like a good lawyer and say, "it depends." I would not be wrong since each case must be examined based on its own set of circumstances and any penal process, not simply one involving confession, is open to unjust prosecution. If sufficient, truly probative direct and indirect evidence exists and the parties to the cause have full exercise of procedural rights, including the defendant's right of defense, we can, of course, say that the possibility for just adjudication exists.

Perhaps the one delict where even this might be doubtful is that of the recording of what is said in confession or the malicious divulging of that matter by means of social media.[45] In such cases, it would seem that the recording itself must serve as the key piece of evidence. However, if the recording was truly made on the occasion of confession, and so contains information gained during its celebration, how can we admit such evidence without violation of the exclusionary rule?

In any case, I want to go further by way of conclusion than "it depends." I suggest that a doubt arises on at least a formal level regarding the possibility of a just adjudication of delicts against the sacrament of penance given the limitations of the current exclusionary rules. I am speaking on the *formal* level. That is, with regard to the procedural norms as they stand and without their concrete application to a specific cause.

How might this be the case? Let me rephrase the question I posed at the beginning of this presentation: Can a just adjudication of *any* penal process take place when that process excludes the possibility for the defendant to confront his accuser? Most legal systems at use in the world today, certainly our own in the United States, would offer an immediate and resounding No to this question; no, it is not possible to conceive of such a process being just.

Our Sixth Amendment to the Constitution guarantees the right in criminal cases and that amendment is based on a common law tradition that is itself based

---

45  *SST* Art. 4 §2. "With due regard for § 1, n. 5, also reserved to the Congregation for the Doctrine of the Faith is the more grave delict which consists in the recording, by whatever technical means, or in the malicious diffusion through communications media, of what is said in sacramental confession, whether true or false, by the confessor or the penitent. Anyone who commits such a delict is to punished according to the gravity of the crime, not excluding, if he be a cleric, dismissal or deposition."

on the Roman Law.[46] We even hear it expressed in the Acts of the Apostles, where Festus discusses the case brought against Saint Paul: "'It is not the custom of the Romans to deliver any man to destruction before the accused meets the accusers face to face, and has opportunity to answer for himself concerning the charge against him.'"[47]

The chorus of "No's" would grow louder if we asked whether the exclusion of all testimony gained on the commission of the crime could still permit a fair penal process. A fair criminal process is not conceivable without sufficient and relevant evidence related directly to the crime. Otherwise, are we saying to the defendant in a violation of the seal case: We will try you for a crime concerning which we will not be able to give you substantial details and during which you will not be able to present many.

Since I am speaking on the formal level – in justice theory rather than justice practice – it is not a matter of holding a penal process, determining whether sufficient evidence exists, and then absolving the defendant if it does not exist, perhaps even due to the exclusionary rule regarding witnesses. On a formal level, we can ask whether it is even conceivable to formulate a criminal process that is in itself just, but that excludes the two elements of proof discussed here.

Perhaps we would not err to argue that at least on the formal level such a penal process should not even take place. Its very framework would be unjust given the possibility of conviction of a defendant who cannot confront an accuser or admit to trial relevant testimony that would acquit him. In the theory of things, as it were, we should never see penal processes take place that have built into them formal elements that are themselves obstacles to justice to the extent that they negatively and substantially impact the right of defense.

That said, I recognize that we do not live in a purely formal world of justice. The material side of things matters greatly. Without the possibility of just trials, we have the impossibility of protecting the innocent faithful and punishing guilty offenders. This, too, would then lead to an injustice. Besides, we saw at least with the case of Father Ignatius perhaps justice result despite the involuntary procedural silence of the defendant. I have served in one role or another in

---

46  As the Sixth Amendment to the U.S. Constitution reads: "In all criminal prosecutions, the accused shall enjoy the right to a speedy and public trial, by an impartial jury of the State and district wherein the crime shall have been committed, which district shall have been previously ascertained by law, and to be informed of the nature and cause of the accusation; to be confronted with the witnesses against him; to have compulsory process for obtaining witnesses in his favor, and to have the Assistance of Counsel for his defence."

47  Acts 25:16 (NIV). For more on the lengthy historical development of the right to confrontation of accusers and witnesses, see: Frank R. Herrmann and Brownlow M. Speer, "Facing the Accuser: Ancient and Medieval Precursors of the Confrontation Clause," *Virginia Journal of International Law* 34 (1994) 481-554.

several penal processes involving an offense against confession, including as a judge. I certainly believe and hope they all had just outcomes. The promotion of the dignity of the sacrament, the protection of the penitent, the guarantee of the right of defense, and the punishment of offenders are each essential to our legal discipline.

Yet, I am still not entirely at ease with the thought that our formal procedural law might not be consonant with an ideal administration of justice. We should not have to wonder, for instance, how our law could hold that the denial of a substantive right of defense leads to nullity of sentence, yet norms governing certain penal processes involving the Sacrament of Penance almost guarantee a substantive denial of that right, but do not lead to such nullity.

In the end, this is where my initial question leaves me: still with a question. I hope this will disappoint no one since it is what I promised at the outset. Nor have I meant to be provocative with my presentation. At the same time, it is my intention today to suggest answers to the questions I leave us with. That is the next step. For that, I will need to dedicate far more thought to what I have begun to outline here; these are first thoughts only. Trials will and should obviously continue and we will, as we always have, strive as best we can to achieve a just outcome based on our procedures, all of which we presume to be fit for achieving that just outcome.

What I do hope results from this contribution is an ongoing examination of our procedural law that allows us to reflect on how it might promote justice and the right of defense ever more forcefully while, at the same time, fully protecting the seal of confession from any harm. Maybe this is wishful thinking and we have the best we can get given the conflicting goods we are trying to uphold. On the other hand, maybe it is time for us to ask a few questions with an earnest hope of revising some aspects of our formal law so that no one escapes justice and justice escapes no one.

\* \* \*

I will conclude my remarks with a very brief postscript. The case against Father Ignatius that I summarized was a real case. In fact, I changed no names or places. Any citation I made came directly from the published acts.[48] What I did not reveal, however, is that this was more of a quasi-judicial process than a true criminal trial. The reason Father Ignatius did not participate is that he had died a few years earlier, on September 22, 1770. The investigation into whether Father Ignatius had directly violated the seal was part of his canonization process.

---

48 See: Sacred Congregation of the Rites, *Positio Super Virtutibus* (Rome: Typographia Rev. Caerae Apostolicae, 1824).

On May 19, 2002, Pope John Paul II spoke these words at the Mass of Canonization of Saint Ignatius of Santhiá: "In the Piedmont of his time, Ignatius of Santhiá was father, confessor, counsellor and teacher of many - priests, religious and lay people - who sought his wise and enlightened guidance. Even today he continues to remind everyone of the values of poverty, simplicity and authentic Christian life."[49]

Although the case of Saint Ignatius of Santhiá still provides a good example of the just resolution of a delict against confession - and the use of the elements of proof to achieve that outcome - even more importantly, perhaps Saint Ignatius can serve as a patron saint for those involved in the resolution of these delicts.

We must without fail promote justice and protect the sanctity of the Sacrament of Penance. We all can agree on that. How this will play out in the cases we now participate in and how it will develop in future years is where I believe fruitful and thoughtful discussion can take place. In any case, we are sure that the intercession of Saint Ignatius can help us greatly in our own ministry of justice in service to the mission of the Church.

---

[49] Homily of John Paul II, May 19, 2002, available at: http://w2.vatican.va/content/john-paul-ii/en/homilies/2002/documents/hf_jp-ii_hom_20020519_canonization.html.

# SEMINAR

## CIRCUMSTANCES ALLOWING THE USE OF THE *PROCESSUS BREVIOR*: SOME EXEGETICAL CONSIDERATIONS
### *Reverend Monsignor John G. Johnson*

Everybody knows that the Fathers of the 2014 Extraordinary Session of the Synod of Bishops expressed concern that then-current procedures for marriage nullity cases did not adequately meet the needs of the people of God.[1] Everybody knows that Pope Frances responded to these concerns by quickly issuing two *motu proprii*, *Mitis Iudex Dominus Iesus*[2] containing revisions to the 1983 Code of Canon Law and *Mitis et misericors Iesus*[3] containing revisions to the Code of Canons of the Eastern Churches. The modifications these documents made in formal procedure were not trivial. For example, the tribunal of the petitioner's domicile or quasi-domicile may now claim competence without first obtaining the consent of the respondent's Judicial Vicar (*MI*, pp. 102-103, revising canon 1672; *MetM*, pp. 136-137, revising canon 1358). In a best-case scenario, this provision shaves weeks off the time necessary for processing a case in first instance. Again, the decision which first recognizes the invalidity of a marriage no longer requires review by an appellate tribunal (*MI*, pp. 108-109, revising c. 1679; *MetM*, pp. 142-143, revising canon 1365). This provision,

---

[1] Cf. "*Relatio Synodi* of the III Extraordinary General Assembly (5 – 19 October 2014)," *The Canon Law Society of Great Britain and Ireland Newsletter* [*CLSGBI Newsletter* in future citations] 181 (March 2015) 24: "47. A great number of synod fathers emphasized the need to make the procedure in cases of nullity more accessible and less time consuming, and, if possible, at no expense. They proposed, among others, the dispensation of the requirement of second instance for confirming sentences; the possibility of establishing an administrative means under the jurisdiction of the diocesan bishop; and a simpler process to be used in cases where nullity is clearly evident."

[2] Pope Francis, Apostolic Letter *Mitis Iudex Dominus Iesus*, 15 August 2015, *Communicationes* 47 (2015) 2: 283-295. The presentation will rely on the Latin and English texts found in P. M. Dugan, L. Navarro, and E. Caparros, eds., *The Reform Enacted by the m.p. Mitis Iudex, Commentaries and Documentation* (Montreal: Wilson & Lafleur, 2016), pp. 92-127. Citations, which will be incorporated directly into the text, will take the form *MI*, p. [n] or, if the reference is to one of the canons, *MI*, canon [n].

[3] Pope Francis, Apostolic Letter *Mitis et misericors Iesus*, 15 August 2015, *Communicationes* 47 (2015) 2: 296-308. The presentation will rely on the Latin and English texts found in Dugan et al., pp. 128-161. Citations, which will be incorporated directly into the text, will take the form *MetM*, p. [n] or, if the reference is to one of the canons, *MetM*, canon [n].

too, significantly reduces the time necessary for a petitioner to establish his/her freedom to marry.[4] Just these two changes enable a tribunal to process a case significantly more quickly than was possible under the two Codes.

Even more notable, however, was the papal creation of a new procedure. Pope Francis wrote, "in simplifying the ordinary process for handling marriage cases, a sort of briefer process was devised... to be applied in those cases where the alleged nullity of marriage is supported by particularly clear arguments" (*MI*, pp. 98-99; cf. also *MetM*, pp. 134-135). Despite striking similarities with the oral contentious process,[5] this "briefer process" is a new institute and will invite careful study by jurists for the foreseeable future.

The purpose of this presentation is to make a small contribution to the discussion of the "briefer process." Its focus will be Article 14 of the "*Ratio procedendi*" which concludes the *motu proprio*. As of the writing of these reflections, not many canonists have had the opportunity of commenting extensively on that norm. I shall therefore take a quasi- or semi-exegetical approach to the Article, accepting the direction the Legislator gives in canon 17, seeking to understand this legal text "according to the proper meaning of the words considered in their text and context." I shall also limit my remarks to *Mitis Iudex*, bearing in mind that the two *motu proprii* are virtually identical.

The nature of the general context of Article 14 seems uncontroversial: the document containing it bears the title, "*Litterae Apostolicae motu proprio datae*" (*MI*, p. 92) and is therefore unquestionably a *legislative* text.[6] It is also unquestionable that the *motu proprio* promulgates laws in the strict sense of the

---

[4] Archbishop Daneels notes "that the suppression of the double conforming affirmative sentence will have the effect that much of the second instance personnel will be freed up to accelerate the first instances processes...." Frans Daneels, "A First Approach to the Reform of the Process for the Declaration of Nullity of Marriage," *The Jurist* 76 (2016) 128. In other words, there will be less work to do (the review of affirmative first-instance decisions will no longer be mandatory) and more people to do it.

[5] There are verbal parallels between canons governing the two procedures. For example, one reads in canon 1676, §1 (governing the *processus brevior*) "*si aestimet eum aliquo fundamento niti*" and "*decreto ad calcem ipsius libellli apposito*," and one finds exactly the same expressions in canon 1659, §1 (governing the oral contentious process). Canon 1684 (governing the *processus brevior*) begins, "*Libelllus quo processus brevior introducitur, praeter ea quae in can. 1504 recensentur, debet....*" Canon 1658, §1 (governing the oral contentious process) begins, "*Libellus quo lis introducitur, praeter ea quae in can. 1504 recensentur, debet....*" The verbal echoes are so exact that one suspects that the drafters of the *motu proprio* used the canons on the oral contentious process as a model. William L. Daniel, "The Abbreviated Matrimonial Process before the Bishop in Cases of 'Manifest Nullity' of Marriage," *The Jurist* 75 (2015) 548-550, provides a more detailed analysis.

[6] Cf., for example, Juan Ignacio Arrieta, *Governance Structures within the Catholic Church* (Montreal: Wilson & Lafleur, 2000), p. 109: "*Apostolic letters* (Litterae apostolicae) *motu proprio*: [are] pontifical laws...."

term: canons which replace their counterparts in the 1983 Code of Canon Law. But it also unquestionable that not everything in a *motu proprio* is a law. For example, the following statement in *Mitis Iudex* is clearly *not* a law: "Through the centuries, the Church, having attained a clearer awareness of the words of Christ, came to and set forth a deeper understanding of the doctrine of the indissolubility of the sacred bond of marriage, developed a system of nullities of matrimonial consent, and put together a judicial process more fitting to the matter so that ecclesiastical discipline might conform more and more to the truth of the faith she was professing" (*MI*, pp. 93-94). Hence, recognizing the legislative character of the document as a whole does not preemptively answer the question, "What sort of statements does the reader find in Article 14?"

The first section of the *motu proprio* consists of discursive prose explaining the background of the pope's decision to revise matrimonial procedures and highlighting the changes he is making. In its middle section are twenty-one canons. The papal signature appears beneath the list of canons. The concluding section of the *motu proprio* is the immediate neighborhood of Article 14. It bears the sub-title, "The way of proceeding in cases regarding the declaration of the nullity of marriage,"[7] and the nature of its Articles has occasioned some perplexity.

One might argue that the Articles, like the canons they complement, are laws.[8] Just above his signature Pope Francis wrote, "Attached and made part hereof[9] are the procedural rules that we consider necessary for the proper and accurate

---

7   The Latin title is "*Ratio procedendi in causis ad matrimonii nullitatem declarandam.*" One might compare the language of canon 31, §1 concerning Instructions: "… *rationes in iisdem [legum praescriptis] exsequendis servandas evolvunt.*"

8   This is the opinion of Joaquin Llobell, "Some Questions Common to the Three Processes for the Declaration of Nullity of Marriage set out in the motu proprio *Mitis Iudex*,", in Dugan et al., eds, *The Reform*, p. 35: "In effect, these rules are of a legislative nature *strictu sensu*: they are authentically laws because produced and promulgated by the Legislator and they introduce innovations in each code." He continues, "The RP could appear to be simply a general executive decree, rather than an i*nstructio*. In effect, the RP do not possess the characteristic typical to *instructions* of being 'given for the use of those whose duty is to see that laws are executed and oblige them in the execution of the laws' (canon 34 §1). General executive decrees, on the contrary, are given for all those to whom a law applies and have as their content the more precise determining of how a law is to be observed (cf. canons 31-33). However, the RP are not a general executive decree either because the legislator himself is the author and, therefore, according to can. 29 they are a law properly speaking…. Certainly, the RP are one part of the entire law promulgated *motu proprio* by the legislator himself."

9   Archbishop Daneels observes that "neither the Latin text nor the Italian contain 'and made part hereof.'" Daneels, *Reform*, p. 120, n. 7. The Latin (presumably, the *official*) text reads, "Praesentibus adnectitur ratio procedendi…"—"To these present [canons] is added the *ratio procedendi*…."

implementation of this new law,[10] which must be observed diligently to foster the good of the faithful. What we have established by means of this *motu proprio*, we deem valid and lasting, notwithstanding any provision to the contrary, even those worthy of meriting most special mention" (*MI*, p. 117). The "attached... procedural rules" are therefore norms of action which the pope promulgated and ordered the faithful to observe "diligently... notwithstanding any provision to the contrary."[11] The pope's language gives the impression that he is legislating.

Even within this brief passage, however, there is some ambiguity: the pope explicitly distinguishes between "the procedural rules" and "this new law." He issues "the procedural rules" to guide "the proper and accurate implementation of this new law." Shortly below this passage is another that compounds the ambiguity. Immediately under the subtitle, "*Ratio procedendi,*" Pope Francis explains that "it has seemed opportune to offer, together with the detailed norms for the application to the matrimonial process, some tools for the work of the tribunals" (*MI*, p. 119). He here distinguishes "detailed norms" and "tools for the work of the tribunals." The structure of the Latin sentence makes the distinction even sharper: "*una cum definitis normis ad processus matrimonialis applicationem*"[12] is separated from "*instrumenta quaedam praebere*" by "*visum est, pro comperta habita Petri Successoris....*" (*MI*, p. 118). Within a few paragraphs, therefore, the pontiff speaks of "this new law," "procedural rules," "detailed norms for the application to the matrimonial process," and "some tools for the work of the tribunal." The expression, *this new law*, obviously denotes the canons the *motu proprio* is promulgating. Do the other three expressions refer to the Articles in the *Ratio procedendi*? And how does one determine which Articles are "detailed norms" and which are only "tools for the work of the tribunal"?

After pondering the matter, experts have offered a range of conclusions about the *nature*, though not the binding force, of the *Ratio procedendi*. Professor Llobell argues that the Articles are laws in the strict sense of the term.[13] For him, the location of the material within the *motu proprio* does not affect its juridic character. Professor Daniel, to the contrary, denies that the norms "are... part of the motu proprio."[14] He maintains that "What is immediately notable about

10 One might compare this with canon 31, §1 concerning "general executory decrees... which define more precisely the manner of applying a law."
11 "Whether or not this formula [viz., "that any and whatsoever provision to the contrary, even 'worthy of most special mention,' was suppressed"] refers also to the attached procedural rules has become a point of discussion among canon lawyers." Daneels, *Reform*, p. 121. If the formula does *not* refer to the procedural rules, then the argument that those rules are laws loses some of its force.
12 Cf. the language of canon 31, §1 "*quibus nempe pressius determinantur modi in lege applicanda servandi.*"
13 Llobell, p. 35.
14 William Daniel, "An Analysis of Pope Francis' 2015 Reform of the Legislation Governing Causes of Nullity of Marriage," *The Jurist* 75 (2015) 456.

the *Ratio procedendi* is its deliberate placement outside of the motu proprio proper.... The function of the *Ratio* as stated by the legislator and as practically observed in the tone of its provisions suggests that it is not legislation but a body of administrative norms."[15] He concludes that the *Ratio* "is... a body of general executory decrees since it is not only directed to those entrusted with executing procedural law in causes of nullity of marriage. It also governs the whole process and the rights of all the faithful acting within it."[16] Cardinal Coccopalmerio, the President of the Pontifical Council for Legislative Texts, offers a third option. "As far as their nature is concerned," he has said, "I think the commentaries which have appeared up to now are agreed that said Rules are simply an Instruction."[17] Professor Jenkins, after surveying the opinions of his brother and sister jurists, concludes that "the consensus among those who have considered the question of the legal status of the PR appears to hold that the 21 articles are part of the substance of the legislative text—with most arguing they hold the same strictly legal character –have the juridic character of legislation, and possibly serve in a similar way as an instruction, although this last point has not found a majority opinion. What cannot help but be noted, however, is how much discussion among experts the legal nature of the PR has engendered. This witnesses primarily to the lack of clarity the legislative text itself presents at times."[18]

Unfortunately, even focusing on the two paragraphs of Article 14 does not solve this problem of the precise categorization of the *Ratio procedendi*.

Although differing in length, the Article's two sentence-long paragraphs are parallel in structure. Both begin with prepositional phrases (*inter* + an accusative) modified by a relative clause echoing the language of one of the canons promulgated by the *motu proprio*. The verb in each sentence is a third person plural present indicative passive of a verb of judging. The major difference between the paragraphs is that the subject of paragraph one is compound and the subject of paragraph two is simple.

---

15  Ibid., p. 459.
16  Ibid., p. 460. Canon 34, §1 specifies that "Instructions... are given for the benefit of those whose duty it is to execute the law...." By contrast, "General executory decrees... define the manner of application or urge the observance of laws" and therefore "bind those who are bound by the laws" (Canon 32). If the *Ratio* addresses, not only "those whose duty it is to execute the law" (e.g., tribunal ministers, bishops, parish priests), but also everyone bound by the law (e.g., the parties to a marriage case), the *Ratio* must have the nature of a general executory decree rather than of an instruction.
17  Francesco Cardinal Coccopalmerio, "The Reform of the Canonical Process for the Declaration of Nullity of Marriage," in Dugan et al., eds., *Reform*, p. 9. Neither Llobell nor Daniel would call the *Ratio procedendi* an Instruction.
18  Ronny E. Jenkins, "Applying Article 14 of *Mitis Iudex Dominus Iesus* to the *Processus Brevior* in Light of the Church's Constant and Common Jurisprudence on Nullity of Consent," *The Jurist* 76 (2016) 238.

Because paragraph two is simpler, it is easier to begin the analysis there. Paragraph two says that certain medical records belong in the category "*instrumenta quae petitionem suffulciunt.*" This expression echoes the language of canon 1684: "The *libellus* introducing the briefer process... must... exhibit, in an attachment, *documenta quibus petitio innitur.*" *Instrumenta* and *documenta* are synonyms. *Suffulcire* means *to prop up* or *to support. Inniti* means *to rest on* or *to be supported by. The documents which support the petition* and *the documents whereby the petition is supported* are virtually identical in meaning. The function of paragraph two of Article 14 is therefore to inform the reader that "all medical records that can clearly render useless the requirement of an *ex officio* expert" are the kind of documents which canon 1684 requires the petitioner to attach to his or her *libellus*. Paragraph two of Article 14 does not impose a new obligation on the petitioner, but it does explain to the petitioner the meaning of the obligation canon 1684 already imposes. If the legislator had included paragraph two of Article 14 as a second paragraph to canon 1684, no one would have had any difficulty in identifying it as a law. On the other hand, if the Signatura had included it in an instruction or a general executory decree, no one would have had any difficulty in identifying it as an administrative norm. Therefore, whether paragraph two of Article 14 is a law or an administrative norm depends on the legal character of its context.

Paragraph one of Article 14 is more of a conundrum. Its verb is the third person plural present indicative passive of *recensere*.[19] From the same root come *censor* and *census*. The census was a kind of list the censor prepared. In preparing the list, the censor did more than count noses; he determined, among other things, which noses were Roman and which of those Roman noses belonged in the Senate. Hence, the activity denoted by *censere* involves weighing as well as counting; it results in evaluating or forming an opinion. *Re-censere* would involve engaging in the activity more than once—to count the collection a second time, for example, or to recheck the figures on one's 1040, or to ensure that nobody on the list of eligible voters was already dead. The legislator appears to be saying[20] that a person who studies the matter intently would include in the

---

19 Canon 1659, §1 uses the very same word, *recensentur*, which translators for the CLSA and The Canon Law Society Trust have rendered *enumerated*.

20 The reason for caution here is the legislator's use of *recurrant* in canon 1683, 2°. *Recurro* should mean something like "to run again" or "to run back." Canon 67, §3 prescribes that when a person doubts whether a rescript is valid, "*recurratur ad rescribentem*" (one should take recourse to the person who issued the rescript). The 1983 Code typically uses *recurrere* to mean, "take recourse to," or, more literally, "to run back to [for clarification or a different answer]." This is obviously not the meaning of the term in the *motu proprio*. The English cognate *recur* means "to occur again," i.e., to happen more than once. But the canon under discussion clearly does not require that the circumstances about which it speaks must happen more than once in a given case before the case is suitable for the briefer process. This leads one to believe that *recurrant* in canon 1683, 2° means no more than *occurrant*; and if that is true, then *recensentur* might mean no more than *censentur*.

category specified by the prepositional phrase the items comprising the subject of the sentence.

The fact that the verb is in the indicative suggests but does not prove that the first paragraph of Article 14 is not a norm of action,[21] but anyone who has read rubrics in the *Roman Missal* knows that the Legislator can and does give orders using the indicative. "The Creed is not said" clearly means, "Don't say the Creed." But if the Legislator had intended to tell the reader, "You must consider these items as examples of the sorts of circumstances allowing the use of the briefer process," he could have done so by adding a single letter—by substituting *recenseantur*, a jussive subjunctive, for *recensentur*.[22] Or he could have used a gerundive. From the way in which the Legislator chooses to express himself one might conclude that he is offering an authoritative opinion rather than imposing an obligation.[23]

Paragraph one of Article 14, like paragraph two, states that certain items belong in a specific category. The language whereby the legislator describes that category—"*rerum et personarum adiuncta quae sinunt causam nullitatis matrimonii ad tramitem processus brevioris iuxta cann. 1683-1687 pertractari*"— refers the reader to canons 1683 ff. Before following up on that reference, however, one might appropriately note what the Article does not say. It does not say that the items constituting the subject of the sentence are new grounds

---

21  For comparison, one might consider canon 1510 of the 1983 Code of Canon Law: "*Conventus, qui citatioriam schedam recipere recuset, vel qui impedit quominus citatio ad se perveniat, legitime citatus habeatur.*" By using the subjunctive the Legislator has imposed an obligation on court personnel: they *should* regard as properly cited a respondent who refuses to accept a citation or makes it impossible for a messenger to deliver a citation.

22  The verb *recenseo* occurs in nine canons in the 1983 Code of Canon Law, always in the form *recensentur*—third person plural present indicative passive. See Xavierius Ochoa, *Index Veborum ac Locutionum Codicis Iuris Canonici* (Rome: Libreria Editrice Vaticana, 1984), p. 406, s.v. In canon 134, §2, in canon 224, in canon 1312, §1, 1, in canon 1334, §2, in canon 1336, §1, 3°, in canon 1336, §2, in canon 1338, §1, in canon 1354, §1, and in canon 1658, §1 *recensentur* means something like *are enumerated* or *are listed*. The lists, in turn, appear to be taxative. The list in Article 14, §1, by contrast, is not.

23  Canon 1079, §4 provides a counter example to canon 1510, above. §2 provides that, if he cannot reach the local Ordinary, a priest or deacon enjoys the faculty of dispensing from certain impediments and from canonical form. §4 reads, "*In casu de quo in §2, loci Ordinarius censetur adire non posse, si tantum per telegraphum vel telephonum id fieri possit.*" The canon makes a statement of fact: the local Ordinary *is* (not *should be*) regarded as unreachable if he can be reached only by telephone or telegraph. This paragraph is clearly a law, but the Legislator expresses it in the indicative. He uses, by the way, *censere*, the root of the same verb he uses in the principal clause of Article 14, §1.

of nullity.[24] In fact, within two of the listed items are three explicit references to existing grounds of nullity (simulation of consent, error that determines the will, defect of the use of reason); and in other items are unmistakable, though implicit, references to existing grounds (avoiding procreation, deceitful concealment, a completely extraneous cause of marriage, physical violence). One infers that *each* of the items of the list points to the occurrence of some standard *caput nullitatis*.[25]

Similarly, the Article does not say that the listed circumstances give rise to a legal presumption in favor of the invalidity of the marriage. Tribunal ministers recall that "A person with a favorable presumption of law is freed from the burden of proof" (canon 1585, CLSA translation). For example, canon 1061, §2 establishes a presumption of law concerning the consummation of marriage: "After a marriage has been celebrated, if the spouses have lived together consummation is presumed until the contrary is proven" (CLSA translation). If Titius can prove that he and Bertha underwent a ceremony of marriage and that they lived together afterwards, he does not have to prove that they consummated the marriage. Similarly, because canon 1101, §1 establishes the legal presumption that "The internal consent of the mind is presumed to conform to the words and signs used in celebrating the marriage" (CLSA translation), Bertha does not have to prove that, when she pronounced her vows, she meant what the words ordinarily express. The language of paragraph one does not echo the language of these or similar canons. If the Legislator had wished to say that the existence of the listed circumstances gives rise to a presumption of law against the validity of the impugned marriage, he would have spoken differently.

---

24 Cf., on this point, Apostolic Tribunal of the Roman Rota, "*Subsidium* for the application of the M.p. *Mitis Iudex Dominus Jesus*," from *The Canon Law Society of Great Britain and Ireland Newsletter* 186 (June 2016) p. 23: "It is necessary to clear away any equivocation in this area: *these circumstances are not, in fact, new grounds of nullity*. We were dealing here simply with situations that the jurisprudence has long enucleated as *symptomatic elements of the invalidity of matrimonial consent*, which can easily be proved by testimonies or documents that can be readily procured. These can present, in some cases, such a factual weight as to suggest evidence of the nullity of the marriage." Subsequent references to this document will take the form: *Subsidium*, p. n.

25 The *Subsidium* speaks of "an error that determines the will (cfr. Can. 1099), or a defect of a valid intention through the exclusion of the marriage itself, or of one of its essential elements or properties (cfr. Can. 1101, §2)" (p. 24), of "simulation of consent, or… a mental reservation about the permanence of the union, or about its exclusivity (p. 24), of "Simulated will… condition, error or deceit" (pp. 24-25), of "a simulated will… contrary to the good of children" (p. 25), of "the refusal of the obligation of faithfulness" (p. 25), of "a deception about a quality which can gravely disturb the consortium of conjugal life" (p. 25), of "the possibility… that one or both of the parties did not really intend marriage" (p. 25), of "Fear caused from the outside" (p. 26), and of "Consensual incapacity due to psychic reasons" (p. 26). The language refers to traditional grounds of nullity.

Nor does paragraph one of Article 14 say that the presence of these listed circumstances guarantees an affirmative decision:[26] canon 1687, §1 acknowledges that the bishop might *not* reach moral certitude and might therefore refer the case back to the tribunal for formal processing.[27] The Article says only that the circumstances it lists *allow a case to be adjudged using the briefer process.*[28]

It may be significant that the verb the Legislator uses in the relative clause is indicative rather than subjunctive—*sinunt* rather than *sinant* or even *sinere possint*. The pope does not say that the items in the subject of the sentence *could allow* or *might allow* the Judicial Vicar to order that the case be processed briefly *coram episcopo*. He says that the items *do allow* the Judicial Vicar to make this determination. On the other hand, he does not say that the items *require* the use of the briefer process.[29] Here, too, the pope's choice of language implies that Article 14, §1 is not a norm of action.

---

[26] Morrisey observes, "The most controversial paragraph in the *Ratio* spells out the types of situations where nullity could be evident. The difficulty will lie in the fact //p. 32// that there will be a temptation to conclude that simply because one or more of these situations exists, the marriage is itself null.... It will be essential to make certain that our courts do not slip into the trap of stating that the simple existence of one or more of these given facts is the equivalent of marriage nullity. The *motu proprio* does not establish new impediments." Francis G. Morrisey, "The *Motu Proprio Mitis Iudex Dominus Iesus*," *The Canon Law Society of Great Britain and Ireland Newsletter* 184 (December 2015) 32-33. Cf. also Jenkins, "Applying," p. 240-241: "...the examples of Art. //p. 240// 14 ... can never be taken in themselves as legally relevant for the invalidation of matrimonial consent. Full proof of nullity arises from all sources of proof, weighed in light of substantive jurisprudence, and not merely from the fact of a recurring circumstance of things or persons has been established."

[27] Professor Jenkins' discussion of this point is apposite: "The manifest nullity of consent present in a petition does not guarantee the ability of the bishop to reach moral certitude regarding the nullity of the marriage. The standard of manifest nullity in the petition is one that allows a type of process to be used. The process, in turn, must now lead to moral certitude regarding nullity of consent. There is no guarantee that the mere attachment of documents, including compelling medical reports, to the petition will result in a finding of nullity. That conclusion can only be drawn once the petition, documents and witnesses (together with all the facts and circumstances, are weighed by the bishop." Jenkins, "Applying," p. 246.

[28] The provisions of canon 1688 provide a parallel. If someone attacks the validity of a marriage on specified grounds—the presence of an undispensed diriment impediment, a defect of canonical form, or the lack of a valid mandate for a proxy—and if "a document subject to no contradiction or exception clearly establishes" the foundation of the allegation, then the judge can omit "the formalities of the ordinary process" and proceed to decision after "the citation of the parties and the intervention of the defender of the bond" (*MI*, p. 115). If certain conditions are verified, the judge may use documentary procedure. By the same token, the presence of the circumstances listed in Article 14 might justify the use of the briefer process.

[29] "This list... in no way offers clear-cut cases for the briefer process." Daneels, *Reform*, p. 131.

Canon 1683, to which Article 14 refers the reader, specifies three essential qualifications of the circumstances in view. In the first place, there must be readily available testimonies and records to prove the existence of these circumstances. Canon 1684 requires the petitioner to indicate in the *libellus* itself "the proofs, which can be immediately collected by the judge" and to attach to the *libellus* "the documents... upon which the petition is based" (*MI*, p. 111). Accordingly, some of the evidence will arrive at the Court with the petition, and the location of the other evidence will be clearly indicated. All of this evidence will be "undisputable, clear, certain, and definite. To a person of average intelligence, knowledge and experience, this evidence neither causes doubt nor needs further explanation."[30] Therefore, the circumstances to which the petition alludes will not need more detailed investigation or analysis. If the Judicial Vicar should need to engage in further research to ascertain whether the circumstances exist, he would not be able to assign the case to the briefer process. Finally, these circumstances must make the invalidity of the marriage manifest.[31]

It also seems relevant that canon 1683, 1° specifies the context within which the Judicial Vicar can interpret these circumstances: either both parties are seeking the annulment of the marriage or else the non-petitioner is at least consenting to the petition.[32] If both parties are seeking the annulment, the Judicial Vicar will have received either a statement from each of them or a joint statement expressing their common understanding of the history of their now-broken relationship. If the non-petitioner is at least consenting to the petition, he or she is at least implicitly endorsing the substance of the petitioner's claim.[33]

Why is this so important? One might use one of the circumstances listed in paragraph one of Article 14 as an illustration. Abortion is a medical procedure. In principle, proof that an woman underwent an abortion should exist in the form of medical records. The aim of every abortion is the removal of an unborn child from a woman's body. Every abortion prevents the birth of at least that particular child. But not everyone who procures an abortion does so to prevent procreation. Consider the case of Bertha who became pregnant in adolescence. Her daughter

---

30 Leszek Adamowicz, "The Circumstances of Things and Persons that can allow a Case for Nullity of Marriage (*Mitis Iudex*—"The way of proceeding...," Art. 14)," *The Canon Law Society of Great Britain and Ireland Newsletter* 188 (December, 2016) 64.
31 Cf. Daneels, *Reform*, p. 132: "Wise and experienced judges may have encountered in their career some rare case in which the nullity of marriage was manifest from the very start.... However, such rare case would have been decided rather quickly anyway by the ordinary process."
32 Cardinal Erdo argues that the "consent" of the non-petitioner embraces the object of the petition, the title of nullity, and the use of the briefer process. Cf. Peter Cardinal Erdo, "Osservazioni sulla nuova regolamentazione del processo matrimoniale," *Periodica* 105 (2016) 640.
33 G. Paolo Montini ("L'Accordo dei Coniugi Quale Presupposto del *Processus Matrimonialis Brevior* [Can. 1683, 1° *MIDI*], *Periodica* 105 [2016] 395-415) disagrees. For him it is sufficient that the non-petitioner consent to the use of the briefer process.

died almost immediately after birth. Shortly after Bertha married Titius, she again became pregnant. Three months into her pregnancy the doctor told the couple that their child was not developing properly. His skull was not forming; and if Bertha carried him to term, he would die during his passage through the birth canal. Bertha and Titius decided to abort their son.

This couple's seeking an abortion had nothing to do with excluding the *bonum prolis* from their marriage. Both parties wanted to have children. Within a year they did have a child. Bertha's seeking an abortion would have been a circumstance justifying the use of the briefer process only if she had done so precisely to avoid bringing a child into the marriage. The Judicial Vicar could know her mindset only if she, acting as petitioner, revealed it to him, or if she, though not petitioning for the annulment, agreed with her former husband's claim that she had acted for that reason. In such a situation the petition itself would contain at least an implicit confession of simulation, the identification of some kind of reason for the simulation, and at least some proof that the abortion took place. One can easily see that such a case is an apt candidate for the briefer process.

This example may show that the parties' concurrence in seeking an annulment provides the sort of context within which the Judicial Vicar can more easily assay the circumstances to which paragraph one of Article 14 refers. Outside that context, the existence of those circumstances might indicate very little about the possible invalidity of the marriage.

With the provisions of canons 1683 and 1684 in mind, I turn to the individual items comprising the subject of the sentence in the first paragraph of Article 14. These items are miscellaneous. Some of the circumstances involve facts or series of facts easily verifiable by documents (for example, an abortion or incarceration or the birth of a child) or by the testimony of knowledgeable witnesses (for example, the length of the conjugal cohabitation or physical violence preceding a wedding). Some of these facts, in turn, are juridically relevant only if coupled with a specific intention (for example, the physical violence must be "inflicted to extort consent"; the "grave contagious illness" must be concealed in order to induce the deceived party to enter the marriage; the *fidei defectus* must be able to give rise to simulation or determining error). In two cases the circumstances are states of a person rather than facts or series of facts: *fidei defectus* and *defectus usus rationis*.

Because the list is so heterogeneous,[34] interpreting it requires item by item study. Before undertaking it, however, one should note that the list is not taxative. The legislator explicitly states this, not once but twice. He prefaces the list with *exempli gratia* and concludes it with *et cetera*. The reader might add other items to the list, and the items on the list are only examples. The open-ended[35] character of the list is arguably a reason not to view Article 14, §1 as a norm of action.

The first item on the list—is *fidei defectus*—is, in my opinion, the most troublesome. The language itself is imprecise: exactly what does the Legislator mean by *defectus*?[36] The noun is derived from *deficere* which tends to mean "to fail, to weaken, to run short," or something similar. The noun tends to mean something like a failure or cessation or even an eclipse. Within its context does *defectus* mean *total absence* or only *deficiency*?[37] And what does the Legislator mean by *fidei*? Number 153 of the *Catechism* teaches, "*Faith is a gift from God,*

---

34  Cf. Paolo Moneta, "The Procedural Dynamics of the *Motu Proprio Mitis Iudex*," in Dugan et al., eds., *Reform*, p. 76: "The long series of circumstances and facts indicated in this provision are miscellaneous. Each is quite different from the other, and variously linked to different grounds of nullity. There is no real point trying to find any common ground between them, since some of them are only exemplary...."

35  Cf. Daneels, *Reform*, p. 131: "...article 14, §1 of the procedural rules... offers an open-ended list of circumstances of things and persons that could allow a case to be handled by the briefer process."

36  According to Ochoa (p. 131, s.v.), *defectus* occurs in eight canons in the 1983 Code of Canon Law: (1) canon 1095, 2° ("The following are incapable of contracting marriage:... those who suffer from a grave lack [*defectu*] of judgment..."); (2) canon 1159, §1 ("A marriage invalid because of a defect [*defectum*] of consent..."); (3) canon 1159, §2 ("If the defect [*defectus*] of the consent cannot be proven..."); (4) canon 1159, §3 ("If the defect [*defectus*] of consent can be proven..."); (5) canon 1480, §2 ("But in the case of the absence [*defectus*] or negligence of the representative..."); (6) canon 1680 ("In cases concerning impotence or defect [*defectu*] of consent because of mental illness..."); (7) canon 1686 ("if the existence of a diriment impediment or a defect [*defectu*] of legitimate form should be certainly evident..."); and (8) 1687, §1 ("If the defender of the bond prudently judges that ... the lack [*defectum*] of dispensation is not certain..."). In two of these instances *defectus* must mean *lack* or *absence*: canon 1480, §2 deals with a party's *lack* of adequate representation; and canon 1687, §1 deals with the *lack* of a dispensation. But canon 1686 cannot be dealing with the situation in which there was a total *lack* of canonical form: *Dignitas connubii*, Article 5, §3 made clear what many canonists already knew: the standard prenuptial investigation rather than a tribunal intervention was sufficient to establish the freedom to marry of someone who had participated in a *lack* of form marriage. Canon 1095, 2° appears to address the situation of a person whose discretion of judgment was not proportionate to the seriousness of marriage rather than a person who had no discretion of judgment whatsoever. In canonical language, therefore, sometimes *defectus* can mean *lack* and sometimes *insufficiency* or *deficiency*.

37  Roch Pagé wonders whether "'defect of faith'... Is ... the same as a lack of faith? Or is it rather an imperfect faith?... Are there degrees in faith? If so, what degree will support or cause a ground of nullity?" in "Questions Regarding the Motu Proprio *Mitis Iudex Dominus Iesus*," *The Jurist* 75 (2015) 610.

*a supernatural virtue infused by him.*" How would a human being—other than Jesus, of course—know whether God had given the gift of faith to anyone else? The *Catechism* continues, "… it is no less true that believing is an authentically human act" (n. 154). Does *defectus fidei* refer to the human response to God's offer of grace? Inasmuch as such a response might be evident in a person's behavior, it might not be impossible for a judge to discover, at the end of a painstaking investigation, that a given individual had not made it;[38] but the *motu proprio* assumes that the Judicial Vicar (*MI*, canon 1685) will make this determination at the beginning of the process on the basis of the formal petition and any attached documents (*MI*, canon 1684). How easily could he do so, especially if *defectus fidei* means *an insufficiency of faith*? What standard would he use in making such a judgment?[39]

Furthermore, the Legislator did not write that any kind of *defectus fidei* was a circumstance suggesting that a marriage is invalid; he wrote that "*is … defectus qui gignere potest simulationem consensus vel errorem voluntatem determinantem.*" Only that sort of *defectus fidei* which *can* spawn an invalidating deficiency in consent constitutes a circumstance that allows the use of the briefer process. Even so, the relative clause itself gives rise to questions. Can a defect of faith which *could have caused* a person to simulate but did not do so nonetheless be a circumstance suggesting the invalidity of a marriage? The language of canon 1098 might provide a parallel here: if someone is inveigled into marriage by a fraud concerning some quality of the other spouse "*quae suapte natura consortium vitae coniugalis graviter perturbare potest,*" the victim marries invalidly. The phrasing of the canon does not require that the presence or absence of the quality in question actually did disrupt the common life. It requires only that the quality be of such a nature that its presence or absence

---

[38] Cf. Daneels, *Reform*, p. 131, n. 26: "…in such cases the nullity of marriage is generally not at all evident from the outset…."

[39] The author is reminded here of criticisms Monsignor Ralph Brown voiced to the use of "inadequate consent" as a ground of nullity: "…the problem that (for me) has arisen about the so-called grounds of lack of commitment or inadequate consent was that to prove such a ground it is necessary in some way to try to measure the amount of thrust given to a person's consent; i.e., was it strong enough…. The amount of thrust has to be measured, and manifestly to enable any set of Judges to do this it is necessary to have some sort of yardstick or *minimum quid*; without it, one is floundering in mere guesswork." Ralph Brown, "Inadequate Consent or Lack of Commitment: Authentic Grounds for Nullity," *Studia canonica* 9 (1975) 263-264. Brown was speaking about the difficulty of making a judgment at the end of the process. *A fortiori*, it would be difficult for a Judicial Vicar to measure the "thrust" or "strength" or "adequacy" of an individual's faith *before undertaking an investigation*. Even more, he would be making this measurement in the belief that the question does "not demand a more accurate inquiry or investigation" (*MI*, canon 1683, 2°).

*could* seriously perturb conjugal life.[40] Is this passage in Article 14, §1 saying something similar—does it mean that a Judicial Vicar could assign a case to the briefer process if there were sufficient evidence (of whatever sort) of a *defectus fidei* irrespective of whether that lack or deficiency actually caused simulation or determining error? The wording of the Article allows such a reading. The drafters of the *motu proprio* could have precluded such a reading very easily: instead of using a relative clause, they could have used a participial construction (*defectus fidei simulationem consensus vel errorem voluntatem determinantem gignens—a defect of faith engendering simulation...*) or they could have shifted focus from the absence/insufficiency of faith to the consensual deficiencies caused thereby (*simulatio consensus vel error voluntatem determinantem ex fidei defectu generatus—simulation or error engendered by a defect of faith*).[41]

Professor Jenkins highlights a potentially more serious difficulty with this circumstance: "Since the use of the briefer process requires the attachment of documents or records to the petition that manifest nullity of consent, we can ask what type of documents would suffice to establish this.... We might think of an official document that records a formal defection from the faith."[42] On the other hand, there are reasons for defecting formally from the faith that might reveal nothing about one's marital intentions (for example, gaining exemption from taxation); and a person could formally leave the Catholic Church without thereby abandoning all of the values cherished by Catholics, just as one might join an atheistic or anti-Christian society while still intending to be faithful to one's spouse or to remain married for life. It is fairly easy to prove that one has been baptized. Proving that one has no faith or only a little bit of faith is not.

The phrasing of the second item on the list, "*brevitas convictus coniugalis*," is unequivocal. The inclusion of this circumstance is an outcropping of a major change in jurisprudence during living memory. In January of 1944 a Rotal *turnus coram* Wynen issued a negative decision in a case in which the Petitioner had made clear before the wedding his intention of not establishing a common life with the Respondent.[43] The Respondent suffered from tuberculosis, and the Petitioner considered her symptoms repulsive. The Petitioner's behavior after

---

40 One might imagine a marriage that has collapsed because the husband drinks. During the divorce proceedings, the wife discovered that her estranged spouse had spent time in the penitentiary for drug dealing. If she could establish in a church court that he had deliberately concealed his past in order to inveigle her into marrying him, could not the judge rule the marriage invalid on grounds of *dolus* despite the fact that his deceit did not precipitate the divorce?

41 The *Subsidium*, after accurately citing Article 14 ("*A lack of faith that can generate a simulation of consent or an error determining the will*"), explains it as if the text were differently worded: "The text refers to a lack of faith that leads to a *false understanding* of marriage or to an induced simulation" (*Subsidium*, p. 24). The text of the *motu proprio* reads "that CAN generate," NOT "that GENERATES."

42 Jenkins, "Applying," pp. 249-250.

43 *Coram* Wynen, 22 January 1944, *RRT Decisiones* 36 (1944) 55-78.

the marriage was consistent with the intentions he had revealed beforehand. The Rota nevertheless concluded that the absence of conjugal life, even if intended at the time of the marriage, does not prove the invalidity of a marriage.

By contrast, on 16 March 2007 a *turnus coram* Verginelli found a marriage to be invalid "only on the ground of exclusion of the communion of life... on the part of the Respondent."[44] The evidence convinced the Rota that the Respondent had entered the marriage with no intention of establishing a common life: "Even before the canonical ceremony" the Prelate Fathers "detected in the man an intention not to establish a life with the petitioner that is properly conjugal."[45] If the deliberate exclusion of the common life were not invalidating (the standard view seventy years ago), then the mere brevity of the common life would not strongly suggest that the marriage is invalid. On the other hand, if the deliberate exclusion of the common life is a form of simulation, then the brevity of the common life might well provoke suspicions about the validity of the marriage.

How long a bride and groom lived together is a question of fact that should be susceptible of proof. In some cases, there might even be documentary evidence.[46] For example, if one of the spouses were in the military, his or her service record might show that he or she reported for duty within days of the wedding and that he or she was posted abroad until the other party filed for dissolution of the marriage. Or the divorce decree might contain a civil court's finding about the date on which the couple definitively separated. Most of the time, however, I suspect that only testimony will establish the length of the common life. Canon 1678, §1 now allows a judge to accept as "full proof" "a judicial confession and the declarations of the parties." This might allow the Judicial Vicar to consider the parties' statements in their formal petition as sufficient evidence of how briefly they cohabited.[47]

A qualification is in order here: Rotal Auditors do not invariably regard short marital cohabitation as indicative of marital invalidity. They have issued

---

44 *Coram* Verginelli, 16 March 2007, *Studia canonica* 43 (2009) 561.
45 Ibid., p. 560.
46 Cf. Jenkins, "Applying," p. 251: "It is easy enough to present a document that demonstrates a short time of cohabitation, such as some type of official change of residence form."
47 "The new canon 1678, §1 completely reverses the traditional standard for assessing the probative weight of the depositions of the parties. No longer are the parties to the marriage case considered suspect; no longer is it considered unusual that the depositions of the parties might be sufficient of providing full proof. Instead [...] of stipulating that the depositions are capable of providing full proof only when they are fully corroborated by other indices and circumstances, the law now asserts simply that these depositions are capable of providing full proof 'unless other elements are present which weaken them.'" John Beal, "*Mitis Iudex* Canons 1671-1682, 1688-1691: A Commentary," *The Jurist* 75 (2015) 499.

negative decisions in cases in which the common life lasted "Only forty days,"[48] "forty or forty-eight days,"[49] and three months.[50]  At most, the shortness of a marriage may bring to light some deficiency that vitiated consent. A person's immediate departure from the home upon discovery that the spouse has or lacks some important quality, for example, might point to the presence of *dolus* or error of a quality principally and directly intended or even a present condition. Again, speedy departure from the home as soon as the formalities of marriage were complete might indicate that the person underwent the ceremony of marriage without intending to establish a community of life and love with the other. The juridic import (if any) of the speedy cessation of the common life would become clear only within the context of the parties' whole relationship. The Judicial Vicar might readily grasp that context from the materials accompanying the formal petition, but adequately understanding why a marriage was short-lived might also require the "more accurate inquiry or investigation" which the briefer process does not allow (*MI*, canon 1683, 2°).[51]

I have already discussed the third item on the list, *abortus procuratus ad vitandam procreationem*. The phrasing of this term is laudably precise: not every abortion is the sort of circumstance that might allow the use of the briefer procedure, but only an abortion procured for the specific purpose of preventing procreation in the marriage.[52] Documentary evidence of the occurrence of the abortion would certainly exist, whether or not a church court might have access to it; but in determining the reason for the abortion, the Judicial Vicar might have to rely on the statements of the parties or knowledgeable witnesses.[53]

It is unlikely that there would be documentary evidence establishing the occurrence of the fourth item on the list, "an obstinate persistence in an

---

48   Cf. *Coram* Caberletti, 12 June 2003, *RRT Decisiones* 95 (2003) 357.
49   Cf. *Coram*. Erlebach, 27 January 2005, *RRT Decisiones* 97 (2005) 44.
50   *Coram*. Huber, 12 February 2004, *RRT Decisiones* 96 (2004) 115.
51   Cf. Jenkins, "Applying," pp. 250-251: "…the question of brevity serves as an indication of possible nullity and [is] not in itself… a ground of nullity or a presupposition in its favor. In fact, jurisprudence holds that the short length of cohabitation is not itself a manifest indication of nullity…. It is easy enough to present a document that demonstrates a short time of cohabitation…. What is not so easy is finding documents that support the cause behind it."
52   Leszek Adamowicz disapproves of the formulation: "Every abortion (including the complicity in this crime) itself raises the suspicion of some defect of personality (ex. The question of the ability to parent), so the narrowing made in art. 14 of 'The way of proceeding' is even inappropriate." Adamowicz, "Circumstances," p. 67. But not every "defect of personality" (assuming, *arguendo*, that the abortion *proves* rather than merely *suggests* such a defect) makes the invalidity of the marriage "manifest."
53   So Jenkins, "Applying," p. 253: "Proof that [the abortion] was concomitant with the intention not to exchange the right to acts per se apt for the procreation of children… cannot be established by medical records alone. Testimony from qualified witnesses will be necessary, such as medical experts or counselors."

extraconjugal relationship."[54] Demonstrating the existence of such a relationship would almost certainly require testimony from knowledgeable witnesses, preferably the parties to the illicit relationship. The mere existence of the liaison would not nullify a marriage, but its persistence might signal exclusion of the *bonum fidei*.[55] By obstinately maintaining such a relationship during the engagement and immediately after the marriage, the errant fiancé/spouse would be manifesting a refusal to accept the obligation to be faithful to his/her spouse. If the unfaithful fiancé/spouse were the petitioner, then the petition itself would contain both an admission of the long-term affair and a confession of simulation. If he or she were not the petitioner, however, the case could be processed briefly only if his/her consent to the petition implied such a confession.

Sterility and a serious contagious illness are conditions whose existence should be verifiable by medical records. The existence of a child as well as his/her parentage can be verified by a birth certificate or, if necessary, by genetic testing. Most jurisdictions preserve records of incarcerations, and some of those records are public. But sterility or the illness or the child or the imprisonment would not be invalidating in itself. The legislator speaks of their "deceitful concealment." Hence, in order to interpret this passage of Article 14 one must bear in mind the provisions of canon 1098: "Whoever enters marriage deceived by *dolus* perpetrated to obtain consent concerning some quality of the other party which of its very nature can seriously disturb the common life contracts invalidly." The sterility, the serious illness, the children, or the imprisonment would constitute a "quality of the other party which of its very nature can seriously disturb the common life"; but the canon requires more. At the time of the marriage the victim must have been in error about this quality. Someone must have deliberately induced the party into error about it or deliberately kept the party in ignorance about it. And the person who acted deliberately must have acted precisely *ad obtinendum consensum*—in order to inveigle the erring party

---

54 The *Subsidium*, p. 25, does mention "private investigative reports, letters, [and] record of telephonic or electronic communications." Professor Jenkins wonders "how private letters or emails, which must be authenticated, do not require further inquiry." Jenkins, "Applying," p. 254. This author wonders whether the materials to which the *Subsidium* refers could prove the nature of the romantic relationship.

55 "As regards exclusion of conjugal fidelity, it is hardly sufficient to prove that sexual relations with a lover existed before and after marriage, although such proof would be a great *indicium*...." *Coram* Alwan, 21 October 2003, *Rotal Jurisprudence Selected Translations*, Victoria Vondenberger, RSM, ed. (Washington, DC: The Canon Law Society of America, 2011), p. 57. In this very strange case the Rota concluded "that the love of the petitioner towards her lover is proven to have begun before the marriage and to have continued after it;" and "that the petitioner maintained a full and firm intention of continuing the amorous relationship with him"; and "that promptly after the marriage, the petitioner and her lover resumed their relationship" (p. 61). "Continuous and proven love of this kind, along with an amorous relationship both before and after the marriage, proves beyond any ambiguity whatever the exclusion of the good of fidelity on the part of the woman."

into entering the marriage. Canon 1098 alerts the Judicial Vicar that, in order to determine that *celatio dolosa* has occurred, he must know both the mental state of the deceived party and the intention of the deceiver at the time of the marriage.[56]

The phrasing of the next item on the list needed better editing.[57] There is nothing in the Latin corresponding to the English translation "consisting of": *causa contrahendi* and *haud praevisa praegnantia* are both nominative and are therefore parallel. A more literal translation would be, "a cause of contracting altogether extraneous to the conjugal life OR the unforeseen pregnancy of the woman." Perhaps switching the position of the two circumstances will make my point clearer: "the unforeseen pregnancy of the woman or a cause of marrying extraneous to conjugal life." The two circumstances do not function identically in vitiating consent. Current Rotal jurisprudence regards a "cause of marriage completely extraneous to married life" as a species of simulation. By contract, a premarital pregnancy, though only in certain circumstances, can give rise to various defects of consent.

In a decision dating from December of 2004 Defilippi provided a list of various ways to simulate totally. He included the situation of the person "who celebrates the nuptial rite solely and exclusively as a means of pursuing an end which is not marriage itself."[58] Erlebach agreed that "the person who through the external celebration of the nuptial rite is exclusively [determined] on achieving an end altogether different from marriage, which one and only stipulation he/she proposes to himself/herself, therefore having excluded all of the effects of marriage..."[59] is somehow simulating. Pena likewise found that implicit simulation occurs "In... cases [in which] matrimony as such does not form the object of the will of the spouse, whose strongest and principal intent is the pursuit of some end or 'proper' good (*finis operantis*), at no time compatible with the 'juridic cause' (or *finis operis*) of the nuptial covenant itself." It likewise "can also follow even from an exclusive contemplation of some peculiar and extrinsic end, even in itself legitimate and not incompatible with the essence of the covenant; for in this case the will of the subject is absorbed by a totally subjective end... so that the direct intention towards matrimony as such pales, so to speak, and collapses, interiorly exhausted."[60] Serrano agreed that entering marriage solely to accomplish an end "radically incompatible with conjugal love" is a

---

56 Cf. Jenkins, "Applying," p. 256: "Incarceration, grave illness, the existence of children... are all open to proof by documents needing no further investigation. What is not so readily available, especially by documents, is proof that the intent of the deceiver was to gain consent and the impact the deceit had on conjugal life...."
57 Ibid., p. 256: "The phrasing used in the text is a bit awkward...."
58 *Coram* Defilippi, *RRT Decisiones* 95 (2003) 795; he cites a decision c. Stankiewicz of 29 January 1981.
59 *Coram* Erlebach, 5 March 2004, *RRT Decisiones* 96 (2004) 192-193.
60 *Coram* Pena, 6 May 2005, *RRT Decisiones* 97 (2005) 226.

form of simulation, but he preferred to categorize it as exclusion of the *bonum coniugum*.[61] In any event, these citations should be sufficient to document the emerging Rotal consensus that marrying for a reason totally extrinsic to marriage is a form of simulation.

The first paragraph of Article 14 lists this anti-marital cause for contracting, not as something a judge might discover at the end of the annulment investigation, but as a circumstance manifest to the Judicial Vicar from the formal petition.[62] This could be the case only if the *libellus* were accompanied by a credible confession from the alleged simulator, by solid evidence of his/her proportionate reasons for simulating, and by equally solid evidence of circumstances supporting his/her claim. If all of this material were available to the Judicial Vicar at the time of the formal petition, the invalidity of the marriage would indeed be manifest! What form this material might take is less certain.

Unlike "a cause of marriage totally extrinsic to conjugal life," an unexpected premarital pregnancy has less clear juridic implications. Unless one agrees with Justice Ginsberg that pregnancy is itself an impediment to ordinary human activity, one must concede that a premarital pregnancy, whether expected or not, does not invariably prevent a couple from eliciting valid consent. In the presence of other factors, however, the consent of one of the parties might well suffer an invalidating deficiency. For example, if the woman's family reacted to the news of her pregnancy by forcing her or her partner to enter the marriage, the marriage might be invalid by reason of reverential fear. If pregnant woman or her partner chose to enter the marriage solely to legitimate the child, or if the groom underwent the ceremony of marriage solely to buttress his legal rights as the child's father, the marriage might be invalid by reason of simulation. If the situation became so stressful that one of the parties simply could not deliberate about assuming the essential obligations of marriage, the marriage might be invalid by reason of a grave lack of discretion of judgment—or, more precisely, an invalidating lack of internal freedom.[63] There is, in short, no intrinsic connection between an unexpected premarital pregnancy and a specific ground of nullity; nor is it evident that *every* marriage occasioned by an unexpected premarital pregnancy is invalid. To qualify for the use of the briefer process, a petition would need to include more than proof that the bride was pregnant at the time of the ceremony. Exactly what kind of documentation would need to accompany the petition would depend on the nature of the allegation against the validity of

---

61  *Coram* Serrano, 23 January 2004, in *Philippine Canonical Forum* X (2008) 330-331.

62  Jenkins ("Applying," p. 257) observes, "Given the difficulty that arises with proof of total simulation, it is not easy to envision what types of documents needing no further investigation or inquiry will be available here to manifest the nullity of consent in the introductory petition...."

63  "...the discovery of an unexpected pregnancy can often be better judged under the ground of force and fear or even the psychological ground of lack of due discretion." Ibid., p. 256.

the marriage. In some of these situations I find it hard to imagine what kind of documentation could make the nullity of the marriage manifest before the Court even begins to investigate.

One of the least controversial circumstances on the list is *violentia physica ad extorquendum consensum illata*. *Torquere* means *to twist*; and *extorquere* means *to wrench* or *to dislocate*. The reader gets the picture of someone racking the expression of consent out of the poor victim, and the expression *violentia physica* does not weaken that impression. If fear of parental indignation, when causative of marital consent, can vitiate that consent, how much more will the application of physical violence render the subject incapable of marrying validly![64]

Even so, it is not mere pettifoggery to pose a jurisprudential question: in any given case involving physical violence, what is the proper *caput nullitatis*? In the presence of violence a genuinely *human* act can fade into an act of a human being. In such a situation there would be no marital consent at all. Or escaping the pain might be the sole object of the victim's act of consent. In such a situation the proper ground might be simulation. One hopes that quibbling over the proper category would not prevent a bishop or a judge from quickly recognizing the invalidity of the marriage, but one also hopes that the bishop or the judge would be concerned about explaining his conclusion coherently and accurately.

In the light of canon 1103 of the 1983 Code of Canon Law, one might find the participial phrase *ad extorquendum consensum illata* surprising. Unlike canon 1087, §1 of the Pio-Benedictine Code, canon 1103 of the 1983 Code contains the phrase *etiam haud consulto incussum*. By means of this phrase the Legislator alerts the judge that the intention of the person making the threats or inflicting the force is juridically irrelevant. What matters is the intention of the victim: if the victim enters marriage to free himself/herself from the threats or the violence, the victim contracts invalidly irrespective of the intention of the threatener. The language of paragraph one of Article 14, by contrast, directs the Judicial Vicar's attention to the motivation of the person acting violently. One might have expected the *motu proprio* to say something like, "physical violence *causing a person to enter the marriage*" or "physical violence *from which a person takes refuge in marriage*." Monier explained in a 2006 decision, "A relationship of causality **is** ... required between the coercion and [the act of] matrimonial consent.... It is **not** required any more that the fear be inflicted to extort consent..., but it is sufficient that the choice of the marriage be the effect of the coercion."[65] I do not argue that the phrasing of this passage from Article 14 prevents the Judicial Vicar from assigning a case to the briefer process unless the agent of the violence deliberately tortured the victim into the marriage. If

---

64  "In cases in which true and specific acts of violence occur to the harm of the reluctant party, the gravest indication of the invalidity of consent is present." *Subsidium*, p. 26.
65  *Coram* Monier, 14 July 2006, *RRT Decisiones* 98 (2006) 267. For a similar observation see *coram* Boccafola, 21 February 1991, in *Rotal Jurisprudence*, pp. 22-23.

nothing else the *et cetera* might justify his doing so. Here as elsewhere, however, the *motu proprio* might have benefited from more careful polishing.

The final specific item on the list is *defectus usus rationis documentis medicis comprobatus*. Within the *motu proprio* this item refers the reader to Article 14, §2: "all medical records [*documenta medica*] which can evidently render useless the requirement for an *ex officio* expert" should accompany the formal petition (cf. *MI* canon 1684, 3°). The item also echoes canon 1095, 1°: "They are incapable of contracting marriage who lack sufficient use of reason." Such persons are *amentes*—they lack the capacity to posit a genuinely *human* act. On the one hand, the item describes a situation that is painfully obvious: if, together with her *libellus*, Bertha presents to the Court medical records demonstrating that *at the wedding* Titius was incapable of positing a human act, the invalidity of the attempted marriage would indeed be manifest. On the other hand, it describes a situation that is probably very rare. In more than forty years of tribunal ministry I have never encountered a case which the judge decided on grounds of lack of sufficient use of reason.[66]

One cannot overlook the final item in paragraph one of Article 14: "*etc.*" The pope hereby explicitly acknowledges that there are other circumstances of the sort he has listed above. I have the temerity to suggest one, and shall do so by recounting the circumstances of a case recently on my own docket. Adam had two children from a prior marriage. Beth already had four. Children may be cheaper by the dozen, but Beth was unwilling to put that hypothesis to the test. She knew that she was already responsible for the rearing of four children, and she realized that she would become indirectly responsible for two more if she married Adam. Six were more than enough for her. She made it clear during the courtship that there would be no more children if they married. To ensure that there would be no more children, she underwent a tubal ligation a few weeks

---

[66] The *Subsidium* observes, "Consensual incapacity due to psychic reasons generally requires an in-depth scientific investigation…. Nevertheless, there can be instances of the gravest pathologies, duly documented… which, according to well-established jurisprudence, permit handing down a judgment without any shadow of positive doubt concerning the nullity of expressed consent." *Subsidium*, p. 26. Jenkins ("Applying," p. 245) offers "A non-comprehensive list": "… chronic, manifest schizophrenia, bipolar disorder, manifest anti-social personality disorder, central nervous system conditions, and other serious psychiatric or medical conditions that require extensive in patient treatment prior to or at the time of consent." He would exclude from the list: "affective immaturity, depression that does not require clinical treatment, some instances of drug and alcohol addiction, obsessive-compulsive disorders, neuroses, and certainly not non-specific disorders." Is this author being contrarian in observing that, although *diagnoses* of the disorders on this list might be readily available, the specific effect of each disorder on the specific individual at the time of the marriage might not be clear "without any shadow of positive doubt"? For example, the fact that Titius has suffered from childhood from bipolar disorder does not necessarily mean that, at the very moment of the marriage, he was lacking the use of reason.

before the scheduled wedding. A tubal ligation is not a medical procedure than aims directly at treating a disease and indirectly causes sterilization. A tubal ligation aims directly at rendering a woman incapable of conceiving a child. Would not Beth's seeking a tubal ligation, coupled with her premarital confession of unwillingness to have more children, be a circumstance that might allow a Judicial Vicar to route the case through the briefer process?

Academics imagining cases in their studies and tribunal ministers encountering strange situations in court will probably propose more circumstances as we become more adept at implementing *Mitis Iudex*. The risk here is that a desire to seem pastorally sensitive might tempt tribunal ministers into rationalizing our cutting procedural corners. As I have argued earlier, however, the *motu proprio* itself provides an antidote. It explicitly states that the kind of circumstance that justifies the use of the briefer process must render the invalidity of a marriage manifest, must be demonstrable by evidence accompanying the formal petition or easily available to the auditor, must have a meaning that is clear without further investigation, and must be understood against the background of information provided by both parties.

# SEMINAR

## CURRENT PRIESTLY FORMATION: *STATUS QUÆSTIONIS*
### Reverend Robert J. Kaslyn, SJ

**Introduction**

The topic suggested for this presentation, "Priestly Formation: *Status Quæstionis*" in itself raises significant issues, concerns, and questions, from a wide variety of perspectives, including but not limited to recent papal and curial documents, canon law, particular law, theology and the intentionality of priestly formation. These varying perspectives are of equal importance; to provide a logical approach to this presentation, the following paragraph will summarize my approach.

This presentation will offer one perspective on priestly formation in light of contemporary canon law and with the intent to clarify current concerns. *Inter alii*, the presentation will address the teleology of such formation as well as the internal and external forum and confidentiality and with reference to psychological testing; policies on such testing; the authentic interpretation on canon 1041, nn. 4-5 of the *CIC*; the scrutinies required prior to ordination and the concept of personal responsibility of those who approve candidates and who request and receive Sacred Orders.[1]

In 2013, the Congregation for the Clergy released *Directory for the Ministry and the Life of Priests*;[2] the Congregation deemed this update necessary so to include a more contemporary presentation of the "recent rich *Magisterium*."[3] With similar motivation, the same Congregation issued *The Gift of the Priestly Vocation. Ratio Fundamentalis Institutionis Sacerdotalis* in December 2016.[4] The

---

1   This analysis is limited to candidates for the secular presbyterate; the formation of members of institutes of consecrated life and societies of apostolic life leading to the reception of Orders is complicated, for example, by the provisions of particular law and thus would constitute its own study. Also distinct is the formation of candidates for the permanent diaconate, whether for the diocese or for an institute or society.

For the text of the *Codex Iuris Canonici*, see *Code of Canon Law, Latin-English Edition: New English Translation* (Washington, DC: CLSA, 2001).

2   Congregation for the Clergy, *Directory for the Ministry and the Life of Priests* (Città del Vaticano: Libreria editrice Vaticana, 2013).

3   CC, *Directory*, Introduction.

4   Congregation for the Clergy, *The Gift of the Priestly Vocation. Ratio Fundamentalis Institutionis Sacerdotalis* (Vatican City: *L'Osservatore Romano*, December 8, 2016).

Introduction to this revised text first refers to the amended *Ratio Fundamentalis Institutionis Sacerdotalis* promulgated on January 6, 1970 and then states:

> Since then there have been numerous contributions on the theme of the formation of future priests, both on the part of the Universal Church and on the part of the Conferences of Bishops and individual particular Churches. It is necessary above all to recall the Magisterium of the Pontiffs who have guided the Church in this time: Saint John Paul II, to whom we owe the ground-breaking Post-Synodal Apostolic Exhortation *Pastores Dabo Vobis* (25 March 1992); Benedict XVI, author of the Apostolic Letter 'motu proprio' *Ministrorum Institutio* (16 January 2013); and Francis, whose encouragement and suggestions gave rise to the present document.[5]

Both of these documents place strong emphasis on the spiritual formation of those destined to request the sacrament of Orders and the on-going development of their spiritual lives. The *Ratio Fundamentalis* states, "The formation of priests means following a singular 'journey of discipleship', which begins at Baptism, is perfected through the other sacraments of Christian initiation, comes to be appreciated as the center of one's life at the beginning of Seminary formation, and continues through the whole of life."[6] Formation and the various integral elements of formation cannot be interpreted and applied without understanding the very purpose (its teleology) of formation.

## A. The Teleology of Formation

*Ratio Fundamentalis* states unequivocally

> The priestly vocation begins with the gift of divine grace, which is then sealed in sacramental ordination. This gift is expressed over time through the mediation of the Church, which calls and sends in the name of God. At the same time, the personal response develops through a process, which begins with an awareness of the gift received, and matures

---

5   *Ratio Fundamentalis*, Introduction, 1. Pope Benedict XVI through his apostolic letter issued motu proprio *Ministrorum Institutio* January 16, 2013, transferred responsibility for seminaries from the Congregation for Catholic Education to the Congregation for the Clergy.

The essential text on formation is Saint John Paul II, post-synodal exhortation *Pastores Dabo Vobis*, to the Bishops, Clergy and Faithful on the Formation of Priests in the Circumstances of the Present Day, March 25, 1992, in *Origins* 21.45 (April 16, 1992).

6   *Ratio Fundamentalis*, Introduction, 3. See also, CC *Directory*, Introduction: "In light of today's cultural climate it is opportune to recall that the identity of the priest as a man of God is not outmoded and never will be [...]."

gradually with the help of priestly spirituality until it becomes a stable way of life, with its own obligations and rights, and a specific mission accepted by the one ordained.[7]

Priestly formation is necessarily directed to the reception of the sacrament of Orders and to its exercise; on-going formation aims at deepening the priest's relationship with Jesus Christ.[8] Such formation finds its meaning and essence in that sacrament and in particular in the presbyteral order. According to *Lumen gentium* 28, presbyters

> ... by virtue of the sacrament of order [...] are consecrated in the image of Christ, the high and eternal priest (see Heb 5, 1-10; 7, 24; 9, 11-28), as true priests of the new testament, to preach the gospel and nourish the faithful and celebrate divine worship. In their own degree of ministry they share in the office of Christ the one mediator (see 1 Tm 2, 5) and proclaim the divine word to all people.[9]

The conciliar decree *Presbyterorum Ordinis* explains: "As it is joined to the episcopal order, the priesthood shares in the authority with which Christ himself constitutes, sanctifies and rules his body."[10] The same decree notes the dichotomy present in those ordained presbyters: "Their very ministry makes a special claim that they should not conform to this world; but at the same time it demands that they should live in this world among its people."[11] From another perspective, the *Ratio Fundamentalis* expresses the need for a similar balance:

---

7   *Ratio Fundamentalis*, 34. The text also warns against clericalism [33] and the temptation to exercise priestly service as some type of 'lordship' [34].
8   CC, *Directory*, Introduction.
9   Vatican II, dogmatic constitution *Lumen gentium*, November 21, 1964: *AAS* 57 (1965) 34; English translation in *Decrees of the Ecumenical Councils*, ed. Norman P. Tanner, 2 vols. (London and Washington: Sheed & Ward and Georgetown University Press, 1990) 2: 872. See also the introduction to the decree On the Ministry and Life of Priests, *Optatam totius*, October 28, 1965: *AAS* 58 (1966) 713: *"Optatam totius Ecclesiae renovationem probe noscens Sancta Synodus a sacerdotum ministerio, Christi spiritu animato, magna ex parte pendere, gravissimum institutionis sacerdotalis momentum proclamat, eiusque primaria quaedam principia declarat, quibus confirmentur leges iam saeculorum usu probatae in easque nova inducantur, quae huius Sancti Concilii Constitutionibus et Decretis necnon mutatis temporum rationibus respondeant. Quae sacerdotalis conformatio ob ipsam catholici sacerdotii unitatem, omnibus sacerdotibus utriusque cleri et cuiusvis ritus necessaria est."*
10   Vatican II, decree *Presbyterorum ordinis*, December 7, 1965: *AAS* 58 (1966) 992; Tanner, 2: 1044.
11   *PO* 3 *AAS* 58 (1966) 994; Tanner, 2: 1045.

During the process of formation for the ministerial priesthood, the seminarian is a "mystery to himself", in which two aspects of his humanity, that need to be integrated, are intertwined and exist side by side. On the one hand he is characterised by talents and gifts that have been moulded by grace; on the other, he is marked by his limits and fraility. [12]

Grace works with nature, not independently of nature; due cognizance must be given both to grace and to the individual person with his strengths and weaknesses. Formation is the on-going process, aided by grace, by which strengths are fostered. The transition from formation to on-going formation begins with ordination itself and the decision by the bishop to ordain this individual to the [transitional] diaconate and then to the presbyterate. This decision requires moral certainty on the part of the bishop.

## B. Moral Certainty and The Decision to Ordain

Concomitant with spiritual formation and formation in spirituality directed to the sacrament of Orders is the decision of the diocesan bishop to accept a candidate for Orders and to ordain him for the transitional diaconate and then to the presbyterate.[13] Based on the individual's formation, the bishop comes to a decision with moral certainty that this particular man should be ordained for presbyteral service in his diocese.

Canon 973, §3 of the 1917 Codex stated straightforwardly: "*Episcopus sacros ordines nemini conferat quin ex positivis argumentis moraliter certus sit de eius canonica idoneitate; secus non solum gravissime peccat, sed etiam periculo sese committit alienis communicandi peccatis.*"[14] From this perspective and in the context of priestly formation for the celibate life, Blessed Paul VI referred to the importance of the bishop's decision:

12  *Ratio Fundamentalis*, 28.
13  See *CIC* canon 1030: "Only for a canonical cause, even if occult, can the proper bishop or competent major superior forbid admission to the presbyterate to deacons subject to him who are destined to the presbyterate, without prejudice to recourse according to the norm of law." Therefore, the decision to ordain to the transitional diaconate is a decision also to intend to ordain to the presbyter, *dummodo* no canonical cause arises in the interim which would justify withholding presbyteral ordination.
14  *Codex Iuris Canonici Pii X Pontificis Maximi iussu digestus Benedicti Papae XV auctoritate promulgatus* (Rome: Typis Polyglottis Vaticanis, 1917). Pius XI quoted this canon in his encyclical *Ad Catholici Sacerdotii*, December 20, 1935 and states, "'To impose hands lightly,' Our Predecessor St. Leo the Great expounds, 'is to confer the sacerdotal dignity on persons not sufficiently approved: before maturity in age, before merit of obedience, before a time of testing, before trail of knowledge; and to be a partaker of other men's sins is for the ordainer to become as unworthy as the unworthy man whom he ordains;' for as St. John Chrysostom says, 'You who have conferred the dignity upon him must take the responsibility of both his past and his future sins'."

> Those who are discovered to be unfit for physical, psychological or moral reasons should be quickly removed from the path to the priesthood. Let educators appreciate that this is one of their very grave duties. They must neither indulge in false hopes and dangerous illusions nor permit the candidate to nourish these hopes in any way, with resultant damage to himself or to the Church. [...] Nor should anyone pretend that grace supplies for the defects of nature in such a man [*neque exspectandum est, hac in re divinam gratiam ea, quae naturae desirat, subiecturam esse*].[15]

*Ratio fundamentalis* refers to canon 1052 of the *ius vigens* and in that context states that the diocesan bishop "must be sure [...] that, after the investigation has been conducted according to the norm of law, positive arguments have proven the suitability of the candidate (*idoneitatem candidati positivis argumentis esse probatam*) and not simply the absence of problematic situations."[16]

Many of us are familiar with the necessity of moral certainty in reaching a decision concerning whether the evidence in a particular case is sufficient to overturn the presumption of law and declare a certain marriage invalid.[17] That same objective certainty as based upon objective evidence is necessary for a bishop to approve a candidate for the reception of sacred orders.

The bishop, as the one who administers the sacrament or who issues dimissorial letters, expresses his judgment based on verifiable factors and assessments that

---

15 Blessed Pope Paul VI, encyclical *Sacerdotalis Caelibatus*, June 24 1967: *AAS* 59 (1967) 683; English translation from William Woestman, *The Sacraments of Orders and the Clerical State* (Ottawa: Saint Paul University, 1999) "Appendix II. Documents Concerning Clerical Celibacy. Paul VI, Encyclical Letter, *Sacerdotalis caelibatus*, June 24, 1967," 261.

16 *Ratio Fundamentalis*, 206; the source of the quotation is the circular letter from the Congregation for Divine Worship and the Discipline of the Sacraments, *Entre la Mas Delicadas*, November 10, 1997, *Notitiae* 33 (1997) n. 2: l.c. 495. The *Ratio Fundamentalis* continues by noting that the Bishop also possesses "the moral obligation to consider with the greatest attention the final assessment of the community of formators ... Experience has shown that when Ordinaries have not accepted the negative judgment of the community of formators, it has been the cause of great suffering in many cases, both for candidates themselves and for the local Churches." Canon 1052, §§ 1-2 refers simply to the proven or established suitability of the candidate; §3 states: "*Si, his omnibus non obstantibus, ob certas rationes Episcopus dubitat num candidatus sit idoneus ad ordines recipiendos, eundem ne promoveat.*"

17 Pius XII, *Discorso di Sua Santità Pio XII al Tribunale della Sacra Romana Rota*, October 1, 1942. See Vatican web site, Pius XII speeches. Pope Pius situates moral certainty between absolute certainty and quasi-certainty or probability and explicitly states that moral certainty is nonetheless objective, based on objective motives: *Discorso* 3: "*questa certezza va intesa come certezza obbiettiva, cioè basata su motivi oggettivi.*"

he possesses moral certainty concerning the candidate's suitability for ordination. Such a decision requires that the candidate recognize and accept his personal responsibility in the act of requesting ordination (see, e.g., canon 1036), both the sacrament and the clerical state with its obligations and rights. The one who ordains or who issues dimissorial letters has the concomitant responsibility to have moral certainty.[18]

Given that the reception of the sacrament of Orders constitutes the intentionality of priestly formation, I would argue that such moral certainty derives in part through each and every aspect of formation, including but not limited to the topics of this presentation: the practice of confidentiality and recognition of the internal forum and psychological testing of candidates prior to and in the seminary; irregularities and impediments which prevent the reception of orders licitly; the scrutinies for ordination; and acceptance of personal responsibility. Formation in general and in specific should contribute to the bishop's ability to render a decision with moral certainty.

In reference to the last, the Congregation for Divine Worship and the Discipline of the Sacraments issued a circular letter concerning the scrutinies of those destined for Sacred Orders. The letter states in part:

> The fundamental principle in the matter consists in this fact that the competent authority must issue the official call in the name of the Church on the basis of moral certitude that is founded upon positive reasons regarding the suitability of the candidate. [...] admission may not take place if there exists a prudent doubt regarding the candidate's suitability (c. 1052 §3 with c. 1030). By 'prudent doubt' is meant a doubt founded upon facts that are objective and duly verified.[19]

Formation is an on-going process that leads to the reception of the sacrament.

## C. Confidentiality, Internal Forum and External Forum

Essential to the life of the priest is the proper understanding of confidentiality and the essential distinction between the internal and external forums. Seminarians must be taught about the two forums and an integral element in such formation

---

18 See canon 1052 §1 – 2 for reference to the dimissorial letters and §3 which reiterates the importance of the decision of the one who ordains, "If, all these notwithstanding, the bishop doubts for specific reasons whether a candidate is suitable to receive orders, he is not to promote him."
19 For the text, see Woestman, *The Sacrament of Orders*, "Appendix VIII. Congregation for Divine Worship and the Discipline of the Sacraments, Circular Letter on the Scrutinies regarding the Suitability of Candidates for Orders, *Among the most*, November 10, 1997," 372.

is that the seminary itself practice confidentiality and maintain the necessary distinctions. I will approach this complex topic from two perspectives: first, in the abstract, as a constitutive element of formation and the education which the candidate receives in seminary, and second, in the particular, with reference to specific examples of seminary officials' need to observe confidentiality and the strictures of the internal forum.

Violations of the seal of confession do occur and, as required by law, are sent to the Congregation for the Doctrine of the Faith for adjudication. To preclude such incidents, the inviolability of the seal of confession must become second nature to seminarians. A proper understanding of the inviolability of the seal is inter-connected with the concepts of the internal and external forums.

The *Final Report* issued after the visitation of seminaries in the United States stated:

> The internal forum needs to be better safeguarded. There is confusion, in places, as to what the internal forum is (it covers only sacramental confession and spiritual direction; psychological counseling may be confidential, but it is not internal forum). In places, seminarians are being asked to reveal (in formation advising, in psychological counseling, in public confessions of faults, etc.) matters of sin, which belong instead to the internal forum. Other seminaries dilute the confidential nature of the internal forum: the spiritual directors and students are presented with a list of "exceptions" to the confidentiality of spiritual direction (even if it is always emphasized that the seal of confession is inviolable.)[20]

Seminaries must ensure that the students and those who come under the heading of formators understand and practice the distinction between the external and internal forums and the distinction within the latter between the sacramental

---

20 Congregation for Catholic Education, *Final Report, Apostolic Visitation of U.S. Seminaries and Houses of Priestly Formation*, Protocol number 1009/2002, 15 December 2008, *Origins* 38:33 (2009) 526.

internal forum[21] and the non-sacramental internal forum. Such distinctions are indispensable for future confessors.

There are *no* exceptions in revealing matters raised in spiritual direction: canon 240, §2 states "When decisions are made about admitting students to orders or dismissing them from the seminary, the opinion of the spiritual director and confessors can never be sought." The norm is straightforward; under the prohibition falls anything communicated in the internal forum, either sacramental or non-sacramental, and any knowledge obtained through the course of direction or confession. Seminarians do not lose the right to privacy by entering the seminary; as with other rights and obligations of the faithful, such rights are contextualized by ordination but are not lost thereby.[22]

Individuals, especially formators, must maintain carefully the distinction between the internal and external forum and in conjunction with this, the function of the Apostolic Penitentiary (especially in reference to irregularities and the legitimate option of recourse to the Apostolic Penitentiary rather than to a particular Congregation). Seminarians learn by example as well as through academic courses and lectures; in order that in their priestly lives they maintain the seal of confession and confidentiality the process must begin in the seminary.

Canon 240, §2 in reference to spiritual directors and to the confidentiality of their information is related to canon 220: "No one is permitted to harm illegitimately the good reputation which a person possesses nor to injure the right of any person to protect his or her own privacy." Several curial documents reinforce the canon's application to seminarians. Manifestly, an individual presents himself for admission to the seminary with the future intention, if possible, of receiving the sacrament of Orders and thus must cooperate with the

---

21  The seal of confession is inviolable, period. Therefore, I do not accept the argument that the penitent could release the confessor from the obligation of the seal; once voluntary exceptions are allowed, the way is open to involuntary exceptions.

The *Final Report* calls attention to the ambiguous role of formators in seminaries: "Americans involved in diocesan priestly formation have praised the formation – advisor system as the royal road [*sic*] ensuring that seminarians interiorize their formation and are held accountable. Indeed the benefits of the system are obvious. Nevertheless, there are sometimes aspects of the system that invite ambiguity." Ambiguity surrounds the role of the formator in the seminary as distinct to the role of the spiritual director; the *Final Report* recalls that formation advising *is not* spiritual direction; seminarians cannot be obliged to reveal matters of the internal forum to formators; and cases have arisen of formation advisors "*invading*" [*emphasis added*] the internal forum, asking about sin. *Origins*, 525.

22  Canon 215 states that the Christian faithful have the right to associate for certain specific purposes; this right is reiterated in canon 278, §1 (priests have the right and at times are encouraged to associate) and contextualized by paragraph 3 of the same canon: clerics' right to associate does not take precedence over the obligations of their clerical state nor over a specific *munus* entrusted to them by their bishop.

process of admission and assessment in the seminary; nonetheless, "cooperation in the process" does not restrict, much less remove, certain rights the seminarian possesses.

The use of psychological testing fits here within the context of confidentiality and the internal and external forum but also separately, given official statements on this issue. *Ratio Fundamentalis* refers explicitly to the seminarians' right to privacy and in two essential areas.[23] First, and in reference to psychological testing itself, the candidate must give "his previous, informed and free consent in writing"[24] and the candidate "must be guaranteed a free choice from among various experts who possess the requisites indicated."[25]

The second area in which the *Ratio Fundamentalis* refers to the rights of the seminarian is in limiting access to such information:

> Specifically, taking into account what has been said, those authorized to have knowledge of the information provided by the expert are: the Bishop (of the Diocese of the candidate, and the Bishop responsible for the seminary, if different), the Rector (of the Seminary in which formation occurs, and also of the Diocesan seminary, if different), and the Spiritual Director.[26]

Three persons or at most, five, may have access to such evaluations: the Bishop of the candidate; (and, if different, the Bishop responsible for the seminary); the Rector of the formation house (and, if different, the Rector of the Diocesan seminary); and the spiritual director. These three (or five) *alone*, according to *Ratio Fundamentalis*, have access to the expert's information. The last, according to canon 240, §2, is obliged to confidentiality. Formators and formation advisors do not have a right to access to such documentation, nor may they oblige the seminarians to reveal such matter to them. Such an obligation of that which is forbidden by the *Ratio Fundamentalis* is not a good pedagogical technique.

---

23 Essential to the discussion in the *Ratio Fundamentalis* is the following text: Congregation for Catholic Education, *Guidelines for the Use of Psychology in the Admission and Formation of Candidates for the Priesthood,* June 29, 2008. For example, *Ratio Fundamentalis* cites *Guidelines* 12 in reference to the necessity of mutual trust between seminarians and formators (47). Key elements in *Guidelines* have been incorporated into *Ratio Fundamentalis*. For a good overview of the issues involved, see, e.g., Michael Johnson, "Psychology and the Seminarian: Historical Developments and Praxis in the United States," *The Jurist* 76 (2016) 531 – 580, although I do not necessarily agree with all of his conclusions.
24  *Ratio Fundamentalis*, 194.
25  Ibid.
26  Ibid., 195.

## D. Use of Psychological Testing and Confidentiality

The distinctions between the internal and the external forum and the right to confidentiality apply to more than psychological testing (for example, medical testing and results); however, these distinctions must be particularly emphasized in the area of psychological testing.

*Ratio Fundamentalis* positively assesses the assistance which the psychological sciences can provide to candidates and to seminarians and to those with the right to review the resulting documentation. Foundationally and self-evidently

> As a rule, candidates will not be admitted to Seminary who suffer from any pathology, be it manifest or latent (for example, schizophrenia, paranoia, bipolar disorder, paraphiliae, etc.) that could undermine the discretion of judgment of a person and consequently, his ability to assume the obligations of the vocation and the ministry.[27]

In the absence of such pathologies,

> The contribution of the psychological sciences has generally been shown to be a considerable help to formators, as they are responsible for vocational discernment. This scientific contribution allows the character and personality of the candidates to be known better, and it enables formation to be adapted more fittingly to the needs of the individual. *"It is useful for the Rector and other formators to be able to count on the co-operation of experts in the psychological sciences. Such experts [...] cannot be part of the formation team* [sic]. *"*[28]

To reiterate, such experts **cannot** be part of the formation team; further, given that only the bishop or both bishops, rector or both rectors and the spiritual director are the only ones with access to the reports, the spiritual director and seminarian must mutually discuss any specific results that might affect the man's vocation and calling to the sacrament of Orders.

---

27  Ibid., 191, under the heading "Psychological Health". The footnote references by analogy canon 1095 $2^0 - 3^0$. See also canons 1040, $1^0$ in reference to the reception of orders and 1044, §2, $2^0$ in reference to the exercise of orders already received.

28  Ibid., 192. One of the complications of combining a background in psychology / psychiatry and a formation role in seminary or one with such a background holding the office of a superior in an institute or society is the very real temptation to conflate the two roles into one and thereby over-extending the professional role of the individual and simultaneously adapting / altering the formation /superior role into that of an expert.

But as importantly, one legitimate canonical question concerns whether one single, uniform policy by which all candidates must undergo psychological testing as a prerequisite for entering seminary is in accord with the law and with magisterial teaching. Admittedly, the question of required psychological testing is complex and involves numerous issues including but not limited to the areas of theology, canon law, universal and particular law, diocesan policies and psychology and psychiatry themselves.

The current *Ratio Fundamentalis*, 194 states, "In this area the theme of recourse to experts in the psychological sciences in the field of formation for ordained ministry has already in the past been addressed by the Church and by the Holy See." Consider, for example, *Apostolorum Successores* 88 which states

> The complex and difficult situation of young people in today's world requires that the Bishop be particularly attentive in assessing candidates at the time of their admission to seminary. In some difficult cases, when selecting candidates for admission to the seminary, it will be appropriate to ask them to undergo psychological testing, but only *si casus ferat*, because recourse to such means cannot be generalized and must be undertaken with the greatest prudence, so as not to violate the person's right to privacy.[29]

---

29 Congregation for Bishops, *Directory for the Pastoral Ministry of Bishops, Apostolorum Successores*, February 22, 2004 (Città del Vaticano, Libreria Editrice Vaticana, 2004). In reference to "necessary in a case" – *si casus ferat* – the text references (the previous), *Ratio Fundamentalis Institutionis Sacerdotalis*, 39. Paragraph 39 states *"Nello stesso tempo, se sarà il caso, si dovrà far esaminare il loro stato di salute fisica e psichica da medici e da esperti psicologi, tenendo conto delle eventuali ereditarietà familiari"*, that is, if there are questions about the human, moral, spiritual, intellectual candidates of a *particular* candidate in a *specific* case (*nello stesso tempo se sarà il caso*), then the candidate's physical and psychological health should be assessed by professionals. In a discourse *Aux Participants au XIIIe Congrès International de Psychologie Appliquée*, April 10, 1958, *AAS* 50 (1958), Pope Pius XII stated, *"La morale enseigne que les exigences scientifiques ne justifient pas à elles seules n'importe quelle manière d'utiliser les techniques et les méthodes psychologiques, même par des psychologues sérieux et pour des fins utiles. La raison en est que les personnes intéressées aux processus d'investigation psychologique n'ont pas seulement à tenir compte des lois scientifiques, mais aussi de normes transcendantes. En effet, ce qui est d'abord en question, ce n'est pas la psychologie elle-même et ses progrès possibles, mais la personne humaine qui l'utilise, et celle-ci obéit à des normes supérieures, sociales, morales, religieuses."* [275] That is, morality forbids the indiscriminate use of psychological examinations and texts in as much psychology does not *in se* necessarily take into account transcendent norms. Another moral issue was previously raised by the same Pontiff in his allocution *Iis, qui interfuerunt Conventui internationali quinto de Psychotherapia et Psychologia, Romae habito* April 13, 1953 *AAS* 45 (1953): *"Au regard de la moralité, du bien commun en premier lieu, le principe de la discrétion dans l'utilisation de la psychanalyse ne peut être assez souligné. Il s'agit évidemment non pas d'abord de la discrétion du psychanalyste, mais de celle du*

The same phrase – *si casus ferat* – occurs in *Guidelines for the Use of Psychology*; see 5:

> "*Si casus ferat*" — that is, in exceptional cases that present particular difficulties —recourse to experts in the psychological sciences, both before admission to the seminary and during the path of formation, can help the candidate overcome those psychological wounds, and interiorize, in an ever more stable and profound way, the type of life shown by Jesus the Good Shepherd, Head and Bridegroom of the Church.

Both *Guidelines for the Use of Psychology* and *Apostolorum Successores* have a common reference to a *Monitum* issued on July 15, 1961 (see footnote 33); of particular relevance to this discussion is the first sentence of number 4 of the *Monitum*:

> Improbanda est opinio eorum qui autumant praeviam institutionem psychoanalyticam omnino necessariam esse ad recipiendos Ordines Sacros, vel proprie dicta psychoanalytica examina et investigationes subeunda esse candidatis sacerdotii et professionis religiosae.

That, the Holy Office rejects the opinion that a psychological assessment is a necessary prerequisite prior to receiving the sacrament of Orders and/or solemn profession, or, more directly, rejects the requirement that all candidates for Orders and for profession must undergo psychological assessment. [30]

Granted, the *Monitum* was issued in 1961 but contemporary curial teaching — *Apostolorum Successores* (2004); *Guidelines for the Use of Psychology* (2008) and *Ratio Fundamentalis* (2016) — cite the *Monitum* as a source for their

patient, qui souvent ne possède aucunement le droit de disposer de ses secrets." [283] The individual's free will must be recognized, especially in determining that which is chosen to be revealed to others between that which is revealed without consent.

As just noted, *Ratio Fundamentalis* (2016), 194 cites as a source one previous version of the *Relatio Fundamentalis* (1985) 39 which in turn cites a number of sources among which are the following: Blessed Pope Paul VI, encyclical *Sacerdotalis Caelibatus*, 63; Sacred Congregation of the Holy Office, *Monitum, Cum compertum, su alcune false opinioni riguardo ai peccati contro il VI comandamento e sopra gli esami psicoanalitici,* Jul 15, 1961: *AAS* 53 (1961) 571; Congregation for Catholic Education, *Orientamenti educativi per la formazione al celibato sacerdotale*, April 11, 1974, n. 38; *Origins* 4: 5 (June 27, 1974).

30  Paragraph 1 of the *Monitum* refers to canon 129 of the 1917 *Codex*: teaching must be according to Church tradition; Paragraph 2 refers to the important role of censors in reading texts and periodicals which reference the sixth commandment of the Decalogue; Paragraph 3 denies to clerics and religious the *munus* of psychoanalysis.

contemporary position. Therefore a manifest and unavoidable connection exists between the first sentence of the *Monitum*, 4 and current magisterial teaching on psychological testing.[31]

These texts offer a salutary warning that psychological testing is not the infallible guarantor of psychological health. Therefore, the bishop must understand the specific limitations of psychological analysis and testing which — as with other aspects of formation —contribute but not exclusively to the development of moral certitude in reference to sacred Orders.

Further, if a decision is made to utilize such analysis *si casus ferat* in admission to a seminary, the obligations mentioned above — choice among experts; confidentiality of reports; limited access to the reports — must be strictly followed. Canon 18 is applicable here: given that the magisterium recognizes the right to privacy of seminarians, then the specific individuals cited as those to be given access to the results of psychological testing (and they alone) may have such access. No option, much less any need, exists, therefore, for other formators in the seminary to have access to the reports of such testing; seminarians cannot be coerced into allowing such access. Finally, seminarians learn by example as well as through classes; the seminary itself and its faculty and staff must themselves put respect for the law in practice, and not create exceptions to or weaken the effects of norms from competent authority.

### E. Irregularities for the Reception of Orders.

Canon 1041 states: "The following are irregular for receiving orders: 4° a person who has committed voluntary homicide or procured a completed abortion and all those who positively cooperated in either; 5° a person who has mutilated himself or another gravely and maliciously or who has attempted suicide." On June 23, 2015 a plenary session of the Pontifical Council for Legislative Texts discussed whether these specific irregularities for the reception of orders applied only to Catholics or included non-Catholics as well. The Council responded

---

31  Johnson notes that there is an apparent inconsistency between the previous *Ratio Fundamentalis* and *Apostolorum Successores* (note 83, 559). As I argue in the text, the documents taken as a whole would rather argue that the recommended norm is expressed by the phrase *si casus ferat* rather than a common policy requiring such testing for each and every candidate.

affirmatively: the irregularities addressed in numbers 4 and 5 apply both to Catholics and to non-Catholics whether baptized or not.[32]

Irregularities for orders are unique and therefore the canonical and particular contexts are both essential for proper interpretation and application. Impediments are either perpetual, known as impediments in the strict sense, or simple and identified as simple impediments (c. 1040). In the majority of situations, simple impediments cease with time; irregularities require a dispensation. Further consequences ensue: for example, the requirement of a just cause for the dispensation (see canon 90, §1); that which constitutes a "just cause" in the case of an irregularity, commensurate with the norm to be dispensed; and whether current praxis indicates that the dispensation is usually granted or not. [33]

---

32  See http://press.vatican.va/content/salastampa/it/bollettino/pubblico/2016/09/15/0646 /01458.html: "*Interpretatio authentica ad can. 1041, nn. 4-5 CIC. Patres Pontificii Consilii de Legum Textibus proposito in plenario coetu diei 23 Iunii 2015 dubio, quod sequitur, respondendum esse censuerunt ut infra:*

D. Utrum sub locutione "irregulares", de qua in can. 1041 *CIC*, veniant etiam non catholici qui acta in nn. 4 et 5 posuerint.

    R. Affirmative.

*Summus Pontifex Franciscus in Audientia die 31 Maii 2016 infrascripto impertita, de supradictis decisionibus certiorfactus, eas publicari iussit."* Franciscus Card. Coccopalmerio, Praeses; Iohannes Ignatius Arrieta, a Secretis."

The first irregularity, *amentia*, would apply in and of itself to anyone, baptized or not, as would *ligamen* (which is of divine law); only Catholics may commit the delicts of apostasy, heresy and schism; and religious vows and reception of orders by the nature of the matter apply to Catholics.

33  See also canons 1043 (on the obligation to inform competent ecclesiastical authority if one knows of an impediment) and 1046 (the multiplication of irregularities and impediments if they arise from the same cause).

An irregularity for the reception of Orders is not equivalent or analogous to a delict[34] or to an expiatory or medicinal penalty or to sin.[35] As Archbishop Arrieta, Secretary of the PCLT explained:

> The irregularities are prohibitions, for those who have in the past been responsible for reprehensible conduct, from receiving ordination – diaconal, priestly or episcopal – without the necessary dispensation from the Authorities; it is not, therefore, in relation to an offence or an additional punishment, but rather a form of prevention to protect the dignity of the Sacrament and the faithful themselves from those who have in the past engaged in specific illicit forms of conduct (certainly already forgiven, in the majority of cases).[36]

Further, an irregularity affects the licit reception of Orders, not its validity, as distinct to diriment impediments to marriage which affect the valid reception of that sacrament.[37]

I suggest that the Council's extensive interpretation — to include non-Catholics and non-baptized in reference to CIC canon 1040, 4⁰ and 5⁰ and thereby extend the scope of the canon — reflects the importance of the absence of any irregularities or simple impediments in coming to a decision with moral certainty concerning the fitness of a candidate for orders. The purpose of irregularities

---

34 See, for example, canon 1321, §1 *"Nemo punitur, nisi externa legis vel praecepti violatio, ab eo commissa, sit graviter imputabilis ex dolo vel ex culpa."* As one effect, therefore, neither *dolus* nor *culpa* are required to commit the act leading to an irregularity for the reception of orders.

35 Distinguishing between the irregularity and sin is necessary in as much as each has a separate canonical description or definition as well as resolution. Commission of a sin may have occurred in the commission of the act which leads to an irregularity but the Code of Canon Law does not require the commission of a sin in order to incur the irregularity. However, see canon 762, §2 of the *Canons of the Eastern Churches, Latin-English Edition* (Washington, DC: CLSA, 1992) in reference to impediments: "The acts that are mentioned in §1, nn. 2-6 do not produce impediments unless they were serious and external sins perpetrated after baptism [*nisi fuerunt peccata gravia et externa post baptismum perpetrate*]." Numbers 2 to 6 are the same as the irregularities cited in *CIC* 1041, 2⁰ to 6⁰. See the next footnote; Archbishop Arrieta referenced the Eastern Code, stating, "Although substantially similar, the Code of Canons of the Oriental Churches presents a system different to that of the irregularities of the Latin tradition and, therefore, does not give rise to interpretative doubts of this type."

36 See the Vatican News website *News.VA*, "Pontifical Council for Legislative Texts: authentic response to canon 1041, nos. 4-15 *CIC*."

37 See canon 1073 "A diriment impediment renders a person unqualified to contract marriage validly."

arises from the divine origin of the sacrament;[38] irregularities are one means among others to determine whether this individual should receive the sacrament of Orders. The decision to ordain — a decision requiring moral certainty — requires that the individual be judged suitable to receive Orders and serve the People of God as an ordained minister.

From another perspective, irregularities and impediments serve to protect the sacrament of Orders from unworthy recipients and to protect the People of God from unworthy ministers. Canon 213 explicitly states the right of the faithful to receive spiritual assistance, especially the word of God and the sacraments, and canons 834, §2; 835, §2, 836, and 837 (concerning the sanctifying *munus* of the Church) articulate the obligation of ordained ministers to "arouse and enlighten [the] faith diligently" (c. 836). In such a context, canon 18 applies especially to the right of the People of God to receive the spiritual goods of the Church from worthy ministers.[39]

---

[38] See, e.g., *Lumen gentium* 28: "In this way the divinely instituted ecclesiastical ministry is exercised in different orders by those who right from ancient times are called bishops, priests, and deacons." *LG, AAS* 57, 33-34: *"Sic ministerium ecclesiasticum divinitus institutum diversis ordinibus exercetur ab illis qui iam ab antiquo Episcopi, Presbyteri, Diaconi vocantur."* Tanner, 2: 872.

[39] Analogously, see the response concerning canon 1041 3° which states "a person who has attempted marriage, even only civilly, while either impeded personally from entering marriage by a matrimonial bond, sacred orders, or a public perpetual vow of chastity, or with a woman bound by a valid marriage or restricted by the same type of vow". Note the paragraph refers to a matrimonial bond, not to "a valid or putative matrimonial bond". Consider, for example, Titus, baptized Catholic, marries Bertha, baptized Catholic, according to the required form of marriage, etc.; he then divorces Bertha to enter into civil marriage with Eunice. Subsequently, the marriage of Titus and Bertha is declared null by an ecclesiastical tribunal and the marriage of Titus and Eunice validated in the Church. Titus later applies for the permanent diaconate program in his diocese. According to a private response from the Congregations for the Doctrine of the Faith and for Divine Worship and the Discipline of the Sacraments in *Canon Law Digest* 13 (1991 – 1995) 540, canon 1041, 3° does *not* apply ("there is no irregularity. The first canonical marriage has been declared null by the competent ecclesiastical authority; the second marriage (civil) is now canonically a valid marriage") but whether Titus is *suitable* for the reception of Orders is a completely different issue. A separate judgment must be made, however, concerning Titus' marital history; the mere absence of an irregularity does not mean that the individual should be ordained. The private response continued: "However, while there is no canonical impediment, one might ask whether a person with such a confused matrimonial background is really suitable to be a permanent deacon, since a married deacon should be a model for Christian family life."

Depending upon the particular irregularity and its accompanying circumstances, the appropriate Congregation[40] or the diocesan bishop may dispense from the irregularity for a just and reasonable cause commensurate with the law that is dispensed. Important also is recognition of the competency of the Apostolic Penitentiary in occult cases.[41]

The decision to request a dispensation from the diocesan bishop or from the Holy See requires a prudential judgment first and foremost that the evidence thus far indicates that this individual could be a worthy recipient of the sacrament. If the bishop does not yet have the moral certainty that the individual should be ordained, then the bishop should wait before granting or requesting the dispensation.[42] If necessary, the period of formation might need to be extended for the bishop to make a decision and write to the appropriate Congregation. Ultimately, if the bishop must write to the Holy See for the dispensation, he must be able to testify that aside from this particular circumstance this man would be a worthy priest. The competent authority would not wish to grant the dispensation if, all things considered, the man should not be ordained.[43]

---

40  See Congregation of Catholic Education, Letter, "Canons 1040–1049. Dispensation from Irregularities and Impediments for Sacred Orders", *Canon Law Digest* 13 (1991 – 1995), 550 – 551. Noting that "prudence requires an adequate passage of time in order to ascertain that the difficulties which gave rise to the irregularity or impediment have been overcome" prior to considering whether a dispensation should be granted, candidates for orders need an explanation of the canonical norms (CIC 1040 – 1049; *CCEO* 762 – 768 in the context of sacramental theology. "In consideration of this, the Congregation of Catholic Education , *collatis consultis* with the other three Dicasteries mentioned above, has determined to establish that such information be given to candidates for Orders from the beginning of theology and [...] no less than four years prior to the presumable date of Ordination." The other Dicasteries are the Congregation for Institutes of Consecrated Life and Societies of Apostolic Life, for the Evangelization of Peoples and for the Oriental Churches.
41  See *Pastor Bonus* "Art. 117 The competence of the Apostolic Penitentiary regards the internal forum and indulgences. Art. 118 For the internal forum, whether sacramental or non-sacramental, it grants absolutions, dispensations, commutations, validations, condonations, and other favors." At times, the Congregation for the Clergy has refused to grant a dispensation while the Penitentiary has chosen to do so.
42  In as much as the Congregation of Catholic Education wishes "timely requests" for dispensations, the bishop in his *votum* should explicitly state that the delay resulted from the bishop's desire to ensure his proper discernment and then judgment concerning the suitability of the candidate (other than in reference to the matter to be dispensed) indicates that he would be a worthy and suitable priest.
43  Consider requests for dispensations from the obligations of the clerical state; if the individual has already entered into a civil marriage or intends to marry, the *acta* must include evidence that the intended spouse is free to marry. The rescript will not be granted to allow the individual to enter an invalid marriage. See also footnote 39.

## F. Right to a Good Name

Canon 220 succinctly states, "No one is permitted to harm illegitimately the good reputation which a person possesses nor to injure the right of any person to protect his or her own privacy."[44] This right is enjoyed by all the Christian faithful — *De omnium christifidelium obligationibus et iuribus* — even by those who have received the sacrament of Orders. Application to those in the latter juridical state received clarification from the PCLT in a private response.[45]

The question presented to the PCLT concerned the actions of a bishops' conference which had published on its website a list of the names of clerics condemned in a civil or ecclesiastical process related to abuse of minors.[46] In its response, the PCLT noted that canon 220 expresses a principle of the natural law and a prohibition against malice[47] and/or defamation ("... *alle lege naturale e all'imperativo che proibisce la maldicenza e la* defamazione"). "Malice" as unjustified or illegitimate publication is contrasted with justified or legitimate publication; in particular circumstances, the greater good — for example, protection of a particular community — may require the publication of facts not favorable to an individual.

The application of canon 220 therefore requires careful discernment; to publish or not the status of an offender, as in the case presented to the PCLT, must be determined on a case by case basis: in some situations, such publication would be legitimate and in other cases publication would not be justified.[48] Further, the competent ecclesiastical authority to discern such legitimacy is the "Pastor" with the care of the community and/or of the offender; other authorities, such as bishops' conferences, act subsequently to that decision.[49]

---

44 Canon 220. "*Nemini licet bonam famam, qua quis gaudet, illegitime laedere, nec ius cuiusque personae ad propriam intimitatem tuendam violare.*"

45 Pontifical Council for Legislative Texts, *Response*, Prot. No. 15512/2016, September 15, 2016, and signed by His Eminence Francesco Cardinal Coccopalmerio, President, and the Most Reverend Juan Ignacio Arrieta, Secretary.

46 "... *sulla pagina web ... di un elenco contenente i nomi dei chierici condonnati dall'istanza civile o ecclesiastica per abusi sui minori.*"

47 "*Maldicenza*" is translated as malice to accommodate the PCLT definition: "...*la maldicenza riguarda la diffusione di notizie vere, anche quando esse sono pubbliche, se fatto in maniera non giustificata.*" In other words, the fact or facts made public are true but their publication is illegitimate; this differs greatly from the situation where that made public might be or might not be true or is in fact false.

48 Definitely **not** legitimate would be such publication of names of those deceased: "... *in questi casi non può esistere una ragione proporzionata per la lesione della fama.*"

49 "*Inoltre, un giudizio del genere corrisponde al Pastore che ha la cura della comunità o che è responsabile del reo. Di conseguenza, altre istanza di autorità – ad esempio, la conferenza episcopale – possono agire successivamente alla delibera dell'autorità competente.*"

Given the above and in response to the query concerning the publication of a list of offenders: *"In tale senso non pare legittimo motivare la pubblicazione di notizie per motivi di trasparenza e di riparazione (a meno che il soggetto stesso non sia consenziente) perché di fatto tale pubblicazione contraddirebbe il can.220 CIC."* That is, such publication contradicts canon 220 in as much as the reasons presented — transparency and/or reparation for damage caused — and absent the consent of the individual involved do not suffice to legitimize such publication.[50]

I would argue that the PCLT has emphasized an important approach to the interpretation and application of law: when a law requires that the competent authority make a decision concerning a person and a specific situation, that authority must be cautious in applying that decision to all cases that might fall under the provisions of the norm.[51]

In its conclusion, the PCLT response cites references to the right of privacy and good reputation in penal law: the accused is not required to confess or be bound by oath (c. 1728, §2); those involved in the penal process are required to maintain secrecy (c. 1455); remission of a penalty is not divulged save to protect the offender's reputation or to repair scandal (c. 1361, §3) and, *maggior ragione*, the same confidentiality would apply to the imposition of a penalty.

**G. Scrutinies Prior to Ordination**

Canon 1051 begins by stating, "The following prescripts regarding the investigation (a*d scrutinium*) about the qualities required in the one to be ordained are to be observed" and is followed by specific requirements. Canon 1052 requires that the bishop have completed the process of scrutinies according to law (*scrutinio ad normam iuris peracto*).

*Ratio Fundamentalis*, having cited *Apostolorum Successores* 89, describes the process of scrutinies in specific detail:

> The discernment of the suitability of the candidate is known as the "scrutiny". It must be undertaken at certain points, five in fact, along the *iter* of priestly formation: admission to candidacy for Orders; the ministries (of lector and acolyte); diaconate and priesthood. These scrutinies are not merely

---

50 The PCLT notes the absence of particular law enacted by the bishops' conference; if such existed, such might influence the decision of the PCLT.

51 See canon 16 §3 "*Interpretatio autem per modum sententiae iudicialis aut actus administrativi in re peculiari, vim legis non habet et ligat tantum personas atque afficit res pro quibus data est.*" A particular decision issued by competent authority through an individual administrative act may serve as a guide to the praxis, for example, of a curial office, no precedent is established requiring the same decision in a subsequent case.

formal bureaucratic acts that employ standard and generic formulae, but give the authoritative assessment concerning the vocation of a specific person and its development, by those who have been authorized to do so by virtue of their office and in the name of the Church. These scrutinies aim to verify the actual presence of the qualities and personal circumstances of a candidate regarding each of the aforementioned points of the formation *iter*. Accordingly, they must be prepared in writing and contain a motivated evaluation, positive or negative, giving reasons, concerning the journey so far completed by the candidate.[52]

The scrutinies, in as much as they provide "the authoritative assessment," are extremely important for the bishop in coming to a decision with moral certainty that an individual should receive Holy Orders. *Ratio Fundamentalis* lists a number of points essential to each scrutiny, among these is an assessment from those with whom the candidate exercised his pastoral service and notes that it might be useful "to have the contribution of women who know the candidate, thus including female assessment and insight."[53]

As already noted, the Congregation for Divine Worship and the Discipline of the Sacraments issued a circular letter on the scrutinies[54] which concurs with other curial documentation. The letter states unequivocally, "Although the call is a canonical act which pertains to a personal authority, it is clear that such an authority ought not proceed merely on the basis of his convictions or intuitions, but should give a hearing to the opinion of persons and councils and not depart from these except on the strength of well-founded reasons (c. 127, §2, 2º).[55]

The letter also states: "…It should be stressed that cases exist in which there has been negligence and imprudence constituting a grave moral responsibility for subsequent defections, in which grave harm is occasioned to persons and grave damage to the Church."[56] This statement is reiterated, with slightly changed wording, in *Ratio Fundamentalis* 206.

The scrutinies exercise an essential role in the positive or negative assessment by formators concerning a candidate for the reception of Orders; in addition to considering the scrutinies in themselves, the bishop also has "the moral obligation" to consider the final assessment of the formators with "the greatest attention." The norms cited above concerning the right to privacy as well as the

---

52  *Ratio Fundamentalis*, 204.
53  Ibid., 205.
54  See note 19 above.
55  Congregation for Divine Worship, *Scrutinies*, 3.
56  Ibid., 6.

inability of the spiritual director and/or confessor to contribute to this assessment deserves reiteration here.

Essential to the decision to ordain an individual is the responsibility of the bishop and of various formators; essential also is the personal responsibility of the individual, both of the one in formation and the bishop who sponsors and decides that the individual should be ordained and be incardinated into his diocese. Both the Congregation for Divine Worship and Church tradition (see footnote 14) reiterate that the absence of moral certainty could lead to a grave moral responsibility for defections from the priesthood and even sin.

**H. Personal Responsibility**

I am not necessarily an enthusiast of Dr. Pangloss, Candide's teacher who maintains (with a nod towards Leibniz) that everything in the world happens from necessity and all happens for the best, although some of my students might raise questions about that. I did state that in the ideal situation no bishop would need to order one of his incardinated priests to fulfill a specific *munus* under the legal obligation of obedience, and no priest would refuse to fulfill a legitimate request from his bishop. The bishop would know his priests well enough that he would not demand that which the cleric could not fulfill, and the priest would know and trust his bishop enough to willingly assume the *munus* assigned to him.

And yet I suggest (or perhaps dare to suggest) that this ideal is the presupposition of the Code and of various magisterial documents. Fundamentally, the bishop and his priests share in the one sacrament of Orders and thus their unity has a sacramental foundation and is nourished and encouraged through grace; the personal responsibility of the bishop and that of the individual priest must take cognizance of its sacramental basis. More specifically, canon 273 states, "Clerics are bound by a special obligation to show reverence and obedience to the Supreme Pontiff and their own ordinary" which norm is balanced by canon 384:

> With special solicitude, a diocesan bishop is to attend to presbyters and listen to them as assistants and counselors. He is to protect their rights and take care that they correctly fulfill the obligations proper to their state and that the means and institutions which they need to foster spiritual and intellectual life are available to them. He also is to take care that provision is made for their decent support and social assistance, according to the norm of law.

Whether or not we agree with Dr. Pangloss, to implement the ideal set before us —or, rather, to strive to particularize this ideal in a given diocese with this bishop and this presbyterate incardinated in the diocese — then both bishops and priests must be aware of their obligations and rights, *in se* and, for the bishop, in reference his "assistants and counselors" and, for the priests, in conforming their "way of thinking and working with the Bishop and brother priests."

*Apostolorum Successores* states,

> The rapport between a Bishop and his presbyterate needs to be inspired and nourished by charity and a vision of faith, such that their *juridical bonds*, deriving from the divine constitution of the Church, appear as a natural consequence of the spiritual communion each one has with God (cf. *Jn* 13:35). In this way, the apostolic labors of priests will be more fruitful, since their union of will and of intent with the Bishop deepens their union with Christ, who continues his ministry as the invisible head of the Church acting through the visible hierarchy.[57]

The "juridical bond" — most importantly incardination and the legal obligation to obey the bishop[58] — is a consequence of a spiritual reality and not simply an autonomous requirement of canon law. Further, "the Bishop should manifestly hold his priests in esteem, showing them trust and praising them as they deserve. He should respect and require others to respect rights and should defend them against unjust criticism."[59]

The relationship / bond between a bishop and his priests both derives from and manifests the unity of the one sacrament of Orders and therefore is "not merely on account of the obligation of obedience required of clerics in general to their own Ordinary (cfr. can. 273)" or the obligation of "vigilance on the part of the Bishop (cfr. can. 384)."[60] As one consequence, therefore,

> Nevertheless, such a bond of subordination [*tale vincolo di subordinazione*] between the priests and the Bishop is limited to

---

57   *Apostolorum Successores* 76. The source given for the last line is *PO* 14-15.
58   In this context, the obligation of a priest to obey his bishop is *not* equivalent to a vow; see canon 1191, §1 "A vow, that is, a deliberate and free promise made to God about a possible and better good, must be fulfilled by reason of the virtue of religion." See also Pontifical Council for Legislative Texts, "Explanatory Note: Elements to Establish the Area of Canonical Responsibility of the Diocesan Bishop on Clerics Incardinated within the Diocese and who exercise their Ministry within it," *Studies in Church Law* 3 (2007) 29 – 39, which indicates that the bond of obedience to one's bishop is limited to the exercise of presbyteral ministry and therefore is much more limited than a public vow received in the name of the Church by a competent ecclesiastical superior. Confer canons 598 – 601 on vows in institutes of consecrated life.
59   *Apostolorum Successores* 78.
60   Pontifical Council for Legislative Texts, "Explanatory Note," II.

> the area of the exercise of their proper ministry which the priests are to carry out in hierarchical communion with their own Bishop. The diocesan priest, however is not a mere passive executor of the commands received from the Bishop [*Il presbitero diocesano, però non è mero esecutore passive degli ordini ricevuti dal Vescovo*]. In fact, he enjoys a legitimate initiative and a just autonomy [*una legittima iniziativa e di giusta autonomia*].[61]

Thus, the grace of the sacrament and the personal response to that grace constitutes a significant element in the bishop's decision with moral certainty to ordain a specific candidate, as well as in the personal responsibility of the candidate and then cleric which in turn underlies canon 273:

> The right or, inversely, unfaithful, response of the priest to the norms of law and to the directives of the Bishop regarding the priestly state and ministry, does not come under the sphere of the juridical responsibility of the Bishop, but of the priest himself who will answer personally for his own acts, even those performed in the exercise of ministry.[62]

Due emphasis needs to be given to two essential phrases: the diocesan priest "enjoys a legitimate initiative and a just autonomy" and he must "answer personally for his own acts."

In reference to formation and formation for the reception of the sacrament of Orders and for the life of a secular priest incardinated into a particular church, two essential questions arise: first, do seminaries inculcate a proper sense of just autonomy within the concept of canonical obedience to one's bishop? Second, do seminaries inculcate in the seminarians the recognition that each one of them is an adult, who faces choices in life and must account for the choices made; in some cases, to the bishop, in some cases, to God. Recently ordained priests are today often placed in positions with significant responsibilities; certain of the newly ordained benefit from a priest mentor to assist them while others do not. They must act and act responsibly. Too great passivity in the seminary will eventually conflict with the very active and decisive role most newly ordained priests face within a few years of their ordination.

---

61  Ibid. In addition, "Above all, from a strictly juridical-canonical viewpoint, only the sphere of general duties of the proper state and of the ministry of priests can and should be the object of vigilance on the part of the Bishop." Such a perspective is respectful of the bishop's authority and responsibility; the bishop is not understood by canon law to be responsible for his priests twenty-four hours a day, seven days a week, even if secular law wishes to maintain such constant oversight on his part.

62  Ibid., "Explanatory Note", 4a.

## Conclusion

The *Directory for the Formation of Priests* states:

> The ministerial priesthood finds its reason for being in light of this vital and operative union of the Church with Christ. As a result, through this ministry, the Lord continues to accomplish among his People the work which as Head of his Body belongs to him alone. Thus, the ministerial priesthood renders tangible the actual work of Christ, the Head, and bears witness to the fact that Christ has not separated Himself from his Church, but continues to give life to her through his everlasting priesthood. For this reason, the Church considers the ministerial priesthood a *gift* given to Her through the ministry of some of her faithful.[63]

"The ministerial priesthood renders tangible the actual work of Christ, the Head" expresses concisely and unequivocally the rationale underlying priestly formation. Those who receive the sacrament of Orders continue the work of Jesus Christ for the salvation of the world until its consummation when the Lord will come again. But as already noted, the grace of the sacrament of Orders works with nature; due cognizance must be given both to grace but also to the individual person with specific strengths and weaknesses.

*Ratio Fundamentalis* recognizes contemporary difficulties: "The pastoral ministry is a fascinating but arduous endeavor open to misunderstanding and marginalization, and, especially today, subject to fatigue, pessimism, isolation, and at times solitude"[64] and in this context cites Pope Benedict XVI "[..] prayer is not a marginal thing: it is the 'occupation' of the priest to pray, as representative of the people who do not know how to pray or do not find time to pray."[65] The priest must recognize and use the means available to him. For example, the sacrament of Penance may be an "occasion to recognize [the cleric's] own frailties and sins and, above all, to understand and experience the joy of feeling loved and forgiven by the Lord."[66]

Making tangible the work of Christ in the Church which is a pilgrim in the world, subject to the frailties and pain of humanity[67] is ultimately the goal of priestly formation, an ideal which can only be achieved by grace. Priestly formation must consequently form men in prayer open to grace, as the proper

---

63 CC, *Directory*, 1.
64 Ibid., 48.
65 Ibid., quoting from Benedict XVI, *Prayer Vigil at the Conclusion of the Year for Priests*, June 10, 2010.
66 *Ratio Fundamentalis* 106.
67 See *LG* 48, *AAS* 57 (1965) 53, in the chapter entitled "*De indole eschatalogica Ecclesiae peregrinantis eiusque unione cum Ecclesia caelesti*".

context in which the candidate proceeds through the four stages of formation — the human, spiritual, intellectual and pastoral — and then, through discernment, requests the sacrament of Orders and the bishop responds with moral certainty to ordain him.

Moral certainty, recognition and practice of the distinction between the internal and external forms as well as of confidentiality; irregularities and impediments; the scrutinies; and personal responsibility should / must contribute to and particularize the context of prayer and of formation stages in the formation of men destined for the presbyterate. Formation, as with grace itself, is not static but dynamic and is on-going. Candidates for the presbyterate must be prepared for the exercise of priestly ministry in today's contemporary situation through an integrated and coherent formation program.

# SEMINAR

## HARMONY AND SOLICITUDE: RECENT CANONICAL CHANGES AND THE CATHOLIC EASTERN CHURCHES
*Reverend Alexander M. Laschuk*

Just over a century ago in May of 1917 Pope Benedict XV issued two documents which would radically redefine how the Catholic Church functioned. One of these documents, likely more familiar to a group of canonists, was the *motu proprio Providentissima Mater*, by means of which he promulgated the 1917 *Codex iuris canonici*.[1] The second of these, perhaps less familiar, was the *motu proprio Dei providentia*, by means of which he established the Sacred Congregation for the Oriental Church.[2] The establishment of this dicastery was a concrete move to implement that greater respect for the Eastern Churches which was addressed twenty years prior by Leo XIII in *Orientalium dignitas*.[3] In *Dei providentis* Benedict XV writes, "The Church of Jesus Christ is not Latin, nor Greek, nor Slavic, but Catholic; accordingly she makes no difference between her children and whether Greeks, Latins, Slavs or members of all other nations, all are equal in the eyes of the Apostolic See."[4]

The Bishop of Rome has, as defined by the dogmatic constitution on the Church *Lumen gentium*, a function whereby he, "presides over the universal communion of charity and safeguards legitimate differences while taking care that what is particular not only does no harm to unity but rather is conducive to it."[5] It is within this context that Pope Francis, who, "by divine right succeeds blessed Peter in the primacy of the whole church," has shown a constant solicitude for the Churches of the Christian East.[6]

Pope Francis has been a prolific legislator and has issued, to this point in the fifth year of his pontificate, at least twenty-two legislative documents, to say

---

1   Benedict XV, motu proprio *Providentissima Mater,* May 27, 1917: *AAS* 9 (1917) 5-8.
2   Benedict XV, motu proprio *Dei providentia*, May 1, 1917: *AAS* 9 (1917) 529-531.
3   Leo XIII, Apostolic Letter *Orientalium dignitas,* November 30 1894: *ASS* 27 (1894-95) 257-264.
4   Benedict XV, *Dei providentia*: *AAS* 9 (1917) 530.
5   *Lumen gentium* 13; English translation in *Decrees of the Ecumenical Councils,* ed. Norman P. Tanner, 2 vols. (London and Washington: Sheed & Ward and Georgetown University Press, 1990) [hereafter Tanner] 2: 859.
6   *Orientalium ecclesiarum* 3.

nothing of the numerous acts of Roman dicasteries issued with his approval.[7] As a comparison, Pope Benedict XVI issued thirteen such legislative documents in his nearly eight-year pontificate.[8] Pope Francis has repeatedly shown his concern for the Catholic Churches of the Christian East in his legislative endeavors. This legislation has served the function of ensuring that the Eastern Churches are able to, "always preserve their own lawful liturgical rites and way of life."[9] Four such documents will be examined to illustrate this solicitude of the Holy Father: *Pontificia praecepta de clero uxorato orientali* (2014), *Mitis et Misericors Iesus* (2015), *De concordia inter codicis* (2016), and the recent *Letter to the Bishops of India* (2017). These documents will be studied in chronological order of promulgation.

### 1. Pontificia praecepta de clero uxorato orientali

On June 14, 2014 Pope Francis approved a document of the Congregation for the Eastern Churches permitting the expansion of the ordination of married Eastern Catholic men to the priesthood outside of their traditional territories. This is a move of great significance for Eastern Catholics in the so-called diaspora. This document will be examined in two sections: first, an overview of the history of married clergy in the Eastern Catholic Churches, including prohibitions, and second, an overview of the recent papal document.

a) Background

As is well known, the Churches of the Christian East ordains married men to major orders. This practice is common to all the non-Catholic Churches of the Christian East, including some which also admit married men to the episcopacy. The practice of ordaining married men also continued in Eastern communities which rejoined the Catholic communion. For example, the Ukrainian Greco-Catholic Church listed among the thirty-three articles of the Union of Brest the preservation of married clergy.[10] The admission of married men to the priesthood was an uncontested practice amongst Eastern Catholics until the nineteenth century. This change corresponded to the time when Eastern Christians began emigrating from their traditional territories into regions dominated by the Latin Church.

---

7   As listed at "Francesco: Motu proprio", accessed online <http://w2.vatican.va/content/francesco/it/motu_proprio.index.html> October 31, 2017.
8   As listed at "Benedetto XVI: Motu proprio", accessed online <http://w2.vatican.va/content/benedict-xvi/it/motu_proprio.index.html> October 31, 2017.
9   *OE*, 6; Tanner 2: 902.
10  For more on the Union of Brest see Boris Gudziak, *Crisis and Reform: The Kyivan Metropolitanate, the Patriarchate of Constantinople, and the Genesis of the Union of Brest* (Cambridge, MA: Harvard University Press, 1998).

Large numbers of immigrants began arriving in North America from the Austro-Hungarian Empire, many of whom were Eastern Catholics accustomed to the ministry of married presbyters. Clergy soon followed and the first documented married Eastern Catholic priest arrived in the United States in 1884. After presenting himself to the vicar general of the Archdiocese of Philadelphia, Fr Ivan Volianskyi was informed that married priests were not welcome and he would not be granted faculties. He was recalled by his ordinary to Europe in 1889.[11] Another Ruthenian Catholic priest, Fr. Alexis Toth, visited the Latin Archbishop of Saint Paul and Minneapolis, John Ireland, upon arriving in the United States. Fr. Toth was a widower, but did have his children with him. Archbishop Ireland expected Eastern Catholics to amalgamate into the Latin parishes. This dispute led to the eventual excommunication of Fr. Toth.[12] Fr. Toth was received into the struggling Russian Orthodox mission in San Francisco along with an estimated sixty-five parishes and 200,000 Eastern Catholics.[13] The Orthodox Church in America canonized Fr. Toth as St. Alexis of Wilkes-Barre in 1994.

The question of married clergy is estimated to have resulted in several hundred thousand Eastern Catholics becoming Orthodox, the majority from modern Ukraine and Sub-Carpathia. The numbers of Catholics entering Orthodoxy was so great that, at least in Canada, it eliminated all Latin resistance to establishing separate Eastern Christian jurisdictions.[14] While the Holy See established hierarchies for these immigrant Eastern communities in North America, at the same time it was careful to prohibit the activity of married priests.

Beginning in 1913 the Holy See began to issue legislative documents prohibiting the ministry of married clerics outside of their traditional territories. The Sacred Congregation for the Propogation of the Faith issued *Fidelibus ruthenis* in 1913 which not only prohibited the ordination of married men in Canada but also excluded the admission of already ordained married presbyters from other territories, again excepting widowers without their children.[15] This legislation was renewed in 1930 for ten years when the same congregation issued *Graeci-Ruthenis ritus*.[16] This document was itself extended in 1941 for an additional ten years.[17] The Sacred Congregation for the Eastern Church issued

---

11   Victor J. Pospishil, *Ex occidente lex* (Carteret, NJ: St Mary's Religious Action Fund, 1979) 23-24.
12   Pospishil, 25-27.
13   John Binns, *An Introduction to the Christian Orthodox Churches* (Cambridge: Cambridge University Press, 2002) 157.
14   David Motiuk, *Eastern Christians in the New World* (Ottawa: Saint Paul University, 2005) 13-24.
15   Sacred Congregation for the Propagation of the Faith, *Fidelibus ruthenis*, August 18, 1913, 10-12: *AAS* 5 (1913) 395.
16   Sacred Congregation for the Eastern Church, *Graeci-rutheni ritus,* May 24, 1930, 12, 15: *AAS* 22 (1930) 348-349.
17   Motiuk, 125.

*Cum data fuerit* in 1929, indefinitely prohibiting married clergy in the United States of America.[18] The ministry of married presbyters in Australia and South America was prohibited when the Sacred Congregation for the Eastern Church issued *Qua sollerti* in 1929.[19] While some married presbyters were ministering in the so-called diaspora, especially in Eastern Canada, the Holy See considered any ministry by these clandestinely ordained married presbyters as illicit.[20]

In recent years several canonists argued these historical prohibitions were no longer in force. Motiuk argued that since the prohibition for Canada contained in *Graeci-ruthenis ritus* lapsed in 1951 and had not been renewed, and since the prohibitions of both *Qua sollerti* and *Cum data fuerit* both did not apply to Canada, it would seem Canadian bishops could, in good conscience, ordain married candidates.[21] Other canonists argued that the promulgation of the *CCEO* had the result of abrogating this previous legislation globally.[22]

However, while the 1990 *CCEO* provided for married clergy, it also contained provision for prohibitions concerning the ordination of married men in certain territories: "The particular law of each Church *sui iuris* or special norms established by the Apostolic See are to be followed in admitting married men to sacred orders."[23] In 2008, the Congregation for the Eastern Churches examined changing these prohibitions in consultation with the Congregation for the Doctrine of the Faith. The determination was that the obligation of celibacy remained normative for candidates to the priesthood outside the traditional territories, while admitting the possibility of the Holy See granting dispensations in "a concrete and exceptional case."[24] This decision was approved by Pope Benedict XVI.[25] This decision was received with uproar from Orthodox

---

18   Sacred Congregation for the Eastern Church, *Cum data fuerit*, March 1 1929: *AAS* 21 (1929) 152-159.
19   Sacred Congregation for the Eastern Church, *Qua sollerti*, December 23, 1929, 6, 18: *AAS* 22 (1930) 102-103, 105.
20   Motiuk, 127-131.
21   Motiuk, 131.
22   George Nedungatt, ed. *A Guide to the Eastern Code: A Commentary on the Code of Canons of the Eastern Churches*. Kanonika, 10. (Rome: Pontificio Istituto Orientale, 2002) 303, 506; Roman Cholij, "An Eastern Catholic Married Clergy in North America: Recent Changes in Legal Status and Ecclesiological Perspective," *Studia canonica* 31 (1997) 311-339.
23   *CCEO*, c. 758, §3. All translations from the *CCEO* are taken from *Code of Canons of the Eastern Churches: Latin-English Edition, New English Translation*, (Washington, DC: Canon Law Society of America, 2001).
24   Congregation for the Eastern Churches, *Pontificia praecepta de clero uxorato orientali*, June 14, 2014: *AAS* 106 (2014) 496-499. English translation by the author.
25   Ibid.

ecumenical partners.[26] Shortly thereafter, the Prefect of the Congregation for the Eastern Churches reminded Eastern Catholic bishops in the United States that they should be: "'embracing celibacy in respect of the ecclesial context' of the United States where mandatory celibacy is the general rule for priests."[27]

b) The Document

The ordination of married men continued *contra ius* in several jurisdictions. In Canada these ordinations openly occurred since 1994.[28] In February 2014 the ordination of a married Maronite man to the priesthood in the United States occurred with the explicit permission of Pope Francis himself.[29] Unknown to those outside of the curia, Pope Francis had issued a decision on December 23, 2013 where he rescinded any and all such bans against married clergy. This decision was not published in the *Acta Apostolicae Sedis* until June 14, 2014. The document is divided into two sections: first, an introductory note and second, a decision approved by the Holy Father.

The first section, the introductory note, describes the history of the prohibition of the ordination of married men to the priesthood outside the traditional territories. The document notes that all Eastern Catholic Churches, except for the Syro-Malabar and Syro-Malankar, ordain married deacons to the priesthood. The document enumerates the various bans which were considered by the Holy See as in force, namely: *Cum data fuerit, Qua sollerti,* and *Gracei-Rutheni ritus*.[30] The document not only acknowledges that these decisions were motivated by the objections of the Latin hierarchy who considered the presence of married clergy a "grave scandal" to the faithful, but also that, "Deprived of the ministers of their proper rite, an estimated 200,000 Ruthenian faithful joined Orthodox Churches."[31]

---

26   See, for example, North American Orthodox/Catholic Theological Consultation, "Statement of the North American Orthodox/Catholic Theological Consultation on the Occasion of the Eighty-fifth Anniversary of the Promulgation of the Decree *Cum data fuerit*," 6 June 2014, accessed online <http:// www.usccb.org/ news/ 2014/ 14-099.cfm>, October 31, 2017.
27   Cindy Wooden, "Eastern Catholics Have Much to Offer US Church, Cardinal Tells Bishops," *Catholic News Service,* 15 May 2012, accessed online <http://www.catholic-news.com/services/englishnews/2012/eastern-catholics-have-much-to-offer-us-church-cardinal-tells-bishops.cfm>, October 31, 2017.
28   Motiuk, 130-131.
29   Jennifer Brinker, "First Married Man Ordained Priest for U.S. Maronite Church," *National Catholic Reporter,* 28 February 2014, accessed online at <https://www.ncron-line.org/news/parish/first-married-man-ordained-priest-us-maronite-catholic-church>, October 31, 2017.
30   Congregation for the Eastern Churches, *Pontificia praecepta de clero uxorato orientali*.
31   Ibid.

The second part of this document publishes the text of the decision of Pope Francis. In November 2013 at the Apostolic Palace the Congregation for the Eastern Churches met in plenary session and reviewed the restrictions on the ordination of married men to the priesthood. During this session the members of the Congregation petitioned the Roman Pontiff to permit the ministry of married Eastern Catholic priests outside their traditional territories. In an audience granted to the Prefect on 23 December 2013, Pope Francis approved this provision "anything to the contrary notwithstanding".[32] The Eastern Congregation interestingly requested not that the Holy Father grant permission not for the ordination of married men, but instead that the Holy Father "give permission to the respective Church Authorities to allow the ministry of married eastern clergy also outside the traditional eastern territories."[33]

There are three situations provided in this decision. First, in *all* Eastern Catholic ecclesiastical jurisdictions the bishop is given the faculty to ordain married men per the tradition of his particular Church, with the obligation of informing the Latin bishop of the territory prior to the ordination in order to obtain his opinion.[34] Second, in ordinariates for Eastern Catholics lacking their own hierarchies (e.g. Argentina and France), the ordinary is also given this faculty, however in these cases he must inform that nation's episcopal conference as well as the Congregation for the Eastern Churches. Finally, in territories where Eastern Catholics lack structures and are entrusted to the care of the local Latin bishop, the faculty is not provided to the Latin bishop but instead must be sought from the Congregation for the Eastern Churches who will exercise it "in concrete and exceptional cases".[35]

This document is published as an act of the Congregation for the Eastern Churches. However, since this document explicitly derogated from the legislative provisions of *Cum data fuerit, Qua sollerti,* and *Graeci-Rutheni ritus,* and congregations lack legislative power, the decision required the specific approval of Pope Francis to have any juridical effect.[36] This is indicated in the document with the words "anything to the contrary notwithstanding."[37] This document eliminated the previous law and as such is an act of the legislative power of

---

32  Ibid.
33  Ibid.
34  The document indicates that *hierarchs* are given this faculty, which would include the protosyncellus and the syncellus (*CCEO,* c. 984, §2). However, it is obvious the document intends for this faculty to be restricted to the eparchial bishop as it speaks of ordination. See John M. Huels, "Canonical Notes on the Pontifical Precepts on Married Eastern Clergy," *Studia canonica,* 50 (2016) 149.
35  Congregation for the Eastern Churches, *Pontificia praecepta de clero uxorato orientali.*
36  John Paul II, Apostolic constitution *Pastor Bonus*, June 28, 1988, 18: *AAS* 80 (1988) 864.
37  Congregation for the Eastern Churches, *Pontificia praecepta de clero uxorato orientali.*

governance of the Bishop of Rome in his capacity as supreme pastor of the Universal Church.

This document interestingly describes the ability of Eastern Catholic hierarchs to ordain married men as a "faculty". A faculty is most generally a permission to perform an action.[38] This phrase reveals that the ability to ordain married men outside of the patriarchal territory is not understood as being within the rights of the individual Eastern Catholic bishop, but is a delegated permission of the Roman Pontiff. The Roman Pontiff is the supreme judge of interchurch relations and he acts in this capacity by determining when this practice is permissible, despite the historical objections of some members of other Churches *sui iuris*.[39] Among other reasons, Huels postulates this is termed a "faculty" in order to permit the listed conditions for the admission of married men to the presbyterate.[40]

Thanks to the decision of Pope Francis, Eastern Catholic bishops are now able to follow their ancestral traditions and ordain candidates, both celibate and married, for their particular churches. This is an application of the Second Vatican Council's decree on ecumenism: "Far from being an obstacle to the Church's unity, a certain diversity of customs and observances only adds to her splendor, and is of great help in carrying out her mission, as has already been stated."[41] The Roman Pontiff has decided to defer to the tradition of Eastern Catholics instead of the concerns of scandal expressed by some Latin ordinaries.

2. *Mitis et Misericors Iesus*

As is well known, on August 15, 2015 Pope Francis promulgated two *motu proprii* which provided the greatest revision to the matrimonial nullity process in several centuries.[42] Pope Francis indicates in the preamble, "taking into consideration the unique ecclesial and disciplinary structure of the Eastern Churches, we have decided to promulgate norms through a separate *motu proprio* to update the practice of matrimonial processes according to the *Code of Canons of Eastern Churches*."[43] This was a break from that which occurred in

---

38  On the juridic nature of faculties, see John M. Huels, *Empowerment for Ministry: A Complete Manual on Diocesan Faculties for Priests, Deacons, and Lay Ministers* (Mahwah, NJ: Paulist Press, 2003) esp. 3-37.
39  See *Orientalium Ecclesiarum* 4.
40  Huels, "Canonical Notes on the Pontifical Precepts on Married Eastern Clergy," 155.
41  Vatican II, Decree on Ecumenism *Unitatis redintegratio*, 16.
42  FRANCIS, *Mitis et Misericors Iesus*, August 15, 2015, *AAS* 107 (2015) 946-957 [hereafter = *MMI*]. All English translations of this document are taken from the version which is published on the Vatican website at *Mitis et Misericors Iesus*, accessed online <https://w2.vatican.va/ content/ francesco/ en/ motu_proprio/ documents/ papa-francesco-motu-proprio_20150815_mitis-et-misericors-iesus.html> October 31, 2017.
43  *MMI*, preamble.

2002, whereby the Instruction *Dignitas connubii* was issued only for the Latin Church.[44]

a) Background

In 2014 the Third Extraordinary General Assembly of the Synod of Bishops issued its *Relatio Synodi* entitled *The Pastoral Challenges of the Family in the Context of Evangelization*. Within this document, the impetus for the revision of the nullity process is described, "synod fathers emphasized the need to make the procedure in cases of nullity more accessible and less time-consuming, and, if possible, at no expense."[45] The result of these concerns was the revision of canons 1671-1691 of the *Code of Canon Law* and canons 1357-1377 of the *Code of Canons of the Eastern Churches*. Beal has noted, "the unexpected appearance of Pope Francis' apostolic letters *Mitis Iudex* and *Mitis et Misericors Iesus* once again 'upset the applecart' for tribunals and necessitated yet another round of rethinking and retooling of their standard operating procedures."[46] In response to this rethinking, commentaries have abounded; indeed, in the months following the promulgation of these documents there has been a flurry of canonical activity in the form of articles, books, courses, and conferences. To this end, in this study *Mitis et Misericors Iesus* will not be examined on a whole as this has occurred repeatedly in other fora, but instead a specific examination will occur on some themes which are of greater interest for our topic of study.

b) The Document

The document is divided into three sections: a preamble, the revised canons, and the complimentary norms. From this text a first point to be examined is the aid provided to smaller eparchies in providing access to an ecclesiastical tribunal. While this is not something unique to *Mitis et Misericors Iesus*, it does offer specific aids to the situation of Eastern Catholic eparchies in the so-called diaspora, many of which are unable to offer their own matrimonial tribunals in an effective manner. Pope Francis specifically recognizes that the Eastern Churches still need to establish tribunals, and he writes:

> The synods of Eastern Churches, […] , should respect the restored and defended right of organizing judicial power in their own particular churches. The restoration of the proximity between the judge and the faithful will never reach its desired result unless episcopal synods offer encouragement and

---

44  *DC*, art. 1, §1.
45  Third Extraordinary General Assembly of the Synod of Bishops, *Relatio Synodi: The Pastoral Challenges of the Family in the Context of Evangelization,* 18 October 2014, 48.
46  John P. Beal, "The Ordinary Process According to *Mitis Iudex:* Challenges to Our 'Comfort Zone'," *The Jurist* 76 (2016) 161.

assistance to individual bishops so that they may carry out the reform of the matrimonial process.[47]

Previously, the bishop utilizing an eparchial or intereparchial tribunal in place of his own eparchial tribunal was unable to delegate judicial power in specific instances to another tribunal.[48] To obtain the services of a neighbouring tribunal (such as one closer to the domicile of the parties in a specific case), the eparchial bishop needed a rescript of the Apostolic Signatura.[49] However, the law now assigns the faculty of the eparchial bishop to undertake this task on his own initiative.[50] In cases where his particular church is, in fact, more able to administer justice on its own, the eparchial bishop can also withdraw from an interdiocesan tribunal on his own initiative.[51] This should occur when participation in such a tribunal is not necessary and could even hinder the faithful's access to justice, such as through the violation of the principle of proximity. The permission of this Supreme Tribunal can no longer be thought of as a requirement of law. The ability to erect one's own tribunal has been described as a "free and inherent right" in the explanation of the *mens legislatoris*.[52] Courtesy would dictate, however, that even if their permission is not required, the Apostolic Signatura would be informed of these decisions, an action which would aid their assigned task of maintaining vigilance over the administration of justice.[53] It has been stated that the approval of the Holy See is only required for the erection of intereparchial tribunals involving multiple ecclesiastical provinces.[54]

A bishop now has numerous options. First, he can, as the law prefers, establish his own tribunal. This is the case whether his diocese lacks a tribunal or whether it is currently participating in an intereparchial tribunal. If this is not possible, such as due to a shortage of qualified personnel, the bishop can turn towards a neighbouring tribunal in virtue of the faculty assigned to him by *Mitis Iudex*.[55] The permission of the Holy See is only required if he wants to associate with an interdiocesan tribunal involving another ecclesiastical province.[56] The law previously also required permission for the establishment of tribunals of

---

47  *MMI*, preamble.
48  *CIC*/83, c. 135, §3; *CCEO*, c. 985, §3. All citations from the *CIC*/83 are taken from English translation *Code of Canon Law, Latin-English Edition, New English Translation* (Washington, DC: Canon Law Society of America, 1999).
49  *Pastor Bonus*, 124.
50  *MMI*, c. 1359, §2.
51  *MMI*, art. 8, §2.
52  "La 'Mens' del Pontifice sulla Riforma dei Processi matrimoniali," in *L'Osservatore Romano* November 8, 2015, 8.
53  *Pastor Bonus*, 124.
54  La 'Mens' del Pontifice sulla Riforma dei Processi matrimoniali," 8.
55  *MMI*, c. 1359, §2.
56  La 'Mens' del Pontifice sulla Riforma dei Processi matrimoniali", no. 2.

numerous Churches *sui iuris*.[57] This permission would be obtained from the Apostolic Signatura.[58]

This ability to draw on neighboring tribunals is of great assistance to Eastern Catholic Churches, especially those in the so-called diaspora. Frequently in these regions an eparchy is without the resources to establish a tribunal on its own. In these cases, an eparchy can easily make use of another tribunal on a stable basis or associate with another eparchy to establish an intereparchial tribunal. *Mitis et Miericors Jesus* also provides the possibility of an eparchial bishop seeking assistance from another tribunal not on a stable basis but on an *ad hoc* basis. This follows from the fact that if a diocesan or eparchial bishop is able to do the greater (establish a stable competent tribunal), he can certainly do the lesser (designate a tribunal for a single case *ad causam*).[59] In cases where an eparchy is unable to provide the structure of a tribunal, the bishop can designate either a stable tribunal (such as a Latin tribunal near the eparchial see) or a tribunal *ad causam* (such as near the domicile of the parties, respecting the principle of proximity), all without requiring the intervention of the Apostolic Signatura. This intervention was previously required for every instance of prorogation.

A second observation of *Mitis et Misericors Iesus* is the investigation of so-called lack of form marriages. The text in *Mitis et Misericors Iesus* on the documentary process is nearly identical to the text contained in *Mitis Iudex* canons 1688-1690.[60] These norms reflect that which is contained in both the 1983 *CIC* as well as *Dignitas connubii*. This harmony is present even though the previous *CCEO* canons 1372-1374 were not identical to the previous canons 1686-1688 of the Latin Code. Previously, the documentary process was not necessary for those, "who would have been obliged to observe the prescribed form for the celebration of marriage required by law, but who attempted marriage before a civil official or a non-Catholic minister, the pre-nuptial investigation mentioned in can. 784 suffices to prove his or her free status."[61] This canon has been eliminated. The implications of this are that the Pontifical Council for Legislative Texts has replied that, "the nullity of the previous marriage must be declared while observing the norms of the new can. 1374 on the documentary process."[62]

One can note there is no canon in the Latin Code providing an exception to the requirement of using the documentary process as was present in *CCEO*

57   *CCEO*, c.1068, §1.
58   *Pastor Bonus*, 124.
59   Following the legal principle of "Plus semper in se continent, quod est minus." *RJ* in *VI°*, no. 35, also *RJ* in *VI°* no. 53. This interpretation is shared by John Beal, see Beal, "The Ordinary Process According to *Mitis Iudex:* Challenges to Our 'Comfort Zone'," 164.
60   *CIC*/83, cc. 1686-1688; *DC*, art. 295-299; *MMI*, cc.1374-1376; Francis, *Mitis Iudex Dominus Iesus,* August 15, 2015, cc. 1688-1690: *AAS* 107 (2015) 965-966.
61   *CCEO*, c. 1372, §2
62   Pontifical Council for Legislative Texts, Private Reply of 25 November 2015 (Prot. N. 15170/2015); English translation *The Jurist* 76 (2016) 288.

canon 1372, §2 and this practice is based on an authentic interpretation of canon 1686 of the 1983 Code.[63] The Pontifical Council has indicated that this authentic interpretation remains in force for the revised norm of *Mitis Iudex*.[64] There does seem to be a contrast between the two positions.

One can ask whether it was the intent of the legislator to make these individuals now go through a more complicated documentary process when the stated goal of these reforms has been to simplify the nullity process, not make it more complicated. Surely this is a situation of unintended consequences emerging from an omission in legal drafting that has resulted in the need for a future revision or interpretation.

Finally, most commentators have focused on the impact of *Mitis* on the court of second instance, *Mitis et Misericors Iesus* has also clarified the jurisdiction of the Roman Rota. Prior to *Mitis et Misericors Iesus*, commentators debated whether the Sacred Roman Rota served as a court of third instance for Eastern Catholics residing within the patriarchal territory.[65] This followed a reading of *CCEO* c. 1063 which reads, in part, "This tribunal [the ordinary tribunal of the patriarchal Church] is the appellate tribunal in second and further grades with judges serving in rotation, for cases already decided in the lower tribunals."[66] This question is settled in *Mitis et Misericors Iesus* where Pope Francis writes, "it is still necessary to retain the appeal to the ordinary tribunal of the Holy See, namely the Roman Rota, so as to strengthen the bond between the See of Peter and the particular churches".[67] However, any Eastern Catholic matrimonial *iurium* cases connected to appeals at the Roman Rota are to be transferred to the territorial tribunals of third instance, that is, the patriarchal tribunal.[68] This is a clear attempt to balance the right of appeal to the Roman Rota with the principle of subsidiarity, a guiding principle of the Eastern Code.[69] This fact of mentioning that *iurium* cases are to be transferred to the patriarchal tribunals does result in the clear conclusion that all other types of cases appealed by Eastern Catholics to the Roman Rota continue to remain in the Rota's jurisdiction.

---

63  See Pontifical Commission for the Authentic Interpretation of the Code of Canon Law, *Authentic Interpretation,* July 11, 1984, 2: *AAS* 76 (1984) 747.
64  Pontifical Council for Legislative Texts, Private Reply of November 18, 2015 (Prot. N. 15182/2015); English translation *The Jurist* 75 (2015) 669.
65  See, for example, Jobe Abbass, "The Roman Rota and Appeals from Tribunals of the Eastern Patriarchal Churches," *Periodica* 89 (2000) 439-490; *contra*: "Joaquín Llobell, "La competenza della Rota Romana nelle cause delle Chiese cattoliche orientali," *Quaderni dello Studio Rotale*, 18 (2008) 15-57
66  *CCEO* c. 1063, §3.
67  *MMI*, preamble.
68  Francis, *Rescritto "ex Audientia SS.mi" sulla nuova legge del processo matrimoniale*, *L'Osservatore Romano*, December 12, 2015, 8.
69  The principle of subsidiarity is one of the listed guidelines for the revision of the *CCEO*, see: Pontificia commissio codici iuris canonici orientalis recognoscendo, "Guidelines for the Revision of the Code of Oriental Canon Law," 6: *Nuntia* 3 (1976) 21.

3. *De concordia inter codicis*

At the twenty-eighth general congregation of the Synod of Bishops, John Paul II referred to the 1983 Code of Canon Law and the 1990 Code of Canons of the Eastern Churches, together with the 1988 constitution *Pastor Bonus*, as integral parts of the one *Corpus iuris canonici* of the Catholic Church.[70] There were, however, obvious differences between the two codes of canon law. There especially emerged questions at the intersections of these systems of law, such as Latin pastors with Eastern Faithful.[71] What is the obligation of a Latin bishop to Eastern faithful? To what degree is he to support their obligation to preserve their ecclesial identity?[72] To answer some of these questions, on May 31, 2016 Pope Francis issued a *motu proprio* which harmonized various norms between the *Code of Canons of the Eastern Churches* and the *Code of Canon Law*.

a) Background

Among the differences between the *CCEO* and *CIC* relates to the care of a bishop for faithful of another Church *sui iuris*. When he has the faithful of another Church in his care, a Latin bishop, "is to provide for their spiritual needs either through priests or parishes of the same rite or through an episcopal vicar."[73] An Eastern bishop, however, "is bound by the serious obligation of providing everything so that these Christian faithful retain the rite of their respective Church, cherish and observe it as far as possible. He is also to ensure that they foster relations with the superior authority of their Church."[74] This is a much more serious obligation imposed upon the Eastern hierarch. The perceived conflict between these two obligations has been the subject of debate and was as a result submitted to the Pontifical Council for the Interpretation of Legislative Texts in 1999.[75] This relates to the right of the faithful to worship in their own Church *sui iuris*.[76] This was described by John Paul II in the apostolic constitution *Sacri canones* as "the very fundamental right of the human person, namely, of professing the faith in whatever their rite, drawn to a great extent from their very mother's womb."[77] What is the intersection between the right of the faithful and the obligation of the hierarch or ordinary?

b) The Document

---

70 John Paul II, Allocution *Memori animo*, 25 October 1990, 8: *AAS* 83 (1991) 490.
71 On this topic see, for example, Pablo Gefaell (ed.), *Cristiani orientali e pastori latini*, (Milan: Giuffrè Editore, 2012).
72 *OE*, 4; Tanner 2: 901
73 *CIC*/83, c. 383, §2.
74 *CCEO*, c. 193, §1.
75 *Comm* 31 (1999), 50.
76 *OE*, 3, Tanner 2: 901.
77 John Paul II, *Sacri canones*: *AAS* 82 (1990) 1035; English translation in *Code of Canons of the Eastern Churches: Latin-English Edition, New English Translation*, xxii.

This *motu proprio* is structured with a preamble which is followed by eleven articles which modify portions of the *Code of Canon Law*. The preamble identifies the motivating factors of this *motu proprio*. Pope Francis recognizes in the preamble that the *CCEO* and *CIC* provide distinct systems of law. Despite this fact, there are situations which require common pastoral norms, exasperated by the continued increasing presence of Eastern Catholics in territories predominated by the Latin Church.[78] These norms predominantly relate to the administration of the sacraments of marriage and baptism. While the individual norms have been examined in detail in other studies, some general observations will be made.[79]

First, the language describing the individual Churches is clarified. *CIC* canon 111, for example, suffered from poor drafting: that which is uniformly referred to as a Church *sui iuris* in the *CCEO* is described in the first paragraph as a "ritual Church" and in the second paragraph as a "ritual Church *sui iuris*".[80] This has now been changed to Church *sui iuris* uniformly through the nine articles.[81] It is important to recall that the term Church *sui iuris* can also be applied analogously to the Latin Church.[82]

Second, the articles identify numerous *lacunae* which existed in the Latin legislation. For example, a comparison of *CCEO* canon 29 and the previous *CIC* canon 111 show an obvious difference: *CIC* canon 111 did not take into account the situation where only one parent was Catholic. In order to address this issue, article one has added a second paragraph to canon 111 providing a norm that corresponds more closely to that of the *CCEO*. Article 2 provides for the procedure by means of which one transfers their ascription, something contained previously only in the *CCEO*.[83]

Third, the legislation adopts certain additional norms that were peculiar to the *CCEO*. For example, *CCEO* canon 681 allowed for non-Catholics to approach a Catholic minister and seek baptism for their child, providing moral or physical impossibility existed in accessing their own minister.[84] This possibility is now included in the revised *CIC* canon 868.[85] The same is true for the possibility of providing the faculty to marry Eastern non-Catholics.[86]

---

78  Francis, *De concordia inter codicis*, preamble: *AAS* 107 (2015) 602.
79  See Jobe Abbass, "*De Concordia Inter Codicis:* A Commentary," *Studia canonica* 50 (2016) 323-345.
80  *CIC*/83, c. 111.
81  Francis, *De Concordia inter codicis*, 1-3: *AAS* 107 (2015) 603-604.
82  Pontifical Council for Legislative Texts, Explanatory note, December 8, 2011: *Comm.,* 43 (2011) 315-316; English translation Jobe Abbass, "The Explanatory Note Regarding *CCEO* Canon 1: A Commentary," *Studia canonica* 46 (2012) 295.
83  *CCEO*, c. 36.
84  *CCEO*, c. 681, §5.
85  Francis, *De Concordia inter codicis*, 5: *AAS* 107 (2015) 604.
86  Ibid.; *CCEO*, c. 833.

Fourth, the legislation settles a doubt of law. The form for marriage established by the *CCEO* is a sacred rite that includes the intervention of a priest who imparts his blessing.[87] The question arose: can an Eastern Catholic faithful contract a marriage in the Latin Church before a Latin deacon following *CIC* canon 1108, §1? Canonists were divided on the topic. Some argued that the deacon could perform the marriage.[88] Others argued it was excluded by *CCEO* canon 828.[89] Article six has clarified the doubt of law: the new third paragraph of canon 1108 indicates clearly that the blessing of the priest is now required for validity and a deacon cannot receive the consent of a marriage where one party is Eastern Catholic. This required numerous other revisions in order to maintain consistency with this norm.[90]

Finally, it should be observed that the document does not uniformly deal with all the differences between the *CCEO* and *CIC* on these questions. For example, there is an additional difference between *CCEO* canon 29 and *CIC* canon 111: the *CCEO* allowed the parents, by mutual consent, to select to which of the two Churches the child is to be ascribed. This is not an explicit possibility in *CIC* canon 111. However, the Eastern parent could make use of *CCEO* canon 29 which allows for this possibility. There does remain some distinctiveness between the legislation of the Church.

4. Letter to the Bishops of India

Among the functions assigned to the Bishop of Rome by the Second Vatican Council is the direction of the preaching of the Gospel throughout the whole world.[91] This is reflected in canon 57 of the *CCEO*, "The erection, restoration, modification and suppression of patriarchal Churches is reserved to the supreme authority of the Church."[92] Reflecting this function, on October 10, 2017 Pope Francis issued his most recent decision affecting the Catholic Churches of the Christian East. On this day a letter was signed, sent to all bishops in India, on the question of the canonical territory of the Syro-Malabar Church.

---

87  *CCEO*, c. 828, §2.
88  See for example Victor Pospishil, *Eastern Catholic Church Law,* 2nd ed. (New York, St. Maron Publications, 1996) 574.
89  See for example Jobe Abbass, *Two Codes in Comparison*, Kanonika 7 (Rome: Pontificio Istituto Orientale, 2007) 100-103.
90  Francis, *De Concordia inter codicis*, 8-9, 11.
91  See Vatican II, decree *Orientalium ecclesiarum* 3.
92  *CCEO,* c. 57, §1.

a) Background

The Syro-Malabar Catholic Church is a major-archiepiscopal Church *sui iuris*. They trace their roots to the Thomas Christians of India which were in full Eucharistic communion with the Assyrian Church of the East (sometimes pejoratively called the Nestorian Church due to their rejection of the Council of Ephesus in 431). This community began its interaction with Latin Catholicism with the arrival of Portuguese missionaries in the sixteenth century. The Portuguese did not recognize the legitimacy of the Thomas Christians and at the Synod of Damper in 1599, under the presidency of the Portuguese Archbishop of Goa, the Church adopted numerous practices including Latin vestments, clerical celibacy, changes to the Eucharistic liturgy, the establishment of the Inquisition, and the restriction of the episcopacy to Portuguese clerics.[93] European candidates were promoted to the episcopacy in the Syro-Malabar Church until 1896 when the Syro-Malabars were granted their own apostolic exarchates. While under the direction of Western clerics the Syro-Malabar Church numbered only 200,000, they now are over 4,100,000.[94] While they have 2866 parishes, there are 4077 secular priests, another 3543 religious priests, and an incredible 34,147 female religious.[95] It was raised to the status of a major archiepiscopal Church by John Paul II in December 1992.[96]

Despite being an indigenous Indian Church, the activity of the Syro-Malabar Church was restricted to Kerala. The remainder of India was outside of its canonical territory and required extensive cooperation with bishops of the Latin Church along with the Roman dicasteries.[97] While in Kerala the synod of bishops could, for example, establish eparchies, elect bishops, and appoint metropolitans with jurisdictional authority, in the rest of India decisions of the synod of bishops

---

[93] For more on the Synod of Damper see George Nedungatt (ed.), *The Synod of Diamper Revisited,* Kanonika 9 (Rome: Pontificio Istituto Orientale, 2004).

[94] Ronald Roberson, *The Eastern Christian Churches: A Brief Survey,* 6th ed. (Rome: Edizioni «Orientalia Christiana», 1999) 149. Current statistics of 4,100,000 are taken from the annual statistics compiled by Ronald Roberson for the Catholic Near East Welfare Association and available at: Ronald Roberson, *The Eastern Catholic Churches 2016,* accessed online <http://www.cnewa.ca/default.aspx?ID=125&pagetypeID=1&sitecode=HQ&pageno=1>, October 31, 2017. These statistics are based on the *Annuario Pontificio 2016.*

[95] Ronald Roberson, *The Eastern Catholic Churches 2016,* accessed online <http://www.cnewa.ca/default.aspx?ID=125&pagetypeID=1&sitecode=HQ&pageno=1>, October 31, 2017.

[96] John Paul II, *Quae maiori Christifidelium,* December 16, 1992: *AAS* 85 (1993) 398-399.

[97] See for example John Paul II, *Address of His Holiness John Paul II to the Bishops of the Syro-Malabar Church of India,* January 8, 1996, 4: *AAS* 88 (1996) 772.

were restricted to questions of liturgical law.[98] There were, until October 10, 2017, regions of India with no Syro-Malabar bishop and thus the faithful, and their clergy, were under the jurisdiction of the local Latin ordinary. Movement by the Syro-Malabar Church to have missionary eparchies was resisted by the local Latin hierarchy which felt that overlapping Catholic jurisdictions in the North and East of India would suggest Christian division before the Hindu majority.[99] While individual eparchies or exarchates have been erected in other regions (Delhi in 2012 and Bangalore in 2015), many Syro-Malabar faithful remained under the care of Latin ordinaries despite having historical roots in some territories.[100]

b) The Document

The letter of Pope Francis is addressed to the bishops of India, presumably of all three Catholic Churches (Syro-Malabar, Syro-Malankar, and Latin). The letter, issued by the Holy Father himself, is dated October 9, 2017 while having a publication date in the header of October 10, 2017.[101] This document is too recent, obviously, to be published in the *Acta apostolicae sedis* which could provide clarity regarding these dates. The letter is divided into nine sections.

Pope Francis begins his letter with a historical overview of the situation. He examines the Antiochian and Chaldean origins of the Churches in India, to which was later added the Latin Church. Pope Francis notes that India has three Churches *sui iuris,* each providing a distinct expression of the single Faith.[102] Pope Francis places his letter in the context of preserving the Eastern Churches and their distinctive traditions, an obligation both upon them and upon the Holy Father.[103]

After completing this first section relating to the theological motivations for the current document, Pope Francis then enumerates specific factors particular to the situation in India which motivated this decision. Pope Francis recognized that the issue of co-existing jurisdictions which was slowly emerging was "not without problems," yet the fact is that it did not "compromise the mission of the

---

98   *CCEO,* cc. 78, 146, 150. For an overview of the powers possessed by the head of a patriarchal or major archiepiscopal Church along with his synod see Cyril Vasil', "Modificazioni nell'estensione della potesta dei patriarchi: Identifazione dei limiti della loro competenza amministrativa secondo Il CCEO," *Folio canonica* 5 (2002) 296-299.
99   Francis, *Letter to the Bishops of India,* October 9, 2017, 5. Accessed online <http:// press.vatican.va/ content/ salastampa/ en/ bollettino/ pubblico/ 2017/ 10/ 10/ 171010b. html> October 31, 2017.
100  Francis, ibid., 6-7.
101  Francis, *Letter to the Bishops of India,* October 9, 2017, as appears on the Vatican website.
102  Ibid., 1.
103  Ibid., 2-4.

Church" as had been the concern of some Latin bishops.[104] On the contrary, the Holy Father notes that these new structures have resulted in greater missionary efforts in India.[105] It is in response to these reports, especially those filed by the Apostolic Visitator for Syro-Malabars living outside the patriarchal territory, that Pope Francis has issued his decisions.

The decision of the Holy Father is contained in the seventh section of the document. The decision is twofold. First, the Holy Father indicates that he has directed the Congregation for the Eastern Churches to erect two new eparchies and to modify the boundaries of an additional two eparchies, the result of which is that Syro-Malabar Catholics now have proper pastoral care throughout India. Second, the Holy Father has decreed that these four eparchies are to be included within the canonical territory of the Major Archiepiscopal Synod of the Syro-Malabar Church.[106] The Holy Father refers to these decrees but does not include them. The establishment of a new ecclesiastical circumscription generally takes the form of an apostolic constitution. It is assumed that these decrees will be published in the *Acta Apostolicae Sedis*.

Pope Francis concludes the letter with two paragraphs addressing the concerns of the Latin pastors. First, he recognizes the concern of Latin pastors who will lose Syro-Malabar faithful from the Latin Church. However, the Holy Father puts these concerns aside, indicating that this is, "an opportunity for growth in faith and communion with their *sui iuris* Church, in order to preserve the precious heritage of their rite and to pass it on to future generations."[107] Second, he pointedly indicates to the bishops of India that their path, "cannot be that of isolation and separation, but rather of respect and cooperation."[108] He then concludes with a call for collaborative activity between the Churches *sui iuris*, especially in terms of pastoral work, education, and ecumenism.[109] With this document Pope Francis offers an important example of the Bishop of Rome's ministry of acting as arbitrator between the Churches *sui iuris*, a ministry which, "safeguards legitimate differences while taking care that what is particular not only does no harm to unity but rather is conducive to it."[110] This is also a practical application of the Second Vatican Council's assurance not only of the equality of the various Churches, but of their common mission and inherent right, "of preaching the Gospel throughout the whole world (see Mk 16, 15) under the direction of the Roman Pontiff."[111]

---

104 Ibid., 6.
105 Ibid.
106 Ibid., 7.
107 Ibid., 8.
108 Ibid., 9.
109 Ibid.
110 *Lumen gentium* 13
111 *Orientalium ecclesiarum* 3.

5. Conclusions

In his letter to mark the close of the Jubilee Year 2000 John Paul II wrote, "How can we forget in the first place those *specific services to communion* which are *the Petrine ministry* and, closely related to it, *episcopal collegiality*?"[112] This reflects the conciliar teaching that the Bishop of Rome has an important role "as supreme arbiter in inter-church relations".[113] Pope Francis has repeatedly demonstrated his understanding of the Petrine Ministry as being at the service of communion and for the preservation of the Eastern Churches. In each of these four documents examined, to varying degrees, Pope Francis has been examining the relationship between Christians of different Churches *sui iuris*, especially between Eastern and Latin Catholics. The preference has, at times in history, deferred to the *praestantia ritus latinae*.[114] While this has been reprobated on a *theoretical* level for well over a century since *Orientalium dignitas*, several of the documents examined show how a sensitivity for the concerns of the Latin Church has resulted in various levels of restrictions upon the Catholic Churches of the Christian East.

Pope Francis has clearly and repeatedly put an end to this practice. The Second Vatican Council stated clearly regarding the Churches *sui iuris,* "Thus the same churches enjoy equal dignity, so that none of them ranks higher than the others by reason of rite, and they enjoy the same rights and are bound by the same laws."[115] This equality, if it is a true equality, must exist even when one is uncomfortable or has corresponding obligations. This reflects a more fundamental theme in the thought of Pope Francis: the need for the unity of the episcopate. Pope Francis has been firm on this theme, and, for example, when addressing the Latin and Ukrainian Catholic bishops of Ukraine he told them, "The unity of the Episcopate, as well as giving a good example to the People of God, renders an inestimable service to the Nation, both on the cultural and social planes and, above all, on the spiritual plane."[116] It is only when the Churches are allowed to practice their legitimate traditions, certainly under the guidance

---

112 John Paul II, Apostolic letter *Novo millennio ineunte*, January 6, 2001, 44: *AAS* 93 (2001) 297; English translation in John Paul II, Apostolic letter *Novo millennio ineunte* (Vatican City, Libreria editrice Vaticana, 2001) 60. Emphasis in original.
113 *Orientalium ecclesiarum* 4.
114 For a brief overview of the history of the concept of the prestige of the Latin rite see Natale Loda, "Uguale dignità teologica e giuridica delle chiese *sui iuris*," in Luis Okulik (ed.), *Nuove terre e nuove Chiese: Le communità di fedeli orientali in diaspora* (Venice: Marcianum Press, 2008) 40-48.
115 *Orientalium ecclesiarum* 3.
116 Francis, *Address to the Ukrainian Bishops on Their "Ad limina" Visit (Bishops of the Ukrainian Greek Catholic Church, Bishops of Byzantine Rite, and Bishops of the Ukrainian Episcopal Conference)*, 4; accessed online <https://w2.vatican.va/content/francesco/en/speeches/2015/february/documents/papa-francesco_20150220_ad-limina-ucraina.html>, 31 October 2017.

of the Successor of Peter, that we can truly have that diversity which, far from subtracting from the Church, instead can only add to its unity.[117]

---

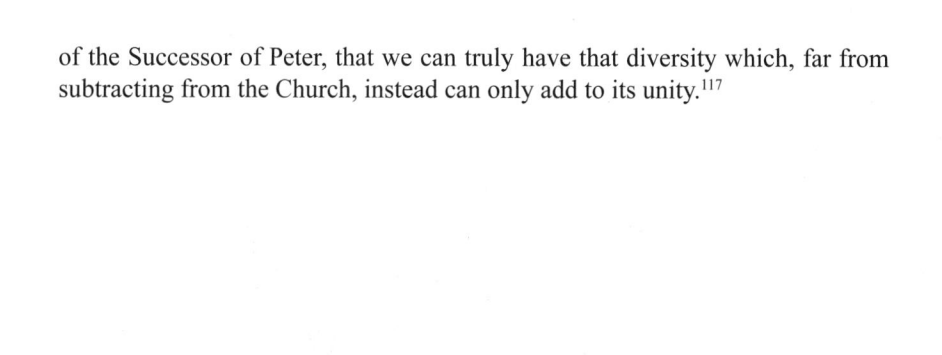

117  Cf. Vatican II, *Lumen gentium* 13: *AAS* 57 (1965) 17.

# Seminar

## Canonical Developments in the Personal Ordinariates Established under the Auspices of the Apostolic Constitution *Anglicanorum Coetibus*

*Most Reverend Steven J. Lopes*

Good Afternoon. I am grateful to the Society for the invitation to speak on the development of the Ordinariate of the Chair of Saint Peter. As you well know, the Ordinariates established under the auspices of the Apostolic Constitution *Anglicanorum coetibus* (2009) are unique juridical structures which provide first for the corporate reunion of Anglican faithful with their pastors into full communion with the Catholic Church. As structures juridically equivalent to dioceses, the Ordinariates are also meant to provide the canonical and ecclesiological "space" within the Catholic Church for the preservation and promotion of a specific liturgical, pastoral, spiritual, intellectual, and organizational patrimony which developed in an Anglican context during a nearly 500-year period of ecclesial separation. In January, the Ordinariate of the Chair of Saint Peter, of which I have the privilege to be the Bishop, will celebrate six years of existence, giving us, I propose, a rather unique experience of building or innovating diocesan structures from scratch. Those structures, if they are to be authentically Catholic, must include provision for the full range of liturgical, sacramental, and pastoral life. I am happy to share with you something of that experience.

Before I go any further, however, I must begin with a caveat: an all-important caveat when addressing the Canon Law Society of America, and that is simply that I am not a canonist. My own academic work is in dogmatic theology, though I do bring to these questions a certain experience, first in having worked at the Congregation for the Doctrine of the Faith during the entire *Anglicanorum coetibus* process—the dialogues, the drafting and publication of the Apostolic Constitution and Complementary Norms, and the subsequent erection and direction of the three Ordinariates (Our Lady of Walsingham in the UK, Chair of Saint Peter in the USA and Canada, Our Lady of the Southern Cross in Australia and the Pacific). I would ask for your understanding and patience, therefore, if some of what I say today lacks the canonical precision or terminology of the other esteemed presenters.

In terms of structure of my presentation, I will begin with a more general reflection on the understanding of the Ordinariate as a Particular Church. To my mind, this is the most important overarching canonical theme in the still-young ecclesial life of the Ordinariates. From this general reflection, I will draw out some implications, questions, and situations, which are not theoretical in nature but part of our daily experience. A second part of my presentation will be less systematic, in that I will attempt to take the 30,000-foot view and articulate some bulletin points on canonical issues and questions that are still open, or have developed in an unexpected way, or are just plain interesting.

Part I: *Understanding the Ordinariate as a Particular Church*

Following the publication of *Anglicanorum coetibus*, I am aware that there was some discussion among canonists as to the nature of the juridical structure of the Ordinariate, specifically whether it is to be understood as a particular Church.[1] Theologically speaking, the issue is rather clear. The necessary elements to any particular Church (a defined portion of the people of God, a bishop, a presbyterate) is well established in the tradition and rearticulated with clarity by the Second Vatican Council in *Christus Dominus* (*CD* #3, 11). While ostensibly more concerned with the relationship with between the universal and particular Church, *Lumen gentium* agrees with this elemental structure, though interestingly adds the Order of Deacons to the essential constitution of the Church (*LG*, 29).

As you all well know, the Code does not include a specific definition of the particular Church *in se*, though Canon 369 comes close with the definition of a Diocese. While Canon 368 maintains that particular Churches are "principally Dioceses," a host of other circumscriptions are listed as being equivalent to Dioceses.[2] These circumscriptions are intended to be ordered and governed as Dioceses, with all the elements of the particular Church, "unless established otherwise." And, just to round out the relevant citations, Can. 372 and Can. 374 § 1 both expressly state that a structure other than a Diocese can be a particular Church, both using the phrase "a diocese or other particular Church." Can. 372 § 2 is the most pertinent to the Ordinariate as it establishes that "in a given territory particular Churches [may be established] distinguished by the rite of the faithful or by some other similar quality."

Questions as to the nature of the Ordinariates established under *Anglicanorum coetibus* are understandable since the juridical figure advanced by the Apostolic

---

1 Cf., for example, Christopher Hill, "An Evaluation of the Apostolic Constitution *Anglicanorum coetibus* in the Current Ecumenical Situation", *Cristianesimo della Storia* 32 (20011) 489-500; Juan Arrieta, "Gli Ordinariati personali," *Ius ecclesiae* 22 (2010) 151-172.
2 *Ecclesiae particolares…sunt inprimis diœceses, quibus, nisi aliud constet, assimilantur…*.

Constitution and Complementary Norms is seemingly new...and we don't generally do new in the Church! There is a tendency to compare this Ordinariate with the hierarchical structures to which it most closely corresponds and extrapolate from there. And so some of the first commentary published by canonists after the publication of *Anglicanorum coetibus* supposed it to be a form of complementary structure to the Diocese such as a military ordinariate or personal prelature, exercising cumulative jurisdiction so that the faithful who are members of the constitutive communities of the Ordinariate are also members of the particular Churches in which they live and work.[3] And yet the Apostolic Constitution goes out of its way to avoid the terminology of cumulative jurisdiction, which is not an oversight. Further, complementary structures, according to *Communionis notio* 16, are established by the Apostolic see "for specific pastoral tasks," a description which even at first blush seems too narrow for the complex purposes cited by the Holy See itself for the erection of the three Ordinariates.

And of course, there is the entire question of the relationship between personality and territoriality as the basis for governance structures in the Church. Here I am simply going to play my "not a canonist" card and avoid any detailed discussion of this particular question. I will, however, reference Saint Bede the Venerable who, it can be said, has a particular resonance in a presentation on the Ordinariates established to preserve and promote the rich patrimony of English Christianity in the Catholic Church. In his *Ecclesiastical History of the English People*, Bede notes that amidst the rather many invasions in 7th century England, it would happen that some pagan tribes would embrace Christianity. As these were by definition mobile communities and therefore without defined territory, bishops were appointed to a particular tribe rather than to a county or city.[4] This is simply to say that, in an Church which has a 20 century history of organizing its institutional life to meet the real pastoral circumstances of real people, that which appears as new is not necessarily unprecedented.

I confess that I have always found the debate as to whether or not the Ordinariates established under *Anglicanorum coetibus* are to be understood as particular Churches to be academic. I know from my own experience working at the Congregation for the Doctrine of the Faith at the time that it was the clear intention of the Holy See to establish a true particular Church with a just autonomy, a structure that would provide the ecclesiological and canonical "space" to preserve the multi-faceted Anglican patrimony central to the identity of these communities while, at the same time—precisely because the Ordinariates are not Ritual Churches *sui iuris*—would provide for their integration and collaboration with the local parishes and Dioceses, thus contributing to the vitality of the

---

3   Cf. Congregation for the Doctrine of the Faith, *Communionis notio*, 16.
4   Bede the Venerable, as cited in Norman Tanner, *New Short History of the Catholic Church* (London—New York: 2011), 73.

Church. The Apostolic Constitution itself provides the basis in law by providing that "Each Ordinariate...is juridically comparable to a diocese" (AC I § 3).

Perhaps because of some of the commentary which appeared shortly after the publication of *Anglicanorum coetibus*, the Decree of Erection of the individual Ordinairates is even more specific about understanding this governance structure as a particular Church. When it says, in no. 1, that "The Personal Ordinariate of the Chair of Saint Peter *ipso iure* possesses juridic personality and is juridically equivalent to a diocese," the decree explicitly cites Canon 372 § 2 about the establishment of a particular Church defined by personality ("the rite of the faithful or by some other similar quality"), even within a defined territory.

This more technical discussion serves as an important background, but I'd like to move now to identifying some implications, questions, and situations which have arisen in this context in the nearly six years since the canonical erection of the Ordinariate of the Chair of Saint Peter.

- The Complementary Norms, which in my view are in need of revision now nearly 10 years after their promulgation, says that the Ordinariate may receive as seminarians "those who belong" to a personal parish of the Ordinariate. What does belong mean? It is the same as canonical membership in the Ordinariate? Does it mean parish registration? If the Ordinariate is a Particular Church, it should interact with the other Particular Churches in the way that all Dioceses must. If, for example, a young man from Evansville comes to college here in Indianapolis, and here discerns his vocation and here integrates himself deeply in the life of the Church, and there here applies to the seminary, is the Archdiocese obligated to send the young man back to his diocese of origin? That is an analogous question. Here is another. Right now, there are 4 young men who are canonical members of the Ordinariate, who are studying for the priesthood for the local dioceses in which they reside. I know them, and have spoken with each, often at length, and support them because their vocational discernment of priesthood is integrally local—the missionary expanse of the Ordinariate requires an openness to mobility that is exceptional in the life of local Churches. I can tell too, that in not one of these cases did the local diocesan bishop speak to me prior to admitting our young men as candidates for priesthood in their dioceses.

- This discussion of Particular Churches is essentially about the interrelationship of the Ordinariate and local Diocese. The Apostolic Constitution itself calls for written agreements between the Ordinariate and the Diocese regarding shared facility use, ministerial assignments of Ordinariate clergy in the Diocese, etc. In our experience, it has been nearly impossible to arrive at written agreements. Part of the reticence might be that clergy assignments in particular morph and develop before the ink is dry. Still, we have nurtured very effective working relationships in many instances, and regular conversation between myself and the local Bishop ensures effective communion and that we are not working at cross purposes.

- When we work closely with the local diocese, we find it to be true what *Anglicanorum coetibus* says about mutual enrichment. Our diversity in liturgical and parochial expression cannot exist without the solid foundation of Catholic faith and sacramental unity. At the same time, our peers have observed that the ministries of our priests within their regions are fruitful, well received, and do articulate different accents and approaches to common pastoral concerns.

- Our Ordinariate faithful have come to Catholic communion willingly, decidedly, and often at great cost. They tend to be zealous in their faith, fervent in their devotion, and already ready to give voice to the hope that is in us (1 Peter 3:15). Other Catholic faithful often find this inspiring and positively challenging, and so it is not uncommon for cradle Catholics to attend Mass at Ordinariate communities on occasion.

Part II: *Issues of Note*

As I mentioned, this section will be less systematic, more of an overview of issues and questions which have arisen, some of which are still open or developing.

*Terminology*

A first issue is basic terminology, both canonical and ecclesiological. This speaks first to our own self-understanding as well as to the "ecclesial perception" of the Ordinariate. As the first part of my presentation indicates, there is some misunderstanding out there about what the Ordinariate is, how it functions, and how it relates to the other local Dioceses. Some of that misunderstanding can be at least meliorated by correct terminology. The Personal Ordinariate of the Chair of Saint Peter—obviously no media or marketing expert was involved in naming the thing, otherwise perhaps we would have avoided taking one abstract concept (Ordinariate) and linking it with another concept (Chair of Saint Peter) which, in the mind of most lay Catholics to say nothing of those outside the Church, remains totally abstract. I completely understand why the Military Ordinariate of the United States had the good sense to petition to have their name changed to the Archdiocese of the Military Services!

Because the name is cumbersome, many attempt to find a verbal shortcut. More often than not, I hear bishops, priests, and lay folks of every stripe call us "the Anglican Ordinariate." This is a problem. My usual quip in response is: whether the Anglicans have an Ordinariate or not I could not say, but all of my people are Roman Catholics. For one thing, the shorthand is ecumenically insensitive to actual Anglicans. To our own clergy and faithful, "Anglican Ordinariate" is actually offensive because it is a subtle way of suggesting that their entrance into full communion is less that total. While our clergy and faithful share a common heritage in English Christianity, they actually come from various jurisdictions and Anglican bodies, of which the Episcopal Church is just one. Some would gladly identify as having come from the Anglo-Catholic "wing" of the Episcopal Church or from one of the "continuing Anglican bodies." Many others, however, identify more readily with the evangelical tradition in Anglicanism. Consequently, the Ordinariate of the Chair of Saint Peter resists shorthand.

There is a similar issue with our form of the sacred liturgy. It is sometimes called a Rite. We are called "the Anglican Use" frequently. Because our liturgy shares many traditional elements and gestures in common with the Extraordinary Form of the Roman Rite, it is thought to be a type of "subset" of that form: "the Extraordinary Form in English" as it is sometimes called. But none of these are either accurate or, honestly, helpful. For one thing, the 1549 *Book of Common Prayer*, a principal source for the Ordinariate Missal, is *older* than the Missal of Saint Pius V, and has its own origins in the Sarum Missal, a variant of the Roman Rite going back to the eleventh century. Our liturgy, given the collective name *Divine Worship* by the Holy See, is more than a collection of liturgical texts and ritual gestures. It is the organic expression of the Church's own *lex orandi* as it was taken up and developed in an Anglican context over the course of nearly five-hundred years of ecclesial separation, and is now reintegrated into Catholic worship as the authoritative expression of a noble patrimony to be shared with the whole Church. As such, it is to be understood as a distinct form of the Roman Rite, as its theological and rubrical context is clearly the Ordinary Form of the Roman Rite.

To this last point, that the rubrical context for Divine Worship is the Ordinary Form of the Roman Rite, this is demonstrated by the fact that the *General Instruction of the Roman Missal* is printed in its entirety at the beginning of the *Divine Worship* Missal. Further, the particular Rubrical Directory of *Divine Worship*: *The Missal* states: "The liturgical norms and principles of the *General Instruction of the Roman Missal* are normative for this expression of the Roman Rite, except where otherwise stipulated in this Directory and in the particular rubrics of *Divine Worship*. This present Directory is intended to provide instructions for those areas in which *Divine Worship* diverges from the R*oman Missal*."[5] This is an understandable canonical framework, since the *General Instruction* is the general framework in law while the particular rubrics that govern *Divine Worship* are a derogation from that universal disposition (and

5   *Divine Worship: The Missal*, Rubrical Directory, no. 7.

hence it is called a Rubrical Directory). This also implies an understanding of the *General Instruction* as something more than a "road map" of rubrics, but rather unfolding the shape and logic of Catholic worship. So even if there is divergence in some of the rubrical practices, there is a much more important theological unity of the Roman Rite which informs this Missal. So ours is a Roman Rite liturgy. Put another way, the Roman Rite subsists in three forms: Ordinary, Extraordinary, and now the Divine Worship or Ordinariate Form.

*Constitutive Communities of the Ordinariate*

In the 18 months following the erection of the Ordinariate of the Chair of Saint Peter, nearly 40 parochial communities entered into full communion with the Catholic Church. These communities varied widely in size, history, experience with Catholic culture, length of catechetical preparation, understanding of ecclesiology and Catholic sacramental practice, etc. The existing parishes of the Pastoral Provision provided at least a backbone of an institutional structure for the Ordinariate, but there was nevertheless a great deal of pressure arising from the fact of so many communities moving into the Ordinariate structure at once. There was a felt moral obligation to take each community as it presented itself, which at times did not allow for the laying of a sufficient structural, administrative or financial foundation, nor sufficient catechetical formation of the lay faithful. Canonically, we were facing not only diverse situations and preexisting structures, but dozens of these at once which afforded no small challenge in discerning the canonical model appropriate in each case. Pastorally, the early development of many of these communities occurred in local situations that were quite distinct one from the other. Some communities, happily, received tremendous support and care from the local diocesan community. Others were easily misunderstood and felt themselves isolated, at times even actively opposed. In the context of this meeting of the CLSA, I would like to give particular mention to one member of the Society, Dr. Margaret Chalmers, who was instrumental in untangling some of the initial mess and weaving together these assorted threads.

Following my ordination in 2016, the Governing Council and I were able to take a more measured approach to the identification of necessary canonical and administrative foundations for each community. On May 31, 2016, we published Architects of Communion (available on our website) which has a two-fold goal. First, it provides clarity as to the structural/canonical *iter* of development: community in formation, Mission, Quasi-parish, and finally Parish. These and only these will be the canonical iterations of the parochial communities of the Ordinariate.

Secondly, the document elaborates for each of these developmental stages a series of metrics (catechetical, financial, administrative, numbers of constitutive families, location, property, etc.). This gives Pastors and their parish and finance councils the tools to plot their own growth and development according to objective plans and criteria, articulated here for the first time in a systematic way. This, I can say, the pastors have welcomed. When a community achieves certain benchmarks, the pastor is able to write a report, offer corresponding documentation, and apply to the Governing Council for the "advancement" of the community to the next canonical figure.

*Tribunal and Canonical Officers*

Article XII of the Apostolic Constitution notes that, for judicial cases, "the competent tribunal is that of the Diocese in which one of the parties is domiciled, unless the Ordinariate has constituted its own tribunal." That the Ordinariate have its own tribunal is indeed the goal, but remains an unattainable goal for at least several years to come. Given that the great majority of our priests have come into full communion from another Ecclesial Community, none will have a canonical background or training. As of yet, the Ordinariate has not been in a position to send one of our priests off for graduate studies in canon law. In addition to the personnel limitations, the financial burden of that is extremely high, especially considering that most of our clergy are married, so it is not just a matter of tuition and board for a celibate priest but the residential and income needs of a family which must be met.

For the moment, then, we rely entirely on the good graces of the local tribunals for our marriage cases. This often works very well. In other instances, our cases seem to go to the back of the line. This takes on added complexity when dealing with groups of people entering into full communion with the Catholic Church. It is not uncommon in a group of, say, 25 to 50 families that there will be 10 to 20 marriages that have issues or need to be regularized. Dealing with that in a responsible way while nurturing the movement of a parochial body into full communion *and* preserving their sense of communion/parish is not always easy.

It is an analogous situation with the appointment of a Judicial Vicar. (Anybody want a job? The pay is terrible, but the work is fun!). By necessity, we have to look outside the Ordinariate for someone to fill that role, and you might imagine that local Diocesan Bishops keep their canonist clergy rather fully engaged. I have been in dialogue with two individuals about that role, both conversations which initially looked very promising, but in both cases the individual decided against accepting the position. So we continue to look.

I do not want to overemphasize the financial component here, but that does become a tremendous hindrance particularly with staffing and personnel issues. It is worth noting that, when a Diocese is at this initial stage, resources are scarce and have to be allocated in terms of need (or perceived need). We began with no central administrative staff, and yet overnight had 42 parishes and parochial communities to look after. There is little opportunity to sit back and think systematically about a priorities list. My predecessor, Monsignor

Jeffrey Steenson, used the image of flying a plane while building it. There is simply no manual for setting up a diocese, and in terms of asking other bishops and chanceries for advice, they are certainly willing but there seems to be little institutional memory in terms of "why" institutional structures were decided upon early on.

Briefly, other issues of note would be:

- There was no provision for the existing Anglican churches which were able to be brought into full communion. One day they were an Anglican parish church, the next day Catholic Mass was being celebrated in them. I will be using the Rite of Dedication of a Church Already in Continuous Use in two of our parishes in November alone.

- When I arrived on scene, the Ordinariate had 7 canonically established Parishes. I discovered, almost by accident, that their pastors had only received 3-year terms of appointment. In addressing this, I further discovered that 6 of the pastors had never been installed in office. The one who had been installed never received a letter of appointment. There are, I learned, various interpretations of what the implications of this could be. Sanations *ad cautelam* are a useful thing.

- We continue to welcome converting Anglican clergy candidates for Holy Orders in the Catholic Church. Each of these cases of married clergy requires a canonical process with the Holy See. We've learned that the gathering of the necessary documentation is something that must be done carefully and never expeditiously or mechanically. At the same time, that documentation presumes a whole other level of engagement with the Candidate and the Candidate's spouse to ensure proper formation, adherence to ecclesiastical discipline, and the right personal disposition needed for the exercise of Sacred Orders.

- We have incardinated four priests and excardinated three with a fourth currently in process. Let me just observe that there is no agreement whatsoever among the dioceses about incardination policy or process. Each situation has been handled in a wildly different fashion. I would have thought that a 3-5 year process was the norm, and so I suppose I am surprised by the *ad hoc* nature of this. I had what I thought was an initial conversation with a bishop, only to receive a decree of excardination of the priest in question the very next week.

Conclusion

Thank you for the invitation to address the Society. I am ever conscious of the great privilege I have been given in my appointment as Bishop of the Ordinariate of the Chair of Saint Peter. The challenges and many practical details of developing structure in an early stage of ecclesial development cannot diminish the fervor of faith, hope, and charity I experience in my priests and people. I suppose much more could be said about matters of interest to canonists, but we do have some time now for questions or discussion. Again, thank you.

# Seminar

## Some Canonical and Pastoral Considerations in Causes of Canonization
### *Jeannine Marino* [1]

...So our communion with the saints joins us to Christ...It is therefore most fitting that we love these friends and coheirs of Jesus Christ, who are also our sisters and brothers and outstanding benefactors, that we give due thanks to God for them, "that we invoke them and that we have recourse to their prayers and helpful assistance to obtain blessings from God through His Son our lord Jesus Christ, who is our Redeemer and Saviour."[2]

Chapter VII of *Lumen gentium* addresses the eschatological nature of the Church: the saving love of Christ, sin and the role of grace in redemption, the Church as the mystical body of Christ, and end times. Yet, mixed in with these weighty doctrinal truths, the Council Fathers teach us about the saints. The saints are our companions, our friends in Christ, whom we love and who love us. We call upon them to help us with our daily struggles, to protect us and guide us as we seek to follow Christ. The saints have gone before us and show us the "safest way by which, through the world's changing patterns...we will be able to attain perfect union with Christ and holiness."[3] Chances are if the average person in the pew was asked to describe the eschatological nature of the Church, even if they knew what eschatological means, they probably would not use the language found in Chapter VII of *Lumen gentium.* But ask any Catholic to name their favorite saint and how that saint has helped, and you will surely hear the

---
1   Assistant Director Evangelization and Catechesis, United States Conference of Catholic Bishops. The thoughts expressed in this article are those of the author alone and are not intended necessarily to represent any official position of the United States Conference of Catholic Bishops.
2   Vatican Council II, *Lumen gentium* 50, November 21, 1964: *AAS* 57 (1965) 56. English translation from *Decrees of the Ecumenical Councils*, ed. Norman P. Tanner (London & Washington: Sheed & Ward and Georgetown University Press, 1990) 890. All subsequent English translations of Vatican II documents are taken from this source unless otherwise indicated.
3   *LG* 50.

same experience that *Lumen gentium* uses to describe the saints. How often do we hear parishioners describe St. Theresa of Lisieux as showing them the way forward little by little, or how St. Michael the Archangel always protects them from harm, and how even fallen away Catholics attest to the constant assistance of St. Jude. The Council Fathers understood the evangelizing power of the saints who capture our imaginations and hearts, showing us the way to holiness through Christ.

The Council Fathers also understood the abuses that creep into the Church's devotion, and urged that these abuses and defects be removed or corrected so that the faithful are instructed in the authentic cult of the saints.[4] One of the post-Councilor responses to curbing abuses and increasing devotion to the saints was the reform of the canonization process itself. The revised norms for canonization sought to simplify the canonization process, and return greater autonomy and authority to the local diocesan bishop in opening and investigating a cause of canonization. As a result, the canonization process now consists of three phases: the diocesan phase, the Roman phase and the judgement of the cause.

The focus of this article will be the diocesan phase of causes of canonization. Since most canonists who work on causes of canonization are involved in the diocesan phase, a properly and carefully instructed diocesan phase is of the upmost concern. Because the Roman phase relies on the evidence, documents and witness testimony, collected in the diocesan phase, a cause of canonization is only successful if the diocesan phase is properly and carefully instructed. In other words, a successful Roman phase and a positive judgement on the sanctity of a person by the Supreme Pontiff builds upon the diocesan phase. To help facilitate the diocesan phase, this article is divided into four parts: Part I: The Current Norms and Their Juridic Nature; Part II: What is Canonizable Holiness and the Object of a Cause; Part III: The Grounds for Canonization and Part IV: Practical Questions When Instructing the Diocesan Phase.

Given the scope of this article, there are some issues that will not be examined such as the history of canonization and the historical development of the current norms. Nor will the theology of sanctity and the liturgical aspects of canonization be examined. Finally, this article will not provide a step by step guide of the diocesan phase or go into detail about the Roman Phase and the role of miracles.[5]

Before getting into the substance of this article, it is important to note that there are two presumptions in the canonization process which are not found in

---

4   *LG* 51.
5   For information about these aspects of the canonization process please see: William H. Woestman, O.M.I., ed., *Canonization: Theology, History, Process,* Second Edition (Ottawa, Canada: Saint Paul University, 2014), and Congregazione delle Cause dei Santi, *Le Cause dei Santi* (Vatican City: Libreria Editrice Vaticana, 2012).

the norms. The first presumption is simply an acknowledgement that there is a tension in the norms. The norms are an attempt to reconcile modern theological and historical methods with the juridic structure of canon law. The attempt to balance theology and canon law is not new. For example, in dealing with penal cases, canonists are asked to strike a balance between justice for the victim and mercy for the perpetrator. When the victim of clergy sex abuse wants the cleric dismissed from the cleric state, but the priest is well into his retirement years and living in a hospice facility, can a life of prayer and penance be an acceptable comprise between justice and mercy? A cause of canonization also seeks to balance these tensions. Can we ever truly know the state of one's soul even with modern historical critical methods to investigate a person's life, and the incredible about of information now available through the internet? How do we balance the juridic requirements of documentary proofs and witness testimony with today's modern world? A cause of canonization requires a careful balance between modern day theological and historical research and juridic precision. This article will highlight some of these tensions.

A second presumption is the Latin maxim: *Quod non est in scriptis aut in actis, non est in mundo. If it is not written in the acts, it doesn't exist!* Everything must be written in the acts. If the norms state that a notary must be appointed, that appointment has to be a written decree that is inserted into the acts. If a person who knew the servant of God has great stories about the Servant of God, their testimony has to be heard, transcribed according the norms for witness testimony in Book VII (cc. 1526-1586) and inserted into the acts. If testimony is not in the acts, the Congregation will not consider it as evidence. Worse still, if the norms require a written decree and the decree is missing from the acts, the Congregation may judge the *acta* juridically invalid. If a decree is missing because of a simple oversight, the Congregation may allow the decree to be submitted after the fact. However, it is a serious matter if decrees are missing because the required acts did not occur.

**Part I: The Current Norms and Their Juridic Nature**

The current norms governing causes of canonization are found in extra-codal texts as well as the norms in the Code of Canon Law and the Code of Canons for the Eastern Churches. Each of the Codes contain one canon on canonization (CIC c. 1403 and CCEO c. 1057). Canon 1403 states that special pontifical law governs causes of canonization, and that the prescripts of the Code "apply to these causes whenever the special pontifical law refers to the universal law or norms are involved which also affect these cases by the very nature of the matter." The extra codal texts in order of promulgation are:

(1) *Divinus Perfectionis Magister,* promulgated by Pope John Paul II on January 25, 1983[6];

(2) *Normae Servandae in Inquisitionibus ab Episcopis Faciendis in Causis Sanctorum* (*Norms to be Observed in Inquiries Made by Bishops in the Causes of Saints*) issued by the Congregation for the Causes of Saints on February 7, 1983[7];

(3) *Sanctorum Mater* (*Instruction for Conducting Diocesan or Eparchial Inquiries in the Causes of Saints*) issued by the Congregation for the Causes of Saints on May 17, 2007[8];

(4) *Rescriptum ex Audientia Sanctissimi: Norme Sull'Amministrazione dei Bene delle Cause di Beatificazione e Canonizzazione* (*Rescript on the Norms for the Administration of the Temporal Goods for Causes of Beatification and Canonization*), promulgated by Pope Francis on March 11, 2016[9];

(5) *'Maiorem hac Dilectionem'. De Oblatione Vitae* (*Greater Love Than This. On the Offering of Life*) issued *motu proprio* by Pope Francis on July 12, 2017.[10]

The majority of this article will focus on the documents *Divinus Perfectionis Magister*, *Normae Servandae*, The *Rescriptum* and *Maiorem hac Dilectionem*,

---

6   John Paul II, apostolic constitution *Divinus Perfectionis Magister,* January 25, 1983: *AAS* 75/1 (1983) 349-355. English translation from Woestman. All subsequent English translations of *Divinus Perfectionis Magister* are taken from this source unless otherwise indicated.
7   Sacred Congregation for the Causes of Saints, *Normae Servandae in Inquisitionibus ab Episcopis Faciendis in Causis Sanctorum,* February 7, 1983: *AAS* 75/1 (1983) 396-403. English translation from Woestman. All subsequent English translations are taken from this source unless otherwise indicated. Abbreviated as *Normae Servandae.*
8   Congregation for the Causes of Saints, *Sanctorum Mater*, May 17, 2007: *AAS* 99 (2007) 465-510. English translation from Woestman.
9   *Rescriptum ex Audientia Sanctissimi: Norme Sull'Amministrazione dei Bene delle Cause di Beatificazione e Canonizzazione, L'Osservatore Romano,* 11 March 2016. The English translation can be found: *L'Osservatore Romano,* Weekly Edition in English, Friday 18 March 2016, and the online edition of *L'Osservatore Romano* has them published here: http://www.osservatoreromano.va/en/news/causes-saints-are-public-good-eng. Abbreviated as *Rescriptum.*
10  *'Maiorem hac Dilectionem' De Oblatione Vitae, L'Osservatore Romano,* 12 July 2017. The English translation can be found: *L'Osservatore Romano,* Weekly Edition in English, Friday 14 July 2017, and *Maiorem* can be found published online here: https://w2.vatican.va/content/francesco/la/motu_proprio/documents/papa-francesco-motu-proprio_20170711_maiorem-hac-dilectionem.html. Abbreviated as *Maiorem hac Dilectionem* or *Maiorem.*

since these documents contain the norms for causes of canonization. *Sanctorum Mater* will be discussed when it offers guidance on the above-mentioned norms.[11]

### *Divinus Perfectionis Magister*

*Divinus Perfectionis Magister* took effect immediately upon promulgation by John Paul II on January 25, 1983, thereby abrogating all previous legislation on causes of canonization.[12] Given that the purpose of *Divinus Perfectionis Magister* is to lay out the entire procedural process for causes of canonization, it is an extremely brief document – only six pages – with little practical guidance. To be fair, *Divinus Perfectionis Magister* does state that further norms detailing and explaining its provisions will follow. The introduction of *Divinus Perfectionis Magister* is a theological treatise on sanctity, the importance of saints in the Church, and a concise history of the canonical process of canonizations. The three other sections in *Divinus Perfectionis Magister* are: Inquiries to Be Made by Bishops, The Sacred Congregation for the Causes of Saints, and Procedure in the Sacred Congregation.

### *Normae Servandae in Inquisitionibus ab Episcopis Faciendis in Causis*

The further norms eluded to in *Divinus Perfectionis Magister* were issued less than a month after *Divinus Perfectionis Magister* and are found in *Normae Servandae*. Issued, on February 7, 1983 by the then Sacred Congregation for Causes of Saints, with John Paul II's approval, the *Normae Servandae* contain thirty-six norms governing the diocesan phase. The norms contained in *Normae Servandae* took effect on the day they were issued.[13] Totaling just seven pages, the *Normae Servandae* expanded on and clarified the provisions of *Divinus Perfectionis Magister*, focusing only on the diocesan phase of the process (there are no additional norms on the Roman phase, or the study and judgment of the case). While there are no formal section titles in *Normae Servandae*, an effective division of the norms could be: a) Initial Phase of the Inquiry (nn.

---

11 There are additional texts that contain norms or clarify existing norms, but these texts will not be examined here since they are concerned with liturgical aspects, miracles, or the Roman phase of the canonization process. These texts have been compiled in the Woestman book including: Decree on the Participation of the Postulator/Vice Postulator at the Sessions of the Diocesan Inquiry, Decree on the Knowledge of the Questionnaires Prior to the Diocesan Inquiry, Instruction for the Transfer of the Body of the Servant of God. Additionally, the Procedures for the Rite of Beatification, the *Regolomento* for the Medical Board, and Istruzione su "Le Reliquie nella Chiesa: Autenticità e Conservazione" issued by the Congregation for the Causes of Saints can be found here: http://www.causesanti.va/content/causadeisanti/it/documenti.html.

12 All previous legislation, including the norms of the 1917 Code and subsequent papal norms previously cited were abrogated except for the Decrees of Urban VIII. The Decrees of Urban VIII are explicitly mentioned in *DPM* 6 as still in force and will be examined below.

13 *NS*, concluding paragraph.

1-12); b) Gathering of Documentary Proofs (nn. 13-14); c) Gathering of Witness Testimony (nn.15-26); and d) Final or Closing Phase of the Inquiry (nn. 27-31 and 36).[14]

### *Sanctorum Mater*

Twenty-five years after promulgating the revised norms of *Divinus Perfectionis Magister* and the *Normae Servandae*, the Congregation for the Causes of Saints issued the instruction *Sanctorum Mater* on May 17, 2007. At just over 50 pages, *Sanctorum Mater* is nearly quadruple the length of *Divinus Perfectionis Magister* and the *Normae Servandae* combined. The introduction of *Sanctorum Mater* states that it is an instruction as understood in canon 34 of the 1983 Code. As an instruction, *Santorum Mater* is meant to clarify the already promulgated law in *Divinus Perfectionis Magister* and *Normae Servandae* and determine the methods to be used to fulfill the law. Instructions are directed to those who are obliged to fulfill the law and, as such, are not new norms, nor do they derogate from existing law.

*Santorum Mater* begins by indicating that its purpose is to "facilitate a closer collaboration in the causes of Saints between the Holy See and the Bishops."[15] It continues, stating that the intention of the document is to "clarify the dispositions of currently existing laws in the causes of Saints, to facilitate their application and indicate the ways of executing them both in recent and in ancient causes. Thus, it is directed to diocesan bishops, to eparchs[16], to those who are equivalent to them in law, and to those who participate in the instruction phase of the Inquiries."[17] Since this instruction is concerned with the diocesan phase alone, it does not contain any clarifications on the Roman phase and, in addition to the Bishop, is meant for petitioners, postulators, promoters of justice, episcopal delegates, notaries, censors and others with a canonical mandate, office or function in a cause of canonization. Besides the Introduction *Santorum Mater* is divided into six parts, plus an appendix: 1) Causes of Beatification and Canonization, 2) Preliminary Phase of the Cause, 3) Instruction of the Cause, 4) Gathering of Documentary Proofs, 5) Gathering of Proofs from Witnesses and 6) Closing of the Inquiry.

The fact that *Sanctorum Mater* is almost four times the length of *Divinus Perfectionis Magister* and the *Normae Servandae* combined indicates that over

---

14   *Normae Servandae* paragraph numbers 32-35 contain norms dealing with the inquiry to be conducted into alleged miracles, which is to be done separately from the diocesan inquiry into virtues/martyrdom. Paragraph 36 prohibits solemn celebrations and panegyric speeches about a Servant of God whose sanctity is being examined.
15   *SM*, Introduction.
16   To avoid repetition from this point forward when the text refers to bishops, it is also referring to eparchs unless otherwise noted.
17   *SM*, Introduction.

the past twenty-five years since the issuing of the first two documents, concerns, issues and questionable practices had arisen that the Congregation hoped to address through the instruction. We will look at some of these questions shortly. *Sanctorum Mater* is a very useful instruction as it provides a step-by-step guide on how to instruct the diocesan phase of a cause of canonization.

### *Rescriptum ex Audientia Sanctissimi: Norme Sull'Amministrazione dei Bene delle Cause di Beatificazione e Canonizzazione*

On March 7, 2016, *Rescriptum ex Audientia Sanctissimi: Norme sull'Amministrazione dei Bene delle Cause di Beatificazione e Canonizzazione* was approved by Pope Francis governing the administration of the temporal goods for causes of canonization. The *Rescriptum* states that these norms are now in force *ad experimentum* for three years. Even though this document is titled *Rescriptum,* and according to canon 59 of the 1983 Code a rescript is an administrative act that grants a privilege, dispensation or other favor, this rescript is normative because it was approved by the Supreme Pontiff.[18] It is therefore obligatory. The *Rescriptum* governs the administration of temporal goods in both the diocesan and Roman phases of causes of canonization.

*Rescriptum ex Audientia Sanctissimi* begins by reminding the parties associated with causes of canonization that the canonical process is complex requiring not only meticulous work but also expenses. It also notes that expenses are incurred during the diocesan phase and the Roman phase and that, even though the Apostolic See covers all expenses related to the Roman phase of a cause, the petitioner is to assist the Apostolic See through a contribution. Additional fees and expenditures are to be carefully overseen so as not to impede the cause. The *Rescriptum* has four additional sections, which outline a new official of the inquiry, the administrator, as well as the duties of the administrator, the oversight of the temporal goods, and the contributions made to the Apostolic See and the solidarity fund. It should be noted that the administrator oversees the funds of a cause. This norm of the *Rescriptum* abrogates *Normae Servandae* 3c which had granted the postulator the duty to oversee the temporal goods of the cause.[19]

---

18   Prior to the 1983 Code rescripts had a broader canonical understanding and were understood as documents containing juridical decisions and norms. For a commentary on the development of rescripts please see, Javier Canosa, "Commentary on Canon 59," *Exegetical Commentary on the Code of Canon Law*, English language edition ed. Ernest Caparros et al. (Chicago and Montréal: Midwest Theological Forum and Wilson & Lafleur, 2004) 1: 588-569.

19   The one exception to the norm of the *Rescriptum* requiring the appointment of an administrator separate from the postulator, is the postulator general. If a religious order has a postulator general, then the postulator general is permitted to oversee the temporal goods of a cause.

*Maiorem hac Dilectionem. De Oblatione Vitae*

On July 12, 2017, Pope Francis issued *motu proprio* the *Apostolic Letter 'Maiorem hac Dilectionem' de Oblatione Vitae*. *Maiorem* has 6 articles and is only 4 pages long, yet it is probably the most significant development to the canonical process of canonizations since the codification of the canonization process in the 1917 Code. Articles 5 and 6 in *Maiorem* simply modified certain paragraphs in *Divinus Perfectionis Magister* and *Normae Servandae* to include the new language concerning the "offering of life" – the new path for canonization. Please note *Maiorem* did not amend *Sanctorum Mater* to include the new language of the offering of life. I believe this is because *Sanctorum Mater* is not a legislative text while *Maiorem*, as a legislative text, is concerned with amending the legislative norms in *Divinus Perfectionis Magister* and *Normae Servandae*. Going forward though, when using *Sanctorum Mater*, the path of "offering of life" should be remembered while reading its instructions. Articles 1-4 of *Maiorem* are the new norms which clearly state there is a new ground for causes of canonization; which is the offering of one's life. This new ground is distinct from the grounds of martyrdom and virtue. We will discuss this new ground, what the 'offering of one's life' could look like and how to proceed using this ground.

**The Canonization Process**

Before we start looking in detail at the diocesan phase, it is helpful to briefly consider the nature of the canonization process. Here is an example of how internal tension can be seen within the current norms. We can say confidently that a cause of canonization is a canonical process, but is it a judicial process or is it an administrative procedure? Or perhaps is it a hybrid — one that combines elements of judicial processes with administrative procedures. Given that Gratian, Benedict XIV, Cardinal Gasparri and the numerous Prefects of the Congregation for the Causes of Saints have been reluctant to answer this question definitively, I am not going to try and answer this question here. I am raising it, however, because even though a cause of canonization uses a very clear canonical structure to instruct the cause, there are still aspects of a cause that are discretionary. For example, it is the right of the bishop to open a cause. He does not have to open a cause, nor does anyone have the right to be named a saint. Furthermore, the bishop has to discern if opening a particular cause truly benefits the Church, ultimately asking if declaring this person a saint would help lead others to Christ? However, once the bishop has decided to move forward with a cause and open it, the cause must follow the strict procedural norms, including how to appoint officials, how to collect and evaluate documentary proofs and how to interview witnesses. When *Divinus Perfectionis Magister* and *Normae Servandae* state that the bishop is to instruct the diocesan phase, 'instruct' does not mean "let's study this issue and see what happens." Instruction means receiving a *libellus*, accepting the *libellus*, appointing officials, collecting proofs and closing the inquiry according to the procedural norms of Book VII. I am pointing out this question of whether or not a cause of canonization is a judicial process, an administrative procedure, or a hybrid because one of the challenges dioceses face when conducting a cause of canonization is understanding which norms are required for validity and which processes are merely helpful to follow. Furthermore, petitioners not familiar with canon law will question why the bishop is doing all this "extra" stuff, when they have already "investigated" the Servant of God's life and they know he or she is saint. The "extra" stuff of a cause of canonization ensures that the holiness of the Servant of God is proven in the external forum. Once the Servant of God's holiness is proven public veneration is granted, thus recognizing that the Servant of God is worthy of imitation. Regardless of whether the canonization process is a judicial processes or administrative procedure, it is a juridic process and, therefore, in order to 'successfully' complete a cause, diocesan personnel must follow the norms of canon law and help non-canonists involved with the cause understand that there is a process that must be followed.

**PART II: What is Canonizable Holiness and the Object of a Cause**

Before a diocese begins a cause of canonization, it is necessary to understand the difference between 'canonizable' holiness and the universal call to holiness. As Vatican II taught us in *Lumen gentium* Chapter V, every one of us is called to holiness – we are all called to be saints. We are all called to live lives imbued with the Christian virtues and to follow Christ in the hopes that when we die we will be reborn into eternal life with God in heaven. What then is the difference between universal holiness and 'canonizable' holiness? Canonizable holiness is found in the lives of those among the Christian Faithful who have lived out the universal call to holiness in a profoundly public way. A profoundly public witness can take the form of martyrdom, heroic virtues or an offering of life. Canonizable holiness describes those Christian witnesses who in life and death imitated more closely Christ. Canonizable holiness provides the Christian Faithful with a witness of how to imitate Christ more closely on earth by martyrdom, living out the Christian virtues or the offering of one's life. There needs to be something in the lives of these men and women, in their death and after their death that the Christian Faithful can relate to, something that makes the Christian faithful want to imitate them, and something that makes the Faithful want to pray for their intercession. And there must be something about their holiness that can help lead all the members of the Church towards holiness.

We all know brothers and sisters in our faith who have personally touched and inspired us to strive for holiness. But these personal witnesses are not always worthy of 'canonizable' holiness. While I believe my grandfather is in heaven, and I am sure you believe the same of your grandparents, that does not mean they are 'canonizable.' Practically, when a bishop is considering opening a cause, the bishop should reflect on the question: Does this person have 'canonizable' holiness? What is it about this person's particular witness to the Christian faith, and particular historical circumstances that will inspire others both in today's and even tomorrow's society to live a holy life? Answering these questions is a process of discernment. Is the reputation of martyrdom, virtues or the offering of life the work of the Holy Spirit calling the Christian Faithful to imitate more closely Christ? If these questions can be answered, one has the basis of a cause. Connected to the concept of canonizable holiness, is the object of a cause.

**Object of a Cause**

The object of a cause would probably come as a surprise to many of the Christian Faithful. When asked, most members of the faithful would probably say the point of a cause of canonization is to canonize the person! But this is not the object of a cause! *Sanctorum Mater* 1.2 clearly defines the object of a canonization process. It is "the gathering of the proofs in order to attain moral certitude on the heroic virtues or the martyrdom of the Servant of God whose beatification and canonization are asked."[20] Now, of course, with Pope Francis' *Maiorem*, we have to add to this sentence of *Sanctorum Mater* the category an "offering of life." The object of a cause, therefore, is not canonization, but having moral certitude regarding the truth about whether a Servant of God was martyred for the faith, led a heroically virtuous life, or offered their life. It may be that a cause of canonization is begun and, in the course of investigating the person's life, death and reputation for intercessory power, the decision is made to halt the cause. Sometimes the decision to halt a cause is due to information gathered during the investigation that has revealed an obstacle to the cause that cannot, at the present time, be removed.

A curious example of halting a cause is the cause of canonization of Fr. Léon Dehon (1843-1925). Fr. Dehon was scheduled to beatified by John Paul II on April 24, 2005. The decree declaring Fr. Dehon's heroically virtuous life was promulgated on April 8, 1997,[21] and the decree declaring a miracle was promulgated on April 19, 2004.[22] However, his beatification was initially postponed due to the illness and subsequent death of John Paul II. Before a new date for the beatification was scheduled, Pope Benedict XVI appointed a special commission at the Secretariat of State to reexamine the writings of Fr. Dehon due to concerns raised by the French episcopacy of newly discovered writings by Fr.

---

20  *SM* 1.2.
21  *Decretum Super Virtutibus Servi Dei Leonis Ioannis a S. Corde,* April 8, 1997: *AAS* 89 (1997) 842-847.
22  *Decretum Super Miraculo Servi Dei Ioannis a S. Corde,* April 19, 2004: *AAS* 97 (2005) 76-78.

Dehon that contained anti-Semitic statements. To date, Fr. Dehon's beatification has not been rescheduled.[23]

This example is illustrative of the principle that *Sanctorum Mater* is trying to make. As noted, the object of a cause of canonization is not canonization but the moral certitude about the person's life, death and reputation for holiness. Sometimes a cause of canonization will result in the beatification and canonization of the Servant of God, and sometimes a cause will result in the moral certainty that a person does not have canonizable holiness. In practice, this concept can be seen when witnesses are called during the diocesan investigation. Well-meaning witnesses will say things like, "I don't want to speak ill of the dead," or "the point of me giving testimony is to prove Father is a saint right, you don't want to hear about the time he cursed out the driver who cut him off do you?" The demands on bishops to rush causes because preliminary materials have been collected and the pressuring by a vocal group must be resisted. Conversely, it should not take 25 years to conduct the diocesan phase, but the bishop and his diocesan canonists should be realistic and frank with the petitioners and faithful. The Christian Faithful should be told in clear language that a cause of canonization is a lengthy process without a guaranteed outcome of sainthood because the purpose is to reach moral certitude about the person's life, death and reputation for holiness.

**PART III: The Grounds for Canonization**

Once the questions surrounding 'canonizable' holiness and the object of a cause have been addressed, the grounds for the cause should be determined. There are currently three grounds for causes of canonization: martyrdom, heroic virtue or the offering of life. There is an argument that there are four grounds: martyrdom, heroic virtue, *equivalent beatification* and the offering of life. The assertion that there are four grounds deserves careful study. Equivalent beatification has existed since the Middle Ages and has traditionally been understood as a derogation from the normal procedural law governing causes of canonization. While equivalent beatification is a derogation from the norm of law, the beatification of an Ancient Blessed is still based on the theological ground of either martyrdom or heroic virtue.[24]

Equivalent beatification is concerned with the Decrees of Urban VIII. Very briefly, Urban VIII's decrees were concerned with two pastoral concerns during

---

23 For more information on the cause of Fr. Dehon please see: "La Béatification du P. Dehon bloquée." La Croix, September 6, 2005. http://www.la-croix.com/Religion/Actualite/La-beatification-du-P.-Dehon-bloquee-_NG_-2005-06-10-509209 (accessed February 10, 2017).
24 Since the equivalent beatification procedure was developed in the Middle Ages, the causes of Ancient Blesseds have proceeded on the theological basis of either martyrdom or heroic virtue. This however, does not rule out the hypothetical possibility of an Ancient Blessed's cause proceeding on the new theological ground of offering of life.

the 17th Century: 1) stopping abuses in the veneration of Servants of God who died with a reputation of holiness, but who were not yet beatified or canonized by the Apostolic See, and 2) reorganizing and updating the process of canonizations. In a series of decrees culminating in the brief *Caelestis Hieruslame Cives* on July 5, 1634, Urban VIII declared that every canonization must follow the ordinary process unless a Servant of God already possessed an illegitimate cult from time immemorial and that this cult could not be eliminated. Time immemorial is understood as 100 years before 1634 when Urban VII issued his final decree. Therefore, causes that wish to proceed using equivalent beatification must prove that the Servant of God enjoyed an illegitimate cult for at least 100 years prior to 1534. When proceeding with a cause using equivalent beatification, the basis of the beatification is still either the martyrdom or heroic virtue of the person in question.

Equivalent beatification has been used by several popes in the 20th and 21st Centuries, including our two most recent popes, Benedict XVI,[25] and Francis.[26] In the US Church, however, it is difficult to think of a cause of canonization that would fit the strict, traditional criteria of an equivalent beatification. Given that even the earliest missionaries did not arrive on the mainland of the US until around 1500, the 100-year time immemorial limit is not possible for US causes.

The majority of causes, therefore, will proceed using the normal canonical procedure based on one of the three grounds that are stated in *Divinus Perfectionis Magister* 1, *Normae Servandae* 7, *and Maiorem hac Dilectionem* 1-4.[27] *Sanctorum Mater* 4.1 explains in greater detail the grounds for martyrdom and heroic virtue:

A cause of canonization is an inquiry into:

---

[25] Benedict XVI used equivalent canonization in 2012 to canonize St. Hildegard of Bingen. Benedict XVI, *Litterae Decretals De Peracta Canonizatione Aequipollente Hildegardis Bingensis,* 10 May 2012: *AAS* 104 (2012) 863-867.

[26] Francis has used equivalent canonization for several saints including: Peter Faber, see Francis, *Litterae Decretales de peracta Canonizatione aequipollenti beati, Petri Favre, S.I.,* 17 Dec. 2013: *AAS* 106 (2014) 607-611, and Marie of the Incarnation (also known as Marie Guyart), see Francis, *Litterae Decretales de peracta Canonizatione aequipollenti beatae Mariae ab Incarnatione,* 13 April 2014: *AAS* 107 (2015) 119-121. Additionally, listed on the Congregation's website (http://www.causesanti.va/content/causadeisanti/it/santi/santi-proclamati-da-francesco.html) as an equivalent canonization by Francis are Angela da Foligno on October 9, 2013, Jose de Anchieta on April 3, 2014, and Bishop Francois de Montmorency-Laval on April 3, 2014. The homily for the canonization of Marie Guyart and Francois de Montomorency-Laval discusses their equivalent canonization and can be found here: Francis, *Homiliae Occasione aequipollentis Canonizationis beatorum Canadensium Francisei de Laval et Mariae ab Incarnatione Guyart Martin,* 12 Oct. 2014: *AAS* 106 (2014) 821-823.

[27] *DPM* 1, NS 7, and *MHD* 1-4.

a Catholic who in life, in death, and after death has enjoyed a reputation of holiness (*fama sanctitatis*) by living all the Christian virtues in an heroic manner; or enjoys a reputation of martyrdom (*fama martyrii*) because, having followed Christ more closely, he has sacrificed his life in the act of martyrdom.[28]

## Martyrdom

The second paragraph of Article 5 in *Sanctorum Mater* states: "The reputation of martyrdom is the opinion that has spread among the faithful about the death endured by the Servant of God for the Faith or for a virtue connected to the Faith."[29] The inquiry into a Servant of God's martyrdom must prove that he or she voluntarily accepted or tolerated death and that his or death was motivated by *in odium fidei*.[30] *Odium fidei* is either hatred of the Catholic faith or hatred of a virtue of the Catholic faith. Martyrdom can be direct (i.e., by shooting, or beheading), or indirect (i.e., as the result of torture), but it must result from or be caused by the Servant of God's Catholic faith in Jesus Christ or the practice of one of the Christian virtues. In short, if you are going to proceed with a cause using this ground, you must prove that the Servant of God was killed because their killer hated the faith.

For example, our first American martyr, Blessed Stanley Rother, was killed during the Guatemalan Civil War. During the Guatemalan Civil War, which lasted over 30 years, the military government and leftist rebels battled over numerous issues including land rights, the rights of indigenous peoples, and the redistribution of wealth. At various points during the war, Church ministers were systematically targeted for torture and murder because the Church and her ministers opposed the often-brutal treatment of the indigenous and impoverished committed by both the government and the rebels. Blessed Rother was killed because he refused to stop ministering to the indigenous people of Santiago Atitlan, and he lived a simple life alongside the people. Fr. Rother helped them farm the land, established irrigation systems and rebuilt houses- all in an effort to make people's lives better and protect their way of life from government and rebel forces seeking to seize their land. His presence was a witness to the faith and a threat to the warring parties. In his homily at Fr. Rother's beatification, Cardinal Angelo Amato said, "From 1971 until 1981, numerous killings of journalists, farmers, catechists, and priests, all falsely accused of communism, took place in Guatemala. This was a real and true time of bloody persecution for the Church. In this situation, Father Rother, aware of the imminent danger

---

28   *SM* 4 §1.
29   *SM* 5 § 2. See also Benedictus XIV, Ponti. Opt. Max., *De Servorum Dei Beatificatione at Beatorum Canonizatione*, in Opera (*Romae: Academiae Liturgicae Conimbricensis Typographi*, 1747) Vol. 1-4, *De Servorum,* II, 39, 7.
30   See also *De Servorum*, III, 11, 1 and III, 13, 1.

to his life, prepared himself for martyrdom, asking the Lord for the strength to face it without fear. He continued, however, to preach the Gospel of love and nonviolence."[31]

When the Archdiocese of Oklahoma City was instructing the diocesan phase, they needed to collect evidence demonstrating that Blessed Rother was not simply killed because he was in the wrong place at the wrong time during a war. The Archdiocese had to prove that Fr. Rother was sought out by the anti-Catholic death squads and killed because he was a priest proclaiming the Gospel and working to better the lives of those he served. To help prove his martyrdom, the historical commission's report contained information about the Guatemalan Civil War and how Catholic ministers were targeted during the war.

**Heroic Virtue**

The Congregation's understanding of heroic virtues found in *Sanctorum Mater* Article 5 is based on the commentary by Benedict XIV: "The reputation of holiness is the opinion that has spread among the faithful about the purity and integrity of life of the Servant of God and about the virtues practiced by him to an heroic degree."[32] The virtues to which the norms and Congregation reference are the theological virtues[33] (faith, hope and charity) as well as the cardinal virtues[34] (prudence, temperance, fortitude, and justice). Although the practice of these virtues is what is demanded of every Christian through one's baptism and life in Christ, in causes of canonization the Church is examining the heroic or unfailing and constant exercise of all these virtues in life's ordinary and extraordinary circumstances. Practically speaking, the practice of heroic virtues does not mean that the Servant of God was perfect. Rather, the Servant of God, through concrete actions day in and day out, did what was expected of them given the Servant of God's state in life. Furthermore, the Servant of God performed those day to day tasks motivated by faith, hope and charity rooted in Christ.[35] The evidence collected in the diocesan phase in the writings of and about the Servant of God, and witness testimony should demonstrate that over time, by practicing the Christian virtues, the Servant of God grew closer to Christ and followed him more closely.

31   Catholic News Agency, "Faithful martyr and missionary Father Stanley Rother beatified in Oklahoma" Published September 23, 2017, Oklahoma City, OK. Accessible: https://www.catholicnewsagency.com/news/faithful-martyr-and-missionary-father-stanley-rother-beatified-in-oklahoma-13669.
32   *SM* 5 § 1. See also *De Servorum* II, 39, 7 and III, 22, 1.
33   John Paul II, *Catechism of the Catholic Church,* 2nd Edition (Libreria Editrice Vaticana, 1994) nos.1812-1829.
34   *CCC* nos.1805-1809.
35   See *Decretum Beatificationis et Canonizationis Venerabilis Servi Dei Ioannis Baptistae Baptistae a Burgundia,* January 5, 1916: *AAS* 8 (1916) 13, and *Decretum Beatificationis et Canonizationis Venerabilis Servi Dei Ioannis Nepomuceni Neumann,* December 3, 1921: *AAS* 14 (1922) 23.

It would be beneficial if there were documentary proofs and witness testimony that can paint a portrait of the Servant of God's entire life. However, the critical years for proving heroic virtues are the last five to ten years of the Servant of God's life. There may be cases, like Mother Lange the founder of the Oblate Sisters of Providence, where very little information is known about a person's early life. That is okay, you can still proceed with the cause and prove heroic virtue. This is possible because holiness is a gradual process that occurs through the constant and consistent practice of the virtues. Even though little is known about Mother Lange's early years, once she arrived in the US and settled in Baltimore there are records about her life and her service to the poor, specifically freed slaves and people of Haitian descent. Once she founded the Oblate Sisters and became the Order's superior, records and testimonials were kept in the Order's archives. These documentary proofs can be used to demonstrate that over time, Mother Lange grew in holiness.

**Offering of Life**

The newest ground for canonization is the "offering of life." Since this ground is so new, there is no jurisprudence or history to help illuminate what this looks like. Rather, canonists must focus on the words of the *motu proprio* to better understand this ground. Pope Francis writes:

> Worthy of special consideration and honour are those Christians who, following more than closely the footsteps and teachings of the Lord Jesus, have voluntarily and freely offered their life for others and persevered with this determination unto death. Certainly the heroic offering of life, inspired and sustained by charity, expresses a true, complete and exemplary imitation of Christ...[36]

Two things are clear from *Maiorem hac Dilectionem*: first, this new ground is distinct from the grounds of martyrdom and heroic virtues, and second, that causes using this ground follow the same canonization procedure. *Maiorem hac Dilectionem* also provides five criteria that must be proved for this ground to be applicable. The Servant of God must have 1) freely and voluntarily offered his or her life and accepted a certain and untimely death, 2) there must be a nexus between the offer of life and the Servant of God's premature death, 3) the Servant of God exercised, at least in an ordinary manner if not in an extraordinary way, the Christian virtues before they offered their life, 4) there is a reputation of holiness and of signs of this after their death, and 5) a miracle is needed for beatification which occurs after the Servant of God's death through his or her intercession.

---

36  *MHD,* Introduction.

Given how new this ground is, the following remarks are going to be theoretical rather than based on proven jurisprudence. It appears that this ground is an attempt to address the very real pastoral problem of those Servants of God who died while exercising one of the Christian virtues, but who was not killed in *odium fidei*. Given how little we know about this new ground, I think the best way to examine it is through an example. Servant of God Fr. Patrick Ryan, of the Diocese of Knoxville, died at age 33 while administrating last rites to those struck with yellow fever during the 1878 epidemic. Fr. Ryan was your average parish priest, doing what priests are called to do every day – celebrate mass, administer the sacraments, teach catechism. By most accounts, Fr. Ryan was a rather ordinary priest. And yet when yellow fever swept through Chattanooga, knowing that he would more than likely contract the disease, he willingly left the safety of his rectory to minister to the sick. He offered them the last rites, and visited grieving families. Within days, he had contracted yellow fever and died. *The Chattanooga Times*, when his body was reinterned from a small parish cemetery to a more prominent cemetery in Chattanooga, wrote, "The brave and faithful priest literally laid down his life in the cause of humanity. Only the morning before he was stricken with the deadly pestilence, the writer met him on his rounds of mercy in the worst infected section of the city. Cheerfully but resolutely he was going from house to house to find what he could do for the sick and needy."[37] Fr. Ryan's cause might be one that could proceed using this ground. Dioceses considering this ground should be mindful, that the diocesan investigation will need to somehow prove that the Servant of God exercised the Christian virtues in an ordinary way, and that the Servant of God met an untimely death because he or she willing gave up his or her life for others. This new ground has the potential to address the real pastoral problem of ordinary Christians who chose the extraordinary path of accepting death so that others might live. It will be interesting to see how the jurisprudence of this ground develops and how the Congregation distinguishes between the ordinary vs. extraordinary exercise of virtues.[38]

Practically speaking, regardless of which ground a cause proceeds with, the diocesan inquiry should be prepared to demonstrate the unique cultural, historical and political landscape during the time when the Servant of God lived. The historical commission's required report is where the unique cultural, historical and political landscape can be described. For example, in Mother Lange's cause, it was important to show Mother Lange not only founded an order of sisters, but that she did this as an immigrant black woman in a slave state before the Emancipation Proclamation. For Fr. Ryan's cause, the instruction of the cause

---

37 Eulogy of Father Patrick Ryan in Chattanooga Times, November 12, 1886 quoted in "The Centenary of Sts. Peter and Paul Parish, Chattanooga." https://www.stspeterand-paulbasilica.com/pages/father-ryan
38 There are several recent causes that hypothetically could proceed on the ground of the offering of life, including Fr. Vincent Capodanno and the Jesuit Scholastic Richie Fernando.

should document how deadly and contagious yellow fever is, the poverty of rural America during his lifetime, how many people Fr. Ryan cared for, and the community's outpouring of grief when he died.

### *Fama Signorum et Fama Miraculorum*

The focus of *Sanctorum Mater* 6 and *Maiorem hac Dilectionem* 2d is the reputation of intercessory power. The diocesan inquiry into the Servant of God's martyrdom, virtues or offering of life also includes investigating his or her reputation of intercessory power, that is, *fama signorum aut fama miraculorum*. This reputation of intercessory power is equated to miracles in *Divinus Perfectionis Magister*.[39] *Sanctorum Mater,* however, states that intercessory power is the "graces and favors received from God through the intercession of the Servant of God."[40] While "intercessory power" certainly can refer to miraculous healings, it also refers to the many spiritual graces and favors the faithful receive from God through the intercession of the Servant of God. For example, the fortitude to face life's daily struggles, the patience to bear wrongs, and charity towards others. The graces and favors demonstrating the faithful's confidence is the Servant of God's intercessory power can best be illustrated by popular piety; the novena to St. Anthony for lost objects or the blessing of throats on the liturgical feast of St. Blaise. Miracles, of course, are necessary for beatification and canonization, and the faithful should certainly be encouraged to pray for miracles, but a reputation of intercessory power means that the faithful also need to pray for the Servant of God's intercession for everyday struggles. The reputation of intercessory power is the divine confirmation of the authenticity of the reputation of martyrdom, heroic virtue or the offering of one's life. The required miracle for beatification and for canonization is divine proof of the ecclesial judgment of the Servant of God's martyrdom, heroic virtues, or the offering of one's life.

A Servant of God proposed for canonization must possess a reputation of holiness among the local community where they lived and died, and hopefully also possess a reputation of holiness among the larger diocesan, national and Universal Church. The reputation of holiness is the belief by a significant portion of the Christian Faithful that the Servant of God in his or her life, death and after death suffered martyrdom, lived all the Christian virtues to a heroic degree, or offered their life, and that he or she is in heaven interceding to the Lord on the community's behalf.

When the norms speak of the diocesan inquiry into the "life and death of the Servant of God," they are referring to basic historical facts (date of birth, date of death, parents' names, date of baptism, etc.) and the facts and circumstances surrounding the Servant of God psychological and religious life (religious, cleric, lay, spouse, etc.) as well as their particular historical and cultural milieu (e.g.,

---
[39] *DPM* 1.
[40] *SM* 6.

U.S., 19th Century, etc.). The "reputation enjoyed after death" then, refers to how, when and what frequency the local community prays to, invokes and venerates the Servant of God. Concretely, the information that needs to be gathered are things like: are there prayer groups that meet in the local community to pray to the Servant of God; are there buildings, roads, parish halls named after the Servant of God; are people in the diocese aware of who the Servant of God is and his or her role in the local Church; is the Servant of God known in the local civic community beyond just the Catholic faithful. If these questions can be answered affirmatively, then a case can be made for the existence of a *fama sanctitatis*.

The diocesan inquiry of the Servant of God not only needs to prove that the *fama sanctitatis* exists, but must also prove that the *fama* is authentic.[41] Before opening a cause, the diocesan bishop must verify that the Servant of God has an authentic and widespread reputation for martyrdom, heroic virtues or an offering of life, and for intercessory power. In order to determine whether this reputation is authentic, the bishop should determine if the reputation has been "stable, continuous, widespread, among trustworthy people," and whether it "exists among a significant portion of the People of God."[42] This understanding of authentic *fama* is derived from c. 2050 §2 of the 1917 Code.[43] The *fama*, furthermore, should not be artificially produced. For the *fama* to be judged genuine, the bishop must determine that the Servant of God's reputation arose spontaneously, and not through conflated human means, and that this reputation has perdured over time among the Christian community and other people of good will.

This is another place where a tension exists. *Fama* is needed and it needs to spread, but the *fama* cannot be artificially inflated. To address this tension, one must keep in mind that there is a difference between evangelization and advertising. Evangelization is the Church's mission, so evangelizing about a local Servant of God and how that person followed Christ is authentic. Advertising miracles for donations, however, is not authentic *fama*. While it can be frustrating that there is no defined standard for how much *fama* is needed, the lack of a standard has its advantages. The prime advantage is that the *fama* can be different for each cause. The same level of devotion to a local Servant of God does not need to equal the devotion to John Paul II, for example. The *fama*, therefore, can be limited to the local diocese and surrounding dioceses, as long as there exists the possibility that the *fama* will continue to spread.

---

41  *SM* 7-8.
42  *SM* 7 § 1-2.
43  1917 *CIC* c. 2050 §2: "Non est necesse ut constet in specie de virtutibus, martyrio, miraculis, sed sufficit ut probetur fama in genere, spontanea, non arte aut diligentia humana procurata, orta ab honestis et gravibus personis, continua, in dies aucta et vigens in praesenti apud maiorem partem populi."

## PART IV: Practical Questions When Instructing the Diocesan Phase

So far, the source of the norms governing canonization, the nature of the process, the possible grounds and the nature of *fama* have been examined in this article. As these issues were presented, some practical and pastoral concerns were highlighted including the content of the historical commission's report, indicators of *fama* and the need to be up front with the Christian Faithful that there is no guarantee that Servant of God will be canonized. For this last section, some general issues bishops and canonists have faced in instructing causes will be examined. Because of limited space, what follows is only a selection of issues and are, by no means, all of challenges faced by dioceses. The issues selected below represent challenges that have been repeatedly voiced by diocesan bishops and their staff.

### To Open a Cause or Not to Open a Cause

One of first questions a diocesan bishop is faced with in any cause of canonization is "Do I open this cause or not?" With the assistance of his diocesan canonists, the bishop should evaluate three elements before opening a cause: 1) the Servant of God's reputation for martyrdom, heroic virtue or offering of life, 2) as well as his or her reputation of intercessory power and 3) the importance of the cause for the Church.[44] The first two factors, have already been examined. *Sanctorum Mater* 8 speaks about the third factor, the "importance of the cause for the Church." In evaluating the importance of a cause to the Church, the bishop is determining if the Servant of God can provide a credible witness to the Universal Church on how to live a virtuous Christian life. Some of the important questions the bishop should ask are: Can they inspire the faithful in this particular culture to follow more closely the Gospel? Can the Servant of God speak to the faithful across cultures? Once the bishop has examined these questions, and has a reasonable belief that they can be answered in the positive, then the third element for opening a cause is satisfied. If, then, the bishop has evaluated all three elements mentioned above and finds a semblance of truth in each, he may decide to either open the cause of canonization or not.

Practically speaking, there are other factors and questions that the bishop will need to take into account when he considers opening a cause. It is important to know, for example, who will be the petitioner. Will the petitioner be the diocese, will it be a religious order, will it be the association or group that the Servant of God founded, or a group of the Christian Faithful established as a Guild.[45] Does the petitioner have the personnel and financial resources to sustain

---
44  *SM* 8.
45  *Normae Servandae* 1a and *Sanctorum Mater* 10 § 2 state that a physical person can be the petitioner. While possible, this is not practical for several reasons. Once such reason, is that it would be very difficult for one person to absorb all the financial costs of a cause.

a lengthy canonization cause? Does the petitioner understand the financial and moral responsibilities of their task? Further, does the petitioner understand that the cause may not result in canonization, or may result in canonization after they, the petitioner, are deceased? Causes take time, which is why it is wiser to have an institution be the petitioner rather than a person. Furthermore, is the petitioner trustworthy? Can the bishop and diocesan staff work with the petitioner in a collaborative way over many years? Canonization is not a quick and easy process, the bishop and petitioner should have a good relationship – it does not have to be a perfect one, but a relationship based on respect and open communication.

Another factor to determine is, whether the petitioner has a postulator? While the petitioner appoints the postulator, the bishop must approve (*approbari debet*) the choice of the postulator. The petitioner and bishop should have a conversation about who would be an acceptable postulator before a postulator is asked and appointed. While it is not required that the postulator be a canonist, it will help the cause proceed more smoothly if the postulator has experience ministering in the institutional church. Does the diocese have canonists who can assist the postulator, as a vice-postulator, if the postulator is not a canonist? If so, remember this diocesan canonist cannot also serve as a member of the diocesan tribunal to instruct the cause.

The need for a trained canonist is essential because the postulator is to gather information before the diocesan phase is opened in a non-judicial manner. The postulator is not to gather all the evidence, interview witnesses and prepare the *acta* of the cause – that is for the tribunal officials. The postulator should be able to know the difference.[46] Just as in a penal case, there is a pre-investigation phase. The assessor should gather information to help the bishop determine if a possible delict occurred. If there is a semblance of truth that a delict may have occurred, then the bishop can initiate a judicial penal process. It is the officials of the penal process who gather the formal evidence, hears witness testimony and the judge who makes a judgement. This same principle applies to causes of canonization and the responsibility of the postulator. If the postulator does gather evidence or interviews witnesses in a judicial manner, the integrity of the cause is at stake. There have been causes that have taken longer than they should have because the postulator interviewed witnesses and then, when the tribunal needed to officially interview them, the witnesses refused, saying that they were already interviewed.[47]

The bishop should ask what qualifications does the postulator have. Have they worked on other causes before, and do they have a sound reputation? Have the petitioner, bishop and diocesan staff met the postulator? Finally, discuss

---

46  See *DPM* 1, 2.1; *NS* 3b.
47  Related to this point, it is important to note for validity that the postulator and vice postulator may not be present at the sessions for the hearing of witnesses.

how much of a stipend, if any, the postulator will charge before opening the cause. Again, causes of canonization take time and there needs to be a good collaborative relationship between the bishop, petitioner and postulator.

Once you have a petitioner and a postulator, the bishop, with the help of his canonists, should review the materials presented by the postulator and petitioner. Does the preliminary investigation conducted by the postulator show a semblance of truth that the Servant of God was martyred, lived a heroic life or offered their life for others?[48] Does it appear that the Christian Faithful believe that the Servant of God is interceding to the Lord on the community's behalf? If there is a semblance of truth to these questions, then open the cause! Accept the *libellus*, appoint members of the tribunal, do the required consultations, appoint members of the historical commission and theological censors and collect witness testimony. If there is not a semblance of truth, or if bishop is unsure, or has lingering questions, do not open the cause. The norms are very clear that it is the sole right of the diocesan bishop to open a cause. The right to open a cause of canonization does not belong to any other private or juridic person in the Church. The diocesan bishop alone decides whether or not to open a cause of canonization.[49]

**Transfer of Competency**

The bishop competent to open a cause of canonization is the diocesan bishop of the territory in which the Servant of God died (Bishop A). If a bishop (Bishop B) wants to instruct a cause and Servant of God died elsewhere, a transfer of competency can be requested. Bishop B should write to Bishop A and ask for the transfer providing some reasons why Bishop B would like to undertake the responsibility of the cause, the merits of the cause and its importance for the Church. Bishop B should also ask for Bishop A's response in writing. Bishop B should remind Bishop A that if he agrees, Bishop B will be forwarding all their correspondence to the Congregation for their approval. If Bishop A is agreeable, Bishop B should then put all the correspondence together and send it to the Prefect of the Congregation. Only the Congregation can approve transfers of competency.[50] If any of this correspondence is not in one of the five languages accepted by the Congregation which are Latin, English, French, Spanish, and Italian then translate the correspondence and make sure you certify the translation.[51]

---

48  Cf. *NS* 3b
49  *DPM* 1; *SM* 20.
50  *SM* 22-24.
51  *SM* 127. This also applies to all other documents in a cause that is not in one of these five languages. At the current time, Portuguese is not one of the languages being accepted by the Congregation.

If the Congregation approves the transfer of competency, the Congregation will notify Bishop B by means of a rescript. The rescript and all letters between Bishops A and B, along with all correspondence with the Congregation related to the transfer of competency, must be included in the *acta*. Finally, be aware that if you obtain a transfer of competency, it does not mean that the relationship between Bishop A and Bishop B is finished. Bishop B may need to send a rogatory commission to Bishop A's diocese to interview witnesses, or Bishop B may need Bishop A to establish a rogatory commission in Bishop A's diocese to interview witnesses. It is always beneficial for there to be a good fraternal relationship between the bishop who has competency and the bishop who wishes to have competency.

**Censors**

There are questions regarding the theological censors, namely, can more than two be appointed, what do the reports need to say, and where can censors be found. The norms say two censors are required, but if the Servant of God's published writing is voluminous, bishops can appoint more than two. If additional censors are appointed, Bishop will have to ensure that each writing is read by at least two censors. The report must state the following: "I as the properly appointed censor, read the following published works by Servant of God and found nothing against faith or morals." *Sanctorum Mater* instructs the diocesan bishop that in addition to this simple statement, it would be helpful if the censors wrote observations about the personality and spirituality of the Servant of God. This report is an important opportunity to demonstrate the virtues and spirituality of the Servant of God. If your diocese has a Catholic college or a diocesan or regional seminary, theological censors could be drawn from the theological faculty. Degreed theologians who have a *mandatum* would surely make a trustworthy censor. The theological censors are to complete their task separately and each is to submit his or her own report. The theological censors are not to function as a "theological commission," only the historical commission acts *in solidum* to submit one report. If the Servant of God has no published works or spiritual writings, theological censors do not need to be appointed. In this case, the bishop must write a declaration on the inexistence of published writings, which must be inserted this declaration into the acts.[52]

**Administrator**

The March 7, 2016, *Rescriptum ex Audientia Sanctissimi,* mandates that all causes of canonization have an administrator to oversee the temporal goods of the cause. The *Rescriptum* is silent on how to appoint this administrator, but following the earlier cited maxim, be sure to appoint this administrator through a written decree that is notarized. Insert this decree into the final *acta*. The diocesan chief financial officer would be qualified to be the administrator. The

---

[52] *SM* 67 and 89.

diocesan bishop should have a good working relationship with the administrator, who should know and understand basic accounting procedures and best practices.

**Conclusion of the Diocesan Phase**

Once you have finished the diocesan phase and the *acta* has been prepared, transcribed and copied, the diocesan phase needs to be closed. The norms require that there be triplicate copies of the *acta*. The original *acta* (archetype) is to be closed and sealed during the last session of the diocesan inquiry, and archetype is to be kept in the diocesan archives. The archetype cannot be opened without the permission of the Congregation. The other two copies of the *acta* (Transcript and Public Copy) are also to be closed and sealed during the last session of the diocesan inquiry, and these two copies are to be sent to the Congregation.[53] The diocesan bishop or episcopal delegate must preside over the closing session. The closing session does not have to be a public mass, but it is appropriate to close the diocesan phase with a mass or prayer service.

At the closing session, the boxes containing the *acta* of the cause should be closed with the diocesan seal. After the closing session, the bishop and Promotor of Justice must affix to the sealed boxes their *vota*. The *vota* should attest to the trust worthiness of the witnesses and the legitimacy of the diocesan acts. However, it is advisable that the bishop and Promotor of Justice offer their opinions about the Servant of God. The Congregation values the opinion of those who instructed the diocesan phase, which is why the *vota* of the bishop or his delegate and the Promoter of Justice are so important.[54] Then the *acta* with the affixed papers are to be transmitted to the Congregation. The norms allow you to either transmit them through the diplomatic pouch of the nunciature or in person through the carrier of the acts.[55] Many bishops have found that transmitting the *acta* in person to the Congregation is also a valuable opportunity. Transmitting the *acta* in person allows the bishop the opportunity to ask any questions regarding the Roman Phase directly to members of the Congregation. The bishop should be accompanied by the Roman postulator, who brings his or her decree of appointment to be given to the Congregation. The diocesan postulator, as well as all participants in the diocesan inquiry, loses his or her office when the diocesan phase is closed. Therefore, you must appoint a Roman postulator. And once you have turned over the diocesan *acta*, make sure there is steady contact with the Roman postulator and the Congregation.

---

53  *NS* 31; *SM* 138 §2 and 145.
54  *SM* 147 § 1
55  Like all other officials of the diocesan phase, the carrier must be appointed and swear an oath. Both the appointment and oath must be included in the form of a written decree.

**Conclusion**

While it is not possible to examine all aspects of the canonization process or the challenges associated with it in this forum, it is hoped that this article has provided a brief overview of the current norms, the difference between canonizable holiness and the universal call to holiness, the object of a cause, the possible grounds for a cause and some practical questions that arise during the diocesan phase. Without a doubt, a cause of canonization is a lengthy process, requiring numerous experts and many hours of meticulous work. Given the complexity and length of a cause, some people have wondered if there are too many saints and if the Church should instead focus on other issues. Responding to this very question, Joseph Cardinal Ratzinger stated, "It would be an absurdity, since in the Church there can never be too many saints. Saint Paul told us unequivocally that we are all called to holiness: 'This is the will of God, your sanctification.' Because of this, the number of saints is, thanks be to God, incomparably greater than the group of individuals given prominence through canonization..."[56]

---

56  Marian Ricci, "I Never Said There Are too Many," in *30 Days,* May 1989, p 18.

# SEMINAR

## CALLED TO BE A MISSIONARY CHURCH: HOW THE MISSIONARY EXPERIENCE CAN INFORM THE NEW EVANGELIZATION
### Reverend Ricardo Martín-Pinillos

As far as I know, the topic of mission and canon law has not been part of any CLSA convention in the past. Despite the Council calling for the Church to be "missionary" in her nature, I do not remember it being part of any of my classes while I was studying canon law.[1] A warning before you continue reading this paper: I am a member of a missionary community, technically a public association of the faithful, and I divide my work between my parish and the chancery in the Archdiocese of Milwaukee. Therefore, my being a missionary and a pastor may have more weight than my being a canonist in this talk.

It is necessary to clarify what kind of mission we are discussing here. As a pastor, I am very aware of recent, very worthwhile efforts to discuss the evangelizing mission of the Catholic Church. We want to remind our clergy and laity alike that we all have a "mission" to evangelize. But this paper is about the missionary activity of the Church *stricto sensu,* which is how the Council understood and used the term *missionary*, and how it is understood in the canons found under the title "The Missionary Action of the Church" in the 1983 Code.[2]

The outline of my remarks is simple. We will take a look at the section of the Code that deals with the missionary activity of the church and apply a minimal exegesis of those canons, including the "who, how, what" of missionary activity. Then, and I am doing this more as a pastor than a canonist, I will discuss how, in my opinion, the missionary experience in missionary territory can be applied in the New Evangelization efforts of the Church in the U.S. and other "developed" societies—a work in which many of us find ourselves immersed. The realities of the New Evangelization in many areas of the country may remind us of the features of missionary territory, such as a smaller number of available priests who have to cover larger areas with more than one faith community, or a more acute need for well-formed lay ministers, or the need to dialogue with a difficult cultural milieu—at best indifferent to our evangelizing efforts.

---

1     E.g., Vatican II, decree *Ad gentes*, 7 December 1965 in *AAS* 58 (1966) 948, n. 2.

2     *CIC* Book III, Title II. This and all subsequent English translations from *Code of Canon Law, Latin-English Edition: New English Translation* (Washington, DC: CLSA, 1998).

*What did the Code mean by mission?*

The Church is indeed missionary everywhere, but what we are discussing here is the mission in *stricto sensu*, also called the mission *ad gentes,* or as other authors have called it, the *ecclesiae plantatio*—the establishment of a (particular) church.

In need of external, verifiably objective situations, the Code considered missionary work *ad gentes* the evangelizing efforts of the Church in territories which were not yet established as formal dioceses. These territories, in the form of apostolic vicariates, apostolic prefectures, and other similar circumscriptions, fall under the responsibility of the Congregation for the Evangelization of Peoples.[3] One of the formal difficulties of this concept is that, as we know, there are many territories that are perfectly constituted as dioceses, some even for centuries, in which the type of work carried out is typically missionary.

Any discussion about the missionary work of the Church must begin in the Gospel:

> All power in heaven and on earth has been given to me. Go, therefore, and make disciples of all nations, baptizing them in the name of the Father, and of the Son, and of the holy Spirit, teaching them to observe all that I have commanded you. And behold, I am with you always, until the end of the age. (Mt 28:18–20, NABRE).

Following the Great Commission, the Council taught that the Church is missionary "by its nature," in her essence. For the Church to be the Church of Christ it has to retain its missionary nature.

*Missionary activity in the Code (cc. 781–792)*

Unlike the 1917 Code, in which the norms regarding the missionary action of the Church were "rather sparse and actually spread throughout,"[4] the 1983 Code put together a whole section on missionary legislation, under the title "*De actione Ecclesiae missionali*" which has been translated as the missionary "action" or "activity" of the Church.

---

3   John Paul II, apostolic constitution *Pastor Bonus*, 28 June 1988: *AAS* 80 (1988) 881, n. 85.
4   O'Reilly, Michael, "Title II: The Missionary Action of the Church [cc. 781–792], in John P. Beal et al., eds., *New Commentary on the Code of Canon Law* (New York/Mahwah, NJ: Paulist Press, 2000) 938.

The section begins with a typical exhortative introductory canon: "Since the whole Church is by its nature missionary and the work of evangelization must be held as a fundamental duty of the people of God, all the Christian faithful, conscious of their responsibility, are to assume their part in missionary work."[5] This initial canon captures the teaching of *Ad gentes*, that the work of the missions is a fundamental duty of *all* of the people of God, who are invited according to their condition (cf. c. 204 §1) to play their own part. This responsibility is fulfilled by direct participation and by prayers, but also by providing the necessary resources for the fulfillment of the missionary apostolate (cc. 791 and 1266.)

The location of this section, in Book III, The Teaching Office of the Church, stresses the priority of preaching the Gospel in missionary work, over but without excluding the offices of sanctifying and governing, to lead people to "the faith, freedom, and peace of Christ by the example of her life and preaching by the sacraments and other means of grace."[6]

*The "who" of missionary activity*

Unlike the 1917 Code, which reserved the oversight of missions to non-Catholics to the Holy See (*CIC*/17 c. 1350 §2), the 1983 Code placed the supreme management and coordination of missionary initiatives with the Roman Pontiff and the College of Bishops (*CIC/83* c. 782). Each bishop is responsible for awakening the missionary consciousness of the faithful in his own church, as each individual church is part of the universal church, participates in its nature and missionary vocation, and should perfectly reflect the image of the universal Church.

The Code did not capture the role that *Ad gentes*[7] gave to episcopal conferences, but it has not prevented national conferences from helping coordinate each bishop's responsibility for missionary work—as our own conference in the U.S. does so faithfully, across several offices.

The Code also issued a particular invitation to members of institutes of consecrated life to engage in missionary action, "in a manner proper to their institute" (c. 783) positively recognizing that religious institutes would be especially equipped to provide the necessary training. The invitation of this canon was renewed with a sense of urgency by John Paul II in *Redemptoris Missio*.[8]

---

5   Canon 781.
6   *AG* 5.
7   *AG* 31 and 38.
8   John Paul II, encyclical letter *Redemptoris Missio*, 7 December 1990: *AAS* 83 (1991) 249–340, esp. n. 69.

The Council (*AG* 18 and 40) included in a significant way institutes of contemplative life (cf. c. 674), which contribute greatly to the conversion and perseverance of those hearing the Gospel for the first time. These institutes are invited to found houses in mission lands and adapt to the religious traditions of those peoples. While not specifically stated, nothing would seem to indicate that this all-encompassing missionary call does not extend to societies of apostolic life, consecrated virgins, and new forms of consecrated life.[9]

In dealing with individuals in missionary work, the Code mentions "missionaries" and defines them as "those whom competent ecclesiastical authority sends to carry out missionary work."[10] It is important to note that prior to the Council and its implementation in the 1983 Code, the term missionary was generally reserved for priests, and the laity were considered "auxiliary missionaries."[11] The 1983 Code also shows here a concern—also present in other sections—for the public recognition of a particular vocation in the church.

There is no need to emphasize here the importance of lay missionaries in carrying out the missionary activity of the Church. The Code emphasizes that these missionaries have to be chosen and sent by the competent authority, and be accepted by the receiving competent authority in the mission territory. Post-conciliar documents have listed requirements for missionaries: sincere intent beyond humanitarianism, health, training, commitment of a certain length, etc.[12]

In terms of "actors," the Code completes the list with the figure of the catechist (c. 785). They are laypersons, presumably "locals," who, under the direction of missionaries and with the proper formation and outstanding in their living of the Christian life, are charged with the responsibility of teaching the Gospel, engaging in liturgical worship, and in carrying out works of charity. These lay catechists are not mere substitutes for priests, but witnesses in their own right to Christ and the Community. *Redemptoris Missio*, quoting number 17 of *Ad gentes*, stated the following about catechists:

> Among the laity who become evangelizers, catechists have a place of honor... "[They are an] army of catechists, both men and women, worthy of praise, to whom missionary work among the nations owes so much. Imbued with the

---

9 We could also include in this list public associations of the faithful, like my own, the Community of Saint Paul. Our foundation was a direct fruit of the inspiration of the Council and the flexibility it brought to religious life. While not technically consecrated, members of the Community of Saint Paul commit for life, and many of them serve in mission territory.
10 Canon 784.
11 O'Reilly, 942.
12 Paul VI, apostolic letter, *Ecclesiae Sanctae*, August 6, 1966: *AAS* 58 (1960) 757-787, esp. III, 24.

apostolic spirit, they make a singular and absolutely necessary contribution to the spread of the faith and of the Church by their strenuous efforts."[13]

*Jurisdiction and governance*

All these agents are sent as "heralds of the gospel" (c.786) until the new churches are fully constituted. According to the legislator, this happens when a new church has suitable resources (spiritual vigor and maturity of faith) and sufficient means, especially material. In the Code, the goal of the mission *ad gentes* was to found Christian communities and develop churches to their full maturity. The mission is not completed until it succeeds in building a new particular church which functions normally in its local setting (*RM* 48, *AG* 19–22).

During this process, mission territories are under the CEP's direct governance (if they belong to the Latin Church), constituted as apostolic prefectures or apostolic vicariates, which in canonical terms are similar to dioceses and whose shepherds are made similar to bishops by the law (see cc. 383, 371 §1). The juridic system is maintained in these territories through the form of *commission*. According to the Council, a church will be considered rooted when it has its own corps of native priests, religious and laity, even if insufficient, and the ministries and institutions necessary to conduct and strengthen the life of the people of God.[14] Then, a bishop is appointed and the work of the church goes from *commission* to *mandate*.

*Inculturation: The "what" of missionary activity*

The object of the mission *ad gentes* is to proclaim the gospel message to those who know not Christ. The Code calls for this proclamation to begin as a "sincere dialogue," that needs to take place "in a manner adapted to [the people's] own temperament and culture" (c. 787). This expression captures the concept of *inculturation*, a process called for by the Council[15] (GS 58) and developed in post-conciliar documents.[16]

---

13  *RM* 73.
14  AG 21,32.
15  E.g., Vatican II, pastoral constitution *Gaudium et spes*, 7 December 1965: *AAS* 58 (1966) 1025–1115, esp. n. 58.
16  E.g, Paul VI, apostolic exhortation *Evangelii Nuntiandi*, 8 December 1976: *AAS* 68 (1976) 5–76, esp. n. 62–63.

The process of inculturation begins by the missionary recognizing the "seeds of the Word"[17] in the culture that he or she is trying to engage. The missionary is called to transmit the values of the Church while at the same time taking the good elements that exist in the culture and renewing them from within. Through inculturation, the Church becomes a more intelligible sign of what she is, and a more effective instrument of mission.[18].

The Fifth General Conference of the Bishops of Latin America and the Caribbean, gathered in Aparecida in 2007, came up with a precise definition of culture and inculturation:

> Culture, understood most broadly, represents the particular way in which human beings and peoples cultivate their relationship to nature and with their fellow humans, with themselves, and with God, so as to attain a fully human existence. As such, [we the bishops] view positively and with true empathy the different forms of culture present in our continent. Faith is only adequately professed, understood, and lived when it makes its way deeply into the cultural substrate of a people.[19]

The slow process of inculturation requires empathy, so that the culture can be understood in dynamic tension with a critical stance, to discover whatever within it is the product of human limitation and sin, also present in cultural manifestations.

Pope Francis, generally recognized as one of the most important contributors in Aparecida, stated in the *Joy of the Gospel* that "the ultimate aim should be that the Gospel, as preached in categories proper to each culture, will create a new synthesis with that particular culture."[20] The Church's mission is not "to spread a religious ideology, much less to propose a lofty ethical teaching. Many movements throughout the world inspire high ideals or ways to live a meaningful life. Through the mission of the Church, Jesus Christ himself continues to evangelize and act; her mission thus makes present in history the *kairos*, the

---

17　Third General Conference of the Bishops of Latin America and the Caribbean at Puebla, "Documento de Puebla," n. 401, http://www.celam.org/documentos/Documento_Conclusivo_Puebla.pdf.
18　*EN* 20.
19　Fifth General Conference of the Bishops of Latin America and the Caribbean at Aparecida, "Concluding Document," n. 476, (http://www.celam.org/aparecida/Ingles.pdf).
20　Francis, apostolic exhortation *Evangelii Gaudium*, 24 November 2013: *AAS* 105 (2013) 1019–1139, at n. 129, in English translation at http://w2.vatican.va/content/francesco/en/apost_exhortations/documents/papa-francesco_esortazione-ap_20131124_evangelii-gaudium.html.

favorable time of salvation. Through the proclamation of the Gospel, the risen Jesus becomes our contemporary."[21]

*Missionary cooperation*

Canon 791 legislates how dioceses in the "developed world" are to support the missionary action of the Church—by promoting missionary vocations, by designating one priest for the promotion of missions, by celebrating an annual day for the missions, and by providing a yearly suitable offering for the missions to be sent to the Holy See.[22] As we know, in the U.S. and elsewhere many dioceses have adopted a "missionary appeal" system, inviting missionaries to speak at parishes and collect funds for the missions.

Many dioceses have also involved themselves in finding new, even more meaningful ways to promote the missions, such as facilitating diocesan or parish level twinning relationships. Out of those efforts, I can witness to the wonderful 35-year-long experience of the twinning between the Archdiocese of Milwaukee and the parish of *La Sagrada Familia* in the Diocese of San Juan de la Maguana, in the Dominican Republic.[23]

As canonists, we can assist our dioceses and our bishops to make sure that our local churches fulfill this obligation to cooperate with the missions—hopefully in more ways than just an annual collection.

*Redemptoris missio:* from *Ad gentes* to the New Evangelization

In 1990, Saint John Paul II issued the encyclical *Redemptoris Missio*, which serves us well as a transition between the understanding of missionary work *stricto sensu* and the context in which many of us find ourselves. In *Redemptoris Missio*, Saint John Paul II described several types of missionary work and minted the term "New Evangelization," calling the whole Church to a re-commitment of all her energies to the mission *ad gentes* and the New Evangelization.[24]

The encyclical describes several missionary situations or stages. First, the mission *ad gentes* that has been described above, in places where Jesus is not known or which lack Christian communities sufficiently mature to be able to incarnate the faith in their own environment and proclaim it to other groups.

---

21  Francis, Message for World Mission Day 2017, n. 3, publication in *AAS* presumably forthcoming, in English translation at https://w2.vatican.va/content/francesco/en/messages/missions/documents/papa-francesco_20170604_giornata-missionaria2017.html.
22  See canon 791.
23  In addition to multiple benefits for both parties, after 35 years and for the first time, a young man from the parish has been admitted to the diocesan seminary in the Archdiocese of Milwaukee.
24  *RM* 3.

Secondly, where we find Christian communities with adequate and solid ecclesial structures, fervent in their faith and in Christian living. They bear witness to the Gospel in their surroundings and have a sense of commitment to the universal mission. In these communities the Church carries out her activity and pastoral care.

Thirdly, there is an intermediate situation, particularly in countries with ancient Christian roots, and occasionally in the younger Churches as well, where entire groups of the baptized have lost a living sense of the faith or even no longer consider themselves members of the Church and live a life far removed from Christ and his Gospel. In this case what is needed is a "new evangelization" or a "re-evangelization."

How can the wisdom acquired from decades of missionary work assist the present-day New Evangelization efforts of the Church, especially in our own context?

In my opinion, we could learn from the mission *ad gentes* in (1) proclaiming the Gospel in missionary style; (2) placing a renewed emphasis on the identification and formation of evangelizing catechists; and (3) learning specifically from the Latin-American experiment of the *comunidades de base* ("base communities," or small Christian communities, also called in some Latin American countries "mission houses") small-group type ministries.

*1. Proclamation in missionary style: focus on the essentials*

In missionary work there is an absolute need to focus on essentials. I cannot find better source for this first application than from the words of Pope Francis himself. In the famous interview with Fr. Spadaro of August 19, 2013, soon after he was elevated to the pontificate, he said,

> The dogmatic and moral teachings of the church are not all equivalent. The church's pastoral ministry cannot be obsessed with the transmission of a disjointed multitude of doctrines to be imposed insistently. Proclamation in a missionary style focuses on the essentials, on the necessary things: this is also what fascinates and attracts more, what makes the heart burn, as it did for the disciples at Emmaus. We have to find a new balance; otherwise even the moral edifice of the church is likely to fall like a house of cards, losing the *freshness* and fragrance of the Gospel. The proposal of the Gospel must be

more simple, profound, radiant. It is from this proposition that the moral consequences then flow.[25]

The Latin American bishops gathered in Aparecida also made the same point when they stated that

> A Catholic faith reduced to mere baggage, to a collection of rules and prohibitions, to fragmented devotional practices, to selective and partial adherence to the truths of the faith, to occasional participation in some sacraments, to the repetition of doctrinal principles, to bland or nervous moralizing, that does not convert the life of the baptized would not withstand the trials of time.[26]

This focus on the essentials may be really understood as an application of the concept of inculturation in our own contemporary context: empathy and dialogue instead of condemnation and confrontation with modern culture. It entails looking at the world in a spirit of humility and dialogue, engaging less in the so-called "culture wars," recognizing the "seeds of the Gospel" present *even* in our industrialized societies.

This can be attained if we avoid what the Holy Father called the "obsession" with the transmission of a multitude of doctrines, and I believe it is an invitation to review our own religious education programming, and its providers—transitioning into my second "proposal."

2. *Emphasis on the identification and formation of missionary catechists*

As many authors are stating today, the baptized are called to be inherently missionary, the way the Church is missionary in her nature. Any individual who has had the opportunity of serving in the missions knows of the importance of identifying catechists in the communities they attend. They are the connection between the missionary and the community, serving as teachers and advisors at once. They are the cornerstones of missionary work, so they should also be the cornerstone of the missionary work of the New Evangelization.

Modern parishes should once again place emphasis on religious education programs that are missionary in focus instead of just teaching children to memorize and recite some prayers. This requires the identification and formation of great catechists, just as we do in missionary work. As it happens in mission

---

25  Spadaro, Anthony, "Interview with Pope Francis," 19 August 2013, in English translation at https://w2.vatican.va/content/francesco/en/speeches/2013/september/documents/papa-francesco_20130921_intervista-spadaro.html.
26  Aparecida, 12.

territory, an essential component of these missionary religious education programs would be the "social work" component—doing at all grades what is usual in Confirmation programs in terms of "social service."

At the risk of oversimplifying and creating misunderstanding, this second application would imply a rebalancing of the effort and finances that the Catholic Church has invested in parochial schools,[27] into the creation and maintenance of more robust and creative religious education programs, with the vital help of great catechists—able, formed and trusted.

*3. Small-group ministries*

Interestingly enough, recent Catholic literature about the New Evangelization recommends the establishment of parish based small-group ministries. There is no healthy Protestant church without this type of ministry. It would be good to remember that the historical origin of this type of ministry is absolutely Catholic, as it is based on the missionary experience of the *comunidades de base* in the Latin-American Catholic Church.[28]

In the words of the bishops in Aparecida,

> In the ecclesial experience of some churches of Latin America and the Caribbean, basic (base) ecclesial communities have been schools that have helped form Christians committed to their faith, disciples and missionaries of the Lord... Puebla noted that small communities, especially basic ecclesial communities, enable the people to have access to greater knowledge of the Word of God, social commitment in the name of the Gospel, the emergence of new lay services, and education of the faith of adults.[29]

These *comunidades de base* started as a response to the relative scarcity of priests,[30] a reality that is becoming even more acutely present in our ministry today. With larger churches hosting thousands of parishioners, small-groups typically hosted in the house of parishioners/facilitators allow individuals to provide pastoral care to one another, hopefully with the coordination and contents provided by the parish pastoral professional staff, helping with the revitalization of parish ministry beyond the participation in the sacraments.

27 In my own parish, the parochial school has a budget of $1,800,000 compared with a budget of $85,000 for the collaborative religious education program of three parishes.
28 The missionary experiment of these basic ecclesial communities has had its detractors, often accused of being too close in structure to communist cells.
29 Aparecida, 128.
30 John Frederick Schwaller, *The History of the Catholic Church in Latin America: From Conquest to Revolution and Beyond* (New York City: NYU Press, 2011) 222.

*Conclusion*

If anything defines missionary work anywhere it is its dynamism and flexibility and its constant invitation to creative solutions to complex problems. I would like to conclude this very imperfect contribution by giving voice again to the Latin American bishops gathered in Aparecida, who proclaimed that,

> The church is called to a deep and profound rethinking of its mission and relaunch it with fidelity and boldness in the new circumstances of Latin America and the world. It cannot retreat in response to those who see only confusion, dangers, and threats, or those who seek to cloak the variety and complexity of situations with a mantle of worn-out ideological slogans, or irresponsible attacks. What is required is confirming, renewing, and revitalizing the newness of the Gospel rooted in our history, out of a personal and community encounter with Jesus Christ that raises up disciples and missionaries.[31]

We are called to be missionaries even in our industrialized societies. We are being called to a profound rethinking of our pastoral action to continue our work to proclaim the freshness of the always new good news of Jesus Christ.

---

31  Aparecida, 11.

# Seminar

## Structural Reorganization of the Metropolitan Appellate Structure and Approval Process
### Very Reverend Joseph L. Newton

With the promulgation of the *motu proprio Mitis iudex Dominus Jesus (Mitis iudex)*, the question of whether to return to the traditional metropolitan tribunal appellate system for some tribunals in the United States became a topic of much discussion. Many tribunals, such as that of the Archdiocese of Indianapolis, had worked within a modified appellate structure. Soon after *Mitis iudex* the bishops of the province of Indiana petitioned the Supreme Tribunal of the Apostolic Signatura to be restored to the traditional metropolitan tribunal appellate system.

This paper will offer an examination of the role of the traditional metropolitan tribunal appellate system in light of *Mitis iudex* and offer practical resources and observations based on the experience of the Province of Indiana as the province returned from a modified metropolitan system to the traditional metropolitan tribunal appellate structure in early 2016.

### The role of the metropolitan tribunal appellate system in light of *Mitis iudex Dominus Iesus*

*Mitis iudex*, establishes in the fifth fundamental criterion, a preference for a restoration of the traditional metropolitan appellate tribunal and recognition of the role of the metropolitan see in a given province. The criteria states:

> It is necessary that the appeal process be restored to the metropolitan see, especially since that duty, insofar as the metropolitan see is the head of the ecclesiastical province, stands out through time as a stable and distinctive sign of synodality in the Church.[1]

---

[1] Pope Francis, motu proprio *Mitis iudex Dominus Jesus*, August 15, 2015. Latin translation from http://w2.vatican.va/content/francesco/la/motu_proprio/documents/papa-francescomotu-proprio_20150815_mitis-iudex-dominus-iesus.html. English translation from http://w2.vatican.va/content/francesco/en/motu_proprio/documents/papa-francescomotu-proprio_20150815_mitis-iudex-dominus-iesus.html. Fundamental Criteria V: " Appellatio ad Sedem Metropolitae restituatur oportet, quippe quod munus per saecula stabile, tamquam provinciae ecclesiasticae capitis, insigne perstat synodalitatis in Ecclesia."

As expressed by Pope Francis, this recognition of synodality and the renewed focus on the role of the bishop as judge in marriage cases,[2] demonstrates a preference for the traditional metropolitan tribunal system. This preference is codified in the revised canon 1673 §6 which states "the tribunal of first instance appeals to the metropolitan tribunal of second instance without prejudice to the prescripts of cann. 1438-1439 and 1444."[3]

Canon 1438 states:

> Without prejudice to the prescript of can. 1444, §1, n. 1:
>
> 1° from the tribunal of a suffragan bishop, appeal is made to the metropolitan tribunal, without prejudice to the prescript of can. 1439;
>
> 2° in cases tried in first instance before the metropolitan, appeal is made to the tribunal which the metropolitan has designated in a stable manner with the approval of the Apostolic See;
>
> 3° for cases tried before a provincial superior, the tribunal of second instance is under the authority of the supreme moderator; for cases tried before the local abbot, the tribunal of second instance is under the authority of the abbot superior of the monastic congregation.[4]

Here, according to canon 1438, 2°, the preference for the appeal of the court of first instance is the metropolitan tribunal.[5] For Pope Francis, this is an expression of synodality and recognition of the role of the bishop in the work of the tribunal. This preference is both expressed in *Mitis iudex*[6] *and in the Subsidium* for the application of the m.p. *Mitis Iudex Dominus Jesus* [hereafter *Subsidium*]

---

2   *Mitis iudex Dominus Jesus*, III.
3   *Codex Iuris Canonici auctoritate Ioannis Pauli PP. II promulgatus* (Vatican City: Libreria Editrice Vaticana, 1983) c. 1673 §6: "A tribunali primae instantiae appellatur ad tribunal metropolitanum secundae instantiae, salvis praescriptis cann. 1438-1439 et 1444." English translation from *Code of Canon Law, Latin-English Edition: New English Translation* (Washington, DC: CLSA, 2001). All subsequent English translations of canons from this code will be taken from this source unless otherwise indicated.
4   C. 1438: "Firmo praescripto can. 1444, § 1, n. 1: 1° a tribunali Episcopi suffraganei appellatur ad tribunal Metropolitae, salvo praescripto can. 1439; 2° in causis in prima instantia pertractatis coram Metropolita fit appellatio ad tribunal quod ipse, probante Sede Apostolica, stabiliter designaverit; 3° pro causis coram Superiore provinciali actis tribunal secundae instantiae est penes supremum Moderatorem; pro causis actis coram Abbate locali, penes Abbatem superiorem congregationis monasticae."
5   C. 1438, 1°.
6   *Mitis iudex Dominus Jesus*, V.

published shortly[7] after the promulgation of *Mitis iudex*, by the Apostolic Tribunal of the Roman Rota. The *Subsidium* states:

> The Bishop exercises his ministry in sacramental communion and of intent with the other members of the episcopal college. A manifestation of this real collegiality is to be found in the ancient institution of ecclesiastical provinces and the function of the Metropolitan. The Episcopal Conferences have a relevant function in assisting the Bishops in the working application of the new matrimonial procedures. For this reason: The right of the Metropolitan, never having been diminished, takes on new force, and from this flows a corollary: *the appeal to the Metropolitan See,* the head of the ecclesiastical province, as a distinctive sign of synodality in the Church. The Ecclesiastical Province, one will recall, is an intermediate jurisdictional instance between the Bishop and the Roman Pontiff.[8]

However, while this was an expressed preference in *Mitis iudex*, it was not a requirement that provinces in a current modified appellate tribunal change to the traditional metropolitan tribunal model. That is this is not a requirement seems apparent by both the choice of Latin used in the fifth fundamental criterion of *Mitis iudex* and also in the prescripts of canons 1438-1439 as mentioned in canon 1673 §6.

The English translation on the Vatican website[9] for the word "*oportet*" as used in the fifth fundamental criterion of *Mitis iudex* is "necessary." Here the word "*oportet*" from which the English cognate "opportune" arises can also mean "it is proper, one should, (or) one ought."[10] Thus, from the language used, it does not seem as those provinces with a modified tribunal structure are required to change to the traditional metropolitan tribunal appellate structure.

While there is a preference for a restoration to the traditional metropolitan appellate tribunal, a modified system can be put in place.[11] For example, the Province of Indiana has five dioceses: the Archdiocese of Indianapolis, the Diocese of Evansville, the Diocese of Fort Wayne-South Bend, the Diocese of Lafayette-in-Indiana, and the Diocese of Gary. Prior to the return to the traditional metropolitan system, the Province of Indiana had a modified metropolitan

---

7   Sacra Romana Rota, *Subsidium* for the application of the M.p. *Mitis Iudex Dominus Jesus*, January 2016: Vatican City.
8   *Subsidium*, 10.
9   http://w2.vatican.va/content/francesco/en/motu_proprio/documents/papa-francesco-motu-proprio_20150815_mitis-iudex-dominus-iesus.html
10  D.P. Simpson. *Cassell's Latin and English Dictionary* (New York City: Hungry Minds, 1987) 155.
11  C. 1438.

system. First instance cases from Indianapolis were appealed to the Lafayette-in-Indiana; Lafayette-in-Indiana appealed to Fort Wayne-South Bend; and Fort Wayne-South Bend appealed to Indianapolis. For their part, Evansville appealed to Gary and Gary appealed to Evansville.

This modified system was put into place with the approval of the Apostolic Signatura in 2003. The procedural canons in 1438-1441, unchanged by *Mitis iudex*, and therefore remain viable, for those dioceses whose appellate structure are a modified metropolitan system, continue to exist until the diocesan parties agree to change; subject to the approval of the Supreme Tribunal of the Apostolic Signatura.

In summary, while a return to the traditional metropolitan appellate structure is preferred, especially as seen as sign of synodality, a province with a modified metropolitan appellate structure is not *contra legem* and continues to function as established by the Apostolic Signatura.

### The Interdiocesan Tribunal

Worth noting in the context of this article is that the interdiocesan tribunal of first instance as established in canon 1423[12] also remain unchanged with the following exception from the *Ratio procedendi* of *Mitis iudex* which states "the bishop can withdraw from an interdiocesan tribunal constituted in accordance with can. 1423."[13] Further elaboration on this point can be found in the *Subsidium*:

> the law now promulgated and clarified by the intention (*mens*) of the Pontiff, gives free and immediate right to the Bishop to withdraw from an existing structure of an inter-diocesan tribunal, if he decides to form his own tribunal or if he chooses a nearer one."[14]

---

12  C. 1423: "§1. With the approval of the Apostolic See, several diocesan bishops can agree to establish a single tribunal of first instance for their dioceses in place of the diocesan tribunals mentioned in cann. 1419-1421. In this case, the group of bishops or a bishop they designate has all the powers which a diocesan bishop has over his own tribunal. §2. The tribunals mentioned in §1 can be established either for any cases whatsoever or only for certain types of cases; §1. Plures dioecesani Episcopi, probante Sede Apostolica, possunt concordes, in locum tribunalium dioecesanorum de quibus in cann. 1419-1421, unicum constituere in suis dioecesibus tribunal primae instantiae; quo in casu ipsorum Episcoporum coetui vel Episcopo ab eisdem designato omnes competunt potestates, quas Episcopus dioecesanus habet circa suum tribunal. §2. Tribunalia, de quibus in § 1, constitui possunt vel ad causas quaslibet vel ad aliqua tantum causarum genera."
13  *Mitis iudex Dominus Jesus*, Art. 8,§ 2.
14  *Subsidium*, 17.

The norms governing the appellate tribunal for the interdiocesan tribunal of first instance remain unchanged, as we have seen above. Noted canonist, John Beal, in his commentary on *Mitis iudex* states:

> This empowerment of bishops to withdraw unilaterally from interdiocesan tribunals applies only to interdiocesan tribunals of first instance, the only ones dealt with in canon 1423. In the United States, several interdiocesan appellate tribunals were established shortly before the provisions of the 1983 code abrogated the American Procedural Norms which had for the previous decade virtually eliminated mandatory appeals of affirmative decisions in marriage nullity cases. The establishment of these interdiocesan tribunals was prompted by concern that the traditional metropolitan appellate system would be unable to deal efficiently with the anticipated volume of appeals. Although these interdiocesan tribunals of second instance were established pursuant to Apostolic Signatura's 1970 Norms on Interdiocesan and Regional Tribunals, they are now governed by canon 1439. Because these tribunals constitute the appellate structure for several dioceses and have effectively replaced the metropolitan tribunal, they cannot be simply dismantled until an alternate appellate structure such as a return to the metropolitan model has been agreed on by all participants.
>
> As a result, the norms of *Mitis Iudex* do not authorize unilateral withdrawals from these interdiocesan appellate tribunals by participating bishops. However, since *Mitis Iudex* encourages that "the appeal to the metropolitan be restored . . . [as] a distinctive sign of collegiality in the church," the desire of bishops currently participating in an interdiocesan appellate court to return to the metropolitan system would surely receive favorable consideration from the Apostolic Signatura.[15]

---

15   John Beal, "*Mitis Judex* Canons 1671-1682, 1688- 1691: A Commentary," *The Jurist* 75 (2015) 531-532.

Therefore with regard to the court of second instance,[16] the diocesan bishop is not free to withdraw from an appellate model without permission of the Supreme Tribunal of the Apostolic Signatura.

### Process, Practical Resources and Observations

Considering the number of automatic appeals to the courts of second instance, the modified metropolitan appellate tribunal system established by the Apostolic Signatura in 2003 worked well for the Province of Indiana. However, after the promulgation of *Mitis iudex*, it soon became readily apparent that returning to the traditional metropolitan system would not only be more suited to the vision of synodality envisioned in *Mitis iudex*, but would also benefit the suffragan dioceses from an economic and personnel perspective.

When Indianapolis was the appeal court for Fort Wayne – South Bend, we would average between 30-40 second instance cases a year, in which the majority were affirmative decisions on automatic appeal. In the last two years, since the return to the traditional metropolitan system, we have averaged 15 appeals total from the four suffragan dioceses in the province. From a practical perspective, since Indianapolis is the largest tribunal in the province, the personnel and budget was already in place to instruct the cases for the province. To date, only one case from Indianapolis has been appealed to our court of second instance.

### Steps to Change an Appellate Tribunal of Second Instance

In order to change the appellate model (whether a return to the traditional metropolitan appellate structure, or to a modified appellate structure), the following processes are required:

1. A letter addressed to the Apostolic Signatura in which the metropolitan bishop and suffragan bishops consent to the proposed change of appellate tribunal (example #1).

---

16  C. 1439 §1: "If a single tribunal of first instance has been established for several dioceses according to the norm of Can. 1423, the conference of bishops must establish a tribunal of second instance with the approval of the Apostolic See unless the dioceses are all suffragan of the same archdiocese; Si quod tribunal primae instantiae unicum pro pluribus dioecesibus, ad normam can. 1423, constitutum sit, Episcoporum conferentia debet tribunal secundae instantiae, probante Sede Apostolica, constituere, nisi dioeceses sint omnes eiusdem archidioecesis suffraganeae. §2. Episcoporum conferentia potest, probante Sede Apostolica, unum vel plura tribunalia secundae instantiae constituere, etiam praeter casus de quibus in § 1. §3. Quod attinet ad tribunalia secundae instantiae, de quibus in §§ 1-2, Episcoporum conferentia vel Episcopus ab ea designatus omnes habent potestates, quae Episcopo dioecesano competunt circa suum tribunal."

2. A letter addressed to the Apostolic Signatura in which the metropolitan bishop has secured the consent of the appellate tribunal for the metropolitan tribunal structure (example #2).

3. Both numbers 1 and 2 require the approval of the Apostolic Signatura. Should these requests be granted, the Apostolic Signatura issues a decree establishing, in this particular case, the traditional metropolitan appellate structure and the appellate tribunal of the metropolitan tribunal (examples #3 and #4).

4. After the Apostolic Signatura grants permission, it is the task of the metropolitan bishop to communicate the approval and decree to the suffragan bishops, and to the appellate tribunal of the metropolitan (examples #5 and #7).

5. Finally, the decree is also communicated to the vicars judicial of the suffragan dioceses and the vicar judicial of the appellate tribunal of the metropolitan (examples #6 and #8).

To give an understanding of the timetable, after consultation with the vicars judicial of the Indiana province, the metropolitan bishop presented the proposal in a meeting of the provincial bishops, who agreed to the proposal. The metropolitan bishop then submitted the letters a month later to the Apostolic Signatura, and approval was received two months after that.

**The Decree**

In the notification of the approval, the effective date communicated to the suffragan dioceses and appellate tribunal of the metropolitan was set as the date of the decree. For causes pending at the time of the decree effective date, the Signatura refers to article 22 of the *Norms for Interdiocesan or Regional or Interregional Tribunals* "by way of analogy" (example 4). The *Norms for Interdiocesan or Regional or Interregional Tribunals* state:

With regard to cases which, on the date of execution of the decree, are pending in the ordinary diocesan tribunals of the respective territorial circuit, these norms shall be observed:

1. Cases which are being acted upon in first instance, should be turned over to the new tribunal of first instance if the issues have not yet been defined in accordance with common law; cases, however, which look to nullity of marriage and are only in the initiatory stage can be turned over to the same tribunal if the consent of each of the spouses and of the defender of the bond is obtained.

On the other hand, if the decree of closing in the case has been already declared and issued, the definitive sentence must be pronounced by the tribunal before which the case was introduced.

In each case appeal is lodged with the new appellate tribunal, without prejudice, however, to the faculty referred to in canon 1599, § 1 , n . 1.

2. With the appropriate changes having been made, the same procedure should be followed in cases which are being acted upon in the appellate level.[17]

From a reading of the *Norms for Interdiocesan or Regional or Interregional Tribunals*, it would appear any causes that were appealed under the modified appellate structure and have not been decreed at joinder of issue would be sent to the new place of appeal, while any remaining causes that have been joined would be completed in the original place of appeal before the change in appellate tribunal.

**Conclusion**

The experience of the province of Indiana returning to the traditional metropolitan tribunal model has been a positive experience which not only honors the synodality envisioned by Pope Francis in *Mitis iudex*, but also has had a practical benefit for the suffragan dioceses in the province, and the metropolitan, by consolidating all appeal cases in one place.

---

17   Supreme Tribunal of the Apostolic Tribunal, *Norms for Interdiocesan or Regional or Interregional Tribunals* (28 Dec, 1970) AAS 63-64: "Quod attinet ad causas die executionis decreti pendentes apud Tribunalia dioecesana ordinaria respectivae circumscriptionis territorialis, haec serventur: 1. Causae quae agitantur in prima instantia, deferantur ad novum Tribunal primae instantiae si dubia nondum fuerint concordata ad normam iuris communis; deferri vero eidem possunt quae nullitatem matrimonii respiciunt et in phasi instructoria versantur, accedente consensu utriusque coniugis et Defensoris vinculi. Sin autem iam editum sit praefatum decretum conclusionis in causa, sententia definitiva proferri debet a Tribunali apud quod causa introducta est. In utroque casu appellatio interponatur apud novum Tribunal appellationis, salva tamen facultate de qua in can. 1599, § 1, n. 1. 2. Idem fiat, congrua congruis referenda, congrua congruis referenda, in causis quae agitantur in gradu appellationis." English translation from *Canon Law Digest* 7: 925-926.

*EXAMPLE 1*

**Sanitized Request to the Supreme Tribunal of the Apostolic Signature by the Ordinaries of the Province Requesting Change to Metropolitan Appellate Tribunal Structure**

[DATE]

Supreme Tribunal of the Apostolic Signatura
Palazzo Della Cancelleria
00120 *Città* del Vaticano

Your Eminence/Excellency:

We, the undersigned Ordinaries of the Province of _____, ask for a modification of the rescript of _____ (Prot. N. _____ SAT) whereby there was established a modified form of the metropolitan system for second instance solely in matrimonial cases.

Since the establishment of the aforementioned second instance system, there have been notable changes in procedural law through the new norms of *Mitis iudex Dominus Iesus*. Thus, to better facilitate these procedural changes, we request the following modification:

*That the modified form of the metropolitan system for second instance in matrimonial cases be restored to the previous metropolitan system, according to canon 1438, in which matrimonial cases appealed in the suffragan dioceses of the province of _____ will be appealed to the Metropolitan Tribunal of the Archdiocese of _____.*

Concerning appeals from the Archdiocese of _____, please find attached a separate letter from the Archbishop of _____ regarding the court of second instance for the Archdiocese of _____. Further, regarding non-matrimonial cases, we are requesting the same arrangement as established in the rescript of _____.

In closing, we take this occasion to express our deepest gratitude to Your Eminence and the staff of the Supreme Tribunal for your assistance to us in these most important matters.

Sincerely yours in Our Lord,


Most Rev. _____
Metropolitan Archbishop


Most Rev.                                    Most Rev.
Suffragan Bishop                      Suffragan Bishop


Chancellor

*EXAMPLE 2*

**Sanitized Request to the Supreme Tribunal of the Apostolic Signature by the Metropolitan Archbishop Requesting A Change to the Appeal Court of the Metropolitan Tribunal if the Request of the Ordinaries of the Province is Granted**

[DATE]

Supreme Tribunal of the Apostolic Signatura
Palazzo Della Cancelleria
00120 *Città* del Vaticano

Your Eminence/Excellency:

The Ordinaries of the Province of _____ have respectfully requested that the modified form of the metropolitan system for second instance in matrimonial cases be restored to the previous metropolitan system according to canon 1438. If this modified system is granted and the matrimonial cases appealed in the suffragan dioceses of the province of _____ are appealed to the Metropolitan Tribunal of the Archdiocese of _____, then the undersigned requests that:

*the appeals from the Archdiocese of _____ be appealed to the court of second instance of the Archdiocese of _____.*

I have conferred with my brother bishop, Archbishop _____ of the Archdiocese of _____, and he is in agreement should this modification be granted.

In closing, I thank Your Eminence and the staff of the Supreme Tribunal for your assistance to in these most important matters.

Sincerely yours in Our Lord,

Most Reverend _____
Metropolitan Archbishop


Chancellor


Cc: [Archbishop of Appellate Tribunal]
    Archbishop of _____

*EXAMPLE 3*

## Sanitized Decree of the Supreme Tribunal of the Apostolic Signatura Restoring the Simple Metropolitan System for Second Instance

Prot. n.

Litteris die _____ datis, Exc.mus Archiepiscopus Metropolita et Exc. mi Episcopi suffraganei Provinciae Ecclesiasticae _____ restitutionem petierunt ordinationis tribunalium de qua in can. 1438, n. 1 pro causis in gradu appellationis pertractandis, designata Tribunali Metropolitano _____ ut foro appellationis pro causis _____ in primo iurisdictionis gradu definitis, iuxta praescriptum can. 1438, n. 2.

Quibus praehabitis,

**SUPREMUM SIGNATURAE APOSTOLICAE TRIBUNAL**

Re sedulo examinata;

Attentis precibus ab Exc.mis Praesulibus porrectis;

Viso decreto die _____ edito (prot. n. _____ SAT), quo novissime immutata est ordinatio tribunalium appellationis in praefata Provincia;

Praehabito consensu Exc.mi Archiepiscopi _____ quoad designationem fori appellationis pro causis iudicialibus _____;
Audito Rev.mo Promotore Iustitiae;

Vi art. 124, n. 2 et 4 Const. Ap. *Pastor bonus* necnon artt. 35, n. 2 et 4 et 115, §§ 1 et 4 H.S.T. *Legis propriae,*

### decrevit:

**Restitui ordinationem tribunalium appellationis de qua in can. 1438, n. I pro Provincia Ecclesiastica _____;**
**Approbari, donec aliter provideatur, designationem Tribunalis Metropolitani _____ utpote fori appellationis pro omnibus causis iudicialibus a Tribunali Metropolitano _____ in prima instantia definitis.**

Quoad regimen causarum die quo hoc decretum vigere incipiet pendentium servetur, saltem ex analogia, praescriptum art. 22 Normarum pro

Tribunalibus Interdioecesanis, vel Regionalibus aut Intenegionalibus ab hac Signatura Apostolica die 28 decembris 1970 editarum (AAS 63 [1971] 492).

Quod notificetur iis quorum interest ad omnes iuris effectus.

Datum Romae, e sede Supremi Signaturae Apostolicae Tribunalis, die _____.

Praefectus

Secretarius

EXAMPLE 4

## An Unofficial Translation[18] of the Decree of the Supreme Tribunal of the Apostolic Signatura Restoring the Simple Metropolitan System for Second Instance

Prot. n.

In a letter dated for _____, His Excellency, the Archbishop Metropolitan, and their Excellencies, the suffragan bishops of the Ecclesiastical Province of _____, have petitioned for the restoration of the tribunal organization mentioned in Canon 1438, 1° for cases to be handled at the level of appeal, having designated the Metropolitan Tribunal of _____ as the form of appeal for causes decided at the first decree of jurisdiction in _____, according to the prescripts of canon 1438, 2°.

Since this has happened,

### THE SUPREME TRIBUNAL OF THE APOSTOLIC SIGNATURA,

Having carefully examined the matter

Taking into account the requests made by Their Excellencies;

Having seen the decree of _____, (prot. n.), by which the order of appeal of the tribunals in the aforementioned Province was most recently changed;

Having received the consent of His Excellency, the Archbishop of _____, concerning the designation as the forum of appeal for judicial cases of _____;

Having heard the Rev. Promoter of Justice;

According to the force of art. 124, n. 2 et 4 of the Apostolic Constitution, *Pastor Bonus* as well as articles 35, n. 2 et 4 et 115, §§ 1 et 4 of the Proper Law of This Supreme Tribunal, has decreed the following:

That there be restored the arrangement of the tribunals of appeal as mentioned in canon 1438, 1° on behalf of the Ecclesiastical Province of _____;

---

18  Unofficial translation by Reverend Monsignor Frederick C. Easton, JCL. Used with permission.

That the designation of the Metropolitan Tribunal of _____ as the form of appeal for all judicial cases decided in first instance by the Metropolitan Tribunal of _____ be approved until otherwise provided for.

As far as the regimen of causes pending on the day in which this decree begins to take effect there is to be observed, at least by analogy, the prescripts of article 22 of the norms for Inter-Diocesan Tribunals, Regional Tribunals and Interregional Tribunals issued by the Apostolic Signatura on 28 December 1970 (AAS 63 [1971] 492).

This decree is to be communicated to those for whom it applies in order to achieve all effects of law.

Given in Rome, from the seat of the Supreme Tribunal of the Apostolic Signatura on the _____.

Prefect

Secretary

*EXAMPLE 5*

**Sanitized Letter of Notification of the Newly Erected Metropolitan Tribunal System to the Bishop of the Suffragan Diocese**

[DATE]

[NAME]
[ADDRESS]
[ADDRESS]

Dear Bishop _____,

On _____, I received a letter from the Apostolic Signature (Prot. N. _____ SAT) granting our request that the Province of _____ be restored to the Metropolitan appellate structure described in can. 1438, n.1. I have attached a copy of the letter, decree, and norms from the Apostolic Signatura, and a translation in English.

After due consultation among the Tribunals of First Instance, we have established that the effective date is the date of the decree which is _____. My judicial vicar, _____, has made provision to contact your judicial vicars to work out the implementation of the appellate structure.

With continued appreciation of our collaboration and with continued prayers for our apostolate, I remain

Sincerely yours in Christ the Redeemer,


Most Reverend _____
Metropolitan Archbishop



Chancellor

*EXAMPLE 6*

**Sanitized Letter of Notification of the Newly Erected Metropolitan Tribunal System to the Judicial Vicar of the Suffragan Diocese**

[DATE]

[NAME]
[ADDRESS]
[ADDRESS]

Dear Father,

On _____, Archbishop _____ received a letter from the Apostolic Signature (Prot. N. _____ SAT) granting the request of the Provincial Bishops of _____ that the Metropolitan appellate structure described in can. 1438, n.1 be restored. I have attached a copy of the letter, decree, and norms from the Apostolic Signatura, and a translation in English.

We have established that the effective date is the date of the decree which is _____. Therefore, from this point on, please forward any appeals of first instance decisions to:

[NAME]
[ADDRESS]
[ADDRESS]

With continued appreciation of our collaboration and with continued prayers for our tribunal service, I remain

Sincerely yours in the Lord,


Vicar Judicial
Metropolitan Archdiocese

**EXAMPLE 7**

**Sanitized Letter of Notification of the Newly Erected Metropolitan Tribunal System to the Archbishop of the Appellate Tribunal**

[DATE]

[NAME]
[ADDRESS]
[ADDRESS]

Dear Archbishop,

On _____, I received a letter from the Apostolic Signature (Prot. N. _____ SAT) granting the request of the Provincial Bishops of _____ that the Metropolitan appellate structure described in can. 1438, n.1 be restored. I have attached a copy of the letter, decree, and norms from the Apostolic Signatura, and a translation in English.

I would like to personally thank you for agreeing to be the appellate tribunal for the Archdiocese of _____. My judicial vicar, _____, has made provision to contact your judicial vicar to work out the implementation of the appellate structure.

With continued appreciation of our collaboration and with continued prayers for our apostolate, I remain

Sincerely yours in Christ the Redeemer,


Most Reverend _____
Metropolitan Archbishop



Chancellor

*EXAMPLE 8*

**Sanitized Letter of Notification of the Newly Erected Metropolitan Tribunal System to the Judicial Vicar of the Appellate Tribunal**

[DATE]

[NAME]
[ADDRESS]
[ADDRESS]

Dear Father,

On _____, Archbishop _____ received a letter from the Apostolic Signature (Prot. N. _____, SAT) granting the request of the Provincial Bishops of _____ that the Metropolitan appellate structure described in can. 1438, n.1 be restored. I have attached a copy of the letter, decree, and norms from the Apostolic Signatura, and a translation in English.

I would like to personally thank you for agreeing to be the appellate tribunal for the Archdiocese of _____. We have established that the effective date is the date of the decree which is _____. Therefore, from this point on, we will be forwarding any appeals of first instance decisions the Archdiocese of _____.

With continued appreciation of our collaboration and with continued prayers for our tribunal service, I remain

Sincerely yours in the Lord,


Vicar Judicial
Metropolitan Tribunal

# Seminar

## Diocesan Administration *Sede Vacante*: Principles and Questions
### Rev. Aaron Nord

Imagine you are the diocesan administrator of the imaginary diocese of Utopia, Missouri. The diocese is vacant; the former bishop has died; you have been elected to administer the diocese *sede vacante*. In the last year before your former bishop died, he merged many of the parishes in the city center of Utopia and consolidated the three diocesan high schools in the city of Utopia into a single campus. The former bishop's plan had foreseen that the newly merged parishes would one day sell the property of the closed parishes that was no longer in use, and the former bishop's plan had foreseen that the diocese would sell the campuses of the closed high schools and use the funds to establish an endowment for the new high school. While the former bishop lived, no one came forward to buy the properties, but the diocese and the parishes have found developers interested in buying the properties. The value of each parish property and each diocesan property is greater than $250,000, the minimum sum set by the USCCB (United States Conference of Catholic Bishops) for a small diocese like Utopia.[1] Can a diocesan administrator authorize the sale of the diocesan properties, following the procedures of canon 1292? Can a diocesan administrator give the permission for the sale of the parish properties, following the procedures of canon 1292?

Let us read the applicable canons. Canon 427 §1 says, "A diocesan administrator is bound by the obligations and possesses the power of a diocesan bishop, excluding those matters which are excepted by their nature or by the law itself".[2] Canon 427 §2 is not applicable: it talks about the procedures after

---

[1] United States Conference of Catholic Bishops, complementary norms *Canon 1292 §1 – Minimum and Maximum sums, Alienation of Church Property*, Nov. 12, 3003 [accessed October 13, 2017], http://www.usccb.org/beliefs-and-teachings/what-we-believe/canon-law/complementary-norms/canon-1292-1-minimum-and-maximum-sums-alienation-of-church-property.cfm.

[2] "Administrator dioecesanus tenetur obligationibus et gaudet potestate Episcopi dioecesani, iis exclusis quae ex rei natura aut ipso iure excipiuntur". All citations from the 1983 Code of Canon Law are from the Canon Law Society of America, *Code of Canon Law, Latin-English Edition, New English Translation* (Washington: Canon Law Society of America, 1998).

a diocesan administrator's election. Canon 428 §1 says, "When a see is vacant, nothing is to be altered".[3] And canon 428 §2 says,

> Those who temporarily care for the governance of the diocese are forbidden to do anything which can be prejudicial in some way to the diocese or episcopal rights. They, and consequently all others, are specifically prohibited, whether personally or through another, from removing or destroying any documents of the diocesan curia or from changing anything in them.[4]

The canons give three basic ideas. First, the diocesan administrator has the power of the diocesan bishop—except where the law or the nature of the thing provides otherwise. A quick glance at the commentary on this canon reveals that the reference to the "nature of the matter" refers to cases where the diocesan administrator is not a bishop. In such a case, the diocesan administrator cannot preform sacraments reserved to bishops, like ordination, though the diocesan administrator can give dimissorial letters permitting his subjects to be ordained by other bishops. Second, the diocesan administrator should not innovate—that is, change—anything in the diocese. Third, the diocesan administrator is prohibited from taking any action which might prejudice the rights of the diocese or the future bishop.

Yet it is not immediately clear how to apply these canons to practical questions facing the diocese of Utopia. Is selling diocesan property no longer in use an innovation, a change? Does that action give prejudice to the rights of the diocese or the coming bishop? Is giving parishes permission to sell their property an innovation, a change? Does that action give prejudice to the rights of the diocese or the coming bishop?

Facing those questions of interpretation, the diocesan administrator might send his canonists to learn what canonical authors have written in commentaries on this topic. His canonist will discover that the authors have different views which when applied to practical questions give different results. For example, Piero Amenta and Roman Walczak hold that the diocesan administrator has only the authority of a local ordinary and so the diocesan administrator is blocked from every action that which the law reserves for diocesan bishops.[5] Canon 1292

---

3   "Sede vacante, nihil innovetur".
4   "Illi qui ad interim dioecesis regimen curant, vetantur quidpiam agere quod vel dioecesi vel episcopalibus iuribus praeiudicium aliquod afferre possit; speciatim prohibentur ipsi, ac proinde alii quicumque, quominus sive per se sive per alium curiae dioecesanae documenta quaelibet subtrahant vel destruant, aut in iis quidquam immutent."
5   Piero Amenta, "Appunti sulla vacanza della sede episcopale" *Apollinaris* 74 (2001) 365; Roman Walczak, *Sede vacante come conseguenza della perdita di un ufficio ecclesiastico nel Codice di Diritto Canonico del 1983* (Rome, Pontificia Università Lateranense, 2008) 194.

reserves the authorization of alienation to the diocesan bishop, so Piero Amenta and Roman Walczak would say that the diocesan administrator cannot authorize the sale of the parish property or of the diocesan property. Ladislas Ziółek distinguishes diocesan property from parish property. Selling the property of the diocese is prohibited, because it gives prejudice to the rights of the future bishop, while giving license to the parishes to sell their property does not give prejudice to the future bishop, because he is not the administrator of that property.[6] Joseph Robert Punderson says that selling property gives prejudice to the diocese, and canon 428 §2 blocks the sale of the sale of diocesan property *sede vacante*, when there is no bishop.[7] Eduardo Molano and Marino Mosconi would prohibit the sales because the administrator's actions would condition in some way the actions of the future bishops—and then one must wonder what other actions might be prohibited, since many actions, even simple ones, in some way condition the actions of the future bishop.[8] Carlos Soler Ferrán makes this comment: "The problem here is that every decision is at the same time innovative and risky. It is not easy to determine the line where acts that fall under this prohibition begin. In principle, grave decisions and those that modify the "structure" of the diocese (for example, a merger of parishes) must be avoided".[9] In this case, however, the mergers have already happened—so perhaps the sale of property would be permitted, or at least not clearly forbidden? To make matters worse, many of these authors say that the general principles laid down by canon 428 admit to exceptions, although different authors give different standards for judging when exceptions are warranted.[10]

I propose to you that the confusion among the commentators is not necessary, because careful attention to the principles which lie at the root of the canonical

6 Ladislas Ziółek, *Sede vacante nihil innovetur: Studium historico-canonicum ad can. 436 C.I.C.* (Rome, Pontificia Università Gregoriana: 1966) 105, 107.
7 Joseph Robert Punderson, *Diocesan Consultors; Development and Present Legislation* (Rome: Pontificia Università Gregoriana: 1988) 274.
8 Marino Mosconi, "'Sede vacante nihil innovetur'. I limiti all'esercizio dell'autorità nella condizione di vacanza della sede", *Quaderni di Diritto Ecclesiale* 17 (2004) 160; Eduardo Molano, "El régimen de la diócesis en situación de sede impedida y de sede vacante", *Ius Canonicum* 21 (1981) 615.
9 "El problema es que toda decisión es, en mayor o menor medida, simultáneamente innovadora y arriesgada; por lo tanto, no es fácil determinar el límite donde empiezan las actuaciones que caen bajo esta prohibición. En principio, las decisiones graves y aquellas que modifiquen la "estructura" de la diócesis (p. ej., una unión de parroquias) deben evitarse", Carlos Soler Ferrán, "Art. 2 De la sede vacante", in *Comentario Exegético al Código de Derecho Canónico*, 2nd ed., edited by Ángel Marzoa Rodríguez, Jorge Miras Pouso, and Rafael Rodrígues-Ocaña, II/1, (Pamplona: Ediciones Universidad de Navarra, 1997) 875. Translation by Ernest Caparros (ed.) in *Exegetical Commentary on the Code of Canon Law II/1: Book II, The People of God, Canons 204-459* (Montréal: Wilson and Lafleur, 2004) 893-923.
10 Roman Walczak, *Sede vacante come conseguenza*, 195; Jospeh Robert Punderson, *Diocesan Consultors*, 273-274; Eduardo Molano, "El régimen de la diócesis", 615; Carlos Soler Ferrán, "Art. 2 De la sede vacante", 875.

tradition gives a clear, balanced, and solid interpretation of canon 427 and canon 428. When canonists read the canons in the light of those principles which motivated past laws given for the vacant diocese, canon 427 and 428 have clear meanings which allow for clear resolutions of practical problems like those facing the diocese of Utopia. Here are my intentions for what follows. First, I will present my solution to the questions facing the diocese of Utopia. Second, I will explain the interpretation and principles behind my solution. Third, I go on to apply the canons to a few other practical questions, such as the question of how to handle a deficit in diocesan budget *sede vacante*. Finally, as an addendum, I will say a few words about two other practical questions that regularly arise in vacant dioceses.

Then let me first respond to the questions facing the diocese of Utopia. On the one hand, the diocesan administrator can give parishes permission to sell their property, because he has the authority of the diocesan bishop (canon 427 §1). Canon 428 §2 does not block the sale of parish property because the property belongs to the parishes, and so neither the future bishop nor the diocese lose any rights when the property is sold (canon 1256). Canon 428 §1 does not block the sale of parish property because the parishes, which are indeed key diocesan structures, have already been merged by the last bishop.[11] On the other hand, the diocesan administrator cannot give permission to sell the former diocesan high schools. While the diocesan administrator has the authority of the diocesan bishop, both canon 428 §1 and canon 428 §2 prohibit selling diocesan property *sede vacante*. Canon 428 §2 prohibits the sale because a sale of diocesan property means the dioceses loses its rights over the property.[12] That gives prejudice to the rights of the diocese. Canon 428 §1 prohibits the sale because the decision to permanently give up valuable diocesan assets for the sake of other goods is a decision which belongs to the diocesan bishop, not to his temporary replacement.[13] Finally, if special circumstance make it urgent to sell diocesan property *sede vacante*, the right solution is not for the diocesan administrator to invoke some exception by reason of necessity or advantage, but for the diocesan administrator to have recourse to the Holy See.[14] The nuncio can give permission for individual acts which go beyond the diocesan administrator's normal authority.[15]

Now please allow me to give my interpretation of the key canons, canon 427 and canon 428. Canon 427 §1 gives the basic law for the vacant diocese. Canon

---

11  Aaron Paul Nord, *Sede Vacante Diocesan Administration* (Rome: Editrice Pontificia Università Gregoriana, 2014) 117-118.
12  Ibid.,113.
13  Ibid., 21-22, 24-26, 119.
14  Ibid., 141-150.
15  Congregation for Bishops, *Index Facultatum Legatis Pontificis tributarum*, n. 3, *Ius Ecclesiae* 12 (2000) 283-286; Congregation for the Evangelization of Peoples, *Index Facultatum Legatis Pontificis in territoriis missionum tributarum*, n. 5, in *Ius Ecclesiae* 12 (2000) 286-288.

427 §1 derives from a principle which I will call the principle of aid, and in accord with the principle of aid, canon 427 §1 gives the diocesan administrator the whole authority of the diocesan bishop. However, the canon 427 itself alerts us that because of the special circumstances of a vacant diocese, other laws will place some special limits on the authority of the diocesan administrator.

Canon 428 §1 gives first and most basic restriction on the diocesan administrator's authority. Canon 428 §2 derives from a principle which I will call the principle of restraint, and in accord with the principle of restraint, canon 428 §1 prohibits the diocesan administrator from innovations, that is, from making changes to key diocesan structures, from making changes to key diocesan directives, and from certain other changes which should only be made by a diocesan bishop, and not by his temporary replacements.[16]

Canon 428 §2 gives a second and more specific restriction on the diocesan administrator's authority. Canon 428 §2 derives from a principle which I will call the principle of defense, and in accord with the principle of defense, canon 428 §2 prohibits the diocesan administrator from taking any action which would give legal prejudice to the diocese or the future bishop. By legal prejudice I do not mean any kind of harm whatsoever, and I do not mean anything which in some way would condition the action of the future diocesan bishop. By legal prejudice I mean something far more specific: the loss of legal rights, or the serious risk of loss of legal rights.[17]

Below I will provide three more examples of how the canons, interpreted in this way, give solid, balanced, clear responses to practical questions. But is this interpretation true? Is this interpretation really what the law means? To answer that question, I need to take a moment to examine the principles which I claim underlie these laws, and to show how they derive from basic problems facing a vacant diocese. Since the principles derive from basic problems facing a vacant diocese, they also appear very early in the canonical tradition. Canon 6 §2 indicates the importance of the canonical tradition for interpreting laws which also appeared in the 1917 Code of Canon Law; indeed, since the 1917 Code itself preserved much older laws for the vacant diocese, interpreting the present law leads the canonist back to some rather venerable texts.

The first principle which I mentioned was the principle of aid. The principle of aid says to those who temporarily care for a vacant diocese, "Continue the work of the bishop when he is absent." The principle of aid comes from the basic situation of the vacant diocese. Diocesan bishops have a very important role in the local church. When there is no diocesan bishop, the good of the faithful would suffer unless there was someone present to temporarily continue the work which is normally done by the diocesan bishop.

16 Nord, *Sede Vacante*, 117-121.
17 Ibid., 111-113.

Appropriately, the principle of aid appears in the oldest texts in the canonical tradition on the law of a vacant diocese, the letters exchanged among St. Cyprian, the priests of his diocese of Carthage, and the priests of the diocese of Rome, which was vacant after the martyrdom of Fabian in the persecution of Decius around 250 A.D. St. Cyprian wrote to his clergy while he was unable to govern Carthage, "I ask you for the sake of your faith and religion to discharge there [in Carthage] both your parts and mine, so that nothing may be lacking either in discipline or diligence."[18] A little later, the clergy of Rome wrote to Cyprian. They wrote,

> Before the constitution of the bishop, we think nothing should be innovated, but we believe the care of the lapsed must be moderately tempered, such that, in the interim, while one waits for God to give us a bishop, the cases of those who can bear the delays of a postponement are held in suspense. But the case of those whose outcome, pressing hard on the end of their life, cannot bear a delay, [such a case,] with penance done and with detestation for their deeds frequently professed – if with tears, if with groans, if with weeping they produce signs of a suffering and truly penitent mind, when no hope of living according to man remains – in the end [such a case can] be helped cautiously and with anxious care. For God himself knows what he will do about such ones and how he will consider the burdens of his judgment, while we, however, anxiously take care lest either impious men praise our spineless easiness or the truly penitent accuse our hard near-cruelty.[19]

---

18 "peto uos pro fide et religione uestra fungamini illic et uestris partibus et meis, ut nihil uel ad disciplinam uel ad diligentiam desit", Cyprian, *Epistula* 5, 1, FFFCCC, , in *Sancti Cypriani Episcopi Epistularium: Ad fidem codicum summa cura selectorum necnon adhibitis editionibus prioribus praecipuis edidit*, edited by Gerardus Frederik Diercks, I, (Turnhout: Typographi Brepols Editores Pontificii, 1999) p. 27.

19 "ante constitutionem episcopi nihil innouandum putauimus, sed lapsorum curam mediocriter temperandam esse credimus, ut interim dum episcopus dari a Deo nobis sustinetur, in suspenso eorum qui moras possunt dilationis sustinere causa teneatur, eorum autem quorum uiate suae finem urgens exitus dilationem non potest ferre, acta paenitentia et professa frequenter suorum detestatione factorum, si lacrimis, si gemitibus, si fletibus dolentis ac uere paenitentis animi signa prodiderint, cum spes uiuendi secundum hominem nulla substiterit, ita demum caute et sollicite subueniri, Deo ipso sciente quid de talibus faciat et qualiter iudicii sui examinet pondera, nobis tamen anxie curantibus ut nec pronam nostram improbi homines laudent facilitatem nec uere paenitentes accusent nostram quasi duram crudelitatem". Cyprian, *Epistula* 30, 8, in *Sancti Cypriani Episcopi Epistularium: Ad fidem codicum summa cura selectorum necnon adhibitis editionibus prioribus praecipuis edidit*, edited by Gerardus Frederik Diercks, I, (Turnhout: Typographi Brepols Editores Pontificii, 1999) pp. 149-150.

St. Cyprian knew that someone had to continue his work while he was absent; the crucial work of a diocesan bishop could not cease altogether; he entrusted this task collectively to the clergy of Carthage. Similarly, while the clergy of Rome held back from resolving important questions, reserving them for the coming bishop, they also governed the dioceses and resolved some of the most pressing cases. Both Cyprian and the clergy of Rome bear witness to the principle of aid: when there is no bishop, someone must come to the aid of the faithful and take up the bishop's important work. In today's law, the principle of aid appears in canon 427 §1: "A diocesan administrator is bound by the obligations and possesses the power of a diocesan bishop".

The second principle which I mentioned was the principle of restraint. The principle of restraint says to those who temporarily care for a vacant diocese, "Restrain your action since you are not the absent bishop." The principle of restraint also comes from the basic situation of the vacant diocese; it is like the obverse of the principle of aid. Since diocesan bishops have a special and unique relationship with their flock, there are some actions which a diocesan bishop rightly takes to aid his flock that are not appropriate to those who temporarily stand in the place of the diocesan bishop.

The principle of restraint also appears in that ancient correspondence from the clergy of Rome to Cyprian. While they did resolve the most pressing cases of the lapsed, they reserved other cases for the future bishop of Rome; in their mind, reconciling the lapsed was a work which belonged in a particular way to the future bishop. While they as the clergy of Rome cared for the diocese in the bishop's absence, still there were some acts which belonged to the future bishop, not to his temporary replacements. In today's law the principle of restraint appears in canon 428 §1: "When a see is vacant, nothing is to be altered".

The third principle which I mentioned was the principle of defense. The principle of defense says to those who temporarily care for a vacant diocese, "Defend the diocese from violations until the bishop is present". The principle of defense is not so fundamental as the principle of aid or the principle of restraint. The principle of defense does not come from the basic situation of the vacant diocese, but does come from a very common experience of the Church: when dioceses are vacant, people try to take advantage of the bishop's absence to do things which they would not attempt if a bishop were present.

That practical experience was noticed early in the life of the Church, and so the principle of defense also appears in some rather early texts, although not so early as Cyprian's letters. For example, the Council of Ancyra in 314. A.D. ordered, "[It seems that the] church should reclaim whatever priests have sold from those things which belong to the church while there was no bishop. But [it seems that] it should be left to the judgment of the bishop whether it is right to receive the price or not, since the yield of the sold goods may return a greater price than the things themselves".[20] In another text, Gregory the Great said that he was unwilling to seem to proceed prejudicially to the rights of a future bishop in resolving a dispute involving a diocese which was vacant; accordingly, he ordered a provisional solution until the future bishop would be named.[21] Both the fathers of Ancrya and Gregory the Great have a special concern to protect the goods and rights of dioceses which are vacant and to preserve those goods and rights unharmed until the arrival of the future bishop. In today's law the principle of defense appears in canon 428 §2: "Those who temporarily care for the governance of the diocese are forbidden to do anything which can be prejudicial in some way to the diocese or episcopal rights".

There is also a principle, a fourth principle which I have not yet mentioned, the principle of continuity. The principle of continuity says to those who temporarily care for a vacant diocese, "Follow the tracks left by the last bishop." Like the principle of defense, the principle of continuity does not come from the basic situation of a vacant diocese, but from a very common experience of the Church: change takes energy and effort. The diocesan administrator should follow the tracks of the last bishop because when the next bishop comes, the new bishop will likely make some changes of his own, rearranging somethings to suit his vision or priorities or preferences. So the diocesan administrator, when possible, should leave things as they are so that the diocese will not waste effort making changes that the new bishop will change again. There are some other considerations that support the principle of continuity, but for the sake of brevity, I will pass over them.[22]

The principle of continuity also appears in an early canonical text. In a letter to Bishop Leontius of Urbinatus who had temporary care of the diocese of Arminum, Gregory the Great rebuked him for removing the officials of the former bishop and replacing them with men loyal to him.[23] Even if Leontius suspected dishonesty among the clerics appointed by the former bishop, Gregory told Leontius that he should have appointed "for the activity also some of your men, so that by alternate care [your men and the native clerics] should be

---

20 "[Visum est] Ex iis quae pertinent ad dominicum, quaecumquae dum non esset episcopus presbyteri vendiderunt, revocare dominicum. Episcopi autem judicio relinqui an oporteat pretium recipere, an non: utpote quod eorum quae sunt vendita, eis ipsis majius pretium reddiderit". Council of Ancrya (314), can. 15, in *Sacrorum Conciliorum nova et apmplissima collection,* II, edited by J.D. Mansi, (Florence, 1758-1927) 515-522.
21 Gregory the Great, *Registrum epistularum,* X, 18, in *S. Gregorii Magni: I. Registrum Epistularum Libri VIII-XIV* edited by Dag Norberg, Corpus Christianorum Series Latina 140/A (Turnholt: Typographi Brepols Editores Pontificii) 847-848.
22 Nord, *Sede Vacante,* 22-24. A fuller explanation of the four principles of the law for the vacant diocese and their interrelations can be found in *idem,* 11-28.
23 Gregory the Great, *Registrum epistularum* V, 48, in *S. Gregorii Magni; I. Registrum Epistularum Libri I-VII,* edited by Dag Norberg, Corpus Christianorum Series Latina 140 (Turnholt: Typographi Brepols Editores Pontificii, 1982) 341-342.

watchmen to each other, making accounts to you in every way".[24] Gregory's concern to keep some continuity in the administration of the diocese, even by a more complicated administration, suggests the importance of following in tracks left by the former bishop. The principle of continuity has only a light presence in today's law. Perhaps one can see it in canon 1018 §2: "A diocesan administrator, apostolic pro-vicar, and apostolic pro-prefect are not to grant dimissorial letters to those who have been denied admission to orders by the diocesan bishop, the apostolic vicar, or the apostolic prefect".[25] Yet this canon might derive as much from the principle of defense as the principle of restraint. In any case, the principle of continuity remains an important practical guideline, and some commentators allude to the principle of continuity as they explain canon 428 §1, *sede vacante nihil innovetur*.[26]

Before discussing additional practical questions, allow me to summarize the key points which I have presented so far. First, the most fundamental law for the vacant see is canon 427 §1. The principle of aid gives the basic need of a vacant diocese; the vacant diocese needs someone to continue the work of the former bishop until a new bishop arrives. Thus, a canonist should expect that the law would give the diocesan administrator almost as much authority as the bishop himself has, and canonists should expect that when the law restricts the authority of the diocesan administrator, the restrictions will have a clear, limited scope.

Second, the two paragraphs of canon 428 are two different laws with different meanings based on different principles. Then canonists should expect that to find two distinct categories of restrictions on the diocesan administrator. True, some actions may be prohibited by both canon 428 §1 and canon 428 §2. But canonists should expect that to find actions that are innovations in the sense prohibited by canon 428 §1 even though those actions do not give prejudice to the rights of the future bishop.

Third, the principle of restraint behind canon 428 §1 is a more fundamental principle than the principle of defense behind canon 428 §2. Thus, canon 428 §1 is the more general law; canon 428 §2 is the more specific law. Why does this matter? Because in canon law, more specific laws derogate from more general laws.[27] Thus, if canon 428 §1 and canon 428 §2 conflict, the more specific law,

---

24 "cum eis quoque homines tuos in actione constitue, ut alterna erga se sollicitudine debeant esse custodes, rationes tibi modis omnibus posituri". Gregory the Great, *Registrum epistularum* V, 48.

25 "Administrator dioecesanus, Provicarius, et Pro-praefectus apostolicus litteras dimissorias ne iis concedat, quibus ab Episcopo dioecesano aut a Vicario vel Praefecto apostolico accessus ad ordines denegatus fuerit."

26 Carlos Soler Ferrán, "Art. 2 De la sede vacante", 876; Ladislas Ziółek, "*Sede vacante nihil innovetur*", 138, Piero Amenta, "Appunti sulla vacanza", 364.

27 "One modifies the generic by the specific", "Generi per speciem derogatur", *Regula Iuris* 34 in VI°.

canon 428 §2 prevails. This point will be helpful in examining the question of budget deficits *sede vacante.*

Fourth, both §1 and §2 of canon 428 are better able to accomplish their purpose, their *ratio legis*, when the restrictions which they impose are specific and limited restrictions. Canon 428 §1 wants to impose self-restraint on the diocesan administrator. The prohibition of this canon is not just directed against bad ideas; even more, it is directed against good ideas that are not appropriate while a diocese is vacant. A specific and limited restriction on the authority of the diocesan administrator shows him what actions are not appropriate in a vacant diocese. A vague and wide-ranging restriction on the diocesan administrator tempts him to with his good-but-inappropriate-in-a-vacant-diocese ideas based on the assertion that such a vague prohibition is no more than a guideline.[28] Canon 428 §2 also imposes restrictions on the diocesan administrator, but in this canon the restrictions are meant to defend the dioceses from actions which a diocesan bishop would recognize as disadvantageous but which might slip through while a diocese is vacant. A specific and limited restriction better corresponds to canon 428 §2's purpose. A specific and limited restriction rebukes "the scoundrel who would steal the goods and rights of the vacant diocese and its bishop. Its clarity strengths the diocesan administrator, the clergy of the dioceses, and the lay faithful in their will to resist such temerity".[29] Moreover, specific and limited restrictions in canon 428 §1 and §2 also allow canon 427 §1 to supply for the basic need of the vacant diocese, that is, the need of the faithful that the diocesan bishop's crucial work continue despite his absence.

In summary, the fundamental laws for the vacant diocese have this basic shape. Canon 427 §1 gives the diocesan administrator the authority of a diocesan bishop, except where limited by more specific laws. While the 1983 Code of Canon Law contains a few very specific limits on this authority—for example, canon 525, 2°—the present law mainly limits diocesan administrators by the two paragraphs of canon 428.

The first paragraph of canon 428, *sede vacante nihil innovetur*, blocks the diocesan administrator from changes that belong specifically to the diocesan bishop by reason of their nature, their purpose, or their mode of proceeding. Acts which are innovations by reason of their nature change key diocesan structures that cooperate with the bishop in his ministry, for example, the parishes of the dioceses or the most important offices of the diocesan curia. Acts which are innovations by reason of the purpose change key diocesan directive which shape the action of the diocese, for example, a diocesan pastoral plan. Acts which are innovations by reason of their way of proceeding would be actions that involve

---

28  The commentary of Carlos Soler Ferrán heads in this direction; Carlos Soler Ferrán, "Art. 2 De la sede vacante", 875-876.
29  Nord, *Sede Vacante*, 112, 133.

decisions whose evaluation should be left to the diocesan bishop, for example, sale of diocesan property or an act which might risk wide-spread scandal.

The second paragraph of canon 428, which prohibits anything that might give prejudice to the rights of the diocese or the future bishop, blocks the diocesan administrator from any action involving legal prejudice, that is, the loss of legal rights for the diocese or bishop. Serious risk of loss—like the risk that arises from entering a trial, for example—is equivalent and also gives legal prejudice. A common way legal rights are lost is by alienation of diocesan property. Such alienations are prohibited *sede vacante*.

Let me now move, as I promised, to more practical questions. The first question which I would like to examine is the question of appointing someone to an ecclesiastical office. Canon 427 §1 shows that the diocesan administrator generally has the full power of a diocesan bishop to make appointments to ecclesiastical offices.[30] Exceptions to this rule arise from canon 525, 2°, which prohibits diocesan administrators from appointing pastors in the first year of the vacancy, and also from canon 481, which shows that the office of vicar generals and episcopal vicar do not exist while the dioceses is vacant.[31] However, canon 428 §1 does not limit the diocesan administrator's authority to appoint to ecclesiastical offices. Canon 428 §1 blocks changes to key diocesan structures themselves, not changes to the people who direct those key diocesan structures. Nor does canon 428 §2 limit the diocesan administrator's authority to appoint to ecclesiastical offices. No prejudice is given to the rights of the future bishop, who may appoint new officeholders the next time the office is vacant and may remove the officeholders appointed by the diocesan administrator if they are deficient in their duties.[32] So diocesan administrators may make appointments to most ecclesiastical offices. However, a prudent diocesan administrator might consider making these appointments provisional, i.e., subject to review of the next bishop. Such an appointment would give the future bishop greater freedom of action, and would be fairer to those appointed to these offices by informing them that their future employment will depend upon the choices of the future bishop.

---

30  The same would apply for offices or positions which are not ecclesiastical offices. Naturally, the diocesan administrator must follow any procedures which the diocesan bishop would have had to follow, for example, canons 1740-1747 for the removal of a pastor.

31  However, the diocesan administrator can give the former vicars general or episcopal vicars delegated authority allowing them to continue their former work; Congregation for Bishops, directory *Apostolorum Successores*, Feb. 22, 2004 (Vatican City: Liberia Editrice Vaticana, 2004), nn. 237, 244; note that the numbering for the English editions of *Apostolorum Successores* differs here from the numbering of the editions in other languages. See also canon 475 §1 and 417.

32  Canons 193, 318 §2, 494 §2, 1740-1752. Canons 162 and 182 §2 show that losing the right to fill an office on a single occasion is different from losing that right absolutely.

The second question which I would like to examine is the question of removing someone from an ecclesiastical office. Canon 427 §1 again shows that the diocesan administrator generally has the full power of the diocesan bishop to remove officeholders from ecclesiastical office.[33] There are again a few laws which give specific exceptions; canon 1420 §5 prohibits a diocesan administrator from removing the judicial vicar or adjutant judicial vicars, and canon 485 places special requirements on the diocesan administrator before he can remove chancellors or other notaries.[34] But canon 428 §1 does not limit the diocesan administrator's authority to remove officeholders from ecclesiastical offices. As noted above, even in the case of an office that directs a key diocesan structure, canon 428 §1 protects the office itself from changes, not the officeholder. Nor does canon 428 §2 limit the diocesan administrator's authority to remove officeholders; the future bishop does not lose a legal right by the removal, for the diocesan bishop can simply reappoint the former officials to the offices which they once held.[35] So diocesan administrators can remove most ecclesiastical officeholders. However, a prudent diocesan administrator should consider that the principle of continuity would urge him to keep in place the same officials appointed by the former bishop.[36]

The third question which I would like to examine is the question of a vacant diocese facing a budget deficit. The question might be particularly difficult in the case in which the former bishop had operated the diocese with a deficit budget. In such a case, especially if the deficit were very large, it might seem that closing the deficit would require such large changes in the diocese as to constitute innovations prohibited by canon 428 §1. Yet taking out more loans to finance a large budget deficit would seem to be prohibited by canon 428 §2. How to resolve this question? Here it is useful to remember that canon 428 §1 is a more general law, that canon 428 §2 is a more specific law, and more specific laws

---

33 The same would apply to offices or positions which are not ecclesiastical offices.
34 Note that canon 184 §1 distinguishes between privation of an ecclesiastical office and removal from an ecclesiastical office. Privation is loss of ecclesiastical office by means of a penalty for a delict; diocesan administrators can cause loss of office by way of privation even for officials whom he cannot remove; Leo Arnold Jaeger, *The Administration of Vacant and Quasi-Vacant Dioceses in the United States: Historical Synopsis of General Legislation and Commentary* (Washington DC: Catholic University of America, 1932) 181, 194; Nord, *Sede Vacante*, 190.
35 This argument relies on the argument presented in the last question that appointing a new official to a vacant office does not give prejudice to the rights of the bishop. However, even if it were true that appointing a new official to some particular office did give prejudice to the rights of the bishop, the removal of that official would not give prejudice to the rights of the bishop as long as the diocesan administrator was careful to make only a temporary and provisional appointment for the discharge of that office. See Aaron Nord, *Sede Vacante*, 192.
36 The letter of Gregory the Great to Bishop Leontius gives even more reasons to be cautious in the removal of officeholders; Gregory the Great, *Registrum epistularum* V, 48. See also Nord, *Sede Vacante*, 196.

override more general laws. Also, one should remember that the principle of continuity is a wise principle, but does not have the force of law; consequently, it cannot override the prohibitions of either canon 428 §1 or canon 428 §2.

These considerations indicate that there are four possible paths a diocesan administrator might take depending on the severity of the budget deficit. First, if the deficit is not great and can be continued without harm to the stable patrimony of the diocese—for example, as might be the case if the diocese has ample savings even beyond its endowments—the principle of continuity would suggest that the diocesan administrator continue in the path taken by the former bishop. Second, if the deficit seems imprudent, then the diocesan administrator should close the deficit while still maintaining continuity with the former bishop's priorities and plans. Third, if the deficit is yet larger, so that it is not possible to close the deficit while maintaining continuity with the former bishop's priorities and plans, then the diocesan administrator should close the budget deficit while avoiding any changes to key diocesan structures. Fourth, if the deficit is so large as to make it impossible to close the deficit without changing some key diocesan structures, then the command of canon 428 §2 overrides the prohibition of canon 428 §1 and authorizes the diocesan administrator even to make those innovations which are needed for the sake of avoiding prejudice to the rights of the diocese and the future bishop.

I hope that these examples show that reading the law for the vacant diocese in the light of the principles of aid, restraint, defense and continuity allows canonists to give clear, balanced, solid answers to the practical questions which arise while dioceses are vacant. I examined some other interesting practical questions in my doctoral dissertation, *Sede Vacante Diocesan Administration*.[37] Before concluding I would like to give attention to two other practical questions. In truth, these last two topics have little connection to canon 427 or canon 428. But each question has so much practical importance that I thought it was worth discussing, even as an afterthought or addendum. The first question regards apostolic administrators. The second questions regard the ordination of deacons in the first year a diocese is vacant.

While a diocesan administrator is elected by the college of consultors and has his authority defined by the Code of Canon Law, an apostolic administrator is appointed directly by the Holy See and has his authority defined by the decree which appointed him. So to understand how his authority is different than a diocesan administrator, one must read the decree which appointed him. I reviewed 41 different decrees appointing apostolic administrators to vacant diocese in the United States between 1974 and 2012. The majority of those decrees resembled something like this:

---

37   Nord, *Sede Vacante*, 151-215.

Congregation for Bishops
[Name of Diocese]
Nomination of Apostolic Administrator
Decree

>To provide for the governance of the Church of [name of dioceses], vacant after the transfer of its last bishop, the Most Rev. [name of former bishop] to the Diocese of [second diocese], the Supreme Pontiff by Divine Providence Pope Benedict XVI, by means of the present decree of the Congregation for Bishops, nominates and constitutes the Most Rev. [name of apostolic administrator] as Apostolic Administrator "sede vacante" to the aforementioned Church from this day and until the new bishop takes canonical possession of the see, and grants him [the apostolic administrator] the rights, duties, and faculties which belong to diocesan Bishops according to the norm of the canons, attentive, however, to those things contained in n. 244 of the directory for the pastoral ministry of Bishops "Apostolorum Successores".
>
>Anything to the contrary notwithstanding.
>Given in Rome from the Office of the Congregation for Bishops, [date]
>
>[Signature of the prefect of the Congregation for Bishops]
>+Seal
>[Signature of the secretary of the Congregation for Bishops][38]

Older decrees did not mention *Apostolorum Successores* n. 244, but otherwise were similar. Please note that in none of the decrees which I reviewed included specific grants of additional faculties. Not one decree said anything like, "the apostolic administrator also has the faculty to merge parishes in the diocese", or "the apostolic administrator also has the faculty to sell diocesan property." But when I looked more deeply, it became clear to me that when the decree said "the rights, duties and faculties which belong to diocesan Bishops", the Holy See indeed meant the authority of a diocesan bishop, not the more limited authority of a diocesan administrator. To be clear: the laws which limit a diocesan administrator, even the most fundamental laws of canon 428 §1 and canon 428 §2, all those laws *do not bind* apostolic administrators appointed by a decree like the one reported above.

Apostolic administrators who have a decree of appointment like the one described above have all the authority that the diocesan bishop would have in

---
38  See Congregation for Bishops, decree *Elpasensis*, Feb. 2, 2012, prot. n. 970/2011.

a diocese which is not vacant. Such an apostolic administrator, if he feels it is needed, can appointed pastors even in the first year the diocese is vacant, despite canon 525, 2°. Such an apostolic administrator can sell diocesan property, merge parishes, or rewrite the diocesan pastoral plan, despite canon 428. Such an apostolic administrator can take all these actions in virtue of the authority already granted him in his decree of appointment, without need to have recourse to the Holy See.

Three observations convinced me that the decrees should be interpreted in this way. First, the plain words of the decree suggest this interpretation. The apostolic administrator is given the authority of a diocesan bishop. Canon 36 §1 indicates that administrative decrees are read according to the common manner of speaking.

Second, there were two decrees which gave apostolic administrators a different level of authority, namely, the "rights, duties, and faculties which belong to diocesan Administrators by the norm of the sacred canons".[39] In some cases the Holy See specifically gave the apostolic administrator the authority of a diocesan administrator; therefore, if the Holy See in other cases had wanted the apostolic administrators to have the authority of a diocesan administrator, the Holy See would have said so. The Holy See gave them the authority of diocesan bishops because the Holy See wanted them to have more authority than a diocesan administrator has.

Third, in some cases I obtained the decrees by which the Holy See appointed apostolic administrators to dioceses where the vacancy took place during a moment of crisis.[40] Even in those cases, the decrees of appointment did not give any special authorizations or additional faculties. Instead, those decrees simply gave the apostolic administrator the authority of a diocesan bishop. It seems that when sending an apostolic administrator to a diocese facing a crisis, the Holy See would want to give him all the authority needed to prepare for the

---

39  «eique iura, officia et facultates tribuit quae Administratoribus dioecesanis, ad normam sacrorum canonum competunt». Congregation for Bishops, decree *Helenensis*, Aug. 1, 2003, prot. n. 418/03; Congregation for Bishops, decree *Camdensis*, Oct. 3, 2003, prot. n. 595/03. I am also aware of a letter from the pontifical legate which suggested that an apostolic administrator had been given the authority of a local ordinary, but I was unable to obtain the decree of appointment; Apostolic Delegation United States of America, letter to John Cardinal Carberry, July 27, 1979, prot. n. 156/79/6.

40  Cf. Congregation for Bishops, decree *Fresnensis*, June 30, 1991, prot. n. 452/91; Congregation for Bishops, decree *Sanctae Fidei in America Septentrionali*, Apr. 6, 1993, prot. n. 321/92; Congregation for Bishops, decree *Litoris Palmensis*, May 29, 1998, prot. n. 477/98; Congregation for Bishops., decree *Litoris Palmensis*, Mar. 13, 2002, prot. n. 235/02. In one other similar case the decree of the Congregation of Bishops used a stylistic variation which did not seem to change the decree of authority which the Holy See intended to give the apostolic administrator; see Congregation for Bishops, decree *Phoenicensis*, June 18, 2003, prot. n. 564/03; Nord, *Sede Vacante*, 234-235.

next bishop. The Holy See accomplished its intent by a decree that gave the administrator the power of a diocesan bishop. Here is yet more evidence that the other decrees which name apostolic administrators with the authority of diocesan bishops intend to do what they say, so that those apostolic administrators have more authority than a diocesan administrator would have.

In conclusion then, many apostolic administrators can treat the laws given for vacant diocese as only guidelines; they are not held to them as laws. To my mind, this shows the importance of realizing that the laws for the vacant dioceses are rooted in fundamental and longstanding canonical principles, the principles of aid, restraint, and defense. Even an apostolic administrator with the full authority of a diocesan bishop might do well to consider carefully these principles before taking actions which the law for the vacant see would normally prevent.

Finally, a word about the ordination of deacons in the first year of a vacancy. On a first glance, canon 1018 §1, 2° would seem to authorize diocesan administrators to give dimissorial letters to men seeking ordination to the deaconate even during the first year a diocese is vacant, and some commentators take this position.[41] Others, however, look to canon 272, which forbids excardination and incardination in the first years of a vacancy.[42] Those commentators hold that by reason of canon 272, diocesan administrators in the first year of the vacancy may give dimissorial letters only to deacons seeking ordination to the priesthood, not to lay men seeking ordination to the deaconate, because the ordination of a deacon would incardinate someone new into the diocese.

However, a closer examination shows that canon 272 does not apply. Canonical authors under the 1917 Code of Canon law distinguished between first incardination (which occurs today when a man is ordained a deacon) and derived incardination (which occurs when a bishop gives incardination to a cleric

---

41  Robert J. Geisinger, "Title VI: Orders [cc. 1008-1054]." in *New Commentary on the Code of Canon Law*, edited by John P. Beal, James A. Coriden, and Thomas J. Green (New York: Paulist Press, 2000) 1199; Jean Lepoutel, "Appel aux Ordres et Ordinations pendant la vacance du siège episcopal", *Les cahiers du droit ecclésial* 5 (1984-1994) 87; William H. Woestman, "Canons 272 and 1018: The Diocesan Administrator and Dimissorial Letters for the Diaconate" in *Roman Replies and CLSA Advisory Opinions 1998*, edited by Kevin W. Vann and James I. Donlon (Washington, DC: Canon Law Society of America, 1998) 51; Raymond Leo Burke, letter to the Most Rev. Robert J. Hermann, Feb. 24, 2009.
42  Michael J. Mullaney, *Incardination and the Universal Dimension of Priestly Ministry; A Comparison Between CIC 17 and CIC 83* (Rome: Editrice Pontificia Università Gregoriana, 2002) 188; Gianfranco Ghirlanda, *Il diritto nella Chiesa misterio di comunione; Compendio di diritto ecclesiale* (Rome: Editrice Pontificia Università Gregoriana) 332; James H. Provost, "Canon 266 and 272; Ordination to the Diaconate by a Diocesan Administrator" in *Roman Replies and CLSA Advisory Opinions 1997*, edited by Kevin W. Vann and James I. Donlon (Washington DC: Canon Law Society of America, 1997) 35-36.

who is already incardinated somewhere else). The words of canon 272 suggest that it refers to only derived incardination, not first incardination. The canon first mentions excardination, then incardination.[43] That order would be strange if the canon referred to first incardination, because a man must be incardinated somewhere before he can be excardinated from that place. But the order of the canon's words makes perfect sense if the canon refers to derived incardination, because an already incardinated cleric must be given permission to excardinate from his present diocese before he can be incardinated into any other diocese (canons 267 and 269). More importantly, an examination of the 1917 Code of Canon Law shows that the phrase "excardination and incardination" is a phrase which always refers to derived incardination, not first incardination.[44] It is a term of art for derived incardination. Then canon 6 §2 shows that when the 1983 Code of Canon Law uses this phrase in canon 272, it intended to prohibit only derived incardination, not first incardination. Thus, the prohibition of canon 272 does not prevent diocesan administrators from giving dimissiorial letters in accord with canon 1018 §1, 2° to men seeking ordination to the deaconate, even if the diocese has not been vacant for a year.[45]

In conclusion, I note that this resolution of the question about ordinations of deacons in the first year of the vacancy, though relying on an exegesis of canon 272, still is harmonious with an interpretation of canon 427 §1 and canon 428 according to the principles of law for a vacant diocese. Today, many dioceses need all the good clerics that they can get; so it makes sense that a diocesan administrator, in harmony with canon 427 §1 and the principle of aid, could ordain deacons even in the first year of the vacancy, so that this urgent need of the faithful may be supplied. On the other hand, no transitional or permanent deacon, whatever his opinion of himself may be, is a key diocesan structure. Thus an ordination of a new deacon is not an innovation of the sort prohibited by canon 428 §1 and the principle of restraint. Finally, canon 428 §2, in accord with the principle of defense, prohibits something specific, the loss of legal rights, and the ordination of a new deacon does not involve this sort of prejudice. The principles of law for the vacant diocese once again show their usefulness as a framework for answering practical questions.

---

43  "Excardinationem et incardinationem".
44  Canons 112, 113, 114, 116 and 969 §2 from the 1917 Code of Canon Law.
45  See also Nord, *Sede Vacante,* 198-208.

# Seminar

## Social Media and Its Relationship to the *Communio*
### *Matthew Palmer*

Social media, in many ways, has become the go to marketing efforts for organizations throughout the world. My journey to that realm, at first, seemed unnatural. I was a sports writer covering the NFL and Major League Baseball during my 20s. The world of Facebook, Twitter and Instagram is mostly thought of as a place to simply, "hang out" and connect with friends. Go deeper, however, and there is always a common theme: people are active seekers of the interesting and the sharable.

The skills I had as a storyteller transferred over, albeit for much shorter attention spans.

Historically, the Catholic Church has grown and thrived as it has adjusted to the latest evangelization tools. From the printed word, to radio and to television, the Church has made the move when it has needed to be somewhere.

Now, more than ever, the Church needs to cement its place online, both to attract new members and to solidify unity within the faithful. Recent Pew Statistics show that 79 percent of online Americans are on industry leader Facebook and 68 percent of all adults are there as well. Instagram, the picture and video mobile app, is the second most popular social media destination with 28 percent of Americans using it. Fifth-nine percent of 18 to 29-year-old people use Instagram. Twenty percent of Internet users have a Twitter, which has some of the most influential people in the world as regular users. President Donald Trump and Pope Francis have nearly 100 million Twitter followers between them and they wield that influence through consistent messaging that drives their audience to action.

The ability to change the world can happen in 140 characters.

Pew stats show nearly 100 percent of teens are online and more than 91 percent do it on mobile device. A quarter of teens are online constantly and 75 percent of them have a cell phone. The amount of text messages sent between them daily is staggering. They are constantly sending and receiving information daily, but, often, are not seeking or sharing their faith. They seek truth online in almost every area except faith. Only 20 percent of Americans share their faith online. According to Pew, 56 percent of Americans say that belief in God is necessary to be moral and have good values. Seventy-three percent of people ages 18 to 29 say that faith in God is necessary to be a moral person.

Almost every other aspect of a person's life is online – including their passion for sports, reading, politics. In a polarized culture where deeply personal conversations can happen between two strangers, it's happening on a much smaller scale in faith circles. When people do engage in their religion online, they do it in much the same way as they do with other things: in a partisan fashion. They look to group their faith much like their politics online, as if there are sides. Often, people have found echo chambers that don't necessarily help them grow in their faith, but affirm how they already feel in their lives, no matter where that stands on the factual plane.

The Church has made large strides during the last five years, following the lead of Pope Francis and Pope-emeritus Benedict XVI in evangelizing efforts on social media. More needs to be done. People, including professional Catholics, must feel emboldened to engage in the culture of encounter.

So, what does social media need?

- Truth
- Compassion
- Authenticity
- Consistency
- Courage
- A Reflection of the beauty of the Church

Following the example of Pope Francis, members of the Church can make that difference. Eighty-seven percent of American Catholics have a favorable view of him and 70 percent of Americans share that view as well. He uses social media to remind people of the basics of the faith. He cuts through the partisan arguments. "Fake News" is a Catholic problem as much as it is a secular issue. People are twisting the Church, the Pope and the teachings of the faith to fit their agenda. False headlines and stories are shared on social media regularly to parse out things said by the Church. This is often called, "Click-bait."

Things like this happen where there is an education void. What can change that? Real expertise of people like canon lawyers and their voices. If you're not on social media, find the one that you like. Test them out. Be a listener, see what the conversation is like and seek it out. Follow people and influencers to see why they have been able to curate such a following. There is room for you, your ministry and voice. Develop your voice.

At the United States Conference of Catholic Bishops, there are more than 200,000 followers. We have, at times, reached more than three million people in a week thanks to creative use of videos, images, graphics and more. At the core, people share and connect when we share truth and inspiration. That's what people share from secular outlets often.

For us, the goal is to support the mission of the bishops. Your organization or person mission should follow the same strategy. We reached more than 50 million people and engaged 1.5 million people in 2017 by leaning in to our mission of speaking out for the poor and immigrants and sharing the truth of the Church.

We do this because there are 2,000 years of evangelization embedded in our religious DNA. It compels us to seek and share the truth. The need is real. We can't sit on the sidelines while the culture becomes increasingly secularized. In the marketplace of ideas, we need to view ourselves as competing for souls.

Using live functions on Facebook, Twitter and Instagram have allowed the USCCB to become more interactive with our followers, giving people insight into what we do and what we believe. It also enables our audience to feel like they are part of a larger conversation because they are. Doing podcasts is a simple way to share expertise. Sit down, hit record and share your knowledge.

Ultimately, that's what people want. They need to feel like they're receiving information from someone who cares about them and has actual knowledge. Social media isn't a one-way street. It's a conversation and Catholics need to be part of it and brings others along.

# Seminar

## Reception into Full Communion of those in Irregular Marriages: Pastoral Realties and a Canonical Solution
### *Monsignor Michael A. Souckar*

**Introduction**

In his nearly five years as pontiff, Pope Francis has repeatedly and in various contexts spoken of the fact that the Church is and must always be a missionary Church. He has also made the virtue of mercy a hallmark of his ministry as Bishop of Rome and Pastor of the Universal Church. The recently celebrated Extraordinary Jubilee Year of Mercy, which this year's Convention recalls, invited us to contemplate Jesus Christ who is the face of the Father's mercy. As the Jubilee Year's theme stated, we are to be "merciful like the Father". In these and many other ways, Pope Francis called upon the Church's pastors to reach out to those who live "on the periphery". Emphasizing the Lord's compassion for the outcast and the fact that Christ is our reconciliation, the Holy Father is drawing attention to the need for unity and reconciliation within the Body of Christ. This invitation has garnered the attention of many in the Church and the general population alike. The secular media, in a particular way, is taken aback by the tone of Pope Francis and they have been giving him a listen. The Pope's message and his off the cuff comments have created more than a few headlines.

For many people – both within and outside the Church – one application of this message of being with those on the periphery focuses on the question of the admission to Holy Communion of divorced and remarried Catholics. In no way am I qualified to make any kind of significant contribution to the many discussions happening in rectories, classrooms, around dinner tables, in synod halls and during the cocktail hour of the CLSA Convention. Nevertheless, the call of Pope Francis has stirred me to give further thought to a question that was first presented to me by my director when I was writing my doctoral thesis on the reception of baptized Eastern non-Catholics into full communion with the Catholic Church and their ascription to a church *sui iuris*.

The question at hand is the following: What options, if any, are there for baptized non-Catholics who seek full communion with the Catholic Church but are in an irregular marriage? Can they be received into full communion?

Must their marital situation be resolved first? If they can be received into full communion does that mean they can receive the sacraments, especially confirmation and Holy Communion? I suspect that this pastoral reality and its challenges are fairly common to many of us.

I would like to begin this seminar with a discussion on the question of religious liberty and the Church's mission of evangelization. The second section will address who is part of the Church and the elements of being in full communion with the Catholic Church. The third section will look at some lessons from the *Code of Canons of the Eastern Churches* and some limitations of the *Rite of Christian Initiation of Adults*. Finally, I hope all this will lend support to my conclusion that the baptized non-Catholics who are in an irregular marriage are, in fact, free to enter full communion with the Church.

**Religious Liberty and Evangelization**

Almighty God has given every person the desire for truth, beauty and goodness, eternal realities that are perfectly found only in the Blessed Trinity. As Saint Augustine realized when reflecting on his own conversion, the human heart is restless until it rests in God.[1] This natural desire for the transcendent carries a duty to accede to it once it is found and to live one's life in conformity with the truths and virtues which arise from it. It is not enough simply to come to know the truth, to experience goodness, or to contemplate beauty; there must be an exercise of the will to live in accord with what the intellect grasps, either naturally or with the assistance of grace. This fundamental search for God and the desire to live according the reveled truth does not end with the reception of baptism. Rather, the Christian life is marked by continual conversion, renewal and growth in a spiritual pilgrimage of faith. Traveling this pilgrimage are those baptized outside the Catholic Church who freely come to desire full communion with the Catholic Church.

Underlying both the search for God and the obligation to embrace the truth is the freedom of human conscience. Every person must have the psychological, moral, religious and civil freedom to follow his/her conscience in the authentic search for God. While the law cannot regulate the religious pursuit of truth, the Church's legislation does articulate principles and guidelines which safeguard the exercise of the right of freedom of conscience. Coriden argues that human dignity demands that all persons should enjoy the use of their own judgment and freedom in making decisions. "They should be free to base their own actions on their consciences," he says, "and not be coerced by internal (psychological) or external pressures."[2]

---

1   Cf., Saint Augustine, *Confessions*, I, 1.
2   J. Coriden, "The Teaching Function of the Church," in *The New Commentary on the Code of Canon Law*, ed. J. Beal et al. (Paulist Press: New York, NY/Mahwah, NJ: 2000), 912.

The Second Vatican Council addressed the question of human freedom and the pursuit of religious truth in its Declaration on Religious Freedom, *Dignitatis humanae*. In this groundbreaking document, the Council Fathers spoke of religious freedom as a basic human right and called upon all civil authorities to respect and protect that right in civil legislation. There is much in the document that is worthy of discussion, but it is sufficient for the purposes of this presentation to mention only a few foundational principles.

The first principle found in *Dignitatis humanae* is that each person has a right to religious freedom. In reference to religious freedom, the decree states: "Such freedom consists in this, that all should have such immunity from coercion by individuals, or by groups, or by any human power, that no one should be forced to act against his conscience in religious matters, nor prevented from acting according to his conscience, whether in private or in public, whether alone or in association with others, within due limits."[3]

Not only are individuals to be free to follow their consciences in the pursuit of religion, *Dignitatis humanae* also states that the human person has an obligation to follow the truth once it is comprehended. The decree states: "In accordance with their dignity as persons, equipped with reason and free will and endowed with personal responsibility, all are impelled by their own nature and are bound by a moral obligation to seek truth, above all religious truth. They are further bound to hold to the truth once it is known, and to regulate their whole lives by its demands."[4]

In 2007, the Congregation for the Doctrine of the Faith[5] issued a document entitled "Doctrinal Note on Some Aspects of Evangelization". In this document the CDF directly addresses the freedom of the Church to undertake the work of evangelization everywhere in the world. The CDF said that "the mission of the Church is universal and is not restricted to specific regions of the earth."[6] The work of evangelization is not only unrestricted by territory, it also is not restricted to certain persons, namely the unbaptized. In this Doctrinal Note, the CDF speaks of evangelization to include the baptized, especially those who have lapsed in their practice of the faith. Speaking of a narrow and broad use of the term evangelization, the document states: "In its precise sense, evangelization is the *missio ad gentes* directed to those who do not know Christ. In a wider sense, it is used to describe ordinary pastoral work, while the phrase 'new

---

3   *DH*, 2a.
4   Ibid., 2b.
5   Henceforth, CDF.
6   CDF, "Doctrinal Note on Some Aspects of Evangelization," Origins 37 (2007) 461. This, in my judgement, also is a reference to the objections raised by some Orthodox hierarchs to works of evangelization by Catholics in what are known as traditional Orthodox or Eastern territories.

evangelization' designates pastoral outreach to those who no longer practice the Christian faith."[7]

It is this continual preaching of the Gospel that draws the baptized to a deeper relationship with the Lord Jesus Christ and a closer relationship with the Church. In his apostolic letter preparing for the Jubilee Year 2000, *Tertio Millennio Adveniente*, Pope Saint John Paul II spoke of the need for the Church to bring "the liberating message of the Gospel to the men and women of Europe" which he described as "becoming missionary territory" because it was "becoming estranged from its Christian roots."[8] This coming closer to Christ, by the unbaptized and the baptized alike, is what the CDF calls conversion. Again, offering both a precise and expanded use of the term conversion, the Congregation states: "Generally, the term conversion is used in reference to bringing pagans into the Church. However, conversion (*metanoia*), in its precisely Christian meaning, signifies a change in thinking and in acting, as the expression of the new life in Christ proclaimed by faith: a continuous reform of thought and deeds directed at an ever more intense identification with Christ (cf. Gal 2,20), to which the baptized are called before all else."[9] This *metanoia* includes all the baptized – Catholic and non-Catholic alike. We are all to have this "new way of thinking". Is that not what happens along the journey in faith toward full communion with the Catholic Church?

**Evangelization and the Codes of Canon Law**

The *CCEO* has a specific section dedicated to evangelization – Title XIV: The Evangelization of Peoples (cc. 584-594). This is followed by Title XV: The Ecclesial Magisterium (cc. 595-666).[10] By contrast, the *CIC* does not have a section dedicated to evangelization; one must turn to the canons on The Teaching Office of the Church in Book III, especially the introductory canons 747-755 and Title II: The Missionary Action of the Church (cc. 781-792).

The relevant canons in both codes begin with the theological doctrine that the Catholic Church has been commissioned by Christ the Lord and is assisted by the Holy Spirit to preach the Gospel to all peoples and to hand on in its integrity the Catholic faith. This divine mandate empowers the Church to undertake the work of evangelization, a mandate which no human authority can regulate. Canon 747

7   Ibid.
8   Saint John Paul II, apostolic letter, *Tertio Millennio Adveniente*, 57.
9   CDF, "Doctrinal Note on Some Aspects of Evangelization," 9.
10  The placement of the canons on evangelization outside Title XV: The Ecclesial Magisterium is an innovation on the part of the *CCEO*, says Nedungatt. While "the proclamation of the good news is an important element of evangelization and as such it comes under the ecclesial Magisterium", it also includes other activities such as works of witness and charity, dialogue, Christian initiation, etc., especially as found in *AG* 11-18. See, G. Nedungatt, "Evangelization of Peoples," in *A Guide to the Eastern Churches*, G. Nedungatt, ed. (Rome: Edizioni Orientali Christiana 2002) 404-406.

says that "the Church...has the duty and innate right, independent of any human power whatsoever, to preach the gospel to all peoples..." (See also, *CCEO* c. 595 §1). Both codes emphasize the inherent and independent right of the Church to undertake its mission of preaching the Gospel everywhere. Salachas points out that this power is not delegated to the Church by any human entity nor is it a right that is humanly acquired. Rather, it is an intrinsic and divine right, "the very foundation of which is Christ the Lord who entrusted to the Church the deposit of faith found in Tradition and Sacred Scripture."[11]

Because the very essence of the Church is to preach the Gospel, this missionary characteristic is to be found in its various functions of teaching, sanctifying and governing. Consequently, *CCEO* canon 584 §1 rightly states: "Obeying the mandate of Christ to evangelize all peoples, and moved by the grace and charity of the Holy Spirit, the Church recognizes herself to be totally missionary." It is from this broad concept of mission that one can understand the Doctrinal Note on Some Aspects of Evangelization when it states that "the work of ecumenism does not remove the right or take away the responsibility of proclaiming in fullness the Catholic faith to other Christians, who freely wish to receive it."[12] This reflects the very close connection between the mission of the Church and the task of evangelization, even among the baptized.[13]

Not only is the Church free to preach the Gospel but, as discussed above, every person has the natural right of religious freedom to search for the truth and the reciprocal obligation to embrace it once it is found. Surprisingly, neither the *CIC* nor the *CCEO* explicitly declares this fundamental right. Rather, there is something of an understood recognition of this right when the *CCEO* calls upon the Christian faithful to ensure that the exercise of religious freedom is protected. *CCEO* canon 586 states that "all the Christian faithful are to take care that the right to religious freedom is maintained, lest anyone be hindered from embracing the Church by unjust harassment." Canon 748 §1 speaks only of the duty to exercise this right of religious freedom and to act in accord with the truth that comes to be known. It reads: "All persons are bound to seek the truth in those things which regard God and his Church and by virtue of divine law are bound by the obligation and possess the right of embracing and observing the truth which they have come to know."

Given this right of the Church to evangelize and the corresponding obligation of every person to follow the promptings of the Holy Spirit to profess the faith and become part of the Body of Christ, should not the Church be eager to receive

---

11  D. Salachas, *Il magisterio e l'evangelizzazione dei popoli nei Codici latino e orientale*, (Bologna: Edizioni Dehoniae, 2001), 16.
12  CDF, "Doctrinal Note on Some Aspects of Evangelization," 12.
13  For an excellent reflection on this connection between mission and ecumenism, see W. Kasper, *Sacrament of Unity: The Eucharist and the Church*, (New York: Herder and Herder, 2004), especially 142-150.

into full communion those who have come to the faith as a result of her works of evangelization and the grace of Almighty God? If people have a fundamental right of religious freedom, should not the limitation of that right be strictly interpreted?

## Being Part of the Church and Full Communion with the Catholic Church

In one sense, it can be said that being part of the Catholic Church is similar to any other international organization. The Church is composed of persons of various ages, nationalities and cultures who come together for a common purpose. From this perspective, it can be argued that the Church is free to determine its own requirements for membership. At the same time, the Church is divinely established and the very question of who belongs to the Church is determined by the mandate given by Christ the Lord to preach the Gospel to all peoples and to baptize those who accept the Gospel.

Still, one may ask, who is part of the Catholic Church? How does one join the Church? These very questions were posed by Blessed Pope Paul VI who asked pilgrims at a general audience in 1966: "Do I really belong to the Church? Who belongs to it? How is this belonging conferred?" The pope goes on to answer by saying: "At first glance, the reply is an easy one. Everyone knows it. It is through baptism that a person enters the Church." Expanding the question of membership in the Church, Pope Paul VI continued: "Are those who have been baptized, even those who are separated from Catholic unity, in the Church? In the true Church? Yes. This is one of the great truths of Catholic tradition, and the Council has repeatedly confirmed it."[14]

To belong to the Catholic Church is a multi-dimensional reality. It is the position of this author that there are three distinct elements by which a person is part of the Catholic Church. The first is baptism by which one is incorporated into Christ the Lord and made part of the People of God. The second element is full communion with the Catholic Church which is realized by the bonds of the profession of faith, the sacraments and ecclesiastical governance. The third element is ascription to a specific church *sui iuris* out of which arises the practice of the faith according to a particular rite; this includes Christian initiation by the reception of the sacraments. Therefore, all members of the Catholic Church are incorporated, joined and ascribed to the Catholic Church.

### Incorporation into Christ by Baptism

It is through a spiritual rebirth in the waters of baptism that men and women of whatever age are joined to Jesus Christ, numbered among the Christian faithful and so constituted as the people of God. Canon 204 §1 states: "The Christian

---
14 Blessed Paul VI, "Who Belongs to the Church?" in *The Pope Speaks* (11: 1966), 372-373.

faithful are those who, incorporated as they are into Christ through baptism, are constituted as the people of God; and so, participating in their own way in the priestly, prophetic and royal function of Christ, they are called, each according to his or her condition, to exercise the mission which God has entrusted to the Church to fulfill in the world."

Feliciani notes that this understanding of the Christian faithful is only possible because Vatican Council II "redefined the Church as the People of God and so brought about a profound re-evaluation of the meaning of belonging to such a people."[15] It is the fact of baptism which is common to all the Christian faithful and by that very fact that they are identified as belonging to the Church as the People of God. All the rights and duties of the Christian faithful arise as a consequence of baptism.[16] *Unitatis redintegratio* states that despite the things that separate baptized non-Catholics from the Catholic Church "all who have been justified by faith in baptism are members of Christ's body, and have a right to be called Christians, and so are deservedly recognized as sisters and brothers in the Lord by the children of the Catholic Church."[17]

The second paragraph of canon 204 proceeds to set forth the divinely established visible expression of the people of God which is the Church. The canon reads: "This Church, constituted and organized in this world as a society, subsists in the Catholic Church, governed by the successor of Peter and the bishops in communion with him." This definition of the Catholic Church distinguished it from all other churches – including the Orthodox Churches – and ecclesial communities. According to Feliciani, at this juncture the legislator faced a "delicate problem". While the code was to define precisely who belongs to the church, it had to do so within the "climate of ecumenical openness sanctioned by Vatican II."[18] Canon 204 § 2 is the resolution of this "delicate problem".

### Full Communion with the Catholic Church

Canon 205 identifies the essential elements by which the baptized are in full communion with the Catholic Church.[19] The canon reads: "In full communion with the Catholic Church on this earth are those baptized persons who are joined with Christ in its visible structure by the bonds of profession of faith, of the sacraments and of ecclesiastical governance." This definition of who is a member of the Church was a most significant development. Kloppenburg reports

---

15  G. Feliciani, "Christian Faithful: Their Rights and Obligations." in G. Nedungatt, ed., *A Guide to the Eastern Code*, 81.
16  Ibid., 81-82. This contrasts with *CIC/17* Book I: *De Personis* (cc. 87-725) which grouped the Christian faithful according to their state of life, i.e. as clerics, religious and laity.
17  *UR*, 3a.
18  G. Feliciani, "Christian Faithful," 82.
19  See also *CCEO* c. 8.

that the schema for *Lumen gentium* had originally used the restrictive language of Pope Pius XII's encyclical letter *Mystici Corporis* to define who is part of the Church. According to the terminology employed by *Mystici Corporis*, says Kloppenburg, "a person either is or is not a member of the Church, either belongs to the Church or does not, either is or is not within the unity of the Church. There are no gradations of more or less, of perfect or imperfect."[20] That changed when *Lumen gentium* taught that baptized non-Catholics enjoy a real yet imperfect communion with the Catholic Church. *Lumen gentium* states: "They are fully incorporated into the society of the Church who, possessing the Spirit of Christ, accept its whole structure and all the means of salvation that have been established within it, and within its visible framework are united with Christ, who governs it through the supreme pontiff and the bishops, by the bonds of profession of faith, the sacraments, ecclesiastical government and communion."[21]

In the course of drafting *Lumen gentium*, states Barranco, the Council fathers deliberately made a distinction between those who are incorporated (*incorporantur*) into the Church (*LG*, 14) and those who are joined (*coniunguntur*) to the Church (*LG*, 15). The term *incorporatio* is reserved only to Catholics, whereas the term *coniuntio* is used in reference to catechumens and baptized non-Catholics. Furthermore, says Barranco, the use of *coniunctio* in regard to catechumens is active by virtue of their desire for incorporation into the Church. On the other hand, the use of *coniuntio* in reference to non-Catholic Christians is passive. It is the Church which recognizes a sense of unity with non-Catholic Christians because of the baptism they have received. This is so even when the baptized non-Catholic has no desire for union with the Catholic Church.[22] Although the same term *coniunctio* is used for both groups, Barranco concludes that it has differing theological meanings. Whereas the catechumen desires to be incorporated into the Church, for the non-Catholic it is the Church that is aware that he is joined to the Catholic Church by the sanctifying work of the Holy Spirit.[23]

## Three Bonds of Full Communion

Through the bonds of the profession of faith, the sacraments and ecclesiastical governance, the baptized non-Catholic comes into full communion with the

20 B. Kloppenburg, *The Ecclesiology of Vatican II*, (Chicago: Franciscan Herald Press, 1974), 128. As Kloppenburg goes on to say, numerous expressions were put forward to try and explain this idea of degrees of communion in the Church. The suggested expressions included "bonds of perfect unity", "fully and perfectly" and even "basic communion". Eventually, as is well known, the expression "full communion" was accepted and used in several of the documents of Vatican II.
21 *LG*, 14.
22 P. Barranco, *La Incorporación en la Iglesia Mediante el Bautismo y la Profesión de la Fe según el Concilio Vaticano II*, (Rome: Editrice Pontificia Università Gregoriana, 1997) 24-25.
23 Ibid., 25.

Catholic Church. Commenting on the three elements of full communion found in canon 205, Green states that this canon "specifies legally verifiable external criteria for determining who is a Roman Catholic." In this way, the canon "distinguished baptismal incorporation into the Church of Christ and degrees of communion with the Catholic Church."[24] There are additional "criteria for communion" found in *Lumen gentium* which, says Green, were not incorporated into the canon on full communion; for example, a person's possession of the Spirit. These criteria "highlighted the inner spiritual dimension of ecclesial communion…and really transcend what can be expressed in the law."[25]

*CIC* canon 205 and *CCEO* canon 8 do not explicitly define what is meant by the bonds of faith, sacraments and governance. Green offers a few helpful references. As to the bond of faith, Green looks to canon 865 §1 on the necessity of an adult candidate for baptism to be sufficiently instructed on the truths of the faith and Christian obligations. He also cites canon 750 on the obligation of the faithful to believe what is found in the word of God, the deposit of faith, and universal magisterium of the Church.[26] In reference to the bond of sacraments, Green points to the common celebration of the sacraments among all the Catholic faithful throughout the various particular churches within the Catholic communion (cf. c. 840). This "profound link" among Catholics "entails a solidarity with the communities celebrating the sacraments and Christ acting in them."[27] The third bond of communion is that of ecclesiastical governance and, says Green, "presupposes the Church's hierarchically structured character." Arising from this bond of governance is the obligation to the sacred pastors (c. 212 § 1) and maintaining communion among them (cc. 333, 336).[28]

## The Act of Reception into Full Communion with the Catholic Church

*A Lesson from the* CCEO

As to the reception of baptized non-Catholics into full communion with the Catholic Church, the *CCEO* offers some helpful insights. It places nothing more than the minimum obligations. *CCEO* canon 896 states that "no burden is to be imposed, beyond what is necessary." The canon's prescription is faithful both to the instruction of the Apostles found in Sacred Scripture[29] and the teaching of the Second Vatican Council.[30] It should be noted that the canon addresses all

---

24 T. Green, "Changing Ecumenical Horizons: Their Impact on the 1993 Code," *The Jurist* 56: 1 (1996) 433.
25 Ibid, 434.
26 The equivalent canons in the *CCEO*, cc. 682 and 598 respectively, are the same without exception.
27 T. Green, "Changing Ecumenical Horizons: Their Impact on the 1993 Code," 434.
28 Ibid.
29 Cf., Acts 15, 18.
30 Cf., *UR*, 18.

baptized non-Catholics when it speaks of them having been baptized in a non-Catholic church or ecclesial community. Therefore, the obligation not to impose any burden beyond what is necessary applies equally to the Orthodox and non-Orthodox baptized Christian who freely seeks full communion with the Catholic Church.

*CCEO* canon 897, citing *Orientalium ecclesiarum* 25, specifies how the baptized Eastern non-Catholic is received into the Catholic Church. The canon states: "A member of the Christian faithful of an Eastern non-Catholic church is to be received into the Catholic Church with only the profession of the Catholic faith, after a spiritual preparation that is suited to that person's condition."

The canon does not provide a specific formula to be used for the profession of faith, something which historically has differed slightly among the Eastern Catholic churches *sui iuris*. The formula to be used for each Eastern Catholic church *sui iuris* "is proper to its particular tradition and is found in its liturgical books."[31] In the Latin Church *sui iuis* the formula for the profession of faith to enter full communion is: "I believe and profess all that the holy Catholic Church believes, teaches and proclaims to be revealed by God". The profession is then received by the celebrant who states: "N. the Lord receives you into the Catholic Church. His loving kindness has led you here, so that in the unity of the Holy Spirit you may have full communion with us in the faith that you have professed in the presence of his family".[32]

*CCEO* Title XVII also identifies those instances when someone should not be received into full communion with the Catholic Church, or at least when the act of reception is to be deferred. *CCEO* canon 900 §1 states that one "who has not yet completed his or her fourteenth year is not to be received, if the parents are opposed to it." Furthermore, §2 adds that "if grave inconveniences are foreseen either to the Church or to the person," the reception of a minor into the Catholic Church "is to be deferred, unless there is imminent danger of death." Salachas points out that "the canon thus strikes a happy balance between public good and private good, the rights of children and those of parents."[33] It is notable to this author that the *CCEO* does not mention the irregular marital status of the baptized non-Catholic as a reason for either the delay or denial of reception into full communion. This is especially relevant given the reality of "second marriages" among the Orthodox.

---

31 G. Nedungatt, "Ecclesiastical Magisterium," in G. Neungatt ed. *A Guide to the Eastern Code: A Commentary on the Code of Canons of the Eastern Churches*, (Rome, 2002), 463.
32 *RCIA*, 585-586. All citations from *Rite of Christian Initiation of Adults,* (Collegeville, 1988).
33 D. Salachas, "Baptized non-Catholics who enter into full communion," in G. Neungatt, ed., *A Guide to the Eastern Code,* 603.

## Full Christian Initiation and the Limitations of the *RCIA*

Canon 842, §2 speaks of full Christian initiation when it states: "The sacraments of baptism, confirmation and Holy Eucharist are interrelated in such a way that they are required for full Christian initiation." Note that the canon makes no mention of full communion with the Catholic Church. This, I believe, is simply presumed; it has been adequately addressed in the more fundamental canons found on the People of God.

In parish life, one often relies on the *Rite of Christian Initiation of Adults* for not only catechumens but also baptized non-Catholics seeking full communion with the Catholic Church. Many pastors and catechists look forward to the celebration of the Easter Vigil and the sacraments of initiation as the culmination of a faith journey of the catechumens and candidates for full communion or the completion of the sacraments of initiation.

In the order of the ritual, the rite of reception follows the baptism of the catechumens. It is immediately preceded by a renewal of baptismal promises by the entire community and the candidates for full communion and the sprinkling with baptismal water (which at the Easter Vigil was just blessed). Following the profession of faith and the act of reception into full communion, there is the conferral of the sacrament of confirmation. This is, of course, followed by the liturgy of the Eucharist with the first reception of the Holy Eucharist.[34]

There are some facts about the *RCIA* which, I suggest, are easily forgotten and confuse our understanding of the reception into full communion of baptized non-Catholics. First of all, it should not be forgotten that in its original restored form (*editio typica*) the *RCIA* is only for catechumens, i.e., the non-baptized. The combined rites of initiation for catechumens (both adults and children of catechetical age), baptized non-Catholics and even baptized but uncatechized adult Catholics with which we are so familiar is an approved adaptation to meet the pastoral realities in the United States.[35] Because we so often make use of these combined rites – arising from the pastoral realities we experience – it is sometimes forgotten that they are exceptional, not normative. By that I mean that they are adaptations of the *RCIA* model. This is consistent with the *praenotanda* of the *RCIA* which speaks of the steps and stages of the catechumenate as a model applicable to other pastoral situations (e.g. baptized non-Catholics seeking full communion with the Catholic Church). It also should be noted that the RICA was promulgated for the Latin Church *sui iuris* and is not used by the Eastern Catholic churches *sui iuris*. The other important point to remember is that the *RCIA* is a ritual book. As such, its primary purpose is to provide for the celebration of the sacraments of initiation (and associated rites) so that the faithful might not only be in full communion with the Church but also fully initiated.

---

34  *RCIA*, 584-594.
35  Ibid., xii-xiii.

**Canonical Solution**

It is clear from many perspectives that being in full communion with the Catholic Church and full Christian initiation through the reception of the sacraments of baptism, confirmation and Holy Eucharist are intimately connected. At the same time, as this presentation has attempted to demonstrate, Catholic theology and therefore the codes make a significant distinction between the two. With this in mind and returning to the question posed at the beginning of this presentation, it is my conclusion that baptized non-Catholics who are in irregular marriages are free to make a profession of faith and so enter into full communion with the Catholic Church. Given that they already share the sacrament of baptism, upon profession of the faith they are accepting the teachings of the Catholic Church and placing themselves under her governance. These are the three elements of full communion as provided for in canon 205.. Unfortunately, however, these persons are not free to receive the sacraments of confirmation or the Holy Eucharist and so would not be fully initiated. Of course, it is preferred that the reason for the irregularity of the marriage (most often a previous presumably valid marriage) is resolved prior to coming into full communion by a profession of faith so that the person can also be fully initiated. But if that cannot be resolved and the person is adequately prepared, what is to keep them from making a profession of faith and thereby enter full communion with the Catholic Church in response to the promptings of the Holy Spirit in their lives?

My position on reception into full communion might seem less startling if we see it in other contexts. John was baptized a Catholic as an infant but, following his parents' divorce, never received the sacraments of Holy Eucharist or confirmation. He now is in your office because he and Jane wish to marry. Do you consider John to be in full communion with the Catholic Church? Of course, he simply is not fully initiated. Or, take the case of Mary who has was baptized a Catholic and received Holy Eucharist as a child but never received confirmation She and Michael were married in the Church several years ago. After 5 years they separated and divorced because of his multiple infidelities. Mary eventually met Tom and they married civilly. They now have their children in your parish school and wish to convalidate their present civil union. Would anyone question that Mary and Tom are in full communion with the Catholic Church? Surely, Mary would not be asked to join the *RCIA*. All this is to say that we are very comfortable saying that baptized Catholics who are not fully initiated are in full communion with the Catholic Church. This is true because of the bonds of profession of faith, the sacraments and governance. I believe the same can be said of a baptized non-Catholic who makes a profession of faith.

**A Few Practical Items**

It is important to note that this option is not available to catechumens. Because they have not been baptized, catechumens lack that essential bond of the sacraments so as to be in full communion with the Catholic Church. It is worthy to note, however, that according to a private response given by the Sacred Congregation for Doctrine of the Faith on 11 July 1983 to the bishop of Honolulu, the non-baptized who are divorced and remarried can be admitted to the catechumenate, even if the marriage must first be regularized before the reception of the sacraments.[36]

There also is the question of when and within what context the act of reception into full communion should take place. As already discussed, the *RCIA* places the act of reception within the Mass and ordinarily at the Easter Vigil. It could be said that the act of reception into full communion is most appropriately done within the celebration of the Holy Eucharist as that where the faithful share Holy Communion. On the other hand, in the particular circumstance we are dealing with here, since the candidate is not yet able to complete his/her sacramental initiation and so cannot receive Holy Communion, the pastor might judge it more suitable to have the act of reception take place outside of Mass, perhaps at a celebration of Lauds or Vespers. Either way, it seems important that the act of reception into full communion somehow take place when the local parish community has gathered for prayer.[37] It is also worth noting that the Church does not reserve Christian initiation to the Easter Vigil. While the Eater Vigil holds a preeminent place, liturgical norms clearly allow the celebration of the sacraments of initiation on other days.[38] *A fortiori*, the act of reception into full communion can be celebrated outside the Eater Vigil.[39]

## Conclusions

Before offering a final conclusion, allow me to share with you an actual case where the proposal here presented was used. Bill was baptized and raised as a Presbyterian. Some fifteen years ago he met Sally who is a Catholic and received all the sacraments of initiation as a young person. The couple is only married civilly because Sally was previously married in the Church. Several years ago, Bill told Sally and the local Catholic pastor that he was interested in "becoming a Catholic". He joined the parish's *RCIA* catechetical and formation program and found this to be most enriching. As Easter approached, the director of faith formation reminded Bill that because of his irregular marriage he would not be able to join the Church at Easter. Despite repeated encouragements by the pastor, Sally refused to present her previous marriage to the local tribunal for

---

36  Cf., "Divorced and Remarried Persons: Catechumenate and Sacraments," in *Canon Law Digest,* 10 (1986), 139-140.
37  It is my suggestion not to adopt the practice once used for mixed marriages where the ceremony was held privately in the parish rectory or offices.
38  Cf., *RCIA*, 17.
39  Traditionally, the Solemnity of Pentecost has been an occasion for the initiation of new Catholics. Perhaps this feast would be a suitable opportunity for the act of reception into full communion.

a possible declaration of nullity. Nevertheless, for several years now Bill has been attending Mass every Sunday – while never receiving Holy Communion – and otherwise has become active in the parish community. The pastor (who also is a canonist) and I discussed the possibility of Bill making a profession of faith but not completing his sacramental initiation. At first, the pastor was uncomfortable with this proposal. However, after his own study of the matter, he eventually presented to Bill this option. Bill gladly accepted and made a profession of faith at Sunday Mass a few weeks later. The pastor reports that Bill, while still very much desiring to receive confirmation and Holy Eucharist, is thrilled to have been "accepted by the Catholic Church". His long journey of conversion led him to the Catholic faith and he says that he really feels "at home" in the Catholic Church. The parish community also was very happy when Bill made his profession of faith. The pastor relates that no one asked why Bill does not receive Holy Communion. It seems that Bill handles this privately, should anyone inquire. This little anecdote, I suggest, summarizes the pastoral realities which this presentation has attempted to address in a manner that is faithful to the mission and teachings of the Church and her disciplines as found in the codes of canon law.

In conclusion, is Pope Francis' call for a missionary Church that is merciful really saying anything new? I believe that he is merely giving right emphasis to the missionary character of the Church. In asking the church's pastors to reach out to those on the periphery, the Holy Father is reminding us of our most basic mission, to go out to all the world and preach the Good News.[40] The codes of canon law, in service to this missionary Church, acknowledges the right of the Church to evangelize, the right and obligation of the individual to follow his/her conscience in matters of religion and, I would say, not only the possibility but also the freedom of baptized non-Catholics in irregular marriages to come into full communion with the Catholic Church. Whenever the Church does this she is living up to her identity as a Church that is missionary, merciful and just.

---

40  Cf., Mt. 28, 17-20

# Officer's Report

## Report of the President
*Rev. Bruce Miller, JCL*

Who am I? Is a question that has often been in my mind since I first received a call from the Nominations Committee to stand for the election of Vice President / President Elect. I actually did not want to run once the other candidate, Diane Barr, was revealed when the entire ballot was announced. If you do not know, no one is told about the other candidates for office when asked to run. I have great respect for Diane; we had worked together; and I did not want to hurt her or be embarrassed myself.

My purpose is to thank you profusely for electing me; tell you how enjoyable overall the challenging year has been; account for the actions of the Board of Governors, the other officers, and myself; and encourage you to seek the presidency of the CLSA one day.

Allow me to be frank about money. If you take advantage of the opportunities that will come your way, you will not be living high on the Society's ticket or even on those who might invite you. I calculate that I personally spent as much if not more especially since I went to Rome once and Australia and New Zealand on my own. Moreover, it does not seem appropriate to pass on some meal and incidental costs to the CLSA even to the regularly scheduled events.

I must acknowledge that, although it was not the customary year for the CLSA President to visit Australia and New Zealand, the usual courtesies were extended. In turn, I was personally pleased to join their Society.

Generally, you will travel often:

- to Rome once as president or vice president
- to Great Britain and Ireland meeting this year in Rome (combined this year with the Roman visit to save two separate trips
- on the alternate year to the conference for Australia and New Zealand
- yearly to Canada twice, once to their convention and once to visit Saint Paul University in Ottawa where you will present a lecture

- to regional meetings (a member of the BOG may substitute); you may be invited as a presenter
- to several BOG meetings in addition to the ones before and after the Convention
- in response to other invitations that may come your way that are not the responsibility of the CLSA or those who invite you

It has been great fun getting to know and working with the Board of Governors. They are some of the finest people I have ever met and are extremely dedicated to our Society. The presidents of our so-called major sister societies, in alphabetical order, Australia and New Zealand, Canada, and Great Britain and Ireland have become dear friends and close associates. The leadership of the regions of our Society support many who work in the canonical trenches and who are not necessarily our members, but need canonical education, have become great examples. The deans of schools of canon law and officials of Vatican tribunals and the dicasteries have been generous and gracious with their time. The hierarchy has sought counsel and humbly accepted it. In all these encounters at various moments that question has run through my mind, Who am I? The answer is no one except the symbol of this Society and its honorable history.

**TRANSITIONS** Father Roger Keeler left the office of the Executive Coordinator as his three-year contract expired. He is gifted in many ways. The two of us have also had the pleasure of working with A.C.T.S. Missions of San Antonio, Texas. As an appendix to this report, I wish to include the final article he wrote in the *CLSA Newsletter* so that it becomes a part of our *Proceedings 2017*. I wholeheartedly endorse it.

At the beginning of this calendar year, the BOG began to consider its responsibilities since the Executive Coordinator reports to it. Father Keeler wished to return to teaching and the Oblates offered him the opportunity to do so.

Aware that there had been an 18-month search to find Father Keeler, with Sister Sharon Euart, the former Executive Coordinator, making an extraordinary sacrifice as did Colleen Crawford in the interim, the BOG began to reflect on the whole history of the office. It also studied the Constitution, Bylaws, and Position Description of the Executive Coordinator. Over many years, many tasks attributed to the Executive Coordinator had been delegated to the secretary, administrative assistant, office staff, or whatever name was given the staff positions. The Constitution and Bylaws did not dictate, as much as was imagined, about the position of Executive Coordinator.

With clarity, the BOG determined that requiring the Executive Coordinator to live in the Washington area, and to be full-time, significantly decreased the likelihood of applications. In addition, it was clearly desired that the Executive Coordinator focus directly on the production of peer-reviewed, professional academic books to fulfill the expectation and need of the English-speaking world CLSA publications. We determined the Executive Coordinator needed to have a canonical degree and experience in publications. A new office, finally entitled General Secretary, imitating the USCCB, with the person capable of operating a membership organization such as ours with an annual convention was also needed.

In the end, the BOG quickly named Colleen Crawford General Secretary. A search was then begun for a halftime Executive Coordinator. It was great to see nine excellent candidates apply for the job. Eventually, the field was narrowed to three, then two were interviewed. Father Pat Cogan, a former Executive Coordinator, with experience as editor of *Studia Canonica* in the interim, was chosen. Thus, Ms. Crawford, General Secretary and Father Cogan, Executive Coordinator were hired. Both would report to the BOG and would be directly supervised by the President.

While this matter was already fully within the Constitution and the Bylaws, in the last meeting of the BOG, at my initial timely proposal, the BOG elected to seek amendment of the Constitution and the Bylaws to restructure the administrative arm of the CLSA accordingly.

**ROME VISIT** By all accounts, it seems that this was a year of very fine visits. In six cases, the Cardinal Prefect himself met with us, often alone. Formal translation was needed only once. The atmosphere was one of openness with the expressed desire to hear about our concerns and to receive guidance. Again and again we were assured that these offices and tribunals of the Holy See were there to assist the bishops. The officials recognize that the canonists write correspondence for the bishops, but the bishops should sign the correspondence. They should seek guidance, express their desires and should be straightforward in giving their *vota*. Ancillary materials that will make the case clear and evident should be included. Anything that is requested and protocols must be included and followed.

For our part, we offered to be of service if they found it helpful. We encouraged them in whatever other way possible to provide more detailed information by way of outlines, protocols and instructions about exactly what motives and means were required to obtain the results desired.

They each made clear that, if something is needed quickly, a cover page should make known the need simply so that it cannot be missed. The bishop should also write through the papal nuncio who may give answer himself or route the matter to a more appropriate dicastery.

In several instances, we were told of some future plans and projects in confidence. Some have already come to fruition. That who am I? feeling came over me more than once!

**PROCEEDINGS** The *Proceedings 2016* could not have been later. They were delivered to you here, in part, because I did not believe that you would buy the line that they were in the mail! To the BOG it seems necessary to establish certain requirements that will make it mandatory for articles suitable for publication be turned in prior to delivery at future conventions. While Power Points will certainly be encouraged as will other media, these presentations are not acceptable as alternatives to the professional articles required for publication in *Proceedings* and will only be published as addenda.

**OUR NEW WEBSITE IS FUNCTIONING.** There are reasons for its delay, but I will only apologize.

**THE GUIDE BOOK APP** has been another effort to help you enjoy the convention. We especially hope that you will use it to evaluate the talks and each part of the Convention so that you will have a better experience in the future. Your candid expressions of appreciation or exasperation, suggestions or offers of service and advice help the Convention Planning Committee and those who execute their plans.

**THE DATABASE HAS LONG BEEN FUNCTIONING AND CONTINUES AS A FREE MEMBER SERVICE FOR NOW.** It is important that this work continue and that it reach its full potential. It is only in its infancy and many people have sacrificed many hours to get it to this point. I am grateful to everyone. It can only be a true tool of our craft when it contains many more references. As such, this effort will be on-going and never finish.

**YOU HAVE SEEN A NEW CLSA SHIRT FOR SALE. WE ARE CONSIDERING REBRANDING OURSELVES.** In other words, it might be time to replace our logo and the various Scripture verses that have been quoted along with it. Please use your Guide Book App to give us your suggestions on this idea.

**FUTURE CHALLENGES** It truly never crossed my mind that the Society not only played the obvious role it has in the United States, but that it plays an even larger one in the English-speaking canonical world. There was a time when canonists from the US wrote only for the CLSA, were never paid a penny, and never gave a second thought as to how those books would ever reach beyond our borders.

The Board of Governors and the Publications Advisory Board are no doubt tired of hearing me say that we are an international publishing house that must find a way to attract new and clever authors who publish exclusively with us. We must be willing to pay a competitive professional fee to them. Finally, we must compete. Our books must sell all over the world at the relative price, including international delivery that similar books sell in those destinations. Furthermore, our books must be e-books also that meet the requirement that the content cannot be converted to a PDF file with little or no effort and disseminated free of charge. All of our other publications must meet the same standards as does our translation of the Code of Canon Law on the Vatican website. Furthermore, for the same motive we must have contracted with publish on-demand companies so that our books can be purchased locally all over the world at similar prices that the local economy can withstand. We must not only speak about justice, but act justly as we carry out the call to be missionary disciples.

Finally, we would do well to cultivate relationships with the other international English-speaking canon law societies.

Mates, let me tell you how smashing overall this year has been, to use the new jargon I picked up last month in New Zealand and Australia!

I am so grateful to each and all who have guided me. You know how many times I emailed, texted and called you. Each time you changed my mind and heart, I offer in thanksgiving to and for you.

If this is your first Convention or 30th, seek to serve in the presidency of the CLSA one day. You will not regret it.

Thank you for the privilege of serving you.

[ADDENDUM]

# From the Desk of the Executive Coordinator
*Rev. Roger H. Keeler*

After several months of conversation with colleagues and friends, I informed the Board of Governors at its January meeting that I would not be renewing my contract with the Society when it expires on the 1st of August.

It was not an easy decision!

My three years in Washington have been very rich, indeed. I have grown to appreciate the nations' capital and all it has to offer, historically, culturally, and in the proximity to that which impacts both our work as a Society and the mission of the Church around the world.

I have become deeply attached to the community of seminarians and their formation team at Theological College, my home on Michigan Avenue. I am grateful to Father Phillip Brown, *p.s.s.*, our Past-President, for making that available to me.

It has been a joy to serve the People of God at Annunciation Parish on Embassy Row, where I have made many friends. I am indebted to former Board Consultor, Monsignor Charles Antonicelli, for welcoming me there.

It has been a tremendous privilege to work with the Board of Governors as they have sought to steer the activities of the Society with energy, conviction and vision. Past-Presidents Father Phillip Brown, *p.s.s.*, Monsignor Michael Souckar, Father Manuel Viera, OFM, and our current President, Father Bruce Miller, have all been encouraging, supportive and thoroughly dedicated in their leadership. I very much enjoyed collaborating with them.

I have been overwhelmed by the wealth of experience, depth of insight, and sheer magnanimity of our world-wide membership. Meeting so many of you is a lasting gift. The work being done by Society committees is not only fruitful, it has enormous potential going forward.

Mary DeBroeck, Renae Kuettel, Danielle Keith and Renee Nida have, each in their turn, made a solid contribution to the work of the office. My only sadness is that there has not been more time to serve with each of them.

Colleen Crawford is a stalwart and thoroughly professional presence in the Office of the Executive Coordinator. Rarely does one meet the combination of integrity, graciousness, and determination found in her: she will be superb in her new role!

Much has been accomplished these past three years, from moving into a newly renovated office space, to acquiring the technology needed to face future needs with confidence, to seeing how the Office of the Executive Coordinator might function in new ways. Yet there is a great deal yet to be done: the third printing of the Code; exploring the possibilities for a fully interactive electronic version of that text; evaluating our warehousing and distribution needs; making out-of-print editions widely available; addressing publications and new possibilities for ongoing education of canonists; increased collaboration with "Sister Societies" around the globe and with those whose mission it is to further the work of building the Reign of God.

My horizons have been expanded in ways I could never have imagined. Chief among them was the reception Father Bruce Miller, Monsignor John Foster, and I received during our biennial visit to the Holy See in late April and early May of this year. I was continually astonished during those meetings as we sat with cardinals, deans and those who minister with them. Over and over again we asked for our observations, opinions and ideas. On more than one occasion the Society was invited to offer input, suggestions and strategies. I came away with a sense of newfound confidence and assurance that the Canon Law Society of America is a valued, respected and dynamic player on the ecclesiastical stage. I couldn't help but remembering what Pope Francis said in our 2015 meeting with him: "Thank you to all of the Society for what you do. The Church needs you!"

I return to the classroom and relative calm of academic life in San Antonio with a profound sense of gratitude for the privilege of serving the Society these past three years. I echo here what I said at the 2014 Convention in St. Louis: these are indeed interesting, fascinating, oftentimes troubling, and certainly complex times for the Church. However, I believe the Canon Law Society of America is singularly well situated and prepared to study, explore, propose, and actively engage the hard work of assisting the Church in the years ahead.

With the promise of prayers ~

Fr. Roger Keeler*

*Originally published in the CLSA *eNewsletter*, 30 June 2017

# Officer's Report

## Report of the Treasurer
*Sr. Nancy Reynolds, SP, JCL*

It has indeed been an honor for me to serve as your Treasurer this past year since the last convention. I have been assisted by so many people. First of all, Colleen Crawford, our new General Secretary, has gone above and beyond the call of duty to assist me in every way possible. She is extremely skillful and knowledgeable in the area of finances and she certainly knows the workings of the Society in order to keep things running smoothly. The addition of Patrick Cogan, S.A., as Executive Coordinator is also a great asset to me and to the Society.

The invaluable help and encouragement of the Board of Governors and especially the officers has been so beneficial to me.

Nothing would be accomplished with the budget without the help of the Resource and Asset Management Committee. The members of that committee – Dr. Marie Hilliard, Sr. Margaret Stallmeyer, CDP, Msgr. William King, Msgr. John Foster, and Former Treasurer Mentor, Rev. Thomas Cronkleton – gave of their time, talent, energy and studied the budget items and monies available very carefully to come up with the budget we have. I am very grateful to them for their dedication and their work.

Below you will find a bit of an explanation of some of the items that appear in this year's budget. In my report I will give you more of the detail, but this is something you can read prior to the report.

I look forward to interacting with many of you at this annual convention and look forward to serving you for two more years as your Treasurer.

**GENERAL OPERATIONS**

To begin, our performance in General Operations for FY 16-17 is satisfactory. We ended with a slight deficit ($4,400), but by utilizing finds from the Investment Unit, as planned, we broke even. You will note that the amount of money needed to offset the deficit, $4,400, is considerably less than what we had anticipated in the Fiscal Year 2016-2017 Budget ($28,270).

*Income*

The response to the increase in Member Dues was largely positive, insofar as we retained most members. We did not quite meet our budget lines for dues, but the Dues Increase Resolution, which took effect this year, helped bring in nearly $50,000 more income than the previous fiscal year, a necessity in the wake of rising operational expenses.

*Expense*

Our staff compensation was under budget, which is good news. The office functioned without an administrative assistant from mid-December until February, which was an overall cost-savings. We were then able to hire a new administrative assistant from February to June, while simultaneously compensating Danielle Keith for her remote work on the new CLSA website, all while staying under budget.

We were slightly "over" in OEC Expenses, in part because of postage. The office sent a large shipment to the Archives in Notre Dame this year (a backlog of previous years' CLSA data), so this "overage" is not indicative of an anticipated, yearly trend, but rather, a "one-time" circumstance. We also slightly exceeded budget lines in hospitality, office supplies, and rent. While our lease rates remained constant for a period of five years at Saint Paul's College/The Hecker Center, we are subject to a 3% increase in rent every December at Theological College. Necessary provisions have been made for next year's budget to accommodate this increase.

We remain under-budget in Member Services. It is worth noting that Joe McCathran, our auditor, makes adjustments to the Cost of Book Production based on inventory sold in a fiscal year, so we anticipate making appropriate adjustments this upcoming year – that is to say, despite two Proceedings bills being among our anticipated expenses for Fiscal Year 2017-2018, it will not be a straightforward $10,000 expense. He will adjust to reflect unit cost and units sold.

The Board of Governors, while exceeding their budget line for the Rome Trip and Regional Meetings (a topic we have discussed, and for which we have made provisions in FY 2017-2018), are still under-budget overall for FY 2016-2017. This is due to a cost savings on lodging, travel, and meeting space. All Officers remain well-within their budget lines.

Committees were very careful in their financial activity. The Nominations Committee had an in-person meeting, which was necessary for determining the candidates for Board election, and the Resource & Asset Management Committee had a conference call to determine the budget for Fiscal Year 2017-2018. We are grateful that some committees communicated via email and third-party phone conference. Some other committees experienced changes in Committee chair and member composition, and plans for meeting were delayed.

## PUBLICATIONS

It was another tough year for us in Publications, although we fared significantly better than last year. Our expenses were down, but our income was down, too. The good news is, Publications will see a flurry of activity in FY 2017-2018, which should help to offset the existing deficit. We have two publications that are currently on the market (the compilation of Religious Advisory Opinions, and the Penal Law Proceedings), as well as new inventory for the *Code of Canon Law*, Latin-English edition. Moreover, we have a planned third printing/reprinting of the Code which will include *Mitis* and *De Concordia* changes. These books will be printed in addition to our regular book production (*Roman Replies & CLSA Advisory Opinions*; *Proceedings*). As we look toward a new, user-friendly website, we hope to see an increase in usage of the Publication Database, and accordingly, we may be able to plan for future income for subscriptions to the Publication Database from seminaries, universities, libraries, and the like.

## CONVENTIONS

We exceeded budgeted income for General Convention registration and Pre-Convention Workshop Two, (Msgr. Pinto and Father Arokiaraj) which is positive, but for the first time in several years, we had to employ existing Convention surplus (cash flow in Wells Fargo) to offset our overall deficit. Our expenses are due in large part to increasing audiovisual costs (a matter we have long discussed with members and the Board, as we become more reliant on technology during major addresses, workshops, and seminars), and also to the expense of accomodating non-member speakers, foreign officials and dignitaries, and their Convention material needs. As we plan for future Conventions, these expenses are worth further consideration.

## SCHOLARSHIPS

The Annual Appeal was a wonderful success because of the generosity of individual members, religious groups, and regional meetings. Between the Doctoral and Licentiate Scholarship Funds, we raised $12,710 for the year, which is slightly above the donation mark from Fiscal Year 2015-2016. We paid out $10,400 in licentiate scholarships, and based on the licentiate awards of $30,000 (across several semester/years), we have $19,600 remaining for future awards, in addition to the $29,000 sanctioned by the Resource and Asset Management Committee for FY 2017-2018. We have remitted in full the Doctoral Fund awards from FY 2016-2017 to two recipients, so there is no carry-over of previously designated Doctoral Funds for FY 2017-2018.

## INVESTMENTS

There have been no real-time transfers with the newly-established Investment Unit, but as we enter FY 2017-2018, and initiate transfers for the close of books, there will be. We will continue to isolate Investment data so members can see the growth of the funds, and so that we might more clearly track transfers.

CUIT Quarterly Balances, Year Ending 6/30/17

|  | General Operations Investment Fund Balance | Licentiate Scholarship Investment Fund Balance | Doctoral Scholarship Investment Fund Balance |
|---|---|---|---|
| 3/31/2014 | $ 769,264.93 | $ 613,175.11 |  |
| 6/30/2014 | $ 797,237.52 | $ 635,471.89 |  |
| 9/30/2014 | $ 799,740.90 | $ 637,467.28 |  |
| 12/31/2014 | $ 771,084.80 | $ 657,027.00 | $ 53,194.96 |
| 3/31/2015 | $ 770,355.00 | $ 656,405.24 | $ 53,144.65 |
| 6/30/2015 | $ 772,070.92 | $ 657,867.38 | $ 53,262.98 |
| 9/30/2015 | $ 732,067.85 | $ 623,781.50 | $ 50,503.24 |
| 12/31/2015 | $ 753,093.09 | $ 641,696.72 | $ 51,953.68 |
| 3/31/2016 | $ 761,338.72 | $ 648,722.56 | $ 52,522.44 |
| 6/30/2016 | $ 773,041.48 | $ 658,694.29 | $ 53,329.79 |
| 9/30/2016 | $ 809,456.81 | $ 689,723.11 | $ 55,841.99 |
| 12/31/2016 | $ 843,851.76 | $ 719,030.35 | $ 58,214.82 |
| 3/31/2017 | $ 870,332.69 | $ 741,594.29 | $ 60,041.63 |
| 6/30/2017 | $ 883,659.21 | $ 752,949.61 | $ 60,960.97 |

# CANON LAW SOCIETY OF AMERICA

Financial Statements, Supplementary Information and Independent Accountant's Review Report

For the Years Ended
June 30, 2017 and 2016

**LSWG**
Linton Shafer Warfield & Garrett, P.A.
CERTIFIED PUBLIC ACCOUNTANTS

**LSWG**
Certified Public Accountants & Business Consultants

*Accounting for your success since 1965*

## Independent Accountant's Review Report

Board of Governors
Canon Law Society of America
Washington, DC

We have reviewed the accompanying financial statements of Canon Law Society of America (a nonprofit organization), which comprise the statement of financial position as of June 30, 2017 and 2016, and the related statements of activities and changes in net assets, and cash flows for the years then ended, and the related notes to the financial statements. A review includes primarily applying analytical procedures to management's financial data and making inquiries of management. A review is substantially less in scope than an audit, the objective of which is the expression of an opinion regarding the financial statements as a whole. Accordingly, we do not express such an opinion.

### Management's Responsibility for the Financial Statements

Management is responsible for the preparation and fair presentation of these financial statements in accordance with accounting principles generally accepted in the United States of America; this includes the design, implementation, and maintenance of internal control relevant to the preparation and fair presentation of the financial statements that are free from material misstatement whether due to fraud or error.

### Accountant's Responsibility

Our responsibility is to conduct the review engagements in accordance with Statements on Standards for Accounting and Review Services promulgated by the Accounting and Review Services Committee of the AICPA. Those standards require us to perform procedures to obtain limited assurance as a basis for reporting whether we are aware of any material modifications that should be made to the financial statements for them to be in accordance with accounting principles generally accepted in the United States of America. We believe that the results of our procedures provide a reasonable basis for our conclusion.

### Accountant's Conclusion

Based on our review, we are not aware of any material modifications that should be made to the accompanying financial statements in order for them to be in accordance with accounting principles generally accepted in the United States of America.

1803 Research Boulevard, Suite 404 • Rockville, Maryland 20850-6118 • 301-738-8400 • FAX 301-590-9343
ROCKVILLE • FREDERICK
*www.lswgcpa.com*

Supplementary Information

The supplementary information included in the schedules of program services and supporting services is presented for purposes of additional analysis and is not a required part of the basic financial statements. Such information is the responsibility of management and was derived from, and relates directly to, the underlying accounting and other records used to prepare the financial statements. The supplementary information has been subjected to the review procedures applied in our review of the basic financial statements. We are not aware of any material modifications that should be made to the supplementary information. We have not audited the supplementary information and do not express an opinion on such information.

*Linton Shafer Warfield & Garrett*
Rockville, Maryland
February 23, 2018

Linton Shafer Warfield & Garrett, P.A.
Certified Public Accountants & Business Consultants

## CANON LAW SOCIETY OF AMERICA
## Statements of Financial Position
### June 30, 2017 and 2016

|  | 2017 | 2016 |
|---|---:|---:|
| **Assets** | | |
| **Current Assets** | | |
| Cash | $ 107,132 | $ 176,221 |
| Cash - scholarship fund | 8,403 | 10,587 |
| Accounts receivable - other | 3,992 | 5,316 |
| Inventory | 49,230 | 56,224 |
| Prepaid expenses | 14,603 | 18,387 |
| Total Current Assets | 183,360 | 266,735 |
| **Furniture and Equipment - at cost** | | |
| Furniture and equipment | 46,491 | 46,491 |
| Less: accumulated depreciation | (13,328) | (7,797) |
| Furniture and Equipment, Net | 33,163 | 38,694 |
| **Other Assets** | | |
| Security deposit | 2,094 | 2,094 |
| Investments | 883,659 | 773,042 |
| Investment - scholarship fund | 813,911 | 712,024 |
| Total Other Assets | 1,699,664 | 1,487,160 |
| **Total Assets** | $ 1,916,187 | $ 1,792,589 |
| **Liabilities and Net Assets** | | |
| **Current Liabilities** | | |
| Accounts payable | $ 30 | $ 30 |
| Deferred revenue | 8,745 | 42,585 |
| Total Current Liabilities | 8,775 | 42,615 |
| Total Liabilities | 8,775 | 42,615 |
| **Net Assets** | | |
| Unrestricted | | |
| Undesignated | 1,060,670 | 981,550 |
| Board designated - publications | 24,777 | 46,328 |
| Total Unrestricted | 1,085,447 | 1,027,878 |
| Temporarily restricted | 821,965 | 722,096 |
| Total Net Assets | 1,907,412 | 1,749,974 |
| **Total Liabilities and Net Assets** | $ 1,916,187 | $ 1,792,589 |

The accompanying notes are an integral part of these statements.

## CANON LAW SOCIETY OF AMERICA
## Statements of Activities and Changes in Net Assets
### For the Year Ended June 30, 2017

|  | Unrestricted Undesignated | Unrestricted Publications | Unrestricted Total | Temporarily Restricted | Total |
|---|---:|---:|---:|---:|---:|
| **Revenue** | | | | | |
| Membership dues | $ 277,535 | $  - | $ 277,535 | $  - | $ 277,535 |
| Convention, workshops | 186,962 | - | 186,962 | - | 186,962 |
| Sale of publications | - | 37,517 | 37,517 | - | 37,517 |
| Contributions | - | - | - | 12,730 | 12,730 |
| Interest and dividends | 10,411 | - | 10,411 | 9,632 | 20,043 |
| Royalties | - | 6,971 | 6,971 | - | 6,971 |
| Appreciation on fair value of investments | 100,346 | - | 100,346 | 92,425 | 192,771 |
| Net assets released from restrictions | 14,918 | - | 14,918 | (14,918) | - |
| Total Revenue | 590,172 | 44,488 | 634,660 | 99,869 | 734,529 |
| **Expenses** | | | | | |
| **Program Services** | | | | | |
| Publications | - | 56,039 | 56,039 | - | 56,039 |
| Convention, workshops | 198,455 | - | 198,455 | - | 198,455 |
| Membership services | 7,249 | - | 7,249 | - | 7,249 |
| Committees | 4,147 | - | 4,147 | - | 4,147 |
| Holy See and Austrialia | 13,332 | - | 13,332 | - | 13,332 |
| Scholarship fund | 14,918 | - | 14,918 | - | 14,918 |
| Total Program Services | 238,101 | 56,039 | 294,140 | - | 294,140 |
| **Supporting Services** | 282,951 | - | 282,951 | - | 282,951 |
| Total Expenses | 521,052 | 56,039 | 577,091 | - | 577,091 |
| **Inter-fund Transfer** | 10,000 | (10,000) | - | - | - |
| **Changes in Net Assets** | 79,120 | (21,551) | 57,569 | 99,869 | 157,438 |
| Net Assets - Beginning of Year | 981,550 | 46,328 | 1,027,878 | 722,096 | 1,749,974 |
| Net Assets - End of Year | $ 1,060,670 | $ 24,777 | $ 1,085,447 | $ 821,965 | $ 1,907,412 |

The accompanying notes are an integral part of this statement.

## CANON LAW SOCIETY OF AMERICA
## Statements of Activities and Changes in Net Assets
## For the Year Ended June 30, 2016

|  | Unrestricted Undesignated | Unrestricted Publications | Unrestricted Total | Temporarily Restricted | Total |
|---|---|---|---|---|---|
| **Revenue** |  |  |  |  |  |
| Membership dues | $ 231,739 | $ - | $ 231,739 | $ - | $ 231,739 |
| Convention, workshops | 211,314 | - | 211,314 | - | 211,314 |
| Sale of publications | - | 55,178 | 55,178 | - | 55,178 |
| Contributions | - | - | - | 12,337 | 12,337 |
| Interest and dividends | 11,349 | - | 11,349 | 10,546 | 21,895 |
| Royalties | - | 7,260 | 7,260 | - | 7,260 |
| (Depreciation) on fair value of investments | (10,348) | - | (10,348) | (9,531) | (19,879) |
| Net assets released from restrictions | 22,704 | - | 22,704 | (22,704) | - |
| Total Revenue | 466,758 | 62,438 | 529,196 | (9,352) | 519,844 |
| **Expenses** |  |  |  |  |  |
| **Program Services** |  |  |  |  |  |
| Publications | - | 95,412 | 95,412 | - | 95,412 |
| Convention, workshops | 210,873 | - | 210,873 | - | 210,873 |
| Membership services | 12,552 | - | 12,552 | - | 12,552 |
| Committees | 3,437 | - | 3,437 | - | 3,437 |
| Holy See and Austrialia | 7,710 | - | 7,710 | - | 7,710 |
| Scholarship fund | 22,704 | - | 22,704 | - | 22,704 |
| Total Program Services | 257,276 | 95,412 | 352,688 | - | 352,688 |
| **Supporting Services** | 250,294 | - | 250,294 | - | 250,294 |
| Total Expenses | 507,570 | 95,412 | 602,982 | - | 602,982 |
| **Changes in Net Assets** | (40,812) | (32,974) | (73,786) | (9,352) | (83,138) |
| **Net Assets - Beginning of Year** | 1,022,362 | 79,302 | 1,101,664 | 731,448 | 1,833,112 |
| **Net Assets - End of Year** | $ 981,550 | $ 46,328 | $ 1,027,878 | $ 722,096 | $ 1,749,974 |

The accompanying notes are an integral part of this statement.

## CANON LAW SOCIETY OF AMERICA
## Statements of Cash Flows
## For the Years Ended June 30,

| Increase (Decrease) in Cash | 2017 | 2016 |
|---|---:|---:|
| **Cash Flows From Operating Activities** | | |
| Changes in Net Assets | $ 157,438 | $ (83,138) |
| Adjustments to reconcile changes in net assets to net cash provided by (used in) operating activities: | | |
| Depreciation | 5,532 | 4,244 |
| Unrealized (gain) loss on investments | (192,771) | 19,879 |
| Change in assets and liabilities: | | |
| (Increase) Decrease in accounts receivable | 1,324 | 1,099 |
| (Increase) Decrease in prepaid expenses | 3,784 | 1,796 |
| (Increase) Decrease in inventory | 6,994 | 20,466 |
| (Increase) Decrease in security deposit | - | (2,095) |
| Increase (Decrease) in deferred revenue | (33,840) | 27,350 |
| Net Cash Used In Operating Activities | (51,539) | (10,399) |
| **Cash Flows From Investing Activities** | | |
| Purchase of investments | (19,734) | (21,742) |
| Purchase of fixed assets | - | (40,909) |
| Net Cash Used in Investing Activities | (19,734) | (62,651) |
| **(Decrease) in Cash** | (71,273) | (73,050) |
| **Cash Balance - Beginning of Year** | 186,808 | 259,858 |
| **Cash Balance - End of Year** | $ 115,535 | $ 186,808 |
| **Supplemental Disclosures** | | |
| Income taxes paid | $ - | $ - |
| Interest paid | $ - | $ - |

The accompanying notes are an integral part of these statements.

Canon Law Society of America
Notes to Financial Statements
For the Years Ended June 30, 2017 and 2016

1. **Nature of Activities**

   The Canon Law Society of America (CLSA) is a national, not-for-profit corporation, established in November 1939 in Washington DC to promote canonical and pastoral approaches to significant issues within the Roman Catholic Church. In addition to a publication service, CLSA conducts an annual convention and other symposia to promote a better understanding of church law and its pastoral applications. Major sources of gross income are from membership dues, sales of publications and books and annual convention and workshops.

2. **Basis of Financial Statement Presentation**

   According to Financial Accounting Standards Board (FASB) Codification Standards, CLSA is required to report information regarding its financial position and activities according to three classes of net assets:

   (1) **Unrestricted Net Assets** - represents resources that are currently available for support of CLSA's operations.

   (2) **Temporarily Restricted Net Assets** - represents resources that may be utilized only in accordance with the restricted purposes established by donor restrictions and CLSA's bylaws. When a restriction expires, temporarily restricted net assets are reclassified to unrestricted net assets and reported in the statement of activities and changes in net assets as net assets released from restrictions.

   (3) **Permanently Restricted Net Assets** - represents resources for which the principal is to be maintained intact and the income may only be spent in accordance with the intent of the donor. CLSA currently does not have any permanently restricted net assets.

   The financial statements are prepared on the accrual basis of accounting, whereby, revenue is recognized when earned and expenses are recognized when incurred.

3. **Summary of Significant Accounting Policies**

   **Cash** – For purposes of the statement of cash flows, CLSA considers all cash accounts and all highly liquid debt instruments purchased with an initial maturity of three months or less to be cash.

   **Investments** - Investments in marketable securities with readily determinable fair values are reported at their fair values in the statement of financial position. Investment income or loss (including gains and losses on investments, interest and dividends) is included in the statement of activities as an increase or decrease in unrestricted net assets unless the income or loss is restricted by donor or law.

Canon Law Society of America
Notes to Financial Statements
For the Years Ended June 30, 2017 and 2016

3. **Summary of Significant Accounting Policies (Continued)**

Investments consist principally of two mutual funds. Fair value of investments in securities is based on the latest reported sales price at June 30, 2017 and 2016.

**Accounts receivable** - Accounts receivable are stated at the amount management expects to collect from outstanding balances. The provision for uncollectible accounts is based on management's evaluation of the collectability of accounts receivable. CLSA considers accounts receivable to be fully collectible; accordingly, no provision for doubtful accounts is required. Books and publication receivables are considered uncollectible if not collected within 90 days after the sale.

**Inventory** – The inventory of books and publications is valued at cost, on the first-in, first-out method.

**Property and Equipment** - Purchases of furniture and equipment are recorded at cost. CLSA's policy is to capitalize expenditures for equipment purchased in the amount of $1,000 or more. Depreciation is calculated over an estimated useful life of five to ten years using the straight-line method. Depreciation and amortization for the years ended June 30, 2017 and 2016 totaled $5,532 and $4,244.

**Fair Value** – Financial Accounting Standards Board (FASB) Codification Standards defines fair value, establishes a framework for measuring fair value, and expands disclosures about fair value measurements and establishes a hierarchy for valuation inputs.

Fair value is the price that would be received to sell an asset or paid to transfer a liability in an orderly transaction between market participants at the measurement date. A fair value measurement assumes that the transaction to sell the asset or transfer the liability occurs in the principal market for the asset or liability or, in the absence of a principal market, the most advantageous market. Valuation techniques that are consistent with the market, income or cost approach are used to measure fair value.

The fair value hierarchy prioritizes the inputs to valuation techniques used to measure fair value into three broad levels:

- Level 1 - inputs are based upon unadjusted quoted prices for identical instruments traded in active markets.

- Level 2 - inputs are based upon quoted prices for similar instruments in active markets, quoted prices for identical or similar instruments in markets that are not active, and model-based valuation techniques for which all significant assumptions are observable in the market or can be corroborated by observable market data for substantially the full term of the assets or liabilities.

Canon Law Society of America
Notes to Financial Statements
For the Years Ended June 30, 2017 and 2016

3. Summary of Significant Accounting Policies (Continued)

- Level 3 - inputs are generally unobservable and typically reflect management's estimates of assumptions that market participants would use in pricing the asset or liability. The fair values are therefore determined using model-based techniques that include option pricing models, discounted cash flow models, and similar techniques.

**Revenue Recognition** - CLSA bills membership dues annually on a basis which conforms to CLSA's fiscal year-end. Dues, workshop and convention registrations received in advance of the next fiscal year are deferred and recognized as revenue in the subsequent year.

Contributions are recognized when the donor makes a promise to give to the CLSA that is, in substance, unconditional. Contributions received are recorded as unrestricted, temporarily restricted, or permanently restricted support depending on the absence or existence and nature of any donor restrictions. Contributions restricted by the donor are reported as increases in unrestricted net assets if the restrictions are met or expire in the fiscal year in which the contributions are recognized. When a restriction expires, temporarily restricted net assets are reclassified as unrestricted net assets. Revenue from convention and workshop registration fees are recognized when the events take place.

**Tax Status** - CLSA is exempt from federal income tax under Section 501(c)(3) of the Internal Revenue Code. CLSA has not been classified by the Internal Revenue Service as a private foundation. Income which is not related to the exempt purpose, less applicable deductions, is subject to Federal and state corporate income tax. CLSA is covered under a group religious exemption and is not required to file Form 990.

**Expense Allocations** - Directly identifiable expenses are charged to programs and supporting services. Overhead and expenses related to more than one function are not allocated but are included in supporting services.

**Estimates** - In preparing financial statements in conformity with generally accepted accounting principles, management is required to make estimates and assumptions that affect the reported amounts of assets and liabilities, the disclosure of contingent assets and liabilities at the date of the financial statements, and the reported amounts of revenues and expenses during the reporting period. Actual results could differ from those estimates.

**Financial Instruments** – CLSA's financial instruments consist of investments, accounts receivable, accounts payable and accrued expenses. It is management's opinion the CLSA is not exposed to significant interest rate or credit risk arising from these instruments. Unless otherwise noted, the fair values of these financial instruments are market values of these financial instruments, and approximate their carrying values.

## Canon Law Society of America
## Notes to Financial Statements
## For the Years Ended June 30, 2017 and 2016

4. **Investments**

Investments in balanced mutual funds at June 30, 2017 and 2016, which are all considered level 1, consist of the following:

|  | Cost | Market |
|---|---|---|
| Total Investments 6/30/2017 | $ 1,075,009 | $ 1,697,570 |
| Total Investments 6/30/2016 | $ 1,055,276 | $ 1,485,065 |

By fund type at June 30, 2017 and 2016:

|  | 2017 Cost | 2017 Market | 2016 Cost | 2016 Market |
|---|---|---|---|---|
| Unrestricted | $ 535,396 | $ 883,659 | $ 525,124 | $ 773,041 |
| Restricted | 539,613 | 813,911 | 530,152 | 712,024 |
| Total Investments | $ 1,075,009 | $ 1,697,570 | $ 1,055,276 | $ 1,485,065 |

CLSA invests in a professionally managed portfolio that contains balanced mutual funds. Such investments are exposed to various risks such as interest rates, market and credit. Due to the level of risk associated with such investments and the level of uncertainty related to changes in the value of such investments, it is at least reasonably possible that changes in risks in the near term would materially affect investment balances and the amounts reported in the financial statements.

Investment income, which is included in the Statement of Activities for the years ended June 30, 2017 and 2016 is comprised of the following:

|  | 2017 Unrestricted | 2017 Temporarily Restricted | 2016 Unrestricted | 2016 Temporarily Restricted |
|---|---|---|---|---|
| Net unrealized gain (loss) | $ 100,346 | $ 92,425 | $ (10,348) | $ (9,531) |
| Interest and dividends | 10,411 | 9,632 | 11,349 | 10,546 |
| Net Investment Income | $ 110,757 | $ 102,057 | $ 1,001 | $ 1,015 |

Canon Law Society of America
Notes to Financial Statements
For the Years Ended June 30, 2017 and 2016

## 5. Concentration of Credit Risk

CLSA maintains its cash in bank deposit accounts, which at times, may exceed federally insured limits. CLSA has not experienced any losses in such accounts and believes it is not exposed to any significant financial risk on cash.

## 6. Commitments

### Office Lease
CLSA leased office space in Washington DC for a 10 year period ending December 31, 2017 that was terminated by the landlord in fiscal year 2016. In December of 2015 CLSA entered into a new lease for a 10 year period ending November 30, 2025. Monthly rent payments for year one is $2,094. Monthly rent payments for the second through the tenth year will be increased by 3% each December 1. Rent expense for the years ended June 30, 2017 and 2016 were $25,573 and $13,232, respectively. Rent expense for 2016 was reduced by rent termination concessions from the previous landlord of $5,779. Minimum future rental obligations by fiscal year are: 2018 - $26,340; 2019 - $27,130; 2020 - $27,944; 2021 - $28,782; 2022 - $29,646, and $77,509 thereafter.

### Postage Lease
CLSA entered into a fifty-one month lease for a postage machine ending April 30, 2018. The lease payment is $184 per quarter.

## 7. Board Designated Funds

The Board has designated that net income from the sale of publications and books be set aside for use only in the publication activities. As reported on the statement of activities, the net assets from publications decreased in fiscal year 2017 by $21,551 to $24,777. In fiscal year 2016 the publications net assets decreased by $32,974.

Canon Law Society of America
Notes to Financial Statements
For the Years Ended June 30, 2017 and 2016

8. **Temporarily Restricted Net Assets**

The activity in temporarily restricted net assets for fiscal years 2017 and 2016 is as follows:

|  | Scholarship Fund | Doctorial Scholarship | Total |
|---|---|---|---|
| Balance June 30, 2015 | $ 678,185 | $ 53,263 | $ 731,448 |
| Income | 22,102 | 781 | 22,883 |
| Expenses | (22,704) | - | (22,704) |
| Unrealized (loss) on investments | (8,817) | (714) | (9,531) |
| Balance June 30, 2016 | $ 668,766 | $ 53,330 | $ 722,096 |

|  | Scholarship Fund | Doctorial Scholarship | Total |
|---|---|---|---|
| Balance June 30, 2016 | $ 668,766 | $ 53,330 | $ 722,096 |
| Income | 18,908 | 3,454 | 22,362 |
| Expenses | (12,365) | (2,553) | (14,918) |
| Unrealized gain on investments | 85,502 | 6,923 | 92,425 |
| Balance June 30, 2017 | $ 760,811 | $ 61,154 | $ 821,965 |

9. **Annual Meeting Site Reservation Agreements**

CLSA has reserved hotel space for future annual meetings. The terms of these reservation agreements provide that a fee will be assessed to CSLA if the reservation is canceled due to site change, within a specified period prior to the meeting dates.

10. **Executive Coordinator's Contract**

CLSA has contracted with the Executive Coordinator beginning August 1, 2014 and ending August 1, 2017. The Executive Coordinator has notified the Board of his intention not to extend the terms of the employment agreement beyond that date.

11. **Subsequent Events**

Management has evaluated subsequent events through February 23, 2018, the date that the financial statements were available to be issued. There were no significant events to report.

**Supplementary Information**

## CANON LAW SOCIETY OF AMERICA
### Schedules of Program Services
### For the Years Ended June 30,

| | 2017 | 2016 |
|---|---:|---:|
| **Publications** | | |
| Cost of publications sold | $ 8,837 | $ 24,543 |
| Executive coordinator office | 6,199 | 13,591 |
| Royalty expense | 1,405 | 1,562 |
| Advertising | - | 10 |
| Electronic database initiative | - | 12,519 |
| BrightKey | 39,598 | 43,187 |
| Total Publication Expenses | 56,039 | 95,412 |
| **Convention and Pre-convention Workshop** | | |
| Coordination | 106,428 | 141,890 |
| Food service | 3,544 | 2,771 |
| Honoraria | 14,400 | 17,600 |
| Speakers' travel | 12,610 | 2,154 |
| Printing | 8,367 | 5,979 |
| Freight | 1,023 | 1,351 |
| Audio Visual | 29,080 | 20,780 |
| Other | 10,012 | 8,330 |
| Postage | 534 | 105 |
| Convention chair | 2,292 | 1,816 |
| Liturgy | 1,931 | 921 |
| Supplies | 5,236 | 3,779 |
| Convention planning committee | 1,040 | 1,057 |
| Convention company | 1,958 | 2,340 |
| Total Convention and Pre-Convention Workshop | 198,455 | 210,873 |
| **Membership Services** | | |
| Postage | 1,093 | 4,811 |
| Printing | 7 | 3,513 |
| Newsletter | - | 47 |
| Regional meetings | 4,510 | 2,244 |
| Platform service webinar | 1,639 | 1,937 |
| Total Membership Services | 7,249 | 12,552 |
| **Visit to Holy See and Australia Trip** | 13,332 | 7,710 |

Continued

## CANON LAW SOCIETY OF AMERICA
### Schedule of Program Services
### For the Years Ended June 30,

|  | 2017 | 2016 |
|---|---:|---:|
| **Committees** | | |
| Resource & asset management | $ 157 | $ 121 |
| Nominations | 3,394 | 2,674 |
| Laity | - | 217 |
| Other | 596 | 425 |
| Total Committees | 4,147 | 3,437 |
| | | |
| **Scholarship Fund** | | |
| Scholarships paid | 12,948 | 20,574 |
| Scholarships expenses | 1,970 | 2,130 |
| Total Scholarship Fund | 14,918 | 22,704 |
| | | |
| Total Program Services | $ 294,140 | $ 352,688 |

The accompanying notes are an integral part of this schedule.

## CANON LAW SOCIETY OF AMERICA
### Schedules of Supporting Services
### For the Years Ended June 30,

|  | 2017 | 2016 |
|---|---:|---:|
| Board of Governors |  |  |
|   Rental housing | $ 12,051 | $ 11,898 |
|   Travel | 5,969 | 5,141 |
|   Food service | 5,913 | 4,572 |
|   Other expenses | 573 | 576 |
| President | 2,773 | 2,937 |
| Vice President & Treasurer | 469 | 282 |
| Executive Coordinator Office | 224,098 | 207,412 |
| Depreciation expense | 5,532 | 4,244 |
| Rent expense | 25,573 | 13,232 |
|   Total Supporting Services | $ 282,951 | $ 250,294 |

The accompanying notes are an integral part of this schedule.

# ACCOUNT SUMMARY
## *Fiscal Year 2017-2018 Budget*

| | | |
|---|---|---|
| **GENERAL OPERATIONS** | | |
| Income | $ | 288,531 |
| Expenses | $ | 285,865 |
| **Excess/(Deficit)** | **$** | **2,666** |
| **PUBLICATIONS** | | |
| Income | $ | 66,000 |
| Expenses | $ | 66,000 |
| **Excess/(Deficit)** | $ | - |
| **CONVENTIONS** | | |
| Income | $ | 199,895 |
| Expenses | $ | 199,895 |
| **Excess/(Deficit)** | $ | - |
| **Subtotal Gen. Ops., Pub. & Conv. *** | **$** | **2,666** |
| **SCHOLARSHIP FUND** | | |
| Income | $ | 59,900 |
| Expenses | $ | 54,575 |
| **Excess/(Deficit)** | **$** | **5,325** |
| **INVESTMENT UNIT (Note 2)** | | |
| Income | $ | 15,720 |
| Expenses | $ | 29,000 |
| **Excess/(Deficit)** | **$** | **(13,280)** |

Note 1: Since Scholarship income by definition belongs to the Scholarship Fund, it can not be used to balance the overall budget. Hence, the first three CLSA "companies" as a whole need to achieve a balance independently, and the number labeled as "Grand Total" is not a simple "operational" profit. An "Excess" in the Scholarship Fund represents an increase in the fund, which is needed for the fund to grow.

Note 2: Investments are operated on a spending policy based upon the use of up to 5% of the three-year quarterly rolling average of the balance of each individual investment fund, as of December 31 of the prior budget year. Because the spending policies utilize prior years' capital gains, interest, and dividends, and not just the current fiscal year's interests and dividends, the expenses can exceed income for this unit, thus causing a deficit to be reported.

## GENERAL OPERATIONS UNIT SUMMARY *(by fiscal year)*

|  | Budget FY 17-18 | Actual FY 16-17 | Budget FY 16-17 | Actual FY 15-16 | Budget FY 15-16 |
|---|---|---|---|---|---|
| **INCOME** | | | | | |
| **Investment Income** | | | | | |
| Interest/RCT | $ - | $ 139 | $ - | $ 31 | $ - |
| Dividends/CUIT | $ - | $ 10,272 | $ - | $ 11,318 | $ 8,720 |
| **Sub-total** (Not Included in Budgeted Income) | $ - | $ 10,411 | $ - | $ 11,349 | $ 8,720 |
| **Portion of Prior Year Realized Net Asset Increase - ADJUSTED** (Note 1) | | | | $ 30,906 | $ 58,519 |
| **Transfer from Investment Unit (Note 2)** | $ - | $ 4,400 | $ 28,270 | | |
| **Dues Income** | | | | | |
| New Member Dues | $ 11,250 | $ 8,410 | $ 12,000 | $ 10,900 | $ 12,000 |
| Previous YR Member Dues | $ - | $ - | $ - | $ - | $ - |
| Current YR Member Dues | $ 267,281 | $ 269,125 | $ 273,775 | $ 220,839 | $ 220,000 |
| Uncategorized Income | | $ 20 | | | |
| **Sub-total** | $ 278,531 | $ 277,555 | $ 285,775 | $ 231,739 | $ 232,000 |
| **Administrative Fees from Pub** (Note 2) | $ 10,000 | $ 10,000 | $ 10,000 | | |
| **Intensive Workshop Registration** | $ - | $ - | $ 25,000 | $ - | $ 25,000 |
| **Webinar Platform Income** | $ - | $ - | $ - | $ - | $ - |
| **TOTAL INCOME** | $ 288,531 | $ 302,366 | $ 349,045 | $ 273,994 | $ 324,239 |
| **EXPENSES** | | | | | |
| **Staff Compensations and Benefits** | $ 146,960 | $ 187,272 | $ 188,955 | $ 172,146 | $ 175,961 |
| **Service Charges** | | | | | |
| Bank Service Charges | $ 1,050 | $ 1,069 | $ 950 | $ 993 | $ 700 |
| Credit Card Fees | $ 4,000 | $ 4,180 | $ 3,600 | $ 2,644 | $ 3,600 |
| **Sub-total** | $ 5,050 | $ 5,249 | $ 4,550 | $ 3,637 | $ 4,300 |
| **OEC Expenses (acct no.)** | | | | | |

## General Operations Unit Summary *(by fiscal year)*

|  | Budget FY 17-18 | Actual FY 16-17 | Budget FY 16-17 | Actual FY 15-16 | Budget FY 15-16 |
|---|---|---|---|---|---|
| Postage Meter Lease | $ 810 | $ - | $ 800 | $ 810 | $ 900 |
| Postage Meter Supplies | $ 150 | $ 828 | $ 190 | $ 109 | $ 175 |
| Insurance/Workers Comp | $ 1,100 | $ 1,130 | $ 1,100 | $ 1,084 | $ 1,100 |
| Hospitality | $ 1,500 | $ 1,841 | $ 1,500 | $ 1,703 | $ 600 |
| Postage/UPS/FedEx | $ 1,000 | $ 1,199 | $ 600 | $ 979 | $ 500 |
| Office Supplies | $ 2,300 | $ 2,610 | $ 2,300 | $ 3,533 | $ 2,300 |
| Telephone/ISP/DSL | $ 2,300 | $ 2,199 | $ 2,400 | $ 2,893 | $ 3,320 |
| Travel | $ 1,000 | $ 869 | $ 1,000 | $ 516 | $ 1,000 |
| Continuing Education | $ 2,000 | $ 1,026 | $ 2,000 | $ 639 | $ 1,000 |
| Taxes | $ 80 | $ - | $ 80 | $ 80 | $ 80 |
| Furniture & Equipment | $ 1,000 | $ 1,302 | $ 1,000 | $ 588 | $ 1,000 |
| Books and Periodicals | $ 600 | $ 693 | $ 600 | $ 552 | $ 300 |
| Professional Collab. w/ Nat'l Organizations | $ 1,000 | $ - | $ 1,100 | $ 24 | $ 500 |
| IT/Tech Support Services | $ 3,500 | $ 2,871 | $ 4,000 |  |  |
| Rent | $ 26,340 | $ 25,573 | $ 25,133 | $ 13,232 | $ 20,916 |
| Copier Lease | $ - | $ - | $ - | $ - | $ - |
| Copier Maintenance | $ 900 | $ 860 | $ 900 | $ 860 | $ 800 |
| **Sub-total** | **$ 45,580** | **$ 43,000** | **$ 44,703** | **$ 27,603** | **$ 34,491** |
| **Professional Services** |  |  |  |  |  |
| Accountant/Auditor | $ 9,000 | $ 7,600 | $ 9,000 | $ 6,950 | $ 6,750 |
| Web Design & Maintenance | $ 5,000 | $ 6,549 | $ 6,237 | $ 7,310 | $ 6,237 |
| Legal Services | $ 500 | $ - | $ 500 | $ 3,000 | $ 1,500 |
| **Sub-total** | **$ 14,500** | **$ 14,149** | **$ 15,737** | **$ 17,260** | **$ 14,487** |
| **Member Services** |  |  |  |  |  |
| General Postage | $ 1,500 | $ 1,093 | $ 1,200 | $ 1,336 | $ 1,600 |
| Newsletter Postage | $ 50 | $ - | $ 50 | $ 47 | $ 50 |
| *Proceedings* Printing | $ 4,000 | $ - | $ 5,000 | $ 3,513 | $ 5,000 |
| *Proceedings* Postage | $ 4,500 | $ 8 | $ 5,000 | $ 3,475 | $ 5,000 |
| **Sub-total** | **$ 10,050** | **$ 1,100** | **$ 11,250** | **$ 8,370** | **$ 11,650** |
| **Board of Governors, Meetings** |  |  |  |  |  |
| Food | $ 6,000 | $ 5,913 | $ 6,000 | $ 4,572 | $ 6,000 |
| Lodging | $ 14,000 | $ 12,051 | $ 14,000 | $ 11,898 | $ 13,500 |
| Meeting Space | $ 1,000 | $ 539 | $ 1,000 | $ 542 | $ 1,000 |
| Supplies | $ 50 | $ 34 | $ 50 | $ 34 | $ 50 |

## GENERAL OPERATIONS UNIT SUMMARY *(by fiscal year)*

| | Budget FY 17-18 | Actual FY 16-17 | Budget FY 16-17 | Actual FY 15-16 | Budget FY 15-16 |
|---|---|---|---|---|---|
| Travel | $ 9,000 | $ 5,969 | $ 9,000 | $ 5,141 | $ 9,000 |
| Rome or Australia Trip | $ 11,000 | $ 13,332 | $ 11,000 | $ 7,710 | $ 11,000 |
| Regional Canon Law Society Meetings | $ 5,000 | $ 4,510 | $ 2,000 | $ 2,245 | $ 2,000 |
| **Sub-total** | **$ 46,050** | **$ 42,347** | **$ 43,050** | **$ 32,142** | **$ 42,550** |
| **Board of Governors, Officers** | | | | | |
| President | $ 3,800 | $ 2,773 | $ 4,000 | $ 2,937 | $ 4,000 |
| Vice President/Past President | $ 500 | $ - | $ 500 | $ 266 | $ 500 |
| Treasurer/Secretary | $ 500 | $ 469 | $ 500 | $ 16 | $ 500 |
| **Sub-total** | **$ 4,800** | **$ 3,242** | **$ 5,000** | **$ 3,219** | **$ 5,000** |
| **Intensive Workshop Expense** | $ - | $ - | $ 20,000 | $ - | $ 20,000 |
| **Committees** | | | | | |
| *Constitutional Committees (order of Const.)* | | | | | |
| Nominations Committee | $ 2,600 | $ 3,394 | $ 2,600 | $ 2,674 | $ 2,600 |
| Resolutions Committee | $ 150 | $ - | $ 150 | $ 5 | $ 100 |
| Resource & Asset Management | $ 300 | $ 157 | $ 300 | $ - | $ 500 |
| Professional Responsibilities Committee | $ - | $ - | $ - | $ 121 | $ - |
| *Standing Committees (alphabetical)* | | | | | |
| Church Governance Committee | $ 500 | $ - | $ 2,000 | $ - | $ 2,000 |
| Clergy Committee | $ 875 | $ - | $ 500 | $ - | $ 500 |
| Institutes of Consecrated Life Committee | $ 150 | $ - | $ 150 | $ - | $ 150 |
| Laity Committee | $ 500 | $ - | $ 2,000 | $ 218 | $ 3,000 |
| Research & Development | $ 250 | $ - | $ 1,500 | $ - | $ 1,500 |
| Sacramental Law Committee | $ 450 | $ - | $ 1,000 | $ - | $ 1,000 |
| Committee Chair Orientation | $ 600 | $ 596 | $ 500 | $ 420 | $ 450 |
| Approved Cmte. Work Contingency | $ 2,000 | $ - | $ 600 | $ - | $ 1,000 |
| **Sub-total** | **$ 8,375** | **$ 4,147** | **$ 11,300** | **$ 3,437** | **$ 12,800** |

## GENERAL OPERATIONS UNIT SUMMARY *(by fiscal year)*

|  | Budget FY 17-18 | Actual FY 16-17 | Budget FY 16-17 | Actual FY 15-16 | Budget FY 15-16 |
|---|---|---|---|---|---|
| **Miscellaneous** | | | | | |
| Platform Service Expense - Webinar | $ 3,000 | $ 1,639 | $ 3,000 | $ 1,937 | $ 3,000 |
| Depreciation | $ 1,500 | | $ 1,500 | $ 4,243 | |
| **Sub-total** | $ 4,500 | $ 1,639 | $ 4,500 | $ 6,180 | $ 3,000 |
| **Staffing Transition** | $ - | $ 219 | $ - | $ - | $ - |
| **Contingency Fund** | $ - | $ - | | $ - | |
| **TOTAL EXPENSES** | $ 285,865 | $ 302,366 | $ 349,045 | $ 273,994 | $ 324,239 |
| **EXCESS/DEFICIT** | $ 2,666 | $ 0 | $ - | $ 0 | $ - |

Note 1: Use of a portion of prior year realized net asset increase to help offset projected General Operations Deficit. This was suggested by the Accountant/Auditor.

Note 2: This new line item reflects a transfer from Publications to General Operations to cover administrative expenses (incurred by General Operations for Publications activities).

## Publications Unit Summary *(by fiscal year)*

| | Budget FY 17-18 | Actual FY 16-17 | Budget FY 16-17 | Actual FY 15-16 | Budget FY 15-16 |
|---|---|---|---|---|---|
| **INCOME** | | | | | |
| Publication Sales | $ 50,000 | $ 29,381 | $ 60,000 | $ 43,765 | $ 61,925 |
| Reprint Permissions | $ - | $ - | $ - | $ - | $ - |
| Royalty Income | $ 5,000 | $ 6,972 | $ 5,000 | $ 7,260 | $ 4,000 |
| Shipping/Restocking - BrightKey | $ 11,000 | $ 8,135 | $ 11,000 | $ 11,413 | $ 11,000 |
| Database Resolution | | $ - | | | |
| **TOTAL INCOME** | $ 66,000 | $ 44,488 | $ 76,000 | $ 62,438 | $ 76,925 |
| Cost of Goods Sold | | $ 2,596 | | $ 24,543 | |
| **GROSS PROFIT** | $ 66,000 | $ 41,892 | $ 76,000 | $ 37,894 | $ 76,925 |
| | | | | | |
| **EXPENSES** | | | | | |
| **Compensation & Professional Services** | | | | | |
| Staff Salary (Note 1) | $ - | $ - | $ - | $ 5,300 | $ 5,300 |
| Administrative Services (Note 2) | $ 10,000 | $ 10,000 | $ 10,000 | | |
| Accountant (Note 1) | $ - | $ - | $ - | $ 2,250 | $ 2,250 |
| Publications Advisory Board | $ 3,000 | $ 3,558 | $ 2,500 | $ 3,257 | $ 2,500 |
| **Sub-total** | $ 13,000 | $ 13,558 | $ 12,500 | $ 10,807 | $ 10,050 |
| | | | | | |
| **Royalties Paid** | | | | | |
| Royalties/*CCEO* | $ 250 | $ 176 | $ 250 | $ 221 | $ 250 |
| Royalties/*CIC* | $ 1,925 | $ 1,046 | $ 2,000 | $ 1,222 | $ 2,000 |
| Royalties/*Dignitas Connubii* | $ 250 | $ 101 | $ 250 | $ 92 | $ 250 |
| Royalties/*Selected Issues* | $ 100 | $ 82 | $ 100 | $ 27 | $ 100 |
| Royalties/*Reception and Communion* | $ 25 | $ - | $ 25 | $ - | $ 25 |
| **Sub-total** | $ 2,550 | $ 1,405 | $ 2,625 | $ 1,562 | $ 2,625 |
| | | | | | |
| **Publication Expenses** | | | | | |
| Advertising - Printing | $ 100 | $ - | $ 100 | $ 10 | $ 100 |
| Advertising - Electronic | $ 50 | $ - | $ 50 | $ - | $ 50 |
| Book Production | $ 7,000 | $ 2,815 | $ 8,000 | $ - | $ 10,000 |
| Copyright Applications | $ 100 | $ - | $ 100 | $ - | $ 100 |
| Outsourcing - BrightKey | $ 38,000 | $ 39,598 | $ 41,000 | $ 43,187 | $ 38,000 |
| **Sub-total** | $ 45,250 | $ 42,413 | $ 49,250 | $ 43,197 | $ 48,250 |
| | | | | | |
| **Office of the Executive Coordinator** | | | | | |
| Postage | $ 250 | $ 116 | $ 300 | $ 196 | $ 250 |
| Supplies | $ 150 | $ - | $ 150 | $ (51) | $ 150 |
| **Sub-total** | $ 400 | $ 116 | $ 450 | $ 145 | $ 400 |

## PUBLICATIONS UNIT SUMMARY *(by fiscal year)*

|  | Budget FY 17-18 | Actual FY 16-17 | Budget FY 16-17 | Actual FY 15-16 | Budget FY 15-16 |
|---|---|---|---|---|---|
| **Service Charges** | | | | | |
| Bank Service Charges/ Wells Fargo | $ 1,000 | $ 858 | $ 1,000 | $ 912 | $ 600 |
| Credit Card Fees | $ 1,800 | $ 1,447 | $ 2,000 | $ 1,726 | 3,000 |
| **Sub-total** | **$ 2,800** | **$ 2,305** | **$ 3,000** | **$ 2,638** | **3,600** |
| **Miscellaneous** | | | | | |
| Publications Contingencies | $ 500 | $ - | $ 500 | $ - | 500 |
| **Sub-total** | **$ 500** | **$ -** | **$ 500** | **$ -** | **500** |
| Database Resolution | $ 1,500 | $ | $ 2,000 | $ 12,519 | 11,500 |
| **TOTAL EXPENSES** | **$ 66,000** | **$ 59,798** | **$ 70,325** | **$ 70,869** | **76,925** |
| **EXCESS/DEFICIT** | $ - | $ (17,905) | $ 5,675 | $ (32,974) | $ - |

Note 1: These historic line items have now been absorbed by 6052, Administrative Expenses.

Note 2: This new line item reimburses General Operations for Publications Expenses incurred by General Operations.

## CONVENTIONS UNIT SUMMARY *(by fiscal year)*

|  | Budget FY 17-18 | Actual FY 16-17 | Budget FY 16-17 | Actual FY 15-16 | Budget FY 15-16 |
|---|---|---|---|---|---|
| **INCOME** | | | | | |
| Convention Fees (Note 1) | $ 134,000 | $ 138,300 | $ 130,000 | $ 166,550 | $ 128,000 |
| Pre-Convention Workshop 1 Fees (Note 2) | $ 11,000 | $ 6,925 | $ 11,000 | $ 13,125 | $ 11,000 |
| Pre-Convention Workshop 2 Fees | $ 11,000 | $ 27,250 | $ 11,000 | $ 5,825 | $ 11,000 |
| Exhibitors' Fees | $ 2,800 | $ 1,150 | $ 2,800 | $ 3,350 | $ 2,800 |
| Sponsors' Donations | $ - | $ 200 | $ - | $ - | $ - |
| Additional Banquet Fees | $ 720 | $ 1,020 | $ 600 | $ 1,080 | $ 420 |
| Guest Registrations | $ 500 | $ - | $ 500 | $ 1,070 | $ 300 |
| Hotel Room Commission (Note 3) | $ 13,000 | $ 12,117 | $ 13,000 | $ 20,314 | $ 13,000 |
| Surplus from Previous Years (Note 4) | $ 26,875 | $ 10,521 | $ 31,045 | | $ 23,725 |
| **TOTAL INCOME** | **$ 199,895** | **$ 197,483** | **$ 199,945** | **$ 211,314** | **$ 190,245** |
| **EXPENSES** | | | | | |
| **Professional Services** | | | | | |
| General Convention Chair | $ 2,000 | $ 2,292 | $ 2,000 | $ 1,816 | $ 1,300 |
| Convention Liturgy Chair | $ 500 | $ - | $ 500 | $ - | $ 500 |
| Convention Planning Cte | $ 2,000 | $ 1,040 | $ 2,000 | $ 1,057 | $ 2,000 |
| OEC | $ 3,000 | $ 4,261 | $ 2,500 | $ 2,465 | $ 2,200 |
| Convention Company | $ 1,200 | $ 1,958 | $ 1,200 | $ 2,340 | $ 900 |
| **Sub-total** | **$ 8,700** | **$ 9,551** | **$ 8,200** | **$ 7,677** | **$ 6,900** |
| **Pre-Convention** | | | | | |
| Honoraria (Note 9) | $ 6,000 | $ 3,000 | $ 6,000 | $ 6,000 | $ 6,000 |
| Liturgy | $ 500 | $ - | $ 500 | $ 120 | $ 500 |
| Printing | $ 500 | $ 1,309 | $ 100 | $ - | $ 100 |
| Shipping | $ 250 | $ 263 | $ 100 | $ 92 | $ 100 |
| Speaker's Travel & Lodging | $ 2,000 | $ 11,022 | $ 2,000 | $ 1,496 | $ 2,000 |
| Supplies | $ 250 | $ 307 | $ 250 | $ 362 | $ 250 |
| Hospitality/Speaker Dinner (Note 5) | $ 500 | $ 1,065 | $ 500 | $ 175 | $ 500 |
| **Sub-total** | **$ 10,000** | **$ 16,967** | **$ 9,450** | **$ 8,245** | **$ 9,450** |
| **Convention** | | | | | |
| Convention Company/Nix | $ 44,345 | $ 46,120 | $ 44,345 | $ 44,345 | $ 44,345 |
| Convention Hotel (Note 6) | $ 76,000 | $ 60,309 | $ 80,000 | $ 97,545 | $ 76,000 |
| Audio Visual | $ 22,000 | $ 29,080 | $ 20,000 | $ 20,780 | $ 17,000 |
| Food (Note 7) | $ 3,500 | $ 3,544 | $ 3,500 | $ 2,771 | $ 3,500 |
| Honoraria (Note 9) | $ 12,000 | $ 11,400 | $ 12,000 | $ 11,600 | $ 11,400 |
| Liturgy | $ 2,000 | $ 1,931 | $ 1,800 | $ 801 | $ 2,000 |
| Postage | $ 700 | $ 534 | $ 700 | $ 105 | $ 700 |
| Printing | $ 6,000 | $ 6,086 | $ 4,500 | $ 5,979 | $ 4,200 |
| Shipping | $ 1,000 | $ 759 | $ 1,000 | $ 1,259 | $ 700 |

## CONVENTIONS UNIT SUMMARY *(by fiscal year)*

|  | Budget FY 17-18 | Actual FY 16-17 | Budget FY 16-17 | Actual FY 15-16 | Budget FY 15-16 |
|---|---|---|---|---|---|
| Speaker's Travel & Lodging | $ 2,500 | $ 1,588 | $ 2,500 | $ 658 | $ 2,500 |
| Supplies | $ 5,000 | $ 4,929 | $ 6,000 | $ 3,416 | $ 6,000 |
| Telephone/Internet | $ - | $ - | $ - | $ - | $ - |
| Hospitality/Speaker Dinner (Note 8) | $ 1,000 | $ 11 | $ 1,000 | $ 865 | $ 1,000 |
| Other/Contingency | $ 500 | $ - | $ 500 | $ - | $ 500 |
| **Sub-total** | **$ 176,545** | **$ 166,290** | **$ 177,845** | **$ 190,125** | **$ 169,845** |
| **Service Charges** | | | | | |
| Bank Service Charges/Wells Fargo | $ 650 | $ 742 | $ 650 | $ 697 | $ 450 |
| Credit Card Fees | $ 4,000 | $ 3,933 | $ 3,800 | $ 4,128 | $ 3,600 |
| **Sub-total** | **$ 4,650** | **$ 4,675** | **$ 4,450** | **$ 4,825** | **$ 4,050** |
| **TOTAL EXPENSES** | **$ 199,895** | **$ 197,483** | **$ 199,945** | **$ 210,873** | **$ 190,245** |
| **EXCESS/DEFICIT** | **$ -** | **$ (0)** | **$ -** | **$ 441** | **$ -** |

Note 1: FY 2017-2018 Budget assumes 320 attendees @ $400 each.

Note 2: FY 2017-2018 Budget assumes 80 pre-convention attendees (40 per workshop) @ $275 each.

Note 3: This line represents the hotel room commission we receive as a result of the work of Nix; this commission was previously included in the hotel bill.

Note 4: This line item reflects a portion of the surplus in the convention unit from the previous fiscal year. The surplus is used to balance the overall budget. A surplus of $441 exists from FY 15-16 and $19,327 exists from FY 14-15.

Note 5: This is a new line item as of FY 2015-2016, allocated for in-room hospitality and one dinner outing for Pre-Convention Speakers.

Note 6: This item reflects general convention expenses with the contracted hotel, including one lunch for convention attendees.

Note 7: This line item reflects expenses for volunteer snacks, food/liquor for the presidential suite, and the banquet wine.

Note 8: This is a new line item as of FY 2015-2016, allocated for in-room hospitality (all speakers) and one dinner outing (Keynote/Major Speakers).

Note 9: These lines reflect an overall adjustment to honoraria; rates have been doubled. $3,000 will be offered to Pre-Convention Speakers, $1,000 will be offered to the Keynote/Major Speakers, and $600 will be issued to Seminar presenters.

## Scholarship Unit Summary *(by fiscal year)*

|  | Budget FY 17-18 | Actual FY 16-17 | Budget FY 16-17 | Actual FY 15-16 | Budget FY 15-16 |
|---|---|---|---|---|---|
| **INCOME** | | | | | |
| **Investment Income (Automatically Reinvested in Fund)** | | | | | |
| Interest Income/Wells Fargo | $ 100 | $ 171 | $ 100 | $ 90 | $ 120 |
| Dividends/CUIT | $ - | $ 9,461 | $ - | $ 4,735 | $ 7,000 |
| **Sub-Total (Not included in budgeted income)** | **$ 100** | **$ 9,632** | **$ 100** | **$ 4,825** | **$ 7,120** |
| **Previously Designated Funds (Note 1)** | | | | | |
| Licentiate Scholarship Designations | $ 19,600 | $ 2,333 | $ 2,333 | $ 14,000 | $ 14,000 |
| Doctoral Scholarship Designations | $ - | $ - | $ - | $ - | $ - |
| **Sub-Total** | **$ 19,600** | **$ 2,333** | **$ 2,333** | **$ 14,000** | **$ 14,000** |
| **This Year Designated Funds (Note 2)** | | | | | |
| Licentiate Scholarship Designations | $ 29,000 | $ 30,000 | $ 30,000 | $ 7,000 | $ 7,000 |
| Doctoral Scholarship Designations | $ 2,500 | $ 2,500 | $ 2,500 | $ - | $ - |
| **Sub-Total** | **$ 31,500** | **$ 32,500** | **$ 32,500** | **$ 7,000** | **$ 7,000** |
| **Donations to Licentiate Fund** | | | | | |
| Donations with Dues | $ 1,000 | $ 886 | $ 1,500 | $ 1,701 | $ 1,500 |
| Donations from Appeal | $ 4,500 | $ 6,873 | $ 4,500 | $ 6,021 | $ 4,500 |
| Donations from Convention | $ 225 | $ 956 | $ 225 | $ 113 | $ 375 |
| Donations from Reg. Mtgs | $ 750 | $ 1,250 | $ 750 | $ 1,125 | $ 750 |
| **Subtotal - Licentiate Fund Income** | **$ 6,475** | **$ 9,965** | **$ 6,975** | **$ 8,960** | **$ 7,125** |
| **Donations to Doctoral Fund** | | | | | |
| Donations with Dues | $ 500 | $ 229 | $ 500 | $ 866 | $ 500 |
| Donations from Appeal | $ 1,500 | $ 1,898 | $ 1,500 | $ 2,099 | $ 1,500 |
| Donations from Convention | $ 75 | $ 369 | $ 75 | $ 38 | $ 125 |
| Donations from Reg. Mtgs | $ 250 | $ 250 | $ 250 | $ 375 | $ 250 |
| **Subtotal - Doctoral Fund Income** | **$ 2,325** | **$ 2,745** | **$ 2,325** | **$ 3,378** | **$ 2,375** |
| **Sub-Total, Donations Income** | **$ 8,800** | **$ 12,710** | **$ 9,300** | **$ 12,337** | **$ 9,500** |
| **TOTAL INCOME** | **$ 59,900** | **$ 57,175** | **$ 44,233** | **$ 38,162** | **$ 37,620** |

## Scholarship Unit Summary *(by fiscal year)*

| EXPENSES | | | | | |
|---|---:|---:|---:|---:|---:|
| **Service Charges** | | | | | |
| Money Market Fees/Wells Fargo | $ 1,800 | $ 1,473 | $ 1,500 | $ 788 | $ 1,500 |
| **Sub-total** | **$ 1,800** | **$ 1,473** | **$ 1,500** | **$ 788** | **$ 1,500** |
| | | | | | |
| **Postage** | | | | | |
| General Postage | $ 25 | $ 3 | $ 25 | $ 8 | $ 25 |
| Appeal Postage | $ 800 | $ 494 | $ 800 | $ - | $ 750 |
| **Sub-total** | **$ 825** | **$ 497** | **$ 825** | **$ 8** | **$ 775** |
| | | | | | |
| **Printing** | | | | | |
| General Printing | $ 100 | $ - | $ 100 | $ - | $ 100 |
| Appeal Printing | $ 750 | $ - | $ 250 | $ - | $ 500 |
| **Sub-total** | **$ 850** | **$ -** | **$ 350** | **$ -** | **$ 600** |
| | | | | | |
| **Scholarships** | | | | | |
| Current Awards - Licentiate Fund (Note 3) | $ 48,600 | $ 10,396 | $ 30,000 | $ 6,263 | $ 24,000 |
| Current Awards - Doctoral Fund (Note 3) | $ 2,500 | $ 2,553 | $ 2,500 | $ 1,974 | $ 2,500 |
| **Sub-total** | **$ 51,100** | **$ 12,948** | **$ 32,500** | **$ 8,237** | **$ 26,500** |
| | | | | | |
| **TOTAL EXPENSES** | **$ 54,575** | **$ 14,918** | **$ 35,175** | **$ 9,033** | **$ 29,375** |
| | | | | | |
| **EXCESS/DEFICIT** | **$ 5,325** | **$ 42,257** | **$ 9,058** | **$ 29,129** | **$ 8,245** |

Note 1: These are future funds to give out and transfers within Scholarship accounts, as such they are not included in the annual Scholarship budget. Income and expenses in FY 16-17 become income and expenses for FY 17-18.

Note 2: Beginning FY 16-17, these funds reflect from a transfer from the Investment Unit to the Scholarship Unit as per the Spending Policy for investments for the Scholarships.

Note 3: This line is calculated using the 5% rolling averages of the resepctive CUIT funds over three years. The amount determined for Licentiate awards is $29,000. The amount determined for a doctoral award is $2,500.

## INVESTMENT UNIT SUMMARY *(by fiscal year)*

|  | Budget FY 17-18 |
|---|---|
| **INCOME** |  |
| **General Operations Income** |  |
| Interest Income | $ - |
| Dividends/CUIT | $ 8,720 |
| Transfers from General Operations | $ - |
| **Sub-Total** | **$ 8,720** |
|  |  |
| **Licentiate Scholarship Income** |  |
| Interest Income | $ - |
| Dividends/CUIT | $ 6,500 |
| Transfer of Licentiate Donations | $ - |
| **Sub-Total** | **$ 6,500** |
|  |  |
| **Doctoral Scholarship Income** |  |
| Interest Income | $ - |
| Dividends/CUIT | $ 500 |
| Transfer of Doctoral Donations | $ - |
| **Sub-Total** | **$ 500** |
|  |  |
| **TOTAL INCOME** | **$ 15,720** |
|  |  |
| **EXPENSES** |  |
| **General Operations Expenses** |  |
| Transfer to General Operations | $ - |
| **Sub-Total** | **$ -** |
|  |  |
| **Licentiate Scholarship Expenses** |  |
| Transfer for Licentiate Scholarships | $ 29,000 |
| **Sub-Total** | **$ 29,000** |
|  |  |
| **Doctoral Scholarship Expenses** |  |
| Transfer for Doctoral Scholarships | $ 2,500 |
| **Sub-Total** |  |
|  |  |
| **TOTAL EXPENSES** | **$ 29,000** |
|  |  |
| **EXCESS/DEFICIT** | **$ (13,280)** |

## GENERAL OPERATIONS: BALANCE SHEET WITH PREV YEAR COMPARISON
### As of June 30, 2017

|  | Jun 30, 17 | Jun 30, 16 |
|---|---:|---:|
| **ASSETS** | | |
|   **Current Assets** | | |
|     **Checking/Savings** | | |
|       1000 · Cash in Wells Fargo - Gen Ops | -91,088.71 | -52,373.86 |
|       1013 · RCT Flex Cash Fund | 24,158.67 | 24,020.07 |
|       1014 · CUIT Balanced Fund | 883,659.21 | 773,041.48 |
|     **Total Checking/Savings** | 816,729.17 | 744,687.69 |
|     **Other Current Assets** | | |
|       1050 · Due - Pub to Gen Ops | 4,029.87 | 4,029.87 |
|       1050.1 · Contribution to Pub | 8,432.00 | 8,432.00 |
|       1051 · Due - Conv to Gen Ops | 527.02 | 527.02 |
|       1052 · Due - Sch to Gen Ops | 321.43 | 321.43 |
|     **Total Other Current Assets** | 13,310.32 | 13,310.32 |
|   **Total Current Assets** | 830,039.49 | 757,998.01 |
|   **Fixed Assets** | | |
|     1060 · Furniture and Equipment | 46,490.64 | 46,490.64 |
|     1062 · Accumulated Depreciation | -7,796.50 | -7,796.50 |
|   **Total Fixed Assets** | 38,694.14 | 38,694.14 |
|   **Other Assets** | | |
|     1073 · Prepaid Expenses - Other | 954.00 | 586.75 |
|     1074 · Pre-paid Website Costs | 2,511.07 | 6,548.85 |
|     1078 · Prepaid USPS/Meter Charges | 1,715.56 | 1,695.89 |
|     1080 · Security Deposits | 2,094.40 | 2,094.40 |
|   **Total Other Assets** | 7,275.03 | 10,925.89 |
| **TOTAL ASSETS** | **876,008.66** | **807,618.04** |
| **LIABILITIES & EQUITY** | | |
|   **Liabilities** | | |
|     **Current Liabilities** | | |
|       **Other Current Liabilities** | | |
|         2005 · Deferred Income | 5,395.00 | 32,950.00 |
|         2050 · Due - Gen Ops to Pub | 79.06 | 79.06 |
|         2052 · Due - Gen Ops to Sch | 4,028.86 | 4,028.86 |
|       **Total Other Current Liabilities** | 9,502.92 | 37,057.92 |
|     **Total Current Liabilities** | 9,502.92 | 37,057.92 |
|   **Total Liabilities** | 9,502.92 | 37,057.92 |
|   **Equity** | | |
|     2080 · Gen Ops Net Assets | 514,066.61 | 514,066.61 |
|     2083 · Board Designated Net Assets | -101,206.61 | -101,206.61 |
|     3010 · Unrestricted-retained earnings | 407,700.12 | 448,849.92 |
|     6501 · Transfer to Other Funds, per JM | -50,000.00 | -50,000.00 |
|     Net Income | 95,945.62 | -41,149.80 |
|   **Total Equity** | 866,505.74 | 770,560.12 |
| **TOTAL LIABILITIES & EQUITY** | **876,008.66** | **807,618.04** |

## Publications: Balance Sheet with Prev Year Comparison
*As of June 30, 2017*

|  | Jun 30, 17 | Jun 30, 16 |
|---|---:|---:|
| **ASSETS** | | |
|   **Current Assets** | | |
|     **Checking/Savings** | | |
|       1000 · Cash in Wells Fargo - Pub | 76,278.66 | 92,388.64 |
|     **Total Checking/Savings** | 76,278.66 | 92,388.64 |
|     **Other Current Assets** | | |
|       1050 · Due - Gen Ops to Pub | -18,813.66 | -18,813.66 |
|       1051 · Due - Conv to Pub | 2,381.85 | 2,381.85 |
|       1100 · Accounts Receivable - BrightKey | 3,066.66 | 4,535.45 |
|       1200 · Inventory - Books & CDs | 65,738.83 | 68,334.92 |
|       1201 · Prepaid Book Costs | -12,110.07 | -12,110.07 |
|       1851 · BrKey - Prepaid Postage | 7,354.77 | 5,085.38 |
|     **Total Other Current Assets** | 47,618.38 | 49,413.87 |
|   **Total Current Assets** | 123,897.04 | 141,802.51 |
| **TOTAL ASSETS** | **123,897.04** | **141,802.51** |
| **LIABILITIES & EQUITY** | | |
|   **Liabilities** | | |
|     **Current Liabilities** | | |
|       **Other Current Liabilities** | | |
|         2050 · Due - Pub to Gen Ops | -15,516.27 | -15,516.27 |
|         2050.1 · Contribution fromGen Ops to Pub | 9,746.20 | 9,746.20 |
|       **Total Other Current Liabilities** | -5,770.07 | -5,770.07 |
|     **Total Current Liabilities** | -5,770.07 | -5,770.07 |
|   **Total Liabilities** | -5,770.07 | -5,770.07 |
|   **Equity** | | |
|     2830 · Board Designated Net Assets | 156,471.63 | 156,471.63 |
|     3010 · Unrestricted-retained earnings | -8,899.05 | 24,035.39 |
|     Net Income | -17,905.47 | -32,934.44 |
|   **Total Equity** | 129,667.11 | 147,572.58 |
| **TOTAL LIABILITIES & EQUITY** | **123,897.04** | **141,802.51** |

## Conventions: Balance Sheet with Prev Year Comparison
## *As of June 30, 2017*

|  | Jun 30, 17 | Jun 30, 16 |
|---|---:|---:|
| **ASSETS** | | |
|   **Current Assets** | | |
|     **Checking/Savings** | | |
|       1000 · Cash in Wells Fargo - Conv | 97,926.55 | 112,330.14 |
|     **Total Checking/Savings** | 97,926.55 | 112,330.14 |
|     **Other Current Assets** | | |
|       1720 · Prepaid Expenses | | |
|         1720.2 · Prepaid Exp - Convention | 1,629.74 | 2,474.97 |
|         1720.3 · Prepaid Exp - Conv Comm | 0.00 | 1,039.88 |
|         1720.4 · Prepaid Exp - Conv Chair | 437.40 | 955.00 |
|       **Total 1720 · Prepaid Expenses** | 2,067.14 | 4,469.85 |
|     **Total Other Current Assets** | 2,067.14 | 4,469.85 |
|   **Total Current Assets** | 99,993.69 | 116,799.99 |
| **TOTAL ASSETS** | **99,993.69** | **116,799.99** |
| **LIABILITIES & EQUITY** | | |
|   **Liabilities** | | |
|     **Current Liabilities** | | |
|       **Other Current Liabilities** | | |
|         1730 · Deferred Income (Convention) | | |
|           1730.01 · Def Inc - Conv Reg | 2,800.00 | 8,475.00 |
|           1730.03 · Def Inc - Pre-Conv Fees - W2 | 550.00 | 1,100.00 |
|           1730.06 · Def Inc - Guest Banquet Fees | 0.00 | 60.00 |
|         **Total 1730 · Deferred Income (Convention)** | 3,350.00 | 9,635.00 |
|         2051 · Due - Conv to Pub | 2,381.85 | 2,381.85 |
|       **Total Other Current Liabilities** | 5,731.85 | 12,016.85 |
|     **Total Current Liabilities** | 5,731.85 | 12,016.85 |
|   **Total Liabilities** | 5,731.85 | 12,016.85 |
|   **Equity** | | |
|     2800 · Convention Net Assets | 19,644.21 | 19,644.21 |
|     3900 · Retained Earnings | 85,138.93 | 84,697.57 |
|     Net Income | -10,521.30 | 441.36 |
|   **Total Equity** | 94,261.84 | 104,783.14 |
| **TOTAL LIABILITIES & EQUITY** | **99,993.69** | **116,799.99** |

## Scholarship: Balance Sheet with Prev Year Comparison
### As of June 30, 2017

|  | Jun 30, 17 | Jun 30, 16 |
|---|---:|---:|
| **ASSETS** | | |
|   **Current Assets** | | |
|     **Checking/Savings** | | |
|       1000 · Cash in Wells Fargo - Sch | 8,403.24 | 10,586.65 |
|     **Total Checking/Savings** | 8,403.24 | 10,586.65 |
|     **Other Current Assets** | | |
|       1050 · Due - Gen Ops to Sch | -46,908.00 | -46,908.00 |
|       1710 · Prepaid Expenses | | |
|         1710.1 · Pre-paid Awards | 7,000.00 | 7,000.00 |
|       **Total 1710 · Prepaid Expenses** | 7,000.00 | 7,000.00 |
|     **Total Other Current Assets** | -39,908.00 | -39,908.00 |
|   **Total Current Assets** | -31,504.76 | -29,321.35 |
|   **Other Assets** | | |
|     1046 · CUIT Balanced Fund - Licentiate | 752,949.61 | 658,694.29 |
|     1047 · CUIT Balanced Fund - Doctoral | 60,960.97 | 53,329.79 |
|   **Total Other Assets** | 813,910.58 | 712,024.08 |
| **TOTAL ASSETS** | **782,405.82** | **682,702.73** |
| **LIABILITIES & EQUITY** | | |
|   **Liabilities** | | |
|     **Current Liabilities** | | |
|       **Accounts Payable** | | |
|         2001 · *Accounts Payable | | |
|           2000.1 · Accounts Payable - Scholarship | -27,000.00 | -27,000.00 |
|         **Total 2001 · *Accounts Payable** | -27,000.00 | -27,000.00 |
|       **Total Accounts Payable** | -27,000.00 | -27,000.00 |
|       **Other Current Liabilities** | | |
|         2000 · Accounts Payable | 27,000.00 | 27,000.00 |
|         2050 · Due - Sch to Gen Ops | -18,709.92 | -35,064.33 |
|         2052 · Due - Sch to Conv | -32,965.00 | -16,465.00 |
|         2525 · Schaaf Project (Int Sch) | 30.00 | 30.00 |
|       **Total Other Current Liabilities** | -24,644.92 | -24,499.33 |
|     **Total Current Liabilities** | -51,644.92 | -51,499.33 |
|   **Total Liabilities** | -51,644.92 | -51,499.33 |
|   **Equity** | | |
|     3002 · Scholarship Net Assets | 411,376.47 | 411,376.47 |
|     3010 · Unrestricted-retained earnings | 322,825.59 | 325,176.50 |
|     Net Income | 99,848.68 | -2,350.91 |
|   **Total Equity** | 834,050.74 | 734,202.06 |
| **TOTAL LIABILITIES & EQUITY** | **782,405.82** | **682,702.73** |

## INVESTMENTS: PROFIT & LOSS
*As of June 30, 2017*

|  | **July 2016 through June 2017** |
|---|---:|
|  | Jul '16 - Jun 17 |
| **Income** |  |
|   4000 · Investment Income |  |
|     4010 · Interest/Dividends |  |
|       4011 · General Ops - Interest/Dividend | 5,126.58 |
|       4012 · Licentiate - Interest/Dividend | 4,289.79 |
|       4013 · Doctoral - Interest/Dividend | 347.31 |
|     Total 4010 · Interest/Dividends | 9,763.68 |
|     4020 · Unrealized Gains/Losses |  |
|       4021 · General Ops - Gains/Loss | 105,629.75 |
|       4022 · Licentiate - Gains/Loss | 89,965.53 |
|       4023 · Doctoral - Gains/Loss | 7,283.87 |
|     Total 4020 · Unrealized Gains/Losses | 202,879.15 |
|   Total 4000 · Investment Income | 212,642.83 |
| **Total Income** | 212,642.83 |
| **Expense** | 0.00 |
| **Net Income** | **212,642.83** |

# Report of the Executive Coordinator
## Rev. Patrick J. Cogan, S.A., JCD

The Board of Governors recently restructured the national office of the CLSA. The position of the Executive Coordinator is now a part-time position with a primary focus on publications. Since beginning the position on August 1, 2017, energies have been devoted to preparing several publications: *Proceedings 2016*, *Roman Replies and CLSA Advisory Opinions 2017*, and a new edition of the *Code of Canon Law*, which will incorporate into the text itself recent documents from Rome that have amended the Code. This has been a careful process, which has required using approved translations from Rome.

The publications area of the CLSA is also entering soon into a new phase of electronic publishing. Already a pastoral resource has been offered electronically, and plans are to also offer other CLSA publications electronically, including the Codes. Presently various electronic formats are being considered.

Also, there has been some expansion of the marketing of the publications, especially to other canon law societies around the world and also to various civil law organizations. Hopefully this will result in increased sales and income.

The CLSA continues to be the largest publisher of canon law texts in English. Our Codes are used throughout the world and the canonical community and others frequently ask about new publications.

# REPORT OF THE GENERAL SECRETARY
*Colleen Crawford*

I have had the unique privilege of serving (and observing) the Canon Law Society of America for several years, from the vantage of daily office administration and quarterly Board meetings, to the flurry of the Convention and the comfortable reliability of an annual calendar. Unequivocally, the greatest fruit has come from personal interactions with members – opportunities to grow not only in my understanding of canon law and the historic record of the Society, but also to witness the academic, administrative, and pastoral contributions and talents of the membership, and by extension, the Church.

It is with keen attention to member services, a renewed commitment to timely administration, and thoughtful consideration for how we might retain and grow the CLSA membership that I have accepted the role of General Secretary. My sincere hope is that we, as an administrative office, will fulfill and anticipate member needs, and that we will continue to expand the resources (electronic and otherwise) that will aid future canonists, associates, and students. I look forward to collaborating with our new Executive Coordinator, Fr. Patrick Cogan, S.A., to achieve these goals.

We will continue the search for administrative support after the Convention's conclusion, with the intention of hiring a new assistant. The preferred candidate will have experience in formatting and layout design, web administration and management, and other areas of technical expertise. In the interim, I am pleased to report that we contracted with a new accountant, Mary Nguyen, beginning in early September. Mary is a familiar face in McCormick Pavilion and currently splits her time between Christian Brothers Conference, the Conference for Catechetical Leadership, and the CLSA. Moving forward, she and I will work with Sr. Nancy and Joe McCathran, our auditor, to streamline banking and accounting practice.

I will conclude by gratefully acknowledging the trust the Board has placed in me. I remain deeply appreciative of the patience and understanding members have extended in the wake of staffing transition, and moving forward, I invite you – the members – to contact me with any administrative questions. As ever, the office will strive to balance transparency, efficiency, and pastoral concern.

# Constitutional Committee Reports

**Committee:** NOMINATIONS
**Constituted:** Constitution, Article X
**Mandate:** This is a standing committee of the Society. Its mandate is:

1. To submit to the active members, at least one month prior to the date of election, the names of nominees as provided for in Article IX of this Constitution.
2. To formulate and recommend to the Board of Governors plans for maintaining and increasing membership in the Society. Revise all proposals so that the meaning of each is clear. (*Article X*)

**Membership:** Chair: Jay Conzemius, JCL (term expires October, 2017)
Rev. Msgr. Michael Padazinski (term expires October, 2018)
Sr. Victoria Vondenberger, RSM (term expires October, 2019)
Rev. Manuel Viera, OFM (term expires October, 2017)

## ANNUAL REPORT

The committee met February 1-3, 2017, at the Society's offices to propose a list of candidates for election to various offices at the CLSA Annual Business meeting in October of 2017. Fortunately, the work of the committee was successful and a full slate of candidates was gathered by February 3rd and forwarded to Fr. Bruce Miller, President of the CLSA.

The nominees are as follows:

**Vice-President/President-Elect:**
- Zabrina Decker, Archdiocese of Milwaukee
- Fr. Pat Cooney, OSB, Archdiocese of Indianapolis

**Secretary:**
- Margaret Poll-Chalmers, Diocese of Birmingham
- Tim Olson, Diocese of Fargo

**Consultor:**
- Christina Hip-Flores, Diocese of Camden
- Fr. Peter Akpoghiran, Archdiocese of New Orleans
- Dr. Chad Glendinning, University of Ottawa
- Fr. Joseph Abraham, Diocese of Reno

The committee members feel very hopeful about this group of candidates' abilities to provide a great future vision for the Society. In addition, the group well represents the Society's growing diversity.

If you have questions about the candidates, please feel free to contact me. I have previously notified Fr. Roger Keeler and Colleen Crawford at the Executive Coordinator's office about this slate of candidates, so they can make sure that the candidates are contacted about the need for a CV and a few details concerning the election at next year's convention.

Respectfully submitted,
Jay Conzemius

---

**Committee:** RESOLUTIONS
**Constituted:** Constitution, Art. X.
**Mandate:**

1. To solicit, develop and draft proposed resolutions which will express the concerns of the Canon Law Society of America;
2. To consult with the membership at large and, in particular with the Board of Governors, the standing and ad hoc committees of the society, and the organizers of the convention;
3. To formulate resolutions on given points in response to requests of the members of the Society;
4. To compose differences in the formulation of similar proposals and to revise all the proposals so the meaning of each is clear; (and)
5. To encourage resolutions which authentically express in a positive way the activities and concerns of the Society.

**Membership:** Mr. Timothy Olson (chair)
Rev. Jaroslaw Skrzypek
Ms. Nwazi B. Nyirenda
*Consultative Members:* Msgr. Michael Souckar; Fr. Peter Mangum

### ANNUAL REPORT

There is nothing to report at the present time. The Resolutions Committee will hear and process resolutions during the 2017 Convention.

Respectfully submitted,
Timothy Olson

---

**Committee:** RESOURCE AND ASSET MANAGEMENT
**Constituted:** Constitution, Article X, as last amended in 2008 and 2013
**Old Committee Structure:** Committees on Budget, Investment and Scholarship Fund.
**Mandate:** The functions of the Committee on Resource and Asset Management shall be:

1. To develop a comprehensive budge for all the activities of the Society and report on the funding available for projects;
2. To submit the proposed budget for the coming fiscal year to the Board of governors for approval at its springs meeting;
3. To conserve, invest and disburse the monies of the Scholarship Fund in accord with the criteria established by the Society; (and)
4. To advise the Treasurer on all matters pertaining to the Society's investments. (Article X, 7)

**Membership:** The Committee of Resource and Asset Management shall consist of the Vice-President, the Treasurer, and a senior consultor and two additional members appointed by the President. The Treasurer shall act as Chair of this committee. (Article X, 2)

**Members:** Sr. Nancy Reynolds, SP (chair)
Msgr. Bill King
Dr. Marie T. Hilliard
Sr. Margaret A. Stallmeyer, CDP
Msgr. John J. M. Foster (*ex officio*)

### ANNUAL REPORT

The RAM Commitee met via conference call and appoved the budget for Fiscal Year 2017-2018. The budget will be presented in conjunction with the Report of the Treasurer.

| | |
|---|---|
| **Committee:** | PROFESSIONAL RESPONSIBILITY |
| **Constituted:** | Constitution, Article X, as last amended in 1995, and the Code of Professional Responsibilities, canon 9c(1), d(1) |
| **Mandate:** | The mandate of the Committee is: |

1. Regarding complaints:
   a) To receive complaints of any party aggrieved with respect to provisions of the *Code of Professional Responsibility* originally adopted by the CLSA in October, 1983, and its can. 9d(i);
   b) To make an initial finding that the complaint is not frivolous but is serious in character; (and)
   c) By majority vote to refer the matter to the hearing officers.
2. To issue advisory opinions and decisions on the application of the *Code of Professional Responsibility*; (and)
3. To advise on all other questions concerning the professional responsibility of canonists (can. 9d(i) of the PR Code).

**Membership:** Patricia M. Dugan (chair)
Dr. Marie T. Hilliard *(ex officio)*
Rev. Manuel Viera, OFM *(ex officio)*
H. Roberta Small (hearing officer)
Very Rev. Phillip J. Brown, *pss* (hearing officer)
Sr. Marie A. Breitenbeck, OP (hearing officer)

## ANNUAL REPORT

There have been no complaints lodged and so I am glad to report there is no activity to report at this time.

Respectfully submitted,
Patricia M. Dugan

# ON-GOING COMMITTEE REPORTS

**Committee:** CHURCH GOVERNANCE
**Constituted:** 2009
**Mandate:** It is the function of the Committee on Church Governance:

1. To initiate as needed any projects pertinent to the study of canon law pertaining to Church structures and governance or the implementation thereof, including but not limited to the following: (a) diocesan and parish temporalities; (b) consultative bodies; (c) diocesan and parish structures; (d) power of governance; (e) comparative law issues; (f) Eastern canon law and institutions
2. To oversee projects referred to the committee by the BOG;
3. To oversee its subcommittees working on projects concerning Church governance; (and)
4. To collaborate with national organizations and other groups dealing with issues of Church governance.

**Membership:** Mary Santi
Carlos Venegas
Michael Sinclair
Rev. Joseph L. Newton
Mary C. Edlund
Msgr. John Renken
Dr. Gerald T. Jorgensen

Eastern Law Committee: Chorbishop John D. Faris
Former President Mentor: Msgr. F. Stephen Pedone
BOG Liaison: Rev. Kenneth A. Riley

### ANNUAL REPORT

*Editor's Note:* A new Chair-elect of the Committee on Church Governance was proposed at the end of June 2017, following a vacancy on the committee and resignation from the previous chair. The Committee has not had the opportunity to meet, and as such, there is nothing to report.

---

**Committee:** CLERGY
**Constituted:** 2009
**Mandate:** It is the function of the Committee on Clergy:

1. To initiate as needed any projects pertinent to the study of canon law pertaining to the life and ministry of bishops, priests and deacons or the

implementation thereof, including, but not limited to, the following: (a) canonical issues related to the sexual abuse of minors, (b) clergy personnel issues and resources, (c) advocacy for clergy in penal cases;
2. To oversee projects referred to the committee by the BOG;
3. To oversee its subcommittees working on projects concerning clergy; and
4. To collaborate with national organizations and other groups dealing with clergy issues.

**Membership:** Fr. Garry Giroux (chair)
Chorbishop John Faris
Deacon Daniel Laurita
Deacon Daniel Welter
Fr. Georges de Laire
Fr. Lou Vallone
Fr. Luke Millette
Fr. William Elder

BOG Liasion: Fr. John Donovan
Former President Mentor: Msgr. Fred Easton

## ANNUAL REPORT

The Committee on Clergy met, via *Skype*, on January 16, 2017, March 9, 2017, June 5, 2017 and August 31, 2017.

At its organizational meeting on January 16, 2017, it was reported by Fr. John Donovan that the BOG had a project proposal for the Committee. Based on Fr. James Conn's 2016 Convention seminar on Letters of Suitability, the BOG suggested the Committee consider developing an alternative process for verifying the suitability of clerics. At that same meeting, Msgr. Fred Easton also recommended the Committee consider organizing and offering a workshop to prepare advocates for penal and administrative cases. The last such workshop was sponsored by the CLSA in 2009.

While other projects were proposed and discussed at the January 16th meeting, the Committee unanimously agreed to adopt as its projects for 2017 the development of an alternative to Letters of Suitability and the organization of a workshop for advocates in penal and administrative cases.

Fr. Louis Vallone, a member of the Committee on Clergy, explained to the membership his efforts in developing a system which, as an alternative to Letters of Suitability, would simplify the verification of clergy suitability. Fr. Vallone generously shared his work on this subject with the Committee.

Over the course of the next five months the *Clergy Suitability ID* project was developed, discussed, critiqued and refined. At the June 5$^{th}$ meeting, the Committee unanimously agreed that the project was sufficiently mature to be sent to the BOG for its evaluation and comment at their August 28-30 meeting. Pending a review from the BOG, the Committee will move forward with this project.

Aside from the membership of the Committee on Clergy, Msgr. Ricardo Bass and Fr. Paul Golden, CM assisted in the development and organization of the workshop to prepare advocates for penal and administrative cases. Following a variety of meetings and email exchanges, Fr. Roger Keeler, the CLSA Executive Coordinator, recommended to the BOG that consideration be given to offering the Committee on Clergy's workshop for advocates as a Pre-Convention Workshop at the 2017 Convention. The recommendation was accepted.

The basics of the project are as follows:

> Title: *Advocacy and the Right of Defense: In Service of Justice and Truth*
>
> Description: This workshop will explore the role of the advocate, including the preliminary investigation, protecting the rights of the accused and associated topics. The presentations will reflect the perspective and experience of both advocates and of the Promoter of Justice of the Congregation of the Doctrine of the Faith. The speakers will form a panel, and after each presentation the panel members will share their comments and experiences. There will be time for questions from participants. This workshop is offered to train new and beginning advocates, but it is also open to all members of the Society who want further development in this area.
>
> Presenters: Daniel Smilanic, J.C.D., Frederick Easton, J.C.L. and Robert Geisinger, S.J., J.C.D.
>
> The Committee on Clergy understands this workshop as a 'springboard' to ongoing efforts at the appropriate formation of personnel for penal and administrative processes.

The Committee on Clergy will be meeting during the Convention in Indianapolis to evaluate the Pre-Convention Workshop and begin its planning for the 2018 year.

Respectfully submitted,
Fr. Garry B. Giroux

**Committee:** CONVENTION PLANNING
**Constituted:** Constituted 1971
**Mandate:** Previous Committee Structure – Committees on Convention Planning (Constitutional) and Convention Liturgies

1. To receive from the Board of Governors the approved general theme of the next Convention as well as any suggestions from the Committee on Research & Development for the development of the theme;
2. To recommend to the BOG, in accord with the general theme, topics for major addresses, seminars or other presentations at a future Convention, as well as a list of potential speakers and the honoraria for such speakers;
3. Following BOG approval, to arrange for the speakers, addresses and seminars for the annual Convention;
4. To plan all Convention liturgies and prayer services;
5. To review the evaluations of the most recent Convention and assist the Convention Chairperson in planning future arrangements, as needed.

**Membership:** A chair and three active members of the Society, appointed by the President, each with staggered three year terms, the Executive Coordinator *ex officio*, and the Past President *ex officio*.

**Membership:** Rev. Jamin Scott David (chair), *2019*
Rev. James Conn, SJ, *2018*
Mrs. Rita Ferko Joyce, *2020*
Rev. Patrick Cogan, SA, *Ex Officio – Executive Coordinator*
Rev. Manuel Viera, OFM, *Ex Officio – Past President*

### REPORT TO THE BOARD OF GOVERNORS, AUGUST 2017

The Committee on Convention Planning met on 08 August 2017 at the Towne Place Suites Baltimore/BWI Airport in Linthicum, Maryland. All members of the committee were present, and Colleen Crawford was also invited to participate in the proceedings of this meeting. New committee member Rita Joyce was welcomed along with incoming Executive Coordinator Father Patrick Cogan. After quick introductions including an overview of each member's participation on this committee historically, Father David reviewed the functions of the committee with its members.

Evaluations of the Major Addresses and Seminars from the 2016 Convention in Houston were reviewed and discussed. The committee was surprised at the sparse number of evaluations that were returned. They request of the Board of Governors (BOG) that at upcoming conventions, announcements be made and participants be reminded of the necessity of evaluating presentations and speakers as these evaluations are essential in convention planning and this committee's work.

Committee members also discussed the types of presenters that would be best employed in our upcoming conventions. Some members noted that there has been an inclination to invite speakers of high profile but a preference should be given, rather, to someone who is engaged in canonical praxis and who is skilled in the law.

Much time was then spent on reviewing the theme for the 2018 Convention to be held in Phoenix, Arizona developed by the Research and Development Committee and subsequently approved by the Board of Governors. The working theme as presented to the Committee on Convention Planning is *Canonical Equity: In Practice with a Vision for the Future.* Admittedly, the specificity of this theme created much dialogue regarding its thrust and whether or not it is timely in nature. A predominate question in this discussion was *"Is the issue of equity something inherent in the law itself or something 'over and above' the law?"*

Much of the remainder of the meeting was spent developing topics for keynote addresses and seminars based upon input provided in evaluations, recommended topics from the Research and Development Committee and the Board of Governors, and other suggestions provided by general CLSA membership. The committee formally recommends the following presentations and potential speakers for the 2018 CLSA Convention in Phoenix, Arizona (see attached). Once approval of the major address and seminar themes and speakers has been realized, the committee members will contact various speakers to arrange for them to speak at the 2018 convention. The Committee on Convention Planning also offers its assistance to the Board of Governors once they have determined themes and speakers for the 2018 pre-convention workshops.

The extremely productive business meeting concluded with the group planning another meeting at the Towne Place Suites at BWI to take place on 09 January 2018 to plan for the 2019 convention to be held in Atlantic City, New Jersey. The committee chair requests that the Board of Governors approve the recommended convention theme for 2019 before the 2018 Convention Planning meeting and that the report of the Research and Development Committee be forwarded to the Convention Planning chair to assist in proper planning before this time.

Respectfully submitted,
Rev. Jamin Scott David, JCL

2018 CLSA Convention Program
## CANONICAL EQUITY: IN PRACTICE WITH A VISION FOR THE FUTURE
08-11 October 2018
Phoenix, Arizona

*Editor's Note*: The Board of Governors approved, with some modifications, the program submitted by the Committee for Convention Planning in late August 2017.

---

**Committee:** INSTITUTES OF CONSECRATED LIFE AND SOCIETIES OF APOSTOLIC LIFE
**Constituted:** 2010
**Mandate:** The mandate of the Committee is:

1. To initiate as needed any projects pertinent to the study of canon law pertaining to the life and ministry of Institutes of Consecrated and Apostolic Life or the implementation thereof, including but not limited to the following:
    a) Sponsorship;
    b) Mergers and restructuring institutes;
    c) Governance;
    d) Membership;
    e) New forms of consecrated life.

2. To oversee projects referred to the committee by the Board of Governors;

3. To oversee its subcommittees working on projects concerning Consecrated and Apostolic Life;

4. To collaborate with national organizations and other groups dealing with issues of Consecrated and Apostolic Life.

**Membership:**  Sr. Karla Felix-Rivera (chair)
Dr. Eileen Jaramillo
Christina Hip-Flores
Rev. Joseph M. Arsenault, SSA
Sr. Eloise Rosenblatt, RSM
Adela Maria Kim
Rev. Richard A. Wahl, CSB
Rev. John Chrysostom Kozlowski, OP

Former President Mentor: Rev. Paul Golden, CM
Board of Governors Liasion: Sr. Nancy Reynolds, SP

## ANNUAL REPORT

1. This past year, this committee grew in membership and we are privileged to have members representing various paths of life: members of religious institutes (1 woman and 2 ordained men), a member of an ecclesial family of consecrated life of apostolic right, a consecrated virgin, and 2 lay women. This is both a richness and a challenge since not all members are able to be present in our conference calls.

2. After working with our Former President Mentor and much brainstorming as a committee, we submitted a project proposal to the BOG in January 2017. We were very happy to receive a green light from the BOG, through Fr. Roger Keeler in February, 2017. At the moment, this committee is developing a canonical commentary for superiors and vicars/delegates for consecrated life addressing the steps of a member's incorporation into institutes of consecrated life, which include topics on vocational discernment, novitiate, temporal vow period, final incorporation. Such a handbook will also include a section for consecrated virgins and new ecclesial families of consecrated life. To this end, this committee held two conference call since February (April 4, 2017 and July 17, 2017) and we hope to meet once again prior to this year's CLSA National Convention in October, 2017.

3. The BOG, through Fr. Keeler, asked this committee to look into the possibility of collaborating with the Laity Committee in writing on issues pertaining to lay associations with consecrated members. Sr. Karla Felix-Rivera and Amy Tadlock spoke with their respective committees in the Spring 2017. The final conclusion is that such work is not possible at this moment; members of the consecrated and apostolic life committee did not show interest since they prefer to focus on the initial formation handbook project.

4. Contributing to the CLSA by writing Advisory Opinions and offering workshops at National Conventions is important to this committee. Various members committed to sending in articles and proposals to the BOG.

Respectfully submitted,
Sr. Karla Felix-Rivera, VDMF

**Committee:** LAITY
**Constituted:** 2009
**Mandate:**

1. To initiate as needed any projects pertinent to the study of canon law pertaining to the life and ministry of lay persons or the implementation thereof, including, but not limited to, the following:
   a. Lay ecclesial ministry;
   b. Collaboration with clergy;
   c. Rights of the lay faithful;
2. To oversee projects referred to the committee by the BOG;
3. To oversee its subcommittees working on projects concerning the laity, (and)
4. To collaborate with national organizations and other groups dealing with the role of the laity in the Church.

**Membership:** Ms. Amy Tadlock, *chair* (2018)
Ms. Anne Bryant (2017)
Mr. Stephen Garbitelli (2017)
Rev. Michael J. Bradley (2017)
Mr. Matthew Glover (2018)
Mr. J. Michael Ritty (2018)
Rev. Mark Payne (2018)
Sr. Margaret Ramsden (2019)

## ANNUAL REPORT

Since the 2016 Annual Convention of the Canon Law Society of America, the Laity Committee has been in conversation with the Consecrated Life Committee about the possibility of a joint project focused on the development of resources on Associations of the Faithful. The Laity Committee will meet at the 2017 Annual CLSA Convention to discuss this and other projects on the role of the laity within the Church, especially as it pertains to the field of canon law.

Respectfully Submitted,
Amy L. Tadlock, Chair

**Committee:** PUBLICATIONS ADVISORY BOARD (PAB)
**Constituted:** Board of Governors, 2007
**Mandate:** The mandate of the Board is:

1. To advise the Board of Governors about all aspects of current, periodic and proposed CLSA publication projects, including financial, literary, educational and marketing issues.
2. To monitor the progress of all CLSA publication projects.
3. To implement the procedures for peer review of CLSA publications.
4. To make the final recommendation to the Board of Governors regarding specific publications.
5. To review the coordination and management of the CLSA's publications activity on the part of the Office of the Executive Coordinator.
6. To provide a written report to the CLSA membership at the annual convention.

**Membership:** Sharon Euart, *chair* (term ends 2019)
Patrick Cogan (term ends 10/17)
Patrick Cooney (term ends 10/20)
Paul Hartmann (term ends 10/18)
Susan Mulheron (term ends 10/20)
Rita Joyce, R&D chair (*ex officio* - term ends 10/17)
John Alesandro, consultant

## ANNUAL REPORT

*Meetings*

The PAB met four times during the year – conference calls in October 2016 and April, 2017 and in-person meetings in February and June 2017 at the Marriott Towne Place Suites BWI. The frequency of communication helped us address the many issues related to CLSA publications. In addition the chair of PAB participated in conference calls with the Board of Governors in January and April 2017 and in person during the BOG's August 2017 meeting to discuss topics of interest and concern. The members also communicated by conference call and e-mail throughout the year.

*Publications Budget*

At the writing of this report the June 30 actual vs budget figures were not available. However, the May 31 financial report indicated that the CLSA Publications would show a significant deficit at the end of the fiscal year due to delays in book production. PAB noted the lack of expenditures for book production for the fiscal year as of May 31 and expressed concern since manuscripts have been ready for publication. If the delay in the publication for *Proceedings* 2016 has been caused by the fact that texts have not been submitted in a timely manner, PAB recommends that office procedures be modified by requiring a drop-dead timeline after which the entry will be dropped and no honorarium paid to the speaker. The PAB is concerned that the late publication of *Proceedings* 2016 may seriously impact members' appreciation of the book as a member service. PAB recommends that a discussion of the policy issues related to publication of *Proceedings* take place as a future time.

Throughout the year PAB reported to and discussed with the Board of Governors its concerns regarding the challenges facing the Society in the area of publications and offered suggestions, in particular, to improve the timeliness of book production of approved manuscripts as well as potential initiatives for electronic book production and the relationship with the CLSA distributor BrightKey. The PAB has recommended a joint meeting of the PAB with the staff of the OEC as soon as possible after the new structure is initiated.

Among the anticipated publications during the past year were the 2014 *Penal Proceedings* and the new resource *Advisory Opinions on Consecrated Life*. It is expected that both will be available in late July along with the 2016 *Proceedings*. In addition, PAB is working with Fr. Aaron Nord on a pastoral resource on "Diocesan and Apostolic Administrators." The text is being reviewed by three members of the Society and observations will be sent to Fr. Nord when all the reviews are completed. Other considerations for publication include a pastoral resource on current topics on Church Finance by the Research & Development Committee. This resource would be a successor to the out-of-print and somewhat outdated *Church Finance Handbook*. The CLSA Sacramental Law Committee is considering a *Vademecum on Mitis Iudex*.

*Inventory*

PAB continues to monitor and manage the CLSA inventory, reducing it when there is little likelihood of additional sales of any significance, particularly for older publications, in order to consolidate the volumes into fewer pallets and thereby reduce monthly storage expenses at *Bright Key*. This is an ongoing task, which involves PAB's collaboration with the Office of the Executive Coordinator and the staff of *Bright Key*. PAB anticipates making available to CLSA members (at no cost except for postage) copies of older publications in the inventory (e.g., *CLD*, 10-14, *Proceedings* 2001-2013). PAB continues to review the inventory in conjunction with the progress on status of the database ingestion and for the continuity in the fulfillment process for available publications.

*CLSA Resource Database*

The PAB receives frequent updates on the status of the Research Database from Msgr. Jack Alesandro. Recent developments include:

- Volume "15" represents new material issued after the publication of CLD 14. Msgr. John Renken is regularly providing new documents for ingestion into the database. "Volume 15" will probably cover about five years' worth of documents. This will be followed by an electronic "Volume 16" and so forth, in an ongoing effort to keep the database current.
- Other data to be ingested will include: all *Advisory Opinions,* all *Proceedings*
- The order of the ongoing ingestion: pre-1983 Code CLD volumes 1-10; material published since Volume 14; material relevant to earlier volumes of CLD that was not included at the time of publication; Latin and Eastern codes.

PAB acknowledges with gratitude the work of Msgr. Alesandro for his leadership on this project; Msgr. John Renken for his coordination of the data gathering process; Rev. Mark Gantley for his coordination of the ingestion process with Alex Padmos; and for Cathy Gilligan and all the CLSA members who has assisted with the ingestion of material for the database.

PAB has extended to all CLSA members the period of free access to the database until July 2018 to allow time for further enhancement of the database based on the suggestions of actual users.

*Code of Canon Law* (Latin)

At the time of preparing this report, the OEC is moving toward a full restock of the Latin code no later than July 31. The production of the Third Printing of the *CIC* has been delayed due to several technical issues including the lack of availability of electronic files, the need for re-pagination due to inclusion of all *Mitis* and *Concordia* changes, Index changes, etc. With the availability of the electronic files, future changes in the Latin code can be made in a more timely fashion.

*Reorganization of OEC*

The PAB discussed the reorganization of the OEC and recommended that there be a meeting of the new Executive Coordinator, the General Secretary and the PAB to discuss the relationship among the parties, clarify the respective responsibilities regarding the publication function of the Society and develop any observations and/or recommendations for the BOG.

Respectfully submitted,
Sr. Sharon Euart, RSM

**Committee:** RESEARCH & DEVELOPMENT
**Constituted:** 2008
**Mandate:** It is the function of the Committee on Research and Development:

To initiate or cooperate in all CLSA research projects such as seminars, symposia and special studies;

1. To design and implement Think Tanks that will allow for diverse views on issues of ecclesial life having canonical implications;
2. To develop and recommend themes for the annual Conventions for submission to the Board of Governors for approval and subsequent referral to the Convention Planning Committee for implementation;
3. To maintain close communication with all the committees of the Society in order to facilitate needed research and discussion;
4. To interact with the Publications Advisory Board in order to assess the current and contemplated publications of the CLSA and offer suggestions and guidance for publication planning

**Membership:** Mrs. Rita Joyce (chair)
Dr. Diane Barr
Rev. Robert Kaslyn, S.J.
Most Rev. Mark O'Connell
Rev. Joseph C. Scheib
Rev. Manuel Rodrigues (volunteer member of committee)
Rev. Monsignor John Foster (*ex-officio*)

## ANNUAL REPORT

**The Research & Development Committee meet via conference call on May 18, 2017.** There were several follow up conversations with individual members as well as emails. There was some additional discussion following the Publications Advisory Board meeting.

Present for the discussion were: Most Reverend Mark O'Connell, Rev. Manuel Rodriquez, Rev. Joseph Scheib, and Rita F. Joyce. Consultation by email: Rev. Robert Kaslyn, Dr. Diane Barr

The purpose of the meeting was twofold:

a) to discuss possible republication of the *Church Finance Handbook*
b) to preliminarily brainstorm themes for the 2019 Convention

There was a consensus that the *Handbook* is a useful tool. However, as two of the original editors proposed, before offering the material in the form of a reprint, it must be updated as the book is 18 years old.

Specifically sections that deal with the Complementary Norms have changed, Also there are numbers of places in the book, at least ten areas where simply "things have changed" such as Chapter 5 – Remuneration of Church Employees. This section needs to be updated in light of civil legal matters.

The basic book has twenty-two chapters and twenty-four authors. There were three original editors, who were also authors. One suggestion was to approach those twenty-four authors that are still alive to see if they are interested in updating their article, or if they would offer the name of someone else who would update their article. Additional sections that could be added are on sponsorship, fundraising, financing of Catholic schools, regionalization, merging or alteration of a parish, reduction to profane use of a church building as some examples. A new detailed Table of Contents would be useful to the end user. It was recommended to keep the glossary as it very helpful and definitions do not change.

If this project is undertaken by the CLSA, if authorized by PAB, several coordinators would be needed to oversee the project. Bishop O'Connell volunteered to discuss and share his knowledge in the newer areas as these are areas that he is familiar with and has worked on in the recent past. Rita Joyce offered to oversee the overall updating with another volunteer should PAB decide it is to be pursued.

It was pointed out that Cardinal de Paolis has written a text on temporal goods in Italian, No one was aware of an English translation. Also Archbishop Schnurr, when he was with the USCCB offered guidelines in 2007 which appear on the USCCB website. Sources recommended to contact were Fr. John Beal and possibly Charles Zek from Villanova University. However, it was also discussed that since there is no remuneration for the project, using persons outside the Society *can prove problematic.* Also, Msgr John Renken published in 2009: *Church Property: A Commentary on Canon Law Governing Temporal Goods in the US and Canada.* Perhaps this text can serve as an alternative to republication.

The second part of the meeting discussed preliminary ideas for **potential themes for the 2019 Convention.** There was not a significant anniversary of any canonical document in 2019 that the members were aware of. Professor Kaslyn pointed out that it is the 90th anniversary of the Lateran Treaty, but other than that he was unaware of any other significant event.

The following ideas were generated:

1. The Pope as legislator both formally and informally. The positive and negative outcomes of informal legislating.
2. Reform of the Curia and its impact upon individual dioceses. (Question as to whether this would happen by 2019?)

3. Salvation of souls – there is a great divide in our own CLSA as well as Church Society as a whole relative to two distinct realities: "there are too many rules-they need to be relaxed" vs. "they are taking away our rules-what is left?"

4. How do you integrate Pope Francis' legacy for the betterment of the Church of the future? How does *Amoris Laetitia* and *Mitus iudex Dominus Iesus* contribute to the manifestation of the divide? Confusion is there, what do we need to do to overcome confusion? Are there instruments that can help facilitate the integration?

5. Contractions/alterations of parishes and their programs from a positive view, a view that brings about a new energy or a new evangelization. Sub theme: Are parishes getting in the way of evangelization? Does the structure of a parish as we know it still make sense?

6. New ecclesial movements in the Church. What are they, how do they help, are they a means of evangelization or something else?

7. Sub theme: Congregation for the Clergy gained supervision of seminaries. Pope Francis, in the new change, made specific mention of integral formation referring not just to seminary formation but post-ordination formation. What could his mean for clergy, for personnel policies, what changes could this bring about?

8. This theme had general "excitement" with the committee because of its boldness and broadness and ability to flesh out the theme with various tracks. *Envisioning a New Code*- "an intellectual exercise." This could be developed as follows: *Significant Emendations in the Code of Canon Law: Current Practice and Future Considerations*. Given that in 1959, some 42 years after the promulgation of the 1917 Code, Pope John XXIII recognized the need for a revision of the Church's law, should a revised code be envisioned after some 34 years?

- Significant emendations in the law have occurred through the pontificates of Saint John Paul II, Pope Benedict XVI and Pope Francis. To what extent do these and other changes require a revised Code? And if so, what possibilities exist for such a Code? (Possibilities for key note / major addresses?)

- Presentations could deal with specific legal changes; granted we are familiar with the changes through the revised marriage law; is it time to review them in light of the tradition and of current praxis? Current Practice; theory behind the law; etc.

- Competency for *ratum non consummatum* cases as well as for nullity of ordination have changed; any developments on either in the new configuration?

- *Pastor Bonus,* which according to John Paul II is one of the three major legal texts of the Church, with the CIC and CCEO, has also been significantly changed. A review of the changes and the impact on the life of the Church might prove useful.
- The changes in the first canons on ordination were effected in order to foster agreement with the Catechism and Lumen gentium. Impact on the sacrament of orders, if any?
- Even a discussion of who changed what and why could prove useful in determining the nature of a universal law Code in the 21$^{st}$ century.

After this meeting, the Chair attended the PAB meeting in June in Baltimore. The following transpired.

As a result of discussion at the PAB meeting, the Chair will take back to the R&D Committee the idea for possibly examining the sections of the *Church Finance Handbook* topics that could together be made into a Pastoral resource stand-alone booklet. Also the idea of separate Pastoral Resources on the following topics will be considered:

1. Altering a Parish, reduction of a sacred space to profane use.
2. Regionalization of Catholic Schools
3. Financing of Catholic Schools & possibly Governance of Schools exploring canonical structures for governance in line with civil structures. Reference was made to a recent governance model used by the Sisters of Mercy Schools called the Mercy Education Systems of the Americas that could be helpful in developing a booklet on structures.

This latter matter of examining the *Handbo*ok for section that could be made into a Pastoral Resource stand alone as well as the three above topics will be brought to the R& D Committee prior to the convention as chairmanship of this committee changes at the convention. Bishop O'Connell has agreed that he will share his knowledge re alteration of parishes, and the Diocese of Pittsburgh is in the midst of a reorganization of parishes. Rita Joyce is willing to explore the possibility of a Pastoral Resource on this subject **or** on the governance and financing of schools as a project of the R&D committee, if there is another volunteer with whom she could share the work, even though she would be cycled off the committee.

**Issues to bring to the attention of the BOG**: Direction on the development of Pastoral Resources in the areas of altering a parish, and or school financing and governance structures from a civil and canonical perspective. Is there an interest in consolidating certain chapters of the Church Finance Handbook to make it a stand-alone resource?

Are there any of the above proposed theme areas that the BOG wishes the committee to develop further? If so, those directions should be given to the successor chair.

Respectfully submitted,
Rita Ferko Joyce

---

**Committee:** Sacramental Law
**Constituted:** 2009
**Mandate:** It is the function of the Committee on Sacramental Law:

1. To initiate as needed any projects pertinent to the study of canon law pertaining the sacramental life of the Church or the implementation thereof;
2. To oversee projects referred to the committee by the BOG;
3. To oversee its subcommittees working on projects concerning the sacramental life of the Church;
4. To offer suggestions to the BOG for marriage topics for pre-convention workshops; (and)
5. To collaborate with national organizations and other groups dealing with the sacramental life of the Church

**Membership:** Dr. Chad Glendinning (chair), 2018
Mrs. Heather Jo Eichholz, 2017
Rev. Robert Sinatra, 2017
Dr. William Daniel, 2018
Rev. Peter Akpoghiran, 2019
Ms. Anna Marie M. Chamblee, 2019
Rev. John Lessard-Thibodeau, 2019
Sr. Maureen A. McPartland, OP, 2019
Rev. Arthur Mollenhauer, 2019
Rev. Shawn P. Tunink, 2019
Rev. Peter O. Eke, 2019
Rev. John Boyle, 2019
Rev. Matthew Furgiuele, 2019
Rev. Mr. Michael Forbes, 2019
Msgr. Dariusz J. Zielonka, 2019
Mr. Timothy Olson, 2019

Former President Mentor: Rev. Daniel Smilanic
BOG Liaison: Rev. Kenneth Riley

## ANNUAL REPORT

All existing members of the sacramental law committee were present at the CLSA convention in Houston in October, 2016. As a result of the successful initiative at this convention, several members expressed an interest in serving on the Sacramental Law Committee. These new members are identified above (with a term expiry of 2019). The committee also welcomes the collaboration of Rev. Daniel Smilanic (past-president mentor) and Rev. Kenneth Riley (BOG liaison). Mr. Jay Conzemius' term expired in 2016. The committee wishes to express its gratitude for his contribution over the past several years.

The principal initiative of the committee remains the collaborative project for the implementation of *Mitis Iudex*, formalized between the Canon Law Society of America, the Canadian Canon Law Society, and the Faculty of Canon at Saint Paul University. The intent is to produce a practical resource that could be used by tribunal practitioners for the correct implementation of *Mitis Iudex*. The publication will be divided into two sections: a) a user-friendly step-by-step guide to creating the vademecum for the prejudicial or pastoral inquiry; b) an outline of the procedure for the ordinary and the briefer processes, and ground-specific questionnaires. The publication, aimed for canonists as well as non-canonists, could serve as an aid to formation in parishes and tribunals.

The Sacramental Law Committee is responsible for the first section, that is, matters pertaining to the prejudicial inquiry, up to and including the submission of the *libellus*. The document will consist of the following components: a glossary of terms; a Q&A / FAQ (Frequently Asked Questions); an overview of the Church's teaching on marriage; an overview of special marriage cases; an overview of the grounds of matrimonial nullity; an overview of proofs; a sample *libellus*; and an annotated application form. The committee remains committed to prepare this resource as quickly as possible, but it is anticipated that some additional time will be needed for editing and preparing the final draft.

Respectfully submitted,
Chad Glendinning

# VARIA

## CANON LAW SOCIETY OF AMERICA
## SEVENTY-NINTH ANNUAL BUSINESS MEETING
### Indianapolis, Indiana
### 18 October 2017

**MINUTES**

CALL TO ORDER AND OPENING PRAYER

The Very Reverend Bruce Miller, President, called to order the Seventy-Ninth Annual Business Meeting of the Canon Law Society of America (CLSA), on 18 October 2017 at 11:00 a.m., at The Westin Indianapolis Hotel in Indianapolis, Indiana. He presided over the meeting as Chair.

The Chair then led the assembly in an opening prayer.

Following the opening prayer, it was announced that Ms. Barbara Anne Cusack would serve as Parliamentarian for the Business Meeting, and that *Robert's Rules of Order* would resolve matters not provided for in the CLSA's *Constitution* or *Bylaws*.

The Chair then gave instructions on the voting procedures to be observed for the election of Vice-President/President-Elect, Secretary, and Consultors during the Business Meeting. The procedures were adopted as described by the Chair.

The Chair then reviewed the procedures for addressing the assembly as well as the CLSA's practices for presenting resolutions. The procedures and practices were adopted as presented by the Chair.

The Chair then entertained a motion that Associate Members present at the meeting have the opportunity to address the assembly, as called-for in Article 5.3 of the CLSA's *Constitution*. The motion was seconded and approved by the assembly.

The Chair then noted that the Minutes of the Seventy-Eighth Annual Business Meeting of the CLSA, written by Ms. Mary Gen Blittschau, Secretary, were provided in advance for review as published in *Proceedings* on pages 410-427 as well as having been distributed electronically to the membership. The Chair then called for any corrections to the Minutes as submitted; no corrections were proposed. Therefore, the Chair announced that the Minutes of the Seventy-Eighth Annual Business Meeting stand approved by the assembly.

## ELECTION OF OFFICERS AND CONSULTORS

The Chair called Mr. Jay Conzemius, Chair of the Nominations Committee, to present the slate of nominees for Officers and Consultors. Mr. Jay Conzemius announced the candidates for Officers and Consultors.

Following the introduction of the candidates, the Chair called for nominations from the floor; there were none, and the nominations were closed.

The Chair then read the provisions of the CLSA's *Bylaws* regarding elections. The active members of the CLSA were instructed to cast their votes. The tellers collected the ballots and retired to a separate room to count them. Later in the Business Meeting, Mr. Jay Conzemius returned and informed the Chair of the election results. The Chair then announced that:

### *For the Office of Vice-President/President-Elect*:

223 valid ballots were cast, with 112 votes needed for election. There were no invalid ballots or abstentions. The votes cast were:

Rev. Patrick Cooney, OSB: 108
Dr. Zabrina Decker: 115

The Chair declared an election with Dr. Zabrina Decker selected as Vice-President/President Elect. The election was received with applause.

### *For the Office of Secretary*:

223 valid ballots were cast, with 112 votes needed for election. There were no invalid ballots and 2 abstentions. The votes cast were:

Dr. Margaret Chalmers: 106
Mr. Timothy Olson: 115

The Chair declared an election with Mr. Timothy Olson selected as Secretary. The election was received with applause.

### *For the Office of Consultor*:

223 valid ballots were cast, with 112 votes needed for election. There was one invalid ballot and two abstentions. The votes cast were:

Rev. Joseph C. Abraham: 85
Rev. Peter O. Akpoghiran: 61
Dr. Chad J. Glendinning: 130
Dr. Christina Hip-Flores: 143

The Chair declared an election with Dr. Chad Glendinning and Dr. Christina Hip-Flores selected as Consultors. The election was received with applause.

## REPORTS

### PRESIDENT'S REPORT

The Chair referred the assembly to pages 17-20 of the *2017 Annual Reports Booklet,* distributed at the convention registration, for the full text of the President's Report.

Gratitude for the opportunity to have served the CLSA was expressed by the President who appreciated acting as the representative of the entire membership.

Following the departure of Rev. Roger Keeler, former Executive Coordinator, whose three-year contract expired and his concurrent decision to return to teaching, the Board of Governors considered its responsibilities related to filling that position. It was determined that requiring the Executive Coordinator to reside in the Washington, DC area in addition to serving in a full-time capacity would significantly decrease the number of applications. In addition, a focus on the production of peer-reviewed professional academic publications was deemed as a necessity for that position. Thus, it was determined that, in addition to holding a canonical degree, the Executive Coordinator needs demonstrated experience in the publications arena.

Furthermore, a new office entitled General Secretary, in imitation of the USCCB model, with someone capable of the operation of an organization which hosts an annual convention was needed; Ms. Colleen Crawford was named to serve in that capacity. Then, a search was begun for a half-time Executive Coordinator; nine candidates surfaced. Eventually, Rev. Patrick Cogan, SA, was hired as Executive Coordinator. Both Father Cogan and Ms. Crawford would report to the Board of Governors and be directly supervised by the President.

During the biennial visit to Rome, six Cardinal Prefects met with the CLSA representatives, and assurance that the tribunals and dicasteries of the Holy See were readily available to assist the bishops was stressed. It was noted that the CLSA stands ready to be of humble service to the Holy See.

Submission of convention presentations for publication in *Proceedings* needs to occur in a timely manner so that the information is readily available for study and review.

The new CLSA website is now functioning and is available for viewing at: canonlawsocietyofamerica.org. In addition, the Guidebook app may be downloaded and provides pertinent information about the convention. Suggestions regarding both items are appreciated. Furthermore, the research database on the website makes available a vast amount of canonical information; the effort to augment the material is continually ongoing.

A Canon Law Society of America polo shirt has been available for purchase at the convention; interest in this item will dictate the consideration of sales at next year's meeting. Rebranding is under review; suggestions and opinions about this matter are sought from the membership.

Future challenges for the CLSA include international publishing, surfacing authors, competitive pricing, e-book publishing, and on-demand publication; disseminating canonical information to the world serves as its own ministry of missionary discipleship. The cultivation of a close rapport with other canon law societies remains a priority.

The Chair then expressed appreciation for the privilege of having served the CLSA during the past year as its president and voiced admiration for the canonical contributions of the entire membership.

No questions or observations regarding the Presidential Report were posed.

## TREASURER'S REPORT

The Chair next invited Sister Nancy Reynolds, SP, Treasurer, to the podium to provide the Treasurer's Report. She noted that the written report is found on pages 22-38 of the *2017 Annual Reports Booklet*.

The auditor's review will be contained in *Proceedings*; at the end of this fiscal year, an audit will occur as is the practice each time a new Executive Coordinator is hired. TD Bank now handles the CLSA accounts.

*Investments Unit:*

For the past fiscal year, General Operations shows $883,659.21 as its balance. The Licentiate Scholarship balance has grown to $752,949.61 while the Doctoral Scholarship balance is $60,960.97.

*General Operations Unit:*

More than a balanced budget is demonstrated with an amount in the excess.

*Publications Unit*

Less income was received than was budgeted. Books which were expected to be published were not; recently, however, four publications have been issued and will realize income. The third edition of the *Code of Canon Law* is slated for publication.

*Conventions Unit*

More than $144,000 in registration fees has been collected for the present convention; pre-convention workshops also afforded more income than originally anticipated.

*Scholarships Unit*

Those who are students are encouraged to apply for a scholarship.

The Treasurer called for questions regarding the report; none were posed.

Following the report of the Treasurer, the Chair then called for any questions in general from the membership; there were none.

## EXECUTIVE COORDINATOR'S REPORT

The Chair then called Reverend Patrick Cogan, SA, to address the assembly. He referred the membership to page 39 of the *2017 Annual Reports Booklet* for the complete text of the report of the Office of the Executive Coordinator.

He noted that he is working from his community's motherhouse which is located north of New York, New York but travels to the CLSA office as needed. Father Cogan expressed gratitude for the opportunity to serve the membership.

## GENERAL SECRETARY'S REPORT

The Chair next called Ms. Colleen Crawford to address the assembly. Ms. Crawford referred the membership to page 40 of the *2017 Annual Reports Booklet* for the complete text of the report of the General Secretary. She then expressed appreciation for the privilege of serving the CLSA and values interaction with the membership so as to be of assistance.

# RESOLUTIONS

The Chair read the applicable CLSA *Bylaws* which govern the proposal of resolutions from the floor and asked if there were any such resolutions to be presented. There being none, he called Mr. Timothy Olson, Chair of the Resolutions Committee, Reverend Monsignor John Foster, Vice-President, and Reverend Jaroslaw Skrzypek, time-keeper, to approach the podium and present the resolution previously submitted to the Resolutions Committee.

One resolution was previously submitted.

The full text of the resolution was projected onto screens in the hall. In addition, printed copies of the resolution were accessible to those in attendance.

Since the resolution concerns amendment of the *Constitution* which requires a two-thirds vote as well as amendment of the *Bylaws* which requires a simple majority, Mr. Olson noted that the vote will be split on the resolution clauses concerning both the *Constitution* and the *Bylaws*.

Since the resolution regards an amendment of the *Constitution*, an attestation from the Secretary, Ms. Mary Gen Blittschau, was made regarding the reception of the requisite documentation at least three months in advance of the Business Meeting.

*Resolution 1*

The Resolutions Committee moved the resolution.

**PROPOSED BY:** Board of Governors

**TITLE:** Constitutional and Bylaw Changes Arising from CLSA Office Restructuring

**STATEMENT OF RATIONALE:**

**WHEREAS,** staffing transition necessitates a reconsideration of duties and responsibilities assigned to administrative personnel;

**AND WHEREAS,** the Board of Governors maintains a supervisory and instructive role in the administration of Society business;

**AND WHEREAS,** the Board of Governors upholds the history of and canonical qualifications for the position of Executive Coordinator, while recognizing a separate and growing need for a position devoted exclusively to administration;

**AND WHEREAS,** the Board of Governors voted to restructure the Office of the Executive Coordinator at its April 2017 meeting, and subsequently publicized Position Descriptions for a part-time Executive Coordinator and full-time General Secretary;

**AND WHEREAS,** proper implementation of this restructuring requires minor amendments to the CLSA *Constitution* and *Bylaws*;

**BE IT RESOLVED THAT** Article VIII of the *Constitution* be amended with the following text:

Reporting to the Board of Governors and supervised by the President, two collaborative positions serve the Office: the Executive Coordinator, who is a degreed canonist, and the General Secretary, who is qualified in organizational management.

Financial provisions for the operation of the office shall be the responsibility of the Board of Governors in the annual budget.

**BE IT FURTHER RESOLVED THAT** all references to an Executive Coordinator appearing in the *Constitution* and the *Bylaws* shall be changed to refer to the Executive Coordinator and the General Secretary, *mutatis mutandis*. All references to the Office of the Executive Coordinator shall be changed to refer to the Administrative Office.

**BE IT FURTHER RESOLVED THAT** Article 16 of the *Bylaws* be amended with the following text:

The General Secretary is the authorized agent for the Canon Law Society of America in all matters, but especially pertaining to those areas denoted in the Position Description, for which such agency is required, unless the Board of Governors or President of the Society shall determine otherwise in particular cases. The Executive Coordinator is also an authorized agent for the Canon Law Society of America in all matters, but especially pertaining to those areas denoted in the Position Description, for which such agency is required, unless the Board of Governors or President of the Society shall determine otherwise in particular cases.

a. The General Secretary shall maintain the Administrative Office.

b. The duties of the General Secretary and the Executive Coordinator shall be defined in their respective Position Descriptions as approved by the Board of Governors.

**IMPLEMENTATION BY MEANS OF:** Modification to the existing language of the *Constitution* and *Bylaws*.

**ANTICIPATED COST:** $0

Very Rev. Bruce Miller of the Diocese of Alexandria and President of the Canon Law Society of America spoke on behalf of the Board of Governors in favor of the resolution regarding both amendments; he referred to the justification for these amendments as explained in his presidential report. He noted that the proposed change is a better approach for the functioning of the CLSA administrative office and is reflective of efficient current praxis.

The Chair requested other interventions in favor of or against the resolution and amendments; no interventions were posed.

The Chair called the question on the resolution to amend the *Constitution*; a count by hand occurred. The resolution was adopted by the membership with the requisite two-thirds majority having voted in favor.

The Chair then called the question on the resolution to amend the *Bylaws*. The resolution was adopted by the membership with the requisite simple majority having voted in favor.

## OLD BUSINESS

The Chair then opened the floor to discuss any Old Business of interest to the assembly; there was none.

## NEW BUSINESS

The Chair opened the floor to discuss any New Business of interest to the assembly; there was none.

## VARIA

### *Greetings by Officials of Canon Law Societies*

The Chair then invited visiting officials of other Canon Law Societies to the podium to address the assembly.

Sister Maria Casey, RSJ, President of the Canon Law Society of Australia and New Zealand, brought cordial greetings to the attendees of this convention. Next year's meeting of the Canon Law Society of Australia and New Zealand will take place in Adelaide, Australia and be held from 3-7 September 2018.

Accomplishments of the CLSANZ include the establishment of an Institute for Tribunal Practice, the annual offering of a canon law course for religious community leaders, publication of its annual convention *Proceedings* as well as twice-yearly editions of *The Canonist*, and collaboration between the Australian Catholic Council for Canon Law and the Australian Catholic Bishops Conference. Sister Maria encouraged the CLSA membership to join the CLSANZ.

Reverend Eric Dunn, President of the Canadian Canon Law Society, shared greetings and expressed gratitude for the opportunity to become acquainted with members of the CLSA. All were invited to attend the convention of the Canadian Canon Law Society to be held in Sydney, Nova Scotia. Fr. Dunn has served over the past three years, and his term concludes at the convention next week. He recalled the generous assistance which was received from the Canon Law Society of America over fifty-two years ago when the Canadian Canon Law Society was established.

Reverend Paul Churchill, President of the Canon Law Society of Great Britain and Ireland, shared cordial greetings and thanked the Canon Law Society of America for its many publications which advance the study of canon law. Attendees were invited to the annual conference which will be held from 14-18 May 2018 in Harrogate, England at The Old Swan Hotel.

## ADJOURNMENT

There being no further business, the Chair entertained a motion to adjourn the meeting. The motion was seconded, and passed unanimously.

At 12:22 p.m., Very Reverend Bruce Miller thanked many and formally closed the Seventy-Ninth Business Meeting of the Canon Law Society of America.

Respectfully submitted,
Ms. Mary Gen Blittschau
Secretary

# VARIA

## CONVENTION MASS HOMILY
## FEAST OF SAINT LUKE
*Reverend Bruce Miller, JCL*

It is indeed appropriate for the first reading for this evening to come from Paul's Second Letter to Timothy and mentions his good friend and companion Luke whose feast we celebrate today. It also mentions those who have abandoned him and gone other directions. It is disputed whether Paul himself or one who knows him quite well has written this letter; whether he is in prison or not; and whether it is his last. This pastoral epistle nonetheless gives us the opportunity to begin to reflect not only on Luke but on our relationships, that have been built through canonical experience.

When I come to a CLSA convention, I am looking forward to seeing my friends and companions that I have known now for many years. Some I have known since seminary, others since canon law school, yet others were met at various conventions, seminars, workshops, committees, and the work of advocacy or ad hoc appointments to tribunals. Some have been my teachers, and some I have taught others come to my aid often by phone or email. We have shared documents. We have literally traveled the world. In some cases, we have been not only coworkers in the vineyard but simply good friends on vacation. Seeing each other has brought us joy as we come together.

At the same time, being here together reminds us of those who have passed on; those who gone before us; those who because of age or infirmity are no longer able to be with us; those whose canonical or legal status or personal choice removes them from our midst. Whatever the reason, we are reminded by their absence of them and regret not seeing them.

It may even be the case that a few we once cherished have become to us as Alexander the coppersmith was to Paul. Still suffering we are not yet able to put the past behind us; we would want to avoid the danger and the pain.

I would be remiss if I did not acknowledge how excited I am to be here with you in Indianapolis. My best friend from canon law school, Paul Shikany came from here and his judicial vicar at the time Fred Easton and the Indianapolis staff always included me as I came to conventions as the sole representative of my small diocese. Even when it is not expected or planned, and Paul and Fred are not with them, I have providentially realized that I am in their midst. The last time was in the open seating for the concelebrants in St. Peter's Square the day following Cardinal Tobin's reception of the Red Hat.

Moreover, you would be amazed at how similar the dispensation system and all the tribunal documents in the Diocese of Alexandria looked when I began that office 31 years ago! The dispensation system has not changed much!

We all can identify with the human relations St. Paul spells out in his letter to Timothy. We all have our stories.

On this feast of Saint Luke, what the letter to Timothy makes clear is that Luke was Paul's companion until the end. It is for that reason when reading the Acts of the Apostles, one discovers that the latter half could be retitled the Acts of St. Paul since Luke from personal experience or Paul's testimony could detail his ministry.

Interestingly, it does not seem that Saint Luke is content to chronicle history or directly mimic the teaching of St. Paul. It is especially to be noted that he does not struggle with the precise moment of the end time and the return of Jesus.

In the gospel pericope today chosen for his Feast, relationships are celebrated. So as not to miss the point, it is heralded in the response to the Psalm, "Your friends make known, O Lord, the glorious splendor of your Kingdom."

Thus, the sending by Jesus of the 72 in pairs, as our translation has it, or the 70 in pairs as do other translations, is precisely about the announcement of the principle purpose of Jesus' mission found in Mark 1:15 "the kingdom of God is at hand; repent, and believe in the gospel". We are all called and sent as "missionary disciples" as friends of the Lord and supporting one another even eliciting the help of those we are sent to help to form community.

Mark 1:15 and the phrase that ends today's gospel, "The Kingdom of God is at hand for you" can seem to point to a time far, far away or pie in the sky but that obscures the full meaning of the good news that the presence of Jesus is "at hand"! It is within reach! It is not out there. It is here and now when the glorious splendor of God's love is to be made known though the community, the family of the Church.

> The Church's deepest nature is expressed in her three-fold responsibility: of proclaiming the word of God (*kerygma-martyria*), celebrating the sacraments (*leitourgia*), and exercising the ministry of charity (*diakonia*). These duties presuppose each other and are inseparable. For the Church, charity is not a kind of welfare activity which could equally

well be left to others, but is a part of her nature, an indispensable expression of her very being.

The Church is God's family in the world. In this family, no one ought to go without the necessities of life. Yet at the same time *caritas - agape* extends beyond the frontiers of the Church. The parable of the Good Samaritan remains as a standard which imposes universal love towards the needy whom we encounter "by chance" (cf. Lk 10:31), whoever they may be. Without in any way detracting from this commandment of universal love, the Church also has a specific responsibility: within the ecclesial family no member should suffer through being in need. The teaching of the Letter to the Galatians is emphatic: "So then, as we have opportunity, let us do good to all, and especially to those who are of the household of faith" (6:10). (#25 *Deus Caritas Est,* Benedict XVI, 25 December 2005).

# VARIA

## ROLE OF LAW CITATION
*Reverend Bruce Miller, JCL*

First, I would like to invite the past recipients of the Role of Law Award to come forward so that we may recognize them. Please join me in acknowledging and honoring them again.

I ask them to come forward and to remain standing around the podium during this presentation so that we may visualize the wonderful company of our distinguished membership that our honoree joins this evening. We will take the traditional picture and then have them seated during the traditional address.

Each year, the Canon Law Society of America presents the distinguished Role of Law Award to a member esteemed in the field of canon law.

The person honored with this award is respected by the members of the Canon Law Society of America as someone who embodies the purpose of the Society, a group of men and women of faith who minister justice and mercy in the Church through its legal structures.

This prestigious award is perhaps the highest honor that can be bestowed on anyone: to be chosen by one's peers in a field as superior among them.

The by-laws of the Society direct the Board of Governors to select a person who demonstrates in his or her life and ministry the following specific characteristics: embodiment of a pastoral attitude, commitment to research and study, participation in the development of law, response to needs and practical assistance, facilitation of dialogue and the interchange of ideas within the Society and with other groups.

Tonight we present this award for the 45th time to a colleague in the field of canon law who is indeed highly esteemed.

Let's begin the intrigue of hearing who this year's honoree might be.

Knowing nothing at the time about canon law, the canonist we honor tonight was first published as a 6th grade student after winning a national essay contest on visiting a shrine for *Our Sunday Visitor*. That essay began, "When you visit a shrine you must always leave sometime. But there is one shrine you always have with you. That shrine is your soul." This evidenced, even then, that this canonist had no grave defect of discretion of judgment and already knew, "the supreme law of the Church is the good of souls (c. 1572)".

With no shipwreck at the beginning of nationwide authorship, it is not surprising that many publications continued. This canonist authored a book about marriage, has published more than 50 articles and edited three books about canon law. Our honoree has given more than 60 presentations about canon law locally, regionally, nationally and internationally, as well as a CLSA webinar.

Here is some adminicular evidence not to be overlooked. Jesuit trained in the spiritual exercises of St. Ignatius, our canonist has directed retreats since the late 1970s and offers on-going spiritual direction.

It will come as no surprise that the customary bachelor and master degrees were earned with a membership in a fraternity along the way. I found interesting some of the other courses taken: futurology, film and sociology. Additionally, our honoree has visited and assisted missions in South Africa and Mozambique on three occasions. Then, our recipient helped raise over a quarter of a million dollars in grants for the work there with refugees and those suffering from AIDS.

By the way, I learned by accident last month at the meeting of the Canon Law Society Australia and New Zealand that the honoree's mum is Australian in a casual conversation. So, I am sure that a few just determined who that person might be.

Enough suspense. From 1988 to 1990 the JCB and the JCL degrees were earned from the University of St. Paul, Ottawa, Canada.

The canonist we honor tonight served as a member of the CLSA American Jurisprudence Committee, as Chair of the Marriage Research Committee, as Chair of the Sacramental Law Committee, as Press Officer for the 2000 convention, as a CLSA Hearing Officer, as a member of the Board of Governors, as CLSA Secretary, and currently serves on the Nominations Committee.

Our honoree was part of the 2014 CLSA Task Force I chaired that submitted to the Holy See suggestions for changes in marriage procedural law and most recently was a co-chair of the 2017 CLSA Task Force that responded to questions from the Pontifical Commission for the Protection of Minors about the Application of Canon law in Cases of Sexual Abuse of Minors or Vulnerable Adults.

This canonist works as a Defender of the Bond for the Diocese of Saginaw, Michigan and worked for many years as Defender of the Bond for the Diocese of Winona, Minnesota, currently serving Winona, as needed, as Promoter of Justice.

In 2010, the member we honor tonight began a cost-free consultation group to assist those with questions about religious law. You have seen some of the responses published in *Roman Replies and Advisory Opinions.*

Our honoree teaches canon law at the Athenaeum of Ohio, Mt. St. Mary's Seminary of the West, teaches Tribunal Training through the Lay Pastoral Ministry Program at the seminary to prepare procurator/advocates to assist parishioners to present marriage cases and also chairs the Review Board for the Franciscan Province of St. John the Baptist.

If you still do not know who we honor tonight, maybe it will help if I tell you that she was an eighth-grade cheerleader! No?

Then, after completing high school in three years, this canonist entered the Sisters of Mercy in 1963.

She has worked as Defender of the Bond and Promoter of Justice for the Archdiocese of Cincinnati where she has been Tribunal Director since 1991.

I am thrilled to announce formally on behalf of the Board of Governors that the 45th recipient of the 2017 Role of Law Award of the Canon Law Society of America is Sr. Vicki Vondenberger.

# Varia

## Role of Law Response
### *Sr. Victoria Vondenberger, RSM*

I am honored to receive this award and I am grateful for this opportunity to speak to you. This is a dinner speech and the teacher in me wants you to know, as I proceed, how much more there is to come so I offer a menu for this banquet of words. I hope to whet your appetites with Moses, then offer a balanced main course and, for dessert, invite you into the pie of truth. On your table is a bookmark of related images.[1]

*Appetizer: Moses and the Law*

In the prayer space in my bedroom stands a small statue of Moses which I found in a thrift store. This "old" high school teacher, of course, still has sticky tack and magic markers which I used to craft his missing hand. Now Moses not only guards the law with one hand but his new hand holds a walking staff to move into the future. The tablets of the law held by Moses' perfect hand are solid and form a tradition we canonists treasure. Add flames and you have the logo of CLSA. Today especially, we need that new staff to lead into the future, particularly when we see much of our world moving away from structure and institutions like the Church. We need to lead God's people to the promised future of hope (Jer. 29: 19). Do I have clear answers about how we will do this? No. But I trust us to discern together how to move forward within the law and lead God's people in right directions.

*Main course: Balancing the Scales of Justice*

As we discern the path to that future of hope we need to reconcile opposites or perhaps realize they are not so opposite after all. We must balance values like the three pairs of goods we will consider this evening: Tradition and Innovation, Justice and Mercy, "Us" and "Them." Dualism has plagued the thinking of our Church at least since the Gnostic heresy in the 2nd century. Belief that flesh is in conflict with spirit continues to war against the theology of Incarnation. I call us tonight to move beyond dualism, avoiding an "either-or" mentality while choosing to embrace a "both-and" perspective.

---

1 Bookmark created by graphic design artist Gert Stefanko, Associate of the Sisters of Mercy of the Americas, South Central Community: gstefanko@aol.com

Rev. Lawrence Wrenn was the 4th person to receive this Role of Law Award in 1976, forty-one years ago. Ten years later, he wrote about goods we need to balance in tribunal ministry. I use his ideas each year with my canon law student at the seminary. Last year, Wrenn's article was published anew in a free ebook.[2] I experience those tensions not only in tribunal procedures but also within us. With the hands of Moses we already considered one pair of the goods to balance which Wrenn names: Tradition and Innovation. It can be frightening to risk something new in our lives. I was a parish organist beginning in 8th grade which, before Vatican II, often meant singing solo which scared me a lot at the time. During the first Mass I played, I was so scared about singing *a capella* that when the priest turned around from the altar and extended his hands, *I* sang *Dominus vobiscum*. Startled, Father Anselm Boeke jerked his gaze to the choir loft and sang in response *et cum spiritu tuo* then quickly turned back to the altar while his whole chasuble shook as he tried to muffle his laughter. Over the years I honestly forgot that moment of teenage embarrassment until Father Boeke reminded everyone at the celebration of my silver jubilee as a Sister of Mercy in 1988, the year I went to study canon law. Moving into change can be frightening and embarrassing but picture the tension between risking innovation and holding on to tradition evenly balanced in the scales of justice. From childhood, I paid attention to St. Thomas Aquinas because his feast day was celebrated on my birthday, March 7th. One of his teachings is *virtus stat in medio* (virtue stands in the middle). I think that applies to Wrenn's list and other tensions in our lives and our ministries.

Consider justice and mercy (the theme of this convention). I am frequently asked how I reconcile being a Sister of Mercy with being a minister of justice in our Church.[3] For some people, mercy and justice seem opposed. If justice involves only dispensing deserved punishment for wrongdoing, and if mercy means only pardoning earned punishment, those virtues would be in conflict. But we who follow Jesus and the Gospel do not make an "either-or" choice here. We strive for both. If we relieve the suffering of a person who is poor with a sandwich from our soup kitchen (mercy) without striving to correct the unjust social systems which caused the hunger (justice), we are neither merciful nor just. Mercy without justice can lead to dependency and entitlement, increasing the power of the giver over the one in need. Justice without mercy can lead to

---

[2] Lawrence Wrenn, Reflections on the History of Procedural Law, Lawrence Wrenn, Smashwords Edition, 2017): Article 6, "In Search of a Balanced Procedural law in Marriage Nullity Cases," previously published in *The Jurist* 46 (1986): 2, pp. 602-623 and Lawrence G. Wrenn, *Procedures* (Washington, DC: Canon Law Society of America, 1987), Appendix One, pp. 86-101.

[3] Archdiocese of Cincinnati, *The Catholic Telegraph*, February 2016, "Justice and Mercy Meet in Tribunal Ministry" page 43; also included in *The MAST Journal* (Mercy Association in Scripture and Theology) Vol 23, No. 3 "Pope Francis and Changes in the Tribunal Process: A Canonist's Perspective" pages 40-44.

hardened hearts and cold, impersonal treatment of others. Virtue stands in the middle.

In 2009 I was privileged to be part of a panel of six US canonists at Santa Croce in Rome presenting our experiences of penal law. Inspired by Wrenn's balancing of tensions, I described the role of the Promoter of Justice as the responsibility to balance the rights of all those involved in a penal process,[4] balancing justice and mercy.

The third pair of goods I have chosen to consider tonight is "us" and "them" which leads us to dessert.

*Dessert: the Pie of Truth*

There are painful divisions today in our world, in our Church and even in this canon law society. Sometimes that results in an "us" and "them" dualistic mentality where "we", of course, are completely correct with God on our side while "they" are totally wrong. Do you remember the harsh debate during our 2015 convention? Resolution # 5 was proposed in response to the revised procedures for marriage cases which had not yet even taken effect. Canonists I respect argued vehemently for both sides. What concerned me was the adversarial, defensive, fearful and even disrespectful, tenor of that debate. That experience leads me to offer tonight the pie of truth. During twenty years of teaching high school, I developed the image of the pie of truth to invite my students not to be so convinced of their own opinions that they could not hear truth in opposing views.

What we see depends on where we stand. Picture a large pie cut into wedges of various sizes. Add to that image a small center circle toward which each piece of the pie is cut. Your perspective about anything is one slice of the pie. Tonight I invite us to consider the perspectives of those opposed to our views. No matter how small your wedge may be, it touches a part of the core. Your slice of the pie, your perspective, offers a unique view of what is ultimate truth or wisdom… or God.

If I stand in my piece of the pie and look over at yours, your viewpoint is crooked or skewed. But, if I am secure enough in what I believe, I could accept the grace to leave my perspective and step over into your piece of the pie. Standing in your piece of the pie, I see more of the core of truth because I have added your perspective to my own. That is the gift of respectful dialogue. But it takes a lot of courage to risk stepping out of my beliefs, my convictions, my prejudices, and my biases, and into your viewpoint. It takes God's grace. I

---

4    Victoria Vondenberger, "Balancing Rights: Role of the Promoter of Justice, *Towards Future Developments in Penal Law: U.S. Theory and Practice*, Patricia M. Dugan, ed., (Montréal: Wilson and LaFleur, Gratianus series, 2010: 55-82.

sometimes close my mind to new truth, fearing the changes a new insight might cause in my life. We tend to resist change, to demonize the different and fear the new. It can be very challenging to allow even God's Spirit to call me out of what is comfortable. We are told that Jesus came to comfort the afflicted but Jesus also came to afflict the comfortable. Are we willing to leave our comfort zones? I hope so.

In our appetizer tonight, the statue of Moses called us to respect tradition while risking innovation. The main course of this talk called us move out of dualism as we balance tensions between goods such as justice and mercy. Now we are about to finish our dessert where we were called to move beyond the dualism of "us" and "them." How about some dancing after dinner tonight? I have a small magnet I bought in a market in a poor township while visiting Mercy missions in South Africa. It proclaims: "hope is the ability to hear the music of the future – faith is the courage to dance to it in the present." Often, hope calls us to a future that is not yet clear to us.

When she responded to the music of the future she heard in prayer, Catherine McAuley did not want to start a religious order but the structure of religious life proved to be the best way in 1831 Dublin for Catherine to answer God's call to serve those who are poor, those who are ill, and those who are uneducated, so she founded the Sisters of Mercy. We Sisters of Mercy make a fourth vow of service because of that call to ministry which was at the core of Catherine's call to Mercy. In the midst of ministry, Catherine McAuley instructed the early Sisters of Mercy that it is critical to stay focused on God who is the Center, just as it is important for us as canonists to keep our focus on the *salus animarum* (canon 1752). Catherine's exact words are, "We have one solid comfort amidst this little tripping about: our hearts can always be in the same place, centered in God -- for whom alone we go forward -- or stay back."[5]

As we prayerfully seek the music of hope for the future unfolding in our lives, our world and our Church, we are called to dance to that music right now in faith. Catherine McAuley liked to dance which probably led to her words describing our daily lives as "tripping about." As a musician as well as a canonist, I hear the divine music of the future calling us, together, more deeply into the center of the pie of truth. I pray that the Divine Lawgiver will grace each of us with enough humility that we will have the courage to step into the insights of each other so that, together, we will create a balance of justice and mercy in our ministries, so that we will behold more of God who is on our midst. Like the two hands of my little statue of Moses balancing innovation and tradition, Catherine McAuley calls her followers to let our focus on God help us know when to go forward and when to stay back. As canonists, we also are called to balance innovation and tradition as we move forward together, not dividing ourselves into us and them.

---

5    Mary C. Sullivan, ed., *The Correspondence of Catherine McAuley, 1818-1841* (Washington: The Catholic University of American Press, 2004) p.332.

As we leave this dinner, dancing into a future of hope: "We have one solid comfort amidst this little tripping about: our hearts can always be in the same place, centered in God -- for whom alone we go forward -- or stay back."
Thank you.

# VARIA

## U.S. TRIBUNAL STATISTICS
*2016*

Since 1975, the CLSA has published Tribunal Statistics annually in *Proceedings*. These statistics are provided voluntarily by participating tribunal offices in the United States. Tribunals were asked to submit a copy of the report sent annually to the Apostolic Signatura, as well as some basic financial information. Submissions came by mail to the Office of the Executive Coordinator or by online entry via clsa.org. This electronic change, implemented several years ago, has resulted in a more accurate comparison of statistics among U.S. tribunals.

The requested template for Tribunal Statistics for calendar year 2016 was modified by Executive Coordinator Roger Keeler, to match more closely new information being asked by the Signatura. The results follow.

## First Instance Tribunal Statistics 2016

| (Arch)Diocese or (Arch)Eparchy | Fees received | Diocesan Subsidy | Annual Tribunal Expenses | Libelli introduced and accepted this year | Libelli rejected | Causes admitted to the ordinary process | Causes admitted to the documentary process | Causes pending at the beginning of the year | Causes admitted this year | Sentences Issued | In favor of the Bond | In favor of nullity | Renunciation | Peremption |
|---|---|---|---|---|---|---|---|---|---|---|---|---|---|---|
| Alexandria | $3,175 | $119,185 | $122,360 | 118 | 2 | 107 | 1 | 31 | 107 | 39 | 0 | 39 | 0 | 0 |
| Altoona-Johnstown | | $80,000 | $70,000 | 74 | 0 | 73 | 0 | 58 | 73 | 63 | 0 | 63 | 3 | 3 |
| Baltimore | | | | 285 | 51 | 285 | 17 | 138 | 285 | 260 | 4 | 256 | 2 | 1 |
| Baton Rouge | $8,925 | $230,374 | $239,299 | 236 | 2 | 211 | 24 | 107 | 211 | 224 | 1 | 223 | 0 | 4 |
| Beaumont | | | | 77 | 0 | 77 | 13 | 25 | 77 | | | | 4 | 0 |
| Birmingham | $17,755 | $209,250 | $280,904 | 88 | 0 | 84 | 11 | 102 | 84 | 76 | 1 | 75 | 2 | 3 |
| Boston | $ - | | | 225 | 0 | 177 | 0 | 145 | 177 | 158 | 1 | 157 | 4 | 3 |
| Bridgeport | $ - | $204,504 | $212,268 | 61 | 5 | 61 | | | | | | | | |
| Brooklyn | $46,450 | $354,206 | $400,456 | 179 | 0 | 179 | 0 | 87 | 179 | 88 | 0 | 88 | 2 | 0 |
| Brownsville | $ - | $86,000 | $85,346 | 144 | 0 | 93 | 284 | 98 | 93 | 93 | 6 | 87 | 0 | 0 |
| Buffalo | $ - | $311,210 | $347,683 | 74 | 0 | 74 | 0 | 39 | 74 | 88 | 0 | 88 | 0 | 0 |
| Burlington | $ - | $ - | 55, 879 | 33 | 0 | 30 | 2 | 48 | 33 | 52 | 12 | 40 | 2 | 1 |
| Camden | $77,400 | $262,340 | $339,740 | 83 | 3 | 77 | 0 | 146 | 77 | 55 | 2 | 53 | 0 | 3 |
| Charles | | | | 66 | 0 | 66 | 12 | 71 | 66 | 75 | 2 | 73 | | |
| Charlotte | $57,305 | $406,995 | $464,300 | 380 | 0 | 162 | 218 | 89 | 162 | 155 | 7 | 148 | 1 | 2 |
| Cheyenne | $ - | $142,812 | $142,812 | 93 | 1 | 92 | 8 | 55 | 92 | 49 | 0 | 49 | 1 | 4 |
| Chicago | $236,945 | $875,755 | $236,945 | 403 | 0 | 403 | 13 | 314 | 403 | 397 | 397 | 0 | 2 | 9 |
| Cleveland | $ - | $1 | $771,410 | 310 | 0 | 309 | 15 | 283 | 309 | 248 | 1 | 247 | 9 | 5 |
| Colorado Springs | $16,635 | $266,901 | $283,536 | 32 | 3 | 26 | 6 | 41 | 26 | 21 | 2 | 19 | 1 | 0 |
| Columbus | $ - | $612,517 | $661,174 | 212 | 0 | 201 | 10 | 127 | 212 | 136 | 3 | 133 | 6 | 3 |
| Covington | $ - | $246,890 | $246,890 | 120 | 2 | 105 | 5 | 65 | 105 | | 81 | | 0 | 0 |
| Davenport | $ - | $142,456 | $133,665 | 94 | 0 | 72 | 8 | 80 | 72 | 68 | 0 | 68 | 2 | 11 |

## First Instance Tribunal Statistics 2016

| (Arch)Diocese or (Arch)Eparchy | Fees received | Diocesan Subsidy | Annual Tribunal Expenses | Libelli introduced and accepted this year | Libelli rejected | Causes admitted to the ordinary process | Causes admitted to the documentary process | Causes pending at the beginning of the year | Causes admitted this year | Sentences Issued | In favor of the Bond | In favor of nullity | Renunciation | Peremption |
|---|---|---|---|---|---|---|---|---|---|---|---|---|---|---|
| Denver | $123,797 | $ - | $145,465 | 188 | 0 | 188 | 6 | 348 | 188 | 212 | 11 | 201 | 3 | 13 |
| Des Moines | $ - | $113,575 | $113, 575 | 0 | 0 | 97 | 48 | 47 | 97 | 53 | 0 | 53 | 7 | 3 |
| Detroit | $35,485 | $684,121 | $719,606 | 300 | 34 | 300 | 2 | 78 | 300 | 301 | 2 | 299 | 0 | 19 |
| Dodge City | $4,000 | $77,841 | $81,841 | 40 | 0 | 38 | 2 | 3 | 38 | 35 | 35 | 0 | 1 | 1 |
| Dubuque | $47,248 | $189,242 | $236,490 | 96 | 0 | 128 | 5 | 106 | 96 | 119 | 0 | 119 | 0 | 9 |
| Duluth | $1,800 | $3,250 | $62,107 | 36 | 2 | 36 | 1 | 38 | 36 | 23 | 2 | 21 | 0 | 0 |
| Evansville | $ - | $182,424 | $182 | 90 | 0 | 88 | 2 | 7 | 88 | 39 | 0 | 39 | 7 | 13 |
| Fairbanks | $1,475 | NA | NA | 8 | 0 | 8 | 0 | 13 | 8 | 8 | 0 | 8 | 0 | 0 |
| Fall River | - | - | - | 59 | 0 | 53 | 0 | 69 | 53 | 49 | 49 | 0 | 2 | 3 |
| Fargo | $1,745 | $308,842 | $312,998 | 57 | 4 | 52 | 5 | 41 | 52 | 55 | 0 | 55 | 2 | 2 |
| Fort Wayne-South Bend | $ - | $348,946 | $348,946 | 177 | 0 | 177 | 2 | 162 | 177 | 68 | 14 | 54 | 10 | 18 |
| Gary | $20,230 | $210,502 | $230,594 | 48 | 0 | 47 | 1 | 112 | 48 | 78 | 2 | 76 | 7 | 9 |
| Grand Rapids | $ - | $146,981 | $146,981 | 120 | 5 | 101 | 10 | 109 | 101 | 96 | 0 | 96 | 8 | 12 |
| Great Falls-Billings | $ - | $52,368 | $52,368 | 22 | 0 | 22 | 22 | 19 | 22 | 16 | 4 | 16 | 1 | 1 |
| Harrisburg | $80,000 | $488,536 | $568,536 | 203 | 0 | 183 | 20 | 244 | 183 | 177 | 175 | 2 | 5 | 3 |
| Hartford | $ - | | | 171 | 6 | 165 | 103 | 87 | 165 | 121 | 22 | 99 | 14 | 0 |
| Helena | $ - | $55,600 | $55,600 | 43 | 0 | 36 | 6 | 136 | 36 | 97 | 0 | 97 | 0 | 9 |
| Honolulu | $ - | $97,667 | $97,667 | 91 | 0 | 87 | 4 | 27 | 87 | 80 | 1 | 79 | 0 | 2 |
| Houma-Thibodaux | $ - | $83,000 | $83, 000 | 94 | 0 | 92 | 1 | 26 | 92 | 31 | 0 | 31 | 0 | 0 |
| Indianapolis | $ - | | | 273 | 16 | 201 | 5 | 149 | 201 | 86 | 1 | 85 | 4 | 6 |
| Jefferson City | $ - | $168,488 | $168,488 | 97 | 21 | 97 | 15 | 125 | 97 | 115 | 0 | 115 | 2 | 6 |

## First Instance Tribunal Statistics 2016

| (Arch)Diocese or (Arch)Eparchy | Fees received | Diocesan Subsidy | Annual Tribunal Expenses | Libelli introduced and accepted this year | Libelli rejected | Causes admitted to the ordinary process | Causes admitted to the documentary process | Causes pending at the beginning of the year | Causes admitted this year | Sentences Issued | In favor of the Bond | In favor of nullity | Renunciation | Peremption |
|---|---|---|---|---|---|---|---|---|---|---|---|---|---|---|
| Kansas City in Kansas | $17,270 | $257,742 | $275,012 | 225 | 0 | 205 | 18 | 225 | 205 | 160 | 1 | 159 | 3 | 23 |
| Kansas City-St. Joseph | | | | 147 | 0 | 132 | 15 | 123 | 132 | 91 | 0 | 91 | 0 | 3 |
| Lake Charles | $19,845 | $208,665 | $228,510 | 66 | 0 | 66 | 12 | 71 | 66 | 75 | 2 | 73 | 0 | 1 |
| Lansing | $2,425 | $222 | $219 | 132 | 1 | 132 | 12 | 72 | 132 | 142 | 4 | 138 | 5 | 5 |
| Lexington | $ - | $243 | $243 | 78 | 3 | 75 | 12 | 32 | 75 | 68 | 1 | 67 | 2 | 2 |
| Little Rock | $3,825 | $203,425 | $207,250 | 184 | 2 | 182 | 40 | 73 | 182 | 98 | 4 | 94 | 7 | 5 |
| Louisville | $10,800 | $325,699 | $336,039 | 150 | 0 | 134 | 16 | 18 | 134 | 137 | 0 | 137 | 1 | 0 |
| Madison | $10,725 | $282,353 | $293,078 | 48 | 2 | 44 | 4 | 37 | 44 | 38 | 24 | 14 | 2 | 1 |
| Marquette | $ - | $46,615 | $46,615 | 53 | 0 | 52 | 0 | 26 | 52 | 49 | 1 | 49 | 0 | 0 |
| Metuchen | $54,175 | $331,820 | $385,995 | 102 | 1 | 100 | 2 | 123 | 100 | 81 | 0 | 81 | 2 | 1 |
| Miami | | | | 233 | 0 | 233 | 4 | 186 | 233 | 169 | 16 | 153 | 5 | 18 |
| Military Services | $24,670 | $228,236 | $252,906 | 96 | 0 | 96 | 10 | 105 | 96 | 110 | 1 | 109 | 1 | 2 |
| Milwaukee | $78,643 | $606,509 | $685,152 | 221 | 3 | 201 | 0 | 223 | 201 | 184 | 0 | 184 | 16 | 13 |
| New Orleans | $32,712 | $423,425 | $456,137 | 213 | 1 | 187 | 13 | 148 | 187 | 162 | 9 | 153 | 0 | 0 |
| New York | $18,059 | $1,243,397 | $1,293,111 | 345 | 11 | 342 | 3 | 157 | 342 | 228 | 31 | 197 | 2 | 9 |
| Norwich | $ - | $245,351 | $245,351 | 65 | 0 | 65 | 1 | 40 | 65 | 58 | 0 | 58 | 0 | 0 |
| Oakland | | | | 133 | 5 | 106 | 9 | 115 | 106 | 96 | 2 | 95 | 6 | 4 |
| Ogdensburg | $ - | $67,874 | $67,874 | 51 | 0 | 51 | 8 | 32 | 51 | 47 | 1 | 38 | 8 | 0 |
| Oklahoma City | $ - | $178,000 | $178,000 | 241 | 0 | 241 | 0 | 149 | 241 | 237 | 218 | 19 | 0 | 11 |
| Omaha | $10,265 | $352,307 | $362,572 | 154 | 0 | 151 | 0 | 240 | 151 | 179 | 30 | 149 | 3 | 7 |
| Palm Beach | $30,000 | $398,000 | $428,000 | 105 | 2 | 105 | 17 | 52 | 107 | 107 | 2 | 105 | 1 | 3 |

## First Instance Tribunal Statistics 2016

| (Arch)Diocese or (Arch)Eparchy | Fees received | Diocesan Subsidy | Annual Tribunal Expenses | Libelli introduced and accepted this year | Libelli rejected | Causes admitted to the ordinary process | Causes admitted to the documentary process | Causes pending at the beginning of the year | Causes admitted this year | Sentences Issued | In favor of the Bond | In favor of nullity | Renunciation | Peremption |
|---|---|---|---|---|---|---|---|---|---|---|---|---|---|---|
| Parma, Byz. Eparchy | | | | 3 | 0 | 3 | 0 | 2 | 3 | 4 | 1 | 3 | 0 | 0 |
| Paterson | $44,150 | $288,541 | $332,691 | 109 | 0 | 109 | 1 | 116 | 109 | 78 | 2 | 76 | 8 | 6 |
| Philadelphia, Ukrainian Archeparchy | $3,250 | $ 6,247 | $9,497 | 11 | 2 | 9 | 6 | 0 | 9 | 9 | 0 | 9 | 2 | 0 |
| Phoenix | $ - | $ - | $ - | 206 | 0 | 195 | 11 | 265 | 195 | 144 | 26 | 118 | 6 | 12 |
| Portland in Oregon | $30,548 | $279,910 | $310,458 | 178 | 1 | 178 | 5 | 170 | 178 | 115 | 6 | 109 | 5 | 8 |
| Raleigh | | $226,882 | $240,856 | 205 | 0 | 185 | 20 | 168 | 185 | 168 | 0 | 168 | 8 | 4 |
| Rapid City | $1,854 | $92,730 | $94,574 | 27 | 0 | 26 | 30 | 30 | 27 | 25 | | 24 | 2 | 3 |
| Reno | $4,450 | $145,960 | $150,410 | 93 | 0 | 37 | 56 | 54 | 37 | 31 | 0 | 31 | 1 | 2 |
| Rochester | $ - | $187,551 | $187,551 | 96 | 0 | 96 | 1 | 70 | 96 | 100 | 1 | 99 | 4 | 2 |
| Rockville Centre | $42,850 | $414,253 | $457,103 | 452 | 0 | 440 | 6 | 493 | 440 | 227 | 0 | 227 | 5 | 25 |
| Sacramento | | | | 133 | | 130 | 3 | 97 | 133 | 147 | 14 | 106 | 12 | 15 |
| Saginaw | $2,925 | $113,932 | $116,857 | 100 | 0 | 90 | 9 | 36 | 90 | 75 | 0 | 75 | 1 | 2 |
| Saint Paul & Minneapolis | $81,000 | $1,010,000 | $1,091,000 | 146 | 2 | 142 | 4 | 282 | 142 | 253 | 38 | 215 | 2 | 8 |
| Salina | | | $133,300 | 47 | 1 | 46 | 2 | 40 | 46 | 51 | 1 | 50 | 0 | 2 |
| Salt Lake City | $13,727 | $111,633 | $125,360 | 95 | 0 | 90 | 0 | 12 | 90 | 93 | 2 | 93 | 0 | 1 |
| San Bernardino | $ - | $ - | $ - | 270 | 0 | 261 | 7 | 261 | 261 | 189 | 11 | 178 | 7 | 6 |
| San Jose | $57,405 | $467,873 | $525,278 | 104 | 0 | 98 | 143 | 80 | 98 | 90 | 1 | 89 | 0 | 0 |
| Savannah | | | | 190 | 1 | 92 | 91 | 36 | 92 | 96 | 81 | 15 | 0 | 1 |

## First Instance Tribunal Statistics 2016

| (Arch)Diocese or (Arch)Eparchy | Fees received | Diocesan Subsidy | Annual Tribunal Expenses | Libelli introduced and accepted this year | Libelli rejected | Causes admitted to the ordinary process | Causes admitted to the documentary process | Causes pending at the beginning of the year | Causes admitted this year | Sentences Issued | In favor of the Bond | In favor of nullity | Renunciation | Peremption |
|---|---|---|---|---|---|---|---|---|---|---|---|---|---|---|
| Scranton | $ - | $328,974 | $328,974 | 185 | 0 | 185 | 1 | 48 | 185 | 125 | 123 | 2 | 2 | 4 |
| Seattle | $28,042 | $495,052 | $613,408 | 248 | 2 | 217 | 31 | 215 | 217 | 180 | 1 | 179 | 7 | 3 |
| Sioux City | $9,545 | $144,810 | $154,355 | 70 | 1 | 70 | 0 | 58 | 70 | 75 | 0 | 75 | 3 | 6 |
| Sioux Falls | | | | 94 | 1 | 94 | 2 | 67 | 94 | 63 | 1 | 62 | 4 | 4 |
| Spokane | $12,510 | $23,965 | $36,475 | 56 | | 54 | 7 | 6 | 54 | 56 | | 56 | 0 | |
| Springfield in Illinois | $43,993 | $92,326 | $136,319 | 144 | 2 | 142 | 92 | 128 | 144 | 110 | 6 | 99 | 2 | 3 |
| Springfield, MA | | | | 100 | 0 | 100 | 0 | 54 | 100 | 18 | | 18 | | 3 |
| Stamford, Ukr. Eparchy | $200 | | $300 | | | | | 4 | | | | | | |
| St. Louis | $154,859 | $394,135 | $548,994 | 189 | 1 | 181 | 7 | 313 | 181 | 206 | 34 | 172 | 5 | 23 |
| Steubenville | $ - | $80,161 | $81,661 | 37 | 0 | 35 | 0 | 20 | 35 | 46 | 0 | 46 | 1 | 0 |
| Stockton | $62,595 | $95,575 | $158,170 | 65 | 0 | 65 | 3 | 43 | 65 | 43 | 1 | 42 | 2 | 1 |
| Superior | $9,650 | $95,168 | $104,818 | 40 | 0 | 40 | 0 | 27 | 40 | 42 | 0 | 42 | 1 | 0 |
| Syracuse | $ - | $64,351 | $64,351 | 0 | 0 | 0 | 0 | 18 | 126 | 117 | 1 | 116 | 3 | 2 |
| Tulsa | $ - | $71,300 | $71,300 | 79 | 0 | 79 | 66 | 9 | 82 | 81 | 0 | 81 | 0 | 1 |
| Tyler | $5,185 | $170,252 | $175,437 | 85 | 10 | 85 | 10 | 47 | 85 | 81 | 4 | 77 | 1 | 6 |
| Victoria | | $1 | | 78 | 0 | 76 | 2 | 13 | 76 | 62 | 62 | | 1 | |
| Wheeling-Charleston | $ - | $ - | $ - | 0 | 0 | 0 | 10 | 116 | 60 | 53 | 5 | 48 | 0 | 0 |
| Wichita | $52,206 | $71,825 | $124,031 | 224 | 0 | 214 | 10 | 285 | 214 | 189 | 2 | 187 | 1 | 1 |
| Worcester | $34,041 | $114,274 | $148,315 | 79 | 0 | 72 | 7 | 60 | 72 | 94 | 1 | 93 | 0 | 2 |
| Youngstown | $1,197 | $314,885 | $316,883 | 118 | 0 | 118 | 61 | 72 | 75 | 75 | 0 | 75 | 0 | 0 |

## Second Instance Tribunal Statistics 2016

| (Arch)Diocese or (Arch) Eparchy | Causes admitted to the briefer process | Causes pending at the beginning of the year | Sentences issued by the Bishop in favor of nullity | Causes remitted to the ordinary process | Appealed to the Bishop mentioned in can. 1687, 3, MIDI | Appealed to the Roman Rota | Causes pending at the end of the year |
|---|---|---|---|---|---|---|---|
| Alexandria | 10 | 0 | 10 | 0 | 0 | 0 | 0 |
| Altoona-Johnstown | 1 | 0 | 1 | 0 | 0 | 0 | 0 |
| Baton Rouge | 1 | 2 | 3 | 0 | 0 | 0 | 0 |
| Boston | 48 | 0 | 37 | 6 | 0 | 0 | 5 |
| Burlington | 4 | 0 | 2 | 0 |  |  | 2 |
| Chicago | 47 | 0 | 8 | 11 | 0 | 0 | 28 |
| Cleveland | 1 | 0 | 0 | 0 | 0 | 0 | 1 |
| Colorado Springs | 4 | 0 | 1 | 0 | 0 | 1 | 3 |
| Columbus | 1 | 0 | 1 | 0 | 0 | 0 | 0 |
| Covington | 10 | 0 | 7 | 0 | 0 | 0 | 3 |
| Davenport | 14 | 5 | 16 | 1 | 0 | 0 | 1 |
| Denver | 2 | 0 | 2 | 0 | 0 | 0 | 0 |
| Detroit | 1 | 0 | 0 | 1 | 0 | 0 | 0 |
| Fall River | 6 | 1 | 3 | 1 | 0 | 0 | 3 |
| Helena | 1 | 0 | 1 | 0 | 0 | 0 | 0 |
| Houma-Thibodaux | 1 | 0 | 1 | 0 | 0 | 0 | 0 |
| Indianapolis | 3 | 0 | 3 | 0 | 0 | 0 | 0 |
| Kansas City in Kansas | 2 | 0 | 2 | 0 | 0 | 0 | 0 |
| Marquette | 1 | 0 | 1 | 0 | 0 | 0 | 0 |
| Milwaukee | 20 | 0 | 14 | 4 | 0 | 0 | 2 |
| New Orleans | 12 | 2 | 9 | 0 | 0 | 0 | 5 |
| Oakland | 18 | 0 | 18 | 0 | 0 | 0 | 0 |
| Omaha | 3 | 0 | 3 | 0 | 0 | 0 | 0 |
| Saginaw | 1 | 0 | 1 | 0 | 0 | 0 | 0 |
| Salt Lake City | 5 | 7 | 5 | 0 | 0 | 0 | 2 |
| San Bernardino | 2 | 0 | 1 | 0 | 0 | 0 | 1 |

## Second Instance Tribunal Statistics 2016

| (Arch)Diocese or (Arch) Eparchy | Causes admitted to the briefer process | Causes pending at the beginning of the year | Sentences issued by the Bishop in favor of nullity | Causes remitted to the ordinary process | Appealed to the Bishop mentioned in can. 1687, 3, MIDI | Appealed to the Roman Rota | Causes pending at the end of the year |
|---|---|---|---|---|---|---|---|
| San Jose | 6 | 0 | 4 | 0 | 0 | 0 | 2 |
| Savannah | 6 | 1 | 3 | 2 | 0 | 0 | 1 |
| Spokane | 2 |   | 2 |   |   |   |   |
| St. Louis | 1 |   |   | 1 |   |   |   |
| Steubenville | 2 | 0 | 2 | 0 | 0 | 0 | 0 |
| Tulsa | 3 | 1 | 4 | 0 | 0 | 0 | 0 |

# VARIA

## Contributors

Rev. John Beal, JCD, Ordinary Professor of Canon Law, The Catholic University of America, Washington, DC

Most Rev. Msgr. Kenneth Boccafola, JCD, Prelate Auditor (Retired), Roman Rota

Sr. Maria Casey, RSJ, JCD, PhD, Canon Law Consultant, Croydon, NSW, Australia

Dr. Barbara Anne Cusack, JCD, Chancellor, Archdiocese of Milwaukee, Wisconsin

Sr. Sharon Euart, RSM, JCD, Executive Director, Resource Center for Religious Institutes, Silver Spring, Maryland.

Prof. Massimo Faggioli, PhD, Professor of Theology and Religious Studies, Villanova University, Pennsylvania

Rev. Robert J. Geisinger, SJ, JCD, Promoter of Justice, Congregation for the Doctrine of the Faith, Vatican City.

Rev. Msgr. Ronny E. Jenkins, STL, JCD, Dean, School of Canon Law, The Catholic University of America, Washington, DC

Rev. Msgr. John G. Johnson, MA, JCD, Pastor, Our Lady of Peace Parish, Columbus, Ohio; Judge, Diocese of Columbus, Ohio and adjunct professor of canon law at the Pontifical College Josephinum

Rev. Robert Kaslyn, SJ, JCD, Professor of Canon Law, The Catholic University of America, Washington, DC

Rev. Alexander M. Laschuk, JCD, PhD, Judicial Vicar of the Eparchy of Toronto and Eastern Canada and Adjutant Judicial Vicar of the Toronto Regional Tribunal

Most Rev. Steven J. Lopes, STD, Bishop, Ordinariate of the Chair of Saint Peter

Ms. Jeannine Marino, JCL, Assistant Director, Secretariat of Evangelization and Catechesis, United States Conference of Catholic Bishops, Washington, DC

Rev. Ricardo Martin-Pinillos, JCL, Vice Chancellor, Archdiocese of Milwaukee, Wisconsin

Very Rev. Joseph L. Newton, JCL, Vicar Judicial, Archdiocese of Indianapolis, Indiana

Rev. Aaron Nord, JCD, Adjutant Judicial Vicar, Archdiocese of St. Louis, Missouri

Mr. Matthew Palmer, Assistant Director for Digital Strategy, United States Conference of Catholic Bishops, Washington, DC

Rev. Msgr. Michael A. Souckar, JCD, Pastor and Adjutant Judicial Vicar, Archdiocese of Miami, Florida

# Varia

## 2017 List of Participants

Joseph Abraham
  Reno, NV
Peter Akpoghiran
  New Orleans, LA
Timothy Alkire
  Lafayette, IN
Krystyna Amborski
  San Francisco, CA
John R. Amos
  Traverse City, MI
Bruce Ansems
  Kansas City, KS
William Anton
  Plainview, TX
Charles Antonicelli
  Washington, DC
Gary Applegate
  Kansas City, KS
Arockiadas Arokiasamy
  Lexington, KY
Christopher Armstrong
  Washington, DC
Joseph Arsenault
  Kansas City, KS
Joseph Augustine
  Charleston, WV
Brian Austin
  Brookville, IN
Kevin Badeaux
  Port Arthur, TX
Marc Balestrieri
  Memphis, TN
Diane Barr
  Baltimore, MD
Virginia Bartolac
  Kansas City, KS

Mary Ann Bartolac
  Leeward, KS
James Bartoloma
  Camden, NJ
Anthony Bawyn
  Seattle, WA
John Beal
  Erie, PA
John Bell
  Plano/Allen, TX
Brian Belongia
  Green Bay, WI
Barbara Bettwy
  Harrisburg, PA
Remek Blaszkowski
  Boynton Beach, FL
Mary Gen Blittschau
  Evansville, IN
Kenneth Boccafola
  Islandia, NY
Celeste Boda
  Owensboro, KY
Bob Boharic
  Riverside, IL
Frank Bollich
  Austin, TX
Richard Bona
  Cleveland, OH
Douglass Bond
  Rockford, IL
James Bonke
  Indianapolis, IN
E. Scott Borgman
  Newport Beach, CA
John Boyle
  Portland, OR

Michael Bradley
  Chicago, IL
Sean Bransfield
  Philadelphia, PA
Christopher Brashears
  Oklahoma City, OK
Cecilia Brennan
  Olympia, WA
Steven Brown
  Cincinnati, OH
Anne Bryant
  Houston, TX
James Burke
  Boston, MA
Michael Burke
  Orlando, FL
Justin Byrne
  Oklahoma City, OK
Jeffrey Cabral
  Fall River, MA
Jesus Cabrera
  Milwaukee, WI
Carl Caldwell
  Cleveland, OH
Steven Callahan
  San Diego, CA
Luis O. Capacetti
  Atlanta, GA
Giovanni Capucci
  Denver, CO
Gregory Caridi
  Houston, TX
Michael Cariglio
  Youngstown, OH
Maria Casey
  President, CLSANZ

David Castronovo
  Savannah, GA
Anthony Celino
  El Paso, TX
Martin Celuch
  Youngstown, OH
Krikor Chahin
  San Antonio, TX
Margaret Chalmers
  Birmingham, AL
Anna Marie Chamblee
  Fort Worth, TX
Paul Churchill
  President, CLSGB&I
J. Michael Clark
  Owensboro, KY
John Cody
  Columbus, OH
Oscar Coelho
  Albuquerque, NM
Patrick Cogan
  Garrison, NY
R. Daniel Conlon
  Joliet, IL
James Conn, S.J.
  Boston, MA
Jay Conzemius
  Pittsburgh, PA
Patrick Cooney
  Owensboro, KY
James Coriden
  Washington, DC
Paul Counce
  Baton Rouge, LA
J. Douglas Courville
  Lafayette, LA
John Crerand
  Columbus, OH
Thomas Cronkleton
  Cheyenne, WY
Barbara Anne Cusack
  Milwaukee, WI
Paul Czarnota
  Detroit, MI

Brendan Daly
  Auckland
William Daniel
  Washington, DC
Jamin David
  Baton Rouge, LA
Georges de Laire
  Manchester, NH
Zabrina Decker
  Milwaukee, WI
David Deibel
  Monterey, CA
Andrew DeKeyser
  Lafayette, IN
Robert DeLand
  Saginaw, MI
Brian Dellaert
  Dubuque, IA
Albert Dello Russo
  Palm Beach, FL
Frank Del Prete
  Newark, NJ
Louis DeNinno
  Pittsburgh, PA
John Dermond
  Trenton, NJ
William Dhein
  La Crosse, WI
Javier Diaz
  Trenton, NJ
John Dickinson
  Portland, ME
Lawrence DiNardo
  Pittsburgh, PA
Stephen Doktorczyk
  Stanton, CA
Francis Dolan
  Chicago, IL
John Donovan
  Syracuse, NY
Patricia Dugan
  Philadelphia, PA
Eric Dunn
  President, CCLS

Stephen Duquaine
  Lafayette, IN
Frederick Easton
  Bloomington, IN
Mary Edlund
  Dallas, TX
Heather Eichholz
  Sioux Falls, SD
Peter Eke
  Gaylord, MI
William Elder
  Lake Charles, LA
Martins Emeh
  Houston, TX
Rev. Erik Esparza
  San Bernardino, CA
Arthur Espelage
  Tucson, AZ
Sharon Euart
  Silver Spring, MD
Massimo Faggioli
  Villanova, PA
John Faris
  Utica, NY
Robert Fath
  Fairbanks, AK
Peter Faulk
  Alexandria, LA
Thomas P. Feeney
  Corpus Christi, TX
Mario Ferrante
  Italy
Christopher Ferrer
  Austin, TX
Victor Finelli
  Allentown, PA
Michael Forbes
  Austin, TX
Debbie Foreman
  Lake Charles, LA
Kenneth Fortener
  New Hope, KY
John Foster
  Washington, DC

Thomas Fransiscus
Reno, NV
Christopher Fraser
Phoenix, AZ
Matthew Frisoni
Albany, NY
Toti Fuentebella
Aruba
Matthew Furgiuele
Gaylord, MI
Christopher Fusco
Metuchen, NJ
Gerardo Galaviz
Los Angeles, CA
Stephen Garbitelli
Portland, OR
Jose Garcia
Houston, TX
Vincent Gardiner
Cleveland, OH
Joseph Gehret
Indianapolis, IN
Robert Geisinger
Rome, Italy
John Giel
Orlando, FL
J. Fernando Gil
Orlando, FL
Daniel Gill
Kansas City, MO
M. Margaret Gillett
Dallas, TX
Garry Giroux
Ogdensburg, NY
Chad Glendinning
Ottawa, ON
Matthew Glover
Little Rock, AR
Raymond Goehring
Lansing, MI
Heidi Gonzales
Detroit, MI
James Goodwin
Fargo, ND

Jason Gray
Peoria, IL
Thomas Green
Washington, DC
Jason Gries
Evansville, IN
Janice Grochowsky
Dodge City, KS
Ralph Gross
Milwaukee, WI
David Gross
Grand Rapids, MI
Kathleen Hahn
Grand Island, NE
Steven Hancock
Denver, CO
Edward Hankiewicz
Grand Rapids, MI
Paul B. Hartmann
Milwaukee, WI
Robert Hayes
San Jose, CA
Bernard Hebda
Saint Paul, MN
Marie Hilliard
Philadelphia, PA
Christina Hip-Flores
Camden, NJ
Timothy Hoag
Rapid City, SD
Thuan Hoang
San Francisco, CA
Christopher House
Springfield, IL
Thomas Howard
Austin, TX
David Howard
Cincinnati, OH
Annette Hrywna
Windsor, ON
Jeffrey Huber
San Antonio, TX
David Hudgins
Lansing, MI

Robert Hyde
Syracuse, NY
Francisca Igweilo
Denver, CO
Hilary Ike
Columbus, OH
James Innocenzi
Trenton, NJ
Matthew Iwuji
Austin, TX
Eileen Jaramillo
Lansing, MI
Lynn Jarrell
Louisville, KY
Chanel Jeanty
Miami, FL
Ronny Jenkins
Washington, DC
Lawrence John
Amarillo, TX
Michael Johnson
Saint Paul, MN
John Johnson
Columbus, OH
Gerald Jorgensen
Dubuque, IA
Saju Joseph
San Jose, CA
Michael Joyce
St. Louis, MO
Rita Joyce
Pittsburgh, PA
Thomas Kadera
Wheatland, WY
Christopher Kadrmas
Bismarck, ND
Samuel J. Kalu
Lafayette, IN
Robert Kaslyn
Washington, DC
Nicholas Kastenholz
St. Louis, MO
Kenneth Kaucheck
Bloomfield Hills, MI

Daniel Ketter
  Atlanta, GA
Adela Maria Kim
  Peoria, IL
R. Anne Kirby
  Dallas, TX
Robert Kitsmiller
  Columbus, OH
David Klein
  Camden, NJ
Daniela Knepper
  Muskego, WI
Jose Kochuparambil
  Lubbock, TX
John Chrysostom Kozlowski
  Washington, DC
Christine Kub
  Chicago, IL
Thomas Kunz
  Pittsburgh, PA
Bonnie Landry
  Lake Charles, LA
Alexander Laschuk
  Toronto, ON
Daniel Laurita
  Athens, AL
Raphael Lee
  Newark, NJ
Adrian Lee
  Hamilton, ON
William Leser
  Northridge, CA
John Lessard-Thibodeau
  Springfield, MA
Andres Ligot
  San Jose, CA
John List
  Lexington, KY
Beatriz Livingston
  Kansas City, MO
Douglas Loecke
  Dubuque, IA
Edward Lohse
  Erie, PA

Steven Lopes
  Houston, TX
Douglas Lucia
  Ogdensburg, NY
Paul Luniw
  Terryville, CT
Vinh Luu
  New Orleans, LA
Gregory Luyet
  Little Rock, AR
Elyn Macek
  Atlanta, GA
Paul Madrid
  Austin, TX
Sandra Makowski
  Charleston, SC
Charles Mangan
  Sioux Falls, SD
Salvatore Manganello
  Buffalo, NY
Jeannine Marino
  Washington, DC
Kurt Martens
  Washington, DC
Ricardo Martin
  Milwaukee, WI
David Masello
  Warren, RI
Paul Matenaer
  Madison, WI
Joseph Matt
  Kansas City, MO
Reynaldo Matunog
  Los Angeles, CA
Alberto Maullon
  Houston, TX
Michael Mazza
  Milwaukee, WI
Robert McBride
  Newark, NJ
Joseph McCabe
  Diocese of Hong Kong
Rose McDermott
  Trenton, NJ

Wendy McGrath
  Manchester, NH
Maureen McPartland
  Dubuque, IA
Mark Mealey
  Wilmington, DE
Jeffrey Meeuwsen
  Portland, OR
George Michalek
  Lansing, MI
Ken Mikulcik
  Russellville, KY
Pamela Miller
  Cheyenne, WY
Bruce Miller
  Alexandria, LA
Richard Millette
  Houston, TX
Edith Miranda
  Oklahoma City, OK
Christopher Moore
  Baltimore, MD
Francis Morrisey
  Ottawa, ON
Laura Morrison
  Camden, NJ
Peter Mottola
  Rochester, NY
Patrick Mullins
  Brisbane, Australia
Martin Mwongyera
  Peoria, IL
James Nall
  Belleville, IL
Luis Navarro
  Stockton, CA
Joseph Newton
  Indianapolis, IN
Francis Nguyen
  Oklahoma City, OK
Kevin Niehoff
  Grand Rapids, MI
Aaron Nord
  St. Louis, MO

Nwazi Nyirenda
  Austin, TX
Benedict O'Cinnsealaigh
  Cincinnati, OH
Linda O'Gara
  Lafayette, IN
Kathryn Olsen
  Oklahoma City, OK
Timothy Olson
  Fargo, ND
Anthony Omenihu
  New York, NY
Jose Opalda
  Baltimore, MD
Roch Pagé
  Ottawa, ON
William Palladino
  Boston, MA
Matthew Palmer
  Washington, DC
Carl Pallasch
  Chicago, IL
Duaine Pamment
  Laingsburg, MI
Thomas Paprocki
  Springfield, IL
John Payne
  Lake Charles, LA
Louanne Payne
  Owensboro, KY
Mark Payne
  Milwaukee, WI
F. Stephen Pedone
  Worcester, MA
Lori Peery
  Bigfoot, TX
Anthony Pileggi
  Kansas City, MO
Jaimes Ponce
  Colorado Springs, CO
Andrea Ponzone
  Boston, MA
Frank Pugliese
  San Diego, CA

Daniel Quinan
  Saint Paul, MN
Gerry Quinn
  St. Louis, MO
Steven Raica
  Gaylord, MI
Marco Rajkovich
  Nicholasville, KY
Margaret Ramsden
  Orange, CA
Lawrence Rasaian
  Tyler, TX
Michael Ravenkamp
  San Diego, CA
Amalraj Rayappan
  Portland, OR
Ann Rehrauer
  Green Bay, WI
John Renken
  Ottawa, ON
Nancy Reynolds
  Louisville, KY
J. Patrick Reynolds
  Owensboro, KY
Mark Richards
  Sacramento, CA
George Rigazzi
  Oklahoma City, OK
Kenneth Riley
  Kansas City, MO
J. Michael Ritty
  Feura Bush, NY
Giovanni Rizzo
  Newark, NJ
Manuel Rodriguez
  Brooklyn, NY
Carolyn Roeber
  Seattle, WA
Meg Romano-Hogan
  Dallas, TX
Brian Romanowski
  Norwich, CT
Eloise Rosenblatt
  San Jose, CA

Rebecca Ruesch
  Washington, DC
Caesar Russo
  St. Augustine, FL
Mark Rutherford
  Williamston, MI
Robert Sanson
  Cleveland, OH
Mary Santi
  Seattle, WA
Noel Sanvicente
  Sunnyvale, CA
Edward Schaefer
  St. Rose, IL
Joseph Scheib
  Pittsburgh, PA
Phillip Schweda
  Venice, FL
Julianne Shanklin
  Boston, MA
Tracey Sharp
  Los Angeles, CA
Donetta Shaw
  Kansas City, MO
Richard Shewman
  Erie, PA
Langes Silva
  Salt Lake City, UT
Robert Sinatra
  Camden, NJ
Christopher Siuzdak
  Portland, ME
Jaroslaw Skrzypek
  New Madrid, MO
Daniel Smilanic
  Chicago, IL
Peter Smith
  Portland, OR
Rosemary Smith
  Atlanta, GA
Elizabeth Sondag
  Omaha, NE
Michael Souckar
  Coral Springs, FL

Anthony St. Louis-Sanchez
   Denver, CO
Ronald Stake
   Chicago, IL
Margaret Stallmeyer
   Covington, KY
Sahaya Stanly F
   Grand Rapids, MI
Richard Stansberry
   Oklahoma City, OK
Anne-Therese Stephens
   Fort Wayne, IN
Karen Sullivan-Kight
   Jacksonville, FL
Thomas Sundaram
   Houston, TX
David Szatkowski
   Chicago IL
Andrew Szymakowski
   Sisters, OR
Amy Tadlock
   Saint Paul, MN
Michael Taylor
   Manchester, NH
Maurice Thompson
   Milwaukee, WI
Charles Thompson
   Indianapolis, IN
Nancy Thompson
   Indianapolis, IN
Mathew Thundathil
   Miami Shores, FL
Anh Tran
   Fort Worth, TX
Gregory Trawick
   Cadiz, KY
Ann Tully
   Indianapolis, IN
Ted Tumicki
   Jewett City, CT
Sebastian Tumusiime
   Peoria, IL
John Vaughan
   Owensboro, KY
Andrew Vaughn
   Milwaukee, WI
Siobhan Verbeek
   Washington, DC
Manuel Viera
   Tucson, AZ
Ruben Villarreal
   Lake Charles, LA
Victoria Vondenberger
   Cincinnati, OH
A. David Warriner
   New Orleans, LA
Joseph Waters
   St. Petersburg, F
Julian Wellspring
   Australia
Daniel Welter
   Chicago, IL
Adam Westphal
   Des Moines, IA
D. Reginald Whitt
   Baltimore, MD
Gregory Wielunski
   Miami Shores, FL
Paul Wienhoff
   Mascoutah, IL
Barry Windholtz
   Cincinnati, OH
Thomas Wisniewski
   Darby, PA
Nicholas Wolfla
   Louisville, KY
Geri Woodward
   New Orleans, LA
Gary Yanus
   Cleveland, OH
Adam Zajac
   Cleveland, OH
David Zimmer
   Linton, ND